SIR WILLIAM LAIRD CLOWES was born in 1865 and made his reputation as naval correspondent of *The Times* between 1890 and 1895. He was a member of the Navy League and involved in the agitation for greater naval resources, and his anonymous articles which appeared in the *Daily Graphic* in 1893 undoubtedly influenced the naval Estimates.

He wrote and compiled this seven-volume history of the Royal Navy between 1897 and 1903, involving a number of distinguished contemporary writers to assist him. From America he employed Captain Mahan, author of *The Influence of Sea Power upon History*, and Theodore Roosevelt who covered the history of the war with the United States. Sir Clements Markham, President of the Royal Geographical Society, dealt with the history of voyages and discoveries, and H W Wilson, author of *Battleships in Action*, described many of the minor naval operations.

Semerciergravure   Printed in Paris

George, Lord Anson.
Admiral of the Fleet.
From the Engraving by Mc Ardell after the Portrait by Reynolds,
shewing Anson in the earliest Admiral's Uniform.

Sampson Low Marston and Company L.td London

The Royal Navy

A History

From the Earliest Times to the Present

By

Wm. Laird Clowes

Fellow of King's College, London; Gold Medallist U.S. Naval Institute;
Hon. Member of the R.U.S. Institution

Assisted by

Sir Clements Markham, K.C.B., F.R.S.
Captain A. T. Mahan, U.S.N.
Mr. H. W. Wilson
Col. Theodore Roosevelt, late Assist. Sec. U.S. Navy
Mr. L. Carr Laughton
etc.

Vol. III.

CHATHAM PUBLISHING

LONDON

PUBLISHER'S NOTE
In the original edition the four photogravure plates and
the first full-page illustration faced the text pages as
listed on page XVII. In this edition these illustrations
are collected at the back of the book after page 564, in
the order in which they appeared in the first edition.

Published in 1996 by
Chatham Publishing,
1 & 2 Faulkner's Alley, Cowcross Street,
London EC1M 6DD

Chatham Publishing is an imprint of
Gerald Duckworth and Co Ltd

First published in 1898 by
Sampson Low, Marston and Company

ISBN 1 86176 012 4

INTRODUCTION TO VOLUME III.

SOME of the causes which contributed to delay the appearance of
the second volume of this History of the Royal Navy, have contributed to delay the appearance of this, the third. The progress
of the work has, as before, been hampered by my ill-health and
my enforced residence in the high Alps during the greater part
of the year. A certain amount of delay, moreover, has resulted
indirectly from the recent war between the United States and
Spain. Captain A. T. Mahan, whose critical narrative of the
major operations of the War of the American Revolution fills
about a third of the present volume, was employed in the service
of his country [1] at Washington during the late conflict, and was
thus prevented for a time from devoting his attention to other
matters. So much of the delay as has been caused by his pre-
occupation will, I am sure, be readily forgiven, seeing that he
has now been able to revise proofs, etc., which must otherwise
have been sent to press without his final *imprimatur*. This book
has much to say concerning the beginnings and the early exploits
of the United States' Navy, which, in the days of Hull and
Decatur, proved itself to be as capable and chivalrous an
opponent as Great Britain ever had to meet upon the seas, and
which since,—and not only in the days of Tatnall,—has shown
itself as true and loyal a friend to Britain and her Navy, in peace
time, as it was gallant a foe in war. I cannot, therefore, refrain
from expressing here a sentiment which, in the course of the late
short but brilliant struggle, must have welled up often in the

[1] I should mention that my other American collaborator, Mr. Theodore Roosevelt,
resigned his appointment as Assistant Secretary of the U. S. Navy, in order to take an
active part in the war, and, having obtained a commission as Lieut.-Colonel of the now
famous " Rough Riders," fought with very distinguished bravery before Santiago-
de Cuba. He has since been elected Governor of the State of New York.

heart of many a Briton. We triumph wherever the race wins
fresh glories ; and we feel proud in the thought that the victory
has been gained by men speaking our speech, bearing our names,
sharing our blood, and inspired by the traditions bequeathed equally
to both nations by Howard, Drake, Hawkins, Blake, Boscawen and
Hawke. Not to us has it fallen in these recent years to illustrate
those traditions, and to add to them fresh epics. Yet, since our
brothers of the New World have shown themselves at Manilla and
Santiago the same men that they were at Mobile and New Orleans,
we are surely justified in hoping that we, should the hour for action
come again, shall be able to prove that our branch of the old stock
retains, in a similar manner, the old grit and the old sea virtues.

Although, as I have said, the progress of the work continues to
be somewhat delayed by my personal disabilities, I am not conscious
that the book suffers in any other way in consequence of my ill-
health. Thanks to my numerous and indefatigable helpers and
correspondents, I am not, in spite of my necessary absence from
home, obliged to forego reference to any documents, state papers, or
books which ought to be consulted. Happily, too, most of the
materials for my part of the work were collected, and, to some
extent, set in order, ere I became a prisoner here ; and although, of
course, I still very often have to appeal for further particulars to the
public libraries, the Record Office, private muniment rooms, and
other storehouses of fact, there is, I find, remarkably little supplementary research of this kind which cannot be carried out for me
by my assistants. It is a longer process, and a costlier, but not, I
hope, a less effective one.

I make this explanation because some friendly critics who have
been so good as to point out certain small errors of omission or
commission in the previous volumes, have generously hinted their
conviction that, were I not the invalid I unfortunately am, these
errors would not have appeared. If I really believed that my state
of health were incompatible with the carrying out of the work in
hand, I should assuredly try to find someone else to take over my
duties and responsibilities. But the fact is that such errors as I
have had brought to my notice,—and fortunately they are neither
serious nor numerous,—are inevitable imperfections in any book of
this nature ; for, paradoxical though it be, I can safely assert that
in nothing is it so impossible to attain to absolute correctness and
finality as in a critical record of historic facts. The difficulty

would beset me equally, were I sound instead of sick, and in London instead of in Switzerland. There are conflicts of evidence which appear irreconcilable; there are original authorities which cannot be laid hands upon, or which even the most studiously careful will by chance overlook; and there are many questions, the discussion of which cannot be seriously attempted in a work to which limits have been set. I am sure that some at least of the critics to whom I have alluded, have made the mistake of supposing that it is because of my condition and my position that I have ignored this witness' testimony on a court-martial, have seemed to pay little or no heed to the statements contained in that document, or have failed to enter upon such and such an interesting, but wide point of criticism. I am obliged to say that such shortcomings as are to be found in these volumes are due, for the most part, to very different causes. Firstly, I am restrained by the space at my command from touching upon many subjects with which I should otherwise like to deal at length, and from entering upon long discussions as to the credibility of evidence. The same consideration even obliges me to omit many footnotes and references which I should otherwise gladly include. Secondly, I am guided by the conviction that anyone who aspires to complete a book so voluminous as this History, must perforce proceed upon principles somewhat similar to those which Dr. Johnson sketched in a very famous passage.

"Failures," he wrote, "however frequent, may admit of extenuation and apology. To have attempted much is always laudable, even when the enterprise is above the strength that undertakes it. To deliberate whenever I doubted, to enquire whenever I was ignorant, would have protracted the undertaking without end, and perhaps without improvement. I saw that one enquiry only gave occasion to another, that book referred to book, that to search was not always to find, and to find was not always to be informed; and that thus to pursue perfection was, like the first inhabitants of Arcadia, to chase the sun, which, when they had reached the hill where he seemed to rest, was still beheld at the same distance from them."

If, to put matters in other words, one were determined, in an undertaking of this kind, to be content with nothing short of absolute completeness and finality, neither the initiator, nor, after his death, any of his successors, would live long enough to finish the work. I make bold to recommend this reflection to all my critics, and especially to one of them, who, in his review of my second volume, said, speaking of the account there given of the first Dutch War (1652–54), that it was "premature." I do not doubt that it will be possible, say a hundred years hence, to write a better and completer history of that war than can be written now; but to admit so much is surely not the same thing as to agree that a history, carefully written now, and illustrated with scores of previously unpublished facts, is written too soon. It is surely not " premature " to brush away even a single published error or misconception concerning the course of our naval history ; and, I think, I may safely say that this volume and those volumes which have preceded it,—although they, too, possibly contain many errors on minor points,—give, upon the whole, a much fairer and more accurate version of that history than has been hitherto presented. One dares not hope for—much less can one wait for,—absolute finality. But, by means of an undertaking planned and carried out as this one is, in accordance with the principles set forth in my General Preface, one may at least be instrumental in enlarging general knowledge of a great subject, and in rendering impossible the future acceptation of some of the gross and astonishing misstatements on naval matters which one finds in almost every English history. I have no wish to say here anything unkind about any of my brother men of letters: but I cannot abstain from citing from one particular book a few misstatements of the sort to which I allude, in order that it may be seen that the present work is not " premature," and that there does exist already a real necessity for something of the kind. I speak of a book, dealing with English history generally, and consisting of upwards of eleven hundred large pages of small type. It bears the imprint of reputable publishers ; and upon the title-page are the names of two distinguished university men, one of whom is described as a lecturer on modern history, and the other as a late professor on history, in a well-known English college. The second edition of this book, dated 1885, is responsible for the following extraordinary statements, among others.

Of Admiral Edward Vernon (1), it is said that he was a " rear-admiral at twenty-four," and that he " failed in his attempt to seize Porto Bello, from an insufficiency of force." The truth is that Vernon was made a vice-admiral in 1739, when he was fifty-five, that he had never before held flag-rank, and that, far from failing at Puerto Bello, he brilliantly captured that place on November 22nd, 1739, " with six ships only," as may be seen on reference to pp. 54–57 of the present volume.

Surely there is some unconscious *suppressio veri* in the assertion that, " foiled in his attempt to catch the Spanish treasure-ship,

Anson sailed westward from America with the *Centurion*, his sole remaining ship, and arrived at Spithead in June 1744." The story of what really happened, and of how the Manilla galleon was taken, will be found on p. 323 of this volume.

Episodes, localities, and individuals are curiously jumbled and confused in the following passage :—" On the 1st of June, 1794, the division of the Channel fleet commanded by Lord Howe attacked and utterly defeated the French fleet off the Hyères Islands. In this action Hood played a conspicuous part, and in the following August he was created Baron Bridport, in the Irish peerage." It is true, of course, that a great battle was fought on " The Glorious First of June," 1794 ; but it was fought, not off the Hyères Islands, which lie near Toulon, in the Mediterranean, but off Ushant, near the mouth of the British Channel. The only important action fought off Hyères during the war of 1793–1802 was fought in July, 1795, by a British fleet under Admiral William Hotham (1). That force was not a division of the Channel fleet, nor were the French utterly defeated on the occasion. Moreover, Lord Bridport was not upon the scene.

Rodney is described as "the son of a naval officer of some renown." Henry Rodney, his father, is usually supposed, nevertheless, to have been a country gentleman, living at Walton-on-Thames. It is further said of Rodney that, while he was residing in France, " offers were made by the French to tempt him to desert his country ; but he rejected the overtures, and was rewarded in 1778 by being promoted to be an admiral." It is news that promotion in the Navy has ever been a reward for a flag-officer's refusal to become a traitor : yet, seeing that when Rodney was made an Admiral of the White, on January 29th, 1782, he was still in France, and that, according to the generally accepted story, he owed his ability to return to England to the fact that a French gentleman lent him the necessary money, it is difficult to believe that the authorities at Whitehall, if they had ever suspected him of treasonable proclivities, could have felt sure, when they promoted him, that their suspicions were baseless.

Of Sir Charles Napier it is said : " in 1829 he was employed off the coast of Portugal in the *Galatea*. He supported the Constitutionalists ; defeated the fleet of Don Miguel, and settled Donna Maria on the throne. Don Pedro was unbounded in his gratitude : created him Viscount of Cape St. Vincent ; gave him all the

Portuguese orders, and named him admiral-in-chief." From this it would certainly appear to the ordinary reader that, while commanding H.M.S. *Galatea*, Napier took an active part in the internal affairs of Portugal and defeated Don Miguel; and that, in consequence of his action, he was given command of Don Pedro's fleet. Yet, in fact, Napier quitted the *Galatea* early in 1832; succeeded Sartorius in command of Don Pedro's fleet in 1833, and did not, until he was already serving in that capacity, defeat Don Miguel.

I might, if it were worth while, cite scores of other misstatements, equally astonishing, from the book in question, and from other recent works dealing with English history. Surely, when such misstatements are being circulated broadcast, it is not "premature" to put forward a Naval History which, though it may possibly contain errors on obscure points of fact or criticism, and though it make no pretence to be absolutely complete and final, has been, at least, prepared with a vast amount of care, which is the outcome of reference,—not, of course, to all existing original authorities, but to many thousands of unpublished documents, private and public, and to many thousands of printed histories, biographies, official papers, Navy lists, pamphlets and periodicals; and which has involved research in, and, in some cases, special journeys to, not merely many parts of England, but also France, America, Spain, Holland, Russia, Denmark and Italy.

For Chapters XXVI, XXVII, and XXX, of the present volume, and for the appendix and some of the notes to Chapter XXXI, I am directly responsible. Sir Clements Markham contributes Chapter XXIX; Captain Mahan, Chapter XXXI, and Mr. L. Carr Laughton, Chapter XXVIII, and the appendix thereto.

Captain Mahan desires me to express here, on his behalf, very cordial thanks to Professor J. K. Laughton, R.N., who has kindly assisted him in many ways in the preparation of Chapter XXXI, in the present volume.[1] With regard to that chapter, I ought to point out that the plan, on p. 375, of the naval attack on Fort Moultrie, Charleston, in 1776, will be found to differ, in some small and unimportant details, from Captain Mahan's description of the dispositions of the ships and of the guns in the works. Seeing, however, that the plan in question is based upon a contemporary drawing

---

[1] " He kindly placed at my disposal numerous notes made by him at the Record Office. These have been of great, and indeed of indispensable assistance in the narrative."—Letter of Captain Mahan to W. L. C.

made upon the spot by a British naval officer, and intended to accompany and illustrate the dispatch of Commodore Sir Peter Parker (1), I have deemed it to be of more than sufficient interest to warrant its reproduction. For its inclusion, however, Captain Mahan is not responsible. Among other supplementary illustrations which I have ventured to add to his chapter, is the valuable note on p. 396. It is but a brief note ; but it represents the results of many days' labour ; and we should not have been able to obtain the figures contained in it, had we not had the co-operation of Colonel H. Hozier, Secretary of Lloyd's, who most kindly allowed some of the clerks in his office to compile the table from the original documents.

To Lord Vernon, for information concerning his distinguished kinsman, Admiral Edward Vernon (1), and to Captain Thomas Suckling, R.N. (retd.), I desire also to express special thanks.

I regret that, owing to the fact that more than one chapter of the present volume has extended to greater length than was originally intended, I have found it impossible to conclude the history of the period 1762–1793 with Mr. H. W. Wilson's account of the minor operations of the War of American Revolution. That account will form the first chapter of Vol. IV, which, since most of it is already in type, will, I hope, be in a condition for publication very early in the year 1899.

W. L. C.

Davos-am-Platz, Switzerland.
Nov. 1898.

ERRATA.

The reader is requested to correct the following errors, the presence of which was not discovered until after the greater part of the volume had been sent to press.

P.   9, *at end of the table, in the two lower lines, under* Cables,
    for Diameter of bower cables, *read* Circumference of bower cables.

P. 373, *line* 4 *from bottom,*
    for Captain James Reid, *read* Commander James Reid.
    „   *line* 2 *from bottom,*
    for Christopher, *read* Tobias.

P. 380, *line* 5,
    for Admiral Lord Howe, *read* Vice-Admiral Lord Howe.

P. 387, *line* 21,
    for Caulfield, *read* Caulfeild.

P. 406, *in table in note, under* Vigilant,
    for Com. Hugh Cloberry Christian, *read* Com. Brabazon Christian

P. 471, *line* 18,
    for Thomas Graves (1), *read* Thomas Graves (2).

P. 473, *line* 25,
    for Caulfield, *read* Caulfeild.
    „   *line* 26,
    for Bonovier, *read* Bonavia.

P. 474, *line* 2 *from bottom,*
    for Caulfield, *read* Caulfeild.

P. 505, *in* 2*nd col. of table,*
    for Capt. George Murray, *read* Capt. Hon. George Murray.
    for Capt. Robert Sutton, *read* Capt. Robert Manners Sutton.

P. 538, *line* 14,
    for Richard Hughes, Bart. (2), *read* Richard Hughes (3), Bart.
    „   *in first foot-note,*
    for Richard Hughes, Bart. (1), *read* Richard Hughes (2), Bart.

P. 546, *in* 3*rd col. of note,*
    for Heros, *read* Héros.

P. 550, *in line* 8 *of* 4*th col. of table,*
    for Lapallière, *read* Lapellière.

P. 554, *line* 35,
    for Batacalo, *read* Batticaloa.

P. 557, *line* 12,
    for Batacalo, *read* Batticaloa.

CONTENTS.

VOLUME III.

——◆——

CHAPTER XXXI.

PUBLISHER'S NOTE
The photogravure plates and the first full-page illustration listed below appear
in this edition at the back of the book, after page 564.

LIST OF ILLUSTRATIONS.

VOLUME III.

———◆———

FULL-PAGE PHOTOGRAVURES.

FULL-PAGE ILLUSTRATIONS.

ILLUSTRATIONS IN THE TEXT.

NAVAL HISTORY.

CHAPTER XXVI.

CIVIL HISTORY OF THE ROYAL NAVY, 1714–1762.

Administration of the Navy—The Admiralty Board—The Sick and Wounded Board—
The Admiralty Buildings—The Navy Office—The Navy Pay Office—First Lords
and Secretaries of the Admiralty, and Principal Officers of the Navy, 1714–1762—
Naval Expenditure—Increase in various classes of ships—State of the fleet in 1714,
1727, 1752 and 1760—The introduction of the true frigate—The dimensions of ships
—Complements—Small arms—Anchors—Cables—Method of computing tonnage
—Service ordnance—The armament of ships—Some typical men-of-war—Cost of
men-of-war in 1719, 1733 and 1741—Hadley's quadrant—Harrison's timekeeper
—Coppering—Sail-cloth—The Eddystone Light—Lighthouses—Lightships—The
King's Regulations and Admiralty Instructions—Pilots—Smugglers—Vernon on
smugglers and their dangers—Repression of piracy—The Articles of War—
Greenwich Hospital—The encouragement of seamen—Prize money—Bounties to
seamen—Pay and half-pay—Officers' servants—Promotion to flag-rank—Superannuation of Captains—The establishment of uniform for officers—The rough life
of the service—The character of officers—Immorality on the lower deck—Health
of the Navy.

URING the period 1714–1762 very little change
took place in the character of the machinery
whereby the Royal Navy was administered. That
machinery had attained a certain degree of perfection,
and was in fairly good working order. The Act of
William and Mary,[1] which specified and defined the
functions of the Commissioners for executing the office of Lord High
Admiral of England, continued to be the authority in virtue of which
the Admiralty Board acted; and the patent granted to her Admiralty
Board by Queen Anne was substantially reproduced from time to
time as fresh Boards succeeded one another. In the civil department, the most important alteration was the appointment, in
1740, of a Sick and Wounded Board. The sick and hurt seamen
of the Navy had been looked after by a Commission in the reign

[1] 2 W. & M., sess. 2, c. 2.

of William III. ; but in 1692 the business had been transferred to the Commissioners of the Register Office, and thence, in 1702, to another separate Commission, which had lasted until 1713. Thereafter, for some years, things remained unsettled; but in 1740, in consequence of the war with Spain, a Commission was specially granted to three persons, who were entrusted not only with the care of sick and wounded seamen, but also with the superintendence of medical stores supplied for the use of the Navy, the management of naval hospitals ashore and afloat, the examination and appointment of naval surgeons, and the maintenance and exchange of prisoners of war. From 1745 to 1749, this Board consisted of four instead of three Commissioners ; from 1749 to 1755, of two only ; from April to November, 1755, of three, as at first; and from 1755 to 1763, of four. Its offices were on Tower Hill.

The old Admiralty buildings at Wallingford House fell into decay about the year 1722, when the office of the Commissioners was temporarily transferred to a house in St. James's Square. The older part of the present Admiralty buildings in Whitehall, was completed and occupied in 1725, though not until 1760 was the colonnade or screen built across the street-side of the court-yard to mitigate the unpleasant effect produced by the attenuated proportions of the columns on the western side of the square. The Navy Office remained during the period at the corner of Seething Lane and Crutched Friars ; and the Navy Pay Office was in Old Broad Street.

The succession of the more important administrative officers was as follows :—

FIRST LORD OF THE ADMIRALTY.

Oct. 14, 1714. Edward, Earl of Orford, Admiral.
Ap.   16, 1717. James, Earl of Berkeley, Admiral.
Aug. 2, 1727. George, Viscount Torrington, Admiral.
June 21, 1733. Sir Charles Wager, Kt., Admiral.
Mar. 19, 1742. Daniel, Earl of Winchelsea.
Dec. 1744. John, Duke of Bedford.
Feb. 20, 1748. John, Earl of Sandwich.
June 22, 1751. George, Lord Anson, Admiral.
Nov. 20, 1756. Richard, Earl Temple.
Ap.   1757. Daniel, Earl of Winchelsea.
June 30, 1757. George, Lord Anson, Admiral.
June 19, 1762. George, Earl of Halifax.
Oct. 16, 1762. George Grenville.

SECRETARY OF THE ADMIRALTY.

Josiah Burchett.

1742. Thomas Corbett.

1751. John Clevland (with, as assistant and deputy, John Milnes).

TREASURER OF THE NAVY.

John Aislabie.
	1718.	Richard Hampden.
	1720.	Sir Geo. Byng, Kt., Adm.
	1724.	Hon. Henry Pattee Byng.
	1725.	William Corbett.
	1734.	Arthur Onslow.
Feb.	1742.	Thomas Clutterbuck.
Dec.	1742.	Sir Charles Wager, Kt., Admiral.
	1743.	Sir John Rushout, Bart.
	1744.	George Doddington.
	1749.	Hon. Henry Bilson Legge.
	1754.	George Grenville.
	1755.	George Doddington.
	1756.	George Grenville.
April	1757.	George Doddington.
June	1757.	George Grenville.
	1762.	William Wildman, Viscount Barrington.

CONTROLLER OF THE NAVY.

Sir Charles Wager, Kt., Rear-Admiral.
April	1718.	Thomas Swanton (1), Captain, R.N.
Jan.	1722.	James Mighells, Vice-Admiral.
Mar.	1734.	Richard Haddock (2), Captain, R.N.
Mar. 22,	1749.	Savage Mostyn, Captain, R.N.
Feb.	1755.	Edward Falkingham (1), Captain, R.N.
Nov.	1755.	Charles Saunders, Captain, R.N.
June	1756.	Digby Dent (2), Captain, R.N.
Dec.	1756.	George Cockburne, Captain, R.N.

SURVEYOR OF THE NAVY.

William Lee.
Mar.	1715.	Jacob Ackworth.
June	1746.	Joseph Allin.
Aug.	1755.	{Thomas Slade. {William Bateley

CLERK OF THE ACTS.

Samuel Atkins.
May	1719.	Tempest Holmes.
Sept.	1726.	Thomas Pearce.
April	1743.	John Clevland.
Aug.	1746.	Robert Osborne.
July	1747.	Daniel Devert.
Jan.	1761.	Timothy Brett.
Mar.	1761.	Edward Mason.

CONTROLLER OF THE TREASURER'S ACCOUNTS.

Dennis Liddell.
Nov.	1717.	Richard Burton.
Aug. 17,	1727.	Sir George Saunders, Kt., Captain and Rear-Adm.
Feb.	1735.	George Purvis, Captain, R.N.
Mar.	1740.	John Philipson.
Dec.	1743.	William Corbett.
Aug.	1753.	Richard Hall.
Mar.	1761.	Timothy Brett.

CONTROLLER OF THE VICTUALLING ACCOUNTS.

Benjamin Timewell.
Nov.	1714.	Richard Burton.
Nov.	1717.	John Fawler.
June	1744.	Francis Gashry.
July	1747.	Robert Osborne.

CONTROLLER OF THE STOREKEEPER'S ACCOUNTS.

Thomas Jennings, Captain, R.N.
Nov.	1714.	Charles Cornwall, Captain, R.N.
July	1716.	Thomas Swanton (1), Captain, R.N.
April	1718.	William Cleveland, Captain, R.N.
May	1732.	Robert Byng.
May	1739.	John Philipson.
Mar.	1740.	George Crowle.
Mar.	1752.	Richard Hall.
Aug.	1753.	George Adams.
Mar.	1761.	Hon. William Bateman, Captain, R.N.

EXTRA COMMISSIONERS.

Isaac Townesend, Captain, R.N.

Lawrence Wright, Captain, R.N.

Nov.	1714.	John Fawler.
Dec.	1717.	Thomas Colby.
Jan.	1727.	Sir George Saunders, Kt., Captain, R.N.
May	1729.	Sir Isaac Townesend, Kt., Captain, R.N.
May	1731.	Robert Byng.
May	1732.	Lord Vere Beauclerk, Captain, R.N.
May	1738.	George Crowle.
Mar.	1740.	Francis Gashry.
April	6, 1743.	James Compton, Captain, R.N.
April	6, 1743.	Alexander Geddes, Captain, R.N.
Jan.	1744.	James Oswald.
May	1746.	Edward Falkingham (1), Captain, R.N.
July	1747.	John Russell.
Feb.	1755.	Thomas Cooper, Captain, R.N.
Nov.	1755.	Arthur Scott, Captain, R.N.
Mar.	1756.	Digby Dent (2), Captain, R.N.
May	1756.	Hon. William Bateman, Captain, R.N.
Dec.	1756.	Digby Dent (2), Captain, R.N. (again).
Jan.	1761.	Edward Mason.
Mar.	1761.	Sir Richard Temple.
Mar.	1761.	Sir John Bentley, Captain, R.N.

COMMISSIONERS AT H.M. DOCK-YARDS, ETC.

Chatham :—

Nov.	1714	James Littleton, Captain and Rear-Admiral.
Mar.	1722.	Thomas Kempthorne, Captain, R.N.
July	1736.	Thomas Mathews, Captain, R.N.
April	1742.	Charles Brown, Captain, R.N.

June	1754.	Arthur Scott, Captain, R.N.
Nov.	1755.	Thomas Cooper, Captain, R.N.
Jan.	1761.	Thomas Hanway, Captain, R.N.

Portsmouth :—

Nov.	1714.	Isaac Townesend, Captain, R.N.
May	1729.	Richard Hughes (1), Captain, R.N.
Feb.	1754.	Richard Hughes (2), Captain, R.N. (Bart. 1773).

Plymouth :—

Nov.	1714.	Sir William Jumper, Kt., Captain, R.N.
Mar.	1715.	Thomas Swanton, Captain, R.N.
July	1716.	Francis Dove, Captain, R.N.
April	1726.	Sir Nicholas Trevanion, Kt., Captain, R.N.
Dec.	9, 1737.	Matthew Norris, Captain, R.N.
Jan.	1739.	Philip Vanbrugh, Captain, R.N.
Oct.	1753.	Frederick Rogers, Captain, R.N. (Bart. 1773).

Deptford and Woolwich[1] *:—*

Henry Greenhill.

May 26, 1744.		Thomas Whorwood, Captain, R.N.
Jan.	1745.	Edward Falkingham (1), Captain, R.N.
May	1746.	James Compton, Captain, R.N.
Dec.	1747.	William Davies, Captain, R.N.

Gibraltar and Minorca :—

Dec. 10, 1742.		Edward Falkingham (1), Captain, R.N.
June 29, 1744.		Thomas Trefusis, Captain, R.N.
Feb. 25, 1747.		John Towry, Captain, R.N.
June 22, 1756.		Charles Colby, Captain, R.N.

---

[1] The business of these Yards was conducted by the Commissioners in London, after the death of Captain Davies on February 16th, 1759.

The following statement of the sums annually voted by Parliament for the " extra " and for the " ordinary " expenses of the Royal Navy, and of the number of seamen and Marines authorised for each year, is taken from Derrick's ' Memoirs of the Rise and Progress of the Royal Navy.'[1] It should be explained that the money voted under the head of " extra," was almost invariably used for building or repairing ships, for providing furniture and stores for such vessels, or for improving the Royal Dockyards ; but that, occasionally, portions of the money were employed for the replenishment of the supplies of hemp, timber, etc., when the quantities in hand happened to be low, and for other special services :—

Year.	Extra.	Ordinary.	No. of Seamen and Marines.[1]	Year.	Extra.	Ordinary	No. of Seamen and Marines.[1]
	£	£			£	£	
1715	237,277	233,471	{(a) 10,000 / (b) 16,000}	1739	..	222,689	12,000
1716	230,623	233,849	10,000	1740	..	199,704	35,000
1717	200,761	226,799	10,000	1741	..	184,691	40,000
1718	165,317	224,857	10,000	1742	..	188,756	40,000
1719	88,494	212,638	13,500	1743	..	188,558	40,000
1720	79,723	217,918	13,500	1744	..	192,834	40,000
1721	50,200	219,049	10,000	1745	..	200,479	40,000
1722	..	218,799	7,000	1746	..	198,048	40,000
1723	..	216,388	10,000	1747	..	196,259	40,000
1724	..	214,622	10,000	1748	..	208,827	40,000
1725	..	214,295	10,000	1749	..	285,878	17,000
1726	..	212,181	10,000	1750	197,896	293,625	10,000
1727	..	199,071	20,000	1751	140,257	290,302	8,000
1728	..	205,561	15,000	1752	100,000	277,718	10,000
1729	..	206,025	15,000	1753	..	280,206	10,000
1730	120,618	213,168	10,000	1754	100,000	278,747	10,000
1731	..	212,034	10,000	1755	100,000	280,288	12,000
1732	60,000	212,885	8,000	1756	200,000	219,021	50,000
1733	104,003	211,495	8,000	1757	200,000	223,939	55,000
1734	..	202,670	20,000	1758	200,000	224,421	60,000
1735	..	198,914	30,000	1759	200,000	238,491	60,000
1736	30,167	217,269	15,000	1760	200,000	232,629	70,000
1737	50,000	219,201	10,000	1761	200,000	258,624	70,000
1738	40,000	222,885	{(c) 10,000 / (d) 20,000}	1762	200,000	272,226	70,000

[1] The cost of these was in addition to the sums specified in the "Extra" and "Ordinary" columns.

(a) Number to Midsummer. (b) Number from Midsummer to December 31st. (c) Number to April 10th. (d) Number from April 10th to December 31st.

For several years after the death of Queen Anne, the number of ships belonging to the Royal Navy showed no increase, but rather a slight diminution. Nevertheless there was, even in those days, an increase in the total tonnage. But, from the death of George I.

[1] 4to. London, 1806.

onwards, the Navy grew enormously   There was no tendency to add to the number of the first and second rates—vessels which were only useful for special purposes, and which, as late as the middle of the eighteenth century,[1] it was customary to lay up every winter.   Of the third, fifth, and sixth rates, and of the sloops, on the other hand, increasingly greater numbers were built. The third rates were the vessels which experience showed to be, upon the whole, most serviceable for the line-of-battle.   The fifth and sixth rates were the ships with which the country found it could best deal with the enemy's cruisers ; and the sloops were

THE FRENCH *Invincible*, 74.   THE SPANISH *Glorioso*, 74.
Taken by Vice-Admiral Anson, 1747.   *Taken by the* Russell, 80, 1747.
(*From the drawings by Charnock.*)

the natural foes of small privateers, and the natural agents for the general policing of the seas.   That the number of fourth rates did not increase is attributable to the gradual discovery of the fact that fifty and sixty-gun ships, while too small and light for the line-of-battle, were too large and heavy for ordinary cruising purposes.   They continued to be built in small numbers, chiefly because they were suitable craft for service in the colonies, and, as flagships, on the less important stations, in war, and almost everywhere in peace ; and, because they continued to be built, they occasionally found their way into the line-of-battle.   But occupying,

[1] Vernon's correspondence with the Admiralty in 1745 is full of references to the danger of keeping three-deckers at sea during the winter months.

as they did, an intermediate position between the line-of-battleships and the regular cruisers, and belonging positively to neither, their value was limited in both directions.

The " state " of the fleet at four different dates during the period now under review is given below :—

RATES OR CLASSES.	Death of Queen Anne. Aug. 12th, 1714.		Death of George I. June 10th, 1727.		Peace. Dec. 31st, 1752.		Death of George II. Oct. 25th, 1760.	
	No.	Burthen Tons.	No.	Burthen Tons.	No.	Burthen Tons.	No.	Burthen Tons.
First-rates, 100 guns . . .	7	11,703	7	12,945	5	9,602	5	9,958
Second-rates, 84 to 90 guns .	13	19,323	13	20,125	13	21,250	13	22,825
Third-rates, 64 to 80 guns .	42	47,768	40	47,958	47	65,277	74	109,494
Fourth-rates, 50 [1] to 60 guns .	69	51,379	64	50,754	67	69,155	63	67,901
Ships of the line, or of 50 guns and upwards	131	130,173	124	131,782	132	165,284	155	210,177
Fifth-rates, 30 to 44 guns .	42	19,836	27	15,065	39	28,813	54	39,173
Sixth-rates, 10 [2] to 30 guns .	25	6,631	27	9,760	39	19,129	61	31,618
Sloops, 8 to 20 guns . . .	7	869	13	1,390	34	8,036	55	12,859
Bombs	4	597	2	417	4	1,104	14	4,117
Fireships	1	263	3	1,057	..	..	8	2,337
Busses	..	..	..	..	..	..	3	242
Storeships	1	516	1	546	1	678	2	1,554
Hospital ships.	..	..	1	532	..	..	3	2,791
Yachts	15	1,521	12	1,378	10	1,195	12	1,518
Hoys, lighters, transports .	13	1,009	14	1,216	23	2,037	33	2,761
Hulks	8	5,774	9	7,719	9	8,648	12	11,957
Ships under the line, or of less than 50 guns . . .	116	37,046	109	39,080	159	69,640	257	110,927
Total ships of all classes .	247	167,219	233	170,862	291	234,924	412	321,104

[1] The 50-gun ships were not counted as of the line-of-battle after about 1756.

[2] Most ships of under 20 guns were counted as sloops, *i.e.*, Commanders' commands, after about 1750.

The Seven Years' War (1756–1762) saw the introduction to the service of a class of vessel which, for nearly a hundred years afterwards, was of the highest value. This was the regular frigate, built to cruise at good speed, and carrying a reasonably heavy armament on one deck. There had previously been no vessels that thoroughly fulfilled this ideal. The forty-four, and even the forty-gun ships of an earlier date were cramped two-deckers ; and below them, until after 1745, there was nothing more formidable than the wretched twenty-gun ship, carrying nine-pounders as her heaviest weapons. Genuine frigates, mounting twenty-eight guns, began to be built about 1748 ; but still no larger gun than the nine-pounder found a place in them. The twelve-pounder thirty-two-gun frigate appeared at about the same time, the earliest examples being the *Adventure* (1741), and *Diana, Juno, Southampton*, and *Vestal* (1757). Then came the twelve-pounder thirty-six-gun frigates, the best British fighting cruisers of the days before the accession of George III. The first of these, the *Pallas* and the *Brilliant*, were built under the superintendence of Sir Thomas Slade in 1757. Yet even they were inferior to thirty-six-gun frigates which were in possession of the French at about the same time. In a table given hereafter, the student will find materials for comparing the British *Brilliant*, 36, of 1757 with the French *Aurore*, which was captured from her original owners in 1758, and added to the Royal Navy as the *Aurora*, 36.

THE *Terrible* 74. TAKEN FROM THE FRENCH, 1747.

(*From a drawing by John Charnock.*)

The first half of the eighteenth century witnessed repeated efforts to establish unvarying standards of size, tonnage, and armament for each of the classes of men-of-war then in most general use. At least two of these efforts—those of 1719 and of 1745—met with considerable success ; and the rules tentatively adopted in each of those years were for some time largely, though not exclusively, adhered to in the construction of ships. But it was probably discovered that to aim at rigorous uniformity was to check improvement ; and, after about the year 1755, all efforts in this direction were wisely relinquished. Seeing, however, that many vessels were built according to these successive " establishments," it may not be deemed improper to give here some particulars of them :—

	Date of Establishment	No. of guns	Three-deckers			Two-deckers							24	20
			100	98 and 90	80	74	70	64	60	53	44	40		
Established Dimensions	1719	Length on gundeck, ft. in.	174 0	164 0	158 0	..	151 0	..	144 0	134 0	..	124 0	..	106 0
		Length of keel for tonnage,[1] ft. in.	140 7	132 5	128 2	..	123 2	..	117 7	109 8	..	101 8	..	87 9
		Breadth, extreme, ft. in.	50 0	47 2	44 6	..	41 6	..	39 0	36 0	..	33 2	..	28 4
		Depth in hold, ft. in.	20 0	18 10	18 2	..	17 4	..	16 5	15 2	..	14 0	..	9 2
		Burthen in tons	1869	1566	1350	..	1128	..	951	755	..	594	..	374
	1733	Length on gundeck, ft. in.	174 0	166 0	158 0	..	151 0	..	144 0	134 0	124 0	..	..	106 0
		Length of keel for tonnage, ft. in.	140 7	134 1	127 8	..	122 0	..	116 4	108 3	100 3	..	..	85 8
		Breadth, extreme, ft. in.	50 0	47 9	45 5	..	43 5	..	41 5	38 6	35 8	..	..	30 6
		Depth in hold, ft. in.	20 6	19 6	18 7	..	17 9	..	16 11	15 9	14 6	..	..	9 5
		Burthen in tons	1869	1623	1400	..	1224	..	1068	853	678	..	..	429
	1741	Length on gundeck, ft. in.	175 0	168 0	161 0	..	154 0	..	147 0	140 0	126 0	..	..	112 0
		Length of keel for tonnage, ft. in.	142 4	137 0	130 10	..	125 5	..	119 9	113 9	102 6	..	..	91 6
		Breadth, extreme, ft. in.	50 0	48 0	46 0	..	44 0	..	42 0	40 0	36 0	..	..	32 0
		Depth in hold, ft. in.	21 0	20 2	19 4	..	18 11	..	18 1	17 2½	15 5½	..	..	11 0
		Burthen in tons	1892	1679	1472	..	1291	..	1123	968	706	..	..	498
	1745	Length on gundeck, ft. in.	178 0	170 0	165 0	..	160 0	..	150 0	144 0	133 0	..	113 0	
		Length of keel for tonnage, ft. in.	144 6½	138 4	134 10¼	..	131 4	..	123 0¼	117 8½	108 10	..	93 4	
		Breadth, extreme, ft. in.	51 0	48 6	47 0	..	45 0	..	42 8	41 0	37 6	..	32 0	
		Depth in hold, ft. in.	21 6	20 6	20 0	..	19 4	..	18 6	17 8	16 0	..	11 0	
		Burthen in tons	2000	1730	1585	..	1414	..	1191	1052	814	..	508	
Men	1719	Complement of men	780	680	520	..	440	..	365	280	..	190	..	130
	1733	,, ,, ,,	850	750	600	..	480	..	400	300	250	..	..	140
	1741	,, ,, ,,	850	750	600	..	480	..	400	300	250	..	..	140
	1745	,, ,, ,,	850	750	650	600	520	470	420	350	280	..	160	..
Arms	1745	Muskets, bayonets, cartridge-boxes	200	200	200	..	..	180	..	120	100	..	..	80
		Pairs of pistols	50	50	50	..	..	50	..	40	30	..	..	20
		Pole-axes (boarding-axes)	50	50	50	..	..	50	..	40	35	..	..	50
		Swords (cutlasses) with belts	200	200	200	..	..	200	..	140	120	..	..	80
		Hand grenades	200	200	200	..	..	180	..	100	100	..	..	100
Anchors	1719	Weight of bower anchors, cwts.	77	67·5	61·5	..	51·5	..	46·5	39·5	..	31·5	..	21
	1745	Weight of bower anchors, cwts.	81	73·5	69·5	69·5	58·7	..	53	49	40·5	..	29·5	
Cables	1719	Diameter of bower cables, in.	23	22	21	..	19·5	..	18·5	17·5	..	16	..	14
	1745	Diameter of bower cables, in.	24	23	22	22	21	..	20	19	17·5	..	15	

[1] In 1719 the method of determining the length of keel for tonnage, and the rule for computing tonnage, were settled by the Lords of the Admiralty as follows :—

" On a straight line with the lower part of the rabbit of the keel erect a perpendicular or square line to the upper edge of the wing transom, at the afterpart of the plank ; and, at the stern, to the forepart of the plank at $\frac{5}{8}$ths part of the height of the wing transom. The length between the said perpendiculars, added to $\frac{1}{24}$th of the extreme breadth (allowing for the stern and stern post without the rabbit), from which subtract $\frac{3}{5}$ths of the height of the wing transom for the rake abaft, and also $\frac{3}{5}$ths of tue main breadth for the rake afore, leaves the length of the keel for tonnage. Multiply this by the breadth, and the product by half the breadth, and divide by 94. The result gives the tonnage."

A simpler and more commonly-used method, both before and after the official adoption of the above highly-conventional formula, was : to multiply the length of the keel into the extreme breadth of the ship within-board, taken along the midship beam, and to multiply the product by the depth of the hold from the plank joining to the keelson upwards to the main deck ; and to divide the last product by 94. The result gave the burthen in tons. *See* Derrick ; ' Mems. of the Roy. Navy,' 301 ; Falconer, ' Dict. of the Marine ' ; Willett, in ' Archæologia,' ii. 154. The last erroneously says that the number to be divided by was 96.

The establishments of 1733 and 1741 were proposed, but never officially adopted. Many ships were nevertheless built in accordance with them.

The establishment of 1745 was generally adhered to for about ten years. There was never afterwards any regular establishment so far as dimensions were concerned.

The mode in which these and other vessels of the period were armed can be seen at a glance on reference to the tables on the following pages.

Although practically all the ships of the Navy were armed according to a regular "establishment" as thus indicated, many vessels were built upon lines which differed from any of the "establishments" for dimensions and tonnage ; and it is therefore well to give particulars of a few craft, both British built ships and prizes taken from the enemy and added to the service, which may be regarded either as typical specimens of the best home constructions of the time, or as models, the capture of which drew the attention of British constructors to points wherein foreign designers excelled them. These will be found on page 12.

The estimated cost of building and equipping a ship of each of the principal classes, and of storing her with eight months' boatswain's and carpenter's stores, according to the Navy Board Regulations, was, in 1719, 1733, and 1741 respectively :—

		1719			1733			1741		
RATE.	GUNS.	COST OF		Total Cost ready for Sea.	COST OF		Total Cost ready for Sea.	COST OF		Total Cost ready for Sea.
		Hull, Masts and Yards.	Rigging and Stores.		Hull, Masts and Yards.	Rigging and Stores.		Hull, Masts and Yards.	Rigging and Stores.	
		£	£	£	£	£	£	£	£	£
I	100	32,707	7,476	40,183	32,725	7,957	40,682	33,110	8,050	41,151
II	90	26,622	6,264	32,886	27,591	6,897	34,488	28,543	7,135	35,678
III	80	21,937	5,400	27,337	22,750	5,950	28,700	23,920	6,256	30,176
	70	17,202	4,512	21,714	18,666	5,202	23,868	19,687	5,488	25,175
IV	60	14,027	3,804	17,831	15,753	4,539	20,292	16,564	4,786	21,350
	50	10,192	3,020	13,212	11,753	3,625	15,140	13,064	4,117	17,185
V	40	6,355	2,356	8,731	7,254	2,881	10,135	7,554	3,003	10,557
VI	20	3,216	1,496	4,712	3,689	1,823	5,512	4,282	2,117	6,399

Many improvements which increased the material efficiency of the Royal Navy were made in the period 1714–1762. One of these was the invention of the reflecting quadrant, an invention usually associated with the name of Doctor Hadley, and introduced by him

PARTICULARS OF SERVICE GUNS (ESTABLISHMENT OF 1743).[1]

NATURE.[2]	Length.		Weight.	Calibre.	CHARGES.								Windage Allowance.
					Proof.		Service.		Saluting.		Scaling.		
	Ft.	In.	Cwt.	In.	Lb.	oz.	Lb.	oz.	Lb.	oz.	Lb.	oz.	In.
42-pounder	10	0	65	7·03	25	0	17	0	11	4	3	4	·35
32-pounder	9	6	55	6·43	21	8	14	0	9	4	2	12	·33
24-pounder (a)	9	6	50	5·84	18	0	11	0	7	0	2	0	·30
,, (b)	9	0	46	,,	,,		,,		,,		,,		,,
18-pounder (a)	9	6	42	5·3	15	0	9	0	6	0	1	8	·27
,, (b)	9	0	39	,,	,,		,,		,,		,,		,,
12-pounder (a)	9	6	36	4·64	12	0	6	0	4	12	1	0	·24
,, (b)	9	0	32	,,	,,		,,		,,		,,		,,
,, (c)	8	6	31	,,	,,		,,		,,		,,		,,
9-pounder (a)	9	0	28·5	4·22	9	0	4	8	4	0		12	·22
,, (b)	8	6	27	,,	,,		,,		,,		,,		,,
,, (c)	8	0	26	,,	,,		,,		,,		,,		,,
,, (d)	7	6	24	,,	,,		,,		,,		,,		,,
,, (e)	7	0	23	,,	,,		,,		,,		,,		,,
6-pounder (a)	9	0	24·5	3·67	6	0	3	0	3	0		8	·19
,, (b)	8	6	22	,,	,,		,,		,,		,,		,,
,, (c)	8	0	21	,,	,,		,,		,,		,,		,,
,, (d)	7	6	20	,,	,,		,,		,,		,,		,
,, (e)	7	0	19	,,	,,		,,		,,		,,		,,
,, (f)	6	6	17	,,	,,		,,		,,		,,		,,
4-pounder	..	..	..	3·22	4	0	2	0	2	0		6	·18
3-pounder	4	6	7	2·91	3	0	1	8	1	8		4	·14
½-pounder[3]	3	6	1·5	1·69		8		4		4		1	

[1] From Mountaine, 'Practical Sea-Gunner's Companion,' 1747.

[2] The reference letters in this column refer to the similar letters employed in the next table (Disposition of Guns).

[3] These were swivels, usually mounted on the bulwarks, etc., and sometimes referred to as patereroes.

DISPOSITION OF THE GUNS IN THE VARIOUS CLASSES OF H. M. SHIPS, 1716, 1743, 1757.

CLASSES OF SHIPS.	Date of Establishment.	Lower Deck.		Middle Deck.		Upper Deck.		Quarter Deck.		Forecastle.	
		No.	Prs.	No.	Prs.	No.	Prs.	No.	Prs.	No.	Prs.
100 guns.	1716	28	42 or 32	28	24	28	12	12	6	4	6
,, ,,	1743	28	42	28	24 (a)	28	12 (a)	12	6 (c)	4	6 (a)
,, ,,	1757	28	42	28	24	28	12	12	6	4	6
90 ,, (large class)	1757	28	32	30	18	30	12	..	..	2	9
,, ,, (ordinary class)	1716	26	32	26	18	26	9	10	6	2	6
,, ,, ,, ,,	1743	26	32	26	18 (a)	26	12 (b)	10	6 (a)	2	6 (c)
,, ,, ,, ,,	1757	26	32	26	18	26	12	10	6	2	6
80 ,, (large class)	1757	26	32	26	18	24	9	4	6	..	..
,, ,, (ordinary class)	1716	26	32	26	12	24	6	4	6	..	..
,, ,, ,, ,,	1743	26	32	26	18 (b)	24	9 (a)	4	6 (d)	..	..
,, ,, ,, ,,	1757	26	32	26	12	24	6	4	6	..	..
74 ,, (large class)	1757	28	32	..	..	30	24	12	9	4	9
,, ,, (ordinary class)	1757	28	32	..	..	28	18	14	9	4	9
70 ,,	1716	26	24	..	..	26	12	14	6	4	6
,, ,,	1757	28	32	..	..	28	18	12	9	2	9
64 ,,	1743	26	32	..	..	26	18 (b)	10	9 (d)	2	9 (b)
,, ,,	1757	26	24	..	..	26	12	10	6	2	6
60 ,, (large class)	1757	26	24	..	..	26	12	8	6	2	6
,, ,, (ordinary class)	1716	24	24	..	..	26	9	8	6	2	6
,, ,, ,, ,,	1757	26	24	..	..	26	12	6	6	2	6
,, ,, (small class)	1757	24	24	..	..	26	9	8	6	2	6
58 ,,	1743	24	24 (a)	..	..	24	12 (a)	8	6 (d)	2	6 (b)
50 ,, (large class)	1757	22	24	..	..	22	12	4	6	2	6

DISPOSITION OF THE GUNS, ETC.—*continued.*

Classes of Ships.	Date of Establishment.	Lower Deck.		Middle Deck.		Upper Deck.		Quarter Deck.		Forecastle.	
		No.	Prs.	No.	Prs.	No.	Prs.	No.	Prs.	No.	Prs.
50 guns (ordinary class) .	1716	22	18	..	..	22	9	4	6	2	6
„ „ „ „ .	1743	22	24 (*b*)	..	..	22	12 (*c*)	4	6 (*e*)	2	6 (*c*)
„ „ „ „ .	1757	22	18	..	..	22	9	4	6	2	6
44 „ (large class) . .	1757	20	18	..	..	22	9	..	..	2	6
„ „ (ordinary class) .	1743	20	18 (*b*)	..	..	20	9 (*c*)	4	6 (*f*)	..	..
„ „ „ „ .	1757	20	18	..	..	20	9	..	..	4	6
40 „	1716	20	12	..	..	20	6	..	..	..	..
36 „	1757	..	..	..	..	26	12	8	6	2	6
32 „	1757	..	..	..	..	26	12	4	6	2	6
30 „	1716	8	9	..	..	20	6	2	4	..	..
28 „	1757	..	..	..	..	24	9	4	3	..	..
24 „	1757	2	9 (*e*)	..	..	20	9 (*e*)	2	3	..	..
20 „	1716	..	..	..	..	20	6	..	..	..	..
„ „	1743	..	..	..	..	20	9	..	..	..	..
„ „	1757	..	..	..	..	20	9	..	..	..	
14 „ (ship-rigged) .	1757	..	..	..	..	14	6	..	..	..	..
12 „ „ .	1757	..	..	..	..	12	4	..	..	..	..
10 „ „ .	1757	..	..	..	..	10	4	..	..	..	..
8 „ „ .	1757	..	..	..	..	8	3	..	..	..	..

TYPICAL SHIPS OF WAR, 1714–1762.

Ship.	Guns.	Date of Launch	Length of Gun Deck.		Length of Keel.		Beam.		Depth.		Burthen in Tons.	Where, and by whom Built.
			ft.	in.	ft.	in.	ft.	in.	ft.	in.		
Royal Sovereign	100	1728	175	0	140	7	50	3½	20	1	1883	Chatham, J. Rosewell.
Royal George .	100	1756	178	0	143	5½	51	9½	21	6	2047	Woolwich, J. Pownall.
Barfleur . .	90	1716	163	0	131	9	47	3	18	6	1565	Deptford.
Blenheim . .	90	1761	176	1	142	3	49	1	21	0	1827	Woolwich, J. Pownall.
Cornwall . .	80	1726	158	0	128	2	44	6	18	2	1350	Deptford.
Princess Amelia	80	1757	165	0	133	0	47	3	20	0	1579	Woolwich, J. Pownall.
Invincible . .	74	*1747	171	3	139	0½	49	3	21	3	1793	*Taken from the French.
Terrible. . .	74	*1747	164	1	133	11	47	3	20	7½	1590	*Taken from the French.
Mars . . .	74	1759	165	6	134	4	46	3	19	9	1556	Woolwich, J. Pownall.
Princesa . .	70	*1740	165	1	130	3	49	8	22	3	1709	*Taken from the Spaniards.
Monmouth . .	70	1742	151	0	123	2	43	5	17	9	1225	Deptford.
Dorsetshire . .	70	1757	162	0	134	4⅜	44	10	19	8	1436	Portsmouth, E. Allen.
Captain. . .	64	1743	151	0	122	0	43	6	17	9	1230	Woolwich, J. Holland.
Plymouth . .	60	1722	144	7	118	0	39	0	16	5	954	Chatham.
Ripon . . .	60	1758	155	5	128	0	42	7	18	7	1242	Woolwich, J. Pownall.
Conquistador .	60	*1762	155	9	128	6	43	3	19	3	1278	*Taken from the Spaniards.
Oxford . . .	50	1727	134	6	109	10	36	3	15	2	767	Portsmouth.
Romney . . .	50	1752	146	0	120	8½	30	4½	17	2	1046	Woolwich, J. Harris.
Ludlow Castle .	44	1744	126	10⅝	103	8	36	3	15	5½	725	Thames.
Phœnix . . .	44	1759	140	9	116	10¾	37	1⅜	16	0	856	Thames, M. Batson.
Brilliant . .	36	1757	128	4	106	2⅝	35	8	12	4	718	Plymouth.
Aurora . . .	36	*1758	144	0	118	9	38	8½	15	2	946	*Taken from the French.
Juno . . .	32	1757	127	10	107	0⅛	34	3	11	10	667	Thames, Alexander.
Crescent. . .	32	*1758	130	5	107	6½	35	9	11	2	731	*Taken from the French.
Coventry . .	28	1757	118	4¾	97	0½	34	0⅞	10	6	599	Beaulieu, H. Adams.
Dolphin. . .	24	1751	113	0	93	4	32	1	11	0	511	Woolwich, Fellowes.
Gibraltar . .	20	1756	107	8½	88	0	30	4	9	8	430	Beaulieu, H. Adams.
Scorpion . .	14	1746	91	2	74	11½	26	4	12	0	276	Beaulieu.
Furnace, bomb.	14	1740	91	6	73	11¾	26	4	11	0	273	Thames.
Terror, bomb .	8	1759	91	6	74	1¾	27	8	12	1	301	Harwich, Barnard.
Princess Augusta	yt.	1710	73	8	57	7½	22	6¼	9	6	155	Deptford, J. Allen.
Royal Charlotte	yt.	1749	90	0	72	2½	24	7	11	0	232	Deptford, J. Holland.

about 1731.   But after Hadley's death, there was found among his
papers a document in the handwriting of Sir Isaac Newton, containing a drawing and description of an instrument somewhat
similar to Hadley's ; so that, apparently, the credit of the innovation should be divided between these men of science, if not given
altogether to the elder of them.

The efforts which had been made under Queen Anne to induce
inventors to turn their attention to the perfection of methods for
discovering the longitude at sea, were continued ; and in 1753 a new

HADLEY'S QUADRANT.

(From John Robertson's ' Elements of Navigation,' London, 1742.)

Act was passed in furtherance of the desired object.   In 1761 the
Board of Longitude decided to give official trial to the timekeepers
of Mr. Harrison, a watchmaker who had produced a clock or
chronometer of unusual accuracy ; and at the instance of the Board,
the Admiralty placed the *Deptford*, 50, Captain Dudley Digges, at
Mr. Harrison's disposal for the purpose.   The ship, with Harrison
on board, sailed from Portsmouth on November 18th ; and, both at
Madeira and at Jamaica, it was found that the timekeeper which
had been experimented with still showed the correct time.   From
Jamaica, Harrison returned to England in the *Merlin*, 14, Captain

Richard Carteret. On March 23rd, 1762, the *Merlin* fell in with the *Essex*, 64, Captain Alexander Schomberg, which had been off Scilly on the preceding evening. Her reckoning agreed exactly with that of the timekeeper; and on the 26th, when Harrison reached Portsmouth, he found that his instrument, in spite of much shaking owing to bad weather, had lost only 1 minute 54·5 seconds since it had left England more than four months earlier. This result marked a great advance upon anything that had been attained up to that time.

It was at about the same time that the experiment of coppering ships' bottoms to preserve them against the worm was first officially tried in the Navy. In 1761, the *Alarm*, 32, was so treated, but, although the effect was found to be satisfactory, the general introduction of the improvement was impeded for several years, owing to the galvanic action which was set up between the copper and the iron bolts of the vessel's hull, and to the evils which this action wrought. The difficulty was ultimately got over by using only copper fastenings in the under-water portion of ships' hulls; yet it was not until 1783 that this measure of precaution was ordered to be generally adopted, and, until then, copper sheathing, while applied to specimens of every class of ships, was very far from being universal in the service.

To encourage home manufactures, it was enacted in 1746 that every ship built in Great Britain or in the American colonies should, when first prepared for sea, be provided with a suit of sails made of cloth woven in Great Britain, under penalty of £50; and that every sailmaker in Great Britain or the plantations should, upon failing to place his name and address legibly and fully upon each new sail made by him, be fined £10.

After the burning of Rudyard's wooden tower in 1755, the lessees of the Eddystone Light, by the advice of the Royal Society, placed the work of constructing a new lighthouse in the hands of John Smeaton, F.R.S., a distinguished engineer. Smeaton built his tower entirely of stone, dovetailing every block into its neighbours, and so making the column practically solid. Operations were begun on August 5th, 1756; the first stone was formally laid on June 12th, 1757, and the last on August 24th, 1759; and a light from twenty-four candles, weighing five to two pounds,[1] was shown

---

[1] Smeaton invented a timepiece, which struck a single blow every half hour, and so warned the keepers to snuff these candles. The original now belongs to the Corporation of Trinity House.

from the rock on October 16th, 1759, and thenceforward every night until 1810, when the candles gave place to oil lamps and reflectors. Smeaton's tower, it is almost needless to add, remained effective until, in 1879–81, owing to the base on which it stood having been seriously shaken by the sea, a new tower, Douglass's, had to be built on a neighbouring rock. Part of Smeaton's tower was thereupon removed, and reconstructed on Plymouth Hoe.

Several other lighthouses which were in their day triumphs of engineering, were erected during the first half of the eighteenth century. One of the best known towers, that on the island of Skerries, near Holyhead, dates from 1730. At about the same time, also, lightships began to be placed round the coasts. The one first moored in English waters was fitted out in 1731 by Mr. Robert Hamblin for the Nore Sand, at the mouth of the Thames; the next, in 1736, by Mr. Daniel Avery for the Dudgeon Shoal, Norfolk.

Until 1730, every commander-in-chief, with the sanction of the Admiralty, issued his own code of instructions. In that year the volume of material provided by the accumulations of lapsed codes was in some measure digested; many additional instructions were set forth; the principles of naval usage were crystallised; and in 1731 there appeared the first issue of ' The King's Regulations and Admiralty Instructions.' This book has since been revised at intervals, but it remains in substance very much what it was in 1731, and most of the important alterations that have been made in it are merely such as have been necessary to bring it into conformity with modern ideas and modern conditions.[1]

In 1717, the rate of pilotage for pilots of Deal, Dover, and Thanet, taking charge of ships in the Thames and Medway, was fixed by Act of Parliament at ten shillings per foot of draught. The Act was subsequently amended with a view to prevent these pilots, who, of course, possessed exceptional opportunities for smuggling, from engaging in that pursuit. The repression of smuggling, indeed, was a burning question during the whole of the period now under review, and especially in war time. The smuggler, besides being a professional cheater of the revenue, was, of necessity, a man of lax patriotism and easy conscience, and one whose success depended upon his maintenance of good relations with both sides of the

---

[1] 'The King's Regulations and Admiralty Instructions' contain, as it were, the civil code of the Navy. The penal code is supplied by the Naval Discipline Act. *See* p. 17, *infra.*

Channel. He was, consequently, ever available as a spy. The frequency with which he impeded, and sometimes even confounded, the operations of the Navy, appears in the correspondence of several of the flag-officers of the time; and there is very little doubt that the many treacherous betrayals, which, in the reigns of the first two Georges, prevented the secret carrying out of naval plans and combinations, were, as often as not, attributed to grave Jacobite and French sympathisers, when they were really the work of persons owning no more serious political conviction than that he who paid duty was a fool. There are several pregnant references to this subject in the letters of Admiral Edward Vernon, who was in command in the Downs at the time of the young Pretender's descent in 1745. Advocating the more extensive recruiting of the Navy from the seaport towns, he writes of men who "are now thought to be principally employed in the ruin of their country by the smuggling trade, and as daily spies to give the enemy intelligence of our proceedings," and goes on to say :—

"I can't but think it a seasonable time to suggest to their Lordships that there are said to be in this town of Deal not less than two hundred able young men and seafaring people who are known to have no visible way of getting a living but by the infamous trade of smuggling, many keeping a horse and arms to be ready at all calls. At Dover, it is conjectured, there may be four hundred : at Ramsgate and Folkestone, three hundred each. And it is said that, within these three weeks, no less than nine cutters at a time have gone off from Folkestone to Boulogne; and it is conjectured that, from the town of Folkestone only, a thousand pounds a week is run over to Boulogne in the smuggling way. And, about six or seven days past, a Dover cutter landed goods in the night under the Castle, that was carried off by a party of sixty horse, and the cutter supposed to have done it came into Dover pier next day ; and, though most believed it was she, no one proceeded against them in any inquiry about it. This smuggling has converted those employed in it, first from honest, industrious fishermen, to lazy, drunken, and profligate smugglers, and now to dangerous spies on all our proceedings, for the enemy's daily information." [1]

And again :—

"Captain Scott, in the *Badger*, is just returned from his cruise off the coast of Sussex. On the 25th of last month he was informed of a cutter being going from Fairleigh to Boulogne that night; but she was gone over before he could get there. On the 3rd of this month, he got sight of the French dogger privateer, and chased him, and neared him as the other was edging down to get to leeward of him; and, when he got within shot of him, he exchanged some guns with him; but the other, getting afore the wind and hoisting her studding sails as the night was coming on, he soon lost sight of him. He has the repute there of being a confederate with the smugglers, and a convoy to them. I send you enclosed Captain Scott's day's work, when he seized two of the smugglers' boats, in which you have the names of the two reputed notorious

---

[1] Letter of November 13th, 1745. Letter Book in Author's Coll.

smugglers they belong to : which are George Harrison and Zebulon Morphet; and a copy of the Collector of Customs' certificate that they are reputed as such.   And a little before that, above a hundred horse had been upon the shore to carry off goods brought by another cutter ; and, by all accounts, they carry on as great an intercourse with the French now as they did in time of profound peace with them : by which they are undoubtedly their daily spies to inform them of all our proceedings.   I am informed there are lawyers who say, as the laws now stand, such an intercourse with his Majesty's enemies is now by our laws high treason ; and, if so, I should think we want a speedy proclamation to inform these infamous wretches that it is high treason ; and they shall be prosecuted as such ; for, surely, no nation but this would suffer itself to be daily betrayed with impunity."

While smuggling and smugglers' treachery at home engaged the attention of the authorities, piracy required, once more, their energetic interference in the West Indies ; and on September 5th, 1717, a proclamation was issued, offering a pardon for piracies committed before January 5th, 1717, to all such pirates as should surrender themselves within a twelvemonth.   After the expiration of that period of grace, a reward would be paid to any of his Majesty's officers, by sea or land, upon the legal conviction of a pirate taken by him.   The rewards promised were : for a captain (master) £100 ; for any officer from a lieutenant down to a gunner, £40 ; for any inferior officer, £30.   Any private seaman or other man who should deliver up a pirate captain (master) or " commodore," would, upon the offender's conviction, be entitled to £200.

In 1749, there was brought in " a Bill for amending, explaining, and reducing into one Act of Parliament, the laws relating to the Navy."   One of the results of this Bill, had it been passed in its original form, would have been to subject officers on half-pay to martial law.   The measure was, in consequence, strongly opposed and petitioned against.   The upshot was that the obnoxious clauses were deleted.   The Bill then passed ; all older laws for the government of the Navy were repealed ; and, in place of them, the first regular Articles of War [1] were established.   In the same year, another Act authorised the Admiralty for the first time to grant commissions to flag-officers, or officers commanding-in-chief, to assemble courts-martial in foreign parts.

The changes and alterations which more intimately affected the

[1] This was the Consolidation Act of George II. 22.   It was based upon the Act of 13 Car. II. c. 9.   Being found to be too stringent, it was amended in 19 Geo. III. In the amended form, it is the foundation of the existing Articles of War; which, in almost exactly their present guise, date from 1847.   The proper name of the measure is The Naval Discipline Act.   It receives small alterations and amendments from time to time.

personnel of the Royal Navy between 1714 and 1762, were numerous. The more important of those relating chiefly or exclusively to the seamen may be first noted.

In 1735 an Act[1] appropriated the forfeited Derwentwater estates to the completion and support of Greenwich Hospital, and extended the benefits of the Hospital so as to allow maimed merchant seamen to participate more fully in them. A little later two naval Acts were passed. One was for procuring a better supply of seamen to serve in the Navy; for permitting merchant vessels to be navigated by foreign seamen in a proportion not exceeding three-fourths of the crew; and for giving the right of naturalisation to such foreigners, after two years' service in British ships. The other was to prevent the impressment of seamen aged fifty and upwards, or aged less than eighteen; of foreigners serving in merchant vessels; of sea apprentices of under three years' service; and of all persons undergoing their first two years' service at sea.[2] In 1749, Mr. Henry Pelham brought in a Bill to revive the system of registering seamen; but, it being violently opposed, he withdrew it. In 1758, another Bill, brought in by Mr. George Grenville, though opposed in the Upper House, was ultimately carried. It provided in general for the encouragement of naval seamen, and, in particular, for the establishment of more regular and frequent payment of wages; and for enabling seamen to remit money for the support of their wives and families by means of tickets payable in cash on demand by any collector of customs or excise. An Act of 1747 authorised masters of merchant vessels to detain from the wages of their seamen sixpence a month, as a provision for the widows and children of men drowned.

On April 3rd, 1744, a royal declaration assigned to the officers and crews of men-of-war all property in prizes taken by them: and, to the officers and crews of privateers and letters of marque, such a proportion as might be conceded to them by the agreement of the owners. It also provided that shares not claimed within three years should go to Greenwich Hospital.

Bounties to seamen were several times offered. In 1734, the rate was 20*s.* for an able-bodied seaman, and 15*s.* for an able-bodied landsman. In 1740, it was 42*s.* for an able-bodied, and 30*s.* for an ordinary seaman. In 1742, it rose to 100*s.* for an able-bodied, and 60*s.* for an ordinary seaman; and it was further ordered that the

[1] 8 Geo. II. c. 29.   [2] 13 Geo. II. c. 3.

widows of such bounty men as should be killed on service were to be
granted a sum equivalent to a year's pay of their late husbands.   In
the same year, apparently to keep down rivalry, pay in the merchant
service was, for a time, restricted by Act of Parliament to a
maximum of 35s. a month.

The pay of officers remained as it had been at the conclusion of
the period 1660–1714; but the position of officers of nearly every
rank was improved in various ways.   Surgeons were, for the first
time, given half-pay in 1729; and, in 1749, an increased number,
both of surgeons and of masters, were granted half-pay.   The
number then entitled to it was, in each case, fifty, of whom the first
thirty received 2s. 6d., and the remaining twenty, 2s. a day.

The number of domestics and servants allowed to officers had been
considerably reduced at the end of the seventeenth, but was again
increased in the first half of the eighteenth century; and, in 1740, it
stood thus :—[1]

Admiral of the Fleet .	50, of whom 16 only to be borne as servants on the books.
Admiral	30, „ 12 „ „ „
Vice-Admiral . . .	20, „ 10 „ „ „
Rear-Admiral . . .	15, „ 10 „ „ „
Captain	4 per 100 of the complement.
Lieutenant, Master, Second Master, Purser, Surgeon, Chaplain and Cook, each	1, in ships having 60 men or above.
Boatswain, Gunner, Carpenter, each . .	2, in ships having 100 men or upwards, and 1 in ships having between 100 and 60.

This generous allowance of servants permitted captains to take to
sea with them young gentlemen who aspired to the position of
officer; and the better captains usually benefited the service by
having with them a large proportion of "servants" of that kind,
training under their own eyes.   Yet, even captains who were heartily
devoted to the interests of their profession, took with them to sea, in
those days, many retainers of a class that would, nowadays, be
deemed very superfluous in a man-of-war.   Tailors, barbers, footmen
and fiddlers, followed their patron.   As late as 1785, Commodore
Edward Thompson, who, it is true, always had his quarter-deck
crowded with such young gentlemen as were destined, a few years
later, to shine in the front ranks of the service, had a painter on
his personal staff, and used to summon the poor artist on deck at

---

[1] And so remained until April, 1794.

strange hours to record impressions of sunrise effects or nocturnal storms.

In 1718, it was, for the first time, formally ordered that captains should, if duly qualified, be promoted by seniority to flag-rank, and so onward to the rank of full admiral. But since, in those days, the entire flag establishment consisted only of nine officers, viz., an Admiral of the Fleet, an Admiral of the White, an Admiral of the Blue, and Vice and Rear-Admirals of the Red, White and Blue respectively, captains soon began to grow very old ere, in consequence of deaths above them, they became eligible for advancement. If, also, the order had been loyally carried out—which it was not—and had not been followed by other modifications, it would presently have resulted in a flag-list composed exclusively of officers too aged to go afloat. The threatened evil was fended off by the gradual increase of the flag-list in 1743 and subsequent years, and by the provision, in 1747, of arrangements in virtue of which senior captains, indisposed, or too infirm, to accept active flag-rank, might be superannuated as rear-admirals, with pay at the rate of 17s. 6d. a day. The first officers to be superannuated under this scheme were captains of 1713, or, to put it otherwise, captains of thirty-four years' service in that rank. Some of them were septuagenarians.

The establishment of a regular uniform for certain officers of the Royal Navy dates from 1748. Three years earlier, some officers appear to have petitioned the Admiralty for the boon ; and, in 1746, sundry captains, at Anson's wish, prepared tentative coats from which a uniform pattern might be selected. But, though a captain may have designed the uniforms which were finally adopted, King George II. himself decided upon the colours of them. Having noticed the Duchess of Bedford, wife of the First Lord, riding in the Park in a habit of blue, faced with white, his Majesty chose blue and white for the first uniform dress of his officers. The innovation applied only to admirals, captains, commanders, lieutenants, and midshipmen, and the wearing of the new uniform was made compulsory, as regards these ranks, by an order dated April 14th, 1748. But there were difficulties in the way of obedience. Patterns were not sent to foreign stations, nor were the regulations sufficiently explicit to enable officers, by their aid only, to instruct their tailors concerning what was required. It is therefore probable that, for several years, the order was not fully carried out.

Admiralty patterns of these uniforms were lodged at the Navy Office and the Dockyards, but they have not been preserved. A few coats, waistcoats, breeches and hats, for captains and lieutenants, were, however, found at Plymouth, in 1846, and are now in the Royal United Service Institution.

" The hats are three-cornered in shape ; one is trimmed with silver or tarnished gold lace ; and both bear the silk cockade instituted by George I. Lace and frills being then worn, there are no collars to the coats. They are made of thick blue cloth; the lappels, which button back, are blue; but the cuffs of the captain's coats are white, and the sleeves of all are purposely made short to allow the laced sleeves of the white kerseymere waistcoats to show beyond. There are two kinds of buttons, one flat, bearing a rose ; the other round and plain. Although we have not the patterns, pictures of the dress of the admirals and midshipmen have come down to us, the embroidery and lace on those of the flag officers being most elaborate." [1]

Some written advice, given by Edward Thompson,[2] in 1756, to a relative who was about to enter the Navy, throws light upon the condition of young gentlemen in the men-of-war of the time.

" Here," he says, " are no back doors through which you can make your escape, nor any humane bosoms to alleviate your feelings; at once you resign a good table for no table, and a good bed for your length and breadth; nay, it will be thought an indulgence, too, to let you sleep where day ne'er enters, and where fresh air only comes when forced." . . . " Your light for day and night is a small candle, which is often stuck at the side of your platter at meals, for want of a better convenience; your victuals are salt, and often bad ; and, if you vary the mode of dressing them, you must cook yourself. I would recommend you always to have tea and sugar; the rest you must trust to, for you'll scarce find room for any more than your chest and hammock, and the latter at times you must carry upon deck to defend you from small shot, unless you keep one of the sailors in fee with a little brandy (which is a good friend at sea, but always drink it mixed with water.") . . . " Low company is the bane of all young men; but in a man-of-war you have the collected filths of jails. Condemned criminals have the alternative of hanging, or entering on board. There's not a vice committed on shore but is practised here. The scenes of horror and infamy on board of a man-of-war are so many and so great that I think they must rather disgust a mind than allure it. I do not mean, by this advice, to have you appear a dull inactive being, that shudders amidst these horrors. No; I would wish you to see them in their own proper shapes, for, to be hated, they need to be seen." . . . " You will find some little outward appearance of religion—and Sunday prayers!—but the congregation is generally drove together by the boatswain (like sheep by the shepherd), who neither spares oaths nor blows." [3]

---

[1] 'The British Fleet,' 500. The first Admiral's uniform is well shown in the portrait of Lord Anson, forming the title-page to this volume. This was painted between 1748 and 1761.

[2] Died Commodore on the West Coast of Africa, January 17th, 1786. He edited some old writers; wrote plays, stories, and songs; and was a friend, and also probably a benefactor, of Dr. Samuel Johnson.

[3] 'Seaman's Letters,' i. 147.

Concerning subordinate officers, and the abuse of power by
superiors, Thompson wrote :—

" The disagreeable circumstances and situations attending a subaltern officer in the
Navy are so many, and so hard, that, had not the first men in the service passed the
dirty road to preferment to encourage the rest, they would renounce it to a man.   It is
a most mistaken notion that a youth will not be a good officer unless he stoops to the
most menial offices ; to be bedded worse than hogs, and eat less delicacies.   In short,
from having experienced such scenes of filth and infamy, such fatigues and hardships,
they are sufficient to disgust the stoutest and the bravest, for, alas! there is only a little
hope of promotion sprinkled in the cup to make a man swallow more than he digests
the rest of his life.   The state of inferior officers in his Majesty's service is a state of
vassalage, and a lieutenant's preferment the greatest in it ; the change is at once from
a filthy maggot to a shining butterfly.   Many methods might be introduced to make
the lower officers of more consequence on their duty, and their lives more agreeable to
themselves ; for that power of reducing them to sweep the decks, being lodged in the
breast of a captain, is often abused through passion or caprice ; besides, it is too
despotic an authority to exercise on a man who has the feelings of an Englishman.

" We are likewise to recollect that all commanders of men-of-war are not gentlemen, nor men of education.   I know a great part are brave men, but a much greater,
seamen.   I allow the maxim of learning to obey, before we command ourselves ; but
still there is no reason to be vulgar, for we are to consider these young people are the
active machines of duty, the wheels which give motion to the main body ; and it is
absolutely necessary to give them authority in their office to carry on the duties of the
ship : but rendering them low in the eyes of the people creates a contempt for
midshipmen in general, and turns that necessary respect due to them into contempt.

" I propose to warrant this body of officers, and make them answer to the Board of
Admiralty for their conduct.   They should possess a third table in the ship, and have
the countenance of their superiors.   This would enliven their servitude, and make
them of consequence on their duty." [1]

But some improvement was already to be noticed, for Thompson
continues :—

" The last war, a chaw of tobacco, a rattan, and a rope of oaths were sufficient
qualifications to constitute a lieutenant; but now, education and good manners are
the study of all; and so far from effeminacy, that I am of opinion the present race
of officers will as much eclipse the veterans of 1692 as the polite the vulgar." [2]

There was, however, as yet little improvement either in the code
of morals, or in the sanitary provisions on board his Majesty's ships.
There is evidence that, towards the end of the seventeenth century,
women were systematically carried to sea in the proportion of so
many per company of Marines ; and Thompson, writing in the
middle of the eighteenth, after describing the unsavoury persons
and dwellings of the negroes of Antigua, goes on :—

" But bad smells don't hurt the sailor's appetite, each man possessing a temporary
lady, whose pride is her constancy to the man she chooses ; and in this particular they

---

[1] ' Seaman's Letters,' i. 140.   [2] *Ib.* 144.

are strictly so. I have known 350 women sup and sleep on board [1] on a Sunday evening, and return at daybreak to their different plantations." [2]

As for sanitation, suffice it to say, by way of example, in addition to the many cases which will be cited in the two following chapters, that, in 1756, at the time of the outbreak of war with France, when she had been on no long cruise, and had been exposed only to the hardships of a few months of service in the Channel, the *Stirling Castle*, 64, Captain Samuel Cornish, arrived at Portsmouth with four hundred and eighty men, of whom two hundred and twenty-five were the pressed refuse of gaols and scum of streets. She was full of fever and other sickness, and, when the diseased had been sent ashore, but one hundred and sixty men remained for duty. Less than three months later, when, having filled up her complement in England, she had proceeded to New York, Edward Thompson wrote from her : " We have now one hundred and fifty-nine people ill in fluxes, scurvies, and fevers." Two months afterwards, ashore at English Harbour, Antigua, he added—

" I have been long declining with the white flux, and, for recovery, am stuffed into a small room with twenty-six people ; but am now in better health. I officiate as chaplain, and bury eight men in a morning. Fluxes and fevers are the reigning distemper, and both I attribute to the water drunk by the seamen, which is taken out of tanks or cisterns, built by Admiral Knowles. It is all rain water, and covered close up, which, for want of air, breeds poisonous animalculæ, and becomes foul and putrid. The melancholy effects it produces might be in a great manner prevented by boiling the water before it is issued, or ordering the people to do it. This would destroy the vermin, and correct the putrefaction. I am convinced from long observation that most of the distempers in southern climates arise from the water drunk, as ship sicknesses do from the bilge water ; which is evidently proved in leaky ships being always healthful. I therefore recommend to all officers, naval and mercantile, to let in salt water every day, and boil their fresh, for the good of themselves and cargoes."

---

[1] He speaks of H.M.S. *Stirling Castle*, 64, carrying 480 men.
[2] ' Seaman's Letters,' ii. 24.

CHAPTER XXVII.

MILITARY HISTORY OF THE ROYAL NAVY, 1714–1762.

MAJOR OPERATIONS.

Accession of George I.—Trouble with Sweden—Norris to the Baltic—Co-operation with Holland, Denmark, and Russia—A Swedish conspiracy—Byng to the Baltic in 1717—The Quadruple Alliance—Irritation of Spain—Byng to the Mediterranean in 1718—Spanish operations in Sicily—The battle off Cape Passaro—The British and Spanish accounts—Mahan's comments—War with Spain—Projected invasion of England—Dispersal of the Spanish fleet—The Ross-shire fiasco—Reduction of Sicily—Peace with Spain—Norris in the Baltic in 1718—Alliance with Sweden—Norris in the Baltic in 1719, 1720, and 1721—Peace between Russia and Sweden—The Treaty of Vienna—The Treaty of Hannover—Jennings to the coast of Spain—Wager to the Baltic—Hosier to the West Indies—Sickness in the fleet—Death of Hosier, Hopsonn, and St. Loe—Wager relieves Gibraltar—Norris in the Baltic—Death of George I.—The Treaty of Seville—Difficulties in the New World—Norris to Lisbon—Haddock to the Mediterranean—Spanish depredations—Jenkins's ears—Reprisals granted—War with Spain—Anson's expedition—Edward Vernon—Vernon to the West Indies—Capture of Puerto Bello—Enthusiasm in England—Co-operation between France and Spain—Vernon reinforced—France holds her hand—Vernon at Chagres—Vernon again reinforced—Death of Cathcart—Beauclerk and de Boisgeroult—Unsuccessful cruises of Haddock, Balchen, and Norris—Junction of the French and Spanish fleets in the Mediterranean—Vernon's difficulties with Wentworth—Attack upon Cartagena—Early success—Failure of the attempt—Attack on Santiago de Cuba—Abandonment of the plan—Criticism of the scheme—The commanders censured—Projected expedition against Panama—Collapse of the venture—Recall of Vernon and Wentworth—Lestock joins Haddock in the Mediterranean—Lestock's character—Mathews commander-in-chief in the Mediterranean—Friction between Mathews and Lestock—Blockade of Toulon—Martin at Naples—Martin to Alassio—Ogle in the West Indies—Repulse of the attack on La Guayra—Repulse at Puerto Cabello—France supports Spain—Norris in the Channel—Escape of de Roquefeuil—War with France and Spain—The Dutch join Great Britain—Disposition of the fleets—Navarro and de Court leave Toulon—Mathews's action off Toulon—Suspension and trial of Lestock—Trials of captains—The court-martial and the Lord Chief Justice—Trial of Mathews—Rowley in the Mediterranean—Gabaret escapes him—Hardy blockaded—Balchen relieves him—Loss of the *Victory*—Barnet in the East Indies—Davers at Jamaica—French intrigues in North America—Annapolis summoned in vain—Schemes of the Pretender—He lands in Scotland—His escape—Capture of Louisbourg—Townsend to the West Indies—Affairs in the Mediterranean—French failures in North America—Lestock on the coast of France—Peyton and La Bourdonnais—Fall of Madras—Duplicity of Dupleix—Lisle and de Conflans—Disgrace of Mitchell—Medley in the Mediterranean—French expedition to Cape Breton—Anson's action with de La Jonquière—Hawke defeats de L'Elenduère—Trial of Captain Fox—Exhaustion of France—Boscawen to the

East Indies—Failure at Pondicherry—Peace of Aix-la-Chapelle—Surrender of
Madras—Knowles takes Port Louis—Attempt on Santiago de Cuba—Knowles's
victory off Havana—Trial of Knowles—Pocock takes a French convoy—Losses
during the war—Terms of the peace—French aggressions—Keppel to North
America—French designs on Canada—Boscawen to North America—Capture of
the *Alcide* and *Lys*—Threatened invasion—French expedition to Minorca—
Operations against Angria—Success of Holmes—Reconnaissance of Brest—British
weakness in the Mediterranean—Byng ordered to Minorca—Byng's action with
de La Galissonnière—The dispatches—Byng superseded, tried, and executed—
Conclusions on his case—Fall of Minorca—Watson takes Calcutta—Fall of
Chandernagore—D'Aché to the East Indies—Forrest's action with de Kersaint—
Expedition to Louisbourg—Misfortunes of the fleet—The expedition abandoned—
Escape of du Revest—Expedition against Rochefort—Pocock's action off Cudda-
lore—Capitulation of Fort St. David—Pocock's action off Negapatam—With-
drawal of d'Aché—Kempenfelt relieves Madras—Siege and capture of Louisbourg
—Boscawen and du Chaffault—Marsh to West Africa—Keppel takes Goree—
Capture of the *Orphée* and *Foudroyant*—Hawke at Ile d'Aix—Howe's expedition
to the French coast—Capture of Cherbourg—Disaster at St. Cas—Renewed French
preparations—Pocock again engages d'Aché—The Dutch at Chinsura—Failure at
Martinique—Operations at Guadaloupe—The conquest of Canada—Saunders in
the St. Lawrence—Boscawen to the Mediterranean—Boscawen defeats de La Choe
—Rodney off Le Hâvre—Blockade of Brest—Hawke defeats de Conflans—
Blockade of Pondicherry—Hurricane in the East Indies—Fall of Pondicherry—
Norbury's action in the West Indies—French attempt against Quebec—Montreal
occupied—Elliot defeats Thurot—Boscawen and Hawke in Quiberon Bay—
Further operations in the East Indies—Keppel's expedition against Belleisle—The
Family Compact—War with Spain—Capture of Manila—Conquest of Martinique
—Conquest of Grenada and St. Lucia—Pocock reduces Havana—Misfortunes of
Pocock's fleet—De Terney at Newfoundland—Recapture of St. John's—The raid
on Buenos Ayres—Enforcement of the right of search—The Treaty of Fontaine-
bleau—Results of the Seven Years' War.

POPULAR MEDAL COMMEMORATIVE OF MATHEWS'S ACTION OFF TOULON,
FEBRUARY 11TH, 1744, AND OF THE FRUSTRATION OF THE
THREATENED INVASION OF ENGLAND AT ABOUT THE SAME TIME.

*(From an original kindly lent by H.S.H. Captain Prince Louis of
Battenberg, R.N.)*

ALTHOUGH, at
the accession
of George I.,
Great Britain
was at peace
with all the
world, the re-
lations of the
country with
certain north-
ern powers
were far from
being satisfac-
tory; and from
the first it was foreseen that difficulties were likely to arise, and
to call for the active employment of the Navy towards their solution.

Sweden had not yet allied herself with Russia, and was, in fact, still at war with her and with Denmark; and Swedish privateers had seized many British ships which were alleged to contain arms, ammunition, and stores, destined, in contravention of treaty, for the service of the Tsar. Remonstrances had been made by the British minister at Stockholm, but they had produced no results. The Dutch, who had similar causes of complaint against the government of Charles XII., found it equally difficult to obtain either redress or apology ; and it was therefore determined by Great Britain and Holland to despatch a combined fleet to the Baltic in 1715 to intimidate the Swedes, and to convoy, and prevent further undue interference with, the trade.

The British contingent, under Admiral Sir John Norris (B.) and Rear-Admiral Sir Thomas Hardy (B.), was made up of twenty ships of the line, besides a few small craft. It sailed from the Nore on May 18th, and, reaching the Sound on June 10th, there joined the Dutch contingent of twelve sail under Rear-Admiral Lucas de Veth. The merchantmen were escorted to their ports, but nothing of importance happened during the rest of the year. In 1716, Sir John, unwilling to adopt strong measures against Sweden unless he had the gravest reasons for doing so, sent an officer to Stockholm to inquire whether or not the practice of seizing British and Dutch ships was to be persisted in. A vague and ambiguous reply being returned, it was determined by the allied commanders, in pursuance of orders from home, to make a demonstration of an exceptional nature. A Danish squadron lay at Copenhagen. There also lay a Russian squadron under the Tsar Peter himself. After the necessary negotiations had taken place, it was agreed that, while the Dutch, then under Commodore Hendrik Grave, with five British men-of-war, should convoy to their destinations such merchantmen as had followed the fleets, the British, Russian, and Danish squadrons, forming for the moment a single fleet, should proceed up the Baltic, in order to let it be seen that, rather than permit any further meddling with her trade, Great Britain would take active part against Charles XII. The Tsar Peter became, for the nonce, commander-in-chief ; Norris assumed command of the van, and Count Gyldenlöve,[1] the Danish admiral, took the rear under his orders.

---

[1] Ulrich Christian Gyldenlöve, known in England as Count Gueldenlew, was a natural brother of King Frederick IV. of Denmark, and had commanded the Danish fleet at the time of Rooke's operations against Copenhagen in 1700.

The confederate fleet assembled in Kjöge Bay, and thence proceeded to Bornholm, where, learning that the Swedes had retired to Karlskrona, unwilling to hazard an action, the Tsar gave directions that the convoys might continue their voyages to their various ports. He then, with his squadron, sailed to the coast of Mecklenburg. Norris and Gyldenlöve took measures for collecting the homeward-bound trade, most of which joined them at Bornholm on November 9th, and with them entered the roadstead of Copenhagen on the day following. The remaining merchantmen, chiefly Dutch, anchored there on the 12th. Sir John Norris left behind him in the Baltic Captain William Cleveland, with seven ships, to act, if necessary, in concert with the Danes; and, with the rest of the fleet, he returned to England. On his voyage he met with terrible weather, and, although he succeeded in preserving his convoy, he had the misfortune to lose the *Auguste*, 60, and the *Garland*, 24.[1] The fleet arrived at the Nore on November 29th, 1716.

The ostensible reasons for this Baltic expedition have been given above. It must be borne in mind, however, that the situation, as between Great Britain and Sweden, was exacerbated by the fact that George I., besides being King of Great Britain, was Elector of Hannover. In his latter quality he had purchased from Denmark territories which had been conquered from Sweden; and, in order to defend these, he had declared war against Sweden, and carried on the conflict at a time when, in his quality of King of Great Britain, he was at peace with Charles XII. The Swedish monarch did not scruple to charge King George with having prostituted the honour of the British flag in order to serve the interests of Hannover; and, although it may be that Charles, in his natural resentment, failed to do exact justice to his opponent, it cannot be denied that the personal union of the crowns of Great Britain and Hannover, if not in 1715–16, at least on many subsequent occasions, led Great Britain into ventures which, had her own interests only been consulted, she would never have embarked upon.

The irritation of Sweden was increased by Norris's demonstration in the Baltic; and one of the results was that, soon afterwards,

---

[1] So say all historians, but no authority can be found for one part of the statement. The *Auguste*, Captain Robert Johnson, ran ashore, it is true, on November 10th, her captain and most of her people being saved. The *Garland*, however, remained in commission, under Captain Ellis Brand, until February 22nd, 1717; from which fact it may be concluded that, if she went ashore, she did not at once become a total loss. There seems, too, to have been no court-martial. MS. List in Author's Coll.

certain Swedish diplomatists, including the minister in London, associated themselves in plots, having for their object the further- ance of the cause of the Pretender.   The discovery of these intrigues aroused the liveliest indignation throughout Great Britain ; and when Parliament met in 1717, it was formally resolved by the House of Commons to introduce a Bill to authorise the King to prohibit commerce with Sweden " during such time as his Majesty shall think it necessary for the safety and peace of his kingdom."   On

SIR JOHN NORRIS, KT., ADMIRAL OF THE FLEET.
(*From the picture by Sir G. Kneller, by permission of H. C. Norris, Esq.*)

March 2nd, the Bill having in the meantime been passed, a proclamation in accordance with its provisions was made public. To properly enforce the prohibition, it was requisite to send another fleet to the Baltic ; and on March 30th, twenty-one ships of the line, with frigates and fireships, sailed for Copenhagen under Admiral Sir George Byng.   A few days later, though in face of strong opposition, the Government obtained a grant of a quarter of a million sterling to enable the King " to concert such measures with foreign princes and states as may prevent any charge and apprehension from the designs of Sweden for the future."

Byng agreed upon a plan of united action with Denmark, and made various dispositions to ensure the carrying out of the objects for which he had been sent to sea; but his proceedings were, upon the whole, uneventful, the Swedes not venturing outside their ports. Returning at the beginning of winter, he arrived in the mouth of the Thames on November 15th. A note of such small services as were performed by the cruisers of the fleet will be found in the next chapter. In the meantime, thanks largely to the good offices of France and Russia, the difficulties in the north were for the moment smoothed over, although, for many years afterwards, they remained a source of much anxiety and expense to the Court of St. James's.

"But this," says Campbell, " was not the only affair of consequence that employed the thoughts of the administration. We were then in close confederacy with the Emperor and France; and, in conjunction with these Powers, had undertaken to settle the affairs of Europe on a better foundation than the Treaty of Utrecht left them. With this view, the Triple Alliance was concluded on January 4th, 1717; and, that not answering the end expected from it, we next entered, as will be shown, into the famous Quadruple Alliance,[1] which was intended to remedy all these defects, and to fix the general tranquillity for ever. Yet, by unforeseen accidents to which human policy will be always liable, this alliance proved the cause of an immediate war between us and Spain, and, in its consequences, was the source of all the troubles that disturbed Europe from the time of its conclusion [2] to the peace of Aix-la-Chapelle."

The terms of the alliance were decided upon some months before the treaty was actually signed. It was determined that Spain should restore Sardinia to the Emperor, and that the King of Spain should renounce his claim to succeed to the French crown, while the Emperor was to renounce his claim to what had been guaranteed to Philip V. under the Treaty of Utrecht, and Philip was to surrender his claim to the Netherlands and to the Italian possessions of the Emperor. In return for Sicily, the Emperor was to hand over Sardinia to the King of Sicily, and was to recognise the right of the House of Savoy to succeed to the crown of Spain in the event of the failure of the heirs of Philip V. France and Great Britain undertook to assist the Emperor to acquire Sicily; and France and the Empire undertook to maintain the Protestant succession in Great Britain.[3]

[1] Of Great Britain, France, Holland, and the Empire.
[2] August, 1718.
[3] Koch & Schöll, 'Hist. des Traités de Paix.'

The arrangement was excessively displeasing to Spain; and no sooner had the House of Savoy transferred Sicily to the Emperor than Spain, whose policy was then controlled by Cardinal Alberoni, made preparations for attacking that island. Great Britain made corresponding preparations for enforcing the provisions of the still unsigned treaty, and, early in 1718, commissioned a large number of ships. The Spanish minister in London remonstrated. George I. rather bluntly replied that it was not his intention to conceal the object of his armaments, and that he purposed to send Sir George Byng to the Mediterranean with a powerful force " to maintain the neutrality of Italy against those who should seek to disturb it."

In March, 1718, Byng was accordingly appointed Commander-in-Chief in the Mediterranean; and on May 24th he received his written instructions. They were not as explicit as might have been wished; but they appear to have been explained and supplemented in the course of an interview which the Admiral, ere he left London, had with Lords Sunderland and Stanhope, and Mr. Secretary Craggs.[1] He was, upon his arrival upon his station, to inform the King of Spain, the Viceroy of Naples, and the Governor of Milan, that he had been sent to sea to promote all measures that might best contribute to the arrangement of such differences as had arisen between the two crowns, and to the prevention of any further violation of the neutrality of Italy, which he was to see preserved. He was also to enjoin both parties to abstain from acts of hostility, so that negotiations for peace might be begun and concluded. But, should the Spaniards persist, after all, in attacking the Emperor's territory in Italy; or should they land in any part of Italy for that purpose; or should they endeavour to make themselves masters of Italy (which would be a step towards the invasion of the kingdom of Naples), Byng was, to the best of his power, to hinder and obstruct them. If, however, they were already landed, he was to try by amicable means to induce them to abandon their project, and was to offer to help them to withdraw their troops; and, should all his friendly offices prove ineffectual, he was to defend the territories attacked, by keeping company with, or intercepting, Spanish ships and convoys, and, if necessary, by openly opposing them.

Sir George Byng sailed from Spithead on June 15th, 1718, with twenty ships of the line, two fireships, two bomb vessels, a store-

---

[1] *See* a letter from Craggs in Campbell, iv. 348.

ship, a hospital-ship, and two tenders, and, passing Lisbon, sent the *Rupert* in thither for intelligence. Being off Cadiz on June 30th, he despatched the *Superbe* with a letter to the British minister at Madrid, desiring him to inform the King of Spain of the presence of the British fleet, and of the instructions under which it was to act. The Spanish reply, returned after some delay, was curtly to the effect that Byng might execute his sovereign's orders. The

GEORGE BYNG, VISCOUNT TORRINGTON, ADMIRAL OF THE FLEET.

(From T. Houbraken's engraving after the portrait by Sir G. Kneller.)

minister, Colonel Stanhope, continued, almost up to the very outbreak of hostilities, to endeavour to induce Spain to give way; and in the meantime, foreseeing the probable futility of his efforts, he did his best to warn British merchants in the Spanish ports to take such measures as would protect their property against the results of any sudden rupture.

Sir George, who had to contend with unfavourable winds, did

not make Cape Spartel until July 8th. He was there rejoined by the *Rupert* and the *Superbe*, and learnt that Spain had been making great preparations for war, and that a considerable Spanish fleet had quitted Barcelona on June 18th for the eastward. Off Gibraltar, the Admiral was joined by a small division of ships under Vice-Admiral Charles Cornwall. The fleet subsequently watered at Malaga, and thence proceeded to Port Mahon, where it landed troops and took off the soldiers who had been in garrison there. It sailed again on July 25th, upon receipt of news that the Spanish fleet had been sighted on June 30th near Naples ; and on August 1st it anchored in the Bay of Naples. Sir George had previously taken care to apprise the imperial Viceroy, and the governor of Milan, of his arrival in the Mediterranean.

The Spaniards had not been idle. They had landed the Marques de Lede in Sicily ; and, except the citadel of Messina, the whole island had quickly fallen to him with little or no resistance. The citadel was held by Savoyards; and as Savoy, under the terms of the understanding, was presently to surrender Sicily to the Emperor, it could scarcely be expected that the fortress would hold out for long. In these circumstances, the imperial Viceroy of Naples hurriedly embarked two thousand German troops [1] on board the British ships, and requested Sir George Byng to endeavour to throw them into Messina citadel, and the neighbouring Fort Salvatore. The fleet quitted Naples on August 6th, and on August 9th arrived off the Faro of Messina.

The Spaniards were besieging the place which Byng desired to relieve ; but Sir George does not seem to have known how near their fleet was to him. Indeed, he had some reason to suppose that it was endeavouring to avoid him. Instead, therefore, of moving onwards to Messina and striking at once, he sent ashore the Captain of the Fleet, George Saunders, with a letter to the Marques de Lede, proposing a cessation for two months of the operations on shore, and adding that, unless a truce were agreed to, he would use all his force " to prevent further attempts to disturb " the dominions which his master stood engaged to defend. De Lede replied that he had no powers to treat, and that he intended to carry out his orders. Upon receiving this answer, Sir George weighed, with a view to place his fleet in front of Messina and to relieve the garrison of the citadel.

---

[1] These troops, under General Wetzel, were, before the battle off Cape Passaro, set ashore at Reggio.

The story of what followed is given in the formal relations which will be presently printed.

" The engagement which ensued can," says Mahan, " scarcely be called a battle, and, as is apt to happen in such affairs, when the parties are on the verge of war, but war has not actually been declared, there is some doubt as to how far the attack was morally justifiable on the part of the English. It seems pretty sure that Byng was determined beforehand to seize or destroy the Spanish fleet, and that as a military man he was justified by his orders. The Spanish officers had not made up their minds to any line of conduct; they were much inferior in numbers, and, as must always be the case, Alberoni's hastily revived navy had not within the same period reached nearly the efficiency of his army. The English approached threateningly near : one or more Spanish ships opened fire : whereupon the English, being to windward, stood down and made an end of them. A few only escaped. . . ."

The forces in face of one another were, as Captain Mahan indicates, as unequal in numbers as in discipline. Over leaf is a comparative statement of them. The ships of the British fleet are arranged according to Sir George Byng's order of battle, in which the *Canterbury* was to lead with the starboard, and the *Rochester* with the larboard tacks on board. The exact order of the Spaniards cannot be determined.

Sir George Byng, in his despatches,[1] thus describes the events of August 10th, and the following days :—

FROM ON BOARD THE *Barfleur*, OFF OF SYRACUSA,
August 6th (O.S.).

" Early in the morning, on the thirtieth of July,[2] as we were standing in for Messina, we saw two scouts of the Spanish fleet in the Faro, very near us ; and, at the same time, a felucca, coming off from the Calabrian shore, assured us they saw from the hills the Spanish fleet lying by. Upon which the Admiral stood through the Faro after the scouts, judging they would lead us to their fleet; which they did; for, before noon, we had a fair sight of all their ships as they were drawing into line-of-battle.

" On our approach, they went from us large, but in their order of battle, their fleet consisting of six and twenty men-of-war, great and small, two fireships, four bomb vessels, seven galleys, and several ships with stores and provisions.

" The Admiral ordered the *Kent, Superbe, Grafton,* and *Orford,* being the best sailers in the fleet, to make what sail they could to come up with the Spaniards; and that the ships which could get headmost, and nearest to them, should carry the lights usually worn by the Admiral,[3] that he might not lose sight of them in the night; while he made what sail he could, with the rest of the fleet, to keep up with them. It being little wind, the Spanish galleys towed their heaviest sailers all night.

" The thirty-first,[4] in the morning, as soon as it was day, they finding us pretty near up with their fleet, the galleys and smaller ships, with the fireships, bomb vessels,

---

[1] Sent home by his son, Pattee Byng. *Gazette,* No. 6673.

[2] *I.e.* August 10th, N.S.

[3] An Admiral commanding in chief carried three lights on the poop and one light in the main-top.

[4] *I.e.* August 11th, N.S.

BATTLE OFF CAPE PASSARO, AUGUST 11TH, 1718.

BRITISH FLEET.

Ref. No.	Ships.	Guns	Commanders.
1	*Canterbury*	60	Capt. George Walton.
2	*Argyle*	50	„ Coningsby Norbury (1).
3	*Dreadnought*	60	„ William Haddock.
4	*Burford*	70	„ Charles Vanbrugh.
5	*Shrewsbury*	80	V.-Ad. Charles Cornwall (W.). {Capt. John Balchen.
6	*Essex*	70	„ Richard Rowzier.
7	*Ripon*	60	„ Christopher O'Brien.
	Success, st. s.	..	„ Francis Knighton.
	Griffin, f.s.		
8	*Grafton*	70	„ Nicholas Haddock.
9	*Superbe*	60	„ Streynsham Master.
10	*Lenox*	70	„ Charles Strickland.
11	*Barfleur*	90	Admiral Sir George Byng. {Capt. George Saunders (1st). {Richard Lestock (2) (2nd).
12	*Breda*	70	„ Barrows Harris.
13	*Rupert*	60	„ Arthur Field.
14	*Orford*	70	„ Edward Falkingham (1). Com. Samuel Atkins.
	Garland, f.s.	..	
	Looe, hosp. s.		
	Basilisk, bomb.		
	A bomb tender.		
15	*Captain*	70	Capt. Archibald Hamilton (2).
16	*Dunkirk*	60	„ Francis Drake.
17	*Royal Oak*	70	„ Thomas Kempthorne. R.-Adm. George Delavall (B.).
18	*Dorsetshire*	80	Capt. John Furzer.
19	*Kent*	70	„ Thomas Mathews.
20	*Montagu*	60	„ Thomas Beverley.
21	*Charles*, galley	44	„ Philip Vanbrugh.
22	*Rochester*	50	„ Joseph Winder.
	Blast, bomb.		
	A bomb tender.		

SPANISH FLEET.

Ships.	Guns.	Commanders.	T., taken. B., burnt. E., esc ped.
Real San Felipe [1],[4]	74	V.-Ad. Don Antonio Castañeta.	T. by 9 and 19..
Principe de Asturias [1]	70	R.-Ad. Don Fernando Chacon.	T. by 12 and 15.
San Fernando [1]	60	R.-Ad. George Cammock.	E. to Malta.
San Carlos [1]	60	Principe de Chalay.	T. by 19.
Santa Isabela [1]	60	Don Andrea Reggio.	T. by 18.
San Pedro [1]	60	Don Antonio Arriago.	E..
Santa Rosa [1]	60	Don Antonio Gonzales.	T. by 14.
Perla [1]	54	Don Gabriel Alderete.	E. to Malta.
Volante [1]	44	Don Antonio Escudero.	T. by 13 and 20.
Juno [1]	36	Don Pedro Moyana.	T. by 6.
San Luis [2]	60	R.-Ad. Don B. de Guevara.	E. to Malta.
San Juan Bautista [2]	60	Don Francisco Guerrera.	E. to Malta.
Real [3]	60	R.-Ad. Marques de Marí.	T. by Walton's div.
(Unknown) [3]	54	......	B., after capture (?)
San Isidoro [3]	46	Don Manuel Villavicentia.	T. by Walton's div.
Esperança [3]	46	Don J. Delfino y Barlaude.	B. by Marí.
(Unknown) [3]	44	......	E., but B. and sunk at [Messina.
Hermione [3]	44	Don Rodrigo de Torres.	E.
Pore-épic [3]	44	A Frenchman.	T. by Walton's div.
Galera [3]	38	Don Michael de Sada.	E..
Sorpresa [3]	30	Don Francisco Alverera.	E..
Castilla [3]	30	Don Francisco Lenio.	E..
Conde de Toulouse [3]	30	Don J. Goccocea.	E., but T. at Messina.
Tigre [3]	26	M. Cavaigne.	T..
Aguila [3]	24	Don Lucas Masnata.	T. by Walton's div.
San Francisco d'Assis [3]	22	(A Scots ren-gade).	E..
San Fernando Me or [3]	20	......	E., but taken later.
San Juan Menor [3]	20	Don Ignacio Valevale.	E..
Flecha [3]	18	Don Juan Papagena.	E..
(A bomb) [3]	10	......	B. by Marí.
(A bomb) [3]	10	......	B. by Marí.
(A bomb) [3]	...	......	T. by Walton's div.
(A fireship) [3]	...	......	B. by Marí.
(An ordinance st. ship) [3]	...	......	T. by Walton's div.
(Three st. ships) [3]	...	......	B. by Walton's div.
(A settee) [3]	...	......	E. to Palermo.
(Seven galleys) [1]	...	Adm. Don F. de Grimao.	......

[1] The main body of the Spanish fleet.
[2] Had been detached to Malta. Rejoined during the action.
[3] Division of Rear-Admiral the Marques de Marí.
[4] The *Real San Felipe*, upon reaching Port Mahon, was unfortunately blown up by accident, with most of her people.

and storeships, separated from the admiral and bigger ships, and stood in for the shore : after whom the Admiral sent Captain Walton, in the *Canterbury,* with the *Argyle* and six ships more. As those ships were coming up with them, one of the Spaniards [1] fired a broadside at the *Argyle.* The Admiral, seeing those ships engaged with the Spanish, which were making towards the shore, sent orders to Captain Walton to rendezvous, after the action, at Syracusa (where the Viceroy for the King of Sicily was, with a garrison). The like orders he despatched to the flags, and to as many ships as were within his reach, that place being defended against the Spaniards, and being the most proper port on that coast for the fleet to gather together again.

"We held on our chase after the Spanish admiral, with three of his rear-admirals, and the biggest ships, which stayed by their flags till we came near them. The captains of the *Kent, Superbe, Grafton,* and *Orford,* having orders to make what sail they could to place themselves by the four headmost ships, were the first that came up with them. The Spaniards began, by firing their stern-chase[rs] at them : but they, having orders not to fire unless the Spanish ships repeated their firing, made no return at first. But, the Spaniards firing again, the *Orford* attacked the *Santa Rosa,* which, some time after, she took. The *St. Charles* [2] struck next without much opposition, and the *Kent* took possession of her. The *Grafton* attacked the *Prince of Asturias,* formerly called the *Cumberland,*[3] in which was Rear-Admiral Chacon : but, the *Breda* and *Captain* coming up, she left that ship for them to take, which they soon did; and stretched ahead after another sixty-gun ship, which was on her starboard while she was engaging the *Prince of Asturias,* and kept firing her stern-chase into the *Grafton.*

"About one o'clock, the *Kent* and *Superbe* engaged the Spanish admiral,[4] which, with two ships more, fired on them, and made a running fight until about three; when the *Kent,* bearing down upon her, and under her stern, gave her a broadside and went away to leeward of her. Then the *Superbe* put for it, and laid the Spanish Admiral on board, falling on her weather quarter : but the Spanish admiral shifting her helm and avoiding her, the *Superbe* ranged up under her lee quarter ; on which she struck to her. At the same time, the *Barfleur* being within shot of the said Spanish admiral astern, inclining on her weather quarter, one of their rear-admirals,[5] and another sixty-gun ship, which were to windward of the *Barfleur,* bore down and gave her their broadsides, and then clap'd upon a wind, standing in for the land. The Admiral, in the *Barfleur,* stood after them till it was almost night. But, it being little wind, and they galing from her out of reach, he left pursuing them, and stood away to the fleet again ; which he joined two hours after night. The *Essex* took the *Juno ;* the *Montagu* and *Rupert* took the *Volante.* Vice-Admiral Cornwall followed the *Grafton* to support her ; but, it being very little wind and the night coming on, the Spaniard galed away from the *Grafton.*

"Rear-Admiral Delavall, with the *Royal Oak,* chased two ships that went away more leewardly than the rest, (one of them said to be Rear-Admiral Cammock [6]) but we, not having seen them since, know not the success. The ship which suffered most, with us, was the *Grafton,* the captain of which, though he had not the fortune to take

---

[1] The *San Isidoro,* 46.   [2] *San Carlos.*

[3] The *Cumberland,* 80, Captain Richard Edwards (a), had been taken by the French in 1707. *See* Vol. II. p. 513. In Spanish hands she carried a lighter armament than she had been built for.

[4] *Real San Felipe.*   [5] Apparently the *San Luis.*

[6] George Cammock had been a post-captain in the Royal Navy until 1714, and had repeatedly distinguished himself. Owing to his Jacobite leanings, he had been dismissed the service, and had entered that of Spain. The Pretender afterwards appointed him Admiral of the White. He is said to have died in banishment at Ceuta. Charnock, iii. 221.

any particular ship, yet was engaged with several, behaved himself very much like an officer and a seaman, and bid fair for stopping the way of those four ships that he pursued ; who escaped, not through his fault, but failure of wind ; and his own sails and rigging were much shattered."

"FROM ON BOARD THE *Barfleur,* AT SEA,
August 7th (O.S.).

"Just now is returned one of the eight ships which the Admiral sent with Captain Walton to pursue those of Spain that went in with the shore, with a letter[1] from that Captain, dated the fifth instant, giving an account that he, with the said ships, had taken one Spanish rear-admiral of sixty guns, one man-of-war of four and fifty, one of forty,[2] which gave the *Argyle* the first broadside, one of four and twenty, one ship laden with arms, and one bomb-vessel ; and had burnt one man-of-war of four and fifty guns, two of forty each, one of thirty, one fireship, one bomb-vessel, and one settee.[3] At the writing of this letter, Captain Walton was making into Syracusa. The ship which brought this letter saw Rear-Admiral Delavall last night ; who had taken the *Isabela,* a ship of sixty guns, with which he was standing in likewise for Syracusa ; to which place we are now going ; and hope to get in there this night.

"When the Admiral has joined the ships absent from the fleet, and which we judge are now in Syracusa with their prizes, he designs to send Vice-Admiral Cornwall, in the *Argyle,* with seven or eight ships more, to carry the ships taken to Port Mahon, to be secured there till his Majesty's pleasure be known. He will also put ashore, in Sicily, the Spanish admirals and commanding officers, with as many of the common prisoners as will not be necessary to help navigate the ships taken."

What may be regarded as an official Spanish narrative of the battle, and of the circumstances which led up to it, was compiled by the Marques de Beretti-Landi, and published at the Hague. It is interesting, as well as fair, to append the following translation of part of it :—

"On August 9th, in the morning, the English fleet was discovered off the tower of Faro. Towards night it lay by, off Cape della Metelle, opposite the tower in question. The Spanish fleet was at the time in the Strait, but was without the detachment commanded by Rear-Admiral Don B. de Guevara, and some ships and frigates which had been sent to other places. As the intention of the English Admiral in thus approaching was unknown, the Spanish Admiral determined to quit the Strait, and to

---

[1] The letter here alluded to is the famous one which, erroneously, has so often been cited as a model of modest brevity and sailor-like conciseness. As given by Campbell, it runs : "Sir, we have taken and destroyed all the Spanish ships and vessels which were upon the coast, the number as per margin. I am, etc., G. WALTON." Even Mahan, following Campbell and Charnock, accepts this docked version of the letter as genuine, and comments upon its shortness ; yet, as a matter of fact, the real letter is one of some little length, and the above quotation forms only the first paragraph of it. Walton's blunt brevity is as mythical as certain well-known stories which are associated with Fontenoy and Waterloo.

[2] The *San Isidoro,* 46.

[3] Some of the vessels here said to have been burnt by Walton were undoubtedly in reality fired by Mari to save them from capture. It comes, however, almost to the same thing.

collect his forces off Cape Spartivento, taking with him his vessels laden with stores, his object being the better to prepare against the designs of the English, seeing that an officer who had been sent by Sir George Byng to the Marques de Lede had not returned. This officer had had orders to suggest to the Marques a suspension of hostilities for two months; but the Marques had replied that he could do nothing without directions from his Court. And although it was believed that a courier had been despatched with the suggestion to Madrid, the Spaniards were unwilling to risk a surprise from the English fleet, and a resort to such tactics as might be prompted by perfidy.

"On the morning of the 10th, the English fleet advanced further into the Faro, and was saluted by all the Spanish ships and vessels lying there. It is to be here noted that although Admiral Byng had convoyed to Reggio some transports having on board troops [1] of the Archduke, the officer who had been sent to the Marques de Lede declared that this was not for hostile purposes, but merely to secure from any insults the transports which were under his protection.

"The Spanish fleet sent out two light frigates to reconnoitre the English fleet; and although these perceived that the English, whose designs were not understood, made all possible sail to close with the Spaniards, whose Admiral was ignorant whether the English came as friends or as enemies, yet the Spaniards, who were two leagues from the strangers, decided to withdraw towards Cape Passaro under easy sail, in order that there might be no pretence that they anticipated hostilities. Soon afterwards a calm supervened, and thus the ships of both fleets fell among one another; whereupon the Spanish Admiral, witnessing the danger, caused his ships of the line to be towed away from the English with a view to collecting them in one body. Yet he did not permit the galleys to commit any unfriendly act, such as they might have committed with advantage while it remained calm. When the Marques de Mari was near the land and was separated from his consorts in the rear and from the frigates and transports of his division, the weather changed, so that he strove in vain to regain the main body of the Spanish fleet. But the English, with dissimulation, held on their way, trimming their sails so as to secure the wind, and to cut off the Marques de Mari's division. When they had at length succeeded in this, they attacked him with six ships, forcing him to separate from the rest of the fleet and to retire towards the shore. As long as it was possible, the Marques defended himself against seven ships of the line, and, when he was no longer able to resist, he saved his people by running his vessels aground. Some of them were burnt under his own direction: others were taken by the enemy.

"The rest of the English fleet, consisting of seventeen sail of the line, fell upon the *Real San Felipe, Principe de Asturias, San Fernando, San Carlos, Santa Isabela,* and *San Pedro,* and the frigates *Santa Rosa, Perla, Juno,* and *Volante,* which continued to make for Cape Passaro; and as, owing to their inferiority of force, they drew off in line, the English attacked their rearmost ship with four or five vessels, and cut her off. They did the same in succession with other ships, which, in spite of the fact that they made all the sail they could, were unable to avoid being captured. Thus, every Spanish vessel being separately fought by five, six, or seven of the enemy, the English finally subdued the *Real San Felipe,*[2] *Principe de Asturias, San Carlos, Santa Isabela, Santa Rosa, Volante,* and *Juno,* though each offered a bloody and determined resistance.

"While the *Real San Felipe* was engaged with the English, Rear-Admiral Don Balthazar de Guevara returned from Malta with two ships of the line, and, heading for the *Real San Felipe,* passed the English ships which were then alongside her, firing upon each. He then attacked such of Admiral Byng's vessels as followed the *Real*

---

[1] Under General Wetzel.

[2] Admiral Castañeta subsequently died of his wounds at Port Mahon.

San Felipe. These, being very much damaged, drew off in the night, and, after the action, remained fifty leagues at sea for three or four days, not only to repair the Spanish ships which they had captured, and which were most severely mauled, but also to make good their own damages. Admiral Byng, therefore, could not enter Syracuse until August 16th or 17th, and then only with much difficulty." [1]

After giving some account of the services of individual ships and captains, the account continues :—

" Such is the story of the action off Abola, or the Gulf of l'Ariga, in the Malta Channel, between the Spanish and English fleets. The English ships, thanks to ill faith and superior strength, were able to beat the Spanish vessels singly, one by one : but it may be conceived, judging from the defence made by the latter, that, had they acted in unison, the battle might have ended more advantageously for them.

" Immediately after the action, a captain of the English fleet, on behalf of Admiral Byng, arrived to make a complimentary excuse to the Marques de Lede, and to assure him that the Spaniards had been the aggressors, and that the battle ought not to be considered to constitute a rupture, seeing that the English did not take it as doing so. But it was replied that Spain, on the contrary, must hold it to constitute a formal rupture ; and that the Spaniards would do the English all possible damage and ill, by ordering the commencement of reprisals. In pursuance of this, several Spanish vessels, and Don Guevara's division, have already seized certain English ships." [2]

" It is difficult," comments Mahan, " to understand the importance attached by some writers to Byng's action at this time in attacking without regard to the line-of-battle. He had before him a disorderly force, much inferior both in numbers and discipline. His merit seems to lie rather in the readiness to assume a responsibility from which a more scrupulous man might have shrunk ; but in this, and throughout the campaign, he rendered good service to England, whose sea power was again strengthened by the destruction not of an actual but a possible rival; and his services were rewarded by a peerage." [3]

It will be well to conclude the history of the major operations of the Spanish War ere turning to the work done in the meantime by British fleets in the Baltic, where a state of unrest continued for several years.

Sir George Byng, after having taken measures to enable the imperial troops to attack the Spaniards in Sicily, and to gradually make themselves masters of the island, proceeded to Malta, and brought away some Sicilian galleys, which, under the Marchese de Rivarole, had been blockaded there by Rear-Admiral Cammock. He returned to Naples on November 2nd. In the interval, Rear-Admiral Guevara, as related in the narrative of the Marques de Beretti-Landi, entered Cadiz, and seized all the English ships there, while

---

[1] There are, of course, discrepancies between the Spanish and the British accounts as here given; but, upon the whole, the two agree unusually well.

[2] For the translation, I am indebted to Dr. Henry Lopes.

[3] Not, however, until September 9th, 1721, when he was made Baron Byng of Southill, and Viscount Torrington.

British merchants and their effects were laid hands upon in Malaga and other ports of Spain. Reprisals followed immediately, yet war was not formally declared until December 17th, 1718.

Spain, though weak, was exasperated and obdurate, and was even more unwilling than at first to accept the terms dictated to her by the Quadruple Alliance. She therefore collected a considerable armament at Cadiz and Corunna, and boldly projected an invasion of the west of England by troops to be led by James Butler, the attainted Duke of Ormonde. A fleet, under Admiral of the Fleet James, Earl of Berkeley,[1] and Admiral Sir John Norris, was fitted out, and cruised in the Channel in April; and troops were concentrated, especially in the west country and in Ireland; but, long

MEDAL COMMEMORATIVE OF BYNG'S VICTORY OFF CAPE PASSARO.
(From an original kindly lent by H.S.H. Captain Prince Louis of Battenberg, R.N.)

ere these preparations had been completed, the Spanish expedition had been dispersed by a violent and long-continued storm, and the scheme had been rendered abortive. Three frigates and five transports, however, conveying, among others, the Earls of Marischal and Seaforth, and the Marquis of Tullibardine, persisted in their design, and, pushing on to the coast of Ross-shire, there landed about four hundred men. These were joined by fifteen or sixteen hundred Jacobite Scots; but they had no success. Their depôt at Donan Castle was taken and destroyed by the *Worcester*, *Enterprise*, and *Flamborough*, and they themselves were soon afterwards defeated

[1] So appointed on March 21st, 1719. He was then also Vice-Admiral of Great Britain and First Lord of the Admiralty, and he hoisted his flag with no fewer than three captains under him, viz., Vice-Admiral James Littleton (1st); Captain Francis Hosier (2nd, or Captain of the Fleet); and the captain of the flagship.

at Glenshiel, whereupon the Spanish auxiliaries surrendered at discretion.

Sir George Byng sailed from Port Mahon for Naples early in the spring of 1719, and, thenceforward, co-operated with the Imperialists in the complete reduction of Sicily. In August, when that reduction was nearly accomplished, a dispute arose between the Admiral and the allies as to the disposal of the Spanish ships that still lay in the ports of the island. As a settlement of the question, so far as it concerned the ships at Messina, Sir George proposed to General Count de Merci, the Imperialist commander, that a battery should be erected, and that the vessels should be destroyed at their anchors. De Merci pleaded lack of orders; but Byng, insisting that no commander needed specific instructions to destroy the property of an enemy, gained his point, in spite of the opposition of the Savoyards; and most of the ships were duly bombarded and burnt or sunk. The citadel of Messina, and the remaining vessels, were handed over to the Imperialists by capitulation on October 7th, 1719. The Spanish troops in the island were not permitted to evacuate it, and were kept, by the fleet on the one hand, and by the Imperialists on the other, in much discomfort; and this fact, combined with the persuasive force of an expedition which was fitted out against Vigo under Vice-Admiral Mighells and Viscount Cobham, and which will be described in the next chapter, at length induced the King of Spain to agree with the Quadruple Alliance. A cessation of arms resulted in February, 1720; and, soon afterwards, both Sicily and Sardinia were evacuated under the terms of a convention, the former going to the Empire, and the latter to Savoy.[1] Thus the objects for which Great Britain had entered into the war were attained. The wisdom of British interference is a matter which it is unnecessary here to discuss.

The difficulties with Sweden, suspended for the moment in 1717, again became acute in 1718, and led to the dispatch of Admiral Sir John Norris once more to the Baltic. He sailed from the mouth of the Thames on April 28th, and from Solebay on May 1st, with a squadron composed of ten sail of the line,[2] a bomb ketch, and a

[1] Authorities for the War of the Quadruple Alliance : 'Account of the Exped. of the Brit. Fleet to Sicily'; 'Annals of K. George IV.'; 'Historical Register'; 'Corps Univ. Diplomatique,' viii. pt. I.; Chandler's 'Debates,' v. and vi.; 'Merc. Hist. et Pol.' xliv. and xlv.; 'Mém. pour servir à l'Hist. de l'Espagne,' iii.; Letters of Earl Stanhope, Alberoni, Beretti-Landi, etc.; *London Gazette.*

[2] *Cumberland,* 80, (flag), Captain William Faulknor; *Buckingham,* 70, Captain

fireship, with Rear-Admiral James Mighells as second in command, and with a number of merchantmen in convoy. Upon his arrival off Copenhagen, he was joined by a Danish squadron, with which he cruised to the northward ; but as the Swedes, upon his approach, shut themselves up in their ports, no naval action resulted.   Sweden was, however, by no means intimidated by the action of the Allies. She made peace with the Tsar ; and, having thus freed herself from anxiety in one direction, turned with renewed energy to prosecute the land war with Denmark, whose territories she invaded with two considerable armies.   In this campaign, although it was upon the whole successful, Sweden suffered the loss of her brave but quixotic king.   Charles XII. was killed by a cannon ball at the siege of Frederikshald on December 11th, 1718.   Sir John Norris, with the fleet, had returned to England in the month of October.

After the death of Charles XII. and the accession of Queen Ulrica Eleanora [1] the policy of Sweden changed.   She entered upon very friendly relations with Great Britain, and, on the other hand, was attacked by her late ally and Great Britain's old friend, Peter the Great.   The Russians ravaged the Swedish coasts until, a fresh British fleet having been entrusted to the command of Sir John Norris in June, and having joined the Swedish fleet in September, 1719, the enemy was obliged to take refuge in the harbour of Reval. A little later, the old quarrel between Sweden and Denmark was settled by British mediation : [2] but when Norris, in order to avoid being frozen up there, left the Baltic in November, Sweden and Russia remained unreconciled, in spite of the efforts which had been made by Lord Carteret—afterwards Earl Granville—the British minister at Stockholm, to pacify them.

In 1720 Russia's attitude continued as before, and Sir John Norris went back to the Baltic to protect Sweden during the open weather.   He sailed on April 16th ; was joined in May by a Swedish squadron under Admiral Baron Wachtmeister ; and, after cruising off

---

Tudor Trevor ; *Hampton Court,* 70, Captain Robert Coleman ; *Prince Frederick,* 70, Captain Covill Mayne ; *Salisbury,* 50, Captain John Cockburne (1) ; *Defiance,* 60, Captain Joseph Soanes ; *Winchester,* 50, Captain James Campbell (1) ; *Guernsey,* 50, Captain Charles Hardy (1) ; and *Windsor,* 60, Captain Francis Piercy. These were afterwards joined by a few other vessels.

Whose consort, Friedrich of Hessen-Cassel, was presently chosen king, to the great annoyance of Russia.

[2] Though the formal treaty of peace was not signed until the summer of 1720.

Reval, returned to England in November.[1] In 1721, Sir John was
employed in the same way, his mission being, however, not only to
protect Sweden, but also to lend moral support to the mediatory
efforts of the British minister at Stockholm. He sailed from the
Nore on April 13th with a fleet of twenty-one ships of the line, two
fireships, three bombs, and two tenders, and with Rear-Admiral
Francis Hosier (W.), and Rear-Admiral Edward Hopsonn (B.), in
command under him. His appearance in the Baltic undoubtedly
favoured the conclusion of peace between the belligerents : and on
September 10th hostilities between Sweden and Russia were
formally terminated by the Treaty of Nystadt. Sir John dropped
anchor at the Nore on October 20th. During these various expeditions to the north he seldom had occasion to fire a gun in anger,
and his proceedings were throughout of an uneventful and un-
exciting character ; yet, thanks to his tact, patience, and diplomatic
ability, and to the recognised strength and efficiency of the forces
under him, he was able to exercise a very weighty influence upon
the councils of the northern powers, and to peaceably bring about
results which a less capable officer might have failed to secure even
by fighting for them.

From 1721 onwards, for four or five years, the Navy had no
great tasks assigned to it ; but the Treaty of Vienna, concluded on
April 20th, 1725, between Spain and Austria, introduced new
sources of trouble to Europe. By a secret article of that treaty,
marriages between the houses of Spain and Austria were arranged,
and both countries pledged themselves to assist the restoration of
the Stuarts, and to compel, if necessary by force, the retrocession of
Gibraltar and Minorca to Spain. To oppose these schemes, Great
Britain, France, and Prussia entered, on September 3rd, 1725, into
the Treaty of Hannover ; whereupon, Spain began to intrigue with
Russia ; and, as the Empress Catherine, the successor of Peter the
Great, was by no means amicably disposed towards Great Britain
and her allies, it became advisable, in 1726, not only to send a fleet
to the coast of Spain, but also to dispatch once more a strong force
to the Baltic. In addition to these fleets a squadron was got ready
for the West Indies.

The fleet destined to check the immediate designs of Spain was
entrusted to Admiral Sir John Jennings (W.), who was afterwards

---

[1] In a storm in the North Sea, the *Monck*, 50, Captain the Hon. George Clinton,
was driven ashore near Golston on Nov. 24th, and lost ; but all her people were saved.

joined by Rear-Admiral Edward Hopsonn (R.). Sir John, with nine ships of the line, sailed from St. Helen's on July 20th. The appearance of the British so much disquieted the Spaniards that, for the moment, they abandoned their hostile projects : and in October, Jennings was able to return to England, leaving Hopsonn, with a reduced squadron, as commander-in-chief in the Mediterranean.

The Baltic fleet, under Vice-Admiral Sir Charles Wager (R.) and Rear-Admiral Sir George Walton (B.), consisted of twenty ships of the line, a twenty-gun ship, two fireships, and a hospital ship. It quitted the Nore on April 17th, and, proceeding to Copenhagen and Stockholm, obtained the co-operation of Denmark and the friendly support of Sweden. A Danish squadron, under Rear-Admiral Bille, joined Sir Charles in May, and, with him, proceeded to the Gulf of Finland. The Russians had, in and about Cronstadt, a considerable force under the General-Admiral Apraxine, Vice-Admiral Thomas Gordon,[1] and a rear-admiral said to have been an Englishman : [2] but, although they were much inclined to issue forth and defy the allies, Gordon succeeded in dissuading them from this suicidal course ; and eventually the ships were laid up. Wager displayed throughout great tact and diplomatic ability. In the autumn he, like Jennings, returned to England, anchoring off the Gunfleet on November 1st.

Vice-Admiral Francis Hosier [3] (B.) was given command of the squadron for the West Indies. He sailed from Plymouth on April 9th with seven men-of-war, and, after a tedious passage, arrived off the Bastimentos, near Puerto Bello, on June 6th. He was then or thereafter joined by several vessels which were already on the station, and by others from home. These brought up his total force to a strength of sixteen ships.[4]

[1] Thomas Gordon, a captain of 1705, severed his connection with the British Navy at the death of Queen Anne, and entered that of Russia, in which he was at once given flag-rank. Other Jacobite naval officers, notably the gallant Kenneth, Lord Duffus, took the same service at about the same time.

[2] Some authorities specify him as Rear-Admiral Saunders, an ex-Master and Commander in the British Navy.

[3] Francis Hosier. Commander, 1694. Captain, 1696. Distinguished himself as captain of the *Salisbury*, 1707–1713. Rear-Admiral, 1720. Second in command in the Baltic. Vice-Admiral, 1723. Died Commander-in-Chief in the West Indies, August 23rd, 1727.

[4] *Viz.*, three third-rates, the *Breda, Berwick*, and *Lenox* ; eight fourth-rates, the *Ripon, Leopard, Superbe, Nottingham, Dunkirk, Dragon, Tiger*, and *Portland* ; one fifth-rate, the *Diamond* ; and three sixth-rates, the *Greyhound, Winchelsea*, and *Happy*.

The appearance of the British fleet in the West Indies gave great uneasiness to the Spaniards; and, as soon as it was reported, the treasure-ships, which were then ready to make their voyage to Europe, were unloaded, and their cargo of pieces of eight and other valuables was placed on shore in security, part at Havana and part elsewhere.   The men-of-war which were to have convoyed the treasure-ships were, moreover, laid up at Puerto Bello; and it was determined that, so long as a powerful British force remained in the neighbourhood, no attempt should be made to dispatch the annual flota to Spain; although, of course, the non-arrival of the usual supplies would inevitably put the mother country to immense inconvenience.

The governor of Puerto Bello sent a civil message to the Vice-Admiral desiring to know the reason for the unexpected visit.   The real reason was that the galleons might be watched: but as there lay in Puerto Bello at the time a South Sea Company's ship, the *Royal George*, and as this vessel would probably have been detained if Hosier had at once proclaimed the nature of his mission, the reply returned was to the effect that the fleet had come to convoy the *Royal George*.   The governor thereupon took measures to facilitate the early departure of that ship; and, when she had joined the fleet, he politely requested the Vice-Admiral, seeing that the ostensible reason for the presence of the force had ceased to exist, to withdraw from off the port.   But Hosier then answered that, pending the receipt of further orders, he purposed to remain where he was; and, that his intentions might no longer be in doubt, he stationed a ship of the line within gun-shot of the castle, and suffered no vessel to enter or leave the port without being strictly examined.   He maintained this blockade for six months, his ships in the meanwhile becoming daily more and more distressed by the ravages of epidemic and other diseases; and when, on December 14th, 1726, he proceeded to Jamaica, his command was so completely enfeebled that he had the greatest difficulty in navigating it into harbour.

The Vice-Admiral refreshed his people and, to the best of his ability, made up his weakened complements to their full strength; and in February, 1727, he stood over to Cartagena, where some galleons then lay.   Until August he cruised upon his station; but his instructions were of a nature which prevented him from being of much use to his country.   They authorised him to make reprisals subject to certain restrictions, but not to make war; and although the Spaniards, after a time, began to seize the property of British merchants and to detain and condemn British vessels, Hosier was obliged to content himself with demanding a restitution which the Spaniards refused, and which he was unable to compel.   During that period disease was even more rife throughout the fleet than it had been in the previous year; and, after thousands of officers and men had perished miserably, the misfortunes of the expedition culminated on August 23rd, when Hosier himself died.[1]

His death has been attributed to anxiety and chagrin, but it was, in fact, caused by fever.   Nor is it astonishing that the fleet was then little better than a floating charnel-house.   The most elementary prescriptions of sanitary science seem to have been neglected, and there is perhaps no better illustration of the extraordinary indifference to the simplest laws of health than the fact that in that hot and pestilent climate the Vice-Admiral's body was given a temporary burial-place in the ballast of his flagship, the *Breda*, where it remained, a necessary source of danger to all on board, until it was despatched to England, late in the year, on board H.M. snow *Happy*, Commander Henry Fowkes.   Hosier's death left Captain Edward St. Loe,[2] of the *Superbe*, 60, as senior officer on the station.

St. Loe pursued the same policy as Hosier had followed, and prevented the sailing of the galleons, until he was superseded by Vice-Admiral Edward Hopsonn, who arrived at Jamaica on January 29th, 1728.   Hopsonn died of fever on board his flagship the *Leopard*, 50, on May 8th, leaving St. Loe once more senior officer.   But by that time the difficulties with Spain were in a fair way of adjustment. It was still, however, necessary to keep a large force in the West Indies; and ere it was materially reduced, St. Loe also fell a sacrifice to the climate and to the insanitary condition of the ships. He died on April 22nd, 1729.[3]

It is doubtful whether any other British fleet has ever suffered from disease so severely as that of Hosier suffered in 1726–27.   Its horrible experiences made a deep and lasting impression upon the nation,[4] and it may be hoped that they have had the effect of

---

[1] Hosier had been promoted on August 11th to be Vice-Admiral of the White.   At the time of his death, a commission empowering the Governor of Jamaica to knight him is said to have been on its way out.   Charnock, iii. 139.

[2] St. Loe flew a broad pennant.

[3] Having been promoted on March 4th, 1729, to be Rear-Admiral of the Blue.

[4] *See*, for example, Glover's popular ballad, ' Admiral Hosier's Ghost.'

impressing upon all later British admirals the supreme importance
of taking systematic and rigorous measures for preserving the health
of their men.   During the two years immediately following Hosier's
first arrival off the Bastimentos, the fleet, the nominal complement
of which never, roughly speaking, exceeded 4750 persons,[1] lost, in
addition to two flag officers and seven or eight captains, about fifty
lieutenants, and four thousand subordinate officers and men, by
various forms of sickness.

The attitude of Great Britain with regard to the galleons provoked Spain to make great preparations for a siege of Gibraltar ;
and as that fortress was neither thoroughly armed nor properly
held, corresponding measures had to be taken for its protection.
A squadron of six men-of-war and two sloops [2] was fitted out at
Portsmouth towards the end of 1726 ; seventeen companies of
troops and large quantities of provisions and ammunition were
embarked ; and on December 24th Vice-Admiral Sir Charles
Wager (R.) hoisted his flag in the *Kent*, 70, and took command.
He sailed on January 19th, 1727, and on February 2nd, having
picked up the *Stirling Castle*, 70, on his way out, arrived in
Gibraltar Bay, where he found Rear-Admiral Edward Hopsonn (R.),
who had remained upon the station during the winter.[3]   As the
Spaniards, fifteen thousand strong, were seen to be working hard,
troops, guns, and stores were landed ; but no actual hostilities took
place until after February 10th, when the enemy began a new
battery within half gunshot of some of the defences of the place.
Colonel Jasper Clayton, the Lieutenant-Governor, made a spirited
remonstrance ; but the Conde de las Torres, the Spanish commander-
in-chief, returned an unsatisfactory and truculent answer ; whereupon fire was opened from the Mole Head, and from Prince's

[1] During much of the time the total complement was not more than 3300 officers
and men.   If there had not been at Jamaica plenty of men whose ships happened
to be laid up there owing to the difficulty with Spain, the deficiencies could not
have been made good, and the fleet must literally have become an array of immobile
and impotent hulks.

[2] *Kent*, 70, *Lenox*, 70, *Berwick*, 70, *Royal Oak*, 70, *Portland*, 50, *Tiger*, 50,
Hawk, 6, and *Cruiser*, 6.   The *Torbay*, 80, and *Poole*, fireship, 8, followed on
March 9th.

[3] Hopsonn had with him the *Burford*, 70, *York*, 60, *Winchester*, 50, *Colchester*, 50,
Swallow, 60, *Dursley Galley*, 20, and *Thunder*, bomb, 4.   A few days later the
Solebay, bomb, 6, which had been cruising, joined.   The *Berwick* and *Lenox* were
detached to the West Indies on February 13th, and the *Portland* and *Tiger* on
April 21st.   On the other hand, several fresh vessels arrived from England and
elsewhere at various times.

and Willis's batteries; and Sir Charles Wager, on the evening of the 11th, sent the *Tiger*, 50, *Dursley Galley*, 20, and *Solebay*, bomb, 6, to throw a flanking fire upon the Spanish lines from the eastward.

From that day the Spaniards prosecuted the siege in earnest; but as they had nothing larger than boats and small settees afloat in the Bay, they accomplished very little. Sir Charles, while always leaving a few vessels to enfilade the Spanish attack, frequently cruised in the Strait and off Cadiz; and on those occasions his vessels made prizes of several merchantmen. On March 11th, moreover, the *Royal Oak*, 70, being detached, took the new Spanish man-of-war, *Nuestra Señora del Rosario*, 46, which was on her way from Santander to Cadiz; and, in the meantime, the small craft employed by the enemy within the Bay were from time to time nearly all seized. So matters went on, until, on June 16th, Sir Charles Wager, having heard that the preliminaries of peace had been agreed to, ordered a cessation of hostilities.[1]

" But," says Smollett, " when the siege was on the point of being entirely raised, and the preliminaries ratified in form, Spain started new difficulties and urged new pretensions. The Spaniards insisted that a temporary suspension of arms did not imply an actual raising of the siege of Gibraltar. . . . Upon this, hostilities began between the ships of the two nations; and Sir Charles Wager continued to cruise on the coasts of Spain, after the cessation of arms at Gibraltar. . . . However, after many cavils and delays, the preliminary articles were at last signed at Madrid on February 24th,[2] above eight months after the death of King George the First, by the ministers of the Emperor, England, Spain, France, and the States; which opened the way to the Congress." [3]

Sir Charles Wager, with part of his fleet, reached Spithead on April 9th, on his return from the Mediterranean. During his absence there, Admiral Sir John Norris (B.), Rear-Admiral Salmon Morrice (W.), and Rear-Admiral Robert Hughes (1) (B.), with twelve ships of the line and several smaller ones, made another demonstration in the Baltic, in order to induce the Empress of Russia to refrain from attacking Sweden. The fleet reached Copenhagen on May 12th, 1727, and its appearance in northern waters created so powerful an impression that Russia, in spite of the fact that she had already threatened Sweden in definite terms, laid up her ships and abandoned her designs. Sir John returned without having had occasion to fire a shot.

[1] Sir Charles utilised the leisure which this cessation gave him by proceeding to Tangier, and renewing the peace with Marocco.
[2] 1728.   [3] Begun at Soissons on June 1st, 1728.

The death of George I., which had occurred at Osnabrück on June 11th, 1727, made no difference to the foreign policy of Great Britain. George II., in his first message to Parliament, while expressing a hope that peace would be re-established as a result of the deliberations then in progress, pointed out that it was still necessary to continue the preparations for war. Eleven ships had already been commissioned in January; and, as the sincerity of Spain remained in some doubt, fifteen more were commissioned in June, 1728. When Parliament re-assembled in January, 1729, the Congress at Soissons had failed to devise terms of peace that were satisfactory to all the numerous parties concerned, and the Spaniards in the West Indies were more troublesome than ever to British trade. But the manifest determination of the King to stand by his allies; his plainly-expressed intention to preserve his " undoubted right to Gibraltar and the island of Minorca ";[1] his assurance that he would secure satisfaction for Spanish depredations in the West Indies; and his orders, issued on May 25th, for the commissioning of twenty sail of the line and five frigates,[2] were not without effect; the result being that, by the Treaty of Seville, concluded on November 9th, 1729, Great Britain, Spain, and France, who were subsequently joined by Holland, became defensively allied. Gibraltar was not mentioned in the treaty; and the fact that it was not mentioned was regarded as a tacit renunciation of the claim of Spain to the Rock; but, in some other respects, the settlement was disadvantageous to Great Britain,[3] and, upon the whole, it was beneficial rather to France than to any other country.

During the peace which followed, Admiral Sir Charles Wager,[4] in 1731, assisted the Marques de Mari in convoying a large body of Spanish troops to Leghorn, in order to place Don Carlos de Bourbon in possession of Parma and Piacenza, to which, under the terms of the treaty, the Prince had become entitled by the death of the Duke of Parma. Yet, notwithstanding this friendly co-operation between Great Britain and Spain in Europe, the relations between

---

[1] Answer of the King to the Commons, March 25th, 1729.

[2] These were presently joined at Spithead by fourteen Dutch ships under Vice-Admiral van Sommelsdijck.

[3] It did not, for example, secure satisfaction for the Spanish depredations in the West Indies.

[4] He had his flag in the *Namur*, 90. Rear-Admiral Sir John Balchen, Kt. (W.), in the *Norfolk*, 80, was second in command.

the representatives of the two countries in the New World became ever more and more strained. And even in Europe very menacing clouds arose when, in 1733, the death of Augustus II., Elector of Saxony and King of Poland, brought about a hostile combination of France, Spain, and Sardinia against the Empire. Great Britain, as a necessary measure of precaution, commissioned no fewer than

ADMIRAL NICHOLAS HADDOCK.

*(From Faber's engraving after the painting by T. Gibson,
representing Haddock when Rear-Admiral of the Red, 1735.)*

eighty-six[1] ships of war early in 1734, recalled British sailors from the service of foreign powers, and offered bounties to seamen.

In 1735, a dispute having broken out between Spain and Portugal, the latter power solicited British aid against the Spaniards ; and, in response, a large fleet, under Admiral Sir John Norris, with Vice-Admiral Sir John Balchen (R.), and Rear-Admiral Nicholas

---

[1] Bringing up the total number in commission to one hundred and twenty.

Haddock[1] (W.), was dispatched to Lisbon, sailing from Spithead on May 27th, and reaching the Tagus on June 9th. The demonstration was made not only in the general interests of peace, but also in the particular interests of the many British merchants whose welfare was more or less dependent upon the safety of the then homecoming Portuguese flota from Brazil ; and it was so efficacious that an actual rupture between the two countries was prevented.

Yet Spain was not to be permanently intimidated. After France, going behind the backs of her allies, had patched up, vastly to her own benefit, her differences with the Empire by the treaty of December 28th, 1735, Great Britain, awaking to the fact that she had been neglecting her own peculiar business in order to be ready to intervene on behalf of powers that deserved no such kindness at her hands, once more turned her attention to the outrages which had for years been committed upon her commerce by the Spaniards in the West Indies. In 1737 she sent Rear-Admiral Nicholas Haddock to the Mediterranean with a squadron, the appearance of which was intended to lend weight to the demands which she then felt it necessary to make. Spain haggled and temporised. In reply to an address from the Commons, King George II., on March 6th, 1738, said : " I am fully sensible of the many and unwarrantable depredations committed by the Spaniards,[2] and you may be assured I will make use of the most proper and effectual means that are in my power to procure justice and satisfaction to my injured subjects, and for the future security of their trade and navigation."

Still, however, Spain temporised. A paper presented to Parliament in 1738 showed that since the Treaty of Seville the loss caused to British merchants by the operations of the Spaniards had been upwards of £140,000, that fifty-two British vessels had been taken and plundered by them, and that British seamen had been very cruelly treated. This caused much excitement. Then came the examination by the House of persons who had, or were alleged to have, suffered at the hands of the Spaniards. Among these persons was Richard Jenkins, sometime master of the *Rebecca*, brig, of Glasgow. He declared that his craft had been boarded by a guarda-costa, whose captain had wantonly cut off one of the

---

[1] Nicholas Haddock. Born, 1686. Captain, 1707. Rear-Admiral, 1734. Vice-Admiral, 1741. Admiral, 1744. Died, 1746.

[2] Accounts of some of these, and further notes about Jenkins, will be found in the next chapter.

deponent's ears, and handed it to him with the insolent remark : " Carry this home to the King, your master, whom, if he were present, I would serve in like fashion." " The truth of the story," says Mr. Lecky, " is extremely doubtful." It has even been said that Jenkins lost his ear at the pillory. Yet the indignation aroused by the man's deposition was general ; and popular opinion grew uncontrollable when it became known that, upon having been asked by a member what were his feelings at the moment of the outrage, Jenkins had replied : " I recommended my soul to God, and my cause to my country."

Spain at length agreed to make some reparation, and to settle outstanding differences. The convention to this effect was submitted to Parliament in 1739, and, after a most stormy debate, approved of ; yet, when the time came for it to be carried out, fresh difficulties cropped up, and Spain, possibly because she had gained by negotiation all the delay which she deemed necessary to enable her to perfect her preparations, silently declined to play her promised part. At about the same time, owing to the precarious state of affairs, the British consuls at Malaga, Alicant, and other Spanish ports, were compelled to advise British merchants and vessels to depart thence with all haste.

Great Britain was to be satisfied only by the adoption of strong measures ; and on July 10th, 1739, the King issued a proclamation in which he set forth that the Spaniards had committed depredations, and that they had promised and failed to make reparation ; and in which he authorised general reprisals and letters of marque against the ships, goods, and subjects of the King of Spain. Half-hearted endeavours were made at the last moment to preserve peace ; but Spain declared that she regarded the making of reprisals as a hostile act ; France reminded the world that she was bound to look upon the enemies of Spain as her own foes ; and Holland averred that, if called upon to do so, she could not but observe the spirit of her treaty of alliance with Great Britain.

The British minister presently withdrew from Madrid, and the Spanish minister from London ; the British squadrons abroad were reinforced ;[1] numerous ships were commissioned ; stringent measures were adopted to procure the necessary number of seamen for the

---

[1] Information as to the state of affairs was also sent to Commodore Charles Brown, who was senior officer at Jamaica, and who at once began reprisals. For an account of them, *see* next chapter.

fleet; letters of marque were announced on July 21st as ready for issue by the Admiralty; and on October 23rd, 1739, war was formally declared against Spain, which put forward her own declaration on November 28th.

The power of Spain was then most vulnerable in the West Indies and the Pacific. An expedition under Captain George Anson, of whose proceedings an account will be found in Chapter XXIX., was prepared for the Pacific, but did not sail until the autumn of 1740. Dispatched primarily for warlike purposes, and originally intended to co-operate with another force under Captain James Cornwall, Anson's command, owing to various adventitious circumstances, gained for its leader an even more brilliant reputation as a navigator than as a fighting officer; and the history of it falls naturally among the chronicles of the great British voyages. But an expedition to the West Indies, which was entrusted to Vice-Admiral Edward Vernon (1), (B.),[1] was, from beginning to end, entirely a fighting venture; and as it was not without effect upon the issue of the war, it may fitly be described here, although it led up to no fleet action, and although it did not, to any appreciable extent, directly strengthen the maritime position of Great Britain.

Edward Vernon was a blunt, well-intentioned, honest, and very popular officer, whose chief service faults were that he could not always control either his tongue or his pen, and that he was too fond of vulgar applause. He had served in the West Indies for several years after his first appointment as a post-captain, and was generally believed to have an intimate acquaintance with the whole of that station and with the weak points of the Spanish position there. He had also been for a long time member of Parliament for Ipswich and for Penryn; and, in the course of one of the debates upon the depredations of the Spaniards, he had taken upon himself to declare in strong terms that the Spanish possessions in the West Indies might be reduced with great ease, and that Puerto Bello,[2] in particular, might be taken by a force of six

___

[1] Edward Vernon was born in 1684, and became a Post-Captain in 1706, and a Vice-Admiral, without having ever been a Rear-Admiral, on July 9th, 1739. Having captured Puerto Bello, etc., in that and the next year, he led an attack upon Cartagena in 1741. In 1745 he attained the rank of Admiral, but, in the following year, owing, among other things, to his fondness for pamphleteering, he was struck off the list of flag-officers. *See* note on p. 111, *infra*. He died in 1757.

[2] Puerto Bello stands on the north side of the Isthmus of Darien, and is abou seventy miles from Panama. It has a considerable bay and good anchorage.

ships of the line.   He said, moreover, that he would gladly venture his life and reputation upon the success of such an enterprise, if only he were permitted to attempt it.   Vernon was popular in the country, and troublesome to the ministry ; and the Government, anxious to be temporarily rid of him, and perhaps equally ready to take credit for his triumph or to rejoice over his disgrace, promoted him, and gave him exactly the mission and force which he had demanded.

ADMIRAL EDWARD VERNON.

(From McArdell's engraving after the portrait by T. Gainsborough, R.A.)

Vernon sailed from Portsmouth on July 24th, 1739,[1] with four ships of seventy guns, three of sixty, one of fifty, and one of forty. Of these, he presently detached three of the seventies, viz., the *Lenox*, Captain Covill Mayne, *Elizabeth*, Captain Edward Falkingham (1), and *Kent*, Captain Thomas Durell (1), to cruise for a month off Cape Ortegal, and to look out for some treasure-ships which were daily expected in Spain.   The vessels were to return afterwards to

[1] He did not, however, leave Plymouth until August 3rd.

England.   He also detached the *Pearl*, 50, Captain the Hon.
Edward Legge, to cruise for three months between Lisbon and
Oporto.   With the rest of his force he crossed the Atlantic, reaching
Jamaica on October 23rd.[1]   There he was joined by the senior
officer already on the station, Commodore Charles Brown, whose
broad pennant was in the *Hampton Court*, 70.

On the voyage out Vernon took every opportunity of disciplining
his men, and of exercising them both at the heavy guns and at small
arms; and there is little doubt that, under his direction, his small
squadron rapidly became, for its size, the most efficient that Great
Britain had sent to sea for many years.

The intelligence received by the Vice-Admiral was to the effect
that the Spanish galleons were about to make rendezvous at
Cartagena, and to proceed thence to Puerto Bello, where they would
exchange their European goods for the gold and silver which had
been sent for the purpose from Panama.   The news that the bullion
was already at Puerto Bello determined Vernon to lose no time in
attacking that place.   He obtained pilots, embarked two hundred
soldiers under Captain Newton, and, on November 5th, 1739, sailed
from Port Royal.[2]   On the following day he issued the following
instructions to his captains :—

"Upon making the land at Puerto Bello, and having a fair wind to favour them,
and daylight for the attempt, to have their ships clear in all respects for immediate
service ; and, on the proper signal, to form themselves into a line of battle, as directed ;
and, being formed, to follow in the same order of battle to the attack, in the manner
hereafter directed.   And as the north shore of the harbour of Puerto Bello is
represented to the Admiral to be a bold steep shore, on which, at the first entrance,
stands the Castillo de Ferro, or Iron Castle, Commodore Brown, and the ships that
follow him, are directed to pass the said fort, within less than a cable's length distant,
giving the enemy as they pass as warm a fire as possible, both from great guns and
musketry.   Then Commodore Brown is to steer away for the Gloria Castle, and anchor
as near as he possibly can to the eastermost part of it, for battering down all the
defences of it, but so as to leave room for Captain Mayne, in the *Worcester*, to anchor
astern of him against the westermost bastion, and to do the same there ; and to follow
such orders as the Commodore may think proper to give him for attacking the said
castle.   Captain Herbert, in the *Norwich*, after giving his fire at the Iron Castle, is to
push on for the castle of San Jerónimo, lying to the eastward of the town, and to
anchor as near it as he possibly can, and batter it down ; and Captain Trevor, in the
Strafford, following the Admiral, to come to an anchor abreast of the eastermost
part of the Iron Castle, so as to leave room for Captain Waterhouse, in the *Princess
Louisa*, to anchor astern of him, for battering the westermost part of the Castle ; and

---

[1] Having called in the meantime at Antigua and St. Kitt's.
[2] With the ships mentioned in the table *infra*, and the *Sheerness*, 20, Captain Miles
Stapleton.   This vessel was presently detached to reconnoitre Cartagena.

continue there till the service is completed, and make themselves masters of it : the youngest officers to follow the further crders of the elder in the further prosecution of the attack : and, if the weather be favourable for it on their going in, each ship, besides having her long-boat towing astern, to have her barge alongside to tow the long-boats away with such part of the soldiers as can conveniently go in them, and to come under the Admiral's stern, for his directing a descent with them, where he shall find it most proper to order it. From the men's inexperience in service, it will be necessary to be as cautious as possible to prevent hurry and confusion, and a fruitless waste of powder and shot. The captains are to give the strictest orders to their respective officers to take the greatest care that no gun is fired but what they, or those they particularly appoint, first see levelled, and direct the firing of ; and that they shall strictly prohibit all their men from hallooing and making irregular noise that will only serve to throw them into confusion, till such time as the service is performed and when they have nothing to do but glory in the victory. Such of the ships as have mortars and cohorns on board are ordered to use them in the attack."

LINE OF BATTLE AT THE ATTACK ON PUERTO BELLO, NOVEMBER 21ST, 1739.

Ships.	Guns.	Men.	Commanders.
Hampton Court . . .	70	495	Commodore Charles Brown. / Captain Digby Dent, (2).
Norwich	50	300	„ Richard Herbert.
Worcester	60	400	„ Perry Mayne.
Burford	70	500	Vice-Admiral Edward Vernon, (B.). / Captain Thomas Watson (1).
Strafford	60	400	„ Thomas Trevor.
Princess Louisa . . .	60	400	„ Thomas Waterhouse.

The squadron sighted Puerto Bello in the night of November 20th, and chased into harbour some small vessels, which apprised the enemy of Vernon's presence on the coast. That he might not be driven to leeward, the Vice-Admiral anchored about six leagues from the shore. Early on the 21st he weighed, and, the wind being easterly,[1] he plied to windward in line of battle ahead. At about 2 P.M., the *Hampton Court*, being close to the Iron Castle, began the attack, and was well seconded by the *Norwich* and *Worcester*. The fire of the enemy, vigorous at first, gradually lessened. Seeing this, Vernon, who was rapidly approaching, signalled for the manned boats to go under his stern, and then ordered them to land beneath the walls of the castle. In the meantime, the *Burford*, which had come abreast of the castle, had received and returned a very heavy fire. The men in her tops forced the enemy to abandon his lower battery, whereupon the landing-party made an assault, and, by climbing into the embrasures upon one another's shoulders, the men entered, and quickly carried the work, most of the defenders of

[1] This prevented the attack from being carried out in the prescribed manner.

which fled to the town, though a few shut themselves up in the
keep, whence they presently shouted appeals for quarter.

By that time night had come on. Owing to the wind, Commodore Brown and his division had been unable to get up the bay and
attack the castles of Gloria and San Jerónimo, and his ships, having
fallen to leeward, were obliged to anchor, ready to proceed at
daybreak should the wind permit.   The *Burford* and *Strafford*,

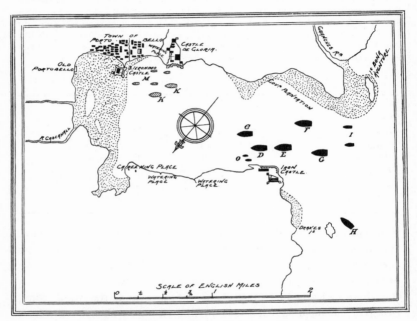

ATTACK ON PUERTO BELLO, NOVEMBER 21ST., 1739.

(From a plan by Com. James Rentone kindly lent by Lord Vernon.)

C. *Worcester.*	H. *Princess Louisa.*
D. *Norwich.*	I. Two tenders.
E. *Burford.*	K. Two Spanish guarda-costas.
F. *Hampton Court.*	M. Three trading sloops.
G. *Strafford.*	O. Boats on their way to land soldiers.

which were just within reach of the heaviest guns in Gloria, were
fired at all night, but received little damage beyond the wounding of
the former's fore topmast.   The fire was returned with effect from
the lower deck of the *Burford*.   Early in the morning of the 22nd,
the Vice-Admiral went on board the *Hampton Court*, and, after he
had consulted with his officers, directed steps to be taken for warping
his ships up the harbour during the night, in order to be able to

attack Gloria and San Jerónimo on the following day. But these measures proved to be unnecessary. The Spanish governor, Don Francisco Martinez de Retez, hoisted a white flag, and sent out a boat with a flag of truce to convey to Vernon the terms on which the place would be surrendered. These terms were deemed inadmissible by the Vice-Admiral, who drew up others which he was prepared to grant. He allowed the governor only a few hours in which to make up his mind; yet, well within the specified time, the terms were accepted. Captain Newton, with two hundred soldiers, was sent to take possession of the town and castles ; and detachments of seamen boarded the vessels in port. The crews of these had, it appeared, landed during the previous night, and committed various outrages. The garrison was allowed to march out with the honours of war, and to carry off two cannon with ten charges of powder for each. The inhabitants were permitted either to remove or to remain, and were promised security for their goods and effects. The ships [1] were surrendered absolutely, though their crews were permitted to retire with their personal effects. And, contingent upon the due performance of all the stipulations, the town, the clergy and the churches were guaranteed protection and immunity in their privileges and properties. [2]

Public money to the amount of ten thousand dollars was found in the place, and at once distributed by Vernon among his men. There were also taken forty pieces of brass cannon, ten brass field-pieces, four brass mortars, and eighteen brass patereroes, besides iron guns, which were destroyed, but not carried off. The fortifications were then demolished—a work which needed the expenditure of one hundred and twenty-two barrels of captured Spanish powder, and which occupied three weeks. [3]

On November 27th, the *Diamond*, 40, Captain Charles Knowles, and on November 29th, the *Windsor*, 60, Captain George Berkeley, and the *Anglesey*, 40, Captain Henry Reddish, joined the flag from the Leeward Islands ; and on December 6th, the *Sheerness*, 20,

---

[1] One of them, a snow, was commissioned as the *Triumph*, sloop, by Commander James Rentone, who was sent home with Vernon's dispatches. Another prize was renamed the *Astræa*, 12.

[2] The loss on the British side during the attack was almost incredibly small, the *Burford* and *Worcester* having each three killed and five wounded, and the *Hampton Court* having one man mortally wounded.

[3] In the service Captain the Hon. Edward Boscawen assisted as a volunteer. His ship, the *Shoreham*, 20, was at the time unfit for sea.

Captain Miles Stapleton, which had been detached to reconnoitre Cartagena, returned. While the Vice-Admiral still lay at Puerto Bello, he sent to Panama a demand for the release of certain servants of the South Sea Company, who were confined in that city; and, although Vernon, being on the wrong side of the isthmus, was scarcely in a position to have backed up his demand by force, the governor, who seems to have been greatly impressed by the easy capture of Puerto Bello, saw fit to comply. The Vice-Admiral sailed on December 13th for Jamaica.

The news of the success was hailed with great joy in England, and Vernon was voted the thanks of both Houses, and the freedom of the City of London in a gold box. Commander James Rentone, the bearer of the intelligence, was presented with two hundred guineas, and made a post-captain. The Ministry realised that it could do nothing more popular than follow up the blow already struck, and it at once arranged to send to Jamaica, if possible in the early autumn, a strong military force composed of two regiments of infantry, and six newly-raised regiments of Marines—the whole under Major-General Lord Cathcart—to be employed by Vice-Admiral Vernon in the prosecution of further designs against the Spaniards in the West Indies and Central America. It was also decided to endeavour to recruit in the North American Colonies a corps of three thousand men, to be commanded by Colonel Spottiswood,[1] and to be sent to Jamaica to strengthen the hands of Lord Cathcart upon his arrival.

In the interval, the Spaniards, thoroughly alarmed for the security of their empire in the New World, sent to the West Indies a strong squadron,[2] with troops and stores, under Admiral Don Rodrigo de Torres. They also prevailed upon France to proclaim not only that she was in strict alliance with Spain, but also that she could not suffer Great Britain to make new settlements or conquests in the West Indies; and this proclamation was succeeded by the dispatch across the Atlantic of three French squadrons. One, of four ships of the line, under the Chevalier de Nesmond, left Brest on July 28th. A second, of eighteen sail, under the Marquis d'Antin, quitted the same port towards the end of August, and, soon after its departure, suffered so severely in a storm, that two or three of its

---

[1] This officer unfortunately died in Virginia ere the troops which he had collected could be embarked.

[2] This sailed from Spain on July 10th, 1740.

best vessels had to return.   The third, of fifteen sail, under the
Marquis de La Roche-Allard, weighed from Toulon on August 25th.
When he had passed the Strait of Gibraltar, the Marquis opened
his orders, and, in pursuance of them, sent back to port four
of his largest ships.   Proceeding with the rest, he made a junction with the other squadrons at Martinique in September and
October.

But the force there assembled was formidable chiefly on paper.
The vessels were not in good condition, and they were both ill-
manned and ill-found.   Many of them had been much damaged by
bad weather ere they arrived ; and when they essayed to move in
company from Martinique to Hispaniola, they fell in with another
storm which caused serious losses, and reduced them to a condition
of impotence.

That they had been sent out to co-operate with Spain is
certain.   But before they had an opportunity of co-operating,
reinforcements had reached Vernon ; and the situation in Europe
had been changed by the death of the Emperor Charles VI., on
October 20th, and by the accession of the Elector of Bavaria as
Charles VII.   France then decided to hold her hand, to recall her
squadrons,[1] and to postpone her definite rupture with Great Britain.
It is not necessary, therefore, to further follow the movements of the
French.   As for the Spanish squadron under Don Rodrigo de
Torres, it reached San Juan de Puerto Rico in a sorely-damaged
condition in September, and there slowly refitted.   In course of time
it went on to Cartagena, threw additional troops into the town, and,
leaving a detachment under Don Blas de Leso in the roadstead,
proceeded to Havana.

Vernon's squadron, on its voyage from Puerto Bello to Jamaica,
was dispersed and shattered by a storm.   All the vessels, nevertheless, reached Port Royal by February 6th, 1740, except the *Triumph*,
sloop, which had foundered off Sambala Keys, but the officers and
men of which had been saved.   The *Greenwich*, 50, Captain Charles
Wyndham, with four bombs, some fireships, and several other
craft, was found in harbour.   The Vice-Admiral did all that lay in
his power to speedily refit his command, but, finding that the
Burford would take some time to prepare for sea, he transferred his
flag from her to the *Strafford*, 60, and sailed on February 25th with
the greater part of his force, leaving the rest of it, under Commodore

[1] Except a few ships left at Hispaniola under the Comte de Roquefeuil.

Charles Brown, for the protection of Jamaica. His determination
was to bombard Cartagena.

On March 1st, the Vice-Admiral sighted the land near Santa
Martha, and, having detached the *Greenwich*, 50, to ply to windward
of that place, to intercept any vessel that might be bound thither, he
bore away ; and, on the evening of the 3rd,[1] anchored in nine fathoms
off Playa Grande, in the open bay before Cartagena.   On the 4th

VICE-ADMIRAL SIR CHARLES KNOWLES.

(From Faber's mezzotint after the portrait by T. Hudson.)

and 5th he reconnoitred the place, and made his dispositions ; and on
the 6th he ordered in the bombs *Alderney*, 8, Commander James
Scott, *Terrible*, 8, Commander Edward Allen, and *Cumberland*, 8,
Commander Thomas Brodrick,[2] with the tenders *Pompey* and
Goodly, and other craft to assist them, to bombard the town.   This

---

[1] On which day he had been joined by the *Falmouth*, 50, Captain William
Douglas.

[2] This officer, who died a Vice-Admiral in 1769, in later life spelt his name
Broderick ; but it was, properly, Brodrick.

they did until 9 A.M. on the 7th, receiving no damage whatsoever, and probably doing little, although they terribly frightened the inhabitants. It is difficult to understand why Vernon made this demonstration, for he knew well that the force which he had with him was insufficient to take the city. It has been suggested that his action was intended as a reply to an insulting letter which he had received from Don Blas de Leso, and this is certainly a plausible explanation, for the quick-tempered Vice-Admiral was ever fully as eager to resent a slight offered to himself as he was to resent one offered to his country. It does not, however, appear that the bombardment of Cartagena assisted, in the slightest degree, the general policy which Vernon had been sent westward to carry out.

From Cartagena he coasted along the Gulf of Darien, exchanging shots with Bocca Chica as he passed, and making observations concerning the defences of the various towns. He detached the *Windsor*, 60, Captain George Berkeley, and the *Greenwich*, 50, Captain Charles Wyndham, to cruise off Cartagena with the object of looking out for the galleons and of intercepting three Spanish ships of war which, he had heard, were about to attempt to join Don Blas de Leso there. Vernon then proceeded to Puerto Bello to refit and water his squadron. He was rejoined on March 13th by the *Diamond*, 40, Captain Charles Knowles,[1] an officer in whom he appears to have reposed exceptional confidence. Knowles was ordered to go on board the *Success*, fireship, 10, Commander Daniel Hore,[2] and, accompanied by one of the tenders, to move round to the mouth of the River Chagres, there to reconnoitre and to make soundings with a view to reporting on the manner in which the fort of San Lorenzo and the town of Chagres might best be attacked. Measures were also taken to blockade the estuary. The Vice-Admiral obtained much information and assistance from an English pirate or buccaneer named Lowther, who, in consequence, received the King's pardon and permission to return home.

On March 22nd the *Strafford*,[3] the *Norwich*, the three bomb ketches, and the small craft, put to sea from Puerto Bello, instructions being left for the other vessels to follow as soon as possible.

---

[1] Charles Knowles. Born, 1702. Captain, 1737. Rear-Admiral, 1747. Commander-in-Chief at Jamaica, 1748. Captured Port Louis, Hispaniola. Defeated Reggio off Havana, October 1st, 1748. Vice-Admiral, 1755. Admiral, 1758. Baronet, 1765, and Rear-Admiral of Great Britain. Served Russia, 1770–1774. Died, 1777.

[2] Or Hoare.

[3] In which the Vice-Admiral still flew his flag.

The *Strafford* met with a slight accident on the passage, and was detained for a few hours, but the *Norwich*, by order, proceeded with the remaining craft, and by 3 P.M. Captain Richard Herbert, with the assistance of Captain Knowles, had not only placed his bombs in position, but had begun to bombard Fort San Lorenzo. The *Diamond* also opened fire in the evening ; and, during the night, the *Strafford*, *Princess Louisa*, and *Falmouth*, arrived and took up their stations.[1] The ships maintained a leisurely fire from their heavier guns until March 24th, when the governor of the place, Don Juan Carlos Gutierrez de Zavallos, surrendered. Captain Knowles took possession in the course of the afternoon.

A large amount of booty, including cocoa, Jesuit's bark, and wool, valued at £70,000, besides plate, etc., was captured. Two guarda-costas, found in the river, were destroyed ; all the brass guns and patereroes[2] in the defences were embarked in the squadron ; and, after the works had been demolished, Vernon quitted the river on March 30th. He was rejoined on the 31st by the *Windsor* and *Greenwich* from before Cartagena, and on April 2nd by his old flagship, the *Burford*, from Jamaica. After making dispositions, which proved to be vain, for intercepting the new Spanish viceroy of Santa Fé, who was on his way out from Ferrol, the Vice-Admiral returned to Jamaica, sending Captain Knowles home with dispatches.

A little later, Vernon, advised from Lisbon of the Spanish preparations for sending out the squadron under Don Rodrigo de Torres, and of the actual departure from Cadiz of a squadron, the supposed destination of which was the West Indies, put to sea again, hoping to fall in with the enemy ; but, having encountered bad weather, and having failed to get any news of his foe, he returned to Port Royal on June 21st. During the summer his cruisers were active, but he was himself detained in port by lack of supplies. On September 5th, however, a number of store-ships, convoyed by the *Defiance*, 60, Captain John Trevor, and the *Tilbury*, 60, reached him, and on October 3rd he was able to put to sea once more. On the 19th he fell in with eight transports, convoyed by the

---

[1] The ships engaged in the attack on Chagres were the *Strafford*, 60, *Princess Louisa*, 60, *Falmouth*, 50, *Norwich*, 50, *Diamond*, 40, *Alderney*, *Terrible*, and *Cumberland*, bombs, and *Pompey* and *Goodly*, tenders. The commanders of all these have already been named. In addition, there were the fireships, *Success*, 10, Commander Daniel Hore, and *Eleanor*, 10, Commander Sir Robert Henley, Bart.

[2] There were eleven brass guns and as many patereroes.

Wolf, sloop, 10, Commander William Dandridge, and laden with troops from North America.[1]   These he escorted to Jamaica.   Soon afterwards he heard of the arrival at Cartagena of Don Rodrigo de Torres, and at Martinique of the Marquis d'Antin ; and not having force sufficient to justify him in risking an encounter at sea with his known enemies, even if they were not assisted by his suspected ones, he remained at Port Royal, anxiously awaiting news of the promised reinforcements from England.

These reinforcements, which included the transports carrying Lord Cathcart's army, were to have been under the orders of Vice-Admiral Sir John Balchen.   But Balchen's division of men-of-war consisted only of one 3rd-rate, five 4th-rates, and one 6th-rate ; and when, after the armament had actually put to sea and had been driven back to port by contrary weather in August, the Ministry learnt what powerful squadrons Spain and France had dispatched across the Atlantic, it was decided to make new arrangements.   Balchen's orders were cancelled, and a very much larger and entirely different squadron, under Sir Chaloner Ogle (1), was appointed to escort the troops.   The change of plan necessarily involved much delay, and it was not until October 26th that the fleet at length sailed.

It cleared the Channel ; but on October 31st, when it was about seventy leagues to the westward of the Start,[2] it met with a heavy gale, in which the *Buckingham*, 70, Captain Cornelius Mitchell, *Prince of Orange*, 70, Captain Henry Osborn, and *Superbe*, 60, Captain the Hon. William Hervey, were so badly damaged that the first had to be sent back to Spithead, and the others had to proceed to Lisbon under convoy of the *Cumberland*, 80, Captain James Stewart. In spite of these deductions the fleet still consisted of upwards of twenty 3rd and 4th-rates, besides several frigates, fire-ships, bombs, etc., under Rear-Admiral Sir Chaloner Ogle (1), Kt. (B.), and Commodore Richard Lestock (2), together with transports carrying about 9000 troops,[3] under Major-General Lord Cathcart, and Brigadier-Generals Thomas Wentworth, John Guise, and William Blakeney.   It anchored on December 19th, 1740, in Prince Rupert's

---

[1] These troops had taken part in the fruitless attack on St. Augustine, Florida, some account of which will be found in the next chapter.

[2] In lat. 17° 54′ W.

[3] *I.e.* the 15th and 24th regiments of foot, six regiments of Marines under Colonels Fleming, Robinson, Lowther, Wynyard, Douglas and Moreton, and some artillery and miscellaneous detachments.

Bay, Dominica ; and, on the following day it had to lament the loss, by dysentery, of the military commander-in-chief.[1]

Sir Chaloner weighed again for St. Kitt's, his general rendez-vous, on December 27th, and thence steered for Jamaica. On the passage thither, being off the western end of Hispaniola, he sighted four large vessels, and signalled to the *Prince Frederick*, 70, Captain Lord Aubrey Beauclerk, *Orford*, 70, Captain Lord Augustus Fitzroy, *Lion*, 60, Captain Charles Cotterell, *Weymouth*, 60, Captain Charles Knowles, and two more ships of the line, to proceed in chase. At 4 P.M. the strangers [2] hoisted French colours ; but as they did not shorten sail, it was 10 P.M. ere the headmost British ship, the *Prince Frederick*, got up with them. She hailed them, first in English and then in French, and then, having failed to get an answer, fired into one of the ships, which promptly returned a broadside. The *Orford* next got into action ; and she and the *Prince Frederick* engaged the chase for about an hour and a half before the remaining ships could approach within gunshot. The *Weymouth* was the third to overhaul the strangers ; and, upon her arrival on the scene, Captain Knowles boarded the *Prince Frederick*, and expressed his conviction that the enemy was French. Lord Aubrey Beauclerk thereupon made the signal to desist ; yet, as the enemy continued firing, the engagement was renewed for about half an hour. At daybreak Lord Aubrey sent an officer on board the senior ship of the chase, and at length it was satisfactorily established that the strangers were indeed French, and not, as Lord Aubrey had at first believed, Spaniards sailing under French colours. The *Prince Frederick* lost four killed and nine wounded ; the *Orford*, seven killed and fourteen wounded ; and the *Weymouth*, two killed ; and all three vessels were much damaged aloft.

The French, who bitterly complained of the manner in which they had been treated, suffered much more severely. They declared that, upon being hailed, they had at once replied ; and modern French writers seriously contend that the true cause of the action was the refusal of their senior officer to send a boat to Lord Aubrey, when he called for one. It is possible, seeing how un-favourable to Great Britain was the attitude of France at the time,

---

[1] Lord Cathcart was succeeded in the command by General Wentworth, a far less experienced and competent officer.

[2] *Ardent*, 64, Captain d'Epinai de Boisgeroult ; *Mercure*, 54, Captain des Herbiers de l'Etenduère ; *Diamant*, 50, Captain de Poisins ; and *Parfaite*, 46, Captain d'Estournel. Guérin, iv. 242. These vessels formed part of d'Antin's squadron.

that neither Ogle nor Lord Aubrey was prepared to exercise much forbearance with the French, and that the action was the result of provocation and irritation on both sides. The squadrons, however, parted with mutual apologies; and Lord Aubrey proceeded to rejoin Sir Chaloner Ogle, who arrived at Jamaica on January 9th, 1741, and there placed himself under the orders of Vice-Admiral Vernon.

It is necessary to return for a time from the West Indies, and to look at the course of events elsewhere.

The outbreak of war had found Rear-Admiral Nicholas Haddock (R.) commander-in-chief in the Mediterranean. Under him was Rear-Admiral Sir Chaloner Ogle (1) (B.). At first, Haddock blockaded the Spaniards in Cadiz, but he was soon drawn off by the foulness of his ships and by the requirements of Minorca, which, it was supposed, might be attacked from other Spanish ports; and while he and Ogle were at Port Mahon, such Spanish ships [1] as had been lying at Cadiz slipped out, under Don Roderigo de Torres, and sailed to Ferrol. Not long afterwards, when it appeared that Minorca was in no danger, and that the Spaniards in the Mediterranean were weaker than had at first been believed, Ogle, with a strong division, was sent home by Haddock. He arrived in England on July 7th, 1740, and, as had been shown, went out later in the year [2] to reinforce Vice-Admiral Vernon. No event of importance occurred in the Mediterranean during the rest of 1740.

Nearer home, much was designed but little was effected. On April 9th, Vice-Admiral John Balchen (R.) was dispatched from Plymouth to intercept a Spanish treasure fleet which, escorted by a squadron under Admiral Pizarro, was on its way home from America. Balchen cruised in the very track which Pizarro had intended to take; but the Spaniards, learning of the British Admiral's station and design, sent out a fast dispatch vessel which, warning Pizarro, caused him to make for Santander by way of the Lizard and Ushant, instead of for Cadiz by way of Madeira, as he had originally purposed. He consequently took his convoy safely into port. To defeat Balchen, Spain in the meantime fitted out and sent to sea a superior force under Admiral Pintado, who, however, failed to find his enemy, and, upon his return, was disgraced. Balchen, against whose conduct no objections were ever alleged,

---

[1] These were they which subsequently proceeded to the West Indies, as has been already related.

[2] He first, however, cruised for a short time under Sir John Norris. *See infra.*

went back to port, having done little but capture the *Princesa*, 70.[1] Later in the year he commanded a squadron in the Channel.

The large concentration of Spanish force at Ferrol, and the knowledge that Spain cherished plans for aiding the Pretender in a descent upon Great Britain or Ireland, led to the assemblage of a large fleet[2] at Spithead. It was entrusted to Admiral-of-the-Fleet Sir John Norris, and, under him, to Admiral Philip Cavendish (B.), and Rear-Admiral Sir Chaloner Ogle (1) (B.). Sir John, who hoisted his flag first in the *Victory*, 100, and afterwards—the *Victory* having been disabled by collision with the *Lion*,[3] 60—in the *Boyne*, 80, had secret instructions; but what they were is, even now, not certainly known. It is supposed by some that he had orders to attack Ferrol, but this is upon the whole unlikely. It is more probable that his force was designed merely to convoy outward-bound merchantmen until clear of the Channel, and to be ready for any special service that might appear desirable. The Admiral of the Fleet took to sea with him as a volunteer Prince William Augustus, Duke of Cumberland,[4] second son of George II. The fleet sailed from St. Helen's on July 10th, but was three times driven back into port by contrary weather: and on August 28th, Sir John, being then in Torbay, hauled down his flag and departed for London with the young Duke.

In 1741 the proceedings of the fleets in home waters were equally uninteresting. In July, and again in October, the Admiral of the Fleet and Admiral Philip Cavendish put to sea with a considerable force and cruised off the north coast of Spain; but, beyond picking up a few small prizes, the command did nothing. It returned to Spithead on November 6th.

In the Mediterranean, Vice-Admiral Haddock, who was from time to time reinforced from England, endeavoured to prevent the junction of a Spanish squadron which lay in Cadiz with the French fleet which lay in Toulon, and to intercept the transport of Spanish troops from Barcelona to Italy. But he failed in both objects. While Haddock was refitting at Gibraltar, the Toulon fleet, under

---

[1] For an account of her capture, *see* next chapter.

[2] Made up of one ship of 100 guns, eight ships of 80, five of 70, seven of 60, and one of 50, besides smaller craft.

[3] The *Victory* carried away her head and bowsprit: the *Lion* lost her foremast, and twenty-eight men who were thrown overboard by the shock.

[4] The victor of Culloden, then in his twentieth year. This short cruise seems to have decided him to adopt a military instead of a naval career.

M. La Bruyère de Court, weighed and steered towards the Strait; and Don Jose Navarro, from Cadiz, issued forth to meet and join hands with it. Haddock suffered Navarro to pass by him,[1] and only went in chase when it was too late to prevent the accomplishment of the junction. His advanced frigates sighted the allies off Cape de Gata on December 7th, 1741, and the British and Spanish fleets were distantly visible one from the other on the following morning; but at that time the junction was actually being effected. The Vice-Admiral called a council of war which, in view of the fact that French neutrality could not be depended upon,[2] judged it inadvisable to continue the pursuit. Soon afterwards the French and Spanish fleets proceeded to Barcelona and embarked 15,000 men, who were thence transported to Orbetello, in Tuscany, there to act against the allies of Great Britain. The ill-success both of Norris and of Haddock was doubtless due rather to the nature of the instructions given to these officers by the Ministry than to any fault on the part of either. Popular indignation rose high, especially when it became known that the passage of Spanish reinforcements to Italy had not been prevented: and the general discontent on this subject contributed much to the fall of Sir Robert Walpole's administration.

In the West Indies, as has been said, Sir Chaloner Ogle joined Vice-Admiral Vernon at Jamaica on January 9th, 1741. A fleet such as had never before been assembled in the waters of the New World was now at the disposal of the British commander, who, unlike his fellow-admirals in Europe, had very full powers to act as he might deem best for the advantage of the service. "Better," says Beatson, "had it been for Great Britain if his powers had been more limited; for, had he been directed to proceed immediately against the Havana, there can be no doubt but he would have succeeded in reducing that place before the hurricane months set in. His instructions pointed strongly at this as the most proper place to commence his operations: and letters from the most able and well informed of his friends[3] in England strongly enforced this idea."

---

[1] Haddock, who had left cruisers to watch Cadiz, seems to have been very ill-served by his scouts.

[2] The Franco-Spanish fleet outnumbered the British by nearly two to one.

[3] " 'Take and hold,' is the cry. This points plainly to Cuba, and if the people of England were to give you instructions, I may venture to say, ninety-nine in a hundred would be for attacking that island." Pulteney to Vernon, August 17, 1740, in ' Letters to an Honest Sailor.'

It would seem that, up to the day of Ogle's arrival, Vernon had formed no distinct plans for the future. He had been looking forward to talking over everything with Lord Cathcart, in whom he had reason for placing the highest confidence. But Cathcart died, and Wentworth, who took his place, was an officer of very inferior ability, for whom Vernon, from the first, entertained dislike and distrust. Wentworth, it is fair to add, did not deserve this. He appears to have been sensible, if not very able; and he was certainly anxious to do for his country the best that lay in his power.

As the result of a council of war held on January 10th,[1] it was determined to proceed with the whole force to windward to observe the motions of the French at Port Louis in Hispaniola. Vernon formed his large fleet into three divisions, one under himself, one under Ogle, and one under Commodore Richard Lestock. Part of the force got out of harbour on January 22nd, but the whole did not make an offing until January 29th. On February 8th it was off Cape Tiburon, the western point of Hispaniola. There the Vice-Admiral was rejoined by the *Wolf*, 10, Commander William Dandridge. She had been sent ahead to gain intelligence, and she reported that there were in Port Louis nineteen large ships, one of which had a flag at the main, and another a broad pennant flying ; but, when the fleet arrived off the place on the 12th, it was found that Dandridge had been mistaken,[2] and that there were in port only some unrigged merchantmen and a large frigate. Three days later Vernon obtained permission from the governor of Port Louis to wood and water the fleet, and learnt that the Marquis d'Antin had returned to Europe. At another council of war it was decided, mainly in deference to Vernon's representations, to attack Cartagena. The fleet, therefore, weighed on January 25th, the *Weymouth*, 60, Captain Charles Knowles, *Experiment*, 20, Captain James Rentone, and a sloop, being sent ahead to sound the coast and to find a safe anchorage for the huge flotilla, which consisted, with the transports, of a hundred and twenty-four sail.

Vernon dropped anchor in the Bay of Playa Grande[3] on March 4th, and at once made such a disposition of his small craft

---

[1] There were present, in addition to Vernon and Ogle, Governor Trelawney of Jamaica, and Generals Wentworth and Guise.

[2] He was misled by a haze which prevailed when he made his reconnaissance.

[3] It is to the windward of Cartagena, between it and Point Canoa.

as to suggest that he intended them to cover a disembarkation of the army. This had the desired effect. It drew a large part of the enemy's troops down to the shore in that neighbourhood, and induced them to begin throwing up intrenchments there.

But no actual attack was made until March 9th, and in the meantime the Spanish garrison of four thousand men, besides negroes and Indians, and the naval force under Don Blas de Leso, perfected its preparations for defence.

The following description of Cartagena, as it then was, is mainly from Beatson :—[1]

The city is in a great measure surrounded by water. It is divided into two unequal parts, the city of Cartagena, and its suburb, called Ximani. The walls of the former are washed by the waves of the Bay of Mexico ; but, on account of some rocks, and perpetual surf, there is no approaching it on that side. The water on the outside of the harbour is seldom smooth, so that landing is at most times difficult. The only entrance to the harbour is upwards of two leagues to the westward of the city, between two narrow peninsulas, the one called Tierra Bomba, the other called the Baradera. This entry is called Boca Chica, or the Little Mouth, and is so narrow that only one ship can enter at a time. It was defended, on the Tierra Bomba side, by a fort called San Luis, a regular square, with four bastions, mounted with eighty-two pieces of cannon and three mortars ; but the counterscarp and glacès were not completed. To this were added Fort San Felipe, mounted with seven guns, and Fort Santiago, of fifteen guns, and a small fort of four guns called Battery de Chamba. These served as outworks to Fort San Luis. On the other side of the harbour's mouth lies a fascine battery,[2] called the Baradera ; and, in a small bay at the back of that, another battery of four guns. And, facing the entrance of the harbour, on a small, flat island, stood Fort San Jose, of twenty-one guns. From this fort to Fort San Luis, a strong boom, made of logs and cables, was laid across, fastened with three large anchors at each end ; and just behind the boom were moored four ships of the line. Beyond this passage lies the great lake or outer harbour of Cartagena, several leagues in circumference, and land-locked on all sides. About mid-way to the town, it grows narrower ; and, within less than a league of it, two points project into the lake from the inner harbour. On the northmost of these was a strong fort called Castillo Grande, being a regular square with four bastions, defended to the land by a wet ditch and glacis proper. The face of the curtain, towards the sea, was covered by a ravelin, and a double line of heavy cannon. The number of guns in this fort was fifty-nine, though there were embrasures for sixty-one. On the opposite point was a horseshoe battery of twelve guns, called Fort Mancinilla. In the middle, between these two forts, is a large shoal with only a few feet of water on it. On each side of this were sunk large ships. At the end of the inner harbour stands the city of Cartagena, on two flat sandy keys or islands, well fortified to the land, and with lakes and morasses running round it. On the fortification of the city are mounted one hundred and sixty guns, and on those of the suburbs, one hundred and forty. South of the city, about a quarter of a mile from the Ximani gate, stands Fort San Lazar, on an eminence about fifty or sixty feet high. It is composed of a square of fifty feet, having three demi-bastions, and two guns in each

---

[1] ' Nav. and Mil. Mems.' iii. 24.

[2] It was for fifteen 24-pounders ; but these seem not to have been mounted until after operations had been begun.

face, one in each flank, and three in each curtain. It completely commands the town ; but there.is a hill about four hundred yards from it which overlooks and commands it entirely.'

Early in the morning of March 9th, Sir Chaloner Ogle, who had shifted his flag from the *Russell*, 80, to the *Jersey*, 60, Captain Peter Lawrence, and who had General Wentworth with him, moved with his division,[1] towards the mouth of the harbour. He was presently followed by Vice-Admiral Vernon and his division,[2] convoying the transports full of troops. The third division,[3] under Commodore Lestock, was left at anchor, so as to distract the attention of the enemy.

The *Princess Amelia*, 80, was specially told off to attack Battery de Chamba, and the *Norfolk*, 80, *Russell*, 80, and *Shrewsbury*, 80, were similarly told off to batter forts Santiago and San Felipe. As the division of Ogle approached, Chamba opened fire, but was soon silenced by the *Princess Amelia*, Captain John Hemmington. At about noon the *Norfolk*, Captain Thomas Graves (1), *Russell*, Captain Harry Norris, and the *Shrewsbury*, Captain Isaac Townsend, anchored in their assigned positions and fired so vigorously that both the forts opposed to them were rendered untenable within an hour. They were then taken possession of by landing parties. Generals Wentworth and Guise, and Colonel Wolfe also landed soon afterwards, and on that day and the 10th, most of the troops were put ashore. These initial successes were gained at little cost. Only six men were killed on board the *Norfolk* and *Russell*, and although the *Shrewsbury* had her cable shot away and fell into a position where she lay for seven hours under a most infernal fire from two or three hundred guns she had but twenty killed and forty wounded. She received, however, two hundred and forty shot in her hull, and of these sixteen were between wind and water.

The following days were employed in landing guns and stores ; in forming a camp in a somewhat ill-chosen position, before Fort San

[1] *Princess Amelia*, 80, *Windsor*, 60, *York*, 60, *Norfolk*, 80, *Russell*, 80, *Shrewsbury*, 80, *Ripon*, 60, *Lichfield*, 50, *Jersey*, 60, *Tilbury*, 60, *Experiment*, 20, *Sheerness*, 20, *Vesuvius*, fireship, *Terrible*, bomb, *Phaeton*, fireship, and *Goodly*, tender.

[2] *Orford*, 70, *Princess Louisa*, 60, *Worcester*, 60, *Chichester*, 80, *Princess Caroline* (flag), 80, *Torbay*, 80, *Strafford*, 60, *Weymouth*, 60, *Deptford*, 60, *Burford*, 70, *Squirrel*, 20, *Shoreham*, 20, *Eleanor*, 10, *Seahorse*, 20, the fireships *Strombolo*, *Success*, *Vulcan* and *Cumberland*, the tender *Pompey*, and a brig.

[3] *Defiance*, 60, *Dunkirk*, 60, *Lion*, 60, *Prince Frederick*, 70, *Boyne*, 80, *Hampton Court*, 70, *Falmouth*, 50, *Montagu*, 60, *Suffolk*, 70, *Astræa*, 12, *Wolf*, 10, the fireships *Ætna* and *Firebrand*, and the *Virgin Queen*, tender.

Luis; and in quarrels between Wentworth and Vernon, who was dissatisfied with the manner in which the engineers did their work, and who used unbecoming language to the military commander-in-chief. As the camp was exposed to the fire of the Spanish fascine battery on the Baradera side, an attack upon this was made on the night of March 19th, when the boats of the fleet, under Captain Thomas Watson (1), of the *Princess Caroline*, Captain Harry Norris, of the *Russell*, and Captain Charles Colby, of the *Boyne*, landed a party of five hundred seamen and soldiers commanded by Captains the Hon. Edward Boscawen, of the *Shoreham*, William Laws, and Thomas Cotes,[1] R.N. The party was put ashore about a mile to leeward of the Baradera Battery, under the very muzzles of a masked battery of five guns that had been thrown up on the beach; but, although a little confused at first by the hot fire which was opened from this, the men promptly rushed it, and then, pushing on, carried the Baradera Battery itself, and, suffering very little loss, spiked the guns, and set the carriages, fascines, platforms, magazines and guard-houses, on fire.

This well-managed exploit relieved the army before San Luis; but there was much sickness in the camp, the works did not progress with the expected rapidity, and Vice-Admiral Vernon grew daily more impatient and irritable. To add to his annoyance, the Spaniards partially refitted the abandoned Baradera Battery, and again began to fire upon the camp from it. They were driven out by the *Ripon*, 60, Captain Thomas Jolly, which later prevented any further attempts from being made to mount guns there. The main British battery opened against Fort San Luis on the morning of the 21st; and on that and the next day a furious fire was maintained on both sides.

On the morning of March 23rd, a general attack upon all the forts and batteries was begun. Commodore Lestock, with the *Boyne*, 80, Captain Charles Colby, *Princess Amelia*, 80, Captain John Hemmington, *Prince Frederick*, 70, Captain Lord Aubrey Beauclerk, *Hampton Court*, 70, Captain Digby Dent (2), *Suffolk*, 70, Captain Thomas Davers, and *Tilbury*, 60, Captain Robert Long, engaged the Spanish forts, batteries and ships,[2] there not being room to bring more vessels to bear upon the enemy's defences. The

---

[1] The military officers were Captains James Murray and Washington.
[2] *Galicia*, 70, flag of Don Blas de Leso; *San Carlos*, 66, *Africa*, 60, and *San Felipe*, 60.

Boyne suffered so severely that she had to be called off at night; the *Prince Frederick*, which lost her captain,[1] and the *Hampton Court*, very much shattered, had to be recalled on the following morning. The other ships did excellent service, and were less injured; yet it was found expedient to withdraw even these on the 24th. During this attack, the chief engineer was mortally wounded : on the other hand, Fort San Luis was breached, and General Wentworth, who went in person to view the effect of the bombardment, determined to assault the place on the night of March 25th.

Vernon undertook to make a diversion on the Baradera side, and, in the afternoon of the 25th, landed Captain Charles Knowles and some seamen near the remains of the fascine battery. The assault was then made with complete success, and with the loss of but a single man. Owing to the fall of Fort San Luis, the Spaniards had to scuttle or burn the *Africa*, *San Carlos*, and *San Felipe*, and they were thrown into so much confusion that Captain Knowles, taking advantage of it, apparently upon his own authority, pulled across to Fort San Jose, on the island, and stormed it without the slightest difficulty. Still unwilling to let slip what seemed to be so splendid an opportunity for dealing serious blows, he, with Captain Thomas Watson, forced a way within the boom, and boarded and took the *Galicia*, 70.[2] They also destroyed the boom, so that on the morning of the 26th part of the British fleet entered the lake. A few days later, it passed up to the narrow entrance leading to the harbour proper,[3] and, upon its approach, the enemy abandoned Castillo Grande, sank two line-of-battleships[4] which had been moored in the channel, and blew up Fort Mancinilla. Such was the general situation on March 31st.[5]

All would, doubtless, have continued to go well, but for the unhappy dissensions between the Vice-Admiral and the General. The siege had caused much disease, especially among the troops, which, on March 25th, had lost about five hundred men, and had about one thousand five hundred more sick on board the hospital-ships *Princess Royal* and *Scarborough*. The fleet was considerably less unhealthy; yet, while the fleet had plenty of water, and, very often, fresh meat

---

[1] Whose place was taken by Captain the Hon. Edward Boscawen.

[2] She was towed out.

[3] Called the Surgidero, or Anchorage.

[4] *Conquistador*, 66, and *Dragón*, 60.

[5] On April 1st Vernon sent home a sanguine dispatch which reached the Duke of Newcastle on May 17th, and caused general exultation.

and turtle, the army sometimes suffered from absolute want. Vernon seems to have forgotten that troops and seamen alike served a common sovereign and a common cause. He took no measures for supplying water to the army; he refused Wentworth's reasonable request that two or three small craft should be told off to catch turtle for the use of the sick; and, speaking generally, his relations with his military colleague were unaccommodating, boisterous, and overbearing. Wentworth, in consequence, became disgusted, and, rather than seek the co-operation of so bearish and dictatorial a man as Vernon, he sometimes stood sullenly aloof, regardless of the magnitude of the public interests involved.

On April 1st the Vice-Admiral moved his bomb-ketches, covered

MEDAL COMMEMORATIVE OF THE DESTRUCTION OF SOME OF THE DEFENCES OF CARTAGENA BY VICE-ADMIRAL EDWARD VERNON, MARCH, 1741.

(From an original kindly lent by H.S.H. Captain Prince Louis of Battenberg, R.N.)

by the *Experiment*, 20, Captain James Rentone, and the *Shoreham*, 20, Captain Thomas Brodrick,[1] into the Surgidero; and Commodore Lestock, who had re-embarked the troops from Tierra Bomba, joined Vernon off Castillo Grande. On the 2nd, three fireships took up their station within the Surgidero in order to protect a projected landing of troops at a place called La Quinta. On the 3rd, the *Weymouth*, 60, Captain Charles Knowles, also passed the narrows; and, early on the morning of the 5th, General Blakeney, with about one thousand five hundred men, was set ashore, and presently pushed forward towards Fort San Lazar, the only remaining outwork of Cartagena. Some resistance was encountered, but the enemy eventually retired. On the 6th, more of the army dis-

---

[1] Who had succeeded Captain the Hon. E. Boscawen.

embarked, and, having joined Blakeney's brigade, encamped with it on a plain about a mile from San Lazar.

On the 7th, a military council of war came to the conclusion that Fort San Lazar ought not to be attempted until a battery should be raised against it, and that the reduction of the work would be greatly facilitated by the co-operation of the bomb-ketches and a ship of the line with the army. Vernon, on being informed of this, testily replied that he strongly disapproved of waiting for the erection of a battery, and that, if a battery should be erected against so paltry a fort, he felt sure that the enemy would not wait for it to be made ready for action ; but, in his answer, he paid no attention to the council's suggestion as to the co-operation of the ships ; nor could Wentworth induce the Vice-Admiral to order his vessels to cover a detachment of troops which had been posted with a view to cutting off communication between Cartagena and the country at its back. In short, it appears that Vernon believed that the army could do, and ought to do, all that remained to be done, and that Wentworth, with wiser intuition, knew that only by co-operation could the desired results be attained. But sickness increased ashore, water grew daily scarcer, and the Spanish defences became hourly more formidable ; and, in an evil moment, at the pressing instance of Vernon, and against the better judgment of some of the land officers, the storming of San Lazar was ordered, and was attempted before daybreak on April 9th. Things were mismanaged ; officers were confused by lack of detailed instructions, and the assault was repulsed with heavy loss.[1]

Operations were continued for two days longer ; but on the 11th a council of land officers decided that, " without a considerable reinforcement from the fleet, it would not be possible to go on with the enterprise." Vernon still shut his ears to the suggestions of his military colleagues ; and when the council, having received from him a very non-pertinent answer, reassembled, it desired that the Vice-Admiral would make arrangements for re-embarking the forces and stores, since it appeared, from his silence concerning the material point, that no reinforcement was to be looked for. On the 14th, after some further interchange of messages, a general council of war, consisting of the sea as well as of the land officers, met on board the flagship. The conference was stormy ; and, in the course of it, Vernon quitted his cabin in a passion. After his departure, Sir

---

[1] The loss was 179 killed ; 459 wounded, many mortally ; and 16 taken prisoners.

Chaloner Ogle gave reasons for objecting to disembark the seamen from the fleet; and Vernon, who sat in his stern-walk within hearing, interjected a remark to the effect that, if the men were set ashore, some of them would infallibly desert to the enemy. The Vice-Admiral then returned to his cabin, and the council unanimously determined that the troops and guns should be re-embarked. In pursuance of this decision, the guns, stores, and baggage were reshipped on the 15th, and the troops, only 3569 of whom remained fit for duty, on the 16th.

Vernon, who may, by that time, have begun to feel uneasy concerning the effect which so signal a miscarriage would have upon his reputation,[1] made a last, but quite useless effort, against the town. Having fitted up his prize, the *Galicia*, as a floating battery of sixteen guns, and having fortified her with earth or sand, he caused her to be warped in as near as possible to the town. During the morning of the 16th, under the command of Captain Daniel Hore, she fired into the place continuously for seven hours. She was then so damaged that she was ordered to cut her cables and drift out of gunshot, but she grounded on a shoal, and had to be abandoned.[2] She lost six killed and fifty-six wounded. But for the happy chance that she grounded, she would probably have sunk with all hands, for she had received twenty shot between wind and water.

As soon as the works which had been already taken had been dismantled and destroyed, the wretched remains of the expedition sailed for Jamaica, where the fleet arrived on May 19th, and where it found a welcome convoy from England awaiting it. Commodore Lestock, with many of the heavier ships[3] and five frigates, was soon afterwards sent home in charge of the trade. Vernon, chiefly in consequence of his dislike to be further associated with Wentworth, wished to go home also; but the ministry, which adroitly flattered him, persuaded him to remain.

---

[1] It is also suggested that Vernon desired to convince General Wentworth, by actual experiment, that ships could not operate with success against the town. But, if so, the experiment was not a fair one. The *Galicia* did not get near the walls because she approached them at the wrong point. Elsewhere there was deep water within pistol-shot of the ramparts. Smollett, vii. 287.

[2] She was subsequently burnt by the British.

[3] *Princess Caroline*, 80, *Russell*, 80, *Norfolk*, 80, *Shrewsbury*, 80, *Princess Amelia*, 80, *Torbay*, 80, *Chichester*, 80, *Hampton Court*, 70, *Burford*, 70, *Windsor*, 60, and *Falmouth*, 50. Vernon transferred his flag to the *Boyne*, 80.

The next attempt of the fleet in the West Indies was against Santiago de Cuba. The home Government would have preferred to see Havana attacked, but the place was strong, and the squadron of Don Rodrigo de Torres lay in the port. Governor Trelawney, of Jamaica, urged an expedition, across the Isthmus of Darien, against Panama, but gave way to the representations of Vernon, Ogle, Wentworth, and Guise, all of whom voted for Santiago de Cuba as the town which, upon the whole, offered the brightest prospects of success. On June 25th, therefore, Captain James Rentone, in the *Ripon*, 60,[1] was dispatched to reconnoitre the harbour and its defences, and on June 30th the fleet[2] put to sea. The Vice-Admiral left at Jamaica the *Suffolk*, 70, *Strafford*, 60, *Dunkirk*, 60, *Bristol*, 50, *Lichfield*, 50, and *Vulcan*, 8, under Captain Thomas Davers, to protect the island and its trade, and ordered the *York*, 60, *Augusta*, 60, and *Deptford*, 60, which were refitting at Port Royal, to be completed for sea, and to be sent after him, as soon as possible.

A spacious harbour lying near the south-east end of Cuba, and then known as Walthenham Bay,[3] was selected as the general rendezvous; and there the expedition dropped anchor on July 18th. This harbour is about sixty-five miles to the eastward of Santiago, which occupies the head of a much smaller bay, and which has a well-defended narrow entrance, closed at that time by means of a substantial boom. Santiago was supposed to be impregnable from seaward, and the leaders of the fleet and army decided to attack it overland from Cumberland Harbour. To facilitate this operation, Vernon despatched some cruisers to watch twelve Spanish sail of the line which lay at Havana, and which constituted a " potential " fleet of decidedly dangerous strength. He also sent other vessels to blockade Santiago; and across the mouth of Cumberland Harbour he stationed six of his largest ships, so that, should any enemy approach, the transports within could not be reached without a

---

[1] Captain Thomas Jolly had died in May. Lord Augustus Fitzroy, of the *Orford*, 70, had also fallen a victim to the climate soon after the arrival of the fleet at Jamaica.

[2] *Boyne*, 80, flag of Vernon, *Cumberland*, 80, flag of Ogle, *Grafton*, 70, *Kent*, 70, *Worcester*, 60, *Tilbury*, 60, *Montagu*, 60, *Chester*, 50, *Tiger*, 50, *Shoreham*, 20, *Experiment*, 20, *Sheerness*, 20, *Alderney*, bomb, *Strombolo*, *Phaeton*, and *Vesuvius*, fireships, *Bonetta* and *Triton*, sloops, *Princess Royal* and *Scarborough*, hospital ships, and *Pompey*, tender, besides about 40 transports carrying 3400 troops.

[3] Re-named Cumberland Harbour by Vernon. It is the bay between Punto de Guantánamo and Caimamera.

severe struggle. But in the meantime Wentworth lost heart. He landed, but he did not go far. The country before him was thickly wooded; his men had rapidly become sickly; he found great difficulty in dragging his guns along with him; and, although Vernon assured him that, if he pressed on, he should find ships before Santiago ready to co-operate with him, the General declined to advance any further. The Vice-Admiral in person went round to Santiago with a view to seeing whether, after all, he could not devise some method of capturing it from the sea; but he was obliged to agree that the venture offered no chances of success. The whole scheme, therefore, was abandoned, the troops being re-embarked on November 20th, and the fleet quitting Cumberland Harbour for Jamaica on November 28th.

This abortive enterprise was as ill-conceived as it was pusillanimously attempted. It was the professed desire of the ministry in England, and of the naval and military chiefs on the spot, to conquer Cuba.[1] Havana was then, as it is now, the capital and heart of the island; and Santiago was a comparatively insignificant place of less strategic and commercial importance than to-day. Yet it was determined to avoid Havana, and to attack Santiago, in spite of the fact that at Havana lay the strong squadron of Don Rodrigo de Torres. Sane strategy would have dictated firstly the annihilation or neutralisation of that formidable " potential " fleet, and secondly the dealing of a blow at the heart instead of at the extremities of the island. That Don Rodrigo lay fast, and did not come out, affords no justification of the British action. He might have elected to come out; and, had he done so, he might, with his superior force, have crushed Vernon, who would have been hampered by the presence of his transports and by the necessity of looking to their safety. As for the pusillanimity with which the descent was attempted, it is sufficient to say that Wentworth lay for about three months, almost inactive, within three or four days' march of Santiago; that there was at no time any considerable body of Spanish troops between him and that city; that the landward defences of Santiago were known to be contemptible; and that the delay involved the sacrifice of more men than would have perished in any active operations that could have been necessary to secure the fall of the place.

---

[1] Settlers were actually invited to cross from North America, and were promised grants of land in the island.—Speech of Gov. Shirley at Boston, Sept. 23rd, 1741. The re-naming of places by the British leaders was also significant.

The Ministry censured both Vernon and Wentworth, yet only with mildness, and chiefly on account of the personal quarrels which had been allowed to spring up between them. The Duke of Newcastle, on October 31st, wrote to Vernon :—

"His Majesty has commanded me to acquaint you and General Wentworth that he sees with great concern the heats and animosities that have arisen between his officers by sea and land, contrary to his orders, whereby the service cannot but greatly suffer ; and I am ordered to recommend to you in the strongest manner carefully to avoid the like for the future, and that, in case of any difference of opinion, all acrimony and warmth of expression should be avoided."

After the collapse of the undertaking had become known in England, neither Admiral nor General received from the Government any much stronger blame than this. Yet one, if not both, should have been recalled. It was obvious, even to their best friends,[1] that they could not work satisfactorily one with the other. Unhappily, they were allowed to embark together upon further adventures.

The transports from Santiago reached Jamaica in safety, while the fleet cruised for a time off Hispaniola in order to protect the arrival of an expected convoy [2] from England. After a time, the Vice-Admiral left part of his force, under Captain Cornelius Mitchell, of the *Kent*, 70, to look for the convoy, and proceeded to Jamaica, where a council of war was held on January 8th, 1742. The council eventually decided to adopt a plan which had been submitted to it by Lowther, the ex-buccaneer, who knew the country well. This involved a landing at Puerto Bello, and a march across the isthmus to Panama, with three thousand soldiers, five hundred negroes, and four hundred friendly Mosquito Indians. But many delays occurred. In the interval, Lowther, in the *Triton*, sloop, convoyed by Captain Henry Dennis in the *Experiment*, went to the Mosquito coast to procure information and to make arrangements with the natives. The *Triton* was for this service disguised as a trader. As for Vernon, who was terribly impatient at the slowness with which the land forces were being got ready, and who had learnt that Spanish reinforcements were on their way to Cartagena, he occupied some of his spare time in making a cruise off Cartagena, with the

---

[1] Pulteney's amiable appeals to Vernon to control his temper were almost pathetic. See especially Pulteney's letter of Nov. 17th, 1741, in 'Letters to an Honest Sailor.'

[2] The convoy, consisting of the *Greenwich*, 50, *St. Albans*, 50, and *Fox*, 20, with transports containing about two thousand troops, reached Jamaica on January 15th, without having sighted Mitchell's squadron.

object of suggesting to the enemy that he was contemplating a new attack upon that place. Sir Chaloner Ogle, who had been left behind at Jamaica to bring on the main body of the expeditionary forces, was not able to sail until the middle of March, 1742. On the 25th of that month, he rejoined the Vice-Admiral, and the fleet [1] then made the best of its way to its destination.

The *Experiment* and *Triton* had been directed to make rendezvous with the fleet off the Bastimentos Islands, in what is now called the Gulf of San Blas. On March 26th, Vernon detached the *Montagu*, Captain William Chambers, to look for those vessels, and to order them, in case they should be fallen in with, to join a detachment which was to land a body of troops at Nombre de Dios, at the head of the gulf of San Blas.[2] The fleet sighted land near the Bastimentos on March 28th, but, seeing nothing of the *Experiment* and *Triton*, passed on to Puerto Bello, and, entering the harbour in line of battle, dropped anchor there before nightfall, without any opposition on the part of the Spanish Governor, who fled with such troops as he had.

Lowther's report, received when the fleet was at Puerto Bello, had the effect of convincing General Wentworth that the design against Panama was impracticable; yet Wentworth was so lacking in tact that, instead of communicating his decision directly to Vernon, he mentioned it casually to Governor Trelawney, the result being that Vernon's first intimation that the expedition was destined to be a failure was conveyed to him in the form of a private request from Trelawney for a passage back to Jamaica. Wentworth's views were formally adopted at a council of war at which seven military officers were present, and were ratified at a general council composed of three military and two naval officers. Vernon and Ogle formed the minority, and could do nothing but acquiesce, although the Vice-Admiral was strongly of opinion that, seeing that Panama had in earlier years been taken from across the isthmus by Sir Henry Morgan with five hundred buccaneers, it might be taken again by the much larger forces which were at the disposal of the British

---

[1] *Boyne*, 80, flag of Vernon, *Cumberland*, 80, flag of Ogle, *Kent*, 70, *Orford*, 70, *Worcester*, 60, *Defiance*, 60, *York*, 60, *Montagu*, 60, *St. Albans*, 50, and *Greenwich*, 50, with three fireships, two hospital ships, and about forty transports. Governor Trelawney, as a colonel, was with the troops.

[2] This landing was never effected. The *Experiment* and *Triton* rejoined the fleet at Puerto Bello.

leaders in 1742. The fleet, therefore, quitted Puerto Bello for
Jamaica on April 3rd, having effected nothing.[1]

Indeed, the only important advance made in the West Indies in
the course of the year was the annexation and settlement of Roatan
Island, in the bay of Honduras, by an expedition[2] from Jamaica
convoyed by the *Lichfield*, 50, Captain James Cusack, and the
Bonetta, sloop, Commander William Lea. Nor is it astonishing
that so little was done. The Admiral and the General were on
worse terms than ever, and their quarrels were taken up by all
around them. Even Ogle and Trelawney fell out. So scandalous
a state of things was terminated, after it had endured far too long,
by the arrival at Jamaica on September 23rd of the *Gibraltar*, 20,
Captain Thorpe Fowke, with orders for both Vernon and Wentworth to return to England. Vernon sailed in the *Boyne*, 80, on
October 18th, leaving Sir Chaloner Ogle in command of the station ;
and Wentworth, with the remnants of the army, departed soon
afterwards, under convoy of the *Defiance*, 60, Captain Daniel Hore,
and the *Worcester*, 60, Captain William Cleland.

In the Mediterranean, where there had been scarcely a large
enough naval force for the due protection of trade, and for the due
observation of the declared and the suspected enemies of Great
Britain, Vice-Admiral Nicholas Haddock had been joined, in
February, 1742, by a considerable reinforcement under Commodore
Richard Lestock (2), who, on March 13th following, was promoted
to be Rear-Admiral of the White.[3] According to Charnock, Lestock,
during this period, " exhibited some proofs of that impatient temper
and improper professional pride which, afterwards becoming infinitely
more apparent, cannot but be condemned even by those who are so
warmly attached to him as to insist that no part of his conduct was
ever injurious or prejudicial to the cause and interests of his native
country."[4] Haddock, owing to ill-health, had to resign his
command and return to England ;[5] and, pending the arrival in the
Mediterranean of his successor, Lestock officiated as commander-in-
chief. Lestock acted with some energy against the enemy, whom

---

[1] The British cruisers were, however, very successful, as will be seen in the next
chapter.

[2] Which reached Roatan on August 23rd.

[3] He was further advanced to be Rear of the Red, on August 9th, 1743, and Vice
of the White, on December 7th, 1743.

[4] .'Biog. Nav.' iii. 340.

[5] Which he reached in the *Roebuck*, 40, on May 26th, 1742.

he obliged to postpone an intended embarkation of troops; but, on the other hand, he again allowed his unfortunate temper to get the better of him. In view of what happened at a later date, it is desirable to reprint here from Charnock [1] an order and certain letters which will explain not only Lestock's peremptory methods, but also his interpretation, at that time, of some of the duties of subordinate commanders when in face of the enemy.

REAR-ADMIRAL LESTOCK TO COMMANDER JAMES HODSELL, OF THE
Ann Galley, FIRESHIP.

"Captain Hodsell: Go to the *Lenox, Nassau, Royal Oak, Romney,* and *Dragon.*[2] Tell them I am the centre from whence the line of battle is to be formed, and, if any ship or ships cannot get into their stations, I am to find remedy for that; but those who can, and do not, get into their stations are blameable; and a line of battle is not to be trifled with nor misunderstood. Go with this yourself to the several captains, from, Sir, your most humble servant, Richard Lestock. *Neptune,* at sea. April 14th, 1742. P.S.—An enemy in sight would not admit of this deliberation."

CAPTAIN CURTIS BARNET, OF THE *Dragon,* TO REAR-ADMIRAL LESTOCK.

"I thought that all the ships of a fleet or squadron were to sail in their proper divisions. I have heard and read of divisions getting late into the line, not in time to have any part in the action; but never knew till now that it was my duty to leave the flag, or officer representing one, in whose division I am, without a particular order or signal. I therefore kept my station in the division, not with a design to trifle with the line of battle. I am, etc., C. Barnet."

REAR-ADMIRAL LESTOCK TO CAPTAIN CURTIS BARNET.

"I have your letter of the 15th inst., in answer to mine I sent you and several other captains by Captain Hodsell on the 14th inst., at the time the signal was out for the line of battle abreast of each other. Your not getting into line when you could have done it, gave me that occasion by the fireship.

"You say you thought that the ships of a fleet or squadron were to sail in their proper divisions; and you have heard and read of divisions getting late into the line, not in time to have any part of the action; but never till now knew that it was your duty to leave the flag, or officer representing one, in whose division you are, without a particular order or signal.

"Let us suppose that you are in a division, and that a signal for the line of battle is made; and that the commanding ship of that division, by bad sailing, could not get into the line, though all the rest of the squadron could have got into the line, but did not. That division makes one-third of the squadron.

"Now: is it your duty to see two-thirds of the squadron sacrificed to the enemy, when you could, but did not, join in the battle? An admiral, in such a case, would either leave the bad sailing ship for one that could get into the action, or would send

---

[1] 'Biog. Nav.' iv. 213 *et seq.* Charnock says: "Mr. Lestock appears in his vehemence of rage to have been guilty of a few literary omissions and mistakes, which we have supplied and corrected." The present editor has adopted some of Charnock's emendations and made others, chiefly with respect to punctuation.

[2] The *Dragon,* 60, Captain Curtis Barnet.

you such orders as should justify you at a court-martial for not coming into the action when you could have done it. Captain Rowley,[1] indeed, has not the power either to shift his ship, or to stop you with him.

"Such an account would tell but ill to our country after the loss of a battle. But I hope such a thing can never happen to an Englishman ; and the punishment inflicted on a breach of the 12th article of the Statute of Charles the Second upon those who withdraw, or keep back, or do not come into the fight and engage, would be what must follow in such a case.

"So I will say no more of trifling nor misunderstanding of a line of battle ; as these are, and must be, the consequences of a not trifling want of duty in the weighing of circumstances in regard to battle : for that is the cause why lines are formed.[2]

"The 13th article of the Fighting Instructions[3] leans that way also. So, having, I think, answered your letter, I am, Sir, your most humble servant, Richard Lestock. *Neptune,* at sea. April 16th, 1742."

CAPTAIN CURTIS BARNET TO REAR-ADMIRAL LESTOCK.

" Dragon, April 16th, 1742.

"Sir,—As you have given yourself the trouble to answer the letter I thought necessary to write in excuse for my continuing in my station in the division of which I am, when you made the signal for the line of battle abreast, and in it are pleased to say : ' Is it your duty to see two-thirds of the squadron sacrificed to the enemy, when you could, and did not, join in the battle ? ' I answer that I should readily concur in punishing rigidly any man who could, and did not, join in the battle. But, as the commanders of divisions will, I imagine, always expect that the captains, in their respective divisions, should, in anything like the late case, take directions from them, and, as we are to suppose every officer of that distinction neither wanting in zeal or capacity, I can make no doubt that such orders would be immediately given as would be most essential for his Majesty's service; and that a signal or order might be expected for the ships to make sail into the line if the commander of the division could not get up with his own ship, and did not think proper to remove into another. Without such an order or a proper signal, I could not in my conscience condemn any man for remaining with his division, or think that he fell under the 12th article of the Statute of Charles the Second, or the 13th of the Fighting Instructions ; for a man in his station cannot be said to withdraw, keep back, or not use his endeavours to engage the enemy in the order the admiral has prescribed. In this manner I should judge, were I to sit at a court-martial on such an occasion ; but in this manner shall no longer act, since you have been pleased to tell me Captain Rowley has not the power to shift his ship or stop me.

"I presume there are instances both of whole divisions going down to the enemy too soon, and of coming in so late as to have no part in the action ; but I never heard that the private captains who kept their stations in those divisions fell under the least censure ; and, as I was neither called nor sent from the division by order or signal, I had no apprehension of being blameable.

---

[1] Afterwards Admiral of the Fleet, Sir William Rowley; then senior officer of Barnet's division. Lestock meant that, as there was no flag-officer of the division, there was no possible question as to what was Barnet's duty.

[2] *I.e.,* "After all, I will not speak of this as trifling, for it is far too light a word to apply to so serious a subject."

[3] "As soon as the Admiral shall hoist a red flag on the flagstaff at the fore-topmast head, and fire a gun, every ship in the fleet is to use their utmost endeavour to engage the enemy, in the order the Admiral has prescribed unto them."

" With regard to what you are pleased to say of seeing the squadron sacrificed to the enemy, that cannot happen while you, Sir, command it, who will never go down to the enemy in an improper manner, with more sail than the principal ships of the line can keep you company. . . ."

Lestock had, undoubtedly, hoped to be continued as commander-in-chief in the Mediterranean ; but Vice-Admiral Thomas Mathews (R.)[1] was appointed to that post on March 25th, 1742, and, having hoisted his flag in the *Namur*, 90, sailed on April 16th,[2] and arrived at Gibraltar on May 7th. Lestock was hurt, and he is said to have foolishly showed his resentment by neglecting to obey instructions to send a frigate to meet Mathews. For this supposed omission Mathews publicly reprimanded Lestock as soon as the two flag-officers met.[3] From that moment the junior seems to have regarded his senior with scarcely-disguised hostility.

Mathews was a good officer, as strict in obeying as he was in enforcing discipline, and a jealous, yet not intemperate, believer in the dignity of the great position to which he had been called by his country. He was, moreover, a highly honourable man, of conspicuous gallantry. Lestock, on the other hand, was ever more ready to enforce than to obey the laws of discipline. In his eyes, his own person was fully as dignified as any rank or place with which his country could invest him. " Unconciliating in his manners, austere when in command, restless when in a subordinate station, he had," says Charnock, " fewer friends than fell to the lot of most men, and that number, which was gradually diminishing, his behaviour never appeared of a nature to recruit." His courage has not been questioned, but his abilities, which were considerable, were contracted and neutralised by a petty meanness of spirit and smallness of view that prevented him from ever commanding either confidence or respect. That Mathews disliked Lestock cannot be gainsaid.[4] Almost every naval officer of the day disliked Lestock.

[1] Thomas Mathews; born, 1676 ; captain, 1703 ; took the *Bien Aimé*, 26, in 1707, and the *Glorieux*, 44, in 1709 ; commanded the *Kent* at Cape Passaro, in 1718 ; Commissioner at Chatham, 1736 ; Vice-Admiral and Commander-in-Chief in the Mediterranean, 1742 ; Admiral, 1743 ; fought a spirited but partial action off Toulon, 1744 ; dismissed the service, 1746; died, 1751.

[2] In company with the *Princess Caroline*, 80, *Norfolk*, 80, and *Bedford*, 70.

[3] Lestock alleged that he had sent a frigate, which had failed to fall in with Mathews. It is admitted that, in this instance, no matter what were the facts as to the frigate, the Vice-Admiral behaved with somewhat unnecessary warmth.

[4] When he accepted his appointment, he stipulated that Lestock should be speedily recalled, but the stipulation was afterwards either forgotten or misunderstood.— Beatson, i. 153.

But Mathews was the last man in the world to allow his private dislikes to interfere with his duty.

The Vice-Admiral met the Rear-Admiral and part of the fleet at Villa Franca on May 27th. He at once instituted a strict watching blockade of Toulon, where a Spanish, as well as a French force, lay. This blockade was maintained chiefly by the division of Lestock, whose headquarters were off Hyères, while Mathews himself remained in reserve at Villa Franca, ready to sail upon the receipt of news that the enemy was at sea. In June, five Spanish galleys, which were to have escorted some Spanish troops to Italy, and which were laden with ammunition and stores, ventured to quit the shelter of Fort Ste. Marguerite, and crept round under the coast as far as the Gulf of St. Tropez. Captain Harry Norris, of the *Kingston*, 60, with a small detachment, blockaded them there, and when, although they were in a neutral port, they fired on him, he effected their destruction.[1] Other Spanish vessels were destroyed at Palamos, Mataro, and elsewhere.

In July, 1742, the Vice-Admiral, who had intelligence that the King of Sicily had dispatched a body of troops to the assistance of the Spaniards in Italy, ordered Commodore William Martin, with a small squadron,[2] to Naples, to endeavour to induce the King to withdraw his forces, and to adhere to a declaration of neutrality. Should the King refuse, Martin was to bombard the city. The squadron arrived, and anchored in the Bay on August 19th; and Martin sent ashore Commander de l'Angle with an ultimatum, and a demand for an answer in half-an-hour, unless, indeed, the King could not be reached within that time. After very little delay, the required assurance was given on the 20th, and the squadron thereupon departed, to the great relief of the Neapolitans. The incident, most creditably managed by Martin, would, perhaps, have had comparatively little importance, had not the same prince who, in 1742, was King of Sicily, become, in 1759, King Carlos III. of Spain. He then remembered against Great Britain the coercion which had been employed against him by the Commodore, and, towards the end of the Seven Years' War, and during the War of

---

[1] For details of this, see next chapter.

[2] *Ipswich*, 70, Commodore William Martin, *Panther*, 50, Captain Solomon Gideon, *Oxford*, 50, Captain Lord Harry Powlett, *Feversham*, 40, Captain Richard Hughes (2), *Dursley Galley*, 20, Commander Merrick de l'Angle; and the bombs, *Carcass*, 8, Lieut. John Bowdler, *Salamander*, 8, Lieut. John Phillipson, and *Terrible*, 8, Lieut. the Hon. George Edgcumbe; besides four tenders.

American Revolution, never ceased to do all that lay in his power to ruin the naval might which had thus humiliated him.

Commodore Martin rejoined the flag, and was soon afterwards again detached to destroy certain storehouses and magazines at Alassio, in the territory of the republic of Genoa. These, which were known to be destined for the use of the Spaniards, were all set on fire by a landing-party from the ships.

In 1743, the blockade of Toulon was continued, and Admiral Mathews, as before, exerted himself to the utmost to hinder the operations of the Spaniards in the Italian peninsula, and the transmission thither of stores and reinforcements from Spain. But the transactions on the station were not of sufficient importance to deserve description in this chapter. They are, therefore, relegated to the next.

One of the first actions of Sir Chaloner Ogle (1) [1] after he had, as has been seen, been left as commander-in-chief in the West Indies, upon Vernon's recall, was to organise an expedition against the Spanish settlements at La Guayra and Puerto Cabello, on the coast of Caracas, in what is now Venezuela. These were reported to be almost defenceless, and to be at the mercy of the fleet. Ogle entrusted the conduct of the expedition to Captain Charles Knowles, in the *Suffolk*, 70, and gave him directions to proceed first to Antigua, there to take under his orders such additional vessels as could be spared, and to embark a certain number of troops. Knowles carried out these instructions, and on February 12th, 1743, sailed for La Guayra. After touching at St. Christopher, he arrived off his port of destination on the 18th.

It is quite true that when Ogle first contemplated the descent upon the coast of Caracas, La Guayra was almost defenceless. Unfortunately, the Admiral suffered his projects to become known, and the Spanish governor of the place, with great promptitude and vigour, thereupon set himself to work to repair the fortifications, to build new ones, to raise extra forces, and to obtain fresh supplies of ammunition. [2]

When, consequently, on February 18th, the squadron began the attack at about midday, a warm and formidable opposition was met

---

[1] Promoted to be Vice-Admiral of the Red on August 9th, and Vice-Admiral of the White on December 7th, 1743.

[2] Some of this ammunition was obtained from the Dutch Governor of Curaçoa, who, by handing it over, committed an unwarrantable breach of the Dutch understanding with Great Britain.

with.   There was a swell which prevented the vessels from
approaching within about a mile from the forts, and the landing of
the troops was found to be impracticable.   Yet, although an attempt
to burn the shipping in harbour, by means of armed boats, failed as
a result of confusion of orders, and although the ships suffered badly,
it looked, at 4 o'clock P.M., as if the fire of the batteries was about
to be silenced.   But at that hour, a chance shot cut the cable of the
Burford, which was anchored at the head of the British line.   The
Burford drove on board the *Norwich*, and forced both her and the
Eltham out of station, the three vessels drifting almost helplessly to
leeward.   This re-encouraged the enemy, and although, up to
nightfall, the attack was pluckily continued, the British, after the
accident, had much the worse of the encounter, and were ultimately
obliged to draw off.   La Guayra was severely damaged ; a magazine
was blown up by a shell from the *Comet*, and about seven hundred
Spaniards were killed and wounded.   Yet, in spite of the gallantry
of the assailants, the day ended with their decisive repulse.   The
composition of Knowles's squadron, and the damage and loss
sustained by each ship, are shown in the following table : —

Ships.	Guns.	Commanders.	Shot received.[1]	Com- plement.	Killed.	Wounded.
Suffolk . .	70	Capt. Charles Knowles . . .	97	380	30	80
Burford .	70	„ Franklin Lushington .	73	380	24	50
Norwich .	50	„ Thomas Gregory (1) . .	7	250	1	11
Advice . .	50	„ Elliot Smith	10	250	7	15
Assistance .	50	„ Smith Callis	41	250	12	71
Eltham .	40	„ Richard Watkins (acting).	44	210	14	55
Lively . .	20	„ Henry Stewart (acting) .	10	120	7	24
Scarborough	20	Commander Lachlin Leslie . .	3	120	..	2
Otter . .	14	„ John Gage . . .	?	45	..	..
Comet, bomb	8	„ Richard Tyrrell . .	?	40	..	..

[1] Shot in the hull only are included.

Captain Lushington, of the *Burford*, a most excellent officer, was
mortally wounded by a chain-shot, which carried off one of his legs
at the thigh.   He died at Curaçoa on February 23rd, two hours
after he had been landed there.   The *Burford*, *Eltham*, and
Assistance, were almost completely disabled; the flagship had
fourteen guns dismounted ; and the squadron, as a whole, was, for
the moment, unserviceable.   It, therefore, proceeded to Curaçoa
to refit.

As soon as he had refitted, and had supplemented his rather reduced forces by taking on board a few Dutch volunteers, Captain Knowles, in pursuance of the Commander-in-Chief's design, turned his attention to Puerto Cabello. He sailed on March 20th, but, owing to a strong lee current, could not anchor in the neighbourhood of his destination until April 15th.

Puerto Cabello was even better prepared to receive him than La Guayra had been. There were in the place three hundred regular troops, twelve hundred seamen belonging to the vessels in port, and a large body of negroes and Indians. The Spaniards had hauled all their smaller craft up to the head of the harbour out of gunshot, and had moored a ship of sixty, and another of forty guns, in good defensive positions, while they had placed a large vessel ready for sinking in the mouth of the harbour. Newly-erected fascine batteries flanked the entrance, and two more, one mounting twelve, and the other seven guns, occupied a low point called Punta Brava. These last, in the opinion of Knowles, were ill-placed, and might be easily taken, and then employed against the fortress itself. He therefore, after having held a council of war, ordered in the *Lively* and *Eltham*, on the afternoon of the 16th, to cannonade the Punta Brava works, and prepared a landing-party, consisting of Dalzell's regiment, all the Marines of the squadron, and four hundred seamen,[1] which, as soon as the batteries should be silenced, was to storm them, while the *Assistance* lay anchored within pistol-shot of the shore to cover a retreat, should one be necessary.

The *Lively* and *Eltham* effected their part of the work by about sunset. All firing then ceased. As it grew dark the storming-party landed, and began to march along the beach towards the batteries, Knowles accompanying the advance in his galley. Just before 11 P.M. the foremost troop seized one of the batteries; but, at that moment, the Spaniards, being alarmed, began to fire from the other works, and, to the mortification of the British leaders, so blind a panic seized the men that they retired pell-mell in the most absolute confusion, and did not regain their self-possession until they were once more on board the ships.

After this disgraceful repulse, another council of war was held on April 21st, and, in pursuance of the resolutions then come to, a general attack from seaward was made upon the place on the morning of the 24th. The *Assistance, Burford, Suffolk,* and

---

[1] The whole being under Major Lucas, of Dalzell's Regiment.

Norwich were told off to batter the main work, and the *Scarborough*, *Lively*, and *Eltham*, to attack the fascine batteries at the entrance of the harbour.   Fire was opened at about 11 A.M., all the ships taking up their stations [1] as well as they possibly could, except the *Norwich*, which apparently hesitated to get into close action. Seeing this, Knowles very promptly sent Captain Henry Stewart (acting), of the *Lively*, to supersede Captain Thomas Gregory, who was put under arrest.[2]   Thenceforward, the engagement was hotly maintained until the close of day, when the enemy's fire slackened, and it became evident that his batteries had suffered severely.   He reopened fire, however, after dark, and so badly mauled the ships— some of which had, by that time, expended nearly all their ammunition—that, soon after 9 P.M., Knowles made the signal to cut cables, and drew off his shattered vessels.

The ships actually engaged in this disastrous affair were, saving the *Advice*, *Otter*, and *Comet*, the same as had been engaged at La Guayra, but some of them were differently commanded.   Captain Richard Watkins had been promoted from the *Eltham* to the *Burford*, *vice* Lushington, killed ; Captain Philip Durell (1) had succeeded Captain Watkins in the *Eltham ;* and, after the supersession of Captain Gregory, Commander John Gage, of the *Otter*, assumed command of the *Lively*.   The loss of the squadron was about two hundred men killed and wounded.   The ships refitted under shelter of the Keys of Barbarat, and were there rejoined by the *Advice*, which had been detached on scouting duty on March 23rd.   On April 28th it was determined that the force was no longer in a condition to attempt anything more against the enemy ; and, after an exchange of prisoners had been carried out, the ships belonging to the Leeward Islands' station [3] returned thither, and the rest of the squadron proceeded to Jamaica.   Captain Knowles, in the autumn, cruised off Martinique, and, soon afterwards, went home to England.

Late in 1743, the excited condition of parties in England, and

---

[1] In this they were impeded by the sinking of the Spanish vessel in the harbour's mouth.

[2] He was later sent to England and court-martialled at Spithead for misbehaviour. (C. M. Sept. 17th, 1743.)   The court dismissed him from the service ; but, after distinguishing himself as a volunteer, he was restored to his rank as from Nov. 12th, 1745. He ended his life in a duel.

[3] Where Commodore (later Vice-Admiral Sir) Peter Warren commanded, with his broad pennant in the *Superbe*, 60.

the widespread dissatisfaction there at the manner in which the interests of Great Britain had, according to the views of many, been sacrificed to those of Hannover, encouraged France to take up an active, instead of a merely benevolent attitude, with reference to the cause of Spain.[1]   France was further encouraged in the same direction by the growing jealousy with which the Emperor, the King of Prussia, and their allies, regarded the pretensions of Maria Theresia, Queen of Hungary, and by the results of the secret negotiations which were set on foot at Frankfurt-on-Main with the object of checking the alleged ambitions of that very able princess. France, therefore, concluded at Fontainebleau an offensive and defensive family alliance with Spain, each party guaranteeing the possessions and claims of the other, and agreeing that no peace should be concluded until the restoration of Gibraltar by Great Britain.   France also despatched reinforcements to the aid of Philip in Savoy; directed M. La Bruyère de Court, Lieutenant-General of the French squadron in Toulon, to co-operate with the Spanish squadron which, under Don Jose Navarro, had so long lain blockaded there by Admiral Mathews; and, early in 1744, sent forth from Brest Lieutenant-General de Roquefeuil, with nineteen men-of-war,[2] to cruise in the Channel.

The objects of France were manifold.   She desired, firstly, to expel Great Britain from the Mediterranean, and then, by sending her own Mediterranean fleet to join her squadrons in the Channel, to annihilate British superiority in those waters as well: she hoped, next, to oblige Great Britain to recall her troops from the Continent, and to desist from supporting on shore the cause of Maria Theresia: and, finally, she looked forward to fomenting revolution in England, and to restoring to the throne the exiled family of Stuart, by means of an invasion from Dunquerque.

The assumption by France of this actively hostile attitude had the happy effect of partially calming the violence of party rage in Great Britain.   The command of the Channel Fleet[3] was given to Admiral of the Fleet Sir John Norris, with Vice-Admiral Sir Charles Hardy (1) (B), and Rear-Admiral William Martin (B), as his

---

[1] The Treaty of Worms, September 1743, leagued together Great Britain, Holland, Austria, Saxony, and Sardinia.   This was met, in October 1743, by the Treaty of Frankfurt, which banded together France, Prussia, Hessen Cassel, and the Pfalz.

[2] These were presently joined by some from Rochefort.

[3] This presently included twenty-five ships of 50 guns and upwards, and twenty-four frigates and small craft.

immediate subordinates. Norris wished to go in search of M. de Roquefeuil, but, it being feared that the latter might possibly pass the British fleet at night, or in thick weather, and so get to Dunquerque, where a French army was awaiting his escort, the Commander-in-Chief was ordered to proceed with his whole strength to the Downs. De Roquefeuil was sighted off the Eddystone on February 3rd, with, it would appear, sixteen ships of fifty guns and upwards, and seven frigates and smaller craft. A little later, believing Norris to have taken refuge in Portsmouth, he detached five vessels, under M. de Barrailh, to Dunquerque, and himself anchored off Dungeness on February 24th.

De Barrailh seems to have passed Norris in the night. The latter, learning of De Roquefeuil's presence to the westward, weighed, and, although the wind was contrary, worked up towards him. At that moment the position of the French was extremely precarious. But, when he was not much more than six miles from the enemy, Norris was obliged by the tide, which made strongly against him, to anchor. De Roquefeuil thereupon got all his anchors apeak, and, as soon as the tide set in his favour, ordered his ships to weigh, and make independently for Brest. Many of the captains were too apprehensive to literally obey the command. Most of them cut or slipped, in order to lose as little time as possible; and, a strong north-westerly gale springing up, they went off at a great rate. The gale increased to a storm, and a fog supervened. The French reached Brest, ship by ship, in a more or less crippled condition, and Norris, hopeless of being able to overtake them, and having himself suffered considerably, returned to the Downs, and thence despatched his three-decked ships to Spithead, where they could lie in greater safety from the weather.[1]

In the meantime, the French flotilla before Dunquerque had experienced the full effects of the storm ; and several transports with troops and stores on board had foundered, or had been driven ashore. When news arrived of the flight of de Roquefeuil, de Barrailh also returned to Brest; and, there being no longer any prospect of a successful invasion of the United Kingdom, the rest of the French troops were disembarked, and the Young Pretender, who had been with them, returned to Paris. De Roquefeuil died on board his flagship, the *Superbe*, 76, on March 8th, and was succeeded in the

---

[1] Sir John Norris soon afterwards hauled down his flag for the last time. He was succeeded in command of the Channel Fleet by Sir John Balchen.

command by the Chef d'Escadre, later Vice-Admiral, Blouet de Camilly, who was directed to guard the French coasts and to detach de Barrailh to cruise off the Scilly Islands. In spite of the nature of these events, war was not formally declared by France until March 20th.[1] A counter-declaration was returned by Great Britain on the 31st [2] of the same month.

The outbreak of formal hostilities enabled the British Government to request Holland, under the stipulations of the treaty, to supply a naval force to co-operate with the British fleets. The States-General had already, in view of war, equipped some ships of forty-four guns and upwards; and they presently sent these and others, a few at a time, to the Downs, under Lieutenant-Admiral Hendrik Grave,[3] in the *Haarlem*, 74, Vice-Admiral Willem 'T Hooft, in the *Dordrecht*, 54, Vice-Admiral Cornelis Schrijver, in the *Damiaten*, 64, and Rear-Admiral Jacob Reijnst, in the *Leeuwenhorst*, 54. As the names and force of the ships are wrongly given in all English histories, they are here copied from De Jonge :—[4]

Haarlem, 72, *Dordrecht*, 54, *Damiaten*, 64, *Leeuwenhorst*, 54, *Delft*, 54, *Assendelft*, 54, *Edam*, 54, *Beekvliet*, 54, *Gorcum*, 44, *Oud Tijlingen*, 44, *Middelburg*, 44, *Gouderak*, 44, *Brederode*, 54,[5] *Tholen*, 64,[5] *Zierikzee*, 64,[5] *Goes*, 64,[5] *Kasteel van Medemblik*, 54,[5] *Ramhorst*, 54,[5] *Prins Friso*, 54,[5] *Vriesland*, 64.[5]

Vice-Admiral Sir Charles Hardy (1) (R) was sent southward with a squadron to escort the trade to Lisbon and some storeships to Gibraltar; Admiral Sir John Balchen and Vice-Admiral William Martin (B) cruised with a fleet in the Channel; and Sir John Balchen subsequently sailed with Martin and Vice-Admiral James Stewart (R) [6] to release Hardy's convoy, which was reported to have been blocked up in the Tagus by a French squadron. A small force, under Commodore Curtis Barnet, was also despatched to the East Indies; and Vice-Admiral Thomas Davers proceeded to the West Indies to relieve Sir Chaloner Ogle. The operations of these officers will be followed later. First, however, some attention must be

---

[1] By ordinance dated March 15th.

[2] By proclamation dated March 29th.

[3] Both Beatson, i. 184, and Hervey, iv. 257, for some unexplained reason, call this officer " Admiral Baccarest, or Baccherest." The contingent was officially styled the Auxiliary Squadron.

[4] 'Nederl. Zeewezen,' iv. 182.

[5] These did not join until late in the year.

[6] Stewart, Hardy, and Martin were not promoted to the ranks here given until June 23rd.

paid to the work of the Navy in the Mediterranean, where the
earliest fleet action of the war was fought.

Admiral Thomas Mathews,[1] being then at Turin,[2] was informed
on December 30th, 1743, that de Roquefeuil had sailed from Brest.
The intelligence was incorrect, but it induced him to suspect that
co-operation between the Brest and Toulon squadrons was intended.
He therefore sent orders to Minorca that all ships there were to put
to sea at once. A little later, he heard that M. La Bruyère de
Court and Don Jose Navarro purposed to quit Toulon together on
January 20th; and, hastening to Villa Franca, he embarked to join
Vice-Admiral Lestock, off Hyères. Upon arriving there early in

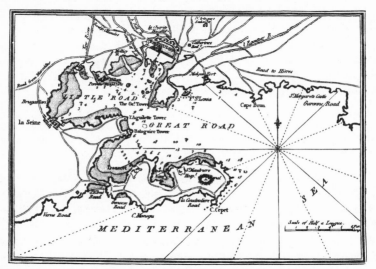

January, 1744, he found himself at the head of only twenty sail
of the line, four of which mounted but fifty guns apiece; but on
the 11th he was reinforced by the *Elizabeth*, 70, *Berwick*, 70,
Princesa, 70, and *Marlborough*, 90; on February 3rd, by the
Somerset, 80, *Warwick*, 60, and *Dragon*, 60; on February 10th, by
the *Boyne*, 80, and *Chichester*, 80, which had been sent out from
England; and on the 11th, on the very eve of the battle, by the
Royal Oak, 70. In the interval, he kept himself admirably informed,
by means of his frigates, of the motions and designs of the enemy.

[1] He was promoted to be Admiral of the White by the *Gazette* of February 18th, 1744.
[2] Where he had been concerting measures with the Sardinian Government for the
defence of the Italian coasts.

On February 9th, the combined fleet appeared under sail in the outer road of Toulon, and there formed a line of battle. Mathews had already unmoored and shortened in cable, and at 10 A.M. he weighed, the wind being westerly. Half an hour afterwards, he formed his line of battle ahead, and then plied to windward between the islands and the mainland, as if inviting the enemy to bear down on him. At night, having stationed cruisers to watch the foe, he

SIR WILLIAM ROWLEY, K.B., ADMIRAL OF THE FLEET.

anchored in Hyères Bay. That evening, when Vice-Admiral Lestock visited his chief on board the *Namur*, Mathews seems to have received him coldly, and to have presently desired him to return to his own ship.

At dawn on February 10th, the British weighed with a land breeze ; and at 7 A.M., the wind being from E. or E.S.E.,[1] Mathews

---

[1] At that time the allies had, or appeared to have, a westerly wind.

signalled for his fleet to draw into line of battle ahead with the wind large, and for Lestock's division to lead with the starboard tacks on board. Both Vice-Admiral Lestock and Rear-Admiral William Rowley repeated the signal, but, as the wind was very light, and there was a heavy swell from the westward, there was much difficulty in getting out of the bay in anything like the prescribed order ; and for some hours many of the ships had to tow with their boats in order to keep clear of one another. The enemy was seen at a distance of twelve or fifteen miles to the S.W. At 1 P.M. Mathews again signalled for the line of battle ahead ; and at 2 P.M. he hoisted a blue flag at the mizzen-topmast head, and fired a gun.[1] He brought to ; the junior flag-officers repeated the signal ; and the whole fleet brought to with the larboard tacks on board. The wind was then so light as to be almost imperceptible, and the swell drove the ships nearer and nearer to the island of Porquerolles. But at 3 P.M., when there was a nearly easterly breeze, Mathews signalled for the line of battle abreast,[2] and then stretched with his division to the south-west, Vice-Admiral Lestock stretching to the west, and Rear-Admiral Rowley making all possible sail with a view to extending the fleet and forming line of battle. Yet, towards evening, most of the ships were still out of station ; Rowley's division was scattered, and was far astern of Mathews's ; and neither Mathews's nor Lestock's division was in line. The allies, on the contrary, were in admirable order, at a distance of between four and five miles, M. de Court being in the centre, M. Gabaret in the van, and Don Jose Navarro in the rear.

Soon after nightfall, Mathews signalled to bring to, the most windwardly ships to do so first and to lie by with their larboard tacks on board. The fleet accordingly brought to close to the allies, and, during the night, lay well in sight of them, the wind varying in the eastern quarter. The *Essex*, 70, and *Winchelsea*, 20, were told off ' to watch the enemy, and to signal intelligence as to any movement on his part ; but these ships do not appear to have observed that, after the moon had set, the allies made sail, and thus

---

[1] " When the fleet is sailing before the wind, and the Admiral would have them bring to with the starboard tacks on board, he will hoist a red flag at the flagstaff on the mizzen-topmast head, and fire a gun ; if to bring to with the larboard tack, a blue flag at the same place, and fire a gun ; and every ship is to answer with the same signal."—' Sailing Instruction,' ix.

[2] Hoisting the Union and a pennant at the mizzen-peak, and firing a gun.— ' Fighting Inst.' ii.

increased their distance from the British, who, in the meantime, had
drifted between the enemy and Toulon, and lay with Cape Sicié
about twelve miles to the N.N.W. At dawn, at least nine miles
intervened between the headmost and the sternmost ships of
Mathews's command; and the various divisions were not in close
order. Neither were the allies as well stationed as M. de Court
must have desired. Not more than six miles, however, represented
the extreme length of their line.

As soon as he realised how far he was from the Admiral, Lestock
on his own responsibility made sail; but when, at 6.30 A.M.,
Mathews ordered the fleet as a whole to do the like, Lestock was
still five miles astern. M. de Court had already signalled for the
line of battle upon a wind; and the allies at that time, now with
their topsails and now with their foresails set, were stretching in
fairly good order to the southward. The British followed, but, says
Beatson :—

"As the rear division was at so great a distance from the centre, and the van not so
close as it should have been, the Admiral, at 7.30 A.M., made the signal for Rear-
Admiral Rowley and his division to make more sail—which signal the Vice-Admiral
repeated; and, soon after, the like signal was made for the Vice-Admiral and his
division. At 8 A.M. the Admiral made the signal for the fleet to draw into a line of
battle, one ship abreast of the other, with a large wind; and, half an hour after, he
made the signal for the fleet to draw into a line of battle, one ship ahead of another.
These signals were repeated by the junior flags."

Yet it took some time to form the line; and, in the meanwhile,
M. de Court seemed inclined to avoid a general action, and to
endeavour to draw the British towards the Strait. Mathews divined
his opponent's intention to be either to escape altogether, or to
proceed without fighting until, reinforced by the squadron from
Brest, he should be in a condition to go into battle with superior
forces in his favour. Mathews was, of course, unwilling to allow
either object to be attained; and it was for that reason that, at
about 11.30 A.M., when, as has been hinted, the order of battle was
still very incompletely formed, the Admiral hoisted the signal to
engage.

The fleets which were about to be opposed one to another were
constituted as follows :—[1]

_____

[1] The lists are taken, with slight alterations, from those in Beatson and Schomberg,
and from the evidence in the courts-martial. It would appear, however, that some of
the Spanish ships practically formed part of the allied centre.

Ships.	Guns.	Men.	Commanders.	Ships.	Guns.	Men.	Commanders.
Van.							
Stirling Castle . .	70	480	Thomas Cooper.	*Borée*	64	650	M. de Damaquart.
Warwick	60	400	Temple West.	*Toulouse* . . .	60	600	
Nassau	70	480	James Lloyd.	*Duc d'Orléans* .	74	800	M. d'Orves.
Barfleur . . .	90	765	Rear-Adm. William Rowley, (R.)	*Espérance* . .	74	820	M. Gabaret (Chef d'Esc.).
				Trident . . .	64	650	M. de Caylus.
			Merrick de l'Angle.	*Alcion* . . .	54	500	M. de Vaudreuil.
Princess Caroline .	80	600	Henry Osborn.	*Aquilon* . . .	48	500	
Berwick	70	480	Edward Hawke.	*Eole*	64	650	M. d'Albert.
Chichester . . .	80	600	William Dilkes.	*Atalante*, 20 .			
Boyne.	80	600	Rowland Frogmore.	A fireship, 8 .			
Kingston	60	400	John Lovet.				
Oxford, 50 . .	..	300	Lord Harry Powlett.				
Feversham, 40 .	..	250	John Watkins (2).				
Winchelsea, 20 .	..	125	William Marsh.				
Centre.							
Dragon	60	400	Charles Watson.	*Furieux* . . .	60	600	M. de Gravier.
Bedford	70	480	Hon. George Townshend.	*Sérieux* . . .	64	650	
Somerset . . .	80	600	George Sclater.	*Ferme*	74	800	M. de Desorquart.
Princesa	74	550	Robert Pett.	*Tigre*	50	550	M. de Saurins-Murat.
Norfolk	80	600	Hon. John Forbes.	*Terrible* . . .	74	850	Adm. de Court.
Namur	90	780	Adm. Thomas Mathews, (B.).	*Saint Esprit* . .	74	800	
				Diamant . . .	50	550	M. de Marrilart.
			John Russel.	*Solide* . . .	64	650	M. de Châteauneuf.
Marlborough. . .	90	750	James Cornwall.	*Fleur*, 20 . .			
Dorsetshire . . .	80	600	George Burrish.	*Zéphyr*, 20 . .			
Essex	70	480	Richard Norris.	A fireship, 8 .			
Rupert	60	400	John Ambrose.	A fireship, 8 .			
Royal Oak . . .	70	480	Edmund Williams.				
Guernsey, 50 . .	..	300	Samuel Cornish.				
Salisbury, 50 . .	..	300	Peter Osborn.				
Dursley Galley, 20	..	125	Giles Richard Vanbrugh.				
Anne Galley f.s., 8	..	45	— Mackie, (Com.).				
Sutherland h.s., 18 . . .	..	100	Alexander Lord Colville, (Com.).				
Rear.							
Dunkirk	60	400	Charles Wager Purvis.	*Oriente* . . .	60	600	Don M. de Vileña.
Cambridge . . .	80	600	Charles Drummond.	*America* . . .	60	600	Don A. Petruche.
Torbay	80	600	John Gascoigne.	*Neptuno* . . .	60	600	Don H. Olivares.
Neptune	90	770	Vice-Adm. R. Lestock, (W.). George Stepney.	*Poder*	60	600	Don R. Errutia.
				Constante. . .	70	750	Don. A. Eturiago.
Russell	80	600	Robert Long.	*Real Felipe* . .	114	1350	Adm. Don Jose Navarro. Don N. Geraldine.[1]
Buckingham. . .	70	480	John Towry.				
Elizabeth. . . .	70	480	Joseph Lingen.	*Hercules* . . .	64	650	Don C. Alvario.
Revenge	70	480	George Berkeley.	*Alción*[2] . . .	58	600	Don J. Rentorin.
Nonsuch, 50 . .	..	300	Edmund Strange.	*Brillante* . . .	60	600	Don B. de la Barrida.
Romney, 50 . .	..	300	Henry Godsalve.	*San Fernando* .	64	650	Conde de Vega Florida.
Diamond, 40 . .	..	250	James Hodsell.	*Sobiero* . . .	60	600	Don J. B. Castro.
Mercury f.s., 8 .	..	45	M. Peadle, (Com.).	*Isabela* . . .	80	900	Don I. Dutabil.
				Volage, 20 . .			
				A fireship, 8 .			

Note.—The *Burford*, 70, Captain Richard Watkins, and several vessels not of the line, were absent from the fleet.

[1] A French officer, Captain Lage de Cueilli, also exercised some executive authority on board.

[2] Some lists omit this vessel, and substitute for her the *Retiro*, 54.

Captain Mahan's account of this action[1] is far too brief to be of much value to the student. What he writes should, however, be here quoted, since it describes in a few words the general lines upon which the battle, such as it was, was fought. After mentioning the issue of the allied fleets from the port of Toulon, he continues :—

"The English fleet, which had been cruising off Hyères in observation, chased, and on the 11th its van and centre came up with the allies; but the rear division was then several miles to windward and astern, quite out of supporting distance. The wind was easterly, both fleets heading to the southward; and the English had the weather-

---

[1] 'Infl. of Sea Power,' 265.

gage. The numbers were nearly equal, the English having twenty-nine to the allied twenty-seven;[1] but this advantage was reversed by the failure of the English rear to join. The course of the Rear-Admiral has been generally attributed to ill-will towards Mathews; for, although he proved that in his separated position he made all sail to join, he did not attack later on when he could, on the plea that the signal for the line of battle was flying at the same time as the signal to engage; meaning that he could not leave the line to fight without disobeying the order to form line. This technical excuse was, however, accepted by the subsequent court-martial. Under the actual condition, Mathews, mortified and harassed by the inaction of his lieutenant, and fearing that the enemy would escape if he delayed longer, made the signal to engage when his own van was abreast the enemy's centre, and at once bore down himself out of the line and attacked with his flagship of ninety guns the largest ship in the enemy's line, the *Royal Philip* of one hundred and ten guns, carrying the flag of the Spanish admiral. In doing this he was bravely supported by his next ahead and astern. The moment of attack seems to have been judiciously chosen; five Spanish ships had straggled far to the rear, leaving their admiral with the support only of his next ahead and astern, while three[2] other Spaniards continued on with the French. The English van stood on, engaging the allied centre, while the allied van was without antagonists. Being thus disengaged, the latter was desirous of tacking to windward of the head of the English line, thus putting it between two fires, but was checked by the intelligent action of the three leading English captains, who, disregarding the signal to bear down, kept their commanding position and stopped the enemy's attempts to double. For this they were cashiered by the court-martial, but afterwards restored. This circumspect but justifiable regard of signals was imitated without any justification by all the English captains of the centre, save the Admiral's seconds already mentioned, as well as by some of those in the van, who kept up a cannonade at long range while their Commander-in-Chief was closely and even furiously engaged. The one marked exception was Captain Hawke, afterwards the distinguished admiral, who imitated the example of his chief, and, after driving his first antagonist out of action, quitted his place in the van, brought to close quarters a fine Spanish ship that had kept at bay five other English ships, and took her—the only prize made that day. The commander of the English van, with his seconds, also behaved with spirit and came to close action. It is unnecessary to describe the battle further. . . ."

After having, at 11.30 A.M., hoisted the signal[3] to engage, Mathews stood on, but overhauled the enemy only very gradually. At 1 P.M., the *Namur* was abreast of the *Real Felipe*, and the *Barfleur*, of the *Terrible*. Half-an-hour later, the *Namur* bore down within pistol-shot of the *Real Felipe*, and began to engage her furiously, and the *Barfleur* presently did the same with the *Terrible*. Lestock's division was still far astern, and to windward, and, according to the evidence at the court-martial, could not have then been up with the centre, unless Mathews had shortened sail and waited for it.

[1] This statement seems to be a little misleading. According to the lists already given, the British had in line twenty-eight ships, and the allies the same number. But, in addition, the British had five 50 and two 40-gun ships, for which the allies had no equivalents. The guns in line on each side were : British, 2080 ; Allies, 1822.

[2] Qy. "four."

[3] This was repeated by Rowley, but not by Lestock, who was at a great distance.

The *Namur* was well supported by the *Marlborough*, which attacked the *Isabela*,[1] and by the *Norfolk*, which attacked the *Constante*. The *Princesa, Bedford, Dragon*, and *Kingston* fired into the *Poder*, and the *Neptuno*,[2] *America*, and *Oriente*, after exchanging rather distant broadsides with the same British ships, passed on with the rear of the French part of the allied fleet. The remaining

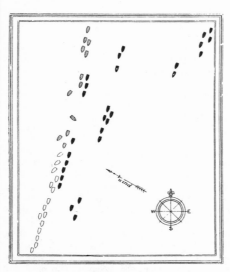

MATHEWS'S ACTION OFF TOULON,
FEBRUARY 11TH, 1744.

British, *black ;* French, *white ;* Spanish, *shaded.*

[Mathews's flagship, the *Namur*, is the centre one of the three rearmost British ships that are closely engaged. Hawke's ship, the *Berwick*, is the rearmost one of the larger closely engaged group. She has already silenced the *Poder*, which lies head to wind astern of her.]

Spanish ships were, at first, considerably astern of their station, but, as the breeze freshened, they came up, and, towards the end of the action, assisted the *Real Felipe*. Lestock made some effort to prevent this, but the wind was still very light with him, and he was also impeded by the swell, so that, although he had all sail set, his efforts were vain.

The *Barfleur*[3] got to close quarters with the *Terrible*, and was much assisted by the *Princess Caroline*[4] and the *Berwick*. The *Chichester* and *Boyne* also threw in their fire, but they were not close enough to the enemy to do much execution. As for the leading ships of the van—the *Stirling Castle, Warwick* and *Nassau*—they did not bear down to the enemy at all, although the signal for them to do so was flying. They chose to disregard it, and to keep their wind, in order, as was afterwards explained or suggested, to prevent the French from doubling upon the head of the British column.

[1] The *Isabela*, which lost nearly three hundred killed and wounded, had by that time moved up to the position next astern of the *Real Felipe*.

[2] The *Neptuno* lost nearly two hundred killed and wounded.

[3] The *Barfleur* had twenty-five killed, and twenty wounded.

[4] The *Princess Caroline* had eight killed, and twenty wounded.

The hottest part of the action was, in the meantime, being waged by the ships immediately about Mathews. The *Norfolk*[1] drove the *Constante* out of the line, a shattered wreck, but was herself too much damaged to pursue her. The *Namur* and *Marlborough* were, at one moment, so close to one another that Mathews, to avoid being fallen on board of by his eager second, was obliged to fill his sails, and draw a little ahead. The *Namur* was then scarcely

ADMIRAL THOMAS MATHEWS.

(From T. Faber's engraving after the portrait by Arnulphi (1743).)

under control, owing to the rough handling which she had received, and could give little help to the *Marlborough*, which, fought by her captain, and afterwards by his nephew, Lieutenant Frederick Cornwall, in the most magnificent manner, was very sorely pressed. None of the vessels immediately astern of her volunteered to assist her in the least, but, keeping their wind, fired fruitlessly at an enemy who was beyond the reach of their shot; and, in spite of

---

[1] The *Norfolk* had nine killed, and thirteen wounded.

H 2

the fact that the Spaniards betrayed every desire to meet them in the most handsome manner, few British captains properly took up the challenge. The most brilliant exception was Captain Edward Hawke, of the *Berwick*, who, noticing how the *Poder* had vainly endeavoured to draw on some of his reluctant colleagues, quitted his station, and bore down upon her. His first broadside did her an immense amount of damage, and, in twenty minutes, when she had lost all her masts, she was glad to strike.

The *Real Felipe* [1] was disabled, but the Spanish ships of the rear were crowding up to her assistance, and Lestock remained afar off, so that it looked as if the British strength about the Spanish admiral would not suffice to compel her to haul down her colours. In these circumstances, Mathews ordered the *Anne Galley*, fireship, to go down and burn the *Real Felipe*, and, seeing that the *Marlborough* [2] was in no condition to help herself, he further signalled for the boats of the British centre to tow her out of the line.

The *Anne Galley* was handled with great ability and gallantry. As she bore down on the *Real Felipe* she was received with a well-directed fire from such guns as that crippled ship could bring to bear, and with a more distant cannonade from the Spanish vessels astern of the flagship. Commander Mackie, match in hand, stood alone upon the deck of his little craft, ready to fire her at the proper moment. Most of his crew were alongside in a boat, which was waiting to take him on board. The rest, by his orders, had taken shelter from the storm of shot that hurtled across the fireship. But the *Anne Galley*, struck repeatedly between wind and water, was already sinking. Moreover, a Spanish launch, crowded with men, was approaching to board her, and tow her clear. Mackie felt that, at all hazards, he must endeavour to destroy the launch, and, in spite of the fact that his decks were littered with loose powder, that his hatches and scuttles were open, and that his funnels [3] were uncapped, he fired his waist guns at the boat. This was fatal. The blast from the guns set fire to the loose powder; and, while the *Anne Galley* was still too far from the *Real Felipe* to seriously damage her, she prematurely blew up, and then sank, carrying down

[1] The *Real Felipe* had about five hundred men killed and wounded.
[2] The *Marlborough* lost Captain Cornwall, and forty-two men killed and one hundred and twenty wounded.
[3] Funnels : in a fireship, tubes leading from the deck to the main body of explosives in the hold.

Commander Mackie, a lieutenant, a mate, a gunner, and two quartermasters.

In the meantime, M. de Court, who, owing to the confusion and smoke, seems to have supposed that the Spaniards were much more closely pressed than was actually the case, tacked to their assistance. Rear-Admiral Rowley tacked too, and followed the allied centre. Very soon afterwards, Mathews, to quote the words of Beatson—

"hauled down the signal to engage the enemy, and also the signal for the line of battle; making the signal to give over chase; but, at half-past five o'clock, he made the signal for the fleet to draw into a line of battle ahead. There was then but little wind, and so great a swell that the ships could only wear. The Admiral wore, and formed the line of battle on the larboard tack. This last manœuvre of the Admiral's appears to have been made with a design to collect his fleet, draw them out of the confusion they were in, and arrange them in a proper order for battle, which he had every reason to think would be speed.ly renewed; the French squadron being now at hand, and in an extremely well-formed line. They crowded, however, to the assistance of the Spaniards. The *Poder*, prize, being dismasted, and being unable to follow the British fleet when they wore, was retaken by the French squadron, she having on board a lieutenant and twenty-three men belonging to the *Berwick*. The *Dorsetshire*, *Essex*, *Rupert*, and *Royal Oak*, wearing at the time the Admiral did, brought them nearer to the sternmost ships of the Spanish squadron, which had by this time joined their admiral in a close line. In passing each other, being on contrary tacks, a short action took place, in which the *Namur*, *Dunki k*, and *C mbridge* joined, but with little execution on either side. Daylight was almost gone, and the British fleet passed on, leaving the confederate fleet astern."

Owing to the condition of the *Namur's* [1] masts, Mathews, at about 8 P.M., shifted his flag from her to the *Russell*, and intimated the fact of the change to Lestock and Rowley. On the morning of the 12th, when the wind was E.N.E., the enemy was seen about twelve miles to the S.W. At about 7 A.M., the *Somerset*, which had become separated from her consorts in the night, fell in with, and for half-an-hour engaged, the *Hercules*, which had likewise straggled from her friends; but, the *Hercules* being assisted by some French ships, the *Somerset* had to draw off and rejoin her division. At 9 A.M. Lestock ordered his squadron to chase to the S.W., and crowded sail ahead of the fleet. At 11 P.M., Mathews signalled for the fleet to draw into line of battle abreast, and then brought to on the starboard tack in order to collect his command. In the afternoon, the British fleet, in admirable order, was going down on the enemy, which was retreating in some confusion before the wind, the Spaniards being ahead of, and to leeward of the French, and the

---

[1] The *Namur* had eight killed and twelve wounded. Among the latter was Captain Russel, who lost his left arm, and who subsequently died at Port Mahon.

Real Felipe still bearing Navarro's flag, although she was in tow of another vessel. As for the *Poder*, she fell so far astern that the enemy fired her to prevent her from again falling into British hands; and, in the course of the following night, she blew up. But, in the meantime, Mathews, at about 5.30 P.M. on the 12th, had ordered his fleet to bring to, there being no more than a light wind from the N.E., and by 10 P.M. that night the enemy was out of sight.

On the 13th, Mathews again chased to the W. and W.S.W.; but at 9 A.M. he ordered the pursuit to be relinquished, his reasons, as afterwards explained, being, that he saw no prospect of bringing the allies to action; that, if he had continued to follow them, he would have been drawn towards the Strait's mouth, and would have left Italy entirely unprotected; and that, as his instructions were stringent as to the protection of Italy, he was unwilling to risk leaving the way clear for the transport thither of a large number of troops which he had reason to believe had been collected for that purpose in the ports of Spain. Yet it was unfortunate that the Admiral did not persist. Had he pressed the chase, he must inevitably either have picked up several of the crippled ships [1] of the allies, or have obliged de Court and Navarro to accept action on disadvantageous terms in order to cover their lame ducks.

After having relinquished the chase, Mathews tried to beat back in the face of strong contrary winds, but failed; so, first showing himself in Rosas Bay, with a view to letting the Spaniards know that he was observing their motions, he ran for Port Mahon. Upon reaching that harbour, he suspended Vice-Admiral Lestock, and sent him to England.

Both in France and Spain, as well as in Great Britain, there was great disgust at the result of the battle off Toulon. In France, Admiral de Court, in consequence of Navarro's representations, was superseded. De Court in a letter to the Bishop of Rennes, who was then Ambassador from France to the Court of Madrid, said, " It was not I, my lord, who forced M. Navarro to fight against all laws of war and prudence; it was not I who separated his ships from him and drove him into danger; but when he had taken so much pains, after all I could do, to get himself beaten, it was I who came to his assistance and gave him the opportunity to get away, which otherwise he never could have had." De Court was at the time an officer of nearly eighty years of age.

---

[1] Four, at least, and probably more, were seriously disabled aloft.

In Great Britain, Lestock's unwillingness to sit quietly under his suspension led to a succession of courts-martial.   These were preceded by an enquiry by the House of Commons, which began on March 12th, 1745, and lasted until the middle of April.   The King was then addressed to order a court-martial into the conduct of Admiral Mathews, Vice-Admiral Lestock, the captains of a number of ships, which had been engaged in the battle off Toulon, and the lieutenants of the *Dorsetshire*.   In his reply his Majesty said, " I am sensible how much depends on preserving an exact discipline in the fleet, and of the necessity there is of bringing to justice such as have failed in their duty on this important occasion."   In the meantime, Mathews, in pursuance of orders from England, had resigned his command and returned home, leaving the fleet under the orders of Vice-Admiral William Rowley.

The court-martial first assembled on board the *London* at Chatham on September 23rd, 1745, under the presidency of Sir Chaloner Ogle (1), Kt., Admiral of the Blue.   The officers brought before it were the lieutenants of the *Dorsetshire*, who were charged with having advised their Captain, Burrish, not to bear down upon the enemy.   They were all acquitted.   On September 25th Burrish's trial began, and sentence was delivered on October 9th.   The court declared, " That by reason of Captain Burrish lying inactive for half-an-hour when he might have assisted the *Marlborough*, and not being in line with the Admiral when he first brought to, he is guilty of a part of the charge exhibited against him, as he did not do his utmost to burn, sink, or destroy the enemy, nor give the proper assistance to the *Marlborough* till after the message he received from the Admiral : that he is guilty on the 12th and 13th Articles of the Fighting Instructions, and that therefore the court adjudge him to be cashiered and forever rendered incapable of being an officer in his Majesty's Navy."   Captain Edmund Williams, of the *Royal Oak*, was next tried on four charges.   The court found that Captain Williams had failed in his duty by not being in line with the Admiral, and by keeping to the windward of the line during the greater part of the action, and not within proper distance to engage with any effect during the most part of the time he was engaged : but, in regard of his long service and his eyesight being very defective and other favourable considerations, the court was unanimously of the opinion that all this greatly weighed in mitigation of the punishment due, and therefore only adjudged him unfit to be employed any more at sea, but recommended him to the Lords Commissioners of the Admiralty to be continued on half-pay according to his seniority. This recommendation their Lordships complied with.[1]

Captain John Ambrose, of the *Rupert*, was tried on October 18th. In his case the court found that he had failed in his duty in not engaging closer while he was engaged, when he had it in his power : but in regard that both before and since the action he had borne the character of a vigilant officer, and that his failure in action seemed to have resulted from mistaken judgment, the court only sentenced him to be cashiered during His Majesty's pleasure, and mulcted of one year's pay for the use of the Chest at Chatham. He was presently restored to his rank, and was in 1750 superannuated as a rear-admiral, dying in 1771. Captain William Dilkes, of the *Chichester*, had to answer the charge of not bearing down and engaging the enemy closer when he had it in his power so to do. The court found the charge proven, and dismissed him from the command of his ship, but he also was afterwards restored to his rank, though relegated to the half-pay list.[2] Captain Frogmore, of the *Boyne*, who was to have been tried with these officers, had died on November 8th, 1744, while still abroad.

At a rather earlier date, Captain Norris, of the *Essex*, who had been accused by his own officers of bad behaviour during the battle, had demanded and obtained a court-martial at Port Mahon, but, as he had previously resigned his command and was on half-pay, the court, after much debate, considered that it had no jurisdiction. The account of the proceedings, and a strongly-worded protest from the accusing officers, having been sent to England, the Admiralty ordered Norris to come home to stand his trial ; but on his way he seized the opportunity to abscond at Gibraltar, thus, it must be feared, admitting his guilt. He died in deserved obscurity.

Vice-Admiral Lestock had brought charges of his own against Captains Robert Pett, George Sclater,[3] Temple West, Thomas Cooper, and James Lloyd. In consequence of his complaints of their misconduct, these five captains were tried in due course. The first two were acquitted, the last three cashiered ; but as the offences of which the latter had been convicted did not reflect

---

[1] Edmund Williams, who was a captain of 1734, subsequently became a super-annuated rear-admiral, and died in 1752.

[2] Captain Dilkes died in 1756.   [3] Or Slaughter.

upon their professional honour or capacity, and as their case was considered a hard one, the King at once restored them to their former rank in the service. After an adjournment of the court, the trial of Vice-Admiral Lestock himself began at Deptford on board the *Prince of Orange,* and, Sir Chaloner Ogle being in ill-health, Rear-Admiral Perry Mayne officiated as president. The other flag-officer in attendance was Rear-Admiral the Hon. John Byng, who, a few years later, was shot for his behaviour in the action off Minorca. Lestock urged in his defence that he could not have engaged without breaking the line, and that he was not authorised to do this because, though the signal for engaging had been made, that for the line-of-battle was still flying. He was unanimously acquitted. The truth is, that he took shelter throughout behind purely technical excuses, which availed him, although he had acted in opposition to the spirit of his earlier correspondence with Barnet, that a subordinate should go to the length of quitting his station, even without orders, for the sake of joining and supporting the main body of the fleet in action. In short, for reasons of his own—and they are not hard to formulate—he chose to forget his broad duty to his country, and his comrades in arms, rather than depart from the narrow letter of his instructions.

During Lestock's trial a very remarkable occurrence happened. On May 15th the president of the court was arrested by virtue of a writ of *capias,* issued by Sir John Willes, Lord Chief Justice of the Common Pleas, in consequence of a verdict which had been obtained by Lieutenant George Frye, of the Marines, against Sir Chaloner Ogle, Rear-Admiral Perry Mayne and others, for false imprisonment and maltreatment in the West Indies, resulting from an illegal sentence passed upon him by a court-martial. The arrest of their president so incensed the members of the court that, oblivious of the fact that the civil law must always of necessity take precedence of the military, they passed resolutions in which they spoke of the Lord Chief Justice of the Common Pleas with violent disrespect. These resolutions they forwarded to the Lords Commissioners of the Admiralty, who laid them before the King. His Majesty was somewhat hastily advised to express his displeasure at the insult which had been offered to the court-martial; but he, like the Lords Commissioners of the Admiralty, had little idea of the great authority vested in the Lord Chief Justice of the Common Pleas, who, as soon as he heard of the

resolutions of the court-martial, promptly ordered each member
of it to be taken into custody.   He was beginning to adopt further
measures to vindicate his office, when the episode was happily put
an end to by the submission of the offending officers.

The trial of Admiral Mathews began on June 16th, 1746, Rear-
Admiral Perry Mayne, as before, being president, and Rear-Admiral
the Hon. John Byng being of the court.   Lestock exhibited fifteen
charges against his superior.   Once more the advocates of a broader
interpretation of the instructions were defeated by the advocates
of the strict letter.   It is perhaps well that in those days it was so,
for, for several years previously, naval discipline had been none too
good.   Mathews, whose anxiety to do his best against the enemies
of his country cannot be denied, though his wisdom may be, heard
his fate on October 22nd, when the following sentence was passed
upon him :—

"The court having examined the witnesses produced, as well in support of the
charge as in behalf of the prisoner, and having thoroughly considered their evidence,
do unanimously resolve that it appears thereby that Thomas Mathews Esq., by divers
breaches of duty, was a principal cause of the miscarriage of his Majesty's fleet in the
Mediterranean in the month of February 1744, and that he falls under the 14th Article
of an Act of the 13th of Charles II., for establishing articles and orders for the better
government of his Majesty's Navy, ships of war and forces by sea : and the court do
unanimously think fit to adjudge the said Thomas Mathews to be cashiered and
rendered incapable of any employ in his Majesty's service."

There is no question that, from a purely legal point of view,
Mathews deserved his punishment, but it is equally undoubted that
Lestock's conduct throughout was really far more reprehensible
than that of the superior officer.   Mathews blundered, but his
intentions were good.   Lestock clung tightly to the dead letter of
his duty ; but his intentions were contemptible, for, in effect, he said
to himself, "My superior is making a mess of this affair.   I will
stick fast to my instructions and let him, and even the fleet and
country, go to ruin before I will strike a blow to help him.   I shall
then be safe, and he, whom I happen to regard as my private enemy,
will pay the penalty." [1]

[1] The minutes of these courts-martial are enormously voluminous, and the
pamphlets called forth by the action off Toulon are extremely numerous.   *See*
especially : 'A Partic. Account of the late Action . . . by an officer in the Fleet,' 8vo,
1744 ; 'Captain Gascoigne's Answer,' etc., 8vo, 1746 ; 'Admiral Mathews's Remarks
on the Evidence,' etc. ; 'Defence made by J. Ambrose,' etc., 8vo, 1745 ; 'Case of
Captain G. Burrish,' etc., 8vo, 1747 ; 'A Narrative of the Proceedings of H.M. Fleet,'
etc., 8vo, 1745 ; 'Vice-Admiral L—st—k's Account,' etc., 1745 ; 'Vice-Admiral
Lestock's Recapitulation,' etc., 1745.

Mathews, after the fight off Toulon, had refitted at Port Mahon, and had then detached Captain Robert Long, with a small division, to cruise off the Italian coast and to intercept supplies for the Spanish army there. Mathews himself put to sea as soon as possible, and on June 14th, 1744, drove ashore and destroyed a number of French transports near Marseilles. In fact he and his cruisers were very active until his return to England in September.

His successor, Vice-Admiral William Rowley, had many objects which he was compelled to keep in view. He had to guard Italy from the French and Spaniards, coming by way of the sea ; he had to observe a French squadron from Brest, which lay at Cadiz ; he had to watch a French fleet at Toulon ; he had to keep his eye on the Spanish squadron at Cartagena; above all, he had to protect British trade. At that time Admiral de Torres was expected in Spain with a valuable convoy of treasure ships from Havana ; and on the other hand, as has been mentioned, Vice-Admiral Sir Charles Hardy (1) had gone southward with a convoy bound for Lisbon and Gibraltar. The French and Spaniards, anxious to facilitate the safe arrival of de Torres, and, if possible, to intercept Hardy, arranged that the Toulon squadron should put to sea, and join with the Spanish at Cartagena, and with the French at Cadiz. Admiral Gabaret, therefore, left Toulon on September 20th with sixteen sail of the line and four frigates. Rowley, who was then at Minorca, with only a part of his forces, did not hear of this till October 7th. He at once put to sea in chase ; and, as soon as he realised that the enemy's plan involved an attempt upon a division of Hardy's convoy, which had reached Gibraltar, Rowley made for Spain. Although he ultimately found the merchantmen safely under the Rock, he thereby managed to miss the enemy.

Hardy had sailed in April 1744, and, having sent his main convoy into the Tagus, whence it was to proceed by divisions to points further south, he returned, and re-anchored at St. Helen's on May 20th. But scarcely had he quitted Lisbon when the transports and store-ships, which he had left there, were blockaded in the river by the French squadron, under M. de Rochambeau, from Brest. As the stores were much needed by the Mediterranean fleet, Admiral Sir John Balchen, with his flag in the *Victory,* and with a considerable force, was detached from the Channel to relieve the blockade. He sailed on July 28th, made several prizes, compelled de Rochambeau to return to Cadiz, and then escorted to Gibraltar that part of the convoy which was subsequently found there by Rowley.

Balchen returned ; but on October 3rd his command was over-taken by a violent storm and was dispersed. Several ships were much damaged and were at times in great danger ; but all of them, except the *Victory*, safely reached Plymouth on October 10th. The *Victory*, which was at that time considered the finest ship in the world, had become separated from her consorts on October 4th, and was never again seen. It is supposed that she struck on the ridge of rocks called the Caskets, near the island of Alderney, seeing that on the night between the 4th and 5th of October the booming of guns was heard, both by the people in charge of the Casket Light and by the inhabitants of Alderney. The wind, however, was so strong that no boat could venture in the direction whence the sounds proceeded. The *Victory's* crew, including her Admiral,[1] her Captain, Samuel Faulknor,[2] her officers, and about fifty young gentlemen volunteers, amounted to upwards of one thousand souls, all of whom perished. The loss of the ship was at that time imputed to some defects in her construction, but it is probable that this really had nothing to do with it, and that the disaster must be attributed solely to the storm and thick weather which prevailed at the time.

Owing to the situation of affairs with France, a small squadron of four ships, under Commodore Curtis Barnet, sent at the request of the directors of the East India Company to the East Indies, had sailed on May 5th, 1744, from Spithead. In January following, after having taken measures to intercept home-coming French ships from China, and after having disguised his own vessel, the *Deptford*, 60, Captain John Phillipson, and the *Preston*, 50, Captain the Earl of Northesk (1), Barnet was so fortunate as to take in the Strait of Banca the French Indiamen *Dauphin*, *Hercule*, and *Jason*, each of 30 guns.

The Commodore had not long left England when the successful return of Commodore Anson suggested to the British Ministry that it might be easy to capture the next treasure-ships bound from Acapulco to Manilla ; and a despatch to that effect was sent to Barnet by the *Lively*, 20, Captain Elliot Elliot. But the activity

---

[1] Sir John Balchen was then in his seventy-sixth year.

[2] A captain of 1736, and a member of one of the most distinguished of British naval families.

and threatening attitude of the French in India prevented the scheme from being carried out; and, after his squadron had taken a few other French ships, Barnet went to Madras and confined himself mainly to observing and harassing the enemy in the Bay of Bengal.

Vice-Admiral Thomas Davers was sent with reinforcements to Jamaica to relieve Sir Chaloner Ogle in 1744; but the French and Spaniards were so strong on that station, and so many battleships were carried home with him by Ogle, that Davers had to restrict himself to the defensive. His cruisers, however, made several prizes and the French failed in their only important enterprise, an attack on Anguilla.

The war which broke out in 1744 was destined to have an important influence on the fate of the British and French empires in North America. At first the French there were very active, and the British were extremely indifferent to their own interests. In consequence of this, the French territories, which had been handed over to Great Britain by the Treaty of Utrecht, were neglected and were badly affected to the new government. They were, indeed, full of active French sympathisers. The natural outcome was a scheme, hatched by the French, to take advantage of the dissatisfaction, and to deprive Great Britain of part at least of her new possessions. M. de Quenel, who was then Governor of Cape Breton, fitted out a small armament from Louisbourg and put it under the command of Captain Duvivier. The native Indians gave, or at least promised to give him some assistance. The armament made first for Canso, where the French arrived on May 11th. They were joined by two hundred Indians, and by many disaffected inhabitants. The place was held by a company of the 40th Regiment, but, as it was indefensible, it presently surrendered. The French demolished such fortifications as existed, and set the place on fire. M. Duvivier, who, in the meantime, had been reinforced by five hundred Indians, proceeded with all his forces to Annapolis Royal. This important position, like Canso, was in a very neglected state; but it was saved by the activity and patriotism of the New Englanders.

Governor Shirley and the Assembly of Massachusetts, well knowing the consequence of Nova Scotia to Great Britain, encouraged the raising in New England of a body of volunteers, which, promptly dispatched to Annapolis, arrived before the French made their appearance. When, therefore, M. Duvivier, who landed

on June 2nd, summoned the town, he was informed that it would
be defended to the last extremity; and, although he made some
preparations for an assault, the strength of the defenders so deeply
impressed him that he finally returned to Louisbourg without
attempting anything further.

This activity of the French suggested to the Governor and
Assembly of New England a project for the conquest of Louisbourg,
which was then the chief French base in North America. A request was made to the home Government to the effect that, as the
necessary naval forces could be sent more quickly from the West
Indies than from England, Commodore Peter Warren might be
detached from the former station to co-operate with a colonial
expedition. To this the Government agreed, and orders were issued
accordingly. The Assembly of Massachusetts raised £27,000 for the
service. Troops were collected and confided to the command of
Mr. William Pepperel, of Kittery, Maine; and, though no fewer
than 3850 volunteers were assembled and sufficient transports and
stores for their accommodation were provided, all was done with so
great secrecy that the enemy seems to have suspected nothing. But
as this expedition did not sail till 1745, the history of its proceedings
must be for the present deferred.

While Great Britain was fully occupied with her foreign foes she
had to contend with not less dangerous enemies at home, for France
in 1745, at a time when the greater part of the British army was on
the Continent, engaged in supporting the schemes of the House of
Austria, suddenly transported the Young Pretender to Scotland.
France did not believe that Prince Charles Edward would be
successful, nor did she ever mean to assist him very actively; but
she realised that he might cause a most useful diversion. With a
slender retinue the Prince embarked at St. Nazaire on board a small
vessel, the *Dentelle*, which was lent him by a Mr. Walsh, who was
a merchant of Nantes but was of Irish extraction. He had arms for
about 2000 men and about £2000 in money, and he sailed on
July 7th. When off Belle Isle he was joined by the *Elisabeth*, 64,
which had orders to escort Prince Charles Edward round Ireland to
the Hebrides. On July 9th, in lat. 47° 57′ N., the little expedition
was discovered by the *Lion*, 58, Captain Piercy Brett (1), which
immediately gave chase. At 5 o'clock the *Lion* ran alongside and
poured a broadside into the *Elisabeth* at short range. The two vessels
continued warmly engaged until 10 o'clock, when the *Lion* had

suffered so severely in her rigging that she was incapable of making sail. The *Elisabeth*, on the contrary, had suffered chiefly in her hull; and, although it is reported that several of her gun-ports were knocked into one, she was able to get away. The smaller vessel at the beginning of the action had endeavoured to assist her consort, but had soon been beaten off by the *Lion's* stern-chasers; and, when she saw that the *Elisabeth* had failed of success, she crowded sail and made her escape. The *Lion*, whose complement was 440 men, lost 55 killed and 107 wounded, of whom seven ultimately died. The French lost 65 killed and 136 dangerously wounded.

Prince Charles pursued his voyage and reached the coast of Lochaber at the end of July. The Young Pretender, on landing, was dissuaded by his best friends from pursuing his adventure; but he persisted, and they then gave way and joined him. For a time he had some success, but he was too fond of pleasure to act with the necessary energy, and presently the British Government began to recover from its first amazement. A regular plan of defence was elaborated. Admiral Edward Vernon (1),[1] with a squadron, was sent

---

[1] It should here be mentioned that Vernon's ultimate disgrace arose out of this appointment of his to the command in the Downs. He had with him but very few ships, and in a letter of November 16th, 1745, to the Earl of Sandwich, he said: "It must have made an odd appearance in the Eye of the World to have seen two Flag-Officers lye so long in the Downs with but one forty-gun ship to form a line of battle with." This paucity of command, combined with the fact that he had no commission as a Commander-in-Chief, was the origin of his discontent. He was also irritated by the conduct of the Admiralty which, in the same letter, he stigmatises in rather strong language. Things came to a head when, on December 1st, Vernon wrote to the Admiralty: "I have read, with great surprise, the long paragraph in your letter informing me their Lordships don't approve of my having appointed a Gunner to the *Poole* when the necessity of the Service required it, and his Mätie's Service must have suffered for the want of it; and acquainting me, it is their Lordships' directions I should withdraw the Warrants that I gave to them for his Majesty's Service. I must say with concern, in answer to it, that I did not expect to have been treated in such a contemptuous manner, and that I can hardly conceive it to be their directions till I see it from under their hands in an Order for me to do it, and shall now entreat the favour of their Lordships that, if they think it deserves an Order, they will please to direct it to my Successor to put in Execution, as I must, in such case, intreat the favour of their Lordships to procure me His Majesty's leave to quit a Command I have long thought too contemptibly treated in regard to the rank I hold for His Majesty's honour and service, and I should rather chuse to serve His Majesty in the capacity of a private man in the Militia, than to permit the rank I hold in His Majesty's Service to be treated with contempt, which I conceive to be neither for our Royal Master's honour or Service. A private Captain over two ships on any foreign service exercises the power of filling up all vacancies under him, and it is for his Mätie's Service he should be empowered to do so. When I attended the Regency, I was spoke to as a person of confidence that was to have had the Chief Command at home. Their Lordships' Orders of the 7th August seem'd to design me for such, tho' that was speedily altered by those of the 14th, and I always

to the Downs to watch the motions of the French at Dunquerque and Calais, and he from time to time detached squadrons under the command of Commodores Thomas Smith and Charles Knowles, who intercepted many small vessels destined for the rebels.   At the

suspected there was something lurking under the avoiding to call me Commander-in-Chief anywhere, but only Admiral of the White, tho', at the same time, Letters had passed thro' my hands, directed to Vice-Admiral Martin (whom, by my first orders, I was to be under my Command), stiling him Commander-in-Chief of His Majesty's Ships in the Soundings. But your letter, Sir, has now explained the whole to me." The controversy led the Admiralty to quote what it believed to be a precedent for its action, whereupon, in a letter of December 6th, Vernon wrote : " I am now come to the last part of your letter in answer to mine of the first, and was pleased to find you had quoted the precedent of Sir John Norris's case in the year 1740. Sir John Norris thought it right to appoint two officers on a vacancy that happened under his command, and, I dare answer for him, would not have thought it right ; but, as he judged it for his Majesty's Service, and that his predecessors had done it before him, and I don't think anyone will say that Lord Orford, Sir George Rooke, Sir Clowdisley Shovell, Lord Aylmer, Lord Berkeley, Lord Torrington, and Sir Charles Wager, have not done the same. Sir John Norris thought it so much a right in him, that, when a person was sent down by the Board to supersede a warrant granted by him, he sent the person back with his warrant, and he was not received while he commanded, but when the service was over, and he returned to town, their Lordships superseded him, so that his acquiescence was necessity, not approbation. And I hope the haughty temper of the noble Lord that presided at the Board at that time, will not be thought a fit precedent to be followed by their Lordships." Again, on December 13th : " As to what I am so politely acquainted with, that their Lordships have appointed a gunner to the *Poole* after my having informed their Lordships that I had warranted the gunner of the *Sheerness* to that ship, I must acquaint you in answer—it was what I little expected— and that I am determined to follow the example of Sir John Norris, and not permit that indignity to be put on me while I remain in command here, but when he arrives, shall civilly send him back again. That officer that don't pique himself on supporting his own honour, and the dignity of the commission he holds under his Majesty, may not be the likeliest to defend the honour of his Prince and the Security of his Country against the face of his enemies, and I will, therefore, never take the fatal step of abandoning my own honour." And on December 14th : " A private Colonel in the Army, who has no command but his regiment, shall be allowed to fill up most of the vacancies for ensigns in his regiment, and the poor slighted admiral bearing his Majesty's flag at main-topmast head, and in actual command, shall be denied the filling up the low vacancy of a gunner ! " The only result of this condition of things was Vernon's supersession, on December 26th. He was succeeded by Vice-Adm. Wm. Martin (1). Immediately after his supersession, he engaged in controversial pamphlet-eering, and, according to general belief, was responsible for two somewhat plain-spoken pamphlets, respectively entitled, ' A Specimen of Naked Truth from a British Sailor,' and ' Some Sensible Advice from a Common Sailor, to whom it might have Concerned, for the Service of the Crown and Country.' He was summoned to the Admiralty to deny the authorship of these productions, but as he did not choose to do so, he was informed, on April 11th, 1746, that the King had been pleased to direct their Lordships to strike his name from the list of flag-officers. Thus ended the service career of a great and honourable officer, who owed his fall to his petulance and pugnacity.—Letter-book in Author's Coll.; the pamphlets above mentioned ; and ' Original Letters to an Honest Sailor ' (published by Vernon after his dismissal from the service).

Nore Captain the Hon. Edward Boscawen commanded: at Plymouth, Captain Savage Mostyn. A further squadron cruised in the Channel under Vice-Admiral William Martin (1); and Rear-Admiral the Hon. John Byng went northward, and, by means of his cruisers, greatly annoyed the rebels on the Scots coast.

The Young Pretender reached Derby, but then lost heart and retreated to await reinforcements. In Scotland for a time he won more successes, but the assured British command of the sea really made his enterprise almost hopeless from the first; for even his private sympathisers in France could not aid him with supplies, such vessels as they dispatched being almost invariably snapped up by British cruisers. Yet individual loyalty, after the disaster at Culloden, saved the Prince from capture, in spite of the fact that the Government had set a price of £30,000 upon his head. He reached the Hebrides, and, after suffering great distresses, was taken on board a French privateer, the *Bellone*, on September 20th, 1746. This vessel had been sent on purpose from St. Malo by some of his French friends. She reached Roscoff, a small port in Brittany, on September 29th, not, however, without having very narrowly escaped capture by a British cruiser in the Channel. It is worth mentioning that she was at least the third vessel which had been sent to Scotland to rescue him. Two large French privateers, one of 34 and the other of 32 guns, had anchored off the coast of Lochaber in the previous April, with the object of picking up fugitives from the rebel army. They had been there discovered by Captain Thomas Noel of the *Greyhound*, 20; but, though he had been joined by the *Baltimore* and *Terror* sloops, and had then attacked them, they had succeeded in beating him off and in carrying away several of the rebel chiefs.

The expedition against Louisbourg assembled at Boston, Massachusetts, and the troops were there embarked, with all the necessary stores, on board eighty transports. It was convoyed by eight privateers of twenty guns, and ten small vessels; and it sailed on March 20th, 1745, arriving at Canso on April 4th. This was immediately after it had become known in New England that Commodore Warren had received orders to co-operate in the undertaking. The expedition reached Canso before the Commodore, and Mr. Pepperel wisely employed his time in exercising and drilling his troops. Meanwhile Mr. John Rous, master of the *Shirley Galley*, the largest of the privateers, proceeded off the harbour of Louisbourg to intercept supplies intended for the place. That he did so was fortunate, for the French Government, hearing of the projected attack, had hastily despatched the *Renommée*, 32, one of its fastest frigates, commanded by the celebrated Kersaint,[1] with dispatches for Louisbourg. On April 18th, she sighted Rous's blockading squadron, which very pluckily attacked her and forced

VICE-ADMIRAL SIR PETER WARREN, K.B.

(*From a lithograph by Ridley in the 'Naval Chronicle*,' 1804.)

her to fly, greatly disabled. In her flight she encountered some transports, which, escorted by a privateer, were on their way to join Pepperel. These she attacked, but the privateer defended them so well that once more she made sail and got away. The *Renommée* had finally to return to France without having effected her purpose.

Commodore Warren's squadron from the West Indies reached

---

[1] A biographical note concerning this gallant officer will be found on pp. 219, 220 of the present volume.

Canso on April 22nd and 23rd, and consisted of His Majesty's ships *Superb*, 60, Captain Thomas Somers, bearing the Commodore's broad pennant; *Eltham*, 40, Captain Philip Durell (1); *Launceston*, 40, Captain Warwick Calmady; and *Mermaid*, 40, Captain James Douglas (1). In the course of the subsequent operations, it was joined by several other vessels. Warren lost no time in landing and in conferring with Mr. Pepperel. Returning on board, he sailed again, and effectually blockaded the harbour of Louisbourg. The troops at Canso were re-embarked on April 29th, conveyed to Gabarus Bay, near Louisbourg, and landed on the morning of the 30th. The French garrison was discontented and mutinous, and its officers were tyrannical and corrupt, so that M. de Chambon, the Governor, feared to attack the invaders after they had inflicted one small check upon him. Thus, the expedition had leisure to establish itself ashore and to rapidly become disciplined and formidable. In the meantime, the *Renommée* had returned to France with the news of what was going on, whereupon the French Government hastily despatched the *Vigilante*, 64, with stores for the threatened fortress. She was, however, intercepted and captured by Warren's squadron on May 19th. A general attack by land and sea upon Louisbourg was imminent, when on June 28th the place surrendered. The British lost during the operations only 101 killed, while the French loss was 300.

With Louisbourg fell the whole of Cape Breton. The conquest was of immense importance. It not only destroyed a nest of French privateers, but it also relieved the British fishermen on the banks of Newfoundland from much dangerous rivalry. Moreover, it had a great moral effect upon the Indians throughout North America. Those who had taken part in it were fittingly and liberally rewarded. Warren was promoted to be Rear-Admiral of the Blue, Governor Shirley, of Massachusetts, was made a colonel, and Mr. William Pepperel, besides also being made a colonel, was created a baronet of Great Britain. Nor were the sailors neglected. The *Shirley Galley* was purchased by the Government, and added to the Navy as a post ship; and her late master, Mr. John Rous, was presented with a post-captain's commission and appointed to her. Finally, the Colonists were reimbursed by Parliament for all the expenses which they had incurred in connection with the expedition.

The despatch of Vice-Admiral Thomas Davers with reinforcements to the West Indies has already been mentioned. Upon the French Ministry hearing of it, it also sent thither a strong reinforcement, under the Chevalier de Caylus, who arrived at Martinique on March 28th, 1745. No sooner was the British Ministry advised of its departure, than it ordered Vice-Admiral William Rowley, then in command in the Mediterranean, to detach to the West Indies a considerable division under Vice-Admiral Isaac Townsend (2), who left Gibraltar on August 2nd, and arrived off Martinique on October 3rd. He fell in, on October 31st, with a squadron of ships of war and store ships, destined to further reinforce the French ; and, chasing it, ultimately took or destroyed upwards of thirty out of about forty sail.

In the Mediterranean, Vice-Admiral William Rowley blockaded the Spaniards in Cartagena, while Rear-Admiral Henry Medley watched the coasts of Italy and prevented supplies from reaching the Spanish Army there. Commodore Henry Osborn observed the French Brest squadron, which lay at Cadiz. When Genoa threw in her lot with the House of Bourbon, Commodore Thomas Cooper was detached to bombard the ports of that Republic, and he caused several of them to suffer very severely. The difficulties of Genoa induced the Corsicans to make an effort to throw off the Genoese yoke and to seek British and Sardinian assistance ; whereupon Commodore Cooper went to Corsica, and on November 17th, 1745, anchored off Bastia. The place was bombarded until the 19th, when the ships relinquished the attack, and withdrew, Cooper despairing of the arrival of the promised Corsican assistance. But his action was a little premature ; for one of the rebel chiefs, the Marchese de Rivarole, had already arrived, and, just after the disappearance of the British, threatened the town with such good effect, that the Chevalier de Mari, the representative of Genoese authority, finding the defences untenable in consequence of the damage that had already been received by them from the British squadron, carried off his garrison by sea. A little later Commodore Cooper sent to Corsica Captain the Hon. George Townshend, who discovered that the Genoese held only a few towns, and that the island was in a fair way of falling into the hands of the patriots.

The success at Louisbourg directed attention to the importance of British interests in North America, and in 1746 suggested fresh undertakings in that quarter. An attack on Quebec was projected, and it was proposed to utilise for the purpose the colonial troops, which had done so well at Cape Breton in the previous year, strengthening them of course by means of large detachments from England. Preparations were made, and troops were assembled at Portsmouth and even embarked; but various causes detained the fleet at Spithead until too late in the season, and the enterprise was, for a time, abandoned. Rumours of the intentions of the Government had, as was usual in those days, promptly reached the ears of the French Ministry, which decided to retaliate for the threatened British invasion of Canada by a descent upon Nova Scotia. In pursuance of this determination a large force was sent across the Atlantic under the Duc d'Anville.

British public opinion had been much attracted by the Quebec idea, and was greatly disgusted by the failure of the expedition to sail. To pacify the people, it was hinted that the troops which had been assembled were not to remain unemployed; and, a little later, as will be seen, they were directed upon the coast of France.

The French fleet of eleven sail of the line and fifty-gun ships, three frigates, three fireships and two bomb-vessels, under the Duc d'Anville, with transports and storeships containing 3500 troops, sailed from Brest on June 22nd, 1746, and arrived off the coast of Nova Scotia on September 10th. But on its passage it was much damaged and weakened by a violent storm. Vice-Admiral Isaac Townsend, who was then at Louisbourg, had with him an inferior force, but had the advantage of assistance from New England, and of a well fortified base. The sudden death of d'Anville depressed the spirits of the French expedition, and although the enemy did land, he soon decided not to prosecute the object for which he had crossed the Atlantic. D'Anville's successor, M. Tournel, a man of impetuous temper, could not agree with the resolutions of the majority of his officers; and, considering that if he retreated he would be dishonoured, he solved his own difficulties by committing suicide, while at the same time he complicated the confusion into which his unfortunate command had fallen. M. de La Jonquière succeeded him: but by that time, owing to delay and neglect, the troops had been almost exterminated by scurvy and by a small-pox epidemic. Some succour was therefore sent to Quebec, and the rest of the expedition, in a very bad case, returned to Europe. On the voyage several of the vessels composing it were snapped up by British cruisers.

The troops which had been assembled at Portsmouth for the undertaking against Quebec were, as has been said transported to

the coast of France.   Command of them had been given to Lieut.-
General the Hon. James St. Clair, chiefly for the reason that,
besides being an excellent officer, he had made a special study of
the military position in Canada.   When the destination of the
expedition was altered, the command, perhaps unwisely, was not
changed.   The fleet destined to convoy the army was entrusted to
Admiral Richard Lestock (B.)   The idea of the Government was
that a descent upon the coast of Brittany might induce the French,
who were very powerful in Flanders, to detach part of the army
which was operating there under Marshal Saxe.   But the affair
was wretchedly managed.   The General had no special knowledge;
the troops were unprepared for the service; and no maps of the
country to be attacked were provided.   St. Clair asked for a map of
Brittany, and the Government sent him, by express, a map of
Gascony.   Nor had the coast been properly reconnoitred.   It was
little known to any of the British naval officers of the time, and
the charts of those days were very indifferent.

Lestock detached Commodore Thomas Cotes to look in at Port
Louis and neighbouring places, and to find some convenient spot
for landing near Lorient.   With the main body of the fleet he
himself sailed from St. Helen's on August 5th, but did not clear
the coast of England until September 14th, nor reach that of France
till September 19th, when Cotes rejoined him.   A landing was in
time effected, and the troops began to advance upon Lorient; but
the country was a close one, and greatly facilitated the guerilla
operations of the French.   Lorient, nevertheless, appeared to be
disposed to treat; and it would no doubt have surrendered to the
British commander if he had been inclined to deal leniently.   Yet
as he would accept all or nothing, the place sturdily prepared to
defend itself.   The siege was begun in a partial and ineffectual way;
but so many necessary supplies were wanting that progress was
very slow, and, though the sailors from the fleet co-operated with
marvellous energy, the enterprise was at last concluded to be
impracticable and the troops were re-embarked, very sickly from
the consequences of exposure, on September 30th.   At a council of
war the project of a landing in Quiberon Bay was discussed and
rejected, but on October 1st, Lestock received so favourable a report
from Captain Thomas Lake of the *Exeter*, of the anchorage there,
that he and General St. Clair decided, in spite of the resolutions of
the council of war, to proceed and there await reinforcements from

England, meanwhile harassing the enemy whenever possible. The fleet sailed, and some troops were landed and works erected ; but, after hesitation and paltering, the forces were re-embarked. Meantime the isles of Houat and Hoëdic had been reduced and the fortifications upon them destroyed. The troops were ultimately sent under convoy to Ireland, and Lestock, with the bulk of the fleet, returned to England. No glory was won, but the expedition partially attained its original object, for orders were actually sent to Marshal Saxe from Paris, directing him to despatch troops to Brittany. These did not, however, reach him until he had so well established his position in Flanders as to be well able to afford to weaken himself.

At the time of the commencement of the active alliance between the French and Spaniards, M. La Bourdonnais, governor of the Isle of France, happened to be at Versailles. He was a most far-sighted administrator and capable soldier, and, had his advice been followed, the fate of India might have been very different from what it has been. He advised his Government to send a strong squadron to the Indian seas, so as to be ready for all eventualities. A squadron of five sail of the line was accordingly collected, and command of it was entrusted to La Bourdonnais himself. He was given great powers over the officers of the French East India Company in India ; and the Company became anxious concerning its rights and privileges as soon as he had sailed. The directors persuaded the French Ministry that hostilities in India were not likely, and that, the representatives of the two countries there being exclusively traders, it was unwise in the highest degree to provoke ill-will where neutrality would, in all probability, be observed if no aggressive measures were taken. The squadron was accordingly recalled ; but La Bourdonnais himself proceeded, and, with the slender resources he possessed, he assembled a motley squadron, which included only one king's ship, the *Achille*, 70. With her and seven other vessels, armed merchantmen, he sailed for the coast of Coromandel.

Commodore Curtis Barnet, who had gone to Madras in the beginning of 1746, would have been a worthy opponent even for so great a man as La Bourdonnais ; and he was preparing to take active measures against the French, when, on April 29th, he died. His successor, Commodore Edward Peyton, was apparently a less energetic and capable officer. He was cruising between Fort St. David and Negapatam when, on June 25th, he sighted the French squadron.[1]   M. La Bourdonnais, though conscious that his ships in strength of armament and in discipline were very inferior to the British, decided to utilise the only superiority which he possessed, the superiority in men, and to attempt to board.   During the earlier part of the day there was little breeze ; and Peyton, who probably grasped the idea of the French admiral, kept as near the wind as possible, so that the two fleets were unable to come to close action.   Not until four in the afternoon did they begin to engage ; and even then the firing was maintained at such a distance that little damage was done to either side.   Peyton might have annihilated his foe had he ventured sufficiently close to take full advantage of the stouter scantling of his ships, and of the heavier guns which they carried.   But he did not attack with dash ; and at dusk the action ceased, the British having lost fourteen men killed and forty-six wounded, and the enemy twenty-seven killed and fifty-three wounded.   The British vessel which suffered chiefly was the *Medway's Prize*.   On the other side, the *Insulaire* was so badly mauled that, immediately after the action, La Bourdonnais had to order her away to repair.   Peyton's behaviour gave great umbrage to the East India Company ; but no one ever brought any specific charge against the commodore.   Commodore Thomas Griffin (1) afterwards superseded him, put him under arrest, and sent him home ; but the matter went no further.

[1] SQUADRONS OF COMMODORE PEYTON AND M. LA BOURDONNAIS IN THE ACTION OF JUNE 25TH, 1746.

BRITISH.			FRENCH.		
Ships.	Guns.	Commanders.	Ships.	Guns pierced for.	Guns mounted.
Medway . .	60	{ Commod. Edward Peyton. { Capt. Henry Rosewell.	*Achille* . .	74	60
			Duc d' Orléans	56	26
Preston . . .	50	„ George, Earl of Northesk.	*Bourbon* . .	56	36
Winchester . .	50	„ Lord Thomas Bertie.	*Neptune* . .	54	34
Harwich . .	50	„ Philip Carteret (1).	*Phénix* . .	54	34
Medway's Prize	40	„ Thomas Griffin (2), actg.	*St. Louis* . .	44	30
Lively . . .	20	{ „ Nathaniel Stephens, { actg.	*Lys* . . .	40	34
			Insulaire .	30	28
	270				282

Some French accounts mention another armed vessel, the *Renommée*, 28, as having been with La Bourdonnais, in addition to the ships named above.   The British official account also mentions a ninth ship, name unknown, mounting, however, 20 guns only. All the French ships, however, except the *Achille*, were merely improvised men-of-war, and were, in that respect, greatly inferior to the British.

The activity of La Bourdonnais was hampered by the jealousy of M. Dupleix, Governor in India for the French East India Company. Dissensions continually arose owing to the natural complications of authority; and the naval commander could obtain scarcely any help from the civil one. La Bourdonnais, nevertheless, made shift to refit, and on July 24th sailed again from Pondicherry and worked to the southward. On August 6th he sighted the British squadron, which was returning from Trincomale, where it had refitted. Peyton avoided action, and, after three days of futile manœuvres, made sail and disappeared. This conduct encouraged La Bourdonnais to plan an attack upon Madras. He was taken ill and had to remain at Pondicherry; but his squadron appeared before the place on August 15th [1] and bombarded it. The guns, however, produced little effect upon the town; nor did the French succeed in an attempt to capture the *Princess Mary*, East Indiaman, which lay in the road.

One of the objects of the British squadron in the East Indies was of course to be a protection to British settlements and British trade; yet it did not proceed to the succour of Madras. Peyton, lying in Pulicat Road, thirty miles to the northward, heard, on August 25th, of what had happened in the previous week; but, instead of going to the rescue of the threatened town, he went to Bengal, his excuse being that the *Medway's Prize* was very leaky and needed repairs. La Bourdonnais was thus induced to proceed. On September 3rd his squadron disembarked troops, and on the 7th a bombardment of Madras by land and sea was begun. On the 10th the place capitulated, upon the understanding that it should subsequently be ransomed. On September 27th, while still before Madras, La Bourdonnais was reinforced by three ships of the line from Europe, the *Centaure*, 74, *Mars*, 56, and *Brillant*, 50. His operations were still hampered by the interference of Dupleix; but, on October 1st, he was able to send off two of his vessels with booty, etc., to Pondicherry. It was fortunate that he did so, for otherwise he would probably have lost almost all his squadron. On the night of October 2nd there was a great storm; and, in the course of it, the *Duc d'Orléans*, *Phénix*, and *Lys* foundered, and about twelve hundred men were lost with them. Two prizes, the *Mermaid* and the *Advice*, shared the same fate, and the flagship, *Achille*, and

---

[1] An account issued by the Hon. E. I. C. says that the enemy appeared at Madras on August 10th.

two other vessels were dismasted.   In fact, every craft in the roadstead either sank or suffered most severely.

In regard to the promised ransom of the town, La Bourdonnais
behaved throughout like a man of honour ; but Dupleix seems
never to have intended that the conditions should be carried out ;
and when La Bourdonnais had gone to Mauritius, on his way home
to France, Dupleix, to the astonishment of many even of his own
officers, caused the treaty to be declared void.   The arrival of
Commodore Thomas Griffin (1) from England soon afterwards, compelled the French to desist from a projected attack on Fort St.
David, and to withdraw nearly all their forces to Pondicherry.

On the Leeward Islands' station, Vice-Admiral Isaac Townsend
commanded at the beginning of 1746 ; but very early in the year
he was ordered to proceed with the greater part of his squadron
to Louisbourg.   He sailed from St. Kitt's in January, and, on his
way, met with so violent a storm that all his ships except two,
the *Princesa* and *Ipswich*, were obliged to return, and those two,
terribly disabled, had to bear away for England.   The *Ipswich*,
which reached Plymouth on April 22nd, was only saved by a
most brilliant display of seamanship, after her crew had suffered
great hardships.

When Vice-Admiral Townsend had refitted, he again sailed for
Louisbourg, leaving Commodore the Hon. Fitzroy Henry Lee in
command in the .West Indies.   Lee was ultimately superseded by
Commodore the Hon. Edward Legge.   Both Lee and Legge were
unfortunate in their attempts to intercept French convoys, several
of which, under the care of M. de Conflans, escaped them.   On
one occasion, as will be seen, Conflans would have come off badly
but for the cowardice of Commodore Cornelius Mitchell.   On
another occasion, he fell in with the British Leeward Islands'
convoy, escorted by the *Severn*, 50, Captain William Lisle, and
the *Woolwich*, 50, Captain Joseph Lingen.   Lisle, who was the
senior officer, ordered the convoy to disperse and each vessel to
shift for herself.   Conflans, in the *Terrible*, 74, with another ship
of the line, chased him, and after three hours' action, obliged the
Severn to strike ; but the *Woolwich* got away, and none of the
convoy were taken.   Lisle's action was considered so creditable
that, after his exchange, he was at once given the command of
a larger ship, the *Vigilant*, 64.

At Jamaica, Vice-Admiral Davers commanded until his death ;

but, being very ill with gout, had to depute Captain Cornelius Mitchell to go in search of M. de Conflans, who was expected with a convoy of ninety merchantmen at Cape François. Mitchell had four sail of the line, a frigate, and a sloop [1]; Conflans had but four vessels in all [2]; and Mitchell's superiority, though small, should, perhaps, have sufficed. Mitchell sighted the convoy on August 3rd off Cape St. Nicolas ; but, as promptly as possible, he ordered his ships to close, and held a council of war. It was thereupon resolved to wait till daylight before bearing down upon the enemy ; but, on the following morning, Mitchell was so backward in bringing on an engagement, in spite of the evident willingness of Conflans, that at 4 P.M. the squadrons had not exchanged a shot. At that hour everything was in his favour, and the breeze was fair ; but he hauled to the wind and shortened sail. The enemy, after he had recovered from his astonishment, gave chase ; and his headmost ship overhauled the *Lenox*, 64, at about 8 P.M., and fought her, without result, for an hour and a half. Mitchell that night ordered his ships to proceed without lights, and laid his course for Jamaica, where, on October 16th, owing to the death of Vice-Admiral Davers, the command devolved upon him. His behaviour having been represented to the Admiralty, he was superseded, and was tried at Jamaica by court-martial on January 28th following. The court convicted him of cowardice and neglect of duty ; but less severe than many of the naval courts of that period, sentenced him only to be mulcted of five years' pay, adjudging him at the same time to be incapable of again serving in the Navy.

In the Mediterranean during 1746 a large fleet, under Vice-Admiral Henry Medley and Rear-Admiral the Hon. John Byng, offered much assistance to the Austrians and their allies, and co-operated with success with the army which, under General Browne, crossed the Var on December 1st. A detachment of small vessels under Captain Hugh Forbes, of the *Phœnix*, 20, and Commander William Martin (2), of the *Terrible*, 6, lent valuable aid to the troops. Medley also blockaded Antibes, assisted in the capture of Ste. Marguerite, and lent help to the insurgents in Corsica.

The year 1747 was upon the whole very successful for Great

---

[1] *Strafford*, 60, Capt. Cornelius Mitchell; *Lenox*, 64, Capt. Peter Lawrence; *Plymouth*, 60, Capt. Digby Dent (2); *Worcester*, 60, Capt. Thomas Andrews (2); *Milford*, 44, Capt. Edward Rich ; and *Drake*, 14, Commander Edward Clark (1).

[2] *Terrible*, 74; *Neptune*, 74; *Alcion*, 50 ; and *Gloire*, 40.

Britain, although it witnessed some check to the cause of Britain's allies in the Mediterranean. The Austrians were obliged, by Marshal Belleisle, to recross the Var; and the Genoese succeeded in defeating the patriots in Corsica, and in driving them to the interior of the island. On the other hand, Vice-Admiral Medley not only maintained the blockade of Cartagena, but also intercepted a French expedition from Toulon to Genoa. Medley died in Vado Bay on August 5th, when Rear-Admiral the Hon. John Byng succeeded to the command.

In the East Indies, Rear-Admiral Thomas Griffin kept M. Dupleix on the defensive, and, at Madras, took and burnt the *Neptune*, 34, which had been left there by M. La Bourdonnais. At Jamaica, Captain Digby Dent (2) commanded until the arrival of Rear-Admiral Charles Knowles. On the Leeward Islands' station, Commodore the Hon. Edward Legge commanded until his death on September 9th, 1747, and was succeeded by Captain George Pocock. On each of these stations the cruisers were successful as well as active, but all the great naval transactions of the year happened on the Atlantic coasts of Europe.

France fitted out two considerable squadrons; one under the Marquis de La Jonquière, intended for the recovery of Cape Breton, and the other under M. Grou de St. Georges, of the French East India Company's service, for co-operation in the conquest of British settlements on the coast of Coromandel. It was arranged that, in order the more surely to escape the dangers presented by British naval superiority in the home seas, the two squadrons should depart from France together and proceed for some distance in company.

The projects of the French were known in England; and a squadron, under Vice-Admiral George Anson and Rear-Admiral Peter Warren, was specially fitted out to checkmate them. The forces which were ultimately opposed one to the other are set forth in the note [1] (p. 125). The French had with them a convoy, which brought the total number of their sail up to thirty-eight. M. de St. Georges left Groix in March, but, after suffering some losses from British cruisers and from very bad weather, had to put into the road of Isle d'Aix. La Jonquière there joined him and the two finally sailed on April 29th. Anson and Warren had left England on April 9th and had proceeded off Cape Finisterre, where, on May 3rd, the Cape bearing S.E., distant twenty-four leagues, they sighted the French. La Jonquière thereupon caused twelve of his best ships to shorten sail and form a line of battle ahead, while the rest stretched to the westward and crowded every possible stitch of canvas. Anson also made signal for a line of battle, believing apparently that he was in the presence of a more formidable squadron than was really before him; but, at Warren's instance, he substituted the signal for a general chase. La Jonquière was but ill-supported. Several of the French East India ships, especially the *Vigilant* and *Modeste*, and later the *Thétis* and *Apollon*, looked to nothing but the idea of saving themselves. It is useless to examine the tactical details of an action of this kind. Suffice to say, that, after a running fight lasting from 4 to 7 P.M., in which several of the French captains behaved with great courage and others conducted themselves with equal cowardice, all the ships which had remained in the French line struck. At 7 P.M. Anson brought to, and detached the *Monmouth*, *Yarmouth* and *Nottingham* in pursuit of the convoy, which then bore W. by S.W., distant about five leagues, and which had been followed and observed during the action by the *Falcon*. These ships captured the *Vigilant*, the *Modeste* and the *Dartmouth*, once a British privateer, together with six of the convoy. Night saved the rest.

---

[1] ACTION BETWEEN VICE-ADMIRAL ANSON AND M. DE LA JONQUIÈRE, MAY 3RD, 1747.

The account of the action, as well as the following list, is based upon the British and French dispatches, and especially upon the papers of La Jonquière in the Archives de la Marine, and upon the report of La Galernerie.

BRITISH.			FRENCH.		
Ships.	Guns.	Commanders.	Ships.	Guns.	Commanders.
Prince George . .	90	Vice-Admiral George Anson. / Capt. John Bentley.	*Diamant* [2] . .	30	Capt. de Hocquart.
			Philibert [2][3] . .	30	,, Larr.
			Vigilant [2][3] . .	20	,, Vauneulon.
Devonshire [1] . .	66	Rear-Admiral Peter Warren. / Capt. Temple West.	*Chimène* [3] . . .	36	,, ?
			Rubis [2] (en flût·) .	52	,, Macarty.
			Jason [2]	50	,, Beccart.
Namur [1]. . . .	74	,, Hon. Edward Boscawen.	*Sérieux* [2] . . .	64	M. de La Jonquière, Capt. d'Aubigny.
Monmouth . .	64	,, Henry Harrison.	*Invincible* [2] . .	74	Capt. Grou de St. Georges.
Prince Frederick .	64	,, Harry Norris.	*Apollon* [2][3] . .	30	,, Noël.
Yarmouth [1] .	64	,, Piercy Brett (1).	*Thétis* [2][3] . . .	22	,, Masson.
Princess Louisa .	60	,, Charles Watson.	*Modeste* [2][3] . . .	18	,, Thiercelin.
Nottingham . .	60	,, Philip de Saumarez.	*Gloire* [2]	40	,, de Saliez.
Defiance [1] . .	60	,, Thomas Grenville.			
Pembroke [1] . .	60	,, Thomas Fincher.			
Windsor [1] . .	60	,, Thomas Hanway.	*Emeraude* [4] . . .	40	,, de la Jonquière de Taffanel.
Centurion [1] . .	50	,, Peter Denis.	*Dartmouth* [2][4] . .	18	,, ?
Falkland . . .	50	,, Bloomfield Barradell.			
Bristol [1] . . .	50	,, Hon. William Montagu.			
Ambuscade . . .	40	,, John Montagu.			
Falcon	10	Commander Richard Gwynn.			
Vulcan (fireship) .	8	Commander William Pettigrew.			

[1] These ships only were engaged.　　　[3] These ships belonged to the French East India Company.
[2] Taken.　　　[4] With the convoy but not in line of battle.

The battle, considering its nature, was a costly one. The French lost about 700 killed and wounded, and the British, 520. Among the French officers killed was Captain de Saliez, and among those wounded were La Jonquière himself and d'Aubigny, his flag captain. On the British side Captain Thomas Grenville, of the *Defiance*, was killed, and Captain Boscawen, of the *Namur*, wounded. The victors found specie to the value of £300,000 on board the prizes. For this service Anson was created a peer, and Warren, a K.B. All the men-of-war taken, and also the East Indiaman *Thétis*, were purchased into the Royal Navy. The name of the *Sérieux* was changed to *Intrepid*, and that of the *Diamant* to *Isis*.

The victory was valuable if not exactly brilliant. Commenting upon it, and upon the other great action of the year, Captain Mahan says :

"Two encounters between English and French squadrons happened during the year 1747, completing the destruction of the French fighting navy. In both cases the English were decidedly superior, and though there was given opportunity for some brilliant fighting by particular captains, and for the display of heroic endurance on the part of the French, greatly outnumbered, but resisting to the last, only one tactical lesson is afforded. This lesson is that, when the enemy, either as the result of battle, or from original inequality, is greatly inferior in force, obliged to fly without standing on the order of his flying, the regard otherwise due to order must be, in a measure at least, dismissed, and a general chase ordered." . . . . "In both cases, the signal was made for a general chase, and the action which resulted was a *mêlée*. There was no opportunity for anything else ; the one thing necessary was to overtake the running enemy, and that could only certainly be done by letting the fastest or best-situated ships get ahead, sure that the speed of the fastest pursuers is better than that of the slowest of the pursued, and that, therefore, either the latter must be abandoned, or the whole force brought to bay."

It would appear that in 1747 the Admiralty had begun to be better served by its intelligence officers than it had been earlier in the war ; and it is not the least merit of the administration that, on several important occasions, it was able to bring superior forces to bear upon its enemies. Anson's success was one result of this foreknowledge ; the success of Captain Thomas Fox, to be noted in the next chapter, was another ; that of Rear-Admiral Edward Hawke, now to be recounted, was a third.

Information was received in England that France was collecting in Basque Road a huge convoy for the West Indies, and that a squadron of men-of-war had sailed from Brest to pick it up and escort it to its destination. Thereupon a squadron, under Hawke, was despatched from Plymouth to intercept it. It left Plymouth Sound on August 9th. The French left Isle d'Aix on October 6th ;

and, on October 14th at 7 A.M., were sighted in lat. 47° 49′ N. and
long. 1° 2′ W., off Finisterre.   Hawke made signal to chase, but at
8 A.M., seeing the enemy's ships to be very numerous, many of them
being large, he, as a measure of prudence, formed a line of battle

COMMEMORATIVE MEDAL OF ANSON'S VICTORY, 1747, AND OF HIS
CIRCUMNAVIGATION OF THE WORLD, 1740–44.

(From an original kindly lent by H.S.H. Captain Prince Louis of Battenberg, R.N.)

ahead.[1]   There were in fact no fewer than 252 merchantmen with
the French squadron.   Commodore de l'Etenduère, who at first
mistook the British for part of his own convoy, no sooner discovered
his mistake than he ordered the merchantmen to make the best of
their way under the care of the *Content*, 64, and himself also formed
a line of battle ahead.   These manœuvres informed Hawke as to

---

[1] ACTION BETWEEN REAR-ADMIRAL HAWKE AND M. DE L'ETENDUÈRE,
OCTOBER 14TH, 1747.

BRITISH.			FRENCH.		
Ships.	Guns.	Commanders.	Ships.	Guns.	Commanders.
Devonshire . . .	66	{ Rear-Admiral Edward Hawke. Capt. John Moore (1).	*Tonnant.* . . .	80	{ M. des Herbiers de l'Etenduère, Chef d'Escadre. Capt. Duchaffault.
Kent	74	,, Thomas Fox.			
Edinburgh . . .	70	,, Thomas Cotes.	*Intrépide* . .	74	,, de Vaudreuil.
Yarmouth . . .	64	,, Charles Saunders.	*Trident* [1] . . .	64	,, d'Amblimont.
Monmouth . . .	64	,, Henry Harrison.	*Terrible* [1] . . .	74	,, du Guay.
Princess Louisa .	60	,, Charles Watson.	*Monarque* [1] . . .	74	,, de La Bedoyère.
Windsor	60	,, Thomas Hanway.	*Severn* [1]	56	,, du Rouret.
Lion	60	,, Arthur Scott.	*Fougueux* [1] . . .	64	,, de Vignault.
Tilbury	60	,, Robert Harland (2).	*Neptune* [1] . . .	74	,, de Fromentières.
Nottingham . .	60	,, Philip de Saumarez.			
Defiance . . .	60	,, John Bentley.	*Castor* [2]	26	,, d'Ossonville.
Eagle	60	{ ,, George Brydges Rodney.	*Content* [2] . . .	64	,, ?
Gloucester . . .	50	,, Philip Durell (1).			
Portland . . .	50	,, Charles Stevens.			
	and some frigates.				

[1] Taken.   [2] With the convoy.

the nature of the force before him, and induced him to haul down
the signal for the line and to again make that for a general chase,
following it half-an-hour later with the signal to engage. A running
fight resulted. The French behaved with great spirit but were overpowered by sheer weight of numbers. They had in line but eight
ships and of these six were taken. Towards night the *Intrépide* and
Tonnant, finding that the day was lost, set all sail with a view
to escaping. Their intention was perceived by the *Yarmouth*,
Nottingham and *Eagle*, which, at the instance of Captain Saunders
of the *Yarmouth*, and on their own responsibility, followed. These
ships engaged the fugitives for an hour, in the course of which
Captain Saumarez [1] of the *Nottingham* fell. The two French ships,
though very badly damaged, succeeded in getting into Brest. At
dark Hawke brought his ships to ; and in the morning, at a council
of war, it was decided, in view of the mauled condition of the British
squadron, not to pursue the convoy. The *Weazel*, sloop, was,
however, despatched to the West Indies, to apprise Commodore
Pocock of the approach of the French ; and thanks to this precaution,
many of their ships were ultimately taken. [2]

The French loss in the action was about 800 killed and wounded,
among the former being Captain de Fromentières of the *Neptune*.
The British lost 154 killed, including Captain Saumarez, and 558
wounded. As nearly all the vessels captured had been dismasted,
it took some time to refit them ; but on October 31st, Hawke had
the satisfaction of carrying them and his squadron into Portsmouth.
A little later he was made a K.B. for his services. All the prizes,
except the *Neptune*, were purchased into the Royal Navy.

Hawke in his despatch had occasion to complain of Captain
Thomas Fox of the *Kent*, who, in the action, when ordered by
signal to make sail ahead after the *Tonnant* and to engage her, had
failed to obey. Captain Fox was consequently tried by court-martial
at Portsmouth on November 25th upon the charge that " he did not
come properly into the fight, nor do his utmost to distress and
damage the enemy, nor assist his Majesty's ships which did."
Fox's personal courage was not impeached ; and there is no doubt

[1] Philip Saumarez, or de Saumarez. Born, 1710. Commander, 1741. Captain,
1743. Killed, as above, October 14th, 1747. He had served with Anson in his voyage
round the world, and had distinguished himself greatly, when already commanding
the *Nottingham*, by his capture of the *Mars*, 64, in 1746. A monument to him is in
Westminster Abbey.

[2] *See* next chapter.

that his failure to obey orders was chiefly due to the faulty system of signals then in use. Both his first lieutenant and his master mistook the signal for close action for one to proceed to the assistance of the Admiral; and he acted accordingly. The trial lasted until December 22nd, when the court came to the conclusion that " he had been guilty of backing his mizen-top-sail and leaving the *Tonnant*, contrary to the 10th and 11th Articles of War." He was acquitted of cowardice, but, because he had paid too much regard to the advice of his officers, contrary to his own better judgment, he was sentenced to be dismissed from the command of the *Kent.* Captain Fox, whose post-captain's commission dated from August 6th, 1737, and who always had been a good officer, was never again employed, but was superannuated as a Rear-Admiral in 1749. He died in 1763.

Criticising the battle, Captain Mahan [1] says :

"If . . . Hawke showed in his attack the judgment and dash which always distinguished that remarkable officer, it may be claimed for Commodore l'Etenduère that fortune, in assigning him the glorious disadvantage of numbers, gave him also the leading part in the drama, and that he failed nobly."

Troude, the French naval critic, remarks [2] of de l'Etenduère that :

" he defended his convoy as on shore a position is defended, when the aim is to save an army corps, or to assure an evolution. He gave himself to be crushed. After an action that lasted from midday to 8 P.M., the convoy was saved, thanks to the obstinacy of the defence, and 250 ships were secured to their owners by the devotion of l'Etenduère, and of the captains under his orders. This devotion cannot be questioned, for eight ships had but few chances of surviving an action with fourteen; and not only did the commander of the eight accept an action which he might possibly have avoided, but also he knew how to inspire his lieutenants with trust in himself, for all supported the fight with honour, and yielded at last, showing the most indisputable proofs of their fine and energetic defence.

" The whole affair," concludes Mahan, " as conducted on both sides, affords an admirable study of how to follow up an advantage, original or secured, and of the results that may be obtained by a gallant, even hopeless defence, for the furtherance of a particular object."

The squadron of Anson and Warren, as well as that of Hawke, cruised in the Channel and Bay after the actions above narrated, and took numerous prizes; but an account of such smaller engagements as were fought in the course of the year may be reserved for the next chapter.

The war had been very costly to France. The French Navy had

---

[1] ' Influence of Sea Power,' 272.
[2] ' Bats. Nav. de la France.'

been almost crushed, and French maritime trade had been almost ruined, though the armies of France had been successful on land. But all the Powers engaged were to some extent weary of the conflict; and it was therefore felt, when a Congress met at Aix-la-Chapelle to consider the terms of an arrangement, that there was every prospect of the conclusion of a satisfactory peace. In the meantime, Great Britain did not relinquish, nor even diminish, her preparations to continue the struggle. In 1748, as in previous years, all ships, as they became ready for sea, were put into commission. Squadrons were sent to cruise at various times in home waters, under Vice-Admirals Sir Peter Warren and Sir Edward Hawke, and Rear-Admiral William Chambers. Commodore the Hon. George Townshend watched the coast of Flanders; Vice-Admiral the Hon. John Byng remained in the Mediterranean; and in the West Indies Rear-Admiral Charles Knowles and Commodore George Pocock, let slip no opportunity of annoying the enemy.

Rear-Admiral the Hon. Edward Boscawen had been sent out in 1747, as Commander-in-Chief, to the East Indies, and had taken with him reinforcements to the station. Before his arrival, Rear-Admiral Thomas Griffin (1) had received three additional ships from England, so that his squadron consisted of three 60's, three 50's, three 40's, and one 20, and was considerably superior to the French force in the same seas. But Mr. Griffin had been outwitted and out-manœuvred by the French commander-in-chief, M. Bouvet, who, in spite of him, had thrown troops into Madras.

The French ministry was warned of Boscawen's departure from England; and M. Dupleix, being advised from home, took such measures as he could to meet the Rear-Admiral, who had with him six ships of the line or 50's, and four smaller craft, and who convoyed eleven ships of the East India Company with 1500 soldiers on board. Boscawen reached the Cape of Good Hope in March, 1748, and was there joined by six Dutch East Indiamen, having on board 400 troops. On May 18th he sailed again, and on June 23rd, after a troublesome voyage, sighted Mauritius, which he had decided to make an attempt upon. The island had been informed by Dupleix of its danger, and was to some extent prepared, though it was but ill garrisoned. On the 25th, after having reconnoitred the coast, Boscawen decided to abandon the project and to proceed to Coromandel. Had he known how few troops were in the island, he would certainly have persisted, and would probably have been successful; for the works, though strong, could not be properly manned.[1]

The Dutch convoy parted company at Mauritius, and proceeded for Batavia; and Boscawen, on June 27th, sailed for Fort St. David (Cuddalore), where he arrived on July 29th. There he met Rear-Admiral Griffin, who, in the meantime, had been promoted to be Vice-Admiral, and who soon afterwards returned to England by way of Trincomale with part of his command.

Besides the naval force, Boscawen had under him many armed East Indiamen, and 3240 troops, including sepoys but not including Marines. Indeed, he was in a position to dispose of 5220 men to act on shore; and, in addition, 2000 native auxiliary cavalry were placed at his service for the contemplated siege of Pondicherry, whither Boscawen presently proceeded. Leaving Captain William Lisle in command of the squadron, he landed to direct the operations on shore. Early in August the army closed round the town, which was closely blockaded from seaward by the *Exeter, Chester, Pembroke* and *Swallow.* An assault upon one of the outlying works was repulsed with loss on August 12th, but the siege was formally begun and some successes were gained. The engineers upon whom Boscawen was obliged to depend were, how-

---

[1] REAR-ADMIRAL THE HON. EDWARD BOSCAWEN'S SQUADRON, WHICH ARRIVED OFF MAURITIUS IN JUNE, 1748.

Ships.	Guns.	Commanders.
Namur	74	{ Rear-Admiral Hon. Edward Boscawen. { Captain Samuel Marshall (1).
Vigilant	64	„ William Lisle.
Deptford	60	„ Thomas Lake.
Pembroke	60	„ Thomas Fincher.
Ruby	50	„ Joseph Knight.
Chester	50	„ Richard Spry.
Deal Castle	24	„ John Lloyd (2).
Swallow	16	Commander John Rowzier.
Basilisk (bomb) . . .	8	„ William Preston.
Apollo (hospital ship) . .	20	Lieutenant Robert Wilson.

The above, proceeding, found on the East Indies Station, the following:—

Exeter	60	Captain Lord Harry Powlett.
York	60	„ Timothy Nucella.
Harwich	50	„ Philip Carteret (1).
Preston	50	„ William Adams (1).
Lively	20	„ Nathaniel Stephens, actg.

in addition to the other vessels, which, upon Boscawen's arrival, returned home or went elsewhere.

ever, incompetent ; and little progress was made, though the *Basilisk,* bomb, threw some shells into the place.   In the operations Ensign Clive, afterwards Lord Clive, gained his first military distinction. As the siege threatened to be a protracted one, Boscawen ordered Captain Lisle to begin a general bombardment from the ships of the squadron ; but, owing to the shallows, these could not approach near enough to do much damage.   The business, however, cost the life of Captain William Adams (1), then commanding the *Harwich.* In the meantime the weather was bad, and the troops were sickly ; and, as the neighbourhood of the town was liable to be completely flooded at the beginning of the rainy season, the siege was raised at the beginning of October, the sick being removed to the ships, and the army retiring overland to Fort St. David.   The expedition cost the lives of 1065 British, and of only about 200 French.   The fiasco reflected no disgrace upon Boscawen, and was entirely due to the incapacity of the engineers and some of the military leaders. Nevertheless, it greatly lowered British prestige with the natives, and led to some serious defections.

Boscawen learned in November of the cessation of hostilities between Great Britain and France, but was ordered to remain on his station until advised of the final conclusion of peace.   Part of the squadron went to Acheen, and part to Trincomale, to avoid the monsoon, and the whole returned in January, 1749, to Fort St. David, where it lay maintaining an observant attitude, while M. Bouvet, with the French forces, lay at Madras, or as it was then often called, Fort St. George, 120 miles to the northward. But the British did not remain wholly idle, and in April ships were detached to assist the East India Company in a war with the King of Tanjore.   While this service was being performed, a violent hurricane wrecked the *Pembroke* and *Namur.*   The former lost her captain,[1] and all hands except fourteen, 330 in all ; the latter lost 520 souls, though the admiral, captain, and a few officers, being on shore, fortunately escaped.   Two East Indiamen were also wrecked. In August, in pursuance of the treaty of Aix-la-Chapelle, which had been concluded on April 18th, 1748, Madras, in a dismantled condition, was surrendered to the British.

In the West Indies, in February, 1748, Rear-Admiral Charles Knowles, with a squadron and detachment of troops, left Port

---

[1] This was on April 13th.   Captain Thomas Fincher's post-commission dated from December 6th, 1745.

Royal to make an attack on Santiago de Cuba; but, the winds
blowing persistently from the north, the ships could not make that
place.   Knowles therefore determined to attack Port Louis, on
the south side of Hispaniola.   The squadron[1] arrived there on

ADMIRAL SIR CHARLES KNOWLES, BART.
(*From an engraving by Ridley.*)

[1] BRITISH SQUADRON AT THE CAPTURE OF PORT LOUIS, HISPANIOLA, 1748.

Ships.	Guns.	Men.	Commanders.
Cornwall . .	80	600	{Rear-Admiral Charles Knowles (B.). {Captain Richard Chadwick.
Plymouth .	60	400	„ Digby Dent (2).
Elizabeth . .	70	480	„ Polycarpus Taylor.
Canterbury .	60	400	„ David Brodie.
Strafford . .	60	400	„ James Rentone.
Warwick . .	60	400	„ Thomas Innes.
Worcester .	60	400	„ Thomas Andrews (2).
Oxford . .	50	300	„ Edmond Toll.
Weazel . .	6	102	
Merlin . .	6	100	

March 8th, and was at once ordered by signal to cannonade the fort, which mounted seventy-eight guns, and was garrisoned by 600 men. A warm engagement resulted, and in the height of it the enemy sent out a fireship, which was designed to fall on board the *Cornwall* or the *Elizabeth*. She was towed off by the boats of the fleet, and left to burn out and explode innocuously. The British boats then boarded and brought away two other craft, which had been prepared as fireships. The action continuing, the Spanish fire after a time languished, and the Rear-Admiral sent a summons to the governor, who, first taking some time for reflection, surrendered upon terms. The place was then taken possession of. The squadron lost only 70 killed and wounded, but among these was Captain Rentone,[1] of the *Strafford*, and Captain William Cust,[2] of the *Boston*, who, with the Rear-Admiral's permission, was serving as a volunteer on board the *Elizabeth*. The enemy lost 160 killed and wounded. With the place were captured three ships, a snow, and three privateer sloops. The fort was burnt, it not being advisable to retain it ; and, the conditions of wind being at length more favourable, the Rear-Admiral decided to prosecute his scheme against Santiago de Cuba.

The place had been much strengthened since the time of Vernon's attack upon it ; and, as the appearance of the British had been anticipated, all possible precautions had been taken. Knowles arrived before the town on April 5th, and, the mode of procedure having been determined, Captain Dent of the *Plymouth*, as senior

---

[1] James Rentone; commander, 1739; captain, 1740.
[2] William Cust; commander, 1746; captain, 1747.

captain, claimed and obtained the honour of leading in. He was seconded by the flagship. When the *Plymouth* had approached close to the harbour's mouth it was seen that the passage was obstructed by a boom, backed by vessels held ready to be used as fireships. The nearest forts were cannonaded and the fire was returned; but Dent, having taken the opinion of his officers, came to the conclusion that it was impracticable to proceed, and so reported to the Rear-Admiral, who thereupon drew off and went back to Jamaica.

Dent's apparent hesitation on this occasion was taken exception to by Knowles; and, in consequence, the captain of the *Plymouth* was court-martialled on his return to England, but he was honourably acquitted.

Later in the year Knowles was informed that the Spanish Plate fleet was expected at Havana from Vera Cruz. He therefore detached Captain Charles Holmes, in the *Lenox*, to convoy a great body of trade, which had been collecting to sail for England; and himself went to cruise off the Tortuga Banks in search of the enemy. The convoy under Holmes sailed from Jamaica on August 25th; and, being prevented from getting through the Windward Passage, had to bear away for the Gulf of Florida. On September 29th it sighted seven large ships, which were presently recognised to be Spanish men-of-war.[1] Holmes signalled the convoy to disperse and to look to its own safety, while he endeavoured to draw the attention of the enemy to his own ship; and, knowing where the Rear-Admiral was cruising at the time, he succeeded, under press of sail, in joining him on the following morning, when he reported what had occurred. Knowles instantly went in quest of the Spaniards,

---

[1] ORDER OF BATTLE OF THE BRITISH AND SPANISH SQUADRONS IN THE ACTION OFF HAVANA, OCTOBER 1ST, 1748.

BRITISH.			SPANISH.		
Ships.	Guns.	Commanders.	Ships.	Guns.	Commanders.
Tilbury	60	Capt. Charles Powlett.	*Invencible* . . .	74	Rear-Admiral Spinola.
Strafford . . .	60	,, David Brodie.	*Conquistador* . .	64	Don de San Justo.
Cornwall . . .	80	{Rear-Admiral Charles Knowles.	*Africa*	74	Vice-Admiral Reggio.
		{Capt. Polycarpus Taylor.	*Dragón*	64	Don de La Paz.
			Nueva España . .	64	Don Barrella.
Lenox	70	,, Charles Holmes.	*Real Familia* . .	64	Don Forrestal.
Warwick . . .	60	,, Thomas Innes.			
Canterbury . . .	60	,, Edward Clark (1).	*Galga*[1]	36	Don Garrecocha.
Oxford[1]	50	,, Edmond Toll.			

[1] Not in the line.

and sighted them early in the morning of October 1st between Tortuga and Havana. The Spaniards at once formed a line; yet the British, though they had the advantage of the wind, edged down only very gradually, and it was 2 o'clock before either side fired. The distance was then too great for much damage to be done, but at about 2.30 P.M., the two squadrons being nearer, a brisk action was begun. The Spaniards seem to have been in good order and close together, but the *Warwick* and *Canterbury* were far astern of station, so that for nearly two hours the British had but four ships opposed to six of the Spanish. During this time the *Cornwall* engaged the *Africa* at pistol range, and was so gallantly received that in half an hour she was obliged to fall astern and quit the line, having lost her main-topmast and received other damage to her rigging. Soon afterwards the *Conquistador*, also much damaged aloft, dropped astern of her consorts and fell nearly where the *Cornwall* lay refitting. Knowles lost no time in attacking her, and quickly killed her captain; but that officer's successor fought the ship bravely until she had thrice been set on fire by shells from the eight cohorns,[1] which the *Cornwall*, unlike most of her class, carried. Not until then did he surrender. The *Lenox* had taken the *Cornwall's* place and had warmly engaged the *Africa;* but other Spanish ships succoured their admiral, and Captain Holmes was hard pressed for about an hour until he was relieved by the *Warwick* and *Canterbury*. The action then became general and fierce, and so continued until about 8 P.M., when the Spanish drew off towards Havana, closely pursued. All, however, escaped except the *Conquistador*. The *Africa*, owing to her damaged condition, had to anchor before she reached port; and, being discovered by the British two days after the action, was burnt by the Spaniards to save her from capture. The enemy lost 86 killed and 197 wounded; the British had 59 killed and 120 wounded. But whilst the Spaniards had several officers of rank included in each category the British had none in either.

Knowles continued to look out for the Plate fleet, but in vain. In the course of time he learnt from a prize that the preliminaries of peace had been concluded and that hostilities were to cease, whereupon he returned to Jamaica. When he went home to England he complained of Holmes for having left the convoy,

---

[1] Cohorn, a small mortar, so named from its inventor, Menno van Coehoorn, the Dutch military engineer (born 1641 ; died 1704).

oblivious of the fact that, had Holmes not rejoined the flag, the victory off Havana could not have been gained. Holmes was most honourably acquitted. On the other hand, some of the captains of the squadron complained of the conduct of the Rear-Admiral, who was in consequence tried on board the *Charlotte* yacht, at Deptford, by a court-martial which sat from the 11th to the 20th December, 1749. It appeared that while Rear-Admiral Knowles was standing for the Spanish fleet he might, by a different disposition of his squadron, have begun the attack simultaneously with six ships, and might have begun it earlier in the day. It appeared too, that, owing to the method which he pursued, he had begun to attack with only four ships. Upon these points the court condemned him ; and it was also of the opinion that, in order properly to conduct and direct the operations of his command, he ought to have shifted his flag from the *Cornwall* to some other vessel, after the former had been disabled. For the rest, the proceedings amply vindicated the Rear-Admiral's personal courage. The sentence was thus worded :

" The court unanimously agree that Rear-Admiral Knowles falls under part of the 14th Article of War, being guilty of negligence, and also under the 23rd Article. The court therefore unanimously adjudge him to be reprimanded for not bringing up the squadron in closer order than he did, and for not beginning the attack with so great a force as he might have done; and also for not shifting his flag, on the *Cornwall's* being disabled."

On the Leeward Islands' Station, Commodore Pocock learned by the arrival of the *Weazel*, sloop, despatched to him by Hawke, of the approach of the large convoy, which had been under the escort of M. de l'Etenduère ; and, although he had not time to collect the whole of his squadron to intercept it, his ships, and the privateers on the station, succeeded in capturing no fewer than thirty-five sail of it.

In the Mediterranean, where Rear-Admiral the Hon. John Byng commanded, the British fleet was too strong for the French and Spanish to attempt at sea anything of importance before the conclusion of the peace. The British hampered the passage of reinforcements to the allied armies at Genoa, by arming a number of small craft and entrusting them to lieutenants, who cruised with great success inshore, and intercepted many transports. On the peace being concluded, Byng returned to England with most of the larger ships of his fleet.

In the home seas Rear-Admiral Sir Edward Hawke went on

a cruise with a considerable squadron in the month of January; and, ere he returned to port, made several prizes, including the *Magnanime*, 74, an account of the capture of which will be found in the next chapter. Rear-Admiral Sir Peter Warren, in April, also went on a cruise; but in May both he and Hawke were recalled to England upon the settlement of the preliminaries of peace.

"In the course of the war," says Beatson,[1] "the British captured from the Spaniards 1249 ships, and from the French 2185, making in all 3434. The Spaniards captured from the British 1360, and the French 1878, making together 3238, being 196 fewer than what had been taken by the British." Yet, in spite of this, the general balance was in favour of Great Britain, for not only were several of the Spanish prizes extraordinarily valuable, but also the British merchant marine, on account of its superior strength, was far better able than either the French or Spanish to suffer great losses without being seriously crippled. The main gain to Great Britain by the war was the reduction of the French navy to proportions which, for the time, were no longer formidable. The peace itself benefited her but little, for, in accordance with it, all conquests made by any of the combatants were to be restored. On the other hand, the point which had been the chief occasion of the war—the right of British ships to navigate the American seas without being searched —was not touched upon, and remained unsettled. The right to the province of Nova Scotia, or Acadia, was to be left to be discussed by commissioners appointed for the purpose. This last matter, never having been properly arranged, was, as will soon be shown, productive of another bloody and expensive war.

The first care of France after the conclusion of peace was to reorganise and revive her navy. Great numbers of ships were laid down at home; and contracts were placed abroad, especially in Sweden, for the construction of others. None of the ambitious projects of King Louis were surrendered. He had merely accepted peace in order the better to prepare for the realisation of his designs. Nor did the French agents invariably take the trouble to obey the spirit of the treaty. As early as 1749 the French Governor of Martinique seized and fortified the neutral island of Tobago; and the place was not evacuated until grave international complications threatened to arise out of the matter. Again, in 1751, the French contemplated aggressions on the West African coast, and only

[1] 'Nav. and Milit. Mems.,' i. 414.

desisted when Captain Matthew Buckle (1), of the *Assistance*, 50, informed M. Perrier de Salvert, the French commodore, that if he persisted in his designs of building a fort at Annamaboe, the British would look upon it as a breach of the peace and would repel force by force.

French aggression in other quarters was not always checked with equal promptitude. M. de La Jonquière, the French commander-in-chief in North America, and M. de La Galissonnière, Governor of Canada, hatched between them a project for tampering with the Indians of North America and for gradually driving British settlers out of that continent; and French officers occupied British territory in Nova Scotia and built forts there. Remonstrances were made, and in 1750 commissioners were appointed to adjust the disputes; but nothing came of their conferences. Still, while Great Britain herself remained almost indifferent, the Colonists at last took up the question. Virginia raised 400 men and £10,000 for the defence of its inland borders, and confided the command of its troops to Major George Washington.[1] The French Canadians, however, in spite of the heroism of the Americans, captured them and their commander on July 3rd. Thereupon the colonial governors held a congress and agreed upon a common plan of defence; and the Ministry at home, shamed into action, sent troops under General Braddock to the assistance of the Colonists. These were convoyed to America in 1754 by two 50-gun ships[2] under Commodore the Hon. Augustus Keppel. Such signs assured the French that, if they persisted in their policy, an open rupture could not but result; and they therefore endeavoured to associate Spain with them in the coming quarrel; but their schemes were foiled by the watchfulness of Sir Benjamin Keene, the British ambassador at Madrid.

In India, where M. Dupleix still governed Pondicherry, the French were as aggressive as elsewhere; and, in consequence, hostilities between the two East India Companies were almost unceasing, so that the peace in that quarter was a merely nominal one. Clive in this contest won great successes and opened up to

---

[1] This was the beginning of the great Washington's military career. See Walpole: ' Mems. of George II.,' i. 347; and ' Corresp.,' iii. 73.

[2] *Centurion*, Capt. the Hon. Aug. Keppel; and *Norwich*, Capt. the Hon. Samuel Barrington. In the latter, Adam Duncan, afterwards Lord Duncan, served as acting lieutenant.—Keppel: ' Life of Keppel,' i. 201.

the British East India Company such a vision of future wealth and glory as induced it to beg the Ministry at home to assist it in preserving its rapidly growing superiority over its French rival. In response the Government in 1754 despatched Rear-Admiral Charles Watson with a force which, as ultimately constituted, consisted of the *Kent*, 70, *Cumberland*, 66, *Tiger*, 60, *Salisbury*, 50, *Bridgewater*, 24, and *Kingfisher*, 16. France at the same time sent out a squadron of nearly equal strength ; but, before the ships arrived, Dupleix had been recalled, and the French in India had adopted a more peaceable policy, which might have led to permanent harmony between the two Companies had not the outbreak of war elsewhere precluded such a consummation.

The despatch of General Braddock to America led France to throw off her mask and to assemble a large expedition at Brest and Rochefort, destined for Canada. Great Britain in reply prepared for war ; and on March 11th, 1755, a proclamation was issued offering bounties for seamen and able-bodied landsmen. On March 14th thirty-five sail of the line and numerous small craft were commissioned ; a hot press for men was instituted in each of the chief ports, and fifty companies of Marines were ordered to be raised.

The French expedition left Brest under the convoy of twenty-five sail of the line, commanded by M. de Macnamara, who, after seeing it fairly to sea, returned with nine sail, leaving the rest of the command to M. Dubois de La Motte, who later detached four sail of the line and two frigates to Louisbourg, and proceeded with the rest of the fleet to Quebec. The British Ministry was only vaguely informed as to these movements, and sent to North America Vice-Admiral the Hon. Edward Boscawen with but eleven sail of the line, a frigate, and a sloop, convoying two regiments. He sailed from Plymouth on April 27th, 1755, with instructions to protect the British colonies and to attack the French squadron wheresoever he should find it. An intimation of what instructions had been given was, at the same time, communicated to the French ambassador, who replied that the king his master would consider the first gun fired at sea in a hostile manner to be a declaration of war. When it became known how greatly superior a French force had gone to America, a reinforcement of six sail of the line and a frigate, under Rear-Admiral Francis Holburne, was sent to Boscawen ; and the necessary arrangements were so quickly made that Holburne sailed on May 11th and joined Boscawen off the Banks of Newfoundland on June 21st.

The military operations in North America of the force under General Braddock need not be followed in detail. Suffice it to say that an American expedition against Niagara Fort miscarried; that Colonel William Johnson, a colonial officer, on his way to occupy Crown Point, defeated a considerable French force which had attacked him; and that Braddock himself, while leading an expedition against Fort Duquesne,[1] was routed and killed. A combined naval and military expedition under Captain John Rous, R.N., and Lieut.-Colonel Monckton, against French forts in Nova Scotia, took Fort Beau Sejour, which was renamed Fort Cumberland, and several other works; and was completely successful with but little loss.

The fleets of Boscawen and Dubois de la Motte did not meet, although four French line-of-battle ships, which had become separated from their consorts, were chased by the British on June 6th. For a time they escaped in a fog; but on June 8th, when the weather cleared, three of the French vessels were again visible and a general chase was ordered. The *Dunkirk*, 60, Captain the Hon. Richard Howe, assisted by the *Torbay*, 74 (Boscawen's flagship), Captain Charles Colby, after a brisk action took the *Alcide*, Captain de Hocquart; and the *Defiance*, 60, Captain Thomas Andrews (2), and *Fougueux*, 64, Captain Richard Spry, took the *Lys*, which, though pierced for 64 guns, had only 22 mounted. The third ship got away owing to the return of the fog.

When Boscawen discovered that the French had safely reached Quebec, and that his own fleet was very sickly, he left Rear-Admiral Holburne with a small squadron to blockade Louisbourg, and went to Halifax to refresh his men. But the epidemic of putrid fever could not be checked; and, before Boscawen, with the main part of his squadron, got home to England, the ships had lost 2000 people. Captain Spry, with a few vessels, was left to winter at Halifax. Boscawen and the rest of the fleet anchored at Spithead on November 4th. It should be added that M. Dubois de la Motte returned to France without adventure, and that the vessels which he had sent into Louisbourg escaped and rejoined him at the time when the British blockading squadron had been driven from its station by bad weather.

---

[1] On the site of what is now Pittsburg.

The capture of the *Alcide* and *Lys* produced great excitement in France, and fanned the flame of war in England; but although hostilities thereupon began, formal war between Great Britain and France was not declared until May 18th, 1756, upon the receipt in London of the news of the French invasion of Minorca.

In the summer of 1755, Rear-Admiral Sir Edward Hawke and Rear-Admiral Temple West, with a strong squadron, put to sea in hopes of intercepting the Comte du Guay, who was expected back from the West Indies after having carried reinforcements to the Leeward Islands. But the enemy avoided them, and re-entered Brest without loss; whereupon Hawke returned to Spithead. The fleet soon afterwards sailed again under Vice-Admiral the Hon. John Byng and Rear-Admiral Temple West, but re-anchored at Spithead on November 21st. When Parliament met in November, the addresses in reply to the speech from the throne were very warlike, and France, which had previously believed that the great body of Englishmen was averse to hostilities, made efforts to negotiate: but too late.

Early in the new year, troops were assembled on the French coast as if for an invasion of Great Britain; and a fleet was collected at Brest. The threat of invasion produced almost a panic in England, and in February the Ministry increased the alarm by issuing a foolish proclamation, ordering the proper officers, in case the French should land, to cause all horses, oxen and other cattle, which were fit for draft or burden and not actually used in the interest and defence of the country, and all other cattle as far as was practicable, and all provisions, to be driven or removed at least twenty miles from the point at which such an attempt should be made. The Government also unwisely detained at home a large fleet, while it left America and the West Indies and the Mediterranean very insufficiently guarded. It did not realise that Great Britain is best protected from invasion by the activity and efficiency of her Navy at sea. France took advantage of the alarm and confusion to quietly embark at Toulon about 16,000 men, under the Duc de Richelieu, and to send them to Minorca, convoyed by a strong squadron under M. de La Galissonnière. The expedition landed at Ciudadella on April 19th.

Before proceeding to give an account of the operations of the war, it may be well to say something of an expedition, which, under Rear-Admiral Charles Watson, rendered valuable service to commerce

by destroying the power of a most dangerous pirate in the East
Indies. This pirate, Tulagee Angria by name, was the representative
of a family which for about a hundred years had committed outrages
on the Mahratta coast, and had acquired both wealth and territory.
Angria was feared not only by the natives of India, but also by
European traders, and even by the East India Company; and he
had extended his authority from the small island stronghold of
Severndroog over a large stretch of coast, which included the town
and port of Geriah. In 1734 Angria had taken the East Indiaman,
Derby, richly laden, and later the *Restoration*, 20, armed ship, and
the French *Jupiter*, 40. He had also ventured to attack Commodore
William Lisle, who had two ships of the line and several other
vessels in company; and he had wrought much damage to the
Dutch trade. He was by origin a Mahratta, but he had thrown off
his allegiance; and the Mahrattas had long urged the East India
Company to assist in effecting his downfall. More than one attempt
had been made to destroy him, but in vain; when, in 1755, an
agreement of the East India Company, the British Government and
the Mahrattas led to the fitting out against the pirate of a force,
which finally secured the desired object. Mr. James, Commodore
of the East India Company's ships in India, sailed in March with
the Company's ships *Protector*, *Swallow*, *Viper*, and *Triumph*, and
attacked and captured Severndroog, afterwards delivering it up to the
Mahrattas. He also took Bencote (Fort Victoria), the most northerly
port in Angria's dominions.

In November Rear-Admiral Watson reached Bombay, and further
operations were begun. James, with the *Protector*, *Revenge*, and
Bombay, went to reconnoitre Geriah, Angria's chief stronghold;
and, upon his return on December 31st, the Rear-Admiral sent His
Majesty's ships *Bridgewater* and *Kingfisher*, with some of the
Company's armed vessels, to cruise off the port. James joined them
on January 27th, 1756, with the *Protector*, and *Guardian ;* and the
Rear-Admiral, with Rear-Admiral George Pocock as second in
command, and with Lieut.-Colonel Clive in command of the troops,
followed with his squadron, arriving on February 12th. In addition
to the King's and Company's ships, there was a contingent of Mahratta
craft, which, however, did little or nothing. Angria, terrified at the
force arrayed against him, fled to the Mahrattas to try to make
terms, and left Geriah under the orders of one of his brothers-in-law.
His offers and promises induced the Mahrattas to withdraw their

active co-operation, in return for an undertaking to put them in possession of the place; and the brother-in-law would have carried out this arrangement but that Watson refused to be satisfied with anything short of the destruction of the pirate's stronghold.

In the afternoon of February 12th, the garrison having refused to surrender, the squadron weighed and stood in in two divisions: one to attack the fort and the other to attack Angria's fleet and dockyard. A brisk cannonade resulted. The shipping was soon burnt, and part of the town was set on fire. After about three hours, the enemy's guns were nearly silenced, and the British guns in consequence ceased also; but, soon afterwards, firing was recommenced, and not until 6.30 P.M., the engagement having begun at about 1.30 P.M., did the pirates cease to make further resistance. Troops were then disembarked under Clive, ready to take possession; and during the night, lest the enemy might again take heart, the bombs occasionally shelled the fort. In the morning Watson summoned the garrison and was refused; whereupon the bombardment was again recommenced. At length a flag of truce was hung out, and an offer of submission was made; but, as it was not complete and unconditional, fire was renewed. The governor then surrendered unconditionally. On the morning of the 14th, Clive marched into the place. Not more than twenty men were killed and wounded on the British side in the affair. The victors found in the fortress two hundred and fifty pieces of cannon, six brass mortars, and a large quantity of stores and ammunition, besides about £100,000 sterling in rupees and £30,000 worth of valuables. Ten Englishmen and three Dutchmen, who had been enslaved by Angria, were released. The pirate fleet which was burnt at Geriah consisted of one ship, eight grabs or galleys, and a large number of armed row-boats called gallivats. At the end of April Watson left the coast of Malabar, and on May 14th arrived off Fort St. David.

In North America the Earl of Loudoun commanded the British land forces, but, before he could take the field, the French had won several successes and had made themselves masters of the British armed vessels on Lake Ontario.

It has been mentioned that Commodore Spry had remained at Nova Scotia after the return of Boscawen to England in 1755. Commodore Charles Holmes, convoying some troops from Cork, was sent out with a reinforcing squadron, and assumed command. With the *Grafton, Nottingham, Hornet* and *Jamaica* he cruised off

Louisbourg in July, and nearly succeeded in cutting off a small French force; and on the following day he fought another French force, which, however, also got away.

On the Leeward Islands' station Commodore Thomas Frankland commanded; and, although he fought no action, and rendered himself very unpopular, his cruisers greatly annoyed the enemy. On the Jamaica station, the squadron was under the orders of Rear-Admiral the Hon. George Townshend; but it was so small that he had to remain almost entirely on the defensive. It, however, prevented the French from carrying out an intended attack on Jamaica.

At home, the threat of invasion continued to cause popular uneasiness, and in January, 1756, Vice-Admiral Henry Osborn was sent to sea with a large squadron to convoy outward-bound merchantmen, and, on his return, to reconnoitre Brest. He would have been better employed in reinforcing the fleet in the Mediterranean, for, although the enemy had sixteen ships of the line in Brest and Rochefort, it was discovered that these could not be ready before May; and in the meanwhile, Great Britain had eight ships of the line and twenty-three frigates quite ready, and thirty-two ships of the line and five frigates nearly ready for sea in the home ports.

Nor was the threat of invasion ever a serious one. The French knew too well that the project at that time was hopeless. Upon the return of Osborn, Vice-Admiral Sir Edward Hawke was sent with a squadron to cruise off Brest, and was reinforced in April by additional ships under Rear-Admiral Francis Holburne. But these precautions were taken too late, for Vice-Admiral d'Aubigny had left Brest for Martinique on January 30th, and M. de Beaussier had sailed on February 19th for San Domingo. Yet Hawke, ere he came back to England in May, made many valuable prizes. He left Holburne to cruise before Brest; and Holburne was presently joined by Vice-Admiral the Hon. Edward Boscawen, who assumed command of the united fleet of eighteen ships of the line, six 50-gun ships and two frigates.

This demonstration naturally induced the French squadron to keep within its harbour; but some of Boscawen's vessels engaged straggling French ships. The invasion scare still continuing, the Vice-Admiral took effectual means to put an end to it. He sent the *Hunter*, cutter, Lieutenant —— Cockburn, to reconnoitre Brest. Mr. Cockburn ran close into the harbour's mouth, and then with

five companions, got into a boat and rowed into the port in the
dark.   He reported that he had found there only nine ships of war
of 50-guns or under and six large merchantmen.   Boscawen and
Holburne returned to England in November, leaving Rear-Admirals
Savage Mostyn and Harry Norris before Brest, chiefly to intercept
such of the enemy's ships as might be coming home from abroad.
The blockading force was afterwards entrusted to Vice-Admiral
Charles Knowles, who came back to port with most of it in
December.   His departure was somewhat premature, in that it
enabled M. de Kersaint to get out with a small force for the coast
of Africa, and M. de Beauffremont to escape with another small
force bound for the West Indies.   It also allowed some small
cruising squadrons to proceed to sea in safety,

The British Ministry was very negligent in the matter of
Minorca.   It is quite clear that as early as October, 1755, it had
received intelligence that the expedition preparing at Toulon was
destined for that island ; and that French reports to the same effect
reached it in November and December, as well as later.[1]   Yet it
took no proper measures for the defence of the place, the reason
apparently being that, at that time, it undervalued the importance of
the position.   The military command of the island was in the hands
of General William Blakeney, an officer in his eighty-second year,
who was so infirm that when Port Mahon was besieged by the Duc
de Richelieu, he, though mentally very active, was obliged to spend
great part of his time in bed.   The garrison also was very weak,
and most of the officers belonging to it were on leave until some
time after the French expedition had sailed from Toulon.   Moreover, the British squadron in the Mediterranean, including as it did
only three ships of the line and a few small craft, was a serious
danger rather than a source of strength.

Yet at length public opinion in England insisted that something
must be done ; and on March 11th, 1756, Vice-Admiral the Hon.
John Byng was appointed to the command of a fleet, which was
then ordered to proceed to Minorca.   The position of second in
command was given to Rear-Admiral Temple West.   But this fleet,
which should have been a large and powerful one, was by no means
of formidable proportions.   It consisted only of ten sail of the line ;
and even those few ships were not fitted out without the greatest
difficulty and friction.   At that late date the Ministry seems to have

---

[1] Resols. of Ho. of Comms., May 3rd, 1757.

been still blind to the importance of Minorca. There were at the moment twenty-seven ships of the line cruising in the Channel and Bay of Biscay, twenty-eight ships of the line in commission at home, and many small craft, which might have been detailed for the service. But Byng was not permitted to utilise any of these, or to draw crews from them; and his mission was evidently regarded as a wholly subsidiary one. He was directed to take on board the absent officers of the Minorca garrison and a reinforcement of troops, consisting of the Royal Regiment of Fusiliers, under the command of Colonel Lord Robert Bertie. To make room for these men, all the Marines belonging to the squadron were sent on shore, with the result that, had Byng been successful in throwing troops into Port Mahon, he would, owing to the absence of Marines from his ships, have been in a condition unfit for subsequently fighting an action at sea.

The Vice-Admiral prepared his fleet with as much dispatch as possible, and sailed from St. Helen's on April 6th, arriving at Gibraltar on May 2nd. He was there joined by some of the ships, which, under Captain the Hon. George Edgcumbe, were already in the Mediterranean; and he received intelligence that the Toulon squadron had landed a French army in Minorca, and that the enemy was already in possession of almost every strong position in the island. Byng communicated to General Fowke, the Governor of Gibraltar, an order from home to the effect that, subject to certain conditions, a detachment from the garrison, equal to a battalion of men, was to be embarked on board the fleet. But General Fowke and his advisers came to the conclusion, firstly, that it would be extremely dangerous, if not impracticable, to throw succour into Port Mahon; and secondly, that the garrison of Gibraltar was already too weak to spare the specified detachment without danger to itself. Yet as the fleet was in great want of men, and as Edgcumbe's ships had left their Marines, and some of their seamen, in Minorca to assist in the work of defence, the Governor permitted 1 captain, 6 subalterns, 9 sergeants, 11 corporals, 5 drummers and 200 privates to embark, it being represented to him that, without such reinforcement, several of the ships would be absolutely unable to go into action.

Captain Edgcumbe, with his little squadron, had been obliged to retire from off Minorca upon the appearance of the French. He had left behind him Captain Carr Scrope of the *Dolphin*, who commanded the naval detachment on shore, and who was to act as signal officer in the event of the appearance of a British squadron before the island. Ere Byng, with an easterly wind, sailed from Gibraltar on May 8th, he had been joined by the whole of Captain Edgcumbe's little force, excepting the *Phœnix*, which had been blockaded at Palma, Majorca, by two French frigates, and which was only able to get out upon the appearance of the British fleet off that island. The wind was for the most part easterly until 9 P.M. on the 18th, when a brisk northerly breeze sprang up; and the squadron, having sailed large all night, sighted Minorca at daybreak next morning. Byng at once sent ahead the *Phœnix*, *Chesterfield* and *Dolphin* to reconnoitre the mouth of Mahon Harbour, to pick up intelligence, and to endeavour to send ashore a letter to General Blakeney. Captain the Hon. Augustus John Hervey, the senior officer of the advanced squadron, drew in with the shore and endeavoured to communicate with the castle of St. Philip; but, before he could effect anything, the enemy's fleet appeared in the S.E., and the detachment had to be recalled.

Vice-Admiral Byng then stood towards the foe and made the signal for a general chase. Both squadrons [1] made sail towards one

[1] THE BRITISH AND FRENCH FLEETS IN THE ACTION OFF MINORCA, MAY 20TH, 1756.

BRITISH.				FRENCH.		
Ships.	Guns.	Commanders.		Ships.	Guns.	Flag-Officers.
Defiance . . .	60	Capt. Thomas Andrews (2).		*Orphée*	64	
Portland [1] . . .	50	,, Patrick Baird.		*Hippopotame* . .	50	
Lancaster . . .	66	,, Hon. George Edgcumbe.		*Redoutable* . . .	74	M. de Glandevez (Chef d'Escadre).
				Sage	64	
Buckingham . .	68	Rear-Admiral Temple West (R).		*Guerrier* . . .	74	
		Capt. Michael Everitt.		*Fier*	50	
Captain	64	,, Charles Catford.		*Foudroyant* . . .	84	M. de La Galissonnière (Lieut.-Général).
Intrepid . . .	64	,, James Young (1).		*Téméraire* . . .	74	
Revenge	64	,, Frederick Cornwall.		*Content*	64	
				Lion	64	
Princess Louisa [1] .	60	,, Thomas Noel.		*Couronne* . . .	74	M. de La Clue (Chef d'Escadre).
Trident	64	,, Philip Durell (1).				
Ramillies . . .	90	Vice-Adm. Hon. John Byng (B). Capt. Arthur Gardiner.		*Triton*	64	
Culloden . . .	74	,, Henry Ward.		FRIGATES, ETC. [4]		
Kingston . . .	60	,, William Parry (2).		*Junon*	46	
FRIGATES, ETC.				*Rose*	26	
				Gracieuse . . .	26	
Deptford [1][2] . . .	50	,, John Amherst.		*Topaze*	24	
Chesterfield [1] . .	40	,, John Lloyd (2).		*Nymphe*	26	
Phœnix [1] . . .	20	,, Hon. Augustus John Hervey.				
Fortune [1] . . .	14	Com. Jervis Maplesden.				
Experiment [1] . .	20	Capt. James Gilchrist.				
Dolphin [1] . . .	20	Com. Benjamin Marlow. [3]				

[1] Were in the Mediterranean under Capt. the Hon. G. Edgcumbe, before Admiral Byng's arrival.

[2] The *Deptford*, having been originally placed in the line between the *Culloden* and the *Kingston*, and then removed from it, was later ordered to take the place of the disabled *Intrepid*.

[3] Capt. Carr Scrope being on service ashore at Port Mahon.

[4] La Galissonnière mentions only four French frigates as having been present.

another; and at 2 P.M. the British Commander-in-Chief made the signal for a line of battle ahead. But, the wind dropping, this order could not be properly carried out. In the meantime he took the precaution of reinforcing such of the ships as were most weakly manned, by means of drafts from the frigates; and he directed that the *Phœnix*, which had been reported as unfit for general service, should be made ready to act as a fireship in case of necessity. At about six o'clock in the evening the enemy advanced in order, with twelve ships of the line and five frigates; the van being commanded by M. Glandevez, the centre by M. de La Galissonnière, and the rear by M. de La Clue. An hour later the French tacked, and went away a distance of about six miles, with a view to gaining the weather-gage; and Byng, to preserve that advantage, tacked likewise On the following morning two tartans, which had been sent out by M. de Richelieu with soldiers to reinforce M. de La Galissonnière, were chased by the British ships, one of them being taken by the *Defiance*, and the other escaping. That morning at daybreak, the weather was hazy, and the enemy was not at once seen; but, a little later, he came in sight in the S.E.

Captain Mahan's account of the action which followed may be here quoted, as it admirably summarises what occurred.

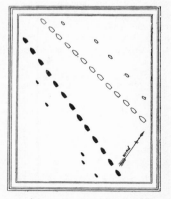

BYNG'S ACTION, MAY 20TH, 1756.

I.—At 2 P.M.

British, *black;* French, *white.*

[The angle of approach was somewhat greater than as shown in the plans.]

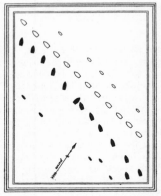

BYNG'S ACTION, MAY 20TH, 1756.

II.—At 2.30 P.M.

British, *black;* French, *white.*

[*Intrepid* should be flying up into the wind. She is here represented as before the wind.]

"The two fleets," he writes, "having sighted each other on the morning of May 20th, were found after a series of manœuvres both on the port tack, with an easterly wind, heading southerly, the French to leeward, between the English and the harbour. Byng ran down in line ahead off the wind, the French remaining by it, so that when the former made the signal to engage, the fleets were not parallel, but formed an angle of from 30° to 40° (Pl. I.). The attack which Byng by his own account meant to make, each ship against its opposite in the enemy's line, difficult to carry out under any circumstances, was here further impeded by the distance between the two rears being much greater than that between the vans ; so that his whole line could not come into action at the same moment. When the signal was made, the van ships kept away in obedience to it, and ran down for the French so nearly head on as to sacrifice their artillery fire in great measure (Pl. II.). They received three raking broadsides and were seriously dismantled aloft. The sixth English ship" (*Intrepid*) "counting from the van, had her foretopmast shot away, flew up into the wind, and came aback, stopping and doubling up the rear of the line (Pl. III.). Then undoubtedly was the time for Byng, having committed himself to the fight, to have set the example and borne down, just as Farragut did at Mobile when his line was confused by the stopping of the next ahead ; but according to the testimony of the flag-captain, Mathews's sentence deterred him. 'You see, Captain Gardiner, that the signal for the line is out, and that I am ahead of the ships *Louisa* and *Trident*' (which in the order should have been ahead of him). 'You would not have me, as admiral of the fleet, run down as if I were going to engage a single ship. It was Mr. Mathews's misfortune to be prejudiced by not carrying down his force together, which I shall endeavour to avoid.' The affair thus became indecisive ; the English van was separated from the rear

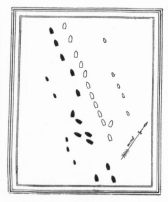

BYNG'S ACTION, MAY 20TH, 1756.

III.—3 P.M.

and got the brunt of the fight.   One French authority blames Galissonnière for not tacking to windward of the enemy's van and crushing it.   Another says he ordered the movement, but that it could not be made from the damage to the rigging ; but this seems improbable, as the only injury the French squadron underwent aloft was the loss of one topsail-yard, whereas the English suffered very badly.   The true reason is probably that given and approved by one of the French authorities on naval warfare.   Galissonnière considered the support of the land attack on Port Mahon paramount to any destruction of the English fleet, though he thereby exposed his own. 'The French navy has always preferred the glory of assuring or preserving a conquest to that, more brilliant perhaps, but actually less real, of taking some ships ; and therein it has approached more nearly the true end that has been proposed in war.'   The justice of this conclusion depends upon the view that is taken of the true end of naval war."[1]

The losses (see following page [1]) in killed and wounded were nearly equal ; but the French lost no officers of rank, whereas in Byng's fleet Captain Andrews, of the *Defiance,* was killed, and Captain Noel, of the *Princess Louisa,* was mortally wounded. The British ships also suffered much more than the French in

[1] 'Infl. of Sea Power upon Hist.,' 286, 287.

their masts, yards and rigging; so much so, in fact, that Byng deemed it right, before venturing to do anything further, to call a council of war on board the *Ramillies*, and to summon to it not only the naval officers, but also several of the land officers who were on board the ships. The questions debated in this council, and the conclusions arrived at, were as follows :—

1. Whether an attack on the French fleet gave any prospect of relieving Mahon ? Resolved : It did not.
2. Whether, if there were no French fleet cruising at Minorca, the British fleet could raise the siege ? Resolved : It could not.
3. Whether Gibraltar would not be in danger, should any accident befall Byng's fleet? Resolved : It would be in danger.
4. Whether an attack by the British fleet in its present state upon that of the French would not endanger Gibraltar, and expose the trade in the Mediterranean to great hazards ? Resolved : It would.
5. Whether it is not rather for His Majesty's service that the fleet should proceed immediately to Gibraltar ? Resolved : It should proceed to Gibraltar.

As a result, the squadron sailed for Gibraltar, and, on the way, occupied itself in repairing such damages as could be repaired at

---

[1] The losses in killed and wounded in the two fleets were as follows :—

BRITISH.			FRENCH.		
Ships.	Killed.	Wounded.	Ships.	Killed.	Wounded.
Defiance	14	45	*Orphée*	10	0
Portland . . .	6	20	*Hippopotame* . .	2	10
Lancaster . . .	1	14	*Redoutable* . . .	0	3
Buckingham . . .	3	7	*Sage*	0	8
Captain	6	30	*Guerrier*	0	43
Intrepid	9	36	*Fier*	0	4
Princess Louisa . .	3	13	*Foudroyant* . . .	2	10
			Téméraire . . .	0	15
			Content	5	19
			Lion	2	7
			Couronne . . .	0	3
			Triton	5	14
Totals . .	42	165	Totals . .	26	136

London Gazette of June 26th, 1756. Lists in Beatson, iii. 118, put the total losses at—British, 43 killed, 168 wounded ; French, 38 killed, 181 wounded. La Galissonnière puts the French loss at 38 killed, and 115 wounded. It may be that 26 French were killed outright, and that 12 more died of their wounds. No two accounts of the number of wounded can be expected to agree exactly, some enumerators naturally including among the wounded men with only slight injuries.

sea. At the Rock the Admiral[1] found reinforcements,[2] which had been sent out to him under Commodore Thomas Broderick,[3] the Ministry, after Byng's departure from England, having apparently realised for the first time the full extent of the danger in the Mediterranean.

It was unfortunate for Byng that the first detailed news of what had happened off Minorca reached the Government through French channels. M. de La Galissonnière's dispatch cannot now be found in the Archives de la Marine in Paris, and possibly it no longer exists ; but a copy of it, or a translation, reached the Secretary of the Admiralty some time before Byng's own dispatch arrived in England ; and upon the former the Government took action, recalling Byng and West, and sending out Vice-Admiral Sir Edward Hawke and Rear-Admiral Charles Saunders to supersede them. The important part of this dispatch of La Galissonnière's [4] is as follows :—

"At half-past two in the afternoon the two squadrons were in line of battle and began the engagement. The English consisted of eighteen sail, of which thirteen were of the line, and ours, of twelve sail of the line and four frigates. The action lasted almost three hours and a half, but was not general during the whole of the time. The English ships that had suffered most from our broadsides got away to the windward, out of gunshot. They continually preserved this advantage that they might keep clear of us as they pleased. After having made their greatest efforts against our rear division, which they found so close and from which they received so hot a fire that they could not break in upon it, they made up their minds to sheer off, and did not appear again during the whole of the next day, the 21st. Speaking generally, none of their ships long withstood the fire of ours. Our vessels suffered but little. They were repaired in the night, and on the following morning were fit for action." . . . "Our total killed was thirty-eight, and wounded one hundred and fifteen."

---

[1] On June 4th, 1756, Byng was promoted to be Admiral of the Blue.

[2] Reinforcement despatched to Admiral the Hon. John Byng under Commodore Broderick :—

Ships.	Guns.	Commanders.
Prince George. .	80	{ Commod. Thomas Broderick. { Capt. Abraham North.
Ipswich . . .	64	„ Richard Tyrrell.
Nassau . . .	64	„ James Sayer.
Hampton Court .	64	„ James Webb.
Isis.	50	„ Edward Wheeler.

[3] This officer, who was born in 1704, and died a Vice-Admiral in 1769, usually spelt his name Broderick. It was, however, properly spelt Brodrick.

[4] As published in the journals of the time.

It may here be pointed out, in passing, that this report makes the British fleet to have been considerably superior to the French, whereas if there were any real difference between them it was only a very slight one; and that it does not agree, in other respects, with the facts as they are now accepted.

Before going further, it is right to print the dispatch which Byng addressed to the Admiralty on May 25th, and in which he gave his version of what had happened. It is right also to say that the Admiralty, after receiving this dispatch, kept it for some time before making it public, and that, when it did publish it, gave it to the world in a mutilated condition. The complete dispatch was printed by Byng after his return to England, and ran as follows :—

Ramillies, off MINORCA, *May 25th*, 1756.

"SIR,—I have the pleasure to desire that you will acquaint their Lordships that, having sailed from Gibraltar the 8th, I got off Mahon the 19th, having been joined by his Majesty's ship PHŒNIX off Majorca two days before, by *whom I had confirmed the intelligence I had received at Gibraltar, of the strength of the French fleet, and of their being off Mahon. His Majesty's colours were still flying at the castle of St. Philip; and I could perceive several bomb-batteries playing on it from different parts. French colours I saw flying on the west part of St. Philip. I dispatched the Phœnix, Chesterfield, and Dolphin ahead, to reconnoitre the harbour's mouth; and Captain Hervey to endeavour to land a letter for General Blakeney, to let him know the fleet was here to his assistance; though every one was of the opinion we could be of no use to him; as, by all accounts, no place was secured for covering a landing, could we have spared the people. The Phœnix was also to make the private signal between Captain Hervey and Captain Scrope, as this latter would undoubtedly come off, if it were practicable, having kept the Dolphin's barge with him: but the enemy's fleet appearing to the south-east, and the wind at the same time coming strong off the land, obliged me to call these ships in, before they could get quite so near the entrance of the harbour as to make sure what batteries or guns might be placed to prevent our having any communication with the castle.* Falling little wind, it was five before I could form my line, or distinguish any of the enemy's motions; and could not judge at all of their force, more than by numbers, which were seventeen, and thirteen appeared large. They at first stood towards us in regular line; and tacked about seven; which I judged was to endeavour to gain the wind of us in the night; so that, being late, I tacked in order to keep the weather-gage of them, as well as to make sure of the land wind in the morning, being very hazy, and not above five leagues from Cape Mola. We tacked off towards the enemy at eleven; and at daylight had no sight of them. But two tartans, with the French private signal, being close in with the rear of our fleet, I sent the PRINCESS LOUISA to chace one, and made signal for the Rear-Admiral, who was nearest the other, to send ships to chase her. The PRINCESS LOUISA, DEFIANCE, and CAPTAIN, became at a great distance; but the DEFIANCE took hers, which had two captains, two lieutenants, and one hundred and two private soldiers, who were sent out the day before with six hundred men on board tartans, to reinforce the French fleet on our appearing off that place. The PHŒNIX, on Captain Hervey's offer, prepared to serve as a fire-ship, but without damaging her as a frigate; till the signal was made to prime, when she was then to scuttle her decks, everything else prepared, as the time and place allowed of.

"The enemy now began to appear from the mast-head. I called in the cruisers; and, when they had joined me, I tacked towards the enemy, and formed the line ahead. I found the French were preparing theirs to leeward, having unsuccessfully endeavoured to weather me. They were twelve large ships of the line, and five frigates.

"As soon as I judged the rear of our fleet the length of their van, we tacked altogether, and immediately made the signal for the ships that led to lead large, and for the DEPTFORD to quit the line, that ours might become equal to theirs. At two I made the signal to engage : I found it was the surest method of ordering every ship to close down on the one that fell to their lot. And here I must express my great satisfaction at the very gallant manner in which the Rear-Admiral set the van the example, by instantly bearing down on the ships he was to engage, with his second, and who occasioned one of the French ships to begin the engagement, which they did by raking ours as they went down. The INTREPID, *unfortunately*, in the very beginning, had her foretopmast shot away ; and as that hung on her foretopsail, and backed it, he had no command of his ship, his fore-tack and all his braces being cut at the same time ; so that he drove on the next ship to him, and obliged that and the ships ahead of me to throw all back. This obliged me to do also for some minutes, to avoid their falling on board me, though not before we had drove our adversary out of the line, who put before the wind, and had several shots fired at him by his own admiral. This not only caused the enemy's centre to be unattacked, but the Rear-Admiral's division rather uncovered for some little time. I sent and called to the ships ahead of me to make sail, and go down on the enemy ; and ordered the CHESTERFIELD to lay by the INTREPID, and the DEPTFORD to supply the INTREPID's place. I found the enemy edged away constantly ; and as they went three feet to our one, they would never permit our closing with them, but took advantage of destroying our rigging ; for though I closed the Rear-Admiral fast, I found that I could not gain close to the enemy, whose van was fairly drove from their line ; but their admiral was joining them, by bearing away.

"By this time it was past six, and the enemy's van and ours were at too great a distance to engage, I perceived some of their ships stretching to the northward ; and I imagined they were going to form a new line. I made the signal for the headmost ships to tack, and those that led before with the larboard tacks to lead with the starboard, that I might, by the first, keep (if possible) the wind of the enemy, and, by the second, between the Rear-Admiral's division and the enemy, as he had suffered most ; as also to cover the INTREPID, which I perceived to be in very bad condition, and whose loss would give the balance very greatly against us, if they attacked us next morning as I expected. I brought to about eight that night to join the INTREPID, and to refit our ships as fast as possible, and continued doing so all night. The next morning we saw nothing of the enemy, though we were still lying to. Mahon was N.N.W. about ten or eleven leagues. I sent cruisers to look out for the *Intrepid* and CHESTERFIELD, who joined me next day. And having, from a state and condition of the squadron brought me in, found, that the CAPTAIN, INTREPID, and DEFIANCE (which latter has lost her captain), were much damaged in their masts, *so that they were in danger of not being able to secure their masts properly at sea ; and also, that the squadron in general were very sickly, many killed and wounded, and nowhere to put a third of their number if I made an hospital of the forty-gun ship, which was not easy at sea ;* I thought it proper in this situation to call a council of war, before I went again to look for the enemy. I desired the attendance of General Stuart, Lord Effingham, and Lord Robert Bertie, and Colonel Cornwallis, that I might collect their opinions upon the present situation *of Minorca and Gibraltar, and make sure of protecting the latter, since it was found impracticable either to succour or relieve the former with the force we had. So, though we may justly claim the victory, yet we are much inferior to the weight of their ships, though the numbers are equal ; and they have the advantage of sending to Minorca their wounded, and getting reinforcements of seamen from their transports, and soldiers from their camp; all which undoubtedly has been done in this time that we have been lying to to refit, and often in sight of Minorca; and their ships have more than once appeared in a line from our mast-heads.*

"*I send their Lordships the resolutions of the council of war, in which there was not the least contention or doubt arose. I hope, indeed, we shall find stores to refit us at Gibraltar; and, if I have any reinforcement, will not lose a moment of time to seek the enemy again, and once more give them battle, though they have a great advantage in being clean ships that go three feet to our one, and therefore have their choice how they will engage us, or if they will at all; and will never let us close them, as their sole view is the disabling our ships, in which they have but too well succeeded, though we obliged them to bear up.*

"I do not send their Lordships the particulars of our losses and damages by this, as it would take me much time; and I am willing none should be lost in letting them know an event of such consequence.

"*I cannot help urging their Lordships for a reinforcement, if none are yet sailed on their knowledge of the enemy's strength in these seas, and which, by very good intelligence, will in a few days be strengthened by four more large ships from Toulon, almost ready to sail, if not sailed, to join these.*

"I dispatch this to Sir Benjamin Keene, by way of Barcelona; and am making the best of my way to *cover* Gibraltar, from which place I propose sending their Lordships a more particular account. I remain, Sir, your most humble servant,—

"J. BYNG.

"Hon. JOHN CLEVLAND, ESQ."

The above dispatch appears to have arrived in England on June 16th; but it was not published in the *London Gazette* until June 26th, and then only with the omission of those passages which are now printed in italics. The omissions, it is clear, were somewhat unfair, and, being calculated to prejudice Byng, they show the bias of the Ministry, which, previously inclined to underrate the importance of Minorca, at length seemed disposed to attach the utmost significance to it. The dispatch is, however, an unsatisfactory one, even as it stands. It is too full of excuses, too apologetic, to be the work of a strong and self-reliant man. It smacks, indeed, more of a Persano than of a Nelson or a Saumarez.

To avoid a break in the narrative, it may here be said that the town of Port Mahon defended itself gallantly, but had to capitulate, on June 29th, on honourable terms. The garrison was sent to England.

Commodore Broderick, with the reinforcement, had reached Gibraltar on June 15th, and was there found by Byng on his arrival there on June 19th. The Admiral at once began preparations to return to Minorca; but, while he was still engaged in these, on July 3rd, the *Antelope*, 50, came in with Vice-Admiral Sir Edward Hawke, Rear-Admiral Charles Saunders, and the order for the supersession of the Commander-in-Chief and Rear-Admiral West.

She had sailed from home on June 16th. Captains Gardiner and Everitt, Captain William Gough (who had been a lieutenant of the *Ramillies*, and who had since been appointed captain of the *Experiment*), and Commander Christopher Basset (who had also been a lieutenant of the *Ramillies* and had been appointed after the action to the command of the *Fortune*), were also recalled, besides other officers, who were required as witnesses in England. The original order to Hawke directed only the supersession of Byng; but after Hawke's departure from England and the receipt of Byng's dispatch of May 25th, the Admiralty decided to go further and to make prisoner of the late·Commander-in-Chief. He sailed for England in the *Antelope*, on July 9th, and, upon arriving at Spithead on July 26th, he was put under arrest. He was landed on August 19th and sent to Greenwich. There he remained in confinement until December 23rd, when he was removed to Portsmouth. His trial began on board the *St. George* in Portsmouth Harbour on December 27th, and continued until January 27th, 1757. On that day sentence was pronounced, and the Admiral was transferred to the *Monarch*, then in harbour.

The court-martial, summoned to try Byng, consisted of Vice-Admiral Thomas Smith (4), who was president, Rear-Admirals Francis Holburne, Harry Norris and Thomas Broderick, and nine captains. After hearing the evidence, the court agreed to thirty-seven resolutions or conclusions, which embodied, among others, the following :—

> That when the British fleet, on the starboard tack, was stretched abreast, or was about abeam, of the enemy's line, Admiral Byng should have caused his ships to tack together, and should have immediately borne right down on the enemy; his van steering for the enemy's van, his rear for its rear, each ship making for the one opposite to her in the enemy's line, under such sail as would have enabled the worst sailer to preserve her station in the line of battle.

> That the Admiral retarded the rear division of the British fleet from closing with and engaging the enemy, by shortening sail, in order that the *Trident* and *Princess Louisa* might regain their stations ahead of the *Ramillies ;* whereas he should have made signals to those ships to make more sail, and should have made so much sail himself as would enable the *Culloden*, the worst sailing ship in the Admiral's division, to keep her station with all her plain sails set, in order to get down to the enemy with as much expedition as possible, and thereby properly support the division of Rear-Admiral West.

> That the Admiral did wrong in ordering the fire of the *Ramillies* to be continued before he had placed her at proper distance from the enemy, inasmuch as he thereby not only threw away his shot, but also occasioned a smoke, which prevented his seeing the motions of the enemy and the positions of the ships immediately ahead of the *Ramillies*.

That after the ships which had received damage in the action had been refitted as
circumstances would permit, the Admiral ought to have returned with his
squadron off Port Mahon, and endeavoured to open communication with the
castle, and to have used every means in his power for its relief, before
returning to Gibraltar.

In short, the court considered that Byng had not done his
utmost to relieve St. Philip's Castle. It also considered that
during the engagement he had not done his utmost to take, sink,
burn, and destroy the ships of the enemy, and to assist such of
his own ships as were engaged; and it resolved that the Admiral
had fallen under the 12th Article of War [1]; and the court decided
that, as the 12th Article of War positively prescribed death, without
leaving any alternative to the discretion of the court under any
variation of circumstances, Admiral Byng should be shot to death,
at such time and on board such ship as the Lords Commissioners
of the Admiralty should direct.

"But," concludes the thirty-seventh resolution, "as it appears by the evidence of
Lord Robert Bertie, Lieutenant-Colonel Smith, Captain Gardiner and other officers
of the ship, who were near the person of the Admiral, that they did not perceive any
backwardness in him during the action, or any marks of fear or confusion, either from
his countenance or behaviour, but that he seemed to give his orders coolly and distinctly, and did not seem wanting in personal courage, and from other circumstances,
the court do not believe that his misconduct arose either from cowardice or disaffection;
and do therefore unanimously think it their duty most earnestly to recommend him as
a proper object of mercy."

The court forwarded the sentence to the Admiralty, with an
accompanying letter signed by all the members. In this the
officers represented the distress of mind which had been occasioned
to them by being obliged to condemn to death, under the 12th
Article of War, a man who might have been guilty of an error of
judgment only; and, for the sake of their consciences, as well
as for Byng's sake, they warmly pleaded for an exercise of
clemency.

In consequence of this letter, and of the recommendation to

___

[1] "Every person in the fleet, who, through cowardice, negligence, or disaffection,
shall, in time of action, withdraw, or keep back, or not come into fight, or engagement,
or shall not do his utmost to take or destroy every ship which it shall be his duty to
engage; and to assist all and every of his Majesty's ships, or those of his allies, which
it shall be his duty to assist and relieve; every such person, so offending, and being
convicted thereof by the sentence of a court-martial, shall suffer death."—Act of
22 George II., Art. 12.

This article superseded one in the Act of 13 Car. II., which, after the word
"death," had the words, "or such other punishment as the circumstances of the offence
shall deserve, and the court-martial shall judge fit."

mercy, the opinion of the twelve Judges was asked for as to the legality of the sentence which had been pronounced. The decision was given on February 14th, 1757, and was to the effect that the sentence was legal. Some of the members of the court then made an effort to save Byng by applying to Parliament to release them from the oath of secrecy, by which they were bound not to reveal the votes or opinions of individual members, upon the allegation that they had something vital to disclose relative to the sentence. Byng was respited, and a Bill for the desired purpose passed the Commons, but was thrown out by the Lords, it not appearing to that House that there was anything material to be divulged. The fact is, that certain members simply desired to be able to make public the fact that, had they realised that the result of their sentence would be the infliction of the death penalty, their sentence would have been other than it was. The severity of the punishment caused Vice-Admiral the Hon. John Forbes, one of the Lords of the Admiralty, to refuse to sign the sentence, and it also induced Rear-Admiral West, who had been offered a command, to decline it, on the plea that although he could answer for his loyalty and good intentions, he could not undertake to be held capitally responsible on all occasions for the correctness of his judgment.

Byng, both during his trial and after his sentence, behaved like a brave man. It was at first ordered that he should be executed on the forecastle of the *Monarch*. This ignominy was, however, spared him at the solicitation of his friends. On March 14th, 1757, the day appointed for the carrying out of the sentence, the Marines of the *Monarch* were drawn up under arms upon the poop, along the gangways, in the waist, and on one side of the quarterdeck. On the other side of the quarterdeck was spread some saw-dust, on which was placed a cushion; and in the middle of the quarter-deck, upon the gratings, a platoon of nine Marines was drawn up in three lines of three. The front and middle lines had their bayonets fixed, as was customary on such occasions. The captains of all the ships in Portsmouth Harbour and at Spithead had been ordered to attend with their boats; but, to avoid crowding, they were directed to lie abreast upon their oars, without coming on board. A little before twelve o'clock, the Admiral retired to his inner cabin for about three minutes, after which the doors of the outer cabin were thrown open, and the Admiral walked from his after cabin with a dignified pace and unmoved countenance. As he passed through the fore cabin, he bowed to his acquaintances there, and, saying to the Marshal of the Admiralty " Come along, my friend," went out upon the quarterdeck.　There, turning to the Marshal, he politely bowed and gave him a paper containing a sober vindication of his position, adding : " Remember, sir, what I have told you relative to this paper."　He next went to the cushion and knelt down.　One of his friends, following him, offered

ADMIRAL THE HON. JOHN BYNG.
(From R. Houston's engraving after the portrait by Hudson.)

to tie the bandage over his eyes, but Byng declined the service and blindfolded himself.　The Marines, in the meantime, advanced two paces and presented their muskets, waiting for the Admiral to give them the signal to fire.　He remained upon his knees for about a minute, apparently praying, and then dropped a handkerchief, the signal agreed upon.　Six of the Marines fired.　One bullet missed ; one passed through the heart ; and four others struck different parts of the body.　The Admiral sank to the deck, dead.

A little later the corpse was put into a coffin ; and in the evening
it was sent on shore to the dockyard, whence it was forwarded to
the family burial place at Southill, in Bedfordshire. His monument
bears this inscription : " To the Perpetual Disgrace of Public
Justice, the Hon. John Byng, Esq., Admiral of the Blue, fell a
Martyr to Political Persecution, March 14th, in the year MDCCLVII ;
when Bravery and Loyalty were insufficient Securities for the Life
and Honour of a Naval Officer."

The tragedy, viewed from nearly every aspect, is to be most
heartily regretted. Byng was neither traitor nor coward ; but he
was not an original genius, and, having seen Mathews punished for
doing a certain thing, he believed that under no circumstances was
it his duty to do anything even remotely of the same kind. His
chief fault was that he was not independent enough, where a great
object was to be gained, to shake himself loose from formulæ and
precedents, and to dash in when occasion allowed him.   Yet, in
one way, the sentence may have been productive of good.   It may
have taught the admirals who followed the unfortunate Byng, that
they must pay more attention to victory than to red tape, and
that not even the most honest devotion to conventional methods
is so great a merit in a naval officer as success against the enemies
of his country.

Sir Edward Hawke, soon after his arrival at Gibraltar, sailed
with the fleet to Minorca, but found that the island had fallen, and
that the French army and fleet had returned to Toulon.   The
enemy had no longer any squadron at sea in the Mediterranean,
and the Vice-Admiral therefore had to confine himself to protecting
British trade and preserving British prestige.   This he did with
conspicuous energy and success.   On December 3rd, 1756, he set
out with part of his fleet for home, leaving Rear-Admiral Charles
Saunders in command.

It has been said that Vice-Admiral Charles Watson, Commander-
in-Chief in the East Indies, arrived off Fort St. David in the middle
of May, 1756. He had not been there long ere he received an
important piece of news, to the effect that six large French East
Indiamen, full of troops, were expected in India, where they were
to be fitted as men-of-war.   Thereupon, in response to an urgent
summons, he went to Madras, where he learnt that the Nawab of
Bengal, Surajah Dowleh, had seized Cassimbazar and Calcutta.
Almost at the same moment Watson received orders from the

Admiralty to return with his squadron[1] to England. He had, however, sufficient strength of character to disregard orders which he knew had been sent to him under misconception of the position in India; and he proceeded at once to the mouth of the Ganges, with a detachment of troops under Lieut.-Colonel Clive. In spite of great difficulties he assembled at Fulta, on December 15th, a force consisting of the *Kent, Tiger, Bridgewater, Salisbury,* and *Kingfisher,* with some ships belonging to the East India Company. He there found Governor Blake and other fugitives from Calcutta, and learnt of the horrible fate of those Europeans who had been less fortunate, and who had been confined in the infamous Black Hole. Watson reinforced his command by the purchase of a craft, which he named the *Thunder,* and fitted as a bomb under the command of Lieutenant Thomas Warwick. The squadron sailed on December 27th; and on the 29th the force was landed, and Fort Bougee-Bougee was attacked. This place was captured by an impromptu assault, brought on by an incursion into the works of a drunken British seaman named Strachan; and on December 30th the white troops were re-embarked, and the squadron proceeded up the river, the sepoys of the Company's service marching parallel with it along the shore.

On January 1st, when the ships entered the channel between Fort Tanna and the battery opposite to it, the enemy abandoned both. The *Salisbury* was left there to bring off the guns from the works, and to demolish the defences, and at night the Vice-Admiral manned and armed the boats of his squadron and sent them a few

---

[1] THE SQUADRON UNDER VICE-ADMIRAL WATSON IN THE EAST INDIES, 1756–1757.

Ships.	Guns.	Commanders.
Kent	70	{ Vice-Adm. Charles Watson (B). { Capt. Henry Speke.
Cumberland . .	66	{ Rear-Adm. George Pocock (R). { Capt. John Harrison.
Tiger	60	„ Thomas Latham.
Salisbury . .	50	„ William Martin (2).
Bridgewater . .	24	„ Henry Smith.
Triton[1] . . .	24	„ Edmund Townley.
Kingfisher . .	14	Com. Richard Toby.
Thunder, bomb[2] .	..	„ Thomas Warwick.
Blaze, fireship[2][3] .	..	Lieut. ?

[1] Arrived from England, after the rest of the squadron had gone to Bengal.
[2] Purchased and armed by the Vice-Admiral in India.
[3] Could not make the Ganges, and had to bear away for Bombay.

miles up the river, where they boarded and burnt some fireships, which had been collected there. Early on the 2nd, Colonel Clive, with the troops, landed and began the march towards Calcutta ; the *Kent, Tiger, Bridgewater,* and *Kingfisher* proceeding as the army advanced. At 9.40 A.M. the enemy opened upon the *Tiger* from their batteries below Calcutta, but abandoned them as the ships drew near. At 10.20 the *Tiger* and *Kent* began a hot cannonade

VICE-ADMIRAL CHARLES WATSON.
(From E. Fisher's engraving after the portrait by Hudson.)

of Fort William, and after two hours drove the defenders out of it. In this action the British lost only nine seamen and three soldiers killed, and twenty-six seamen and five soldiers wounded. Calcutta was at once occupied.

The Vice-Admiral later detached an expedition, the naval part of which was under Captain Richard King (1), who was serving as a volunteer in the squadron, to seize the town of Hugli, thirty miles above Calcutta. Another expedition, under Captain Speke, burnt the enemy's granaries at Gongee, and, assisted by the troops, defeated a body of natives which had attacked them. This action provoked Surajah Dowleh to send a large army against Calcutta. Clive obtained from the Vice-Admiral the aid of a detachment of seamen, under Commander Warwick, and tried to bar the way to the city; but, being misled by his guides in a fog, he had to retreat upon Calcutta. In this affair Lieutenant Lutwidge of the *Salisbury* was mortally wounded, and seventeen seamen were killed and fifteen wounded. Clive, however, quickly regained his former advanced position, and so disconcerted his opponent that the latter sued for a peace, which was concluded on February 9th. The British might undoubtedly have obtained more favourable terms than they did, had they not been anxious to patch up all their differences with the native princes, in order to be able to concentrate the whole of their resources in opposition to the French in India.

These matters having been settled, the Vice-Admiral made preparations for at once attacking Chandernagore; but the French made overtures for the neutrality of the place, and thus to some extent delayed him. Failing in their efforts in this direction, the French began to tamper with Surajah Dowleh. In the meantime, however, Watson and Clive invested Chandernagore. On March 19th, the British boats destroyed some French fireships which were collected near the town. On the 21st, Rear-Admiral Pocock joined the flag; but he had been obliged to leave his own flagship at Ballasore, as she drew too much water to come up the river; and he arrived in a boat. On the 22nd he hoisted his flag in the *Tiger*. On the 23rd there was a general bombardment of the fort from land and water; and, after three hours' hot firing, the French capitulated. The *Salisbury*, owing to an accident, was unable to get into action. The *Kent* lost 19 killed and 49 wounded; the *Tiger*, 13 killed and 50 wounded. Among those hurt was Rear-Admiral Pocock.

The fugitives from Chandernagore were received and sheltered by the Nawab, who acted throughout with great duplicity; and, as the British soon afterwards learnt of a plan of his own discontented subjects to depose him, they determined to aid and abet it. It cannot be pretended that the negotiations to this end were altogether honourable to those Englishmen who were concerned in it; and Vice-Admiral Watson declined to be a party to certain questionable undertakings, which, in pursuance of the resolution, were entered into by Clive and the council; but his name was, without his privity, affixed to the treaty with the malcontents. Clive then attacked the Nawab, and on June 23rd, 1757, defeated him at Plassey. This victory eventually led to the fall and death of Surajah Dowleh, and to the establishment in his place of Meer Jaffier, a nominee of the British. The settlement was barely concluded when, on August 16th, Vice-Admiral Watson died. His part in the foundation of the British Empire in India has scarcely been done justice to, and his loss, just then a serious one, would have been much more severely felt than it was, had he not had as his successor so capable an officer as Rear-Admiral Pocock.

Commodore James, of the East India Company's service, in the *Revenge*, 22, had been stationed off Pondicherry to watch the motions of the enemy, and had been joined there by H.M.S. *Triton*, 24. But these vessels were driven off in September by a strong French squadron; and, since Pocock's ships were in a rather bad condition, and some of them temporarily unfit for action, the situation began to look threatening, especially seeing that an expected British reinforcement, under Commodore Charles Stevens, had been detained at Bombay, and did not actually sail thence for the coast of Coromandel until January 20th, 1758.

Indeed, the French were making great efforts to defend their challenged possessions in India. They had already fitted out an expedition, the naval command of which was given to the Comte d'Aché, and the military, to General Comte de Lally. The squadron consisted of three king's ships, and one ship and a frigate belonging to the French East India Company, with about 1200 troops on board. D'Aché sailed on March 6th, 1757, but was driven back to Brest by a storm, and, while there, was deprived of two of the king's ships, in order that they might be despatched to Canada. Instead of them he received five more East Indiamen. He sailed on May 4th, and on December 18th reached Isle de France, where he found four additional armed East Indiamen. Choosing the best vessels at his disposal, he put to sea with them on January 27th, 1758. The further movements of d'Aché and of Pocock will be referred to later. Operations in other quarters during 1757 must first be followed.

On the Leeward Islands' station, Commodore John Moore (1) relieved Rear-Admiral Thomas Frankland and rendered valuable service in protecting trade. On the Jamaica station, Rear-Admiral

Thomas Cotes was in command, and was not less successful. In the autumn, learning that the French were assembling, at Cape François, a convoy for Europe, he sent the *Augusta, Edinburgh* and *Dreadnought* to cruise off that place to intercept it. This convoy was to be escorted by M. de Kersaint, with a small squadron, which Cotes believed would be little, if at all, superior to that under Captain Arthur Forrest of the *Augusta.* But de Kersaint was reinforced at Cape François, and had in consequence a considerably more powerful command [1] than the British officer. On October 21st, [2] de Kersaint issued forth, hoping by his very appearance in such force to drive Forrest away. The latter, upon the French being signalled, summoned his brother captains on board the *Augusta,* and, when they met him on his quarterdeck, said, " Well, gentlemen, you see they are come out to engage us." Upon which Captain Suckling answered, " I think it would be a pity to disappoint them." Captain Langdon was of the same opinion. "Very well," replied Captain Forrest; "go on board your ships again "; and he at once made the signal to bear down and engage the enemy. The French had seven vessels to the British three. Captain Suckling took the van, Captain Forrest the centre, and Captain Langdon the rear. The action began at about 3.20 P.M., and continued very briskly for two hours and a half, when the French commodore ordered one of his frigates to come and tow him out of the line. Others of his squadron soon followed his example ; and eventually the French made off. The British ships were all much cut up aloft. The *Augusta* lost 9 killed and 29 wounded ; the *Dreadnought,* 9 killed and 30 wounded ; and the *Edinburgh,* 5 killed and 30 wounded. The loss of the French is said

---

[1] THE BRITISH AND FRENCH SQUADRONS ENGAGED ON OCTOBER 21ST, 1757.

BRITISH.			FRENCH.		
Ships.	Guns.	Commanders.	Ships.	Guns.	Commanders.
Augusta. . . .	60	Capt. Arthur Forrest.	*Intrépide* . . .	74	M. de Kersaint.
Dreadnought . .	60	,, Maurice Suckling.	*Sceptre*	74	
Edinburgh . . .	64	,, William Langdon.	*Opiniâtre* . . .	64	
			Greenwich . . .	50	
			Outarde. . . .	44	
			Sauvage	32	
			Licorne	32	

[2] On the same day, forty-eight years later, was fought the battle of Trafalgar. Nelson, before going into action, recalled the fact that the day was the anniversary of his uncle's gallant behaviour, and regarded it as of good omen.

to have exceeded 500 in killed and wounded.   Few pluckier or more
creditable actions have ever been fought ; and it is worth noting
that among the British captains, all of whom greatly distinguished
themselves, one, Maurice Suckling, was a maternal uncle of Lord
Nelson, and Nelson's earliest patron.   Forrest had to bear up for
Jamaica, in order to get his ships refitted.   De Kersaint, in the
meantime, picked up his convoy and sailed for France.   But, at the

CAPTAIN MAURICE SUCKLING, R.N., CONTROLLER OF THE NAVY, 1775–78.

(By permission, from the portrait by Bardwell, in the possession of Capt. Thomas Suckling, R.N.)

very end of his voyage, he met with a severe storm, in which
the *Opiniâtre, Greenwich,* and *Outarde* drove ashore and were
wrecked.

On the North American station Lord Loudoun, the new military
commander-in-chief, had formulated in the autumn of 1756, a plan
for the conquest of Cape Breton ; and, in the winter, the Ministry
at home approved his scheme.   On January 3rd, 1757, he laid
a general embargo on all outward-bound ships in American colonial

ports. His objects were, firstly, to prevent the communication of
intelligence to the enemy ; secondly, to obtain the necessary transports ; and thirdly, to secure additional seamen for his Majesty's
ships. The measure, though perhaps it was wise, produced strong
dissatisfaction both in America and at home ; and, in spite of the
precaution, the French heard of the project. In the early spring,
therefore, they sent a fleet and strong reinforcements to Louisbourg.

Loudoun assembled at New York ninety transports; and,
presently, Sir Charles Hardy (2), Governor of New York, received a
commission as Rear-Admiral, with orders to hoist his flag and co-
operate with the military commander-in-chief. He first hoisted his
flag in the *Nightingale*, 20, but removed it later to the *Sutherland*, 50,
Captain Edward Falkingham (2). The army, consisting of 3500
men, was all embarked by the 25th ; but, just as the fleet was ready
to sail, news arrived that a French squadron, of five ships of the
line and a frigate, was cruising off Halifax. This delayed the
departure of the expedition until the Rear-Admiral had sent two
sloops to reconnoitre. As they saw no enemy, Hardy sailed on
June 5th, and a few days afterwards disembarked his forces for
refreshment and exercise at Halifax, where were found three
infantry regiments and a company of artillery, bringing the total
force up to about 11,000 men.

Loudoun would scarcely have left New York with so feeble
a convoy[1] as that which was available under Hardy, had he not
had reason to expect to meet at Halifax Vice-Admiral Francis
Holburne, with a fleet from England, to support him. But, owing
to mismanagement at home, Holburne did not leave St. Helen's for
Ireland, where he was to pick up troops, until April 16th ; and
sailing from Cork on May 27th, he did not reach Halifax until
July 7th, when the season was almost too far advanced for the safe
commencement of an enterprise which could not but be met with
the most vigorous opposition. Moreover, the French had been
beforehand, and had despatched from Brest a fleet, which, under
M. de Beauffremont, went first to the West Indies, and, proceeding,
entered Louisbourg on June 5th, finding there four sail of the line
which a few days earlier had arrived from Toulon under M. du
Revest. A further reinforcement from Brest, under M. Dubois

---

[1] *Sutherland*, 50, Captain Edward Falkingham (2); *Nightingale*, 20, Captain
James Campbell (2) ; *Kennington*, 20, Captain Dudley Digges ; *Vulture*, 16, Commander
Sampson Salt ; and *Ferret*, 14, Commander Arthur Upton.

de la Motte, sailed on May 3rd, and, evading the British blockade, reached Louisbourg on June 29th, when the united French squadrons included eighteen sail of the line and five frigates, a force much superior to that which Holburne and Hardy were able to dispose of. The town also contained 7000 regular troops. Dubois de la Motte had been expressly ordered to protect Louisbourg, and on no account to hazard an engagement with the British fleet unless he should be in such overwhelming force as to place the question of his success beyond a doubt. It is right to point this out in order to excuse him for having neither annihilated Holburne, nor blockaded the British in Halifax.

Vice-Admiral Holburne sent the *Winchelsea*, 20, Captain John Rous, and other frigates, to look into Louisbourg. Rous returned, and, in consequence of his report, the army was re-embarked on August 1st and 2nd, and a rendezvous was appointed in Gabarus Bay, six miles west of Louisbourg. Rous seems to have underrated the strength of the French forces ; but truer information concerning it was presently received from some papers which had been discovered in a prize. This led to the abandonment of the project. Some regiments remained in Halifax ; others, under convoy, went to the Bay of Fundy, to Fort Cumberland, and to Annapolis Royal ; and the rest, with Loudoun, against whom there was a great outcry, returned to New York.

Holburne, however, was not satisfied, and resolved to reconnoitre Louisbourg for himself. Leaving, therefore, a few vessels for the defence of Halifax, he sailed on August 16th, and arrived before the place on August 20th. Near the harbour's mouth some of his ships got close enough in to draw the fire from the island battery. The Vice-Admiral was thus able to satisfy himself that the strength of the enemy had not been exaggerated. Dubois de la Motte signalled his fleet to unmoor, whereupon the British tacked, stood off, and at nightfall bore away. On September 11th, Holburne was again at Halifax, where he found reinforcements of four sail of the line from England, under Captain Francis Geary.

The original project could not then be persisted in, but Holburne, after watering and rewooding his fleet, which by that time consisted of nineteen sail of the line, two fifty-gun ships, and several frigates, sailed for Louisbourg with the intention of blockading the French, until the approach of winter and shortness of supplies should oblige them to come out and fight him. On September 24th, he was only

about sixty miles south of Louisbourg, when a fresh easterly gale
sprang up. In the night it veered to the southward and blew an
awful hurricane until about 11 A.M. on the 25th. Then, fortunately,
it again veered to the north, otherwise the fleet could scarcely have
been saved from destruction. The *Tilbury*, 60, Captain Henry
Barnsley,[1] who, with nearly all the crew, was lost, struck and went
to pieces. The *Grafton*,[2] 70, Captain Thomas Cornewall, bearing
the broad pennant of Commodore Charles Holmes, also struck, but
was got off. The *Ferret*, 14, Commander Arthur Upton, foundered
with all hands. All the other ships of the fleet were seriously
damaged, no fewer than twelve being dismasted either wholly or in
part. It was the fiercest hurricane ever experienced by anyone then
on the station; and it naturally put an end to Holburne's plan. The
Vice-Admiral sent his most damaged ships direct to England, under
Sir Charles Hardy (2) and Commodore Charles Holmes, and went
with the rest to Halifax, whence, having refitted, he too sailed for
England, leaving a few ships under Captain Lord Colville, of the
Northumberland, 70, to winter at Halifax. Lord Colville had
orders to endeavour, when the season should permit, to prevent
supplies from getting into Louisbourg. The French force there,
however, put to sea at the end of October, and, after suffering from
very bad weather during the voyage, reached Brest at the end of
November.

The proceedings of M. de Kersaint on the Jamaica station have
already been described. Previous to going thither he had cruised
on the coast of Guinea; and, in the absence of any sufficient British
squadron there to oppose him, had taken many prizes. He had also
attempted Cape Coast Castle, but had been beaten off by the resource
and courage of Mr. Bell, the Governor.

In the Mediterranean, Rear-Admiral Charles Saunders, who had
been left in command after the return to England of Sir Edward
Hawke, heard at the end of March that four sail of the line—the
same which later reached Louisbourg—and one frigate, under
M. du Revest, had quitted Toulon. He therefore left Gibraltar on
April 2, 1757, to intercept them with the *Culloden*, 74, *Berwick*, 64,
Princess Louisa, 60, *Guernsey*, 50, and *Portland*, 50. On April 5th,

---

[1] In some Navy Lists of the period this officer appears as Barnsby. He was a
captain of 1748.

[2] She lost her mainmast, foretopmast, and rudder; but the ship was safely steered
to England by means of a jury-rudder devised by Commodore Holmes. (*See* plate.)

at 5 P.M., he sighted the enemy and, being to leeward, formed his line.   At sunset the French did the same, and began to fire at very long range.   The British chased, and gained so much on them that the *Guernsey* and *Princess Louisa* were able to engage ; but in the night the French got away.   Vice-Admiral Henry Osborn arrived with reinforcements in May, and assumed the command ; but, though the trade was well protected and many prizes were taken,

ADMIRAL SIR CHARLES SAUNDERS, K.B.
(*From a portrait in the ' Naval Chronicle,'* 1802.)

no further fleet operations of any importance took place on the station during the year.

It has been said that M. Dubois de la Motte escaped from Brest in May 1757, with nine sail of the line and four frigates, and reached Louisbourg.   He was enabled to escape by the fact that the blockading squadron before the place, under Vice-Admiral Temple West, had been driven from its station by bad weather. West was afterwards relieved by Rear-Admiral Thomas Broderick, who remained cruising till June, when Vice-Admiral the Hon. Edward Boscawen took the command of the squadron for about a month.   Prizes were made, but there was no meeting between the fleets of the two countries.

As the French still notoriously cherished the design of an invasion of England, the Ministry determined if possible to be beforehand and to deal a blow on the French coasts.   A military officer, who had made a short stay at Rochefort before the outbreak of the war, gave information concerning the condition of the defences of that port, which, though supposed to be weak, contained a most valuable dockyard, arsenal, and foundry.   The representations of this officer, Captain Clarke by name, induced the authorities to undertake an expedition against the town, and they were the more readily inclined to adopt this course seeing that nearly the whole of the French army was believed to be employed in Germany, and that but few troops were supposed to be available on the Atlantic seaboard. The scheme was kept secret; but a large squadron was prepared and entrusted to Admiral Sir Edward Hawke (*Ramillies*, 90), Vice-Admiral Charles Knowles (*Neptune*, 90), and Rear-Admiral Broderick (*Princess Amelia*, 80) ; and troops were collected and embarked under Lieut.-General Sir John Mordaunt and Major-Generals Conway and Cornwallis.   The instructions to Sir Edward Hawke were " to attempt, as far as it shall be found practicable, a descent on the coast of France, at or near Rochefort, in order to attack and, by vigorous impression, force that place ; and to burn and destroy to the utmost of his power all such docks, magazines, arsenals and shipping as shall be found there."

The fleet consisted of sixteen sail of the line, besides numerous frigates, small craft, and transports ; and it sailed on September 8th ; but its destination was not known, nor even suspected, by any with it, except the chiefs, until September 14th, when the alteration of course revealed it.

On the 20th Sir Edward Hawke issued orders to Vice-Admiral Knowles, directing him to attack Isle d'Aix ; and at noon the Vice-Admiral proceeded to execute these directions ; but, in doing so, he chased a two-decked French ship, which escaped into the Garonne and gave the alarm.   Early on the 23rd the Vice-Admiral, with the *Neptune*, 90, Captain James Galbraith ; *Magnanime*, 74, Captain the Hon. Richard Howe ; *Barfleur*, 90, Captain Samuel Graves (1) ; *Torbay*, 74, Captain the Hon. Augustus Keppel ; *Royal William*, 84,

Captain Wittewronge Taylor, and two bombs, the *Firedrake* and *Infernal*, attacked the works on Aix. The *Magnanime* got into action within forty yards of the fort, and, she being well seconded by the *Barfleur*, in half an hour the position surrendered. It was taken possession of, and the defences were later destroyed. In the meantime vessels were sent to reconnoitre, and to sound for a suitable place of disembarkation on the mainland; but it was discovered that a landing in any case would be difficult, and that, if opposed, it could scarcely be effected. At a council of war, held on the 25th in the *Neptune*, it was therefore decided not to proceed; but at another council of war, on the 28th, this decision was reversed, and it was determined to attempt an attack, in spite of the fact that the enemy, who had been very active, was then better than ever prepared. Yet when, in the early morning of the 29th, all was ready, the wind blew off shore, and the scheme had finally to be abandoned. On October 1st the fleet sailed for England, and on the 6th arrived at Spithead. The collapse of the expedition, and the waste of money, which its mismanagement by the Government had entailed, caused grave public dissatisfaction.

Almost immediately afterwards a fleet of fifteen sail of the line and several frigates, under Admiral Sir Edward Hawke and Vice-Admiral the Hon. Edward Boscawen, was sent to sea with a view to intercept the home-coming French squadron from Louisbourg. It sailed from Spithead on October 22nd, but, when on its station, was dispersed by a gale; and, before it could regain its assigned position, M. Dubois de la Motte got into Brest unperceived, except by the *Vanguard*, Captain Robert Swanton, which sighted it on November 23rd, and which was engaged by some of the enemy. M. Dubois de la Motte finally called off his chasers for fear of attracting the attention of the British fleet. Hawke and Boscawen, therefore, returned to Spithead on December 15th.

The Earl of Loudoun was in 1758 succeeded as military commander-in-chief in North America by Major-General Abercrombie; and it was determined to begin operations for the year with the siege of Louisbourg. Admiral Boscawen, Rear-Admiral Sir Charles Hardy (2), and Commodore Philip Durell (1), were nominated to the command of the fleet which was designed for the service; and, in January, Hardy sailed in the *Captain*, 64, for Halifax, to assume charge of the ships already there, and with them to blockade Louisbourg as soon as the season should permit. Early in February,

Durell followed him in the *Diana*, 36, to make the necessary local
preparations; and on February 19th Boscawen himself sailed with
the fleet.   After Boscawen's departure, Sir Edward Hawke was
despatched to blockade the French Channel ports, while Commodore
Charles Holmes cruised off the north coast of Holland, and assisted
in obliging the French and their allies to evacuate Emden.   At
the same time, troops were assembled in the Isle of Wight for an

ADMIRAL SIR GEORGE POCOCK, K.B.

(*From an engraving by Ridley, after the portrait by Hudson.*)

intended incursion upon the coast of France, and Admiral Lord
Anson assumed the command of the blockading fleet before Brest,
while a squadron for the descent upon the French coast was collected
under Commodore the Hon. Richard Howe.   It should be added
that reinforcements were sent to India, under Captain Richard
Tiddeman; that a small force under Captain Henry Marsh went to
the west coast of Africa; and that an expedition, ultimately entrusted to Commodore John Moore, sailed later for the West Indies.

Having thus summarised some of the chief naval movements of 1758, we may proceed to give accounts of the squadrons and their principal doings.

In the East Indies Vice-Admiral Pocock was joined in Madras Road, on March 24th, by Commodore Charles Stevens, and, on April 17th, sailed, with the object of getting to windward of Fort St. David, to intercept the French squadron which was expected on the coast. Comte d'Aché had reached Mauritius on December 17th, 1757, and had there joined the small squadron under M. Bouvet, with whom he sailed on January 27th, 1758, and made for the coast of Coromandel; but, owing to the monsoon, he did not anchor off Fort St. David until April 28th. Having eleven vessels, the French cut off the escape of H.M.S. *Bridgewater*, 24, Captain John Stanton, and *Triton*, 24, Captain Thomas Manning, which were lying there, and which, to save them from capture, were run ashore and burnt. D'Aché detached thence the *Comte de Provence*, 74, and the *Diligente*, 24, to carry to Pondicherry M. de Lally, the new governor of the French East India possessions. On the 29th, at 9 A.M., ere the detachment had disappeared, Pocock sighted the French squadron which then consisted of eight[1] ships fit for the line, whereas the British consisted of only seven.[2] Pocock signalled for a general chase; upon which the French weighed and stood out to sea E. by N., with the wind from the S.E. At 12.30 P.M. Pocock got within three miles of the enemy, who waited for him in line of battle ahead. He then hauled down the signal for a general chase and

[1] Nine were actually put into line by the French.

[2] BRITISH AND FRENCH SQUADRONS IN THE ACTION OFF CUDDALORE ON APRIL 29TH, 1758.

BRITISH.			FRENCH.		
Ships.	Guns.	Commanders.	Ships.	Guns.	Commanders.
Tiger	60	Capt. Thomas Latham.	*Bien Aimé* . . .	58[1]	Capt. de La Pallière.
Salisbury . . .	50	,, John Stukley Somerset.	*Vengeur*	54[1]	,, Bouvet (2).
			Condé . . .	44[1]	,, de Rosbau.
Elizabeth . . .	64	Commod. Charles Stevens. Capt. Richard Kempen-felt.	*Duc d'Orléans* . .	56[1]	,, de Surville (2).
			Zodiaque . . .	74	Comte d'Aché. Capt. Gotho.
Yarmouth . . .	64	Vice-Admiral George Pocock. Capt. John Harrison.	*St. Louis* . . .	50[1]	,, Joannis.
			Moras	44[1]	,, Bec de Lièvre.
			Sylphide	36	,, Mahé.
Cumberland . .	56	,, William Brereton.	*Duc de Bourgogne*.	60	,, d'Apret.
Newcastle . . .	50	,, George Legge.			
Weymouth . . .	60	,, Nicholas Vincent.	*Comte de Provence*.	74	,, de La Chaise.
			Diligente . . .	24	
Queenborough . .	24	,, Hon. James Colville.			
Protector, storeship					

[1] Guns actually mounted. Each of these ships could, and later did, carry more.

made that for line of battle ahead, with the ships at a distance of half a cable apart. The *Cumberland* and *Tiger*, sailing badly, did not get into their positions until 2.15, when Pocock bore down on the *Zodiaque*, d'Aché's flagship, which occupied the centre of the French line. The captains of the *Newcastle* and *Weymouth* unfortunately mistook the signal for the line, and did not close up to the ships ahead of them; and, when the Vice-Admiral signalled for closer action, these ships did not obey. The enemy opened fire as the British approached. The *Cumberland* was so long in getting up that the Vice-Admiral, and the three ships ahead of him, had, for some time, had to sustain the whole fire of the French. Yet, Pocock did not return a shot until his ship had hauled up exactly abreast of the *Zodiaque*, and then, at 3.55 P.M., he made the signal to engage.

Commodore Stevens, with the ships ahead of the Vice-Admiral, behaved magnificently, but the three ships astern did not properly support the van. This might have been serious, and even fatal, if there had not been corresponding mistakes and derelictions of duty on the French side. The captain of the *Duc de Bourgogne* took up a post behind the French line, and, in the most cowardly manner, fired across it at the British; and the *Sylphide*, 36, a weak ship, which seems to have improperly found a place in the line, was driven out of it at the first broadside The *Condé* lost her rudder, and was also obliged to fall out. In the van and centre, however, the action was for the most part fought with the greatest determination on both sides. In her somewhat belated attempts to get into action, the *Cumberland* nearly fouled the *Yarmouth*, and forced her to back her topsails, thus obliging the *Newcastle* and the *Weymouth* to back theirs likewise. But when the *Cumberland* had at length gained her station, the *Newcastle* held back, in spite of signals from the Vice-Admiral, and in spite of the *Weymouth's* hailing her to close up; whereupon the *Weymouth* hauled her wind and, passing to windward of the *Newcastle*, got into line ahead of her and quickly obliged the *Moras* to bear away. The *Cumberland* in the meanwhile engaged the *St. Louis*, so materially relieving the *Yarmouth*.

In the height of the engagement explosions of powder on board both the *Zodiaque* and the *Bien Aimé* caused some confusion. D'Aché signalled for those of his ships which had withdrawn to return to the action; but they paid no attention. Still the fight was hot, and the *Tiger* was very hard pressed until she was assisted by the *Salisbury* and *Elizabeth*. As the battle neared its termination, the ship and frigate which had been detached by d'Aché to Pondicherry, and which M. de Lally had refused to allow to return at once, although d'Aché had signalled for them, were coming up; but, the British rear then closing somewhat, and the fugitive French vessels not rejoining, d'Aché at about 6 P.M. bore down to his friends, and then, hauling his wind, made for Pondicherry. His final movement, which seems to be thus rightly interpreted, appeared to Pocock to have a different significance; for he wrote :—

" At half-past four P.M. the rear of the French line had drawn pretty close up to their flagship. Our three rear ships were signalled to engage closer. Soon after, M. d'Aché broke the line and put before the wind. His second astern, who had kept on the *Yarmouth's* quarter most part of the action, then came up alongside, gave his fire, and then bore away; and a few minutes after the enemy's van bore away also."

From this, as Captain Mahan points out, it would appear that the French deliberately, before leaving the scene of the action, effected upon the principal English ship a movement of concentration, defiling past her.[1]

Pocock hauled down the signal to engage, and rehoisted that for a general chase; but such of his ships as had fought well were too disabled to come up with the enemy, and, night approaching, he stood to the southward with a view of keeping to the windward of the enemy, and of being able to engage him in the morning, if the French did not weather the British. With this object he ordered the *Queenborough*, 24, ahead to observe the enemy; and he continued to endeavour to work up after the French until 6 A.M. on May 1st, when, as he lost ground and pursuit appeared to be useless, he anchored three miles south of Sadras.

In this battle, which was fought about twenty-one miles from Lampraavy, the British had lost 29 killed and 89 wounded. At 10 P.M. on the day of the action, the French anchored off Lampraavy. There, owing to the loss of her anchors and to damage to her cables, the *Bien Aimé* drove ashore and was wrecked; all her crew, however, being saved. In the engagement the French had suffered far more severely than the British, having lost 162 killed, and 360 wounded; for the ships had been full of troops and the English fire had been directed, as usual, against the hulls rather than against the rigging. D'Aché afterwards proceeded to Pondicherry, where he landed 1200 sick, and superseded M. d'Apret, captain of the *Duc de Bourgogne*, by M. Bouvet. It seems to have

[1] ' Infl. of Sea Power,' 308.

been chiefly owing to the backwardness of the captains in the British rear that the French were not completely defeated.

At about the time of the action, the French on land had taken Cuddalore, the garrison of which was allowed to retire to Fort .St. David. That place was soon afterwards besieged by M. de Lally. Pocock received some additional men from Madras, including eighty lascars, and, having repaired the worst damages of his ships, tried in vain to work up along the coast. He then stood to sea, and on May 10th had stretched as far south as lat. 9° 30', whence he endeavoured to fetch to the windward of Fort St. David; but, standing in, he met with a strong west wind, and, being unable to get higher than Lampraavy, he anchored there on May 26th. On the 30th he sighted Pondicherry, and saw the French squadron in the road.

D'Aché, upon descrying the British, called a council of war, which decided that the ships should remain moored close under the batteries to await attack; but M. de Lally, arriving from before Fort St. David, insisted that the British should be met at sea, and sent out to the fleet 400 lascars as a reinforcement. As de Lally had the supreme command in India, d'Aché weighed with eight ships of the line and a frigate; yet, instead of bearing down on Pocock, who could not work up to him, he kept his wind and plied for Fort St. David, whither de Lally returned by land to prosecute the siege. But no sooner had de Lally departed than the governor and council of Pondicherry, who had full powers during de Lally's absence, recalled d'Aché to protect their town. This order was most serviceable to the British; for, soon after the return of the French squadron, three valuable East India Company's ships, which must otherwise have been taken, got safely into Madras.

Chiefly owing to the bad sailing of the *Cumberland*, Pocock failed to get up with the French squadron. On the 6th he heard that Fort St. George was likely to be invested; and, realizing that should this be so, his ships would be unable to re-water on the coast, he made for Madras, where he brought his defaulting captains to court-martial. Captain George Legge, of the *Newcastle*, was dismissed the service; Captain Nicholas Vincent, of the *Weymouth*, was dismissed his ship; and Captain William Brereton, of the *Cumberland*, was sentenced to the loss of one year's seniority as a post-captain.

Fort St. David capitulated on June 2nd, and M. de Lally destroyed the place. Had he then gone at once to Madras, he could have

taken it easily; but he delayed, and, in the interval, Fort St. George
was considerably strengthened. Instead of going to Madras, he
attacked Tanjore, in order to obtain payment of some money which
had been promised by the king to M. Dupleix in 1749. Before
Tanjore, his army, weakened by sickness and want of provisions,
was defeated; and, being obliged to raise the siege and to retire,
closely pursued by his native opponents, he had some difficulty in
reaching Carical. On his retreat thither he learnt that d'Aché,
then off Pondicherry, had intimated his intention of proceeding to
Mauritius. He therefore sent to remonstrate with the French
commodore, and was thus able to induce him to postpone his
departure.

Vice-Admiral Pocock refitted, and, on July 25th, sailed with a
favourable wind southward along the shore to seek the enemy. On
the 26th he anchored off Lampraavy, where he took or burnt some
small craft of the enemy. On the evening of the 27th he got within
nine miles of Pondicherry, and saw the French fleet at anchor in
the road. On the 28th, at 10 A.M., the French got under sail and
stood to the southward with a land breeze; on which Pocock
signalled for a general chase; but the enemy kept to windward and
anchored early next morning off Porto Novo. When the land breeze
arose, the French weighed and stood to windward; and at about
8 A.M. were out of sight. In the afternoon Pocock burnt the French
ship *Restitution*, a British prize, off Porto Novo. At 10 A.M. on
August 1st he again sighted d'Aché, who was getting under sail off
Tranquebar, and who soon afterwards formed his line of battle
ahead with starboard tacks on board, and seemed to edge down
towards the British. But when Pocock made sail and stood for the
French, they hauled on a wind. At about 1 P.M., however, they
formed line of battle abreast and bore down on Pocock under easy
sail. He, at 1.30, signalled for a line of battle ahead with the
starboard tacks on board, and stood to the eastward under topsails,
or with the maintopsails square so as to allow his ships to take
station, in waiting for the enemy. At 5 P.M. the French van was
abreast of the British centre at a distance of about two miles. The
enemy stood on till his van was abreast of the British van, and then
kept at about that distance until 6.30, when he hoisted his topsails,
set his courses, and stood to the south-east. Admiral Pocock
signalled to his van to fill and stand on, and made sail to the southward, keeping his line until midnight, when he judged the French

to have tacked. He then signalled the fleet to wear, and stood after the enemy to the westward. But, at daylight on the 2nd, the enemy was not to be seen. In the evening, however, four sails were sighted inshore to the north-west; and on the 3rd, at 5 A.M., the British sighted the French fleet off Negapatam, about three miles to windward, formed in line of battle ahead, with the starboard tacks on board.[1]

Pocock also formed his line of battle ahead on the starboard tack, and stood towards the French; and, seeing that the *Comte de Provence*, 74, led their van, he ordered the *Elizabeth*, 64, to take the place of the *Tiger*, 60, an inferior ship, as the leader of his own line. At 11 A.M., the wind dying away, the British were becalmed; though the enemy still had a light breeze from off the land, and, with it, stood on, their line stretching from east to west. On that course the French passed at right angles so close to the rear of the British that they might almost have cut off the *Cumberland* and *Newcastle*, the sternmost ships. At noon a sea breeze sprang up, and gave Pocock the weather-gage. Both fleets thereupon formed line afresh; and at 12.20 P.M. Pocock signalled to bear down and engage.

The *Elizabeth* and *Comte de Provence* began the action; but, the latter's mizen catching fire, she had to quit the line and cut away the mast. The French charge Pocock with throwing inflammables on board of them; but the Vice-Admiral does not seem to have taken any special measures for setting his opponents on fire, though certainly in this battle they were unusually unfortunate in that respect. The *Elizabeth's* next opponent was the *Duc de Bourgogne*, which, being hardly pressed, would have been assisted by the

---

[1] List of the British and French Squadrons in the Action off Negapatam, on August 3rd, 1758.

BRITISH.			FRENCH.		
Ships.	Guns.	Commanders.	Ships.	Guns.	Commanders.
Yarmouth . . .	64	Vice-Adm. George Pocock. Capt. John Harrison.	*Zodiaque* . . .	74	Comte d'Aché.
			Comte de Provence.	74	Capt. de La Chaise.
			St. Louis . . .	64	
Elizabeth . . .	64	Commod. Charles Stevens. Capt. Richard Kempenfelt.	*Vengeur.* . . .	64	„ de La Pallière.
			Duc d'Orléans . .	60	„ de Surville (2).
			Duc de Bourgogne.	60	„ Bouvet (2).
Tiger.	60	„ Thomas Latham.	*Condé*	50	
Weymouth . . .	60	„ John Stukley Somerset.	*Moras*	50	„ Bec de Lièvre.
			Diligente . . .	24	
Cumberland . .	56	„ William Martin (2).			
Salisbury . . .	50	„ William Brereton.			
Newcastle . . .	50	„ Hon. James Colville.			
Queenborough . .	24	„ Digby Dent (3)			

Zodiaque, had not the latter had her wheel carried away by a shot from the *Yarmouth*, her first antagonist. To repair it, she went under the lee of the *Duc d'Orléans ;* but, as soon as she returned to the line, one of her lower-deck guns burst, and a fire broke out near her powder room. In the consequent confusion, her new steering gear gave way, so causing the ship to fall on board the *Duc d'Orléans ;* and, while the two ships were entangled together, both

REAR-ADMIRAL RICHARD KEMPENFELT.

(From a lithographed engraving by Ridley.)

were heavily cannonaded with impunity by the *Yarmouth* and *Tiger*. By that time the *Condé* and *Moras* had been driven out of the line ; and, at 2.8 P.M., the *Zodiaque* being free, M. d'Aché bore away. He was followed in about a quarter of an hour by the rest of his ships.

Pocock signalled for closer action ; and the retiring enemy was badly mauled as he went off under all possible sail. The signal for a general chase followed ; whereupon the French cut away the boats which most of them had towing astern ; and crowded to the N.N.W.

A running fight was maintained till about 3 P.M., when the French were out of range. Pocock, however, pursued until dark, and, at about 8 P.M., anchored three miles off Carical, while the French pursued their course to Pondicherry.

The fight, considering its indecisive character, was a very bloody one, especially on the side of the French, who lost 250 killed and 600 wounded. The *Zodiaque* alone lost 183 killed or dangerously wounded. On the British side, however, only 31 were killed and 166 wounded. Both d'Aché and Pocock received slight injuries; and Commodore Stevens had a musket wound in his shoulder. Aloft the British suffered more than the French; and, had the weather not been fine, many of them must have lost their masts.

D'Aché refitted at Pondicherry; and, being apprehensive of an attack there, anchored his ships close under the town and forts. Feeling also that he could not, in his then state, again fight the British, and that his remaining on the coast might lead to disaster, he again announced his intention of proceeding to Mauritius. M. de Lally and the French military and civil officers were astounded at this new determination, and endeavoured to dissuade him; but he was supported by his captains, and, having landed 500 marines and seamen to reinforce the army on shore, he sailed for his destination on September 3rd. Pocock could not believe that d'Aché had any idea of withdrawing from the scene of operations, and supposed that he would presently set out on a cruise. The *Queenborough*, 24, was therefore despatched to get news of the French; but she failed to obtain any. The British sailed from Madras on August 20th for Bombay, calling at Trincomale for water. The Admiral ordered the *Revenge*, a Company's ship, to cruise off that port; and she actually sighted, and was chased by, d'Aché on his way to Mauritius; but, though the British put to sea, they could not come up with the enemy. Pocock afterwards continued his voyage to Bombay.

In spite of the withdrawal of d'Aché, between whom and M. de Lally the worst possible relations existed, the latter continued his activity, and on December 14th laid siege to Madras. The town was hard pressed, when, on February 16th, 1759, Captain Richard Kempenfelt, with two twenty-gun ships and six other vessels, containing men and stores, arrived. Early on the 17th de Lally raised the siege, retiring in such haste that he left behind him much of his siege artillery, and large quantities of stores and ammunition. It was a remarkable and dramatic instance of the influence of sea power upon history. Had d'Aché held the sea, and had he been in a position to prevent the arrival of reinforcements and stores, the place must have fallen. The raising of the siege of Madras may be said to mark the beginning of the end of French dreams of empire in India.

On the .Leeward Islands' station, where Commodore John Moore (1) commanded in 1758, no fleet action or engagement of much moment happened during the year; but there was great and commendable activity; and more than one of the transactions in those seas will be found noticed in the next chapter.

On the Jamaica station, likewise, there were very few events of importance, though the enemy's trade suffered severely, thanks to the excellent dispositions of Vice-Admiral Thomas Cotes and to the vigilance of his cruisers.

It has been seen that in North America preparations had been made for a new attack on Louisbourg. Rear-Admiral Sir Charles Hardy (2) placed himself off that port as soon as the season permitted; but, owing to fog and gales, he was unable to prevent the entry into the harbour of M. du Chaffault, who took out a strong squadron from Brest. Du Chaffault, however, fearing to be blockaded, left there six ships of the line and some frigates under M. de Beaussier to assist in the defence, and himself went to Quebec. Hardy only succeeded in intercepting the *Foudroyant*, 22, and a few other French craft bound up the St. Lawrence. The *Foudroyant* pluckily stood a short action with the *Captain*, 64, ere she surrendered. She had on board a large amount of very valuable stores.

Admiral the Hon. Edward Boscawen, who had been appointed to the command of the expedition against Louisbourg, sailed from Portsmouth in February. At the very commencement of his voyage he lost the *Invincible*, 74, Captain John Bentley, which, missing stays, ran on a shoal east of St. Helen's and became a total loss. But the *Dublin*, 74, was as quickly as possible substituted for her by the Admiralty; and she carried out Major-General Jeffrey Amherst, who was to command the military forces. The *Dublin* met Boscawen on May 28th, as he was coming out of Halifax with his fleet; but, being very sickly, she went on into port, while Boscawen with his whole force, numbering in all one hundred and sixty-seven sail of various kinds, made for Gabarus Bay. The fleet was dispersed by bad weather, and the main part of it did not reach the rendezvous until June 2nd. Among the celebrated men who shared in this expedition were George Brydges Rodney, Edward Hughes, later the opponent of Suffren, and James Wolfe, the hero of Quebec.

The French were found to be well prepared, Louisbourg being very thoroughly fortified, especially on the sea face. Between the day of his arrival and January 8th, General Amherst several times caused the troops to be put into the boats, ready for landing ; but on each occasion he was compelled by the state of the surf to desist and to re-embark them. In the interval the enemy was busy on his defences, and never omitted to fire on the ships when they ventured within range. On the 8th the army was again put into the boats ; and it was decided to make three separate attacks. Those on the centre and right were intended as feints or diversions, and were to be made in Freshwater Cove and on White Point respectively. That on the left was to be the real attack. It was made under Brigadier-General Wolfe, under cover of the *Kenning-ton*, 28, Captain Dudley Digges, and *Halifax*, 12. The *Diana*, 36, Captain Alexander Schomberg, *Gramont*, 18, Commander John Stott, and *Shannon*, 36, Captain Charles Meadows,[1] covered the feint in the centre ; and the *Sutherland*, 50, Captain John Rous, and *Squirrel*, 20, Commander John Cleland (1), the feint on the right.

These ships, as soon as they had taken up their stations, began a hot cannonade ; and, a quarter of an hour later, Wolfe's division landed in the steadiest manner through the surf under a heavy fire. Many men were unavoidably drowned through the oversetting of boats, and much ammunition was wetted ; but the troops, fixing their bayonets, drove the defenders from their position near the beach ; and, before night, all the other troops had been landed. Almost immediately afterwards the wind arose, and communication with the fleet was cut off for several days. Siege operations were begun on June 13th, the troops being at first much annoyed by the fire of the French ships in the harbour. The Admiral landed his Marines to assist. On the 28th the enemy sank the *Apollon*, 50, *Fidèle*, 36, *Biche*, 16, and *Chèvre*, 16, in the mouth of the harbour to blockade the entrance ; and on July 9th he made a vigorous but ineffectual night sortie. On July 21st the *Entreprenant*, 74, one of the largest French ships in the harbour, took fire, blew up and set in flames two

---

[1] Properly Medows, but the Navy List spelling is Meadows. This gentleman, afterwards known as Charles Pierrepont, became Viscount Newark and Earl Manvers. He resigned while yet a captain, and died in 1816.

more ships of the line, the *Célèbre*, 64, and the *Capricieux*, 64. All three eventually become total losses. The fire from the two remaining ships of the line being still troublesome, Boscawen, on the night of the 25th, sent into the harbour in boats 600 seamen, under Captains John Laforey and George Balfour; and these, in spite of a very fierce fire from the vessels and batteries, executed their mission. Laforey took the *Prudent*, 74, which, being aground, he burnt. Balfour carried the *Bienfaisant*, 64, and towed her into the north-east harbour. This decided the issue. Boscawen was making preparations to send in six ships of the line, when the

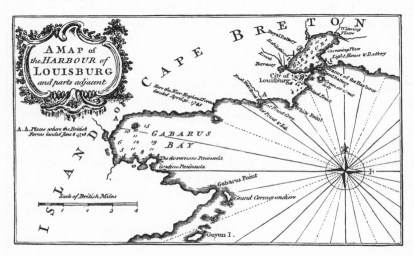

governor proposed terms; and, after a brief correspondence, the place was surrendered on the 26th. About 3600 combatants became prisoners of war; and 216 guns, besides mortars, were taken. With Louisbourg was surrendered, not only the island of Cape Breton, but also that of St. John.[1] Boscawen sent home Captain the Hon. George Edgcumbe with the naval dispatches. The colours which were captured were placed in St. Paul's Cathedral.

Immediately after the fall of the place, Boscawen sent Rear-Admiral Sir Charles Hardy (2), with seven ships of the line, to destroy the French settlements at Miramichi, Gaspée, etc., General Wolfe

---

[1] The island of St. John was renamed Prince Edward's Island in 1799, in honour of Prince Edward, Duke of Kent, and father of H.M. Queen Victoria.

accompanying him.   Some ships were also sent to the island of
St. John, with a garrison for it.   General Amherst, who heard at
about that time of the repulse of Abercrombie at Ticonderoga,
embarked six battalions under convoy of the *Captain*, 64, for
Boston, and then marched for Lake George.   Boscawen left Mr.
Durell, who in the meantime had been promoted to be a Rear-
Admiral, with a part of the squadron, to winter in America, and
himself sailed for England.   On his passage, his squadron became
separated, so that when, on October 27th, as he was entering
the Soundings, he sighted the French squadron returning from
Quebec under M. du Chaffault, he had with him in company only the
Namur, 90, (flag), Captain Matthew Buckle (1), *Royal William*, 84,

COMMEMORATIVE MEDAL OF THE CAPTURE OF LOUISBOURG, 1758.

(From an original kindly lent by H.S.H. Captain Prince Louis of Battenberg, R.N.)

Captain Thomas Evans, *Somerset*, 64, Captain Edward Hughes,
Bienfaisant, 64, Captain George Balfour, *Boreas*, 28, Captain the
Hon. Robert Boyle Walsingham, *Trent*, 28, Captain John Lindsay,
Echo, 28, Captain John Laforey, with two fireships ; and the
Bienfaisant was useless, having but a few rounds of powder on
board.   The French squadron consisted of ·the *Tonnant*, 80,
Intrépide, 74, *Héros*, 74, *Protée*, 64, and *Belliqueux*, 64, besides a
frigate, and the *Carnarvon*, a captured British East Indiaman.   The
enemy, being on the contrary tack, passed the British squadron, very
near, to leeward ; and, in passing, discharged his broadsides.
Some of the British ships returned the fire ; but, the wind blowing
hard, most of the vessels could not open their lower ports ; and
thus, in this partial action, very little damage was done.   Boscawen,
in spite of the superiority of the French, changed his course and

stood after them. The night was very stormy ; but, on the following morning, the enemy was again discovered, though his force
then consisted of only four ships of the line and a frigate, one
ship of the line having evidently lost company in the darkness.
Boscawen also had lost sight of all his frigates. He nevertheless
renewed the chase ; yet, although there was at first no great
distance between the squadrons, the British did not gain ground.
The only prize made was the *Carnarvon*. The rest of the French
ships got away. One of them, the *Belliqueux*, was afterwards taken
off Ilfracombe by the *Antelope*, 50. Boscawen arrived at Spithead
on November 1st.

For their services in North America both Boscawen and Amherst
received the thanks of the House of Commons. The conquest
which had been effected, besides being very important in itself, had
involved a loss to the enemy of six ships of the line and five frigates,[1]
and had deprived France of one of her best fisheries, and of a
valuable station for the privateers which long had preyed on the
coast commerce of the American colonies. It paved the way for
future British successes on the North American continent, and
sounded the death knell of the French dominion there. In fact,
just as the raising of the siege of Madras was the turning point of
the struggle in India, so the capture of Louisbourg was the turning
point of the struggle in North America ; and both results were
brought about by the force of sea power.

It has been said that in 1758 a small squadron under Captain
Henry Marsh was despatched against the French settlements in
West Africa. It is curious to note that this belligerent expedition
was first suggested by a Quaker, Mr. Thomas Cumming, who had
been on the coast, and who knew some of the native princes. One
of these had promised his co-operation against Gorée and Sénégal,
and had undertaken, in case of the success of the adventure, to
grant exclusive trading privileges to British subjects. Cumming
represented that a force of a certain strength would be required for
the service ; but the administration unwisely cut down his estimates,
and repeatedly deferred action, until Mr. Samuel Touchet, an
influential London merchant, warmly seconded the project. The
force finally assigned for the service consisted of the *Harwich*, 50,

---

[1] In addition to the three frigates sunk in the mouth of the harbour by the enemy,
the *Diane* (renamed *Diana*), 36, had been taken by Sir Charles Hardy (2), and the
Echo, 28, had been captured by the *Juno* and *Scarborough*.

Commodore Henry Marsh, the *Nassau*, 64, Captain James Sayer, the *Rye*, 20, Commander Daniel Dering, the *Swan*, 16, Commander Jacob Lobb, and the two eight-gun busses, *London* and *Portsmouth*, Commanders Archibald Millar and James Orrok, together with five small hired vessels carrying from four to eight guns apiece. The troops included 200 Marines under Major Mason, and a detachment of artillery with ten guns and eight mortars. Mr. Cumming accompanied the expedition, which sailed from Plymouth on March 9, 1758.

From Tenerife, where the squadron called for wine and water, Mr. Cumming, in the *Swan*, went on in advance to arrange for assistance from the natives; but, before he could conclude matters, the squadron itself arrived on the coast. Marsh decided not to wait for negotiations, but at once to proceed; and on April 23rd, he reached the mouth of the river Sénégal, and sighted the French flag flying on Fort Louis in midstream, twelve miles above the bar.

The enemy had armed a brig and six sloops, and had placed them above the bar to defend the channel through it. These much annoyed the British boats, which went in to sound. In the meantime troops were put into the small craft. On the 29th the *Swan*, with the busses and armed vessels, weighed and made up the river with a fair wind. The *London*, and some of the small craft, were wrecked on the bar; but no lives were lost; and most of the rest of the vessels got in safely, and made for the enemy's ships, which promptly retired under the guns of the fort. On May 1st the work surrendered; but the actual handing over of the place was delayed, owing to the action of the natives, who, not thinking that their interests had been sufficiently secured, blockaded the French. The difficulty being got over, the fort was occupied. In it ninety-two guns were found; and, with it, sixteen craft of various sizes were given up. The entire estimated value of the capture was about £200,000. Podor, and other stations further up the river, were included in the capitulation. For his services Mr. Cumming was granted a pension during his lifetime. These possessions had long supplied negro slaves to the French settlements in the West Indies; and for that reason their loss was soon severely felt.

Commodore Marsh, leaving a few small vessels on the spot, sailed next to attack Gorée, about ninety miles to the southward. He arrived off the island on May 24th, and at once began a hot cannonade, having anchored his ships with springs on their cables. But he had miscalculated the strength of the defence; and in about two hours and a half he had to signal his little squadron to cut, as the rigging and spars, as well as the hulls, were badly mauled, and about twenty men were killed, and forty wounded. This check was owing purely to the inadequacy of the force employed; and towards the end of the year, the Government sent out a stronger squadron to complete Commodore Marsh's work. In the meantime the *Nassau*, *Swan* and *Portsmouth* returned to England, with such trade as was bound thither; and, later, the *Rye* sailed with a convoy for the Leeward Islands. Marsh himself escorted the trade which was bound for Jamaica.

The new expedition was entrusted to Commodore the Hon. Augustus Keppel, who hoisted his broad pennant in the *Torbay*, 74, Captain Thomas Owen, and who had under him the *Nassau*, 64, Captain James Sayer, the *Fougueux*, Captain Joseph Knight, the *Dunkirk*, 60, Captain the Hon. Robert Digby, the *Lichfield*, 50, Captain Matthew Barton, the *Prince Edward*, 44, Captain William Fortescue, the *Experiment*, 20, Captain John Carter Allen, the *Roman Emperor*, 20, Commander William Newsom, the *Saltash*, 14, Commander Walter Stirling, and the two bombs, *Firedrake*, Commander James Orrok, and *Furnace*, Commander Jonathan Faulknor (1). At Cork he picked up troops, under Lieut.-Colonel Worge, who had been appointed governor of Sénégal; and, after some delay, he finally sailed thence on November 11th, 1758.

In the early morning of November 29th, owing to an error in reckoning caused by bad weather, the *Lichfield* ran ashore on the coast of Marocco, and became a total loss.[1] On the same occasion a transport also went to pieces. On December 28th, after having made a short stay at Santa Cruz, in the Canaries, the squadron sighted Gorée, and at 3 P.M. anchored in the road in eighteen fathoms of water, the island bearing S.W. by S. distant about four miles. The *Saltash* and the transports containing the troops were sent into the bay between Point Gorée and Point Barrabas; and, early on the 29th, the troops from them were disembarked in boats in readiness to land on the island upon signal being made by the Commodore. Most of the ships gradually took up their assigned

---

[1] There was unfortunately some loss of life. The survivors were detained by the Sultan of Marocco until ransomed, with other British subjects, for 170,000 dollars. Captain Barton was tried for the loss of his ship, and honourably acquitted.

positions on the west or leeward side of Gorée, and moored head and stern under a heavy fire. At 9 A.M. the attack was begun by the *Prince Edward;* but the cannonade was not general until about noon, some of the vessels experiencing difficulty in taking up their stations. The bombardment was then rapidly effective ; for, after a brief parley, followed by an almost equally short renewal of the action, the enemy surrendered; whereupon Keppel landed his Marines to take possession. About three hundred French, and many negroes, became prisoners of war. The British loss was inconsiderable. After escorting Colonel Worge to Sénégal, and cruising for a short time off the coast, the Commodore returned to England.

In the Mediterranean Admiral Henry Osborn and Rear-Admiral Charles Saunders commanded. The French had on several occasions discovered the wisdom and advantage of despatching in winter their reinforcements of ships and troops for abroad, since they found that the British blockading squadrons and squadrons of observation were frequently prevented at that season by fogs or bad weather from obtaining touch of the outward-bound detachments. But one of their divisions which, under M. de La Clue, left Toulon in December, 1757, for North America and the West Indies, was forced by the vigilance of Admiral Osborn into Cartagena, and was there blockaded. The French Government, in response to M. de La Clue's representations, sent five ships of the line and a frigate, under M. Duquesne, to endeavour to join him there, and then to assist him in breaking the blockade. Two of the line-of-battleships succeeded in getting in, but the rest of the force was not so fortunate. On February 28th, off Cape de Gata, Osborn at daybreak sighted four strange sail near his fleet, and ordered them to be chased. The French ships separated, but each was pursued. At 7 P.M. the *Revenge*, 64, Captain John Storr, brought the *Orphée*, 64, to action ; and, on the *Berwick*, 64, coming up, the enemy struck. In the *Revenge*, thirty-three were killed and fifty-four wounded, among the latter being Captain Storr. The *Orphée* was but six miles from Cartagena when she hauled down. Meanwhile the *Monmouth*, 64, Captain Arthur Gardiner, the *Swiftsure*, 70, Captain Thomas Stanhope, and the *Hampton Court*, 64, Captain the Hon. Augustus John Hervey, chased the largest of the enemy, the *Foudroyant*, 84, flag ship of Duquesne. The *Monmouth*, being far ahead of her consorts, got up with and engaged the enemy at 8 P.M. and fought her gallantly. When Gardiner fell his place was taken by Lieutenant Robert Carkett,[1] till 12.30 A.M., when the Frenchman's guns were reduced to silence. Not until then was the *Swiftsure* able to get up. Captain Stanhope hailed the foe to know whether she had surrendered, but was answered with a few guns and a volley of small arms, whereupon he poured in a broadside and part of a second, and the enemy promptly surrendered. She had 100 killed and 90 wounded, while the *Monmouth* lost only 28 killed and 79 wounded. It was a magnificently conducted action, and Lieutenant Carkett was deservedly rewarded with the command of the prize. When measured, at Gibraltar, she was found to be 185 feet 3 inches in length from stem to taffrail, and to have a length of keel of 155 feet. She was thus about 12 feet longer than the large British first-rates of her day. Moreover she carried 24 and 42-pounders, whereas the *Monmouth* was armed only with 12 and 24-pounders.

As for the other French vessels, one, the *Oriflamme*, 50, was driven ashore by the *Monarch*, 74, Captain John Montagu, and the *Montagu*, 64, Captain Joshua Rowley. The last, the *Pleiade*, 26, escaped by superior sailing.

Rear-Admiral Saunders was relieved in the spring by Rear-Admiral Thomas Broderick (W.), who went out in the *Prince George*, 80, Captain Joseph Peyton (1), which was unhappily burnt by accident on April 13th with a loss of 485 lives. Osborn continued to blockade the French in Cartagena until he was obliged to go to Gibraltar to refit, leaving only some frigates to look out off the port. M. de La Clue then escaped and returned to Toulon. A little later Osborn, being in bad health, had to resign his command. He was succeeded by Rear-Admiral Broderick.

The part borne by H.M.S. *Seahorse* and *Stombolo*, under Commodore Charles Holmes, in obliging the French and Austrians to evacuate Emden in March, 1758, scarcely merits detailed description here. Suffice it to say that the service was creditably performed. Other events in waters near home must, however, be described at some length.

Learning in the spring of the year that the French were fitting out a considerable squadron to escort a convoy to America from Isle d'Aix, the Admiralty ordered Admiral Sir Edward Hawke to

---

[1] Lieutenant, 1745. Captain, for this service, March 12th, 1758. Commanded *Stirling Castle*, 64, in Byron's action, 1779, and in Rodney's action in the West Indies, 1780, and was lost in her in the hurricane of October 10th, 1780.

endeavour to intercept it. He sailed from Spithead on March 11th
with seven ships of the line and three frigates, and on the night
of April 3rd arrived off the island. At 3 o'clock next morning he
steered for Basque Road, and at daylight sighted a number of
vessels, escorted by three frigates, some miles to windward. He
gave chase but they got into St. Martin, Rhé, except one brig,
which was driven ashore and burnt by the *Hussar*, 28, Captain
John Elliot. At about 4 P.M. Hawke discovered, lying off Aix,
the French men-of-war *Florissant*, 74, *Sphinx*, 64, *Hardi*, 64,
Dragon, 64, and *Warwick*, 60, besides six or seven frigates, and
about forty merchantman, which had on board 3000 troops. At
4.30 the Admiral signalled for a general chase, and at five the
enemy began to slip or cut in great confusion, and to run. At six
the British headmost ships were little more than a gunshot from the
rearmost of the French; but, by that time, when many of the
merchantmen were already aground on the mud, the pursuers
were in very shoal water; and, further pursuit being dangerous,
and night coming on, Hawke anchored abreast of the island. On
the morning of the 5th nearly all the French flotilla were seen
aground four or five miles away, several being on their broadsides.
When the flood made the Admiral sent in the *Intrepid*, 64, Captain
Edward Pratten, and the *Medway*, 60, Captain Charles Proby,
with his best pilots, as far as the water would serve ; and ordered
them to anchor there. They did so in about five fathoms, of which
three fathoms were due to the rise of the tide. The enemy was
very busy in lightening his ships, and in hauling and towing such of
them as could be moved towards the mouth of the River Charente ;
and by evening some of the French men-of-war had been got thither.
The British frigates did what they could, by destroying the buoys
which they had laid down over their jettisoned guns and gear,
to prevent the ultimate salving of the merchant vessels. That day
150 Marines were put ashore on Isle d'Aix ; and, under Captain
Ewer, they destroyed the works there and safely re-embarked.
Hawke sailed on the 6th, having effectually prevented the despatch
of supplies to America, and, it may be, so facilitated the conquest
of Cape Breton and its dependencies.

A greater continental expedition, consisting of two squadrons
of men-of-war, and about 14,000 troops, under Lieut.-General the
Duke of Marlborough, was prepared somewhat later in the year.
One naval squadron, which was designed to directly co-operate

with the army, was entrusted to Commodore the Hon. Richard
Howe. The other squadron, composed of upwards of twenty sail
of the line, was commanded by Admiral Lord Anson, having under
him Admiral Sir Edward Hawke. This force was intended to
cruise off Brest and to prevent any French squadron from interfering with the operations of Howe and Marlborough. As on some
previous occasions, the main object of the projected demonstration
on the coast of France was to divert French attention, and, by
calling off troops from elsewhere, to assist the King of Prussia and
other British allies on shore; but the precise destination of the
armament was kept very secret.

Howe's squadron consisted of one ship of the line, four 50's,
ten frigates, five sloops, two fireships, and two bombs, convoying
one hundred transports, twenty tenders, ten storeships and ten
cutters; together with a number of flat-bottomed boats, which
were carried on board the ships, and which were to be used for
the landing of troops. On May 27th the whole armament was
assembled at Spithead. On June 1st Anson weighed and sailed
to the westward; and Howe soon afterwards made sail and steered
straight across the Channel.

At 8 A.M. on June 2nd, after a stormy but not unfavourable
night, Howe sighted Cape La Hougue. The French were quickly
alarmed, and, from his course, probably formed a shrewd guess as
to his destination. The tides, and the frequent calms which supervened, compelled the British to anchor repeatedly, but on June 5th
the entire force stood into Cancale Bay, six miles east of St. Malo.
At 11 A.M. the Duke of Marlborough went in shore in a cutter to
reconnoitre and was fired at. By 2 P.M. all the fleet was at anchor,
and the signal was made for the flat-bottomed boats to be hoisted
out. Howe shifted his broad pennant to the *Success*, 24, Captain
Paul Henry Ourry, and stood in with the *Rose*, 24, Captain Benjamin
Clive, *Flamborough*, 28, Captain Edward Jekyll, and *Diligence*, 16,
Commander Joseph Eastwood, to silence the batteries, clear the
beach, and cover the landing. This he did, and then signalled for
part of the troops to disembark. The landing was effected in good
order and without loss, in spite of some musketry fire from the
enemy posted on a hill behind Cancale. These sharpshooters, however, soon fled as the troops advanced. More soldiers were afterwards landed, and before dark a large force was ashore. It lay on its
arms for the night. The rest of the army, with the guns and stores,

was landed on the 6th; and, at dawn on the 7th, the whole of it except one brigade, that of Major-General the Hon. George Boscawen, marched away in two columns. It is not intended here to follow the military movements on shore : it is only necessary to say that it was ultimately considered impracticable to attempt St. Malo, and that, after doing a great deal of damage, the army returned and re-embarked on the 11th and 12th. The loss up to that time had not been more than thirty killed and wounded.

Owing to adverse winds, the fleet did not leave Cancale Bay till June 21st; and, after crossing and recrossing the Channel, it was on the 26th close in with Le Hâvre. It was intended to effect a landing near that town; but the enemy was found to be well prepared. On the 29th, therefore, the fleet bore away before the wind for Cherbourg and anchored two miles from it. The batteries on shore fired, doing, however, no harm. Preparations were made for a descent; but, a gale springing up and blowing on shore, there was a very great surf, and, when the weather grew worse, the fleet was in considerable danger. The crowded condition of the ships had begun to breed sickness ; the horses on board were almost starving for want of fodder; and, as nothing was to be gained by waiting, Howe weighed and re-anchored at Spithead on July 1st. The army was immediately landed in the Isle of Wight to refresh itself. In the course of this expedition the French frigate *Guirlande*, 22, was taken by the *Renown*, 32, Captain George Mackenzie, assisted at the last moment by the *Rochester*, 50, Captain Robert Duff.

Some of the troops in the Isle of Wight were sent to reinforce the allied army in Germany ; and the remaining part of the military force was then entrusted to Lieut.-General Thomas Bligh, an officer who, though he had rendered good service, was then too old for the command. The squadron, having refitted and been strengthened by the arrival of the *Montagu*, 60, Captain Joshua Rowley, again sailed on August 1st, when it had re-embarked the troops ; and on August 6th it anchored in Cherbourg Road and was again fired at from the shore. The defences had been improved since the previous visit of the fleet, and many troops were in the town. Howe, who had with him Prince Edward,[1] second son of the Prince of Wales,

---

[1] H.R.H. Edward Augustus. Born, 1739; went to sea, 1758; Captain, June 14th, 1759; created Duke of York and Albany, 1760; Rear-Admiral of the Blue, 1761; second in command in the Channel, with Howe as his flag-captain; Vice-Admiral of the Blue, 1762; Commander-in-Chief in the Mediterranean, 1763; died at Monaco, September 14th, 1767; buried in Henry the Seventh's Chapel at Westminster.

serving as a midshipman, accompanied General Bligh to reconnoitre; and arrangements were made for a landing. The fleet moved to Marais Bay early on the 7th, leaving only a frigate and a bomb before the town. Howe, whose broad pennant was then in the *Pallas*, 36, Captain Archibald Cleveland, signalled to the frigates and small craft to cover the disembarkation. These drove off the enemy, and the troops were put ashore with little opposition. All the infantry had been disembarked by the evening. On the 8th the cavalry and artillery followed, and a march was begun on Cherbourg, six miles to the eastward. The place was entered without any fighting, the enemy retiring from the forts as well as from the town at the approach of the British. By the 15th, the pier, works, magazines, etc., had been destroyed, and the various vessels in harbour had been sunk, burnt, or carried off. On the 16th the army re-embarked, having lost but twenty killed and thirty wounded, although there had been frequent small skirmishes. Cherbourg was not then an important naval station, and the destruction of its harbour was a blow more mortifying than serious to the French.

The fleet sailed on August 17th, and on the 19th anchored in Portland Road. But the authorities were not satisfied with what had been done, and a continuation of the operations was ordered. The fleet, therefore, put to sea again on August 31st, and on September 3rd anchored in the Bay of St. Lunaire, about six miles west of St. Malo. On the following day the army landed and encamped. On the 5th, Bligh detached a small force to burn some shipping at St. Brieuc; and, on the same day, the Commodore and General reconnoitred the bank of the River Rance to see if St. Malo could be attacked on that side. As the west bank was found to be well fortified and held, the design against the town was abandoned. On the day following, at a council of war, the Commodore stated that he did not consider it safe to re-embark the troops in the Bay of St. Lunaire, as the bottom was rocky and the weather threatened to be not good; and he expressed his desire to remove the fleet to the Bay of St. Cas, and to embark the army there.

The troops therefore marched off on the 7th; but, unfortunately, they wasted their time and did not make the best of their way. They were much harassed by small parties of the enemy in woods and hedges, and had frequent encounters with organised bodies of soldiers, losing men continually. On the night of the 9th, the

General, whose intelligence service seems to have been almost non-existent, learnt, to his surprise, of the presence, only three miles from him, of a large force under the Duc d'Aiguillon. The Bay of St. Cas was then only four and a half miles off; and an officer was sent in haste to Howe to inform him that the army would proceed thither as quickly as possible. The Commodore, in the early morning, made as good a disposition of his ships as time permitted, in order to cover the re-embarkation. In the meanwhile, the retreat had begun, but it was 9 P.M. ere the heights above the Bay were gained. The strange error was committed of re-embarking all the guns and horses before the infantry. Nevertheless, by 11 A.M., two-thirds of the army were on board. At about that time the enemy's cavalry and infantry appeared, and opened a battery of guns on those who remained on the beach, doing great execution there and in the boats. Gradually the French descended from the hills; and at last, after a desperate struggle, they seized the village of St. Cas. There were then on shore only about seven hundred British under Major-General Dury, whose dispositions and movements were excessively rash. At length the French got close up to the retiring British, whose ammunition was then exhausted; and a rout followed. Part plunged into the sea, part seized and held a rock on the right of the Bay, whence many were taken off by the boats; but the majority had to surrender. The army lost, in killed, wounded, or taken prisoners, eight hundred and twenty-two officers and men. Of the naval officers who were superintending the embarkation, Captains Joshua Rowley, Jervis Maplesden, and William Paston, and Commander John Elphinstone (1), were taken. The further naval loss, however, was but eight killed and seventeen wounded.

The fleet which, under Lord Anson, was intended to cover the operations under the Hon. Richard Howe and General Bligh, consisted of twenty-two sail of the line and eight frigates. It blockaded Brest and annoyed the enemy's trade, but returned to Plymouth on July 19th, without having encountered the French. Sir Edward Hawke being ill, his place was taken by Rear-Admiral Charles Holmes. The fleet went back to its station on July 22nd, and in August it was joined by a contingent under Vice-Admiral Charles Saunders. The three admirals continued to cruise until the middle of September, by which time the operations against the French Channel ports had been concluded. Anson and Holmes returned

to England, leaving Saunders to blockade Brest and to endeavour
to intercept the French squadron which was expected from Quebec ;
but he did not fall in with it, and himself went back into port in
the middle of December.

In 1759 the French made extraordinary efforts to retrieve their
position at sea, and once more resorted to the old expedient of
threatening an invasion, chiefly with a view to crippling British
activity in distant parts of the world. But the situation of Great
Britain was then in every respect much stronger than in 1756,
when similar tactics had been tried ; and the scheme did not produce
the desired results. British troops were sent from England to the
Continent, to North America, and to the West Indies ; and a most
formidable expedition was organised against Canada ; while, on the
other hand, the French paid so much attention to menacing the
British in the home seas that they almost entirely overlooked
the business of protecting their own dominions abroad.

In the course of the year France assembled three expeditionary
forces : one at Vannes, in Brittany, under the Duc d'Aiguillon,
which was to be convoyed to Ireland by a fleet under M. de Conflans
and M. de La Clue ; one on the coast of Normandy, which was to be
despatched from Le Hâvre against England ; and the smallest of
the three, at Dunquerque, to be convoyed to Scotland or Ireland
by M. Thurot and six frigates and corvettes. To meet these and
other preparations the militia was embodied, and the following dispositions of ships were made. Commodore William Boys watched
Dunquerque ; Admiral Thomas Smith (4) [1] and Commodore Sir Piercy
Brett (1) commanded a force in the Downs ; Rear-Admiral George
Brydges Rodney cruised in the Channel, and kept an eye on the
ports of Normandy ; and Sir Edward Hawke blockaded Brest.
Elsewhere, Boscawen commanded in the Mediterranean ; Rear-
Admiral Samuel Cornish went with reinforcements to the East
Indies ; the squadron on the Leeward Islands' station was
strengthened by a division under Captain Robert Hughes (2), and
by troops under Major-General Hopson ; and Vice-Admiral Charles
Saunders and Major-General Wolfe were despatched against the

---

[1] Thomas Smith was called by the seamen of his day "Tom o' Ten Thousand,"
because, while first lieutenant of the *Gosport*, in the absence of the captain, he compelled
a French frigate in Plymouth Sound to lower her topsails by way of salute. For this
act Lieutenant Smith was court-martialled and dismissed the service, but, on the
following day, both restored and posted. Captain, 1730 ; Rear-Admiral, 1747 ; Vice-
Admiral, 1748 ; president of the court-martial on Byng ; Admiral, 1757 ; died, 1762.

French in Canada. The operations of this important and successful year in the various parts of the world may now be followed in greater detail.

In the East Indies, Vice-Admiral ·Pocock, who had refitted his squadron at Bombay, sailed for the coast of Coromandel on April 7th, endeavouring to get thither in advance of the French fleet, which was expected back from Mauritius. He succeeded in this object, and then cruised to intercept the enemy. On June 30th he was joined by the *Grafton*, 68, and *Sunderland*, 60, with five East Indiamen full of stores, of which he was greatly in need. On August 3rd he sailed for Pondicherry, and, during the rest of the month, cruised off that port, but could learn nothing of the enemy, and was at length obliged by lack of provisions and water to proceed to Trincomale. He sailed again thence on September 1st, having a few days earlier sent the East India Company's frigate, *Revenge*, to cruise off Ceylon and to keep a look-out for the French.

M. d'Aché had reached Mauritius in September, 1758, and had there found a reinforcement of three sail of the line and several French East India Company's ships. But provisions were so scarce that he had to send one of the men-of-war and eight of the Indiamen to South Africa to purchase supplies. These reached Cape Town in January, 1759, and returned to Mauritius in April and May. M. d'Aché was thus enabled to sail on July 17th for Bourbon and Madagascar, to pick up further stores, and thence for India. He reached Batticaloa in Ceylon on August 30th, and, having there learnt something of the movements of the British squadron, sighted it off Point Pedara [1] on September 2nd. His force consisted of eleven sail of the line, besides two frigates ; that of Vice-Admiral Pocock, of only nine sail of the line and one frigate.

On that same day, at about 10 A.M., the *Revenge* signalled to the Vice-Admiral that she saw fifteen [2] sail in the south-east, standing to the north-east. These were the enemy. Pocock signalled for a general chase, and stood towards the French under all possible sail ; but, the wind failing, the British were unable to get up. In spite of his great superiority, d'Aché apparently did all that lay in his power to avoid an action, although Pocock was equally anxious to provoke one. After much fruitless manœuvring the French were lost sight of, and Pocock then stood ·to the north for Pondicherry,

---

[1] Called also Point Palmyra. It is the N.E. point of Ceylon.
[2] It does not appear that there were really more than thirteen.

where he expected to find his foe. He arrived off that place in the
early morning of the 8th, but saw no ships in the roadstead. At
1 P.M., nevertheless, he sighted the enemy's fleet to the south-
east. He was then standing to the northward with a sea breeze.
On the morning of the 9th, the French were again visible ; and
at 2 P.M., the wind springing up, the Vice-Admiral once more
signalled for a general chase. Two hours later the enemy appeared
to have formed a line of battle abreast, and in that formation bore
down. But no action resulted.

At 6 A.M., however, on September 10th, the French bore S.E.
by S., distant eight or nine miles, sailing in line of battle ahead on
the starboard tack. Pocock,[1] in line of battle abreast, bore down
on them with the wind about N.W. by W. At 10 A.M. the enemy
wore, and formed a line of battle ahead on the larboard tack ; and
an hour afterwards Pocock did the same, the *Elizabeth* leading.
The action was begun on the British side by Rear-Admiral Stevens,
who, in the *Grafton,* attacked the *Zodiaque.* The tactics of the
day present no features of special interest ; and the action is
chiefly remarkable for the fury with which it was fought ; for the
fact that, owing to various defects, two of the British ships were
able to take only a very insignificant part in the engagement ; and
because, in the evening, the whole of the superior French squadron
bore away and stood to the S.S.E. under a crowd of sail. Most
of the British ships were far too damaged to be able to pursue ;

---

[1] Order of battle (on the starboard tack) of the British and French squadrons in the
East Indies in the action of September 10th, 1759 :—

BRITISH.			FRENCH.		
Ships.	Guns.	Commanders.	Ships.	Guns.	Commanders.
Elizabeth . . .	64	Capt. Richard Tiddeman.	*Actif*	64	
Newcastle . . .	50	,, Colin Michie.	*Minotaure* . . .	74	
Tiger.	60	,, William Brereton.	*Duc d'Orléans* . .	60	Capt. de Surville (2).
Grafton . . .	68	{Rear-Admiral Charles Stevens (R). Capt. Richard Kempenfelt.	*St. Louis* . . .	60	
			Vengeur . . .	64	,, de La Pallière.
			Zodiaque . . .	74	{Lieut.-General Comte d'Aché.
Yarmouth . . .	66	{Vice-Admiral George Pocock (R). Capt. John Harrison.	*Comte de Provence.*	74	Capt. de La Chaise.
			Duc de Bourgogne.	60	,, Bouvet (2).
Cumberland [1] . .	58	{,, John Stukley Somerset.	*Illustre* .	64	
			Fortune	64	
Salisbury . .	50	,, Digby Dent (3).	*Centaure* . . .	70	,, de Surville (1).
Sunderland. . .	60	{,, Hon. James Colville.			
Weymouth . . .	60	{,, Sir William Baird, Bart.	*Sylphide.* . . .	36	
			Diligente . . .	24	
Queenborough . .	24	,, Robert Kirk.			

[1] Had been a 66-gun ship, but was reduced to a 58 to ease her.

and, having ordered the *Revenge* to observe the motions of the French, Pocock lay to on the larboard tack to enable his most shattered vessels to repair damages. At dawn on September 11th the French were seen in the S.S.E., about twelve miles away, lying to on the larboard tack, the wind being about west. On perceiving the British, they at once wore and brought to on the other tack, and so continued until evening, when they were so far off that they were almost out of sight. At that time, the wind veering to the east, Pocock signalled his ships to wear, and stood under easy sail to the south-west ; the *Sunderland* towing the *Newcastle*, the *Weymouth* the *Tiger*, and the *Elizabeth* the *Cumberland*.

The loss sustained by the French in the engagement was, all things considered, enormous, amounting, as it did, to nearly 1500 killed and wounded. Among the killed were the captains of the *Zodiaque* and *Centaure*, and among the wounded was d'Aché himself. The French made for Pondicherry. The loss on the British side was also very heavy, being 569 killed and wounded, including 184 who were either killed outright or died of their wounds. Among the killed was Captain Colin Michie of the *Newcastle*, and among the wounded were Captain Somerset of the *Cumberland* and Captain Brereton of the *Tiger*.

On September 15th the British anchored in the Road of Negapatam ; and, having hastily completed their refitting, Pocock sailed with his ships again on the 20th. On his way to Madras he had to pass Pondicherry, where the French were lying ; and, unwilling to pass it by night, or to do anything to prevent M. d'Aché from fighting another action, he so arranged matters as to appear off the town at daybreak on September 27th. There he lay with the wind about W.S.W., with his maintopsails to the mast, and with but just sufficient steerage way on his ships for the proper maintenance of the line. Thus the British drifted slowly to leeward, yet not until Pocock had given d'Achè the fullest possible opportunity to come out and fight. But the latter had no such intention ; and, after weighing and making a few meaningless demonstrations, he returned to port and there announced his intention of sailing immediately for Mauritius. He carried out this determination on September 30th, in spite of the anxious remonstrances of the shore authorities, and especially of M. de Lally. His principal motive for thus acting seems to have been his knowledge that Pocock was about to be reinforced by four ships of the line from England.

Pocock, being short of water and stores, and with ships in bad condition, returned to Madras, where he anchored on September 28th.   Thence he sailed on October 16th for Bombay, and on the 17th fell in with Rear-Admiral Samuel Cornish, with three ships of the line, one 50-gun ship,[1] and three East Indiamen, which last, and the troops which had been brought out as reinforcements, were sent on to Madras escorted by the *Queenborough*.   They reached that place on October 27th.   Pocock proceeded to Bombay, and, after making various dispositions, sailed on April 7th, 1760, for England with a very valuable convoy, arriving in the Downs on September 22nd following.   He left behind him Rear-Admirals Stevens and Cornish.

Alluding to this last action, Mahan, after referring to the numerical superiority of the French, says :

"The fruits of victory, however, were with the weaker fleet, for d'Aché returned to Pondicherry and thence sailed on the 1st of the next month for the islands, leaving India to its fate.   From that time the result was certain.   The English continued to receive reinforcements from home, while the French did not; the men opposed to Lally were superior in ability; place after place fell, and in January, 1761, Pondicherry itself surrendered, surrounded by land and cut off from the sea.   This was the end of French power in India; for though Pondicherry and other possessions were restored at the peace, the English tenure there was never again shaken, even under the attacks of the skilful and bold Suffren, who twenty years later met difficulties as great as d'Aché's with a vigour and conduct which the latter at a more hopeful moment failed to show."[2]

Vice-Admiral Pocock was deservedly made a K.B. for his services and promoted to be Admiral of the Blue.

Such naval successes as the French won in the East after the departure of Pocock were confined to the capture of the East India Company's factory at Gombroon in the Persian Gulf, and the reduction of certain British settlements in Sumatra.   These successes

[1] Reinforcement which reached Vice-Admiral Pocock in the East Indies in October, 1759 :—

Ships.		Guns.	Commanders.
Lenox		74	⎰ Rear-Admiral Samuel Cornish (B.). ⎱ Captain Robert Jocelyn.
Duc d'Aquitaine . . .		64	„ Sir William Hewitt, Bart.
York		60	„ Vincent Pearce (2).
Falmouth		50	„ Richard Hughes (3).

[2] 'Infl. of Sea Power,' 310.

were merely raids, without influence on the course of the war or on the future of Franco-British commercial rivalry. The Dutch, seeking to profit by the temporary difficulties of the British, attempted, with seven East Indiamen and some troops from Batavia, to seize Chinsura on the Ganges, but were checkmated by the energy of Colonel Clive, Governor of Bengal, and by the gallantry of the masters of several British East Indiamen, who, under Wilson of the *Calcutta*, took or drove off the enemy on November 24th, 1759, after a sharp action. The captured Dutch vessels were afterwards returned to their owners, on security being given for the payment of £100,000 damages.

The British force on the Leeward Islands' station, under Commodore John Moore, was strengthened by eight ships of the line under Captain Robert Hughes (2), and by troops under Major-General Hopson, in order that the force might reduce some of the French Caribbee Islands, which were supposed to be weakly garrisoned.[1] The troops left England in November, 1758, under convoy of Captain Hughes, and reached Carlisle Bay, Barbados, in January, 1759. There Commodore Moore was met with. On the 13th of that month the whole force sailed for Martinique, and on the afternoon of the 15th entered Fort Royal Bay. On the morning of the 16th the *Bristol*, 50, Captain Leslie, and the *Ripon*, 60, Captain Jekyll, silenced and occupied a fort on Negro Point. The *Winchester*, 50, Captain Le Cras, *Woolwich*, 44, Captain Peter Parker (1), and *Roebuck*, 44, Captain Thomas Lynn, cannonaded the batteries in the Bay of Cas des Navires, where it was intended to disembark troops.

[1] List of the British fleet on the Leeward Islands' station under Commodore John Moore in 1759 :—

Ships.	Guns.	Commanders.	Ships.	Guns.	Commanders.
Cambridge . . .	80	{Commodore John Moore. {Capt. Thomas Burnett.	Woolwich . . .	44	Capt. Peter Parker (1).[3]
St. George . . .	90	,, Clarke Gayton.	Roebuck	44	,, Thomas Lynn.
Norfolk . . .	74	,, Robert Hughes (2).	Ludlow Castle . .	40	,, Edward Clark (1).[4]
Buckingham . .	70	,, Richard Tyrrell.[1]	Renown	32	,, George Mackenzie.
Burford . . .	70	,, James Gambier (1).	Amazon . · . .	26	,, William Norton.
Berwick. . . .	64	,, William Harman.	Rye	20	,, Daniel Dering.
Lion	60	{ ,, William Tre- { lawney.	Bonetta	14	,, Richard King (1).
			Weazel	14	Com. John Boles.
Ripon	60	,, Edward Jekyll.	Antigua	13	,, Weston Varlo.
Panther . . .	60	{ ,, Molyneux Shuld- { ham.	Spy	10	,, William Bayne.
			Kingfisher, bomb .	8	,, Sabine Deacon.
Winchester . . .	50	,, Edward Le Cras.	Falcon, bomb . .	8	,, Mark Robinson (1).
Bristol	50	,, Lachlin Leslie.[2]	Grenado, bomb .	8	,, Samuel Uvedale.
			Infernal, bomb .	8	,, James Mackenzie.

[1] Later, Capt. Lachlin Leslie.   [2] Later, Capt. Peter Parker (1).   [3] Later, Capt. Daniel Dering.
[4] Brought out the second battalion of the Royal Highlanders from Scotland.

The above were eventually joined by the *Lancaster*, 66, Captain Robert Mann (2), the *Emerald*, 28, and the *Griffon*, 28.

A landing was effected at about 4 P.M. under Captains Molyneux Shuldham, James Gambier (1), and Thomas Burnett; and, by the following morning, nearly the whole army was ashore. But against 4400 British, available for the service, there were at least 10,000 French, including their militia; and, after some small operations had been attempted, General Hopson, despairing of success, withdrew his troops to the transports.

The expedition then proceeded to St. Pierre, the capital of the island. But, on his arrival off that place on the 19th, the Commodore did nothing except send in the *Ripon,* 60, Captain Jekyll, to attack some batteries, the reduction of which would not in the least have influenced the general fate of the island. Jekyll was quite unsupported; and, having fought from 2 till 4.30 P.M. with great gallantry and silenced one battery, he was obliged to cut his cable and tow off. The position of the *Ripon* was for some time not unlike that of the *Formidable* under Captain de St. Bon at the attack on Lissa in 1866. She narrowly escaped grounding, and could not entirely get clear till 6 P.M. Jekyll behaved magnificently.

It was then decided to abandon the attempt on Martinique, and to attack Guadeloupe; and on the morning of the 20th the squadron sailed to the northward. By noon on the 22nd it was off Basse Terre. After the town had been reconnoitred and a council of war held, it was determined that on the morning of January 23rd the citadel and various batteries of Basse Terre should be cannonaded and, if possible, silenced, by the *Lion,* 60, Captain William Trelawney, *St. George,* 90, Captain Clarke Gayton, *Norfolk,* 74, Captain Robert Hughes (2), *Cambridge,* 80, Captain Thomas Burnett, bearing the broad pennant of Commodore Moore, *Panther,* 60, Captain Molyneux Shuldham, *Burford,* 70, Captain James Gambier (1), *Berwick,* 64, Captain William Harman, and *Ripon,* 60, Captain Edward Jekyll. The last named got aground, and was again in the greatest danger, until relieved by the *Bristol* and *Roebuck.* At about 5 P.M. the enemy's fire was silenced. Nevertheless, the town was rather wantonly destroyed on the following day by the fire of the four bomb ketches. Indeed, Commodore Moore exerted from the first much unnecessary force. He might have landed his troops a little to the north of the town, and so captured the place, which was open on the land side; but he preferred the useless and risky expedient of opposing his ships to forts. In the action, however, only about thirty men were killed and about sixty wounded, among the latter being Captain Trelawney, of the *Lion*. Commodore Moore, of course, gained his object; and on the 24th the army was put ashore and Basse Terre and Fort Royal were occupied. The advantage was, unfortunately, not pressed; and the French governor retired to the mountainous interior of the island, and was there able to make a most courageous stand for upwards of three months.

During the interval, the Commodore detached the *Roebuck*, 44, Captain Lynn, the *Winchester*, 50, Captain Le Cras, the *Berwick*, 64, Captain Harman, the *Panther*, 60, Captain Shuldham, the *Woolwich*, 44, Captain Dering, and the *Renown*, 32, Captain Mackenzie, under Captain Harman; and this force, on February 13th, made itself master of Port Louis on the Grande Terre side of the island. But the guerilla warfare and comparative inactivity played havoc with the troops. There were great numbers of sick; and many of them had to be sent to Antigua. On February 27th General Hopson died, and was succeeded in the chief military command by Major-General the Hon. John Barrington. This officer was beginning to take somewhat more energetic measures than had previously been displayed, when the army was partially deprived of the assistance of the fleet in consequence of the arrival in the West Indies of M. de Bompart, with five ships of the line and three large frigates, containing troops intended for the relief of the French islands. Commodore Moore felt it necessary to proceed to Prince Rupert's Bay in the Island of Dominica, so that he might be in a position to watch and promptly follow the motions of the enemy, who lay in Great Bay, Fort Royal, Martinique. The operations on shore were thereafter conducted chiefly by the army. The inevitable capitulation was signed on May 1st, M. de Bompart not having interfered. Nevertheless, after Guadeloupe had surrendered, he made a brief descent upon the island, and then, learning the truth, returned to Martinique. Moore heard of this movement of the French squadron, and put to sea in search of the enemy; but he failed to find him, and once more anchored in Prince Rupert's Bay. After the capture of Guadeloupe, General Barrington summoned, and received the surrender of, Marie Galante, the Saintes, La Désirade and Petite Terre. A little later Moore, reinforced by the *Raisonnable*, 64, and the *Nassau*, 64, proceeded to Basse Terre Road, and, on June 25th, despatched part of the army to England under convoy of the *Roebuck*.

Their inferiority of force prevented the French from attempting anything of importance against either the British fleet or the British garrisons in the West Indies; and, as no French fleet put to sea, Moore had subsequently to confine himself to repressing the enemy's privateers and to protecting British trade. On the Jamaica station, where Vice-Admiral Cotes still commanded, the situation was very similar; and, though useful work was done by the cruisers, no event of importance happened.

In North America the plans which had been formulated by the Earl of Loudoun during his commandership-in-chief continued to be carried out after his supersession; and, in pursuance of these, four considerable expeditions were entered upon in 1759, the object of all being the ending of French rule in Canada. Three of these expeditions, one against Fort Niagara, under Brigadier-General Prideaux; one against the French settlements on Lake Erie, under Brigadier-General Stanwix; and one under Major-General Amherst against Crown Point and Ticonderoga, were mainly military. The fourth, under Vice-Admiral Charles Saunders and Major-General Wolfe, against Quebec, was fully as much naval as military. All, however, were parts of a single scheme, which was designed to occupy the French in several quarters simultaneously, and so to prevent them from concentrating their full strength at any one point. The various expeditions were intended ultimately to assist one another; but that all the schemes did not accurately dovetail as originally intended is only natural. That mistakes should be committed and that there should be in some cases lack of fore-sight and of due preparation, were matters of course. Yet, in spite of local insuccesses, the great combined undertaking was in its results triumphant, thanks largely to Saunders and, above all, to Wolfe.

Prideaux's force of about 5000 men started on May 20th from Schenactady up the Mohawk River, and so, amid great difficulties, to Oswego on Lake Ontario; whence, leaving there a detachment, it crossed the lake and reached Niagara on July 6th. In the operations General Prideaux was killed by accident, and the com-mand devolved upon the Colonial colonel, Sir William Johnson, Bart., who, after defeating a relieving force of the enemy, received the surrender of the fort on July 25th. Johnson, being short of ammunition and supplies, then returned to Oswego, where he relinquished his command to Brigadier-General Gage, who built a fort there, while Captain Joshua Loring, R.N., superintended the construction of two large vessels for the navigation and command of Lake Ontario and the River St. Lawrence.

The expedition under General Stanwix was completely successful, but it was so purely a military one that there is no need to describe its operations here.

The expedition under General Amherst against Crown Point and Ticonderoga was in many respects a large and powerful one ; yet it should have included a great number of ship's carpenters, and quantities of supplies for the creation of a naval force on Lake Champlain. This provision was, however, overlooked. About June 1st, the army was assembled at Fort Edward, and on June 11th it marched to the banks of Lake George. Such boats and radeaux as could be built were of an unsatisfactory nature ; but at length a motley flotilla was collected, and the army embarked and proceeded down the Lake. On June 22nd the troops were landed near the Second Narrows and advanced against Ticonderoga, which on the 25th was evacuated and blown up, the enemy retiring on Crown Point. The boats and radeaux were then laboriously got into Lake Champlain. On August 1st, Amherst learnt that Crown Point had been abandoned ; and on the 4th he occupied it. He at once set to work to endeavour to put a suitable naval force on Lake Champlain, so that he might be able to press on and effect a junction with the force under Wolfe. But, owing to the lack of preparations, there were delays ; and, although the French force on the Lake was in part taken or destroyed, the approach of winter obliged Amherst at the end of October to cut short his advance and to return to Crown Point. Thus, both Prideaux and Amherst, who were to have held forth helping hands to Wolfe, failed, perhaps through no fault of their own. Only Stanwix, whose object was rather diversion than actual and immediate co-operation, completely gained his end. It is not the least of Wolfe's merits that, in spite of the lack of expected help, but with the cordial co-operation of the Navy, he brought to a triumphant conclusion the most important and difficult expedition of the four.

Wolfe had with him ten battalions of infantry, three companies of grenadiers and some companies of artillery and rangers, about 9200 men in all. The fleet, which was to convoy and support the force, was under Vice-Admiral Charles Saunders and Rear-Admirals Philip Durell (1) and Charles Holmes, and consisted of twenty sail of the line, two fifty-gun ships and numerous frigates and small craft.[1] Part of this fleet was already on the North American station under Durell, and had wintered at Halifax. As soon as the season permitted, Durell had entered the River St. Lawrence, and on May 23rd got up as far as Isle Bic. Holmes went out from England to Halifax early in the year 1759 to forward preparations; and on February 17th Saunders and Wolfe sailed from Spithead. The main body of the expedition was gradually assembled at Louisbourg in the island of Cape Breton; and there it was joined by the troops in garrison. On June 1st it began to leave the harbour; and on the 23rd the fleet found Rear-Admiral Durell near Isle Coudres, and obtained from him some French pilots whom he had secured by a ruse. Durell, reinforced, was left off Isle Coudres to bar the river, and Saunders, hoisting his flag in the *Stirling Castle*, 64, Captain Michael Everitt, proceeded, and on June 26th anchored off Isle d'Orléans, a few miles below Quebec.

The Marquis de Montcalm, who defended the city, had taken all possible precautions, and had removed the buoys and marks. His main army was about 14,000 strong, and lay at Beauport, to the immediate north-east of Quebec. Detachments of it were posted down the river at points whence it was expected that the advancing

[1] List of the British fleet employed on the expedition to Quebec, 1759:—

Ships.	Guns.	Commanders.	Ships.	Guns.	Commanders.
Neptune . . .	90	Vice-Admiral Charles Saunders (B). Capt. Brodrick Hartwell.	*Trent*	28	Capt. John Lindsay.
			Lizard	28	,, James Doake.
			Echo	28	,, John Laforey.
Princess Amelia .	80	Rear-Admiral Philip Durell (1) (R). Capt. John Bray.	*Lowestoft* . . .	28	,, Joseph Deane.
			Seahorse. . . .	24	,, James Smith.
			Scarborough . .	24	,, John Stott.
Dublin	74	Rear-Admiral Charles Holmes (W). Capt. William Goostrey.	*Eurus*	20	{ John Elphinstone (1).
Royal William. . .	84	,, Hugh Pigot (1).	*Nightingale.* . .	20	{ James Campbell (2).
Terrible	74	,, Richard Collins (1).	*Hind.*	20	,, Robert Bond.
Shrewsbury . .	74	,, Hugh Palliser.	*Squirrel.* . . .	20	,, George Hamilton.
Northumberland .	70	{ ,, Alex. Lord Colville.	*Fowey*	20	{ ,, George Anthony Tonyn.
Vanguard . . .	70	,, Robert Swanton.	*Scorpion.* . . .	14	Com. John Cleland (1).
Devonshire . . .	66	,, William Gordon.	*Porcupine* . . .	14	,, John Jervis.
Orford	66	,, Richard Spry.	*Hunter*	10	{ ,, William Adams (2).
Somerset. . . .	64	,, Edward Hughes.			
Alcide	64	,, James Douglas (1).	*Zephyr*	10	{ ,, William Greenwood.
Bedford	64	,, Thorpe Fowke.			
Captain	64	,, John Amherst.	*Baltimore*, bomb .	8	,, Robert Carpenter.
Trident	64	,, Julian Legge.	*Pelican*, bomb .	8	,, Edward Mountford.
Stirling Castle. .	64	,, Michael Everitt.	*Racehorse*, bomb .	8	,, Francis Richards.
Prince Frederick .	64	,, Robert Routh.	*Vesuvius*, f.s. . .	16	,, James Chads.
Medway . . .	60	,, Charles Proby,	*Cormorant*, f.s. .	16	,, Patrick Mouat.
Pembroke . . .	60	,, John Wheelock.	*Strombolo*, f.s. .	16	Lieut. Richard Smith.
Prince of Orange .	60	,, Samuel Wallis.	*Boscawen*, a.s. . .	16	Com. Charles Douglas.
Centurion . . .	50	,, William Mantell.	*Halifax*, a.s. . .	12	Lieut. ——
Sutherland . . .	50	,, John Rous.	*Rodney*, cutter . .	4	{ Lieut. Hon. Philip Tufton Perceval.
Diana	32	{ ,, Alexander Schomberg.	*Crown*, st.s. . .	18	Com. Joseph Mead.
Richmond . . .	32	{ ,, Thomas Hankerson.	besides transports, etc.		

British could be annoyed. He had also thrown up strong works on the north side of the river, between the River St. Charles and the Falls of Montmorency, and had armed two hulks in the River St. Charles to defend the communications with the army and Quebec. The Governor of the Province, Captain de Vaudreuil, was, however, a naval officer, while the Marquis de Montcalm was a soldier; and there was not a good understanding between them. Montcalm prudently desired to make his preparations with a view to the necessity of a retreat; but de Vaudreuil maintained that such precautions were needless, and that if the whole French force were concentrated on the north side of the river, the worst the British could do would be to demolish some of the houses in the city.

On June 27th, the British army landed on Isle d'Orléans and the French defences were reconnoitred. Towards night the ships were disposed to the best advantage, and measures were taken to prevent damage from the enemy's fireships, which were known to be in readiness higher up. A certain number of Marines had been taken from those ships which had been left at Isle Coudres under Durell, and these were distributed throughout the fleet. At midnight on June 28th, the French sent down seven fireships and two fire rafts; but they were grappled and towed clear by the activity and good conduct of the seamen. Vice-Admiral Saunders then decided to move some of his vessels into the open space of water immediately below the town, known as the Basin of Quebec; and, to afford them some protection, he induced General Wolfe to order the occupation of Point Lévis by Brigadier-General Monckton. The enemy tried to dislodge this force on July 1st by means of floating batteries, but in vain. The batteries were driven back by the fire of the *Trent*, 28, Captain John Lindsay. Ultimately some large ships were stationed a little higher up the river. Above these were frigates; and again above them armed boats rowed guard every night. The enemy thereupon ordered such ships as he had up to Batiscan, sixty miles above Quebec, but kept most of their crews in the city to assist in working the guns. Batteries were erected on Point Lévis to bombard Quebec, and, the works on Isle d'Orléans having been completed, Wolfe, on July 9th, embarked his troops, and under convoy of the *Porcupine*, 14, Commander John Jervis, and the *Boscawen*, armed ship, 16, Commander Charles Douglas, effected a landing on the north shore of the river below the falls of Montmorency.

On July 18th the *Sutherland*, 50, Captain John Rous, the *Squirrel*, 20, Captain George Hamilton, two armed sloops, and two transports, passed the town without loss, and gained the upper river. On July 31st, supported by the fire of the *Centurion*, 50, Captain William Mantell, an attempt was made to land troops below the enemy's entrenchments; but the force had to be drawn off to the beach. Some efforts were then made to destroy the French ships above the town and to open communication with General Amherst, who was supposed to be advancing from Crown Point. The *Lowestoft*, 28, Captain Joseph Deane, the *Hunter*, 10, Commander William Adams (2), two armed sloops, and two storeships, passed up to co-operate; but it was found that the force could not be got further than about thirty miles above Quebec.

On August 29th, the *Seahorse*, 24, Captain James Smith, two more armed sloops, and two more storeships, were sent past the town in preparation for a projected attack on Quebec from the west. Rear-Admiral Holmes took command of the flotilla on the upper river. On the night of September 4th, all the flat-bottomed boats and many vessels passed the town; and as many troops as could be spared were sent up with them. On the evening of the 12th, all the boats remaining below the town were filled with Marines; and on the following morning at break of day they made a feint of landing on the northern shore below the city, under cover of the fire of the frigates and sloops. Troops had been already got into the boats on the upper river, where Wolfe himself then was; and in the starlight they moved still further up, a French corps under M. de Bougainville[1] marching parallel with them along the north bank. An hour before daylight the boats turned and rowed down at great speed, current and ebbing tide being both in their favour, and were followed by the ships. The whole force quite outstripped the French, who attempted to keep up with it. Just as day was breaking the boats arrived eastward of Sillery, a short distance above Cape Diamond, those containing the light infantry falling a little lower down. There the attacking force disembarked at the foot of a woody precipice, scaled the height, and dispersed the guard on the summit;

[1] Louis Antoine de Bougainville. Born, 1729; began life as a lawyer; secretary to the French embassy in London, 1755; had previously, in 1752, been elected a Fellow of the Royal Society for a treatise on the integral calculus; aide-de-camp to Montcalm in Canada; founded a French colony in the Falkland Islands, 1763; circumnavigated the globe, 1766–68; commanded at sea during the war of American Revolution; vice-admiral, 1791; made a senator by Napoleon; died, 1811.

and presently the whole army was pouring up the steep slopes, and forming on the top, to await the approach of the main body of the French, who, under Montcalm, were seen to be in motion.

The action began early. At 8 A.M. the sailors dragged up a gun, which was most useful. By 10 the battle had become very general, the enemy advancing with courage to within thirty yards, but then wavering under the British fire, and being followed up with the bayonet. It was at that time that Wolfe, at the head of the Louisbourg Grenadiers, received a second wound, which proved mortal. The Marquis de Montcalm was also fatally wounded. After some further fighting, the French retreated to the city. General the Hon. George Townshend, who succeeded to the command, fortified the position which had been won. Additional ships were brought up ; and batteries were being erected to bombard Quebec, when, on the 17th, the enemy offered to surrender. The Vice-Admiral and General, and the French commandant, signed the capitulation on the morning of the 18th. Later in the day the upper town was taken possession of by troops under Lieut.-Colonel Murray, and the lower town by seamen, under Captain Hugh Palliser, R.N. The Vice-Admiral's dispatches were sent to England by Captain James Douglas (1), of the *Alcide*, who was knighted by the King, and presented with £500 wherewith to buy a sword. Throughout the British dominions a public thanksgiving was ordered. Wolfe's body was sent home in the *Royal William*, 84, and a monument to his memory was erected at the national expense in Westminster Abbey.

Saunders sent back to England his larger ships under Holmes and Durell, and followed in October, leaving Captain Lord Colville in command, with his own ship (the *Northumberland*, 70), the *Alcide*, 64, the *Trident*, 64, the *Pembroke*, 60, the *Prince of Orange*, 60, and several frigates, in North America. The *Race-horse*, bomb, Commander George Miller (1), and *Porcupine*, 14, Commander John Macartney, were left to winter at Quebec.

After the British fleet had retired, the French ships at Batiscan also fell down the river, waiting at Cape Rouge for a fair wind to carry them past the batteries of Quebec. On November 22nd, three of them, the merchantmen *Soleil Royal*, 24, *Senecterre*, 24, and *Duc de Fronsac*, 24, drove ashore in a gale and were lost. On the 24th, in the night and on the ebb, the rest came down with a favourable breeze ; and, although the garrison was ready for them, and every possible gun was fired at them, they all got past safely except one, another merchantman, the *Elisabeth*, which took the ground on the south side of the river.   Her crew made preparations for blowing her up, and then with the assistance of the crews of the merchant-men *Machault*, 24, and *Chézine*, 22, boarded and carried a British schooner in which they escaped.   On the following morning Com-mander Miller, of the *Racehorse*, went on board the *Elisabeth*, and ordering a light to be struck, inadvertently blew up the ship and destroyed most of his party.   He and his lieutenant survived to be removed, but were so fearfully injured that they died within a few days.

The campaign was a most successful one, chiefly because the French had made but faint efforts to divert British attention from the main objects which were kept in view by Mr. Pitt.   On the other hand, the British would not allow their attention to be diverted in the slightest degree.   Beatson rightly observes that :—

" had M. de Bompart, when he found he could not prevent the island of Guadeloupe from falling into our hands, steered for New York with his squadron, he might have made such an impression there as would have obliged General Amherst either to come himself, or at least to make such a detachment from his army as would perhaps have disabled him from acting on the offensive for the remainder of the campaign.   From New York, M. de Bompart might have gone to Halifax, or St. John's, Newfoundland, or both.   An attack on either of these places would have obliged Admiral Saunders to make such a detachment from his fleet as might have greatly diminished our efforts before Quebec, and, perhaps in the end, would have proved the ruin of the enterprise ; while before such detachment could have been able to overtake M. de Bompart, he might have done his business, and sailed for Europe."

It was of course inevitable, when France was straining all her resources in order to invade Great Britain and Ireland, and when there were no considerable British forces in the Mediterranean, that she should endeavour to collect as large a naval force as possible at Toulon, and then to send it round to join her main fleet at Brest. Vice-Admiral Broderick commanded in the Mediterranean.   Early in the spring of 1759 his small squadron was reinforced by several ships from England, and he received, and was able to carry out, orders to watch Toulon.   But Pitt was not content with merely reinforcing the Mediterranean fleet.   On April 14th, Admiral the Hon. Edward Boscawen, with three more sail of the line and some frigates, left Spithead to take over for a time the chief command on the station, and on April 27th he arrived at Gibraltar.   There he made arrangements as to the dispositions of cruisers and convoys ;

and, sailing on May 3rd, joined Vice-Admiral Broderick off Cape Sicié on May 16th, and assumed the command.

The French squadron prepared at Toulon was in charge of M. de La Clue; and, when the British arrived off the port, it was almost ready for sea. The French were carefully blockaded, or rather, watched with a view to preventing them from leaving without being detected and followed. On June 7th, before they attempted to come out, Boscawen chased two French frigates, and drove them into a fortified bay near Toulon, whither on the 8th, he ordered the *Culloden*, *Conqueror* and *Jersey*, under the orders of Captain Smith Callis, to proceed, and, if possible, destroy them. The ships were gallantly taken in; but, when under the batteries, they were becalmed; and, after a sharp two hours' engagement, they had to be recalled without having accomplished their object. The *Culloden* lost 16 killed and 26 wounded : the *Conqueror*, 2 killed and 4 wounded : and the *Jersey*, 8 killed and 15 wounded; and all the vessels were badly damaged aloft.

The Admiral continued on his station until he was compelled, at the beginning of July, to go to Gibraltar for provisions and repairs. Preferring Salou [1] for watering purposes, he put in there on the 8th, remaining until the 24th; and thus he only reached Gibraltar on August 4th. Meanwhile he ordered the *Lyme*, 24, Captain James Baker, to cruise off Malaga, and the *Gibraltar*, 24, Captain William M'Cleverty, to cruise between Estepona and Ceuta to keep watch for the enemy. On August 17th the latter descried the French fleet, consisting of ten sail of the line, two fifty-gun ships and three frigates, close in under the Barbary shore. Captain M'Cleverty made at once for Gibraltar, and arrived off Europa Point at 7.30 P.M., when he signalled the force and situation of the enemy to the Admiral, who sent off an officer to the *Gibraltar*, ordering her to keep sight of the foe and from time to time to signal to him accordingly. The British squadron was not quite ready for sea, and Boscawen's flag-ship, the *Namur*, in particular, had not so much as a single sail bent. Still, a little before 10 P.M., the whole fleet, of thirteen sail of the line and two fifty-gun ships besides frigates, was out of the bay.

Owing to the haste in which they had gone out, and to the Admiral, after leaving harbour, carrying a press of sail to the westward, the ships were, on the following morning, in two well

---

[1] A few miles south-west of Tarragona.

defined divisions.   The *Warspite, Culloden, Swiftsure, Intrepid, America, Portland,* and *Guernsey,* which had lain at anchor near the *Namur* and had put to sea along with her, were still with her. Vice-Admiral Broderick, in the *Prince*, with the rest of the squadron, was many miles astern.   At 7 A.M. on the 18th,[1] the advanced division sighted the enemy to the westward.   There were then visible only seven sail, and it afterwards proved that the rest had gone, without orders, into Cadiz during the night.   De La Clue first thought that the ships coming up behind him were his own missing vessels ; but he was disabused when Boscawen signalled a general chase to the N.W.   At 9 A.M. the British Admiral ordered his sternmost ships to make more sail.   This soon had the effect of bringing up the Vice-Admiral's division, which enjoyed a fine easterly

---

[1] British and French fleets off Gibraltar in August, 1759 : indicating, the order in which the advanced British ships got into action on August 18th ; the loss suffered by each in the action ; and the fate of the French ships.

BRITISH.					FRENCH.		
Ships.	Guns.	Commanders.	Killed.	Wounded.	Ships.	Guns.	Fate.
6. *Namur* . .	90	Admiral Hon. Edward Boscawen (B). Capt. Matthew Buckle(1)	13	44	*Océan* [2] . .	80	} Burnt.
Prince . .	90	Vice-Admiral Thomas Broderick (B). Capt. Joseph Peyton (1).			*Redoutable* .	74	
					Centaure . .	74	
					Téméraire . .	74	} Taken.
					Modeste . . .	64	
Newark. .	80	,, William Hol- bourne.	..	5	*Souverain* . .	74	} Escaped, Aug. 18–19.
					Guerrier . .	74	
					Fantasque . .	64	
5. *Warspite* .	74	,, John Bentley.	11	40	*Lion* . . .	64	
1. *Culloden* .	74	,, Smith Callis.	4	15	*Triton* . . .	64	} Parted company, Aug. 17–18 ; and entered Cadiz.
Conqueror .	70	,, William Lloyd (1).[1]	2	6	*Fier.* . . .	50	
7. *Swiftsure* .	70	,, Thomas Stanhope.	5	32	*Oriflamme*. .	50	
Edgar . .	64	,, Francis William Drake.					
St. Albans .	64	,, Edward Vernon (2)	6	2	*Chimère* . .	26	
8. *Intrepid* .	60	,, Edward Pratten.	6	10	*Minerve* . .	24	
2. *America* .	60	,, James Kirke.	3	16	*Gracieuse* . .	24	
Princess Louisa .	60	,, Robert Harland (2).[1]					
Jersey . .	60	,, John Barker (1).					
4. *Guernsey* .	50	Lieut. Michael Kearny (acting).	..	14			
3. *Portland* .	50	Capt. Jervis Maplesden.	6	12			
Ambuscade.	40	,, Richard Gwynn.					
Rainbow .	40	,, Christopher Basset.					
Shannon .	36	,, Charles Meadows.					
Active . .	36	,, Herbert Sawyer (1).					
Thetis . .	32	,, John Moutray.					
Lyme . .	24	,, James Baker.					
Gibraltar .	24	,, William M'Cle- verty.					
Glasgow .	24	,, Andrew Wilkinson.					
Sheerness .	24	,, John Clark (1).					
Tartar's Prize.	24	,, Thomas Baillie (1).					
Favourite .	16	Com. Timothy Edwards.					
Gramont .	16	,, Philip Affleck.					
Ætna, f.s. .	8	,, Richard Bickerton.					
Salamander, f.s. . .	8	,, Hon John Leve- son Gower.					

---

[1] Exchanged ships.

[2] Flag of M. de La Clue. Suffren, who was in her, thus became for the second time a prisoner to the British.

breeze, while the enemy had barely enough wind to give them
steerage way.   Thus the British gained on the chase till, at about
1.25 P.M., Boscawen signalled to engage.

At 1.30 P.M. the enemy began to fire at the headmost British
ships as they came up; and since Admiral Boscawen perceived that
the French intended to make off as soon as the breeze should reach
them, he naturally desired that the most advanced ships of his fleet
should push on and attack the enemy's van, to stop their flight until
his remaining ships could get up.   He therefore ordered the *America*
and *Guernsey* to make more sail.   At about 2.30 P.M. the *Culloden*
began to fire on the *Centaure*, the rear ship of the enemy; and, very
soon afterwards, the *America*, *Portland*, *Guernsey* and *Warspite* got
into action.   The wind had by that time dropped altogether, so far
as the ships which were in action were concerned.   The British rear
division, however, still had a breeze, and was thus able to get up in
time to have a share in the victory.

Boscawen, himself, in the *Namur*, was in action with the sternmost ships of the enemy at about 4 o'clock.   The *Swiftsure* and
Intrepid were at that time to windward of him; and, hailing the
former, he ordered her to push on for the enemy's van ship.   By
about 4.30 P.M., the *Namur* was close alongside the *Océan;* and,
when the two had been engaged for about half-an-hour, the *Namur*,
having lost her mizenmast and both topsail yards, was disabled, and
fell astern.   De La Clue made every effort to take full advantage of
this misfortune to the British flagship.   Each of his vessels, except
the *Centaure*, set all possible sail to get away; but the *Centaure* had
been engaged by every ship as she came up, and had stood the brunt
of the fight.   At last, her fore and main topmasts had fallen; and
she was so greatly damaged in every respect that she had no alternative but to strike.

The misfortune to the British flagship did not affect the energy
and activity of the British Admiral, who ordered out his barge and
was rowed at once to the *Newark*, and there hoisted his flag.   But,
by that time, the battle proper had almost ceased, and the pursuit
had begun.   Boscawen continued it during the whole night.   Though
there was a fine breeze, there was also a slight haze; and, under
cover of this, two of the French ships, the *Souverain* and *Guerrier*,
altered their course in the darkness and so escaped.   Thus, at daylight on the 19th only four sail of the enemy were to be seen.   The
British were about three miles astern of them, and about fifteen

miles from Lagos. Once more the wind had almost died away. At about 9 o'clock the *Océan* ran among the breakers, and the three other ships anchored under the Portuguese batteries. Boscawen thereupon sent the *Intrepid* and *America* to destroy the *Océan*, which, in taking the ground, had carried away all her masts. Captain Pratten had anchored ; and he failed to carry out the order ; but Captain Kirke, taking in the *America* very close, discharged a few guns into the enemy at point-blank range, and obliged her to strike. M. de La Clue, who had one leg broken and the other injured, and who eventually died of his wounds at Lagos, had been landed about half-an-hour previously. Captain Kirke took possession of the French flagship ; and having removed such officers and men as were found in her, he set her on fire, deeming it impossible to bring her off. The *Warspite* was ordered in against the *Téméraire*, 74, and succeeded in bringing her out very little damaged. Vice-Admiral Broderick's division went against the remaining two ships, and, after about half-an-hour's action, captured the *Modeste*, 64. The *Redoutable*, 74, having been abandoned, and being found to be bulged, was burnt. In this action the enemy's loss was very severe in killed and wounded. In the *Centaure* alone, about 200 were killed. The loss of the British, on the other hand, was very small, amounting only to 56 killed and 196 wounded.[1]

"The British," says Beatson, "as well as the French Admiral, was not quite well pleased with the behaviour of his captains, some of whom, he thought, did not make sail enough to get up with the van of the enemy's fleet, which the Admiral wished they should attack, in order to retard their flight until the rest of the squadron should be able to join in the action. Others, through mismanagement, he thought, had allowed their ships to fall to leeward, after they had engaged the enemy some time, and therefore could not properly get into action again. But great allowance ought to be made for this, for just as the British ships came up with the enemy's rear, the wind died away. They attacked the enemy on the lee side, in order that they might be able to open their lower ports, some of the ships carrying them very low. Another reason why some of the British ships fell so much to leeward was that the French Admiral, on perceiving Admiral Boscawen in the *Namur*, and some ships along with him, pressing forward to attack his van and centre, made his fleet luff up as much as they possibly could, so as to form a sort of crescent; by which position the whole of his ships in their van and centre were enabled by their fire, not only to assist the rear, but each other, in their endeavours to repel the attack, which they looked for every moment from the British Admiral. By this manœuvre of M. de La Clue's, such of our ships as first got up with the enemy's rear, and to leeward of their line, were thrown out of action; while, for want of sufficient breeze of wind, they could not get into it again. The *Portland*, having lost her foretopmast, dropped astern. The *Intrepid* was to windward of the *Namur*; she did not bear down close enough, but kept aloof, and fired at the enemy across the other ships." [2]

---

[1] Boscawen's Disp. *See* table p. 212, *antea.*   [2] 'Nav. and Mil. Mems.,' ii. 318.

Boscawen, who said of the battle, " It is well but it might have been a great deal better," presently rehoisted his flag in the *Namur*, and despatched Captain Matthew Buckle, in the *Gibraltar*, to England with dispatches. Buckle was graciously received by the King, and presented with £500 to buy a sword. The Admiral himself, as soon as his fleet had repaired damages, returned, in accordance with his instructions, to England, taking with him the *Namur, Warspite, Swiftsure, Intrepid, America* and *Portland*, the *Salamander* and *Ætna* fire-ships, and the prizes *Téméraire* and *Modeste*. These were afterwards followed by the *Edgar, Princess Louisa*, and the prize *Centaure*. Vice-Admiral Broderick, who remained in the Straits, blockaded Cadiz, in which still lay that part of the French squadron which had taken refuge there.

Boscawen's rewards were a membership of the Privy Council and a generalship in the Marines. Captains Bentley, of the *Warspite*, and Stanhope, of the *Swiftsure*, were knighted for their share in the action ; and the three prizes were purchased, and added to the Navy under their French names.

Broderick blockaded Cadiz very closely ; but, on November 9th, he was driven from his station by a storm, and was obliged to send his flagship to Gibraltar to refit, and to hoist his flag on board the *Conqueror*. The *Newark* and *Culloden* had to cut away all their masts, and run for port. Returning off Cadiz, Broderick continued the blockade as before ; but the enemy, though by that time superior in strength, declined to come out and offer him battle. The Vice-Admiral being a second time driven from his station by a storm, the French at length ventured forth, and were happy enough to get safely back to Toulon.

Rear-Admiral George Brydges Rodney was sent in the summer with a light squadron,[1] consisting of one ship of the line, four fifty-gun ships, five frigates, a sloop and six bomb ketches, to endeavour to destroy the flat-bottomed boats, and the supplies which had been

<hr>

[1] Squadron under Rear-Admiral Rodney in the Channel, 1759: *Achilles*, 60, Rear-Admiral George Brydges Rodney, Captain the Hon. Samuel Barrington; *Chatham*, 50, Captain John Lockhart; *Deptford*, 50, Captain John Hollwell; *Isis*, 50, Captain Edward Wheeler; *Norwich*, 50, Captain George Darby; *Brilliant*, 36, Captain Hyde Parker (1); *Juno*, 36, Captain Henry John Philips; *Vestal*, 32, Captain Samuel Hood (1); *Boreas*, 28, Captain Hon. Robert Boyle; *Unicorn*, 28, Captain Thomas Graves (2); *Wolf*, 16, Commander Hugh Bromedge; *Furnace*, bomb, Commander Jonathan Faulknor (1); *Firedrake*, bomb, Commander James Orrok; *Basilisk*, bomb, Commander John Clarke (1); *Mortar*, bomb, Commander Joseph Hunt; *Carcass*, bomb, Commander Charles Inglis (1); and *Blast*, bomb, Commander Thomas Willis.

collected at Le Hâvre for the projected invasion of England. Sailing from St. Helen's on July 2nd, 1759, he anchored on the 3rd in the Road of Le Hâvre, and stationed his bombs in the channel leading to Honfleur. These threw shells into the town, magazines, and boats for fifty consecutive hours, and did immense damage, without receiving any injury worth mentioning. Rodney, with some of his frigates, remained off the port for the rest of the year, and captured numerous prizes.

Admiral Sir Edward Hawke sailed in June, with a fleet of twenty-five sail of the line and many frigates, to blockade or, more strictly, to observe the enemy in Brest. He cruised some leagues at sea, leaving an inshore squadron of his lighter ships, under Captain the Hon. Augustus John Hervey, of the *Monmouth*, 64, close off the port. He also detached Commodore John Reynolds (1), in the *Firm*, 50, with a small squadron, to watch the French transports which had assembled in the river Morbihan in preparation for the invasion of Ireland. When at length the *Firm* became very foul and had to go home to refit, she was relieved by the *Rochester*, Commodore Robert Duff. In the course of the blockade the *Achilles*, 60, Captain the Hon. Samuel Barrington, also had to go home, having run on a rock when in pursuit of some French vessels. It may be mentioned that, during part of the summer, Prince Edward Augustus, afterwards Duke of York, again served as a midshipman, with Captain Lord Howe, in the *Magnanime*, 74.

Numerous brushes with the enemy relieved the tedium of the blockade. On one occasion the French sent out four ships of the line to attack the inshore squadron ; but Hervey, instead of retiring, went to meet them ; and, the fleet making as if to support him, the French withdrew. The intention had been that, if Hervey had drawn off and left the coast clear, the four ships of the line should have gained the mouth of the Morbihan, crushed Duff, and then escorted the French invasion of Ireland. Hervey and the inshore squadron continued very active, and greatly annoyed the enemy, until in October the *Monmouth*, which had become very leaky, had to return to England.

The approach of the season of bad weather seemed to afford the French better opportunities for putting into execution their scheme of invasion, it being impossible, in those days, for a blockading squadron, no matter how strong or how ably commanded, to always maintain its position during the autumn and winter. A violent gale of wind, in fact, forced Hawke from his station on November 9th, and obliged him to put into Torbay. This storm proved the salvation of M. de Bompart, who, with his squadron, was returning from the West Indies, and who must otherwise have been snapped up by the British fleet. Most of the men of his ships were turned over to the fleet under M. de Conflans, who learnt by the arrival of M. de Bompart that the British had been driven from off the port.

With the hope of being able to effect something against Commodore Duff, de Conflans put to sea on November 14th. Hawke on the same day got under way from Torbay, and on the 15th was informed by Captain William M'Cleverty, of the *Gibraltar* (the same who three months earlier had warned Boscawen of the approach of M. de La Clue), that the Brest fleet had sailed, and that it had been seen twenty-four leagues N.W. of Belle Isle, steering S.E. Hawke, with strategical intuition, made for Quiberon Bay with all possible sail, rightly judging that the French would take advantage of their brief liberty in order to make for that neighbourhood, so as to free the transports which were blockaded by Duff in the Morbihan. But he was unable to proceed with the speed he desired. Wind from the S. by E. and S. drove him considerably to the westward and delayed him. On the 19th, however, the wind became fair; and, on that day, Hawke ordered the frigates *Maidstone* and *Coventry* ahead of the fleet, one on the starboard and the other on the larboard bow. Early in the morning of the 20th he also ordered the *Magnanime* ahead to make the land.

The contrary wind which had baffled Hawke also retarded de Conflans, and was instrumental in saving Duff, who received his first news that the Brest fleet had put to sea by Captain Gamaliel Nightingale, of the *Vengeance*, on the morning of the 20th. Nightingale on entering the bay had fired guns to alarm the Commodore. Duff realised at once the danger that was upon him, and immediately made the signal for his ships to cut their cables. In a few minutes they were all under way. He attempted to take them out to sea round the north end of Belle Isle, but, the wind shifting, the *Belliqueux*, 64, Captain Thomas Saumarez, was the only one which escaped by that passage. She was not able to rejoin until three days after the battle. Duff then tried to escape by the south end of the island; and, in doing so, he was observed by de Conflans, who made the signal to chase. The *Chatham*, 50, which sailed very badly, was almost within gunshot of a French seventy-four, when a man

on the main-top-gallant yard of the *Rochester* hailed that he saw a
sail, and, presently, that he saw a fleet. The Commodore quickly
made out what the fleet was, and at once ordered his little squadron
to tack and chase the enemy. At first the French were puzzled by
this change of policy; but, as soon as de Conflans discovered the
cause, he recalled his chasers; and Duff's squadron was thus enabled
in the course of the day to join Sir Edward Hawke.

At about 8.30 A.M. the *Maidstone* signalled that she had sighted
a fleet; and at 9.45 the *Magnanime* announced that the strangers
were enemies. The French were at that time relinquishing the chase
of the Commodore's squadron, and Belle Isle bore E. by N. $\frac{1}{4}$ N.[1]

Hawke instantly made the signal for a line of battle abreast, in
order to draw up his ships; and he followed it soon afterwards with
the signal for the seven ships which were nearest the enemy to

[1] List of the British and French fleets in the action in Quiberon Bay, November
20th, 1759 :—

BRITISH.			FRENCH.		
Ships.	Guns.	Commanders.	Ships.	Guns.	Fate.
Royal George . .	100	Admiral Sir Edward Hawke, K.B. / Capt. John Campbell (1).	*Soleil Royal* . .	80 [2]	Beached and burnt by the French.
Union	90	Vice-Admiral Sir Charles Hardy (2). / Capt. John Evans.	*Tonnant*. . . .	80 [3]	To the Charente.
			Formidable . . .	80 [4]	Taken.
			Orient	80	To the Charente.
			Intrépide . . .	74	
Duke.	90	,, Thomas Graves (2).	*Glorieux* . . .	74	,, Vilaine.
Namur	90	,, Matthew Buckle (1).	*Thesée*	74	Foundered.
Mars	74	Commod. James Young (1).	*Héros*	74	Taken, wrecked, and burnt.
Warspite . . .	74	Capt. Sir John Bentley, Kt.			
Hercules. . . .	74	,, William Fortescue.	*Robuste*	74	To the Vilaine.
Torbay	74	,, Hon. Augustus Keppel.	*Magnifique* . . .	74	,, Charente.
			Juste	70	Wrecked.
Magnanime . .	74	,, Viscount Howe.	*Superbe*	70	Foundered.
Resolution [1]. . .	74	,, Henry Speke.	*Dauphin Royal* .	70	To the Charente.
Hero	74	,, Hon. George Edgcumbe.	*Dragon*	64	
			Northumberland .	64	
Swiftsure . . .	70	,, Sir Thomas Stanhope, Kt.	*Sphinx*	64	,, Vilaine.
			Solitaire . . .	64	
Dorsetshire . . .	70	,, Peter Denis.	*Brillant*. . . .	64	,, Charente.
Burford . . .	70	,, James Gambier (1).	*Éveillé*	64	,, Vilaine.
Chichester . . .	70	,, William Saltren Willett.	*Bizarre*	64	,, Charente.
Temple	70	,, Hon. Washington Shirley.	*Inflexible* . . .	64	,, Vilaine.
Revenge	64	,, John Storr.	*Vestale*	34	
Essex [1]	64	,, Lucius O'Brien.	*Aigrette*	36	,, Vilaine.
Kingston . . .	60	,, Thomas Shirley.	*Calypso*	16	
Intrepid. . . .	60	,, Jervis Maplesden.	*Prince Noir* . .	..	
Montagu . . .	60	,, Joshua Rowley.			
Dunkirk . . .	60	,, Hon. Robert Digby.			
Defiance . . .	60	,, Patrick Baird.			
Rochester . . .	50	,, Robert Duff.			
Portland . . .	50	,, Marriot Arbuthnot.			
Falkland . . .	50	,, Francis Samuel Drake.			
Chatham . . .	50	,, John Lockhart.			
Minerva . . .	32	,, Al-xand r Arthur Hood.			
Venus	36	,, Thomas Harrison (2).			
Vengeance . . .	28	,, Gamaliel Nightingale.			
Coventry . . .	28	,, Francis Burslem.			
Maidstone . . .	28	,, Dudley Digges.			
Sapphire . . .	32	,, John Strachan.			

[1] Wrecked.
[2] Flag of M. de Conflans, Vice-Admiral.
[3] Flag of the Prince de Bauffremont-Listenois, Chef d'Escadre.
[4] Flag of M. St. André du Verger, Chef d'Escadre.

chase, draw into line of battle ahead of him, and endeavour to arrest the French until the remainder of the fleet could get up and bring about a general engagement.

Upon realising that they were in the presence of the British, the enemy fell into some confusion, but, in the course of a short time, seemed to arrive at a determination to fight, and endeavoured to form a line. While they were executing this manœuvre, the British approached very rapidly, the wind being then nearly west. De Conflans then suddenly altered his mind, and, instead of waiting to engage, made off. He was near his own coasts, with the difficulties and dangers of which he was fully acquainted and presumably knew well how to avoid, while the British were on a lee shore, with which they were unfamiliar. The weather was tempestuous and was rapidly growing worse; and the November day would soon end. De Conflans therefore endeavoured to keep his fleet together, and steered right before the wind for the land, which was not more than about twelve miles distant.[1]

The wind, as the short afternoon drew to its close, was variable between N.W. and W.N.W., and blew in heavy squalls. Yet both fleets crowded sail, the French to escape, and the British to overtake them. At 2 P.M. the enemy began to fire at the leading ships of the British fleet; and, half-an-hour later, when the *Warspite* and *Dorsetshire* were close up with the enemy's rear, Hawke made the signal to engage. The British fleet was then to the south of Belle Isle. A little later the *Revenge*, *Magnanime*, *Torbay*, *Montagu*, *Resolution*, *Swiftsure* and *Defiance* got into action, and hotly engaged the French rear. Yet this fact did not prevent the French admiral, who was in the van, from leading round the Cardinals. The *Formidable*, carrying the flag of Rear-Admiral du Verger, was attacked by the *Resolution*, and, in addition, received a broadside or two from every other British ship that passed her; and, having been severely treated, she struck about 4 o'clock. The loss on board of her was terrible, M. du Verger and upwards of two hundred others being killed. The *Formidable* was taken possession of by the *Resolution*. In the meantime, the ships of the British rear were straining to get into action. The *Thesée*, Captain de Kersaint [2] was hotly engaged by the *Magnanime*,

---

[1] For Quiberon Bay and its neighbourhood, *see* chart facing p. 488, in Vol. II.

[2] Guy Simon de Caetnampreu, Comte de Kersaint; born, 1709; entered the navy as a seaman, 1722; lieutenant, 1742; captain, 1745. In *Renommée* captured *Prince*

but was relieved by the disablement of the British ship, which, being fouled by one of her consorts, fell astern. Very soon after-wards the *Thesée* was tackled by the *Torbay* ; and, in the contest which resulted, she capsized and foundered, chiefly owing to the fact that her captain, from motives of self-pride, persisted in fighting his lower deck guns, regardless of the stormy state of the weather. All her crew of about eight hundred men, except twenty, were lost. The *Torbay*, owing to similar causes, was at one time in danger of a like fate ; but Captain Keppel closed his ports in time, and saved her. Another French ship, the *Superbe*, foundered at about the same time.

Owing to the gale, the lee shore, and the gathering darkness, there was at that time great confusion ; and it is almost impossible to tell exactly what happened. But it would appear that after having engaged the *Thesée*, and having been fouled first by the *Warspite* and then by the *Montagu*, Lord Howe, in the *Magnanime*, observed the French *Héros* somewhat disabled to leeward, and, bearing down and ranging alongside, quickly obliged her to strike. The *Héros* anchored, but, owing to the weather, no boat could be sent to take possession of her ; and, later, her captain ran her ashore and landed his crew. As night fell, the enemy's fleet divided ; part, under M. de Beauffremont, the vice-admiral, making to the south-ward within the Four Bank, and probably designing to attract the British into danger.

But Hawke would not be tempted to pursue them. Night was come ; islands, rocks, and shoals were all around ; no pilots were on board ; the charts were indifferent, and the weather was terrible. Hawke, therefore, made the signal to anchor, and came to in fifteen fathoms of water, the Isle de Dumet bearing E. by N. two or three miles distant, the Cardinals W. $\frac{1}{2}$ S., and the steeples of Le Croisic S.E., as was discovered in the morning. Unfortunately, the signal was not taken in, and, consequently, was not obeyed, by many ships of the British fleet. According to the code then in use, the signal to anchor by night was made by firing two guns from the flagship,

---

of Orange. Commanded the *Alcide* in the East Indies. Some French accounts state that the *Thesée* was sunk at Quiberon owing to being run down by Hawke's flagship while de Kersaint was going to the assistance of the *Soleil Royal;* but these are clearly incorrect. The Count's son, who saw his father sink at Quiberon, was later a distinguished naval officer, but, meddling with politics, was guillotined in 1793. He was then a vice-admiral.

without using lights or any other indications to distinguish the particular purpose for which the guns were fired. At a moment when there was still a certain amount of firing going on on all sides, the discharge of two guns from the flagship could of course not be recognised as a signal except by the few vessels which chanced to be so near the Admiral as to be aware that he had anchored. The others either stood out to sea or anchored, as prudence suggested. Had the French only known the dangerous position in which the unsatisfactory nature of the signal book had left their enemy during that stormy night, they might, in the morning of the 21st, have attacked the small body remaining at anchor near Hawke, and perhaps have won a decided and complete victory by the mere strength of superior forces.

The night was dark, and even more boisterous than the evening had been ; but, though guns of distress were heard from all sides, it was not possible to send assistance to anyone. On the morning of the 21st the *Resolution* was seen to be ashore, and the French *Héros* was on the Four Bank. De Conflans's flagship, the *Soleil Royal*, in the obscurity overnight, had come to anchor in the very midst of the British ; and, when at daylight she perceived her situation, she slipped her cable and tried to get away, but presently went ashore near the town of Le Croisic. No sooner was she observed to be in motion than Hawke signalled the *Essex* to slip and pursue her ; but in the ardour of the chase the *Essex* unfortunately got on the Four Bank and was also wrecked. It was seen that, while the French vice-admiral had gone to the southward with part of the fleet, the remainder had stood to the N. and was engaged in the mouth of the river Vilaine in getting out guns, stores, etc., and endeavouring to find a haven up the river. On the 21st and 22nd, by taking advantage of the flood tide and of what wind there was under the land, all of them got into the river, whence several of them could never be brought out again. On the 22nd Hawke ordered the *Soleil Royal* and *Héros* to be set on fire. The French, however, anticipated him by themselves burning the former.

On the British side the number of men killed in the action did not exceed fifty, and only about two hundred and fifty were wounded.[1]

As soon as it became known in England that the French had sailed from Brest, the excitement was great, and every effort was

[1] Hawke's Disp. of November 24th.

made to meet the situation. Rear-Admiral Geary was detached with a reinforcement of ships[1] for Hawke; and other vessels capable of putting to sea were ordered to be in readiness at a moment's notice. Vice-Admiral Charles Saunders, returning from the conquest of Quebec, learnt in the chops of the Channel that the French were out and that Hawke had gone in chase of them. Though he had with him but three ships of the line,[2] he realised so fully that no addition of forces was to be despised, and he had so strong a sense of his duty, that, on his own responsibility, he steered for Quiberon Bay with all the sail he could set. But neither Geary nor Saunders joined Hawke ere the battle. Geary arrived several days too late,

COMMEMORATIVE MEDAL OF HAWKE'S VICTORY IN QUIBERON BAY, 1759.

(From an original kindly lent by H.S.H. Captain Prince Louis of Battenberg, R.N.)

and Saunders, hearing of the issue of the action,[3] altered his course and steered again for England.

Hawke sent home his dispatches by Captain John Campbell (1), who, as Captain Matthew Buckle had been, was graciously received by the King, and presented with £500 to purchase a sword. Hawke himself received the thanks of the House of Commons and a pension of £2000 a year. Nor were other officers who had distinguished themselves during the campaign forgotten. Boscawen, as has already been mentioned, was made General of Marines; Vice-

---

[1] *Sandwich*, 90, Rear-Admiral Francis Geary, Captain Richard Norbury; *Foudroyant*, 84, Captain Richard Tyrrell; *Bienfaisant*, 64, Captain George Balfour; *America*, 60, Captain James Kirke; *Anson*, 60, Captain Matthew Whitwell; *Firm*, 60, Captain John Reynolds (1); and *Juno*, 32, Captain Henry John Philips.

[2] *Somerset*, 64, Vice-Admiral Charles Saunders, Captain Edward Hughes; *Vanguard*, 70, Captain Robert Swanton; and *Devonshire*, 66, Captain William Gordon.

[3] Mahan calls this action "the Trafalgar" of the Seven Years' War. Guérin exclaims: "C'était La Hougue, moins la gloire et l'honneur français sauvés."

Admiral Saunders was made Lieut.-General of Marines, and Captains Sir Piercy Brett (1), Kt., the Hon. Augustus Keppel, and Lord Howe, were made Colonels of Marines.

On the 26th Hawke sent Commodore James Young (1), with a squadron, to anchor in Quiberon Bay, and on the 27th detached Captain the Hon. Augustus Keppel, with a squadron, to Basque Road, to attack such of the enemy as might be found there. But before the latter reached his destination, M. de Beauffremont had lightened his ships and retired up the river Charente, whither the British vessels were unable to follow him. Neither in the Charente nor in the Vilaine could the fugitive ships be reached. Time, however, effected what force could not; for few of the vessels were ever again fit for active service. Hawke was relieved by Boscawen, and returned to England after an absence of ten months.

During the blockade it was notorious that no fleet employed on similar service had ever before been so amply supplied with beer, provisions, and vegetables; but, after the defeat of de Conflans, in consequence chiefly of the adverse state of the weather, supplies failed, and the men were obliged to be put upon short allowance. This gave rise to the well-known satirical lines:—

> " Ere Hawke did bang
> Monsieur Conflans,
> You sent us beef and beer.
> Now Monsieur's beat,
> We've naught to eat,
> Since you have nought to fear."

The small French expedition which had been assembled at Dunquerque for a descent upon Scotland or Ireland, and which was to be convoyed by Thurot, was blockaded throughout the summer and early autumn of 1759 by a squadron [1] under Commodore William Boys, who, however, was driven from his station by a gale in October. Thurot then slipped out and made to the northward, Boys following as soon as possible, but not being able to overtake the enemy, and ultimately having to content himself with cruising

---

[1] Squadron under Commodore William Boys, engaged in the blockade of Dunquerque, etc., 1759: *Preston*, 50, Commodore William Boys, Captain John Evans; *Antelope*, 50, Captain James Webb; *Phœnix*, 44, Captain Christopher Codrington Bethell; *Danae*, 40, Captain Henry Martin (2); *Liverpool*, 32, Captain Richard Knight; *Stag*, 32, Captain Henry Angell; *Argo*, 28, Captain John Bladon Tinker; *Tweed*, 28, Captain William Paston; *Hussar*, 28, Captain Robert Carkett; *Surprise*, 24, Captain Charles Antrobus; *Badger*, 14, Commander Basil Keith; *Alderney*, 12, Commander John Peighin.

off the coast of Scotland with the object of preventing any sudden raid there. As Thurot's destination was unknown, and as there were rumours that he contemplated a blow on some port on the east coast of England, the squadron in the Downs,[1] under Commodore Sir Piercy Brett (1), was ordered to Yarmouth. But Thurot's operations in the British seas did not begin till the following year, and an account of them may for the present be deferred.

During the year 1760 the British squadrons on active service were disposed as follows. Commodore Sir Piercy Brett commanded in the Downs and North Sea; Rear-Admiral George Brydges Rodney cruised in the Channel and blockaded Le Hâvre; Admirals Sir Edward Hawke and the Hon. Edward Boscawen relieved one another in Quiberon Bay, and watched the French vessels in the Vilaine and Charente, at Brest, Lorient, and Rochfort; Commodore Robert Swanton was despatched with reinforcements to Commodore Lord Colville in North America; Captain the Hon. John Byron was sent with a squadron to destroy the fortifications at Louisbourg; Commodore Sir James Douglas (1) relieved Commodore John Moore (1) on the Leeward Islands' station; Rear-Admiral Charles Holmes relieved Vice-Admiral Thomas Cotes at Jamaica; and five additional ships were sent to the East Indies to reinforce Rear-Admirals Charles Stevens and Samuel Cornish. In the Mediterranean Vice-Admiral Charles Saunders succeeded to the command.

In the East Indies, Arcot and Carical, with many other places, were taken from the French, the Marines serving in several instances on shore, and the ships co-operating with the land forces whenever possible. Pondicherry was besieged and blockaded, and in October the boats of the fleet, under Commander William Newsom, acting captain of the *Southsea Castle*, 40, and Lieutenant Isaac Florimond Ourry, brilliantly cut out from under the forts the *Hermione*, 36, and *Baleine*, 32, which were afterwards purchased into the Royal Navy. The rainy season approaching, Rear-Admiral Stevens left five ships of the line, under Captain Robert Haldane, of the *America*, 60, to continue the blockade, and himself sailed on October 23rd for Trincomale. In the mean-

---

[1] Squadron under Commodore Sir Piercy Brett (1), Kt., in the Downs and North Sea, 1759: *Isis*, 50, Commodore Sir Piercy Brett, Kt., Captain Edward Wheeler; *Woolwich*, 40, Captain Daniel Dering; *Aurora*, 36, Captain Samuel Scott; *Alarm*, 32, Captain John Rushworth; *Aquilon*, 28, Captain Chaloner Ogle (2); *Tartar*, 28, Captain John Knight (1); *Solebay*, 24, Captain John Dalrymple; and *Deal Castle*, 24, Captain George Tindall.

time the siege was actively carried on by Lieut.-Colonel Eyre Coote.

On December 25th, Stevens returned with four of his ships of the line, and resumed command off the port. On January 1st, 1761, a violent hurricane burst upon the shipping. Stevens, whose flag was in the *Norfolk*, 74, Captain Richard Kempenfelt, cut his cable, and by gun-signals ordered his captains to do the same; but, owing to the violence of the gale and the amount of spray in the air, the signals were neither heard nor seen. The *Panther*, 60, Captain Philip Affleck, the *America*, 60, Captain Robert Haldane, the *Medway*, 60, Captain John Bladon Tinker, and the *Falmouth*, 50, Captain William Brereton, were dismasted, yet managed to ride out the storm. A worse fate overtook the *Newcastle*, 50, Captain Digby Dent (3), the *Queenborough*, 20, and the *Protector*, fireship, all of which drove ashore and were wrecked about two miles from Pondicherry, though they lost only seven of their crews. Other vessels were even more unfortunate. The *Duc d'Aquitaine*, 64, Captain Sir William Hewitt, Bart., the *Sunderland*, 60, Captain the Hon. James Colville, and the *Drake*, storeship, foundered with all hands, except seven Europeans and seven lascars. The total sacrifice of life was about eleven hundred souls. Stevens, however, resumed his position, and renewed the blockade on January 3rd, and was next day joined by Rear-Admiral Cornish with additional ships from Trincomale. Pondicherry was gradually reduced by famine, until on January 15th it surrendered, and was occupied on the 16th by the Navy and army. Thus ended the French power on the coast of Coromandel.

On the Leeward Islands' and Jamaica stations the enemy was in force too feeble to attempt anything of moment. Indeed, only one action that was fought in the West Indies in 1760 calls for mention here. In the autumn Rear-Admiral Holmes learnt that a French convoy, escorted by five frigates, was about to sail from Cape François for Europe and he despatched the *Hampshire*, 50, Captain Coningsby Norbury (2), the *Boreas*, 28, Captain Samuel Uvedale, and the *Lively*, 20, Captain the Hon. Frederick Lewis Maitland (1), to intercept them. On October 16th the French put to sea, the escort consisting of the vessels mentioned in the note.[1] Next morning at dawn the British ships sighted and

[1] *Sirène*, 32; *Duc de Choiseul*, 32; *Prince Edward*, 32; *Fleur de Lys*, 32; and *Valeur*, 20.

chased them, but closed very slowly until evening, when the breeze freshened. At midnight the *Boreas* engaged the *Sirène*, but, being disabled aloft, fell astern, and could not come up with her again till 2 P.M. on October 18th, off the east end of Cuba. A hot action then began, and at 4.40 P.M. the *Sirène* struck, having lost 80 killed and wounded. The *Boreas* had lost but one killed and one wounded. In the meanwhile the *Hampshire* and *Lively* had been in chase of the other frigates. Soon after daybreak on the 18th, the *Lively*, by using her sweeps, got alongside of the *Valeur*, and, after an hour and a half, forced her to surrender, she having lost 38 killed and 25 wounded, and the *Lively* but two wounded. Both the *Sirène* and *Valeur* were added to the Navy under their own names. The *Hampshire* at 3.30 P.M. got between the *Duc de Choiseul* and the *Prince Edward*, but the former, having the advantage of the wind, got into Port au Paix. The latter ran ashore and struck, but was, nevertheless, subsequently burnt by her crew. On the 19th the *Hampshire* and *Lively* were about to attack the *Fleur de Lys*, which lay in the bay to leeward of Port au Paix, when the enemy saved them the trouble by abandoning and burning the ship.

The conquest of Canada had not been completed when Quebec fell, and the French still cherished hopes of ousting the British and of regaining command of the country. On the other hand, the British were determined to make good their possession. In the winter of 1759–60, a naval force consisting·of the *Onondaga*, 18, *Mohawk*, 16, and several row-galleys and gunboats, was established on Lake Ontario, with a view to transporting an army down the St. Lawrence to Montreal. This army, of about 11,000 men under General Amherst, consisted half of regulars and half of provincial levies, besides Indians, commanded by Sir William Johnson, Bart. It was to be aided by another, of 5000 men, under Colonel Haviland, advancing from Lake Champlain, and by a third, ·under Brigadier-General Murray, advancing from Quebec up the St. Lawrence.

To help these various expeditions, Commodore Lord Colville [1]

---

[1] *Northumberland*, 70, Commodore Lord Colville, Captain William Adams (2); *Alcide*, 64, Captain Thomas Hankerson; *Trident*, 64, Captain Julian Legge; *Pembroke*, 60, Captain John Wheelock; *Prince of Orange*, 60, Captain Samuel Wallis; *Richmond*, 32, Captain John Elphinstone (1); *Eurus*, 20, Captain Nathaniel Bateman; *Porcupine*, 16, Commander John Macartney; and *Racehorse*, bomb, which was already at Quebec. The above wintered in America, and were joined at various times by the *Devonshire*, 66, Captain George Darby; *Norwich*, 50, Captain William M'Cleverty; *Greyhound*, 24, Captain Thomas Francis; and *Lizard*, 28, Captain James Doake.

was directed to enter the St. Lawrence as soon as the season should
allow ; and a reinforcement [1] under Commodore Swanton, consisting
of two sail of the line, three fifty-gun ships, and four frigates, sailed
from England early in the spring.

Knowing of some, at least, of these preparations, the French
made gallant attempts to seize Quebec before the river should be clear
of ice. They sent down the St. Lawrence an army of about 14,000
men under M. de Lévis. General Murray, underrating the force
of the enemy, marched out and attacked him, but was defeated at
Sillery on April 28th. If the French had at once followed up
their advantage, they could probably have taken the place, but
they let slip their chance. Murray was very active in the defence,
and sent the *Racehorse* down the river to look for the fleet and
hasten its arrival. On May 9th the *Lowestoft*, 28, Captain Joseph
Deane, anchored in the Basin, and brought news of the near
approach of Commodore Swanton, who, on the evening of the
15th, arrived in the *Vanguard*, 70, with the *Diana*, 36, Captain
Alexander Schomberg. On the 16th, in response to the expressed
wishes of General Murray, the *Vanguard*, *Diana* and *Lowestoft*
worked up towards the enemy's flotilla in the upper river, and soon
obliged it to retire with the loss of the *Pomone*, 36, which grounded
and was burnt near Cape Diamond, the *Atalante*, 32, which grounded
and was burnt thirty miles higher up, and all the other craft except
a sloop. The active part of this work was done exclusively by the
Diana and *Lowestoft*, while the *Vanguard*, dropping down abreast
of Sillery, enfiladed the enemy's trenches there, and compelled their
abandonment. Indeed, this attack induced M. de Lévis to raise
the siege on the night of the 16th, leaving behind him 44 guns,
10 mortars, and various stores. Unfortunately, the *Lowestoft*,
in returning, struck on a sunken rock and foundered, but without
loss of life. Lord Colville, with his squadron, reached Quebec on
the 18th.

All was then in readiness for the projected advance against
Montreal. General Murray's army was escorted up the river by
the *Penzance*, 40, Captain William Gough, the *Diana*, 32, Captain
Joseph Deane, the *Porcupine*, 16, Commander John Macartney,

---

[1] *Vanguard*, 70, Commodore Robert Swanton; *Kingston*, 60, Captain William
Parry (2); *Rochester*, 50, Captain Thomas Burnett; *Falkland*, 50, Captain Francis
Samuel Drake; *Sutherland*, 50, Captain Benjamin Clive; *Penzance*, 44, Captain William
Gough; *Diana*, 36, Captain Alexander Schomberg; *Vengeance*, 28, Captain Gamaliel
Nightingale; and *Lowestoft*, 28, Captain Joseph Deane.

the *Gaspée*, schooner, 8, and a flotilla of thirty-five small craft, it having embarked in forty transports on June 13th.   Progress was on several occasions challenged by French batteries ; but the various difficulties were slowly overcome.   Behind the main force followed some troops from Louisbourg under Lord Rollo.   In the interval, General Amherst was advancing down the St. Lawrence under the conduct of Captain Joshua Loring, R.N.[1]   In the course of the advance the *Onondaga* was taken by the enemy, and, though retaken, had to be abandoned.   Many boats and some small craft were also lost by the way, owing to the great difficulties of navigation.   On September 6th, however, the Commander-in-Chief's army landed on the upper end of the Island of Montreal, nine miles above the city.   The enemy fled, and Montreal was quickly invested.

As for Colonel Haviland's force, it embarked at Crown Point on August 11th, and, gradually driving the enemy before it, made its way, partly by water and partly by land, to Isle Ste. Thérèse near Montreal, appearing there within a few hours of the arrival of Amherst and Murray in the same neighbourhood.   The co-operation could not have been more exactly timed.

On September 7th a cessation of hostilities was agreed to ; and on September 8th M. de Vaudreuil capitulated and Canada became British.   The final conquest had been prefaced by the capture or destruction by Lord Colville of a large number of French privateers on the St. Lawrence, and by the destruction by Commodore the Hon. John Byron in Chaleur Bay, on July 8th, of the *Machault*, 32, *Bienfaisant*, 22, *Marquis de Marloze*, 16, and several French small craft which had taken refuge there in expectation of chance offering them some opportunity for slipping up the river.

Captain Joseph Deane, R.N., and Major Barré carried home the dispatches announcing the great success.   Each was presented with £500 wherewith to buy a sword.   Byron, who had proceeded on his own responsibility to Chaleur Bay on the service above noted, and who had interrupted for the purpose the business of razing to the ground the fortifications of Louisbourg, subsequently returned and completed that work.

In the Mediterranean, whither Vice-Admiral Charles Saunders

---

[1] Joshua Loring came of a family which had been for some time settled in North America.   Lieutenant, 1745 ; Commander, 1756 ; Captain, 1757 ; chief director of the Naval Department in the Interior, and Commander-in-Chief of the Lake Flotilla, 1759–1762 ; died, 1781.

went as Commander-in-Chief in April, 1760, little of importance happened, owing to the overwhelming superiority of the British naval forces. A French division slipped out of Toulon in June; but the greater part of it was driven by a squadron, under Captain Hugh Palliser, of the *Shrewsbury*, 74, into a port in the island of Candia, and was blockaded there until the British vessels had to withdraw for supplies and repairs, whereupon the enemy got back to Toulon.

The fortunes of M. Thurot must now be followed. Evading Commodore Boys, he left Dunquerque on October 15th, 1759. In his little squadron of six frigates and corvettes, he had thirteen hundred troops under Brigadier-General de Flobert.[1] He first went to Gothenburg in Sweden, partly to procure stores, and partly, no doubt, to baffle pursuit or observation. There he remained for nineteen days, going next to Bergen in Norway. On his way thither, one of his ships, the *Bégon*, was so damaged in a gale as to be obliged to return to France. The *Faucon* also parted company early in the voyage. Thurot quitted Bergen on December 5th, and proceeded, by way of Strömö, in the Faröe Islands, reaching the neighbourhood of the Irish coast on January 25th, 1760. The weather confounded an intended descent near Londonderry, and scattered his squadron, so much so that the *Amaranthe*[2] never rejoined, and returned in some distress to St. Malo. As the ships were by that time all in a sorry plight, and more than one of them was almost mutinous, the captains implored Thurot to abandon the descent. But he refused, and put into Claigeann Bay, in the island of Islay, on February 15th, to refresh.

Thurot left the island on February 19th, and next day anchored in Belfast Lough, opposite Kilroot Point. The town of Carrick-fergus was garrisoned by four newly-raised and weakly companies of the 62nd Regiment under Lieut.-Colonel Jennings. Thurot landed about six hundred men on February 21st, and M. de Flobert, after comparatively little fighting, obliged Colonel Jennings to surrender the castle. The French requisitioned provisions from

---

[1] De Flobert, from the first, threw difficulties in Thurot's way, regarding him with contempt and jealousy. Thurot, as a seaman, probably had no high opinion of the soldier; for, as Laughton points out ('Studs. in Nav. Hist.,' 346), even until quite recent times there was a saying on board ship, "a messmate before a shipmate; a shipmate before a stranger; a stranger before a dog; but—a dog before a soldier."

[2] It is tolerably certain, nevertheless, that the *Amaranthe* could have rejoined, had her captain desired to do so.

the town, and made several small prizes in the Lough, rifling
and afterwards burning them; but de Flobert resisted Thurot's
entreaties to advance and seize Belfast. The whole adventure
cost the French about thirty killed and sixty wounded. The mayor
and some gentlemen were carried on board as hostages, and at
midnight on February 27th, the enemy, having re-embarked, set
sail to return to France.

The Duke of Bedford, Lord Lieutenant of Ireland, upon getting
news of the descent, sent expresses to all the principal ports to
inform the captains of any of H. M. ships that might be there of
what had happened. At Kingsale one of these expresses found
the frigates *Æolus*, *Pallas*, and *Brilliant*,[1] which had been driven
from their station with Hawke's fleet on the coast of France.
These at once put to sea and went north. At Dublin, on the 26th,
the senior officer, Captain John Elliot, learnt that the enemy was
still at Carrickfergus. That same evening, he found himself off the
mouth of Belfast Lough, but, the wind being contrary, he could
not get in. On the 28th, at 4 A.M., he caught sight of the French
as they rounded Copeland Island, and gave chase. "About nine,"
continues Captain Elliot, in his dispatch of February 29th to the
Duke of Bedford, "I got alongside their commodore; and, in a
few minutes, the action became general, and continued very briskly
for an hour and a half, when they all three struck their colours."
The *Maréchal de Belleisle* alone fought well; the *Blonde* and
Terpsichore struck almost as soon as they were engaged. Elliot,
with the prizes, subsequently put into Ramsay, Isle of Man, to
refit. All the vessels were greatly disabled aloft, and the *Maréchal
de Belleisle*, which had suffered most of all, was with difficulty
prevented from sinking.

[1] Squadron which, under M. Thurot, escaped from Dunquerque in 1759; and
squadron which, under Captain John Elliot, met and captured part of it on
February 28th, 1760:—

FRENCH.		BRITISH.				
Ships.	Guns.	Ships.	Guns.	Commanders.	Losses.	
					Killed.	Wounded.
Maréchal de Belleisle . .	44	*Æolus*	32	Capt. John Elliot.	4	15
Blonde	36	*Pallas*	36	,, Michael Clements.	1	5
Terpsichore	24	*Brilliant* . . .	36	,, James Loggie.	0	11
Bégon [1].	36					
Amaranthe [1]	18					
Faucon [1]	18					

[1] Had parted company before the action.

The gallant Thurot,[1] who fell on this occasion, was an opponent who, in his method of carrying on the war, had never shut his eyes to the principles of honour, generosity, and humanity, and who was scarcely less lamented by his British foes than by his own countrymen. The three victorious captains were unanimously voted the thanks of the Irish House of Commons, and the *Blonde* and *Terpsichore* were purchased into the Royal Navy.

Admiral Boscawen, after the return of Sir Edward Hawke, sailed to command the fleet in Quiberon Bay, with his flag in the *Royal William*, and with Rear-Admiral Francis Geary, in the *Sandwich*, as second in command. While he was going to his station, the *Ramillies*, 90, Captain Wittewronge Taylor, of his squadron, went ashore on Bolt Head in a gale and was lost, the crew all perishing except one midshipman and twenty-five men. Boscawen, who was obliged by the heavy weather to return, subsequently shifted his flag to the *Namur*, and proceeded. His cruisers took several prizes; but the enemy's fleet did not—indeed, could not—come out. The blockade prevented the French from sending supplies across the Atlantic, and from interfering with British trade. In August, Sir Edward Hawke, in the *Royal George*, relieved Boscawen, who returned to England on September 1st. This was Boscawen's last service. He died at his house, Hatchlands, near Guildford, on January 10th, 1761.[2] Hawke pursued his predecessor's policy, and was equally successful. Rear-Admiral Rodney, cruising off Le Hâvre, was not less energetic.

An expedition, to be commanded by Commodore the Hon. Augustus Keppel, and to be directed either against Mauritius and Bourbon or against the coast of France, was in preparation when, on October 27th, George II. died. This important event led to so much delay, that on December 13th orders were given for the fleet to return from St. Helen's, where it lay ready for sea, to Spithead, and for the troops on board to be disembarked. For that season the enterprise was given up.

---

[1] François Thurot, born at Nuits, 1726. Son of a small innkeeper; educated by the Jesuits at Dijon; apprenticed to a druggist; surgeon in a privateer, 1744; captured by the British; escaped; devoted himself to privateering; lived for some time in London; given a commission in the French navy; commanded the *Friponne*, and, from 1757, the *Maréchal de Belleisle*. His actions with the *Southampton*, the *Seahorse*, etc., will be found noticed in the next chapter. He was one of the boldest of the French corsairs.

[2] Boscawen was, however, buried in the church of St. Michael, Penkevel, Cornwall, where there is a monument by Rijsbraak to his memory.

By 1760 the enemy's navy had been so nearly annihilated that
but two or three of His Majesty's ships were taken by the French;
and French trade had been so diminished that the British cruisers
made but comparatively few captures—only one hundred and ten
vessels in all. But the British mercantile losses by the ravages
of small privateers were enormous. As many as three hundred
and thirty trading vessels were taken. Few of them, however,
were of any considerable size; and, in spite of the loss, British
trade flourished exceedingly. It was, no doubt, chiefly owing to its
healthy condition that the commercial marine experienced so many
losses.

In 1761 Vice-Admiral Francis Holburne commanded at Ports-
mouth; Commodore Sir Piercy Brett (1) in the Downs; Commodore
Robert Swanton in the Channel; Sir Edward Hawke and Sir
Charles Hardy (2) in Quiberon Bay till March, when Commodore
Keppel took charge of the squadron in the Bay of Biscay; Vice-
Admiral Charles Saunders in the Mediterranean; Commodore Lord
Colville in North America; Rear-Admiral Charles Holmes at
Jamaica; Commodore Sir James Douglas (1), and, at the end of the
year, Rear-Admiral Rodney, on the Leeward Islands' station; and
Rear-Admiral Stevens in the East Indies, until his death, when
the command devolved on Rear-Admiral Cornish.

After the capture of Pondicherry, Mahé was reduced by the
troops under Major Hector Munro, supported by four sail of the
line under Rear-Admiral Cornish. The place surrendered on
February 10th. In May Rear-Admiral Charles Stevens fell a
victim to the unhealthiness of the climate. The French on the
station were by that time practically helpless, and Cornish soon
afterwards went to Bombay to refit. He then proceeded southward
to meet an expedition which he had reason to believe was on its
way out, under Commodore Keppel, to attack Bourbon and
Mauritius; but all idea of this expedition had, in the meantime,
been abandoned. The means taken, however, to apprise Cornish
of the change of plans were not efficacious; and the Rear-Admiral
was actually obliged, by scarcity of supplies, to go back to
Madras without hearing any news from home. Two of his ships,
however, the *York*, 60, Captain Henry Cowell, and the *Chatham*, 54,
Captain Thomas Lynn, being unable to keep with the fleet, had
to bear up for the Cape of Good Hope. There they learned from
the *Terpsichore*, 26, Captain Sir Thomas Adams, Bart., that Keppel

was no longer to be expected; and in due course they carried the intelligence to the Rear-Admiral in India.

On the Leeward Islands' station, Commodore Sir James Douglas (1), who was reinforced by four sail of the line and three frigates,[1] with troops from North America under Lord Rollo, attacked, and, on June 8th, captured, the Island of Dominica. During the rest of the summer, operations were chiefly confined to the protection of trade, and the repression of privateering. Towards the end of the year, it having been determined to prosecute a more active and offensive policy, and to largely increase the force among the West India Islands, Rear-Admiral Rodney was appointed to the command; and on November 22nd he arrived at Carlisle Bay, Barbados, where he was presently joined by the *Téméraire* and *Actæon*, with troops from Belle Isle, and by a military force from North America under Major-General Monckton.

On the Jamaica station there were several single-ship encounters, but no occurrences of first-rate importance. Rear-Admiral Charles Holmes, dying on November 21st, was succeeded in the command by the senior officer, Captain Arthur Forrest, of the *Centaur*, pending the arrival of Sir James Douglas. In North America, likewise, little of moment happened, the chief business of the fleet being to convoy troops to the West Indies. Nor were there any transactions on a large scale in the Mediterranean, although the force there was, towards the end of the year, greatly strengthened by the arrival of a detachment from home under Sir Piercy Brett (1). The French scarcely ventured to put to sea; and, when any of their ships did issue from port, they were almost invariably captured.

Admiral Sir Edward Hawke and Vice-Admiral Sir Charles Hardy (2) remained in the Bay of Biscay, watching the French ships in the Vilaine and Charente; and, to better effect their purpose, stationed an inshore squadron, under Captain James Gambier (1), quite close to the mouth of the Vilaine. Yet, in spite of this precaution, on January 2nd, the night being dark and the breeze fresh, several of the French vessels slipped out thence, and, though chased by Gambier, escaped into Brest. After this evasion, the

---

[1] *Stirling Castle*, 64, Captain Michael Everitt; *Norwich*, 50, Captain William M'Cleverty; *Falkland*, 50, Captain Francis Samuel Drake; *Sutherland*, 50, Captain Julian Legge; *Penzance*, 44, Captain John Boyd (acting); *Repulse*, 32, Captain John Carter Allen; and *Lizard*, 28, Captain James Doake.

blockading force was needlessly large for the work remaining to be done, and in March Hawke returned to England, leaving behind him enough ships to observe the enemy's motions.

The expedition, which had been prepared during the previous year, and had been destined at one time for Bourbon and Mauritius, and later for the coast of France, was again brought forward in 1761, Commodore Hon. Augustus Keppel being appointed to command the sea, and Major-General Studholm Hodgson [1] the land forces. The squadron at first included ten sail of the line, eight frigates, three sloops, three bombs, and two fireships, but was eventually reinforced with five more sail of the line. [2] The army originally consisted of about seven thousand men, [3] but about three thousand more were subsequently sent to the scene of operations.

The expedition [4] sailed from St. Helen's on March 29th, and sighted Belle Isle, [5] which it was designed to attack, on April 6th. That evening Keppel detached six frigates to cruise between the island and the mainland, in order to sever communications. A squadron under Captain Matthew Buckle (1), consisting of thirteen

[1] Later a field-marshal.

[2] British squadron employed under Commodore the Hon. Augustus Keppel in the expedition against Belle Isle, 1761 :—

꜓ Ships.	Guns.	Commanders.	Ships.	Guns.	Commanders.
Valiant	74	{Commod. Hon. Augustus Keppel. {Capt. Adam Duncan.	*Monmouth* [1] . .	64	Capt. John Storr.
			Lynn	44	,, Walter Stirling.
Sandwich . . .	90	,, Richard Norbury.	*Launceston* . . .	44	,, Edmund Affleck.
Dragon	74	{ ,, Hon. Aug. John Hervey.	*Southampton* . .	36	,, Charles Antrobus.
			Mélampe	36	{ ,, William Hotham (1).
Téméraire . . .	74	,, Matthew Barton.	*Adventure* . . .	32	,, Matthew Moore.
Torbay	74	,, William Brett.	*Actæon*	28	,, Paul Henry Ourry.
Swiftsure . . .	70	{ ,, Sir Thomas Stanhope, Kt.	*Flamborough* . .	24	,, Samuel Thompson.
			Aldborough . .	24	,, Mitchell Graham.
Hampton Court .	64	,, Carr Scrope.	*Escort*	14	Com. Charles Ellys.
Essex	64	{ ,, Alexander Schomberg.	*Fly*	10	,, George Gayton.
			Druid	8	{ ,, Hon. John Luttrell.
Prince of Orange .	60	,, Samuel Wallis.			
Achilles	60	{ ,, Hon. Samuel Barrington.	*Firedrake*, b. . .	8	,, James Orrok.
			Infernal, b. . .	8	,, James Mackenzie.
Hero [1]	74	,, William Fortescue.	*Furnace*, b. . .	8	,, James Chaplen.
Buckingham [1] . .	70	,, Peter Parker (1).	*Vesuvius*, f.s. . .	16	,, James Chads.
Burford [1] . . .	70	,, James Gambier (1).	*Ætna*, f.s. . . .	16	{ ,, Michael Henry Pascal.
Chichester [1] . . .	70	{ ,, William Saltren Willett.			

[1] Followed the fleet as reinforcements.

[3] Its nominal force was 9000, but the regiments were incomplete. Hodgson to Albemarle, March 28th, 1761.

[4] For Keppel's secret instructions, see 'Life,' by Hon. and Rev. T. Keppel, i. 302. That biography, however, appears to contain numerous errors.

[5] For Belle Isle and neighbourhood, see chart facing p. 488 of Vol. II.

sail of the line and three frigates,[1] was presently sent to cruise off Brest to prevent the possibility of interference from that quarter. Early on April 7th the fleet passed the south end of the island close in, so as to enable the Commodore and General to reconnoitre, and at noon it anchored in the Road of Palais. The Commodore and General then reconnoitred more closely in a cutter, having first ordered the boats to be hoisted out, and the troops to be made ready to land. They found no place more suitable for a disembarkation than a bay near Point de Locmaria, which they had remarked in the morning. To distract the enemy, a feint of landing was made near Sauzon by a detachment under Captain Sir Thomas Stanhope; and, on the morning of the 8th, the wind being north-east, the real landing in force was made near Port Andro, after the *Prince of Orange, Dragon,* and *Achilles,* with two bombs, had silenced a four-gun battery at the entrance of the bay. Commodore Keppel gave the signal for the disembarkation from the *Prince of Orange,* to which he had shifted his broad pennant from the *Valiant.* The boats were led by Captain Matthew Barton, and, although the enemy offered a most vigorous resistance, the landing was effected at three different places. But the troops found it impossible to hold their ground or to mount the well-defended slopes in front of them, and, after a hot contest, had to retreat with very considerable loss. The retiring boats were covered by the fire from the ships.

Bad weather for several days prevented any renewal of the attempt; but on the 22nd, while two feints were made elsewhere, a new landing was prepared under Major-General John Craufurd at Fort d'Arsic, under cover of the *Sandwich, Dragon, Prince of Orange,* two bombs, and two armed transports; Captain Barton, as before, leading in the boats. The feints were ordered to be made by Brigadier-General Hamilton Lambart, one near St. Foy and the other at Sauzon. Lambart was directed, if he saw any probability of success, to actually land, and to endeavour to hold

---

[1] *Namur,* 90, Captain Matthew Buckle (1); *Union,* 90, Captain Thomas Evans; *Royal William,* 84, Captain Hugh Pigot (1); *Princess Amelia,* 80, Captain John Montagu; *Hero,* 74, Captain William Fortescue; *Fame,* 74, Captain the Hon. John Byron; *Cornwall,* 74, Captain Robert Man (2); *Mars,* 74, Captain Richard Spry; *Bedford,* 64, Captain Joseph Deane; *Prince Frederick,* 64, Captain Jervis Maplesden; *Lion,* 60, Captain Edward Le Cras; *Ripon,* 60, Captain Edward Jekyll; *Unicorn,* 28, Captain Charles Douglas; *Tweed,* 28, Captain William Paston; *Aquilon,* 28, Captain Chaloner Ogle (2).

his own.   This, in fact, he did under cover of the *Swiftsure*, *Hampton Court*, *Essex*, and *Lynn*, and with the assistance of Marines under Lieut.-Colonel Mackenzie and Captain Murray.   As he effected his object before the intended landing at d'Arsic had begun, the division intended to attack that place rowed promptly to Lambart's support, and enabled him to maintain his position and to drive back the enemy.   All the troops were disembarked by 5 P.M., and the French retired before them to Palais.   Batteries were erected against the town on May 2nd, and in the preliminary operations before the place, some Marines, under Captain David Hepburn, greatly distinguished themselves.   On May 13th several advanced redoubts were carried, and the enemy was driven from the town to the citadel, which, from the 16th onwards, was subjected to a furious bombardment.   On June 7th, a large breach had been formed ; and preparations were being made for storming it, when the Chevalier de St. Croix, the governor, offered to surrender. Possession was taken on the 8th.   The British in these operations lost about three hundred and ten killed and five hundred wounded, besides many men who died of disease.   During the whole proceedings the most perfect harmony prevailed between the naval and the military chiefs.[1]   The naval dispatches were sent home by Captain the Hon. Samuel Barrington, who, upon his arrival, was, as was then usual in such cases, presented by the King with £500. The island was held during the remainder of the war.

After the landing on Belle Isle, Keppel, who had been again reinforced, despatched Sir Thomas Stanhope with a squadron[2] to attack such French ships as might be lying in Basque Road, and to destroy the works on Isle d'Aix.   No ships were discovered, but the destruction of the works was satisfactorily accomplished by Captain Peter Parker (1) of the *Buckingham*, in company with the *Monmouth* and *Nassau*, assisted later by the *Actæon*, *Fly* and *Blast*,

---

[1] "I hear some scoundrels have spread a report that the Commodore and I have disagreed.   I believe there never was more friendship and more harmony between two persons since the creation of the world than has subsisted between us. . . . The two services have acted as one corps ever since we left England."   Hodgson to Albemarle, June 8th, 1761.

[2] *Swiftsure*, 70, Captain Sir Thomas Stanhope; *Sandwich*, 90, Captain Richard Norbury; *Trident*, 64, Captain Benjamin Clive; *Buckingham*, 64, Captain Peter Parker (1); *Monmouth*, 64, Captain John Storr; *Nassau*, 64, Captain Maurice Suckling; *Prince of Orange*, 60, Captain Samuel Wallis; *Actæon*, 28, Captain Paul Henry Ourry; *Fly*, 14, Commander George Gayton; *Blast*, bomb, 8, Commander ———; *Furnace*, bomb, 8, Commander James Chaplen.

and by the boats of the squadron. The French prames from the mouth of the Charente endeavoured to interfere with the operations; but the work was completed with very little loss on June 21st and 22nd. Sir Thomas Stanhope continued on the station during the rest of the year, his ships being occasionally relieved. In December, the enemy made an ineffectual attempt to destroy them by means of fireships. Soon afterwards Lord Howe succeeded Stanhope in the command.

It may here be mentioned, although the matter has nothing to

SIR PETER PARKER (1), BART., ADMIRAL OF THE FLEET.

(From an engraving by Ridley after a portrait once in the possession of Mr. Valentine Green.)

do with the military operations of the Navy, that, in August, Lord Anson, as Admiral of the Fleet, hoisted his flag on board the *Royal Charlotte* (ex-*Royal Caroline*), yacht, in order to escort to England the Princess Charlotte of Mecklenburg-Strelitz, who had been promised in marriage to George III., and who landed at Harwich on September 6th. Anson's flag-captain on that occasion was Captain Peter Denis, and the royal yacht was convoyed by the

Nottingham, 60, Captain Samuel Marshall (1), the *Winchester*, 50, Captain John Hale, the *Minerva*, 32, Captain Alexander Arthur Hood, the *Tartar*, 28, Captain John Knight (1), the *Hazard*, 14, Commander the Hon. Henry St. John (1), the *Lynx*, 14, Commander the Hon. Keith Stewart (1), and a number of small yachts.

During the year there was a disposition, on the part of both belligerents, to treat for peace ; but the negotiations broke down, and the prospects of an amicable arrangement were seriously diminished by the signature, on August 15th, 1761, of what is known as the Family Compact, between the rulers of France and Spain.   As soon as news of this was received in England, Pitt desired at once to declare war against Spain, which had for some time previously behaved in a manner not altogether becoming a neutral ; but, being overborne, he resigned.   Had war been declared when Pitt wished, the very rich home-coming Spanish treasure-ships from America might have been seized.   As soon as they were safely in port, Spain took no more pains to disguise her hostility, the consequence being that, by proclamation dated January 2nd, 1762, war was declared by Great Britain, and, by proclamation of January 16th, by Spain.   The Spanish court at once endeavoured to coerce Portugal into joining Spain and France ; but Portugal was loyal to her ancient ally, and manfully stood out, although war was very quickly declared against her as a penalty for her non-compliance.   Substantial British military support was promptly given her, numerous British officers joined her army, and Commanders Joseph Norwood, Thomas Lee (1), and Michael Henry Pascal[1] took service in her Navy.

It was early resolved to deal with Spain in the most vigorous and uncompromising manner.   It has been stated that a large body of troops had been ordered from North America to the West Indies with a view to the reduction of the French Caribbee Islands.   The Ministry determined that these troops should be reinforced from England, and that, after the newly conquered islands should have been properly garrisoned, an expedition should proceed to the attack of Havana.   The command of the army assigned for this service was given to Lieut.-General the Earl of Albemarle.   The command of the squadron was given to Admiral Sir George Pocock, K.B., with, as his second, Commodore the Hon. A. Keppel, the Earl of Albemarle's brother.

---

[1] All these officers, upon their return to England after the peace, were posted.

Another movement induced by the rupture with Spain, was the despatch of Commodore Sir Piercy Brett (1), with a strong reinforcement, to Sir Charles Saunders, K.B.,[1] in the Mediterranean. Sir Edward Hawke, with Rear-Admiral the Duke of York, cruised off the coasts of Spain and Portugal ; and later, the same squadron, under command of Sir Charles Hardy (2) and the Duke of York, left port a second time on the same errand. While arrangements were thus made to attack Spain in the West Indies, and, at the same moment, to distract her attention at home, a small expedition, under command of Brigadier-General Draper, was despatched from India against the Philippine Islands.

On the death of Rear-Admiral Holmes, Sir James Douglas (1) was appointed to the command at Jamaica ; Rear-Admiral Rodney still commanded on the Leeward Islands' station ; and Commodore Lord Colville remained in North America. Commodore Spry cruised with a squadron of observation off Brest, until he was relieved by Commodore Robert Man (2) ; and Commodore Lord Howe lay in Basque Road until he was relieved by Commodore Peter Denis. Admiral Holburne commanded at Portsmouth ; Commodore John Moore (1), in the Downs, and Commodore James Young (1), in the Channel.

Rear-Admiral Cornish continued to command in the East Indies ; but, as the French had neither settlement nor trade there, he had little to do against them. When, therefore, war broke out with Spain, he was able to devote almost his undivided attention to the new enemy. Colonel Draper, afterwards Sir William Draper, K.B., an officer who had distinguished himself at the siege of Madras in 1759, had devoted part of a period of sick leave to inquiring into the condition of the Spanish settlements in the Philippine Islands ; and he had discovered that the defences had been much neglected, and that the Spaniards there trusted rather to their remoteness than to their strength for their protection.[2] Upon the commencement of hostilities, Colonel Draper laid his information before the Ministry, and measures were taken accordingly. He was at once sent to India in the *Argo*, 28, Captain Richard King (1), with instructions for fitting out an expedition against Manilla, and with an appointment as commander-in-chief of the troops to be employed. The expedition ultimately consisted of the 79th Regiment, a company of

---

[1] Vice-Admiral Saunders was so installed, by proxy, on May 26th, 1761.
[2] As they appear to have done again in 1898.

Royal Artillery and miscellaneous bodies, which, with 630 seamen
and 270 Marines from the fleet, brought the total of the available
field army up to about 2300 men, who were embarked in Rear-
Admiral Cornish's squadron and in two East Indiamen.   The
preparations were begun and completed within three weeks.   The
Seahorse, 20, Captain Charles Cathcart Grant, was sent in advance
to intercept any vessels that might be bound for Manilla.   A

ADMIRAL SIR RICHARD KING (1), BART.

(From a lithograph by Ridley, after a miniature.)

division of the fleet, under Commodore Richard Tiddeman, sailed
on July 29th; and the rest, with the exception of the *Falmouth*, 60,
which was left to convoy an Indiaman, followed under the Commander-in-Chief on August 1st.   On August 19th the fleet[1] reached

[1] List of H.M. ships engaged in the expedition against Manilla :—*Norfolk*, 74, Rear-
Admiral Samuel Cornish (Vice-Admiral, October 21st, 1762), Captain Richard Kempen-
felt; *Elizabeth*, 64, Commodore Richard Tiddeman, Captain Isaac Florimond Ourry;
Lenox, 74, Captain Robert Jocelyn; *Grafton*, 68, Captain Hyde Parker (1); *Wey-
mouth*, 60, Captain Richard Collins (2); *America*, 60, Captain Samuel Pitchford;
Panther, 60, Commander George Ourry (acting for Captain William Newsom);

Malacca, and there watered and took on board various supplies. On the 27th it sailed again; and on September 23rd, to the great surprise of the Spaniards, who had not heard of the outbreak of war, it anchored off Manilla. On the 24th the town was summoned, but without result; and, in the afternoon, under cover of the *Argo*, *Seahorse*, and *Seaford*, some troops were landed, in spite of a heavy surf which caused much loss of, and damage to, material. The boats on this occasion were under the direction of Captains Hyde Parker (1), Richard Kempenfelt and William Brereton. There was but slight opposition. The rest of the troops and the Marines were disembarked on the 25th; and on the 26th a brigade of seamen, under Captains Collins, Pitchford and Ourry, reinforced them. On the following days batteries were erected and opened; and on the 29th the *Elizabeth* and *Falmouth* were ordered to co-operate as best they could with the army, by enfilading the enemy's front. By October 5th a practicable breach had been made in the works. Early in the morning of that day this was stormed with success, and the governor and officers were driven to the citadel, which they presently surrendered at discretion. Not only Manilla, but with it also Luzon, and all the Spanish islands, were handed over by the terms of the capitulation. It was arranged that Manilla should be ransomed for four millions of dollars to save it from pillage. Owing, however, to the bad faith of the Spaniards, only half of this amount was ever paid. The conquest, together with most of the prize money, was handed over to the East India Company.

During the operations, Cornish obtained news that a galleon from Acapulco was on her way to Manilla. Accordingly, on October 4th, he despatched the *Panther* and *Argo* to intercept her. These failed to do so; but they succeeded in taking, on October 31st, the *Santisima Trinidad*, which had left Manilla for Acapulco on August 1st, having on board treasure worth about three million dollars. In the meantime, the galleon from Acapulco had arrived at Palapa, in Samar. It was agreed that, subject to certain conditions, she was to be surrendered to the British; but the arrangement was never carried out, and it is probable that much of her rich cargo eventually passed into the hands of private persons, who had no right to it.

Falmouth, 50, Captain William Brereton; *Argo*, 28, Captain Richard King (1); *Seahorse*, 20, Captain Charles Cathcart Grant; *Seaford*, 20, Captain John Peighin; and *Southsea Castle*, store-ship.

The operations before Manilla were less costly than might have been expected. The army lost but 115 killed, drowned and wounded, and the Navy but 35. The only naval officer who was killed was Lieutenant Porter, of the *Norfolk*, but, unfortunately, Commodore Tiddeman was accidentally drowned on the day of the surrender. Captain Richard Kempenfelt was sent home with the naval dispatches. As a reward for the service, Cornish was made a baronet, and Draper a K.B., and each received the thanks of both Houses. The colours taken at Manilla were hung in the chapel of King's College, Cambridge, of which Draper had been a member.

The French empire in North America had ceased to exist; and its disappearance had rendered unnecessary the presence on the spot of part of the large body of troops which had been concerned in the conquest of Canada. As has already been mentioned, it had been decided to employ some of them against the French islands in the West Indies. Rear-Admiral Rodney had left England in October, 1761, and had arrived in Carlisle Bay, Barbados, on November 22nd. He there found part of the squadron under Commodore Sir James Douglas (1), which he speedily detached to blockade Martinique. Troops and transports were in the meantime assembled at Barbados; and an improvised force of armed hired sloops was sent to cruise off St. Eustatia to prevent the Dutch from assisting the French with supplies and provisions. At length, on January 5th, 1762, the fleet,[1] having on board nearly 14,000 troops from England, Belle Isle,

[1] British fleet employed in the expedition against Martinique, etc., 1762 :—

Ships.	Guns.	Commanders.	Ships.	Guns.	Commanders.
Marlborough . .	70	Rear-Admiral G. B. Rodney (B). / Capt. John Hollwell.	*Woolwich* . . .	44	Capt. William Bayne.
Dublin	74	Commod. Sir James Douglas(1). / Capt. Edward Gascoigne.	*Penzance*[1] . . .	44	,, John Boyd.
Foudroyant. . .	84	,, Robert Duff.	*Dover*[1]	40	,, Chaloner Ogle (3).
Dragon[1]. . . .	74	,, Hon. Aug. John Hervey.	*Echo*	32	,, John Laforey.
Téméraire . . .	74	,, Matthew Barton.	*Stag*	32	,, Henry Angell.
Temple	70	,, Lucius O'Brien.	*Repulse*	32	,, John Carter Allen.
Vanguard . . .	70	,, Robert Swanton.	*Actæon*	28	,, Paul Henry Ourry.
Modeste	64	,, Hon. Robt. Boyle Walsingham.	*Crescent* . . .	28	,, Thomas Collingwood.
Stirling Castle . .	64	,, Michael Everitt.	*Lizard*	28	,, James Doake.
Devonshire . . .	64	,, George Darby.	*Levant*	28	,, William Tucker.
Raisonnable . .	64	,, Molyneux Shuldham.	*Nightingale* . .	28	,, James Campbell (2).
Alcide	64	,, Thomas Hankerson	*Fowey*	20	,, Joseph Mead.
Nottingham. . .	60	,, Samuel Marshall(1).	*Greyhound* . . .	20	,, Thomas Francis.
Rochester . . .	50	,, Thomas Burnett.	*Rose*	20	,, Francis Banks (1).
Sutherland . . .	50	,, Ju ian Legge.	*Antigua*. . . .	10	,, John Neale Pleydell Nott.
Norwich[1] . . .	50	,, William M'Cleverty.	*Barbados* . . .	10	Com. Stair Douglas (1).
Falkland . . .	50	,, Francis Samuel Drake.	*Ferret*	16	,, James Alms (1).
			Virgin	12	Capt.
			Zephyr	12	Com. John Botterell.
			Basilisk, bomb[1] .	8	,, Robert Brice.
			Thunder, bomb .	8	Lieut. Robert Haswell.
			Grenado, bomb .	8	,, James Hawker.
			Infernal, bomb .	8	Com. James Mackenzie.

[1] Detached, under Capt. the Hon. Augustus John Hervey, against St. Lucia.

North America and the West India Islands, under Major-General the Hon. Robert Monckton, sailed, and, on the 7th, joined Douglas off Martinique. The coasts of the island had not been properly reconnoitred, nor had the ships adequate charts on board. The configuration of the island and the nature of its defences rendered it desirable to land the troops as close as possible to the places at which they were to be employed. But, at first, this fact was not realised ; and Rodney, while detaching only a small squadron to the Great Bay of Fort Royal, detached another to La Trinité to make a feint, and himself anchored with the bulk of his force in St. Anne's Bay. A division, under Sir James Douglas, silenced the batteries there, and landed the troops, losing, however, the *Raisonnable*, owing to the ignorance of her pilot. But it was soon found that the march across to Fort Royal from St. Anne's Bay would be an undertaking too difficult to be entered upon. The works which had been erected at St. Anne's were therefore blown up, the troops were re-embarked, and the whole force proceeded to Fort Royal Bay.

The order of the attack having been arranged, the ships went to their stations early on the morning of the 16th, opening fire upon the batteries and silencing them by noon, soon after which the troops were landed in three divisions in Cas des Navires Bay, under conduct of Captains Molyneux Shuldham, Robert Swanton and the Hon. Augustus John Hervey. By sunset two-thirds of the army were on shore ; and the rest, with 900 Marines, followed next morning. The distance to Fort Royal was not great, only about five or six miles ; but the country was terribly difficult, and the defenders fought well from behind every rock and tree, as well as within artificial works of all kinds. The necessary guns were, however, dragged to the front, thanks mainly to the energy of the seamen of the fleet ; and on January 24th, a preliminary attack was made by a body of troops advancing along the coast parallel with a detachment of a 1000 seamen in boats ; and the enemy was driven back. On the 25th, the batteries began to bombard the citadel ; and on the 27th the key to the whole position was taken. Yet the citadel did not surrender until February 4th, and not until February 16th was the whole island in possession of the British. Captain Darby, of the *Devonshire*, and Major Gates, later a general in the army of the revolting American Colonists, carried home the dispatches announcing the capture of Fort Royal ; and each received from the King the usual compliment of £500. The British loss during the operations amounted to about 500 killed and wounded.

Even before the conquest had been completed, Rodney detached Captain Swanton to blockade Grenada; and, when Martinique had surrendered, Swanton was reinforced by vessels conveying troops. These reached Grenada on March 3rd; and on the following day the island was summoned; but the governor refused to comply. The inhabitants, however, ignored him, and capitulated on the 4th; and the governor himself was obliged to surrender at discretion on the 5th. With Grenada fell the Grenadines. Swanton, leaving a garrison, returned to Martinique.

On February 24th Captain the Hon. Augustus John Hervey had been similarly detached against St. Lucia. But he could not satisfy himself as to the enemy's strength; and, to discover it, he disguised himself as a midshipman, and, in the capacity of an interpreter, accompanied the officer whom he sent to summon the governor, M. de Longueville. That gentleman refused to surrender; yet Hervey learnt so much during his visit that, on the following day, he made preparations for taking his ships into the harbour. No sooner did the governor notice signs of their intention to approach than he capitulated.

Hervey was next about to proceed to St. Vincent to assure the Caribs that their neutrality would be maintained, and that the French would be no longer suffered to interfere with them, when he was recalled by Rodney, in consequence of news having been received that a French squadron of seven sail of the line and four frigates,[1] under M. de Blenac, with seven battalions of troops, had escaped from Brest, owing to Commodore Spry having been driven from his station off that port; and that it was on its way to relieve the French West India Islands. Spry had detached the *Aquilon*, 28, Captain Chaloner Ogle (2), with this intelligence to Rodney. But, before the arrival of Spry's dispatch, the French squadron had been sighted on March 8th, on the windward side of Martinique. It lay to off the coast until the 10th, when it stood for Dominica.

Rodney summoned his detached division to a rendezvous off the Salines, and, with Sir James Douglas (1), went in search of the enemy; but without result. When he had collected his whole force and had

---

[1] *Duc de Bourgogne*, 80; *Défenseur*, 74; *Hector*, 74; *Diadème*, 74; *Protée*, 64; *Dragon*, 64; *Brillant*, 64; *Zéphyr*, 32; *Diligente*, 32; *Opale*, 26; *Calypso*, 16.

been assured that the French had gone to Cape François, he returned to Martinique to water. He there found the *Aquilon*, from which he learnt trustworthy details of M. de Blenac's strength. He already knew, thanks to early information sent him by Commander George Johnstone, commanding the *Hornet* on the Lisbon station, of the rupture with Spain; and he was thus enabled to attack the Spanish trade in the West Indies before the Spaniards themselves knew that war had broken out. This important intelligence had been brought to him by a small French privateer prize, which Johnstone had entrusted to the *Hornet's* master, Mr., afterwards Captain, John M'Laurin. At Martinique Rodney also heard that a strong Spanish squadron had arrived at Havana and that Jamaica was believed to be threatened. He therefore sent a frigate to warn Captain Arthur Forrest, who, as senior officer, had succeeded Rear-Admiral Holmes on the Jamaica station, and to desire him to join the main fleet off Cape St. Nicolas, whither he himself intended to proceed.

He was, however, not quite ready to sail when, on March 26th, the *Richmond*, Captain John Elphinstone (1), arrived from England with orders for him and General Monckton to postpone further operations pending the appearance of Admiral Sir George Pocock, who had been commissioned to conduct a secret expedition on an important scale. This did not prevent Rodney from sending Sir James Douglas (1),[1] with ten sail of the line, to the Jamaica station with directions to bring Forrest's squadron thence as soon as possible, and to join Pocock. He also sent Captain Swanton, with a division, to cruise off the Spanish Main, and himself went to St. Pierre, Martinique, sending a frigate to meet Pocock at Barbados, where Sir George arrived on board the *Namur* on April 20th. Pocock sailed again on the 24th, joined Rodney at Cas des Navires on the 26th, and, with the greater part of the fleet, proceeded on May 6th for Havana, leaving Rodney in charge of the Leeward Islands.

On the Jamaica station Captain Forrest was, of course, super-

---

[1] *Dublin*, 74, Commodore Sir James Douglas (1), Captain Edward Gascoigne; *Culloden*, 74, Captain John Barker (1); *Dragon*, 74, Captain Hon. Aug. John Hervey; *Téméraire*, 74, Captain Matthew Barton; *Temple*, 70, Captain Julian Legge; *Devonshire*, 64, Captain Samuel Marshall (1); *Alcide*, 64, Captain Thomas Hankerson; *Stirling Castle*, 64, Captain James Campbell (2); *Nottingham*, 60, Captain Thomas Collingwood; *Sutherland*, 50, Captain Michael Everitt; *Dover*, 40, Captain Chaloner Ogle (3); *Thunder*, bomb, Commander Robert Haswell; and *Grenado*, bomb.

seded by the arrival of Sir James Douglas (1), who despatched a squadron under Captain Hon. Augustus John Hervey[1] to blockade M. de Blenac at Cape François, until the whole Jamaica squadron should be ready to join Pocock at Cape St. Nicolas.

The Havana expedition, when complete, included about 15,500 men, the whole commanded by George, Earl of Albemarle. The strength of the fleet will be found set forth in the note.[2] After leaving Martinique the expedition was joined in the Mona passage on May 8th by Captain Hon. Augustus John Hervey, and, having arrived off Cape St. Nicolas on the 18th, was there reinforced on the 23rd by Sir James Douglas from Jamaica.

It was open to Pocock either to sail by the south side of Cuba, along the track of the galleons, round the west end of the island and

---

[1] *Dragon*, 74, Captain Hon. A. J. Hervey; *Téméraire*, 74, Captain Matthew Barton; *Stirling Castle*, 64, Captain James Campbell (2); *Alcide*, 64, Captain Thomas Hankerson; *Defiance*, 60, Captain George Mackenzie; *Nottingham*, 60, Captain Thomas Collingwood; *Pembroke*, 60, Captain John Wheelock; *Dover*, 40, Captain Chaloner Ogle (3); *Trent*, 28, Captain John Lindsay; and *Port Mahon*, 20, Captain Thomas Lemprière.

[2] Fleet under Sir George Pocock at the reduction of Havana, and on the Jamaica station, 1762:—

Ships.	Guns.	Commanders.	Ships.	Guns.	Commanders.
Namur	90	Admiral Sir George Pocock, K.B. (B). Capt. John Harrison.	*Dover*	40	Capt. Chaloner Ogle (3).
			Enterprise[4]. . .	40	,, John Houlton.
Valiant	74	Commod. Hon. Augustus Keppel. Capt. Adam Duncan.	*Richmond* . . .	32	{ ,, John Elphinstone (1).
			Alarm	32	{ ,, James Alms (1) (acting).
Cambridge[4] . .	80	,, William Goostrey.	*Echo*	28	,, John Lendrick.
Culloden. . . .	74	,, John Barker.	*Lizard*[2]	28	,, Francis Banks (1).
Téméraire . . .	74	,, Matthew Barton.	*Trent*	28	,, John Lindsay.
Dragon	74	{ ,, Hon. Augustus John Hervey.	*Cerberus*[1] . . .	28	,, Charles Webber.
			Boreas	28	,, Samuel Uvedale.
Centaur[1] . . .	74	,, Thomas Lemprière.	*Mercury* . . .	24	{ ,, Samuel Granston Goodall.
Dublin[3] . . .	74	,,´ Edward Gascoigne.			
Marlborough . .	70	,, Thomas Burnett.	*Rose*	20	{ ,, John Neale Pleydell Nott.
Temple . . .	70	,, Julian Legge.			
Orford . . .	66	,, Marriot Arbuthnot.	*Port Mahon* . .	20	,, Richard Bickerton.
Devonshire . .	64	,, Samuel Marshall (1).	*Fowey*	20	,, Joseph Mead.
Belleisle	64	,, Joseph Knight.	*Glasgow* . . .	20	,, Richard Carteret.
Edgar	64	{ ,, Francis William Drake.	*Bonetta*	16	Com. Lancelot Holmes.
Alcide[1]	64	,, Thomas Hankerson.	*Cygnet*	16	{ ,, Hon. Charles Napier (1).
Hampton Court .	64	,, Alexander Innes.			
Stirling Castle . .	64	{ ,, James Campbell (2).	*Merlin*	16	{ ,, William Francis Bourke.
Pembroke . . .	60	,, John Wheelock.	*Porcupine*[2] . .	16	,, James Harmood.
Ripon	60	,, Edward Jekyll.	*Barbados* . . .	14	,, James Hawker.
Nottingham . .	60	{ ,, Thomas Collingwood.	*Viper*	14	,, John Urry.
			Port Royal . .	14	,, Stair Douglas (1).
Defiance	60	,, George Mackenzie.	*Ferret*	14	Lieut. Peter Clarke.
Intrepid[2] . . .	60	,, John Hale.	*Lurcher*, cutter	14	,, —— Walker.
Centurion[3][4] . .	50	,, James Galbraith.	*Thunder*, bomb .	8	Com. Robert Haswell.
Deptford . . .	50	,, Dudley Digges.	*Grenado*, bomb .	8	
Sutherland[1] . .	50	,, Michael Everitt.	*Basilisk*, bomb. .	8	,, —— Lowfield.
Hampshire . . .	50	,, Arthur Usher.			
Penzance[4] . . .	40	,, Philip Boteler.	besides storeships, hospital ships, and transports.		

---

[1] Joined after the siege had begun.   [2] Escorted troops from North America.
[3] Some time with the broad pennant of Commodore Sir James Douglas.
[4] Escorted convoys from Jamaica to England.

so beat down to Havana, or to steer along the north side of Cuba through the Old Strait of Bahama. The former was the easier, though the longer, course ; the latter was the shorter, though it was somewhat difficult and even hazardous, the channel being narrow and intricate. But the Admiral chose it, since time was precious, and since it was important as early as possible to secure the only passage by which the French could send supplies to Havana. Pocock despatched Sir James Douglas in the *Centurion* to Jamaica to bring stores thence, and to hasten forward such ships as were still there ; and on the 27th, with his huge fleet of about two hundred sail, the Admiral bore away for the Old Strait of Bahama. The precautions which he took are described in a letter which, on June 14th, he addressed to the secretary of the Admiralty. He placed boats on the most dangerous shoals on each hand to act as marks ; and he records that he was greatly assisted in the navigation by Anson's chart, which he found very correct. During the passage, two Spanish vessels, the *Thetis*, 22, and *Fénix*, storeship, were captured by the *Alarm*, Captain James Alms (1).

The Strait was passed on June 5th ; and on the morning of the 6th the fleet was brought to about fifteen miles east of Havana, so that directions might be given to the captains as to the landing. The conduct of this operation was entrusted to Commodore the Hon. Augustus Keppel, who had under him six sail of the line and some frigates. At 2 P.M. the Admiral bore away with thirteen sail of the line, two frigates, the bombs, and thirty-six victuallers and storeships, and ran down towards the harbour, in which he saw twelve Spanish sail of the line [1] and several merchantmen. On the

[1] Spanish men-of-war taken or destroyed during the expedition against Havana, 1762 :—

	Ships.	Guns.	Commanders.	Fate.
At Havana.	*Tigre*.	70	{ Marqués del Real Trasporte. { Don J. Y. Madariaga.	} Surrendered with the city.
	Reina	70	,, L. de Velasco.	
	Soberano . . .	70	,, J. del Postigo.	
	Infante	70	,, F. de Medina.	
	Neptuno	70	,, P. Bermudez.	Sunk at mouth of harbour.
	Aquilón	70	Marqués Gonzales.	Surrendered with the city.
	Asia	64	Don F. Garganta.	Sunk at mouth of harbour.
	America . . .	60	,, J. Antonio.	Surrendered with the city. Renamed *Moro*.
	Europa	60	,, J. Vincente.	Sunk at mouth of harbour.
	Conquistador . .	60	,, P. Castejon.	
	San Genaro . .	60	} Not in Commission.	} Surrendered with the city.
	San Antonio . .	60		
	Venganza . . .	26	Don D. Argote.	Taken by *Defiance* at Mariel, May 28.
	Thetis	22	,, J. Porlier.	,, *Alarm* in the Strait, June 3.
	Marie	18	,, D. Bonechea.	,, *Defiance* at Mariel. May 28.
	Fénix, st.s. . .	..	..	,, *Alarm* in the Strait, May 28.

Two unfinished ships upon the stocks were destroyed.

following morning, the 7th, he made a feint of landing the Marines
about four miles to the west of Havana, while the Earl of Albemarle,
with the whole army, landed without opposition between the rivers
Boca Nao and Coximar, six miles east of Moro Castle, under the
conduct of Captains Hervey, Barton, Drake, Arbuthnot, Jekyll, and
Wheelock, R.N.   After it had landed, the enemy made some show
of fight, especially when the troops were about to cross the river
Coximar; but the foe was dispersed by the fire of the *Mercury*,
Bonetta, and *Dragon*.   A detachment of seamen and 900 Marines
were landed to co-operate.

On July 1st, after some progress had been made with the siege,
the *Cambridge*, *Dragon*, and *Marlborough* were ordered to cannonade
Moro; and at about 8 A.M. they began a heavy fire, which was well
returned till 2 P.M.   The vessels were all so much damaged that,
one after another, they had to be called off.   The *Cambridge* lost
24 killed and 95 wounded; the *Dragon*, 16 killed and 37 wounded;
and the *Marlborough*, 2 killed and 8 wounded.   Among the killed in
the *Cambridge* was Captain Goostrey, whose place was afterwards
taken by Captain Lindsay of the *Trent*.   As this mode of procedure
was found to be too costly, the further bombardment of the defences
was left mainly to the shore batteries, which, aided by mines, made
a practicable breach in the Moro by July 30th.   On that day the
castle was carried by storm.   In the struggle the commandant, the
gallant Don Luis de Velasco, was mortally wounded.   In honour of
his defence, there has ever since been a ship named the *Velasco* in
the Spanish navy.   The vessels in the harbour took part in the
operations, but were of little avail.

Upon the fall of Moro the siege was pressed, and, on August 11th,
after a particularly heavy bombardment, flags of truce were hung
out on shore and in the Spanish flagship.   A little later another flag
was sent to the British headquarters; negotiations were entered
upon; and, after some delay, the capitulation was signed on the
13th, and part of the works was taken possession of by the British
on the 14th.

The specie, stores, and valuables found in the place were worth
about £3,000,000 sterling; and with the city were also taken nine
sail of the line.   Two others lying on the stocks had been burnt,
and three more, besides a large galleon, had been sunk in the mouth
of the harbour.[1]   On the other hand, the British killed, wounded,

----

[1] For the names and force of these, see note p. 247.

and missing numbered no fewer than 1790 ; and many other lives were lost owing to the unwholesomeness of the climate and the hardships of the siege. The naval dispatches were sent home by Captain the Hon. Augustus John Hervey, in the *Dragon*, which on her passage had the good fortune to capture a French ship valued at £30,000.

During the siege several Spanish vessels were taken on the coast. On July 24th the *Chesterfield*, 40, and four transports with reinforcements of troops from North America, were lost at Cayo Confite, but the people were saved. Lieutenant Walker, commanding the *Lurcher*, cutter, going on June 13th up the Chorera River out of mere curiosity, had the misfortune to be killed. The prize money divided amounted to about £736,000. Its division caused much heart-burning, the shares of the Admiral and general being each £122,697 10s. 6d. ; while the share of a captain R.N. was but £1600 10s. 10d., of a petty officer only £17 5s. 3d., and of a seaman or Marine not more than £3 14s. 9¼d. It was felt, and perhaps with reason, that the administration permitted the commanding officers to appropriate far too large a share of the spoils to themselves.

The fall of Havana, apart from its intrinsic significance, had almost the importance of a great naval victory, owing to the large number of Spanish sail of the line which shared the fate of the city. The military conduct of the siege by the Earl of Albemarle has been blamed, chiefly because, instead of attacking the city where it was weak, he attacked Moro and Punta Fort, which were strong, but which, nevertheless, must have quickly fallen had the city itself been taken. But although there may be justice in this criticism, it does not appear that anything can be urged against Pocock's conduct of his part of the business ; unless indeed, it be admitted that he was wrong to oppose his ships to the Moro on July 1st. For the rest, the co-operation between the Navy and army was thoroughly loyal and smooth ; and the behaviour of both was admirable.

Sir George Pocock delivered up the command of the fleet to the Hon. Augustus Keppel, who by that time had been promoted to be a Rear-Admiral of the Blue ; and, with the *Namur*, *Culloden*, *Temple*, *Devonshire*, *Marlborough*, *Infante*, *San Genaro*, *Asunción*,[1] and several other Spanish prizes and about fifty transports, sailed for England on November 3rd. About six hundred miles west of Land's

---

[1] A prize merchantman.

End, the squadron was dispersed by a very violent gale from the eastward. Twelve of the transports foundered, though their crews were happily saved. The *Temple* came to a similar end. The *Culloden* and *Devonshire* would probably have fared likewise, had they not thrown overboard many of their guns. Part of the fleet made Kingsale. The other part, which kept the sea, suffered terrible privations from famine, thirst and sickness. So anxious did the Admiralty become, that it sent out several frigates to search for Sir George ; who, however, safely reached Spithead on January 13th, 1763. The *San Genaro*, one of the ships which had put into Kingsale, came to grief when at length she anchored in the Downs. She was overtaken by another storm, and was cast away. The *Marlborough* lost company with the Admiral early on the voyage ; but she, too, met with very heavy weather, and, owing to leaks, was obliged to put before the wind, throw her guns overboard, and keep her crew at the pumps until November 29th, when her people were taken off by the *Antelope*, 50, Captain Thomas Graves (2), which was on her voyage home from Newfoundland. The *Marlborough*, after having been abandoned, was destroyed. Rear-Admiral Keppel sent home the rest of the Spanish prizes under Captain Arbuthnot of the *Orford*, together with the *Centaur, Dublin, Alcide, Hampton Court, Edgar* and some frigates ; and, after having acted with energy upon the station until the peace, he remained to deliver up Havana on July 7th, 1763, in accordance with the provisions of the treaty. Some of his vessels then proceeded to Florida to take over that province : and Keppel himself went to Jamaica, where he was presently relieved by Rear-Admiral Sir William Burnaby.

In the meantime, the French, taking advantage of the large withdrawal of troops to the West Indies, of the defenceless condition of Newfoundland, and of a fog in the Channel, despatched from Brest, under M. de Ternay, a squadron, which, with 1500 troops under Comte d'Haussonville, evaded Sir Edward Hawke, crossed the Atlantic, entered the harbour of St. John's on June 24th and quickly took the town. On its way, this fleet fell in with three combined convoys of great value, which it might easily have taken had it not preferred the ulterior object of the expedition, and had it not been deterred by the bold front offered to it by Captain Joshua Rowley, of the *Superb*, 74, who had with him the *Gosport*, 44, Captain John Jervis, and the *Danae*, 38, Captain Henry Martin (2). The capture of this convoy would have done Great Britain far

more damage at that moment than the capture of Newfoundland.
Captain Thomas Graves (2), governor of the island, who lay at
Placentia in the *Antelope*, 50, at once sent news of the French
descent to Commodore Lord Colville, at Halifax. Colville sailed to
the relief of the island, and joined Graves; and on August 25th,
M. de Ternay found himself blockaded in St. John's. On
September 11th, troops arrived from Louisbourg, and were landed;
and the enemy was driven back; but on the 16th, the blockading
ships being driven from their station by a westerly gale, M. de
Ternay slipped his cables and got away. A relieving squadron had
been sent from England in the meantime under Captain Hugh
Palliser, but de Ternay managed to avoid this force also. After his
departure, the condition of the French was, of course, hopeless;
and on September 18th Comte d'Haussonville capitulated.

A little expedition of 1762 deserves some mention here in spite
of the fact that the Royal Navy had very little part in it, and that
it had no important results. It was an adventure which, in a
degree, recalls some of the exploits of the Elizabethan era, in that
it was a warlike undertaking by private persons, countenanced,
however, by the administration, and that it was aimed against the
Spanish power in America. A company of British noblemen and
merchants came to the conclusion that an attack upon the province
of Buenos Ayres might be both useful to the nation and lucrative
to the adventurers. They purchased from the Admiralty H.M. ships
Kingston, 50 (which they renamed *Lord Clive*), and *Ambuscade*, 28 ;
and they placed these under the orders of Mr. Macnamara, an
officer of the East India Company's marine. They further obtained
the co-operation of two Portuguese vessels, in which were embarked
five hundred soldiers. The little squadron, which also included
five store ships, sailed for Rio de Janeiro, where the final preparations were made, and, proceeding, entered the River Plate on
November 2nd. Macnamara found that the Spaniards were better
situated for defence than he had expected. An attempt was made
on Nova Colonia, which had been captured by the Spaniards from
the Portuguese : but it was not successful. In a second attack, on
January 6th, 1763, the *Lord Clive* took fire and burnt to the water's
edge, her people, however, fighting her to the very last. Of her crew
of three hundred and fifty, two hundred and seventy-two, including
Macnamara, perished. The *Ambuscade*, though terribly mauled,
managed to get back to Rio. It should be added that the gallant

Spaniards treated with the greatest generosity those survivors of the *Lord Clive* who fell into their hands, and, instead of regarding them as enemies, treated them as guests whom misfortune had cast upon their shores.

The year witnessed no events of great importance in the Mediterranean; where Sir Charles Saunders was strongly reinforced by a squadron under Sir Piercy Brett (1). Some exceedingly valuable prizes were made on the station; but the fleets of the belligerents did not meet. Sir Charles Saunders, and most of the ships returned to England at the peace, leaving Rear-Admiral Sir Piercy Brett to take possession of Minorca. Brett was subsequently relieved by Commodore Thomas Harrison (2).

It has been already mentioned that M. de Blenac got out of Brest, and sailed for Martinique during a temporary absence from his station of Commodore Spry, owing to heavy weather. Spry chased; but, his provisions threatening to give out, he had to return to England, having first sent the *Aquilon* to warn Rodney of what had happened. During the year the other occurrences in waters near home were mainly confined to the monotonous blockading of the enemy's ports, and to the capture of their cruisers. Commodore Lord Howe lay in Basque Road, watching Rochefort and the mouth of the Charente, until he was relieved by Commodore Peter Denis. When M. de Ternay escaped from Brest, the fleet under Sir Edward Hawke and the Duke of York went in pursuit, but missed him. This fleet, then under Sir Charles Hardy (2), cruised again in September and October, and once more in November, but accomplished nothing. The cruisers of Commodore Robert Man (2), who succeeded Spry off Brest; of Commodore James Young (1), who commanded in the Channel; and of Commodore John Moore (1), who commanded in the Downs, made various prizes; but the details of these, and of other minor captures, will be fittingly given in the next chapter. One episode, in which the force under Commodore Moore was concerned, may, however, be noticed here.

The Dutch had for some time been supplying the enemies of Great Britain with provisions and stores; and the British cruisers, in consequence, vigilantly searched their merchantmen. The States General, resenting this, commissioned some men-of-war to protect the illicit trade; and, in September, a Dutch flotilla of four merchantmen, convoyed by a 36-gun frigate, was fallen in with by the *Hunter*, sloop, which, being refused permission to search, and being too weak to enforce her demands, returned to Moore. He sent the *Diana*, 32, Captain William Adams (2), the *Chester*, 50, Captain William Hay, the *Hunter*, 14, Commander James Ferguson, and the *Trial*, 14, Commander James Cunningham, with orders to do what was necessary. Adams found the Dutchmen, and demanded to know what the convoy had on board. The Dutch captain again refused to allow a search, and declared that he would fight rather than permit it ; whereupon Adams sent boats to board each merchantman. The Dutch fired a gun at the leading boat, and wounded a man in her. Adams retaliated by firing a gun at the frigate, which replied with a broadside. This brought about an action, which, in fifteen minutes, resulted in all the Dutch ships submitting. They were taken into the Downs. The merchantmen, being found to have on board stores for the French navy, were detained ; but the frigate, which had lost four killed and five wounded, was dismissed.

During this last year of the contest the enemy took but two British men-of-war, a sloop and a bomb ketch. The list of the men-of-war taken by the British will be found in the appendix. The French merchantmen and privateers taken numbered 120 ; and, as in previous years, their value was greatly in excess of that of the British privateers and merchantmen captured, though the number of the latter was considerably greater. Towards the close of the campaign the French had very few vessels at sea ; and their trade was ruined. The Spanish power afloat was never great enough to be a serious menace.

The first overtures for peace came from France to Great Britain through the Sardinian envoy in London. In consequence of them, the Duke of Bedford was sent to Paris, and the Duc de Nivernois came to England, with full powers ; and on November 3rd, 1762, the preliminaries of peace, between Great Britain on the one side and France and Spain on the other, were signed at Fontainebleau. The terms were scarcely proportionate to the measure of the successes which had been gained by Great Britain during the war. She acquired Canada, St. John's, Cape Breton, and that part of what was then called Louisiana, east of the Mississippi, except New Orleans, together with the right of free navigation of the Mississippi. France received permission, subject to certain conditions, to fish on the banks of Newfoundland, and was given the islands of St. Pierre and Miquelon as fish-curing stations. Spain relinquished her claim to

fish on the banks of Newfoundland; and undertook to restore to
Portugal any places which she might have conquered from that
power, and to cede Florida to Great Britain. But Great Britain
was to restore Havana and its dependencies. Martinique, Guadeloupe, and Marie Galante also, were to be given back to France,
which, in addition, obtained St. Lucia, previously a neutral island.
Great Britain retained Grenada and the Grenadines, and received
the formerly neutral islands of Dominica, St. Vincent and Tobago.
She also had Minorca restored to her and kept Sénégal; but she
restored Belle Isle and Gorée to France. The fortifications of
Dunquerque, should, it was agreed, be demolished. In Asia, Great
Britain had to restore the conquests made from France; but France
was to erect no fortifications in her possessions within the province
of Bengal. Louisiana west of the Mississippi was ceded by France
to Spain.

The terms of the treaty, though honourable, could not be considered as particularly advantageous to Great Britain, seeing that
her maritime superiority in 1762 was such that she might have
seized, and kept, almost what she would. The definitive treaty was
signed at Paris on February 10th, 1763; and so ended the Seven
Years' War.

Commenting upon the settlement, Mahan writes :—

"The nation at large and Pitt, the favourite of the nation, were bitterly opposed to
the terms of the treaty. 'France,' said Pitt, 'is chiefly formidable to us as a maritime
and commercial power. What we gain in this respect is valuable to us above all
through the injury to her which results from it. You leave to France the possibility
of reviving her navy.' In truth, from the point of view of sea-power and of the
national jealousies which the spirit of that age sanctioned, these words, though
illiberal, were strictly justifiable. The restoration to France of her colonies in the
West Indies and her stations in India, together with the valuable right of fishery in
her former American possessions, put before her the possibility and inducement to
restore her shipping, her commerce, and her navy, and thus tended to recall her from
the path of continental ambition which had been so fatal to her interests, and in the
same proportion favourable to the unprecedented growth of England's power upon the
ocean. The opposition, and indeed some of the ministry, also thought that so commanding and important a position as Havana was poorly paid for by the cession of the
then desolate and unproductive region called Florida. Puerto Rico was suggested,
Florida accepted. There were other minor points of difference, into which it is
unnecessary to enter. It can scarcely be denied that with the commanding military
control of the sea held by England, grasping as she now did so many important
positions, with her navy overwhelmingly superior in numbers, and her commercial
and internal condition very thriving, more rigorous terms might easily have been
exacted and would have been prudent. The ministry defended their eagerness and
spirit of concession on the ground of the enormous growth of the debt, which then
amounted to £122,000,000, a sum from every point of view much greater then than
now; but while this draft upon the future was fully justified by the success of the

war, it also imperatively demanded that the utmost advantages which the military situation made obtainable, should be exacted. This the ministry failed to do. . . Nevertheless, the gains of England were very great, not only in territorial increase, nor yet in maritime preponderance, but in the prestige and position achieved in the eyes of the nations, now fully opened to her great resources and mighty power. To these results, won by the sea, the issue of the continental war offered a singular and suggestive contrast. France had already withdrawn, along with England, from all share in that strife, and peace between the other parties to it was signed five days after the Peace of Paris. The terms of the peace were simply the *status quo ante bellum.* By the estimate of the King of Prussia, one hundred and eighty thousand of his soldiers had fallen or died in this war, out of a kingdom of five million souls; while the losses of Prussia, Austria, and France aggregated four hundred and sixty thousand men. The result was simply that things remained as they were."

CHAPTER XXVIII.

MILITARY HISTORY OF THE ROYAL NAVY, 1714–1762.

Minor Operations.

L. CARR LAUGHTON.

Richard Lestock—" The Fifteen "—Moorish Pirates—Exploits of the *Hind* and the *Bridgewater*—Piracy in the West—Edward Thatch, *alias* " Blackbeard "—Bartholomew Roberts—Chaloner Ogle off Cape Lopez—Mighells at Vigo—Smugglers and guarda-costas—The right of search—Salt gathering at the Tortugas —Stuart and illicit trading—Fandino—Reprisals—The *Shoreham's* prizes—The *Princesa* taken—Pearce and Oglethorpe at St. Augustine—Barnet and de Caylus —The West Indies—Loss of the *Tiger*—Loss of the *Tilbury*—Callis at St. Tropez —Martin at Ajaccio—Naval disasters—The *Northumberland* taken—The hurricane at Jamaica—Mostyn's fiasco—Capture of the *Eléphant*—The *Anglesey* taken—Lieut. Baker Phillips—The privateers—Successes of " The Royal Family "—The *Jersey* and the *St. Esprit*—M. de Lage—The *Nottingham* and the *Mars*—The *Alexander* and the *Solebay*—The *Portland* and the *Auguste*—Fox and de La Motte—Captures and losses—Commodore Pocock's successes—George Walker—Capture of the *Magnanime*—The *Chesterfield*—Piracy—The *Blandford*—Capture of the *Espérance*—The *Warwick* taken—The Chausey Islands—Fortunatus Wright—A repulse at Algeciras—Captain John Lockhart—" Error of Judgment " —Loss of the *Greenwich* and the *Merlin*—Destruction of the *Aquilon* and the *Alcion*—Captures—Privateers—Thurot—Capture of the *Emeraude*—Disasters—Burning of the *Prince George*—Capture of the *Raisonnable*—Captain Brodrick Hartwell—The *Winchelsea* taken—The *Buckingham* and the *Florissant*—The *Vestal* and the *Bellone*—Capture of the *Danaé*—The *Achilles* and the *Comte de St. Florentine*—The *Aréthuse* taken—Indecisive actions—Convoys—Adventures of the *Diadème*—Sinking of the *Cumberland*—The *Unicorn* and the *Vestale*—The *Richmond* and the *Félicité*—The *Minerva* and the *Warwick*—The *Ripon* and the *Achille*—Captures—Capture of the *Achille* and *Bouffonne*—The *Bellona* and the *Courageux*—Last captures of the war.

FOR several years after 1715, the sending of a fleet to the Baltic became, as has been already shown, a species of annual exercise. All these expeditions were barren of serious fighting, and there is little to be said of them here. In 1717, however, when the fleet was under Sir George Byng, it was found that, although the Swedish men-of-war still kept in port, considerable annoyance was occasioned to British trade by the numerous privateers. Against these Sir George detached various cruisers, of which none was so successful as the *Panther*, 50, Captain Richard Lestock (2). Many privateers were sent home; but none of them was of any great force, the average scarcely running to ten small guns and sixty men per ship. The matter, indeed, is chiefly worth noticing because it was in this way that Lestock, a man whose subsequent behaviour rendered him notorious, began to come to the front. His activity on these cruises attracted Byng's attention, and gained him the name of a zealous officer. Sir George, in consequence, chose him to command his flagship in the Mediterranean campaign of the following year. The subsequent Baltic campaigns were less active even than the campaign of 1717.

Nearer home, and on the Barbary coasts, meanwhile, the Navy was finding work to do; in the one case in connection with the pro-Stuart rising, in the other, with the recrudescence of piracy. The Pretender landed in December, 1715, and in the middle of January, 1716, Sir John Jennings, Admiral of the White, was appointed to the command of a squadron of ten ships wherewith to cruise on the east coast and in the Firth of Forth. Other ships cruised on the west coast, also for the suppression of the rebels, while others again were kept in the Channel to restrain sympathetic Frenchmen. A body of French officers, trying to escape from Peterhead, was driven back; but in spite of all precautions, the Pretender himself contrived to get away safely. Some imputation of negligence not unnaturally fell upon the Navy; but the Government was satisfied that reasonable diligence had been shown, and published in the *Gazette* the following :—

"The *Royal Anne*, galley, *Pearl*, *Port Mahon*, *Deal Castle* and *Phœnix* are returned from cruising, it appears by the journal of Captain Stuart,[1] that he had early intelligence of the Pretender having put to sea, in a clean-tallowed French snow, which rowed out of the harbour and close in along shore a good way with her sails furled. The *Port Mahon* lay all that night within two leagues of the harbour's mouth, but 'twas so dark there was no seeing a ship a quarter of a mile distant."[2]

Every precaution, indeed, seems to have been taken by the refugees; and it may be added that they appear to have been

[1] The Hon. Charles Stuart; born, 1681; Captain, 1704; Rear-Admiral, 1729; Vice-Admiral, 1733; died, 1740.

[2] Quoted in Lediard, 867.

aware of the disposition of the various cruisers. Leaving Montrose, the snow stretched across to the coast of Norway, whence she coasted southward and made Gravelines in safety. The Chevalier de St. George testified his gratitude and appreciation by knighting Mark Forrester, her master. In spite of their failure to intercept this snow, the English ships did good, if unostentatious, work in helping to stamp out the embers of the revolt, chiefly, of course, by co-operating with the troops when they chanced to touch the shore.

Piracy in the Mediterranean continued to demand considerable attention, but was at length dealt with by the Admiralty on something like a rational. system. In other words, there were ships constantly cruising against the Barbary pirates ; and there was thus avoided the great and often bootless expense incurred by the fitting out of occasional expeditions on a large scale. The reign is marked by no such fight as that of Captain Kempthorne of the *Mary Rose* in 1669; but cruisers detached, first by John Baker and after him by Charles Cornwall, the officers in command on the station, did efficient service. Of these the *Hind*, 20, Captain Arthur Delgarno, in May, 1716, took one Sallee rover, and, in October following, another, of 24 guns. This latter ship resisted for two and a half hours before she struck, and then promptly sank, taking down with her all but thirty-eight of her men. The *Bridge-water*, also, in the same year, drove two Sallee ships, each of 16 guns, ashore near their own port. The Barbary pirates, however, though a real nuisance, were not the only one of the kind, nor, indeed, were they so serious an obstacle to commerce as they had been in the seventeenth century. This was, as has been mentioned, partly due to the constant watch kept upon their movements. A more formidable species of piracy, the piracy of romance, flourished on the Spanish Main, and spread thence over the high seas. The doings of the notorious Kidd have been recorded ; the history of William Dampier shows with what ease British seamen drifted into this evil course of life ; and it will be easily understood that the Sir Francis Verneys and the Wards of the era preferred to join the successors of Sawkins, primarily to plunder the Spaniard, rather than to turn renegade and prey on their own countrymen in the Mediterranean. But though piracy in the West was a growing source of anxiety, the bulk of its exponents confined their attentions with some strictness to foreign flags, and some of them, notably Sir Henry Morgan, compared not unfavourably with the gentleman adventurers of the Elizabethan age. Kidd, it has been shown, was a decided exception; Avery was another; and so also was Edward Thatch, commonly called Teach, or, more commonly still, from his appearance, " Blackbeard." [1] Born in Bristol about 1675, he had, through the War of the Spanish Succession, served in privateers, and he did not turn his hand to piracy till the end of 1716. It is notorious that the pirates of fact enjoyed, to an even greater degree than their brethren of fiction, the short life and merry one supposed to belong to men of their calling; and for his enjoyment of existence, as well as for his egregious brutality, Thatch stands forth from among many short-lived contemporaries. About the end of 1717, he took a large Guineaman, which he named the *Queen Anne's Revenge*, and in which he went cruising, after having mounted her with forty guns. One of the first incidents of his cruise was the falling in with H.M.S. *Scarborough*, 20, which he beat off after a fight lasting for some hours. The governor of Carolina entered into a league with him, and he chose the coasts of that colony and of Virginia as his scene of operations, and continued haunting their creeks and preying on the merchants, whether at sea or ashore, till they petitioned the governor of Virginia to rid them of the pest. The governor took counsel with the captains of the *Lyme*, 20, and *Pearl*, 40, and concerted a scheme by which Lieut. Robert Maynard,[2] of the *Pearl*, was to command two small sloops against Blackbeard, who had got rid of his great ships, and was lurking in a sloop in Ocracoke Inlet, one of the entrances to Pamlico Sound. The sloops under Maynard's command mounted no heavy guns, while the pirates were known to be well armed in that respect; but, on the other hand, the sloops had sweeps, which their enemy had not. Maynard rowed into the passage on November 21st, 1718, and with great difficulty, after lightening his vessel, got close to Thatch, who had run aground. Meanwhile, the pirate sloop floated, and by a broadside of langridge, did great damage among Maynard's men, who were much exposed by the lowness in the waist of their ship. Maynard thereupon kept his men below as much as possible ; upon which Blackbeard, thinking

---

[1] In Johnson's ' Lives of the most Notorious Pirates,' he appears as Teach. In official papers he is Thatch.

[2] Died, a captain of 1740, in 1750.

that there were few left to deal with, boarded at the head of fifteen men. The rival commanders engaged hand to hand, and the fight went stubbornly on, as usual in such cases, till the pirate's death. Besides those killed, fifteen pirates were taken, and of them thirteen were hanged.[1] That Thatch had so few men with him was owing to his having marooned or otherwise got rid of the bulk of his company shortly before in consequence of a dispute as to the distribution of prize-money.

There was no lack of men to carry on the abominable work; but even of the best known of these desperadoes, such as Stede Bonnet, Edward England, John Rackam, and Howel Davis, none arrests the attention in such a degree as Bartholomew Roberts.[2] Roberts was, in 1718, mate of a ship which was plundered by pirates on the Guinea coast, and, joining his captors, was elected to the command on the death of Howel Davis, their captain. He cruised with considerable success from Brazil to Newfoundland, and, in 1721, crossed over to the African coast, where, amongst other prizes, he took a large ship belonging to the Royal Africa Company. To this ship he turned over, named her the *Royal Fortune*, mounted forty guns in her, and with a 32-gun ship, under a man named Skyrm, and a 24, continued his cruise. His luck continued good till on February 21st, 1722, when he and Skyrm lay anchored under Cape Lopez, there came down on him H.M.S. *Swallow*, 60, Captain Chaloner Ogle (1), which, since the preceding year, had been on that coast. Ogle knew with whom he had to deal; and when Skyrm, taking him for a merchantman, slipped in chase, he bore away out of earshot of the *Royal Fortune*. He then turned upon Skyrm, and, after a sharp encounter, took him. Returning to Cape Lopez and hoisting the French flag, he lured Roberts into attacking him. Roberts, overmatched and taken by surprise, made a desperate fight, which did not cease till he himself had been killed. Of 262 prisoners taken it is well to

---

[1] Of the two who escaped the gallows one was Israel Hands, the master, who at the time of the action was ashore recovering from a wound received from Thatch, who had a trick of blowing out his cabin lights and firing cross-handed under the table. Another practice of Blackbeard's was to light sulphur in the ship's hold, and to try who could longest withstand the fumes. This was by way of enlivening a dull cruise.

[2] Roberts is said to have been the original of Scott's Cleveland in 'The Pirate,' but the career of the real does not agree with that of the ideal. The doings of Roberts, as chronicled in Charles Johnson's 'General History of the Most Notorious Pirates,' are, so far as can be ascertained, substantially correct.

notice that 52 were hanged, and that only 77 were acquitted on trial.
The captured ships were taken to England, where they were
bestowed on Ogle,[1] who also for this good piece of work received
the honour of knighthood.

In the latter end of July, 1719, preparations were making in
England for a secret expedition against Spain. About fifty transports were got together to convey a force of four thousand men
under Viscount Cobham ; and, meanwhile, a small squadron was
sent ahead under Commodore Sir Robert Johnson, in the *Weymouth*,
to co-operate with the French who were then engaged in the siege
of San Sebastian. In the beginning of August, some French troops
and two hundred seamen were landed by the squadron at Fort San
Antonio. Owing to the strength of the batteries at the entrance
to the harbour, the force was landed some distance to the westward,
advancing from which direction, it destroyed the fortifications and
spiked the guns in the harbour. On September 15th, Johnson,
in the *Weymouth*, having the *Winchester* and *Dursley Galley* in
company, heard that there were two Spanish men-of-war and a
large merchantman lying in Rivadéo. Accordingly the *Weymouth*
and *Winchester* appeared off the port on the following day ; boats
were sent in to take soundings; and the two ships anchored alongside
the enemy and abreast of a battery of eight guns. The battery
was taken, the men-of-war were destroyed, and the merchantman
was brought off. In the meantime, the main expedition had sailed
and was looking for Johnson off the Spanish coast, in hopes of
gaining information from him. This force was commanded by
Vice-Admiral James Mighells, who, detached by Berkeley in the
spring, had learnt of the dispersal of the Spanish fleet intended for
the invasion of Scotland. The object now before Mighells, and
the soldiers under Cobham whom he convoyed, was to proceed to
Vigo and retaliate for this intended insult. Sailing from St. Helen's
on September 21st, 1719, the expedition made Vigo on the 29th
without being joined by Johnson. The fleet at once entered the
harbour and landed the troops about three miles from the town.
On October 1st, the army occupied a strong position under the
walls ; whereupon the enemy spiked the guns in their batteries
and withdrew to the citadel. A bomb ketch was brought up on
the 3rd ; but as she could do little, owing to the greatness of the
range, some forty odd mortars were put ashore ; and on the 4th,

---

[1] Captains' Letters, O 2.

Fort San Sebastian, which had been occupied, was armed with
heavy guns from the fleet. The citadel, upon that, surrendered,
its garrison of four hundred and sixty-nine officers and men
marching out on the 10th. The town, it was decided, could not
be held; but a large quantity of guns, small arms, and ammunition,
which had been collected for the invasion of England, was taken
and brought home. Seven ships, also, were seized in the harbour,
of which three were fitting out for privateers. On the 14th, the
ships reduced Ponte Vedra, at the upper end of the harbour.
There, too, many guns were found; so that the total number
brought home was one hundred and ninety iron and thirty brass
heavy guns, with ten thousand stand of small arms, two thousand
barrels of powder, and other warlike stores. On November 11th,
Vice-Admiral Mighells put into Falmouth with the *Enterprize*,
Kingsale, and *Biddeford,* and with most of the transports. The
expedition had been prompt and successful : it had fully attained its
object ; and by sickness, desertion, and the sword it had lost no
more than three hundred men.

The difficulties experienced by British merchants in the Spanish
settlements of the west were a heritage of the days of Elizabeth, and
were by no means smoothed away by the many treaties which had
been entered into between the two nations.[1] It is not possible here
to enter into an examination of these treaties; let it suffice to say
that, by forbidding, save under the harshest restrictions, all traffic,
except, of course, that in negroes, which had been granted by the
Assiento, they put a premium on smuggling. We know the traditional attitude of English and Spaniards to one another in the
New World, and we have noticed the growth of piracy, testifying to
the existence of a considerable proportion of unsettled spirits among
the British inhabitants of the American colonies. When we consider both the evergreen national hatred, and the bitterness with
which the guarda costas must have regarded the enterprising and
unscrupulous smugglers, we cannot wonder at the tales of brutality
on the part of the Spaniards; but we must also be prepared to
believe that the Spaniards spoke the truth when they insisted that
the British traders of the islands were not always the lambs
they professed to be, and were, in many cases, but little removed
from pirates. There always has been ill-feeling about the right of

[1] The texts of these treaties will be found at length in Rousset de Missy, 'Recueil
Historique'; and in Jean Dumont, 'Corps Universel Diplomatique,' vol. viii.

search—probably there always will be—nor are we to believe that a guarda costa, boarding a Jamaica smuggler in 1720, acted with such civility as we expect from the Customs' House nowadays. On the contrary, as he often had considerable difficulty in catching his suspect, he was prone to try to catch him where he could, and to scruple little whether he caught him in Spanish waters or on the high seas. Such was the state of affairs, and it is clear that it was bound, sooner or later, to lead to war. Before passing on to the war itself, it will be interesting to examine in some detail one or two of the incidents that thus led up to it.

In the latter part of 1728, a Spanish guarda costa sighted and bore down on the *Dursley Galley*, 20, mistaking her for a merchantman, and with the intention of searching her. Naturally, the *Dursley Galley* did not bring to, and the Spaniard opened fire, which the British ship warmly returned. After a short fight, in which the guarda costa lost five men killed and twenty wounded, the Spaniard surrendered. That she was shortly afterwards released was due simply to the fact that there was no reason for keeping her, and Lediard [1] is undoubtedly wrong when he points to this as illustrative of the difference between Spanish and English methods. As will presently be shown, British ships that were detained were, at any rate in most cases, legally detained as being smugglers. The next incident to be mentioned was connected with the vexed question of the gathering of salt at the Tortugas. It must be remembered that the right to gather salt,[2] like the right to cut logwood at Campeche, was denied to the English by the Spaniards, although, in point of fact, it had actually been acknowledged by the Convention of Madrid. Early in 1733, a fleet of British ships under escort of the *Scarborough*, 20, Captain Thomas Durell (1),[3] was loading salt at the Tortugas, when there came down on it two Spanish men-of-war, one of sixty, and the other of seventy guns.[4] Four of the merchantmen, viz., the *Catherine*, *Two Sisters*, *Hopewell*, and *Three Brothers*, were taken at the outset before the *Scarborough* could cover her convoy; but after that she managed to engage the attention of the Spaniards so well that the rest of the salt ships made good their escape.

A point that is apt to be passed over in such an account as this is that two Spanish ships of the line were quite equal to making mince-

[1] Lediard, 913.   [3] Captains' Letters, D 4.
[2] Rousset de Missy, i. 441.   [4] Beatson, i. 22.

meat of the *Scarborough* first and of her convoy afterwards, had they been so inclined.   It would appear, then, that the Spaniards, whose force seems to be exaggerated, and who were probably heavy coast-guard cruisers, believed themselves to be engaging merely in the reprisals customary in those parts, and that, when they found that they had before them a King's ship, they refused to fight her for fear of involving themselves in serious diplomatic entanglements.

Whether the guarda costas are to be regarded as privateers or not, there is interest in a letter written from Jamaica by Commodore Edward St. Loe, to Burchett, at the Admiralty, in May, 1728.[1] Complaining that Spanish privateers infested the Jamaican coasts, he said :—

"It's my opinion I could go in and destroy most of them had I but His Majesty's permission.   They, according to my notion, are no better than pirates, having no commission for what they do, save from the governor of the place."

This is the opinion of a man qualified to judge.   It may be tempered by that of another naval officer who commanded on that station, and who certainly held no brief for the Spaniards.   This was Rear-Admiral the Hon. Charles Stuart, who was sent out to Jamaica in the *Lion* on December 9th, 1729, to take over the command of the station in succession to St. Loe.   Stuart seems to have begun his commission with the prevailing belief that the fault lay with the Spaniards, but his attitude changed somewhat as time went on, and as his knowledge of the British merchants increased. Writing on October 12th, 1731, to the Duke of Newcastle, he admitted that the British carried on the trade at their own risk, and that the ships were good prize if taken.   This, he said, led them to retaliate by robbing such Spaniards as they could overpower, and he added :—

"I can assure you that the sloops that sail from this island manned and armed on that illicit trade, have more than once bragged to me of having murdered seven or eight Spaniards on their own shore.   I can't help observing that I believe I am the first military person who has stood up in the defence of peace and quietness, and for delivering up vessels, against a parcel of men who call themselves merchants, but they are no better than pedlars, and one of them formerly in jail for piracy."

His plea for peace and quietness may have been merely the outcome of his knowledge that, as the British had by far the greater number of ships in those seas, reprisals would be a losing game.   That truth was abundantly evidenced when war broke out; for from September,

[1] Home Office Records, Admiralty, No. 66, quoted in 'Eng. Hist. Rev.,' iv. 741.

1739, to November, 1741, the Spaniards took 331 British ships as against only 231 of their own which they lost.[1]

On September 12th, 1731, Stuart wrote to the governor of Havana a strong letter of complaint. It had been hoped that a better condition of affairs was about to begin, as the King of Spain, in response to pressure from England, had sent instructions to his colonial governors to mitigate their harshness to British traders. But this proclamation was bound to be without effect, for it exempted from its protection all such ships as were engaged in the illicit trade, while leaving it to the governors concerned to draw the necessary distinction between legal and illegal traffic.[2] So it was that Stuart never lacked cause of complaint, and, in the instance cited,[3] made mention "particularly of one Fandino, and others who have committed the most cruel piratical outrages . . . particularly about the 20th April last, sailed out of your harbour in one of those guarda costas, and met a ship of this island,[4] bound for England . . ." and so forth, giving the well-known traditional details of the notorious Jenkins case. He ended this letter with, " The king, my master, having reason to believe that these repeated insults on his subjects could never be continued but by the connivance of the several Spanish governors in these parts, is determined to endeavour to put a stop to these piratical proceedings." But at the same time he was much attacked by the merchants, who objected strongly to his saying that they exaggerated their case, and who resented his interference with their illicit trade, and his endeavours to repress their cruelties.

Juan de Leon Fandino, probably more from the accident of his having handled Jenkins than for any other reason, stands out from among the guarda costa officers. On September 9th, 1731, he detained and plundered the *Prince William*, William Joy, master, but this ship was released a month later. Not so the *Dolphin*, Benjamin Carkett, master, which was taken by Fandino in July, and sent into Havana. She was adjudged legal prize, as the governor wrote to Stuart; but he added that he intended to chastise Spanish privateers,

---

[1] Lists in *Gent. Mag.* 1741, pp. 689–698.

[2] Beatson, i. 15.

[3] This letter, taken from Home Office Records, Admiralty, No. 69, is printed in 'Eng. Hist. Rev.,' vol. iv.

[4] Jenkins's ship, the *Rebecca*, is not here mentioned by name, but is identified with this vessel by a list of ships taken or plundered by the Spaniards down to December, 1737. The *Rebecca* was taken on April 9th, which in the new style would be the 20th.

who were now no longer necessary, and whose commissions he had revoked. Stuart, however, must stop ships coming from Jamaica to Cuba, where British and Dutch ships were then to be found all through the year.

What ultimately became of Fandino falls into its place here, though chronologically the story should be postponed. On June 4th, 1742, among the Bahamas, Captain Thomas Frankland, of the *Rose*, fell in with, and chased, four ships, which showed British colours.[1] He chased under the same, and, overhauling them, fired a gun.[1] The chase then hoisted the Spanish flag, and fought him furiously, using all sorts of missiles, from broadsides of shot to poisoned arrows. Frankland, however, held his fire for the fourth ship, a snow, which seemed the strongest, giving the others only a few guns as they chanced to bear. The first three sheered off badly hulled.

"I then endeavoured," says Frankland, "to lay the snow aboard, which she shunned with the utmost caution, maintaining a warm fire till I had torn her almost to rags, the commander having determined rather to sink than strike, for reasons you'll hereafter be sensible of: but in about four hours the people, in opposition to the captain, hauled down the colours."

The prize mounted ten carriage guns, as many swivels, and had a crew of over eighty men.

"The captain is Juan de Leon Fandino. . . . He is the man that commanded the guard of coast out of the Havana that took Jenkins when his ears were cut off. . . . Not but such a desperado with his crew of Indians, Mulattoes and Negroes could have acted as he did, for we were at least two hours within pistol shot of him keeping a constant fire."

So much for a story which has long been accounted a myth, both from its intrinsic improbability, and from the circumstance that Jenkins, like other merchant skippers who gave evidence before the House of Commons in 1738, was not on oath.[2]

In 1739, as has been seen, reprisals were ordered, and instructions to that effect were sent out to Commodore Charles Brown at Jamaica, whose broad pennant was then flying in the *Hampton Court*.[3] The bearer of this dispatch was the Hon. Edward Boscawen, of the *Shoreham*, who joined Brown at Port Royal on August 6th, and,

---

[1] Captains' Letters, F.

[2] Mr. Lecky's opinion of the truth of the story is given on page 51 of this volume; and neither Stuart's nor Frankland's letter really goes far towards contradicting that opinion.—W. L. C.

[3] The *Hampton Court's* log is of little value; details of the cruise will be found in the Commodore's log, bound up with his dispatches in Admirals' Dispatches 1738–1742, Jamaica, in the Public Record Office.

after whose accession, the squadron consisted, besides the two ships named, of the *Falmouth, Diamond, Torrington, Windsor* and *Drake*. Brown at once proceeded to carry out his orders, and on the following day the *Drake* and the *Hampton Court's* barge brought in a schooner. On the 14th the whole squadron left Port Royal, and proceeded round Cuba on a cruise, during which, owing to the scarcity of Spanish ships, they did no great amount of damage, but managed to collect reliable information as to the strength and distribution of Spanish men-of-war in those seas. On September 3rd, Captain Charles Knowles, of the *Diamond*, was detached in pursuit of a strange sail, and did not rejoin. The *Shoreham* was the most successful ship of the squadron. In her, Boscawen reconnoitred Havana, and, near that port, destroyed two sloops and took another, while a little later, about September 15th, he landed at Porto Maria, and burnt a large quantity of timber and other stores. He was there attacked by two half galleys and a sloop, but they kept in such shoal water that the *Shoreham*, though hulled more than once, could not get close enough to harm them. Meanwhile, a small fort between Matanzas and Havana was destroyed. Brown, having stayed for twelve days off Havana in hopes of falling in with a Spanish squadron, learnt that none was expected, and, leaving the *Windsor* and *Falmouth* to cruise there till the end of the month, proceeded round the western end of the island, and, on October 28th, anchored in Port Royal. There he found the *Diamond*, which had made two captures—a ship and a brigantine, said to be worth £30,000. These, with two other small sloops taken, and a few large canoes, represent the total damage done. In Port Royal lay Vernon's squadron, to which Brown had by that time become attached.

Active warfare was at first entirely confined to the West Indies ; and in European seas the first action of importance took place when the *Princesa*, 64, six hundred men, of the Spanish Ferrol squadron, fell in with the *Lenox, Kent,* and *Orford,* which had been detached from Vice-Admiral John Balchen's squadron. These three ships, with the *St. Albans* and *Ripon*, had been cruising to intercept a convoy of treasure ships under Pizarro, but saw nothing of them. Pizarro, for his success on this service, was appointed immediately to command the expedition which was sent out to round Cape Horn and to act as a check on Anson. The *Princesa* was sighted at 9 A.M. on April 8th, 1740, and was at once chased by the three ships, viz., *Lenox*, 70, Captain Covill Mayne, *Kent*, 70, Captain Thomas

Durell (1), and *Orford*, 70, Captain Lord Augustus Fitzroy (1).[1]
The chase was then under French colours; but, when the *Orford*
drew up soon after half-past ten, she hoisted Spanish.   About eleven
the *Lenox* also drew close up, and opened fire with her chase-guns,
being soon followed by the *Orford*.   All three ships came into close
action and gave her many broadsides, for the most part within pistol
shot; but she made a most stubborn defence, and, though she became
ungovernable, owing to the loss of her foretopmast, early in the engagement, she proved capable of a great deal of passive resistance.   In
explanation of this it was pointed out at the time that she was more
heavily armed than the British 70's.   The Spanish establishment was,
24-prs. on the lower deck, 18-prs. on the upper deck, and 8-prs. on the
quarter deck and forecastle, as against 24, 12, and 6-prs. in the British
Navy; but it is possible that the *Princesa* may have had heavier guns
mounted.   She was moreover of very stout scantling, and, having small
portholes, was, defensively at any rate, a most powerful ship.   It has
also been suggested that, as a fresh breeze was blowing, the British
ships could not use their lower deck guns.   This was not so.   Covill
Mayne makes special mention of sending the enemy broadsides from
his lower, upper, and quarter-deck guns.   The reports clash somewhat; but, roughly, the middle part of the action seems to have
been fought with the *Princesa* out of hand, the *Kent* on her larboard
beam, and the *Lenox* or *Orford* on her starboard side, and the third
ship always under her stern, raking her fore and aft.   In the afternoon the *Orford* had her fore rigging so much disabled that she
dropped astern and had to lie to to knot and splice; but meanwhile
the raking fire from the *Lenox* had carried away the *Princesa's* main
and mizen masts.   The *Orford*, having repaired damages, drew up
again; and thereupon the enemy struck her colours, having maintained an almost hopeless struggle with the utmost gallantry for
close on seven hours.   Not unnaturally Lord Augustus Fitzroy
claimed that she had struck to him, and sent the first boat on board,
following closely himself.   To Covill Mayne's indignation he
received the sword of her commander, Don Pablo Agustin de
Aguirre, and took charge of her papers.   There was some angry
protest, but the matter seems to have blown over.   The prize, rated
as a 70, continued for some years as one of the best two-deckers in
the British Navy.

The next operation that falls within the scheme of this chapter

[1] Captains' Letters, vols. M 9, and F 5.

was not so satisfactory to British pride. General Oglethorpe, commanding the troops on the North American station, conceived the notion that it would be to His Majesty's service to take St. Augustine, in Florida.[1] Accordingly he consulted with the General Assembly of Carolina, asking what troops could be spared to him; and he also gained the adherence to his plan of Captain Vincent Pearce (1), of the *Flamborough*, the Commodore on the station. The project was first suggested to Pearce in January, 1740; but the general found some difficulty in putting it on a working basis, and it was not till April that he renewed his request for the co-operation of his ships. These were :—

Ships.	Guns.	Commanders.
Flamborough . . .	20	Captain Vincent Pearce (1).
Hector	44	„ Sir Yelverton Peyton, Bart.
Squirrel	20	„ Peter Warren.
Phœnix	20	„ Charles Fanshaw.
Tartar	22	„ the Hon. George Townshend.
Spence	6[1]	„ William Laws.
Wolf	8	Commander William Dandridge.
Hawk	6[2]	
and a schooner.	8	

[1] and ten swivels.   [2] and four swivels.

When Oglethorpe's request was finally made the squadron was just on the point of starting on a cruise, and was therefore in perfect readiness for immediate action. The *Squirrel* was sent off St. Augustine pending the arrival of the rest of the force; and she was annoyed by six half-galleys that lay there, and which, during calms and light winds, proved of considerable service to the Spaniards. The *Wolf* was sent on to join Warren towards the end of April, and on the 28th the *Squirrel* took a sloop belonging to the king of Spain. This prize mounted eight 4-prs. and six swivels, and had eight thousand pieces of eight on board. In May the *Hector* and *Spence* joined the ships off the bar of St. Augustine, Pearce meanwhile lying in St. John's River co-operating with the troops then on the advance from the northward. Two small forts, St. Francis de Pupa and Fort Diego, were taken by Oglethorpe, who then returned to the mouth of the St. John's River, whence on May 31st a general advance was made. On June 1st Pearce proceeded off St. Augustine, and found the Spaniards getting away their guns from a battery on the Island of St. Eustatia. He

[1] Captains' Letters, vol. P 8.

promptly sent in his boats, ordering the *Wolf* and *Spence* to cover the attack; but the enemy gave no trouble, making off into the harbour on the approach of the boats.   On June 5th it was decided at a council of war that the ships could remain on that coast till July 5th; on the 7th there was another skirmish with the galleys; and on the 13th the island was occupied by two hundred seamen and as many soldiers.   Two days later Colonel Palmer was killed at Fort Moosa and his party driven back; a serious reverse which gave the enemy free communication to the landward. Meanwhile guns were brought into position on the island, and two small craft were fitted to serve against the galleys, there being so little water on the bar that the ships could not get in.   On June 20th the governor was summoned to surrender, but promptly refused.   Deserters soon afterwards came into the British camp with news that the galleys were very badly manned and could easily be taken.   As it had been discovered that the range was so great that the guns on the island could have little effect, a council of war was held with the view of seeing whether this information should be acted upon.   Pearce, however, was averse from taking the risk: possibly he had doubts of the deserters; and he persisted in his refusal though the land officers offered to put one hundred soldiers into the boats to take the places of those seamen who were absent in the batteries ashore.   On this Colonel Vanderdussen pointed out how badly off the troops would be when the ships left the coast; for the galleys would cut their communications.   Pearce found that there was no port near where he could lay his ships up for the hurricane season; and, not being too well manned, he had to refuse a request that he would leave two hundred seamen to reinforce the troops.   It was by that time July; and the moment had come when, in accordance with the council of war of June 5th, the ships were to leave the coast.   Without any friction, therefore, between Oglethorpe and Pearce, it was decided that nothing further could be done,[1] and on the 5th the whole force withdrew, the ships covering it from any attempt on the part of the galleys.

In July, 1741, Captain Curtis Barnet, of the *Dragon*, 60, was detached from Vice-Admiral Nicolas Haddock's squadron with the two 44-gun ships, *Feversham* and *Folkestone*, and with orders to cruise in the neighbourhood of the Strait of Gibraltar.   Being off

[1] Bound up with Pearce's letters are his log for three months, the minutes of the councils of war, and letters from Oglethorpe, Vanderdussen, Peyton and others.

Cape Spartel on the 25th of the month he chased and came up with
three ships, which he had reason to believe were two Spanish
register ships under convoy of a frigate. The *Feversham* had fallen
astern, and the other two ships did not come up with the strangers
till after dark. Barnet hailed to know what they were, and was
answered that they were Frenchmen from Martinique. He explained
that he was an English man-of-war, and that it was his duty to
satisfy himself that they were not Spaniards ; but, to his demand
that his boat should be allowed to board them, he received no
response save incivilities. Finding that he could do nothing by
talking, and being confirmed in his belief that the ships were really
Spanish, he opened fire, after due warning. The ships were, however, really French, being the *Borée*, 62, the *Aquilon*, 46, and the
Flore, 26,[1] under the command of Captain de Caylus, in the first
named. A brisk action ensued, and the British ships, as the *Feversham* was still far astern, being somewhat at a disadvantage, soon
found themselves obliged to lie to for half an hour to knot and splice.
In the morning, they and their consort again came up with the
Frenchman, and a boat was sent on board the *Borée* under a flag of
truce. The truth at once appeared ; but it also appeared that the
ships, being on their way from the West Indies, and knowing the
state of relations between the two countries, were under the conviction that war had broken out. Barnet's lieutenant was requested to
swear before the French officers whether this were the case or not,
and was able to satisfy them that the two monarchies were still at
peace. It is hard to say that either Barnet or De Caylus was to
blame ; but the trouble might have been avoided had M. de
Pardaillan, the captain of the *Aquilon*, been less suspicious of a
British ship ranging alongside cleared for action. The blame really
lay with the government which, though knowing that war was
inevitable, hesitated to declare it. As it was, the ships parted with
mutual apologies, and with a loss in killed of eleven men on the
British side, and of about thirty-five, among whom was M. de
Pardaillan, on board the French ships. All the vessels, moreover,
had their masts and rigging much cut.

Meanwhile, in the West Indies, several of the cruisers which
were detached by Vernon had better fortune than the main fleet.
Some fell in with register ships of considerable value, and others did
good service by capturing dispatch vessels. Of these latter the

[1] Froude, i. 289.   [2] Barnet's letter in Beatson, iii. 31.

Worcester, 60, took a Spanish 24-gun ship bearing dispatches to the viceroy of Mexico, and the *Squirrel*, 20, Captain Peter Warren, captured a large privateer belonging to Santiago de Cuba. It is said that the importance of this prize lay in information gained from her papers that the French squadron, under M. d'Antin at Port Louis, was intended to join with the Spaniards at Havana.[1] Be that as it may, M. d'Antin's squadron was rendered ineffective by putrid fever,[2] and the breach with France was postponed. Captures in the West Indies, as in home waters, were frequent; but so great was the number of the enemy's privateers, and so large the number of British merchantmen, that the balance was not in favour of Great Britain; and the London merchants, dissatisfied with the conduct of the war, fell to petitioning Parliament for a redress of grievances.[3]

Early in the next year the *Tiger*, 50, Captain Edward Herbert (1), was lost on a key near Tortuga. The crew got safely ashore with a quantity of stores and provisions, and raised on the island a fortification, in which they mounted twenty of the ship's guns. It was well that they did so, for the Spaniards, hearing of the misadventure, sent the *Fuerte*, 60, to capture them. She was, however, lost in the attempt, and the *Tiger's* men, after two months on the island, managed in their boats to take a sloop, in which they reached Jamaica. Though several prizes of value were made during the year, 1742, there was only one that calls for note. This was the guarda costa already mentioned, commanded by Fandino, the man who is alleged to have ill-treated Jenkins, and whose capture has been described as a fitting conclusion to the Jenkins episode.[4]

The Spaniards at that time sent out a new governor to Cartagena, and with him a reinforcement of over a thousand men. The troops were in five ships of the Caracas company, of which two mounted 40, two 30, and the fifth 12 guns. The squadron was dispersed by a hurricane, and two of the ships were lost, while the others, one of the 40's and both the 30's, fell in on April 12th, 1742, with the *Eltham*, 40, Captain Edward Smith, and the *Lively*, 20, Commander Henry Stewart. After some hours' hard fighting, night ended the engagement, and the Spaniards bore up for Puerto Rico. As they had lost in killed and wounded some six hundred men,

---

[1] Beatson, i. 115.
[2] Poissonnier Desperrières, 'Maladies des gens de Mer,' p. 295.
[3] Beatson, i. 121–25. See also *Gent. Mag.* 1741, pp. 689–698.
[4] See above, pp. 51 and 266.

including the new governor among the former, it[1] may be said that the reinforcement had been practically annihilated.

On September 21st, 1742, the Navy sustained a heavy loss in the destruction of the *Tilbury*, 60, Captain Peter Lawrence, by fire, off Hispaniola.　The cause of the accident was a drunken scuffle; and the whole of the story, down to the loss of one hundred men, corresponds almost exactly with that of the destruction of the *Paragon* during Penn's return from the West Indies in June, 1655.[2]

The destruction of five Spanish galleys at St. Tropez in June, 1742, was a spirited piece of service.　Captain Richard Norris, of the *Kingston*, 60, had been detached, with the *Oxford*, 50, and *Duke*, fireship, in company, to blockade them; but as St. Tropez, being a French port, was neutral, there would have been no attack had not the galleys been so ill-advised as to fire upon the British.　On June 13th, therefore, Norris gave orders to Commander Smith Callis, of the *Duke*, to go in and do his utmost to destroy the galleys at the mole. Callis went in on the 14th, and fired his ship with such good effect, that the whole of the five were destroyed.　So rapidly did he carry out his orders that nothing was saved from the *Duke*, not even the ship's or officers' papers.[3]　For his success, Callis was posted to the *Assistance*.

Early in 1743, Vice-Admiral Thomas Mathews, hearing that the Spanish ship *San Isidoro*, 70, was lying in the Bay of Ajaccio, sent in the *Ipswich*, 70, Captain William Martin (1), *Revenge*, 70, Captain George Berkeley, and the *Anne Galley*, fireship, to bring her out. Her captain refused to yield to the odds arrayed against him, and opened fire, but finding it impossible to hold the ship, he ordered her to be burnt.　She blew up before all her people had been taken out of her, and a considerable number of men perished.

Apart from this piece of work, there was little done in the Mediterranean, though the cruisers continued to send in prizes, and to annoy the enemy's coast.　In June, however, the enemy contrived so far to avoid the blockading squadron as to carry fifteen shiploads of warlike stores from Majorca to Genoa for the use of the army in Italy.　Mathews at once appeared off that port with six sail of the line, and overawed the Genoese into sending the supplies back to Corsica, there to lie till the conclusion of the war.

[1] Beatson, i. 149.
[2] See above, Vol. II. p. 208.
[3] Captains' Letters, C 14.　Callis to Thomas Corbett, August 11th, 1742.

The following year, 1744, was very far from being a fortunate one for the British navy. The fiasco off Toulon was supplemented by the capture of the *Seaford,* 20, *Solebay,* 20, and *Grampus,* 14, by de Rochambeau, by the throwing away of the *Northumberland,* 70, and by the loss, through stress of weather, of the *Victory,* 100,[1] *Orford,* 70, *Colchester,* 50, *St. Albans,* 50, *Greenwich,* 50, and other ships of less value. Against this tale of disaster we could oppose merely the capture of the *Médée,* 26, on April 27th, by the *Dreadnought,* 50, Captain the Hon. Edward Boscawen,[2] and *Grampus,* 14, which formed part of the fleet of Vice-Admiral Sir Charles Hardy (1), off the coast of Portugal.

Of these misfortunes that requiring most particular notice here is the loss of the *Northumberland.* This ship, commanded by Captain Thomas Watson (1), was detached in chase of a strange sail on May 8th by the Vice-Admiral, who was then homeward bound from the Tagus. In view of the sequel, it is worth remembering that Watson was a good and brave officer, favourably known in the service for his work as Vernon's flag-captain at Puerto Bello and Cartagena. But his skull had been fractured, and his mind impaired, so that " a small matter of liquor rendered him quite out of order, which was his unhappy fate that day." [3] The weather grew thick, the chase was lost sight of, and the signal was made for the *Northumberland's* recall ; but Watson held on. Soon three sail were made out to leeward, and as he bore down on them under a press of sail, it was seen that they were two two-decked ships and a frigate. They were, in point of fact, the

Ships.	Guns.	Commanders.
Content . . .	64	Captain de Conflans.
Mars	64	,, du Perrier.
Vénus	26	,, d'Aché.

The French ships lay to under topsails, while the *Northumberland* bore down on them. Properly handled, the British ship would have

[1] See the previous chapter.
[2] Boscawen's nickname in the service dates from this time. The seamen transferred the name of the ship to the man ; and he went through life as " Old Dreadnought."
[3] 'A true and authentic Narrative of the action between the *Northumberland* and three French men of war' . . . . By an Eye Witness. 8vo, 1745.

had them at a disadvantage, for they were widely separated, and the *Content*, a mile to windward of her consorts, made no attempt to rejoin them.   Watson, therefore, had the option of disabling her before the others could interfere, or of following the counsel of his master, Dixon, who advised him to stand close-hauled to the north-ward [1] under a press of sail, and so to lead the enemy across the course of the British fleet.   This advice was disregarded, and no reasonable nor customary measures were taken to put the ship into a fit state for action.

"We bore down so precipitately that our small sails were not stowed, nor top-gallant sails furled, before the enemy began to fire on us, and at the same time we had the cabins to clear away ; the hammocks were not stowed as they should be; in short we had nothing in order."

Instead of engaging the weathermost ship, the *Content*, Watson ran down to leeward without answering her fire, and so had to deal at once with his three enemies.   Even then, there was no real reason why the ship should be taken, for the French gunnery was so extremely bad that she was little hurt, and had but few men killed. But Watson fell early in the action, none of the lieutenants were on deck to take command, and the Master ordered the colours to be struck, though there was fight enough left both in the ship and in her crew.   The *Northumberland* was taken into Brest, and till the 1st of June, 1794, for fifty years, the trophy name found a place on French navy lists.   When the officers returned to England from their captivity, a court-martial was held.   The first lieutenant, Thomas Craven, was honourably acquitted, but Dixon, the master, was condemned for surrendering the ship.   The court took into consideration the good advice which he had given his captain before the action, and sentenced him only to be imprisoned for life in the Marshalsea.   The court found also "that Captain Watson had behaved very rashly and inconsiderately, to which was owing chiefly the loss of her "; but death had settled his account.[2]

The hurricane that devastated Jamaica on October 20th was one of the most violent upon record.   Admiral Sir Chaloner Ogle (1) was at sea with a great part of the fleet, and so escaped its fury; but eight ships of the Royal Navy, besides a great number of merchant-men, were either wrecked or driven ashore.   The *Greenwich*, 50,

[1] The wind was westerly.
[2] Minutes of Court Martial held at Portsmouth on February 1st, 1744–5.   R. O. vol. 27.

Captain Edward Allen, was sunk, with the loss of her captain, a lieutenant, and seventy men; the *Lark*, hulk,[1] sank, and one hundred and ten men with her; and the *St. Albans*, 50, Captain William Knight, *Bonetta*, sloop, Commander William Lea, and *Thunder*, bomb, were also total losses. The *Prince of Orange*, 60, *Montagu*, 60, and *Experiment*, 20, went ashore, but were got off again.[2] The history of the year at sea was about as disheartening as possible; and 1745 saw no marked improvement.

On January 6th, 1745, four sail of the line, the *Hampton Court*, 70, Captain Savage Mostyn; *Captain*, 70, Captain Thomas Griffin (1); *Sunderland*, 60, Captain John Brett; and *Dreadnought*, 60, Captain Thorpe Fowke, cruising off Ushant, sighted and gave chase to three French ships to the north-east. These were the *Neptune*, 74, and *Fleuron*, 64, homeward bound from Martinique, with a vast quantity of specie on board, worth four millions sterling, it is said, and in company with the privateer *Mars*, George Walker, master, which they had captured two days before. As the captain of the *Fleuron* told Walker, who was a prisoner on board his ship, the French commodore had made a great mistake in interrupting his journey to Brest for so trifling an object as the *Mars*. This was hardly complimentary to Walker, who at that time, with Fortunatus Wright, did as much to uphold British prestige at sea as any captains of the Royal Navy; but it was true, and, had the two French ships fallen, they would richly have deserved their fate. As it was, they were not captured; and the story, as disclosed in the subsequent court-martial,[3] and in an able comment thereon addressed to the House of Commons,[4] is very unpleasant reading.

It is desirable here to enter into the matter in some detail, for it shows the alarming state to which British naval prestige had fallen, and it explains the necessity for the new Naval Discipline Act of 1749.

The French ships, after their long passage, were both sickly and foul, and the English, with a fresh southerly breeze, gradually crept up. The *Captain*, the leading ship, kept away after the *Mars*, and took possession of her at dusk, leaving the others to continue the

---

[1] Formerly a 44-gun ship.
[2] Beatson, i. 193.
[3] Minutes of the Court Martial, etc. 1745, 8vo.
[4] 'An Enquiry into the Conduct of Captain Mostyn, being remarks on the Minutes of the Court Martial, etc. Humbly addressed to the Hon. House of Commons by a Sea Officer.' 1745, 8vo.

chase. The *Sunderland* carried away her main topmast, and dropped astern; but at sunset the *Hampton Court* was close up with the enemy. The *Dreadnought*, sailing very badly, could not quite get up, and Mostyn shortened sail to wait for her. All through the night and during the next day, the position continued the same, the *Dreadnought* sailing no faster than the chase and the *Hampton Court* not engaging without her. At last, after ranging abreast of the *Neptune*, but out of gunshot to windward, Mostyn decided that nothing could be done, and left the French to carry their valuable cargo into Brest.[1] Of course the two ships ought to have been taken. Griffin, who was senior officer, had no business to bear away after the *Mars*; yet, apart from that, it was Mostyn's duty to have engaged as soon as he came up, and to have detained the enemy till the *Dreadnought* could get into action. Griffin, at the court-martial, stated that when he bore away he believed the *Mars* alone to be a ship of war and the other two to be merchantmen under her convoy. He was accordingly acquitted; but, as the other three ships had no doubt whatever as to the nature of the *Neptune* and *Fleuron*, and as the *Captain* was nearest to them, the opinion of the service was unfavourable to the commanding officer of the ship last named. As for Mostyn, the evidence went that, in the fresh breeze that was blowing, the *Hampton Court's* lower deck ports could not be opened, while both the enemy's ships could fight all their guns, to leeward as well as to windward. It was further stated that the *Hampton Court* lay along so much that shot from her upper deck guns, at extreme elevation, would have struck the water fifty yards from their muzzles. This, however, was mere conjecture, and does not explain why not a shot was tried. It might have been possible to knock away a spar, and to give the *Dreadnought* a chance of coming into action. As to the Frenchman's lower deck guns being run out to leeward, the writer of the appeal to the House of Commons [2] points out that the witness who swore to this fact proved too much. Those on board the *Hampton Court*, in her position to windward, were not in a condition to see whether the enemy's lee ports were open or not. There was no cross-examination; and the Court decided that Mostyn " had done his duty as an experienced good officer, and as a man of courage

---

[1] The *Fleuron* was, however, blown up in Brest harbour before her treasure could be taken out of her.

[2] Believed to be Vernon.

and conduct." It is difficult to believe that this decision was come to without bias. At any rate, it by no means satisfied public opinion ; and, a year later, the *Hampton Court*, with Mostyn still in command, went out of Portsmouth Harbour to the cry of " All's well ! there's no Frenchman in the way." [1]

On February 20th following, the *Chester*, 50, Captain Francis Geary, and *Sunderland*, 60, Captain John Brett, fell in in the Soundings with the *Eléphant*, 20, then on her way home from the Mississippi, and having twenty-four thousand pieces of eight on board. They chased, shot away her main topmast, and captured her. This was but a mere flicker of success, closely to be followed by another loss and by another unsatisfactory court-martial.

On March 28th, the *Anglesey*, 44, Captain Jacob Elton, one of the ships cruising to command the entrance of the Channel, put out of Kingsale, whither she had been to land some sick, amongst whom was her first lieutenant. On the following day, a fresh westerly breeze blowing, a large sail was sighted to windward. Elton, making sure that she was his consort the *Augusta*, piped to dinner, and paid no further heed. Meanwhile, the stranger came down fast ; but it was not till she was close to the *Anglesey* that, yawing slightly, she showed French ornamentation on her quarter. Then all was hurry and confusion. Elton, to gain time, ordered the foresail to be set ; but the only effect of this manœuvre was to bury the lee lower deck ports in the sea and almost to swamp the ship. The enemy, which proved to be the *Apollon*, 50, belonging to the French navy, but fitted out by private adventurers, ran close under the stern of the *Anglesey* and rounded-to on her lee quarter, pouring in a heavy fire. Elton and the Master fell at the first discharge, and the command devolved on the second lieutenant, Baker Phillips. The decks were not cleared ; the ship was half-full of water ; and sixty men were dead or wounded. Phillips could not order the helm to be put up without falling aboard a ship as full of men as his was of water ; so, taking hasty counsel with Taafe, the third lieutenant, he decided that no effective resistance could be offered, and ordered the colours to be struck. It is difficult to see what else Phillips could have done. William Hutchinson, " the Mariner," laid down that a ship attacked as the *Anglesey* was ought to be box-hauled, and to pass under the enemy's stern raking him, as the

[1] Charnock, iv. 431.

Serapis subsequently did in the course of her action with the *Bonhomme Richard*. But in 1745 Phillips could not have had the advantage of a study of Hutchinson's ' Treatise on Practical Seamanship '; and, being a young man and inexperienced, he acted as most other men in his position would have done. The ship was lost by being engaged to leeward. The subsequent court-martial [1]—

" was unanimously of opinion that Captain Elton, deceased, did not give timely directions for getting his ship clear or in a proper posture of defence, nor did he afterwards behave like an officer or a seaman, which was the cause of the ship being left to Lieutenant Phillips in such distress and confusion. And that Lieutenant Baker Phillips, late second lieutenant of the said ship, by not endeavouring to the utmost of his power after Captain Elton's death to put the ship in order of fighting, not encouraging the inferior officers and common men to fight courageously, and by yielding to the enemy, falls under part of the tenth article. They do sentence him to death, to be shot by a platoon of musqueteers on the forecastle, . . . but . . . having regard to the distress and confusion the ship was in when he came to the command, and being a young man and unexperienced, they beg leave to recommend him for mercy."

The recommendation was ignored, and the sentence was duly carried into effect. It is difficult to say what was the reason of this, and it has been suggested in explanation that there was a suspicion that Phillips was in the pay of the Young Pretender. No hint of this appears in the minutes of the court-martial; but it must be remembered that the terror of an invasion was at that time very great, and that men may be swayed by motives which they do not acknowledge even to themselves. Whether as a result of this court-martial or not, it remains to be recorded that not a ship wavered in her allegiance, though there were undoubted Jacobites in the fleet.[2] The one action of the year that had a direct bearing on the result, the engagement between the *Lion* and the French ship *Elisabeth*, has already been described.[3]

A number of valuable prizes continued to be made, chiefly in the West Indies. The greatest success fell to the privateers ; but in December, 1744, the *Rose*, 20, Captain Thomas Frankland, had fallen in with and taken the treasure-ship *Concepción*, bound from Cartagena to Havana. The prize mounted twenty guns and had a large crew ; but her value lay in the enormously rich cargo which, after a stubborn fight, became the property of the British. As she was not condemned

---

[1] 25th and 26th June, 1745. P. R. O., vol 28.

[2] *Vide e.g.,* P. R. O. Courts-martial, vol. 29. Lieutenant William Johnston, for treason, July 15th, 1745.

[3] *Supra,* Chap. XXVII., p. 110.

by legal process, the exact value of her lading is unknown. It will be enough, however, to say that it consisted chiefly of gold, silver, and jewels, and that such additional finds as 20,000 and 30,000 pistoles, made after the ship had been cleared, were looked on by comparison as trifles. The privateers which harmed the enemy most at that time were the *Prince Frederick, Duke,* and *Prince George,* fitted out by a London firm in the summer of 1745, and cruising under one James Talbot, master of the first-named, as commodore.[1] The profit resulting from this single cruise, £700,000, was so enormous as to tempt the merchants to repeat their scheme ; and the ships were sent to sea again in the following year under George Walker. Subsequently to his capture by the *Fleuron,* Walker had commanded the privateer *Boscawen,* which, as the French royal frigate *Médée,* had been the first prize of the war, and had been renamed in honour of her captor.

The French West India trade of 1745 went out under the convoy of the *Magnanime,* 74, and other ships of war. Vice-Admiral Isaac Townsend had, however, received news concerning the convoy, and, on October 31st, intercepted it off Martinique. Townsend, in the *Lenox,* together with the *Dreadnought* and *Ipswich,* engaged the men-of-war, while the smaller ships were sent off in chase of the flying merchantmen. Several of these latter were picked up to leeward or were driven ashore, but the men-of-war escaped by taking refuge under the batteries.[2]

In the Mediterranean, meanwhile, the only action of importance was that between the *Jersey,* 60, Captain Charles Hardy (2), detached from Captain Henry Osborn's squadron, and the *St. Esprit,* 74. The action was very severe, lasting for two hours and a half, at the end of which time both ships were crippled. The *St. Esprit* returned to Cadiz with the loss of her foremast and bowsprit, and with twenty men killed.

It has been said that the *Apollon* was a royal ship in private employ. This hiring out of the State's ships was by no means an uncommon practice with the French ; and, on the break up of their main fleet subsequent to the battle off Toulon, it was carried out on a considerable scale. M. de Lage, a man whose chief merit lay in his self-assertiveness, succeeded in obtaining from the Admiral of France an acting commission as commodore, with authority to fit

---

[1] Beatson, i. 294 ; J. K. Laughton : ' Studies in Naval History,' p. 237.
[2] Beatson, i. 286.

out a squadron at his own expense. The crews were to be raised from the government lists of seamen and marines, but were to be paid by de Lage. But the men had a peculiar dislike to the adventurer, and would not volunteer; and it was with the greatest difficulty that, after a hot press, two ships of the line and two frigates got to sea in April, 1745. These were the *Ferme*, 74, *Oriflamme*, 54, *Diane*, 30, and *Volage*, 30. Three times did de Lage put to sea, and three times was he driven in by bad weather. On each return to port numbers of men deserted, and finally he had to pay off the *Ferme*. With the three ships that were left, he put to sea for the last attempt at the end of March, 1746. On the 29th he was sighted by Commodore the Hon. George Townshend, who had with him at that time the *Bedford*, 70, and *Essex*, 70, and two bombs, but who, contenting himself with a distant view, chose to believe that the enemy was of superior force, and declined to engage.[1] De Lage stood over to the coast of Spain where, on April 4th, off Cape St. Martin, the *Volage*, which had chased out of sight of the squadron, was taken, after an obstinate resistance, by Captain John Fawler, of the *Stirling Castle*, 70. On the following morning her consorts hove in sight; and Fawler, believing himself to be in no fit condition to engage them, cut adrift the prize, which he had taken in tow. She was therefore retaken, and with her, a lieutenant and twenty-five men. Fawler was tried by court-martial at Gibraltar on October 6th and 7th following; and the court, though it acquitted him for not engaging de Lage, condemned him for not destroying the prize, which, as he had had possession of her all night and had learnt from the prisoners that her consorts were in the neighbourhood, he should and could have done.

When de La Jonquière, driven out of America by putrid fever and small-pox, was on his way back to Europe, he had a narrow escape from falling in with Anson, then in command in the Channel. Indeed, so near were the fleets to one another that the French ship, *Mercure*, 56, doing duty as a hospital, was taken, when but a little separated from the main body. Two other ships failed to reach France; the *Ferme*, 54, which had been sent to Quebec with military stores, and which had fallen in with the British blockading squadron, and the *Mars*, 64, which had been driven by stress of weather to Martinique. Thence, after refitting, she had sailed for

---

[1] Court-martial on Townshend, February 9th, 1746–47. P. R. O., vol. 30.

home ; but she was seventy-five men short of her complement and very sickly, so that, when she fell in, on October 11th, 1746, with the *Nottingham*, 60, Captain Philip de Saumarez, cruising to the south-west of Cape Clear, she was not in a condition to make effective resistance.   The fight was, nevertheless, maintained for two hours, ere the *Mars*, reduced to a wreck, with twelve men killed and forty wounded, as against three killed and sixteen wounded in the *Nottingham*, struck.   But for the fineness of the weather it would have been impossible to send her in.   She was added to the Navy.

In 1746, the privateers on both sides continued to have a good share in the hard knocks, and from time to time did excellent service.   There are two of their exploits which specially claim mention.   On April 10th the *Alexander* privateer, one hundred and forty men, Phillips master, was cruising off Rhé, when she saw a frigate, with a store ship in company, standing into St. Martin. This was the *Solebay*, 20 guns and two hundred and thirty men, which had been taken by de Rochambeau on the Portuguese coast nearly two years before.   Phillips boarded her athwart the bowsprit, at the very entrance to the road, and carried her, killing fifteen of her men.   Phillips, like Walker, was kept out of the King's service, which he was desirous of entering, by the stringency of the regulations, and had to be content with an acknowledgment of five hundred guineas and a gold medal.   The second instance occurred on May 1st, when, as has been briefly noted in the previous chapter, H.M.S. *Greyhound*, 20, with the sloops *Baltimore* and *Terror*, fell in off the west coast of Scotland with two heavy French privateers of 32 and 34 guns respectively.   The British were severely handled and beaten off, and Commander the Hon. Richard Howe (afterwards Earl Howe), then of the *Baltimore*, was badly wounded.

On February 9th, 1746, the *Portland*, 50, Captain Charles Stevens, cruising in the Soundings, fell in with and engaged the French *Auguste*, 50, four hundred and seventy men.

"After two-and-a-half hours' close action," wrote Stevens, "she struck, having fifty killed, ninety-four wounded, all her masts so shattered that they went by the board, and so many shot in the hull, that, with the late hard easterly wind, I was obliged to put away with her before it a hundred leagues to the westward, and am now towing her for Plymouth." [1]

The *Portland* had five men killed and thirteen wounded, and lost her main yard.[2]   The *Auguste* was bought into the service, and,

[1] J. K. Laughton : 'Studies in Naval History,' p. 255.   [2] Charnock, v. 229.

as the *Portland's Prize*, cruised with success. On November 19th of the same year, in company with the *Winchelsea*, 20, the *Portland* sighted the *Subtile*, 26. The *Winchelsea*, in which Samuel (afterwards Viscount) Hood was then a lieutenant, outsailed her consort, and, after a very severe action, fought the chase to a standstill, so that, on the *Portland's* coming up, the Frenchman struck immediately.[1] The rest of the doings of single ships and light squadrons in European waters during the year may be dismissed with a mere reference to the destruction of the *Ardent*, 64, which was chased ashore in Quiberon Bay in November by Lestock's squadron when returning from its fruitless descent on Lorient.

Before Anson's victory of May 3rd, there was little done at sea in 1747 ; and, after it, the enemy began to show great signs of that exhaustion which, consequent on their second defeat in October, put an end to the war. Anson's work was well supplemented when Captain Thomas Fox, of the *Kent*, 74, having put to sea with a small squadron in April, fell in, to the westward of the Bay of Biscay, on June 20th, with the large fleet of French West Indiamen which he had long been anxiously awaiting. The merchantmen were under the convoy of M. Dubois de La Motte, whose force consisted of three sail of the line and a frigate, a force inferior indeed to the six ships [2] of Fox's squadron but not so far inferior as to justify the flight which followed. M. de La Jonquière, in his encounter with Anson, had earned the gratitude of his country by deliberately giving himself to be crushed that he might save his convoy ; de La Motte shrank from the sacrifice, and took his men-of-war unscathed into Brest, while, of the West Indiamen, about fifty, to the value of upwards of a million, were picked up either by Fox himself or by Rear-Admiral Sir Peter Warren's squadron to leeward.

On the following day the *Etoile*, 46, escorting five merchantmen, was driven ashore at Cape Finisterre by Sir Peter Warren, and was burnt.[3] A few days later, an attempt to execute a somewhat similar exploit ended in disaster. The *Maidstone*, 60, Captain the Hon. Augustus Keppel, which had been cruising in the Soundings and in the Bay of Biscay, chased an enemy's ship inshore at Belle

[1] The *Subtile* was added to the Royal Navy as the *Amazon*.

[2] *Kent*, 74, Captain Thomas Fox; *Hampton Court*, 70, Captain Savage Mostyn; *Eagle*, 60, Captain George Brydges Rodney ; *Lion*, 60, Captain Arthur Scott; *Chester*, 50, Captain Philip Durell (1); *Hector*, 44, Captain Thomas Stanhope ; with the fireships *Pluto* and *Dolphin*.

[3] Troude, i. 318 ; Beatson, i. 372 ; Charnock, iv. 187.

Isle on June 27th. Venturing too close in, the *Maidstone* ran aground and became a total wreck; and Keppel and his men were made prisoners of war.

Other captures of note made during the course of the summer in European waters were those of the *Bellone*, *Loup*, and *Renommée*. The *Bellone*, a 36-gun frigate bound from Nantes to the East Indies, was taken by the *Edinburgh*, *Eagle*, and *Nottingham*, was bought into the service as the *Bellona*, and was at once sent out to cruise, with Captain the Hon. Samuel Barrington in command. The *Loup* had been the British sloop *Wolf*, taken by the French two years earlier. It is interesting to notice that she was captured by the *Amazon*, 26, which, as has been mentioned, was originally the French *Subtile*. The *Wolf*, in French hands, had been used as a privateer, but resumed her duties as a 14-gun sloop in the British Navy, curiously enough, under the orders of Commander George Vachell, who had had her before her capture in 1745.[1] The *Amazon*, whose captain was Samuel Faulknor (2), son of that Samuel Faulknor (1) who had perished with Balchen in the *Victory* in 1744, continuing her cruise, fell in, on September 12th, with the *Renommée*, 32. A severe but indecisive action followed, and left both ships badly crippled. They parted company in the night, but, next day, the *Renommée*, having the further misfortune to fall in with the *Dover*, 50, Captain the Hon. Washington Shirley, was taken, and, with her, M. de Conflans, who was going out in her to take over the government of San Domingo.

The French force under M. de l'Etenduère, which suffered defeat on October 14th, 1747, at the hands of Hawke, had under its convoy a large fleet of merchantmen for the West Indies. Hawke, after the battle, was not in a fit state to pursue the convoy, but, with admirable promptness, at once victualled the *Weazel*, sloop, and despatched her to warn Captain George Pocock, who had succeeded Captain the Hon. Edward Legge as commodore on the West India station, of its approach. Thanks to this promptness, Pocock, though his squadron was scattered when the news reached him, was able to capture many of the merchantmen. The *Captain* took eight, the *Dreadnought* six, the *Dragon* five, the *Ludlow Castle* another, and the privateers on the station ten more. The twenty taken by Pocock were valued at £100,000.[2]

---

[1] He was lost with her off the Irish coast in January, 1749.

[2] Beatson, i. 368 and 408.

It still remains to describe the most noteworthy of the minor actions of the year 1747.[1] Mention has already been made of George Walker, a man who would have done credit to any service, and who was kept out of the Navy only by the regulations which made it impossible to offer him therein any command which he would be likely to accept. His fortune on two or three occasions brought him into close contact with the Royal Navy, but never more closely than in the present instance. Walker, it has been seen, took over Talbot's squadron of privateers on the latter's retirement. He enlarged it, and, like his predecessor, cruised with great success against the enemy's commerce. On October 6th, 1747, the " Royal Family," so called because all the ships composing it were named after members of the reigning house, were standing out of Lagos Bay when a large ship was sighted coming in towards Cape St. Vincent. They immediately gave chase; and the stranger bore away to the westward, being, like the British ships, in some doubt as to the enemy's force. She was, in fact, the *Glorioso*, a Spanish 74, which had previously landed at Ferrol about three millions of treasure from the Spanish Main, and was then bound to Cadiz. She was a fine powerful ship, though, as was general in that service, she carried no heavier guns than 24-pounders. This was not her first hostile meeting during the voyage, for on July 14th she had fallen in at the Azores with the *Lark*, 40, Captain John Crookshanks, and *Warwick*, 60, Captain Robert Erskine. The *Warwick* had attacked but, left unsupported, had been beaten to a standstill; and the *Glorioso* had made off. For this fiasco, Crookshanks, who was the senior officer, was cashiered. A few days later the Spaniard had met with the *Oxford*, 50, with the *Shoreham*, 24, and *Falcon*, 14, in company; but they had made room for her as being of superior force.

It was now for Walker to try his hand. He believed that there was treasure still on board; but when, at about noon on the 6th, he overhauled the chase, his frigate, the *King George*, 32, was alone. It had fallen flat calm, and the rest of the "Royal Family" had not been able to get up, so that the *King George* and the *Glorioso* lay looking at one another, each uncertain as to what the other was. In the evening a breeze arose, and the *Glorioso* headed in-

---

[1] J. K. Laughton : 'Studies in Naval History,' pp. 239 *sqq.* P. R. O. Courts-martial, vol. 32, December 28th, 1747, on Smith Callis of the *Oxford*, and, February 1st, 1748, on Crookshanks of the *Lark*.

shore, followed by the privateer which, on closing, hailed for information. The Spaniard answered with a cross-question, and, on finding that the ship alongside was British, poured in a broadside, which was returned at once ; and the ships ran slowly in to the land, engaged yard-arm to yard-arm. There have been instances enough of frigates attacking ships of the line ; the capture of the *Guillaume Tell* in 1800 was directly due to the embarrassing attentions of the *Penelope ;* and no small share of Edward Pellew's great name is due to the manner in which, in the *Indefatigable*, 44, he hung on to the *Droits de l'Homme* in a gale of wind on a lee shore, till he left her a hopeless wreck. But this is the only instance in which a frigate, in a smooth sea and fine weather, voluntarily placed herself, yard-arm to yard-arm, with a ship of the line ; and not the least wonder of it is that the frigate was only a privateer. Fortunately for the *King George*, many of the enemy's shot either went over her or took effect in her spars ; yet, in spite of that, after some hours her position began to be critical. On one of her consorts, the *Prince Frederick*, coming up, however, the *Glorioso* took to flight. On the morning of the 8th, the *King George* was too disabled to pursue, and the *Prince Frederick*, with two other ships of the squadron, was making sail after the chase when a large vessel was seen coming up from the eastward. She was made out to be British, and Walker at once sent to explain the situation to her captain. She was the *Russell*, 80, Captain Matthew Buckle (1), homeward bound from the Mediterranean, but with only half a crew on board ; and, even of these, some were sick. As the *Russell* crowded sail in pursuit the chase was seen to be sharply engaged with some vessel unknown which presently blew up. It was thought at first that she was the *Prince Frederick*, but she was in reality the *Dartmouth*, 50, Captain James Hamilton (2), which had been drawn to the scene of action by the firing of the previous night. Out of her crew of three hundred only fourteen, including a lieutenant, were saved. Shortly afterwards the *Russell* in her turn came up, and began a hot action which lasted for five hours, at the end of which time the enemy's main-top mast went overboard and she struck. So short-handed was the *Russell* that the number of the prisoners was a serious embarrassment, and many of them had to be sent away in the privateers.

Towards the end of 1747 Captain Dubois de La Motte went out to San Domingo with a convoy of merchantmen. His force consisted of the *Magnanime*, 64, and a new *Etoile*, 42. On November 18th four British men-of-war were seen,[1] of which one mounted 60 and another 50 guns. From these M. de La Motte protected his convoy. There was some desultory firing, and the merchantmen, with the exception of six, got safely away. No sooner was the *Magnanime* back in France, than she was ordered to the East Indies, bearing the broad pennant of Commodore the Marquis d'Albert.[2] On January 31st, 1748, she was sighted in the north-west by the fleet then cruising under Hawke to the westward of Ushant. The *Magnanime* had been partially dismasted in a gale a few days previously, and was then on her way back to Brest to refit. Directly she was sighted, the *Nottingham*, 60, Captain Robert Harland (2), was detached in chase; but, immediately afterwards, it became apparent that the enemy was a ship of force, and the *Portland*, 50, Captain Charles Stevens, was also ordered to follow her. The *Nottingham* was engaged for nearly an hour before Stevens could come up, and suffered somewhat severely, losing in all sixteen men killed and eighteen wounded. The loss of the *Portland* was only four men wounded, its smallness being due to the disabled condition of the French ship, which allowed the *Portland* to keep on her quarter and rake her at will. After a stubborn resistance, lasting for six hours, the enemy struck, having lost, out of a crew of six hundred and eighty-six men, forty-five killed and one hundred and five wounded. The prize was a very fine ship, and was added to the British Navy under her old name. Her capture was the last one of importance in the war.

The 10th of October, 1748, was marked by the mutiny of the *Chesterfield*, 40, which was stationed on the coast of Africa. On the date named, while the ship lay off Cape Coast Castle, and the captain, O'Brien Dudley, and others were ashore, Lieutenant Samuel Couchman organised a rising, and, persuading the lieutenant of Marines, the carpenter, and thirty men to join him, got possession of the ship. The boatswain, Mr. Gastrien, was of those on board the most zealous in his attempts first to dissuade, and afterwards to

---

[1] This is on the authority of Troude, i. 319. Beatson makes no mention of it, and as Troude gives no English names it is hard to say what the ships were.

[2] Troude, i. 321. There is some doubt as to the date of the capture of the *Magnanime*, but as she had been in the West Indies in December, January 31st, the latest date given, seems the most probable. *Cf.* Beatson, i. 409.

overpower, the mutineers ; but had Couchman and his party been men in any way equal to the risky part which they had set themselves to play, there can be no doubt that it would have gone very hard indeed with the boatswain and the loyal party. The mutineers, however, having first tried to reason a few more into joining them, and having failed, left the well-disposed members of the crew to roam about the ship and concert plans at their leisure. On the 12th, therefore, the boatswain took counsel with the gunner, who was ill in his cabin, and, thus getting hold of twenty pistols, armed a few resolute men and recovered the ship. A court-martial was held on board the *Invincible* at Portsmouth on June 26th, 1749, to inquire into alleged neglect of duty on the part of Captain O'Brien Dudley, and to examine into the reasons for his being ashore with so many of his officers to the detriment of the service. Captain Dudley proved that there had been no cause to suspect latent mutiny, and that he and his officers were ashore on duty. He and they were, accordingly, acquitted of all blame. As for Couchman and John Morgan, the lieutenant of Marines, they were tried on the 28th and 30th respectively, and both were condemned to be shot. On the 10th July six men were tried for the same offence, and of them two were acquitted and the rest hanged.[1]

Till the outbreak of the next war the Navy had little to do, and, as was usually the case in a time of comparative quiet, it turned its attention to the Mediterranean pirates. A small squadron was sent out, with Captain the Hon. Augustus Keppel in the *Centurion*, 50, as Commodore. Keppel had a special mission to the Dey of Algier, to treat with him, or, if necessary, to force him to restrain his piratical cruisers ; and the story told [2] is that the Dey professed astonishment that the King of England should have sent a beardless boy to treat with him. Keppel, who was twenty-six, was, no doubt, nettled, and is said to have answered : " Had my master supposed that wisdom was measured by length of beard, he would have sent your Deyship a he-goat." When the angry Dey threatened his visitor with death, Keppel, pointing to his squadron, is said to have explained that there were enough of his countrymen there to honour him with a glorious funeral pyre. Whether there be truth in the story or not,

[1] P. R. O. Courts-martial, vol. 33. See also Beatson, iii. 89.
[2] A suspiciously similar story is told of the behaviour of the Bey of Tripoli to Shovell in 1675. There is no reference to the affair in the Hon. and Rev. Thomas Keppel's 'Life' of his relative.—W. L. C.

the fact stands that in June, 1751, the difficulties were smoothed over, and that Keppel returned to England in the following month and paid off.

It was not until after some months of unofficial hostilities in North America, and until after the receipt in England of Boscawen's dispatch relative to the capture of the *Alcide* and *Lys*, that the Seven Years' War was fairly set on foot.

Thus far the British had been the gainers in the struggle that still awaited a formal initiation. They had taken two ships, and they had lost but one, the *Mars*, 64, which had grounded while going into harbour at Halifax on the return thither of Boscawen's squadron at the end of June; and which it had been impossible to get off again. Soon afterwards, on the night of August 13th, 1755, the *Blandford*, 20, Captain Richard Watkins, when on her way to South Carolina, fell in off Brest with a French squadron homeward bound from the West Indies under M. du Guay. She did what she could to get away, and, even when surrounded, attempted some resistance; but the British 20-gun frigate of that period was "a pigmy with a pop-gun armament;" and she was easily taken possession of and sent into Nantes.[1] The sequel is curious as testifying to a tardy zeal on the part of the French to avert the consequences of their aggressions. With a parade of regard for legality, the *Blandford* was restored by the French Government; but Great Britain was not thus readily appeased, and she quickly retaliated by capturing the *Espérance*, commanded by Comte de Bouvet. That ship, nominally a 74, but having only twenty-four guns mounted, was on her way home from Louisbourg, when on November 13th, 1755, she fell in with Byng's fleet, which had sailed from Spithead a month before. The *Orford*, 64, Captain Charles Stevens, was ordered to chase, and soon began a close action, in which the *Revenge*, 64, Captain Frederick Cornwall, presently joined. The *Espérance*, however, made a stout resistance, and did not strike till the squadron began to draw up. She was an old ship, and had been so severely handled that, considering the badness of the weather, it was judged useless to try to keep her afloat. She had lost ninety killed and wounded out of a total of three hundred. Her surviving people were, therefore, taken out of her, and she was set on fire. This was on the 15th, when it was first possible to send a boat on board her, although she had been

---

[1] P. R. O. Court-martial on Watkins, October 6th, 1755. Vol. 36.

making signals of distress ever since her capture on the 13th. Byng wrote [1] concerning her :—

"She was in the most distressed condition I ever saw a ship, extremely leaky and not able to carry any sail, having only her lower masts standing and foretopmast, and not one yard across except the spritsail yard."

On March 11th, 1756, still prior to the declaration of war, the *Warwick*, 60, was taken by the French near Martinique. Seeing that, according to a French account,[2] this ship was taken by a frigate, it is interesting to turn to the story of the affair as given by her commander, Captain Molyneux Shuldham, at the subsequent court-martial.[3] The *Warwick* had been detached on December 21st, 1755, by Commodore Thomas Frankland, to cruise in the neighbourhood of Martinique ; and shortly after reaching her station she began to be very sickly. As, however, the sickness began to decrease, and as there was no information of any French ships of force being in those waters, Shuldham resolved to continue his cruise.

On March 11th, at daybreak, three sail were sighted, and, they being obviously of superior force, and the private signal being unanswered, the *Warwick* bore away under a press of sail. The strangers were, in fact, the French 74-gun ship *Prudent*, and the two frigates *Atalante* and *Zéphyr*, then on their way out from France under the command of Captain d'Aubigny of the *Prudent*. The *Warwick* was one of the smallest of her class, was a dull sailer, had less than three hundred men fit for service, and was so crank that she could rarely use her lower deck guns. As there was a heavy sea running, she was unable to use them on the occasion in question ; and she had to rely almost entirely on the 9-pounders of her upper deck and quarter-deck. The *Atalante*, 34, Captain du Chaffault, was the first to come up with the chase, and, hanging on her quarter, out of reach of her weather broadside, kept up a galling fire. The wind shifted in a hard squall ; both ships were taken aback ; and before the *Warwick*, whose rigging was much cut, could pay off her head, the *Prudent* drew close up and opened fire. Shuldham ordered the great guns to play upon the commodore only, and the small-arm men to keep up their fire on the *Atalante ;* but it was

---

[1] Admiral's Dispatches, Channel Fleet, vol. 2. Byng, November 19th, 1755.
[2] Troude, i. 338.
[3] P. R. O. Courts-martial, vol. 38, March 27th, 1758.

still impossible to use the lower deck guns, the ship being half swamped ; and after half an hour more, being defenceless and unmanageable, she struck her flag.   Shuldham remained a prisoner of war for two years, and on his release was adjudged by the court-martial, held to inquire into the loss, to have done his duty.

An indecisive action was fought on May 17th, 1756, between the *Colchester*, 50, and *Lyme*, 28, Captains Lucius O'Brien and Edward Vernon (2), on the one hand, and the French ships *Aquilon*, 50, and *Fidèle*,[1] 26, on the other.   The French ships were standing in for Rochefort in charge of a convoy, when, quite near the forts, they were sighted by the British and chased.   The convoy was ordered to make the best of its way, and the men-of-war gave battle to cover its retreat.   The ships paired off, the *Colchester* engaging the *Aquilon*, while the frigates fought it out together ; but so equal were the forces on both sides, that; when they parted by mutual consent, and with heavy loss, no definite result had been arrived at as the outcome of seven hours' hard pounding.

A small expedition, planned and carried into effect during the summer of 1756, deserves mention on account of the relief which it afforded to British trade in the Channel.   The enemy was busy fortifying the Chausey Islands, which lie off Granville, being influenced thereto by the fact that the islands afforded a refuge to the St. Malo privateers, and were also close to the Channel Islands, upon which the French had designs.   It was desirable that the fortifications should not be proceeded with, and Captain the Hon. Richard Howe, of the *Dunkirk*, 60, was sent with a small squadron, consisting of a 20-gun frigate and some small craft, to put a stop to the work. With Howe went three hundred men of the Jersey garrison ; but there was no fighting, for the French commandant, after some dispute about terms, was content to respect the force arrayed against him, and to surrender on the conditions offered.   The fortifications were immediately destroyed.   The conquest, small though it was, would not have been so easily effected, had all the works been completed, for the situation was strong ; and the approach to it was difficult, and wholly exposed to the fire of the fort, which was designed to mount thirty guns.[2]

---

[1] Troude, i. 339, calls her *Cybèle*, but there was no ship of the name in the French Navy List.   O'Brien, in his report to Boscawen (Admiral's Dispatches, Channel Fleet vol. 4), called her *Lafiddelle*.

[2] Beatson, i. 520.

Consequent upon Byng's action, there was a lull in the Mediterranean. The French had no fleet at sea there; and Hawke's command was for the most part uneventful. Its most interesting episode was one which brought him into contact with Fortunatus Wright,[1] the most noteworthy of all the British privateers who ever plied in the Mediterranean. At the outbreak of the war Wright was at Leghorn, where he had been building a small vessel in readiness for emergencies. But Tuscan sympathies were so entirely French that Wright, when on the point of sailing, found himself strictly limited as to the force he might embark. However, he got outside the port, took on board more guns and men from ships which had sailed under his convoy, and at once beat off a large French privateer which was cruising in readiness to intercept him. Following this, he put back to Leghorn to refit, but was at once ordered, or rather forced, to bring his ship inside the mole, where she was detained on a charge of having violated the neutrality of the port. A diplomatic squabble began, and was continued until Captain Sir William Burnaby appeared on the scene. Wright had contrived to let Hawke know how matters stood; and Hawke had immediately despatched Burnaby, in the *Jersey*, 60, together with the *Iris*, 50, to set matters straight. The mission of Sir William was to convoy the trade from Leghorn, and to see the *St. George*, Wright's ship, safe out of that port. To the representations of the governor and the Austrian or French sympathies of that officer, Burnaby had nothing to say; but he made it abundantly clear that he was authorized, and in a position, to repel force by force, should any resistance be offered; and the *Jersey*, the *Iris*, the *St. George*, and the merchantmen went out of Leghorn in peace.

Another somewhat invidious piece of service that fell to the lot of Sir Edward Hawke was the cutting out, from under the guns of the Spanish port of Algeciras, of a British merchantman which had been carried thither by a French privateer. The Spaniards were, like the Tuscans, strongly French in their sympathies; and, after refusing to order the French ship and her prize out of their port, they helped the privateer to pour a murderous fire into the attacking boats. The boats lost one hundred and fifty men killed and wounded, but the ship went back to Gibraltar with them, and the memory of the affair stood over until 1762.

[1] Gomer Williams: 'Liverpool Privateers.' J. K. Laughton: 'Studies in Naval History.'

The only other captures of men-of-war made during 1756, were, on the one hand those of the *Arc en Ciel*, 50, and *Chariot Royal*, 36, in July and March respectively, the vessels being at the time engaged in carrying stores to Louisbourg, and on the other, that of the small brig *Adventure*, mounting six 3-pounders. After a stout resistance, she struck to the privateer *Infernal* of Havre. But many privateers of force were taken; and in that kind of service Captain John Lockhart,[1] of the *Tartar*, made a great name both for energy and for success. The *Tartar* was a frigate of 28 guns and 180 men, and Lockhart, who was appointed to her in March, 1756, continued cruising in her for two years, during which time he took many large privateers of equal or superior force. Among these were the *Cerf* of 22 guns and 211 men, the *Grand Gidéon* of 26 guns and 190 men, and the *Mont Ozier*, of La Rochelle, of 20 guns and 170 men. In engaging the last named, Lockhart was severely wounded, but no sooner had he rejoined his ship, after an absence of two months, than he took off Dunnose the *Duc d'Aiguillon* of St. Malo, of 26 guns and 254 men. These are but some of the many large prizes made by the *Tartar*.

In February, 1757, while Lockhart was ashore wounded, the ship went out under the command of her first lieutenant, Thomas Baillie (1), and took the *Victoire*, privateer, of Le Hâvre, of 26 guns and 230 men, which was bought into the Royal Navy under the name of the *Tartar's Prize*. The *Gramont*, 18, taken in the following October, was bought in under her own name, as also was the *Mélampe*, the finest of all the *Tartar's* prizes. This ship was taken, after a long chase and a stubborn action, early in November. She was of 700 tons, mounted 36 guns, and had a crew of 320 men.[2] Her capture proved to be the last of the achievements of Lockhart while a frigate captain, for the Admiralty testified its appreciation of his successful cruising by moving him into a fifty-gun ship, and so limited his activity.

At the very end of 1756 there occurred an incident, which, though of no great importance in itself, throws some light on the interpretation of the Naval Discipline Act, and has in consequence some bearing on the fate of Byng. It is an instance of what a court-martial accepted as an " error of judgment," and as such is recommended to the attention of those who have been led to believe that it was merely for an " error of judgment " that Byng suffered. On

---

[1] Afterwards Sir John Lockhart Ross, Bart.   [2] Beatson, ii. 77.

the morning of December 27th, Captain Thomas Graves (2)[1] in the *Sheerness*, frigate, discovered a large ship making for Brest. There was some doubt as to what the stranger was; for it was known that French ships of the line were in the neighbourhood, and the vessel in question looked as if she might be one of them. The weight of opinion on board the *Sheerness* was to the effect that the enemy was a sixty-gun ship, and it was well seen that she was just ending a long voyage and was very foul. The Frenchman tried to get away before dawn, but, when she discovered the *Sheerness's* force, she shortened sail to wait for her. In point of fact, the enemy was only an East Indiaman, and the court, satisfied on that point, decided that Graves, who kept away, ought to have gone down and discovered her force by engaging her. His holding aloof was not attributed to negligence, disaffection, or cowardice. It was agreed, however, that he had laid too great a stress on his orders, to carry intelligence to Vice-Admiral Sir Charles Knowles; that his fault was an " error of judgment; " and that his case fell under the thirty-sixth article. He was, in consequence, publicly reprimanded by the president of the court.

On March 16th, 1757, being then off Cape Cabron, San Domingo, the *Greenwich*, 50, Captain Robert Roddam, saw to windward eight large vessels. She made sail from them, and they gave chase; and eventually, on the 18th, the three leading ships came up with her and opened fire. These were the *Diadème*, 74, *Eveillé*, 64, and a frigate. The *Greenwich* was quite hemmed in, and at length, seeing that her position was hopeless, she struck.[2] The prize was fitted out against us, and fought against Forrest on October 21st of the same year, but, being sent back to France after the action, was lost near Brest. Another vessel captured from the Royal Navy during the year was the *Merlin*, 10, which struck to the French privateer *Machault*, 30, on April 19th. Commander John Cleland (1), of the *Merlin*, was endeavouring to rejoin a convoy from which he had been separated, when the privateer bore down upon him.[3] It had been, and was still blowing hard; and the *Merlin*, as was usual with ships of her class, had her decks full of water, and had quite enough to do to look after herself. The guns were all secured fore and aft; and, save with small arms, it was impossible to make any resistance.

[1] Afterwards Admiral Lord Graves.

[2] P. R. O. Courts-martial, vol. 37, July 14th, 1757.

[3] *Ib.*, vol. 37, July 5th, 1757.

The prize did not remain long with the French, being retaken in the autumn by the *Lancaster* and *Dunkirk*.

During the whole of the year 1757, though British squadrons were constantly cruising on the enemy's coast, there was no meeting of fleets. The captures of armed ships by our cruisers were numerous enough, but the vessels taken were, in almost every instance, privateers. There were exceptions however. The *Aquilon* and *Alcion* were destroyed, and the *Emeraude, Hermione, Bien Acquise* and the French East India Company's ship *Duc d'Aquitaine*, manned and armed as a ship of war, were taken. The *Aquilon*, 50, was met, on May 14th, by the *Antelope*, 50, Captain Alexander Arthur Hood, which was cruising off Brest. After a short action the *Aquilon* was run on the rocks of Audierne Bay, where she became a total wreck. The *Duc d'Aquitaine*, for a Company's ship, was most powerful, mounting as she did fifty 18-pounders on two decks and having a crew of nearly five hundred men. On the night of May 30th the *Eagle*, 60, Captain Hugh Palliser, and the *Medway*, 60, Captain Charles Proby, sighted her in the Bay of Biscay. She had landed her cargo at Lisbon, and was then on her way round to Lorient. At daylight the *Medway* shortened sail to clear ship, and the *Eagle*, passing ahead of her, engaged at close range. The *Medway* was foul and could not get up at once, the result being that, when she did reach the scene of action, she was too late. The enemy had been beaten to a standstill, and had lost her main and mizen masts together with fifty men killed; and she struck her flag as the *Medway* came up. Charnock[1] says that she had ninety-seven shot holes through both sides, which would seem to imply that, in the thickness of her planking, she differed considerably from a ship built exclusively for war purposes; but the Admiralty thought her stout enough, and ordered her to be bought into the service. Another French man-of-war destroyed during the year was the *Nymphe*, 36, which was driven ashore at Majorca by the *Hampton Court*.

In the account given of the captures of privateers during 1756 it will have been noticed that the majority of the prizes were vessels of considerable force. In fact, it may be said that the beginning of the Seven Years' War saw a great increase in the size of the average French privateer. During the remainder of the struggle, this increase in size was maintained: for, as the French navy grew

---

[1] Biog. Nav., v. 487.

more and more exhausted, there was ever more and more work for private venture, seeing that the growing British commerce proved an ever more and more tempting bait. France, in short, sought to use the authorised and officially encouraged privateer, instead of the national vessel, as the cheapest weapon for a *guerre de course.* This Great Britain never did. Her privateer was always a supplementary, and often a much-suspected, cruiser. Of the privateers taken during the year 1757, there were many representatives of the large class. For instance, the *Invincible* of St. Malo, which fell to the *Unicorn*, 26, Captain John Rawling,[1] after a stubborn fight, was a 24-gun frigate, and had been cruising with a consort mounting eighteen guns. Again, the *Comte de Gramont*, not to be confounded with the ship taken in the previous year, was a frigate of thirty-six guns and three hundred and seventy men. She was taken by the *Lancaster*, Captain the Hon. George Edgcumbe, and the *Dunkirk*, Captain the Hon. Richard Howe. If it be needful to multiply instances of the strength of these privateers, mention may be made of the *Télémaque*, 26, taken by the *Experiment*, 24, Captain John Strachan ; of the *Vainqueur*, 24, taken by the *Ambuscade*, 32, Captain Richard Gwynn ; and of another 26-gun ship, taken by the *Fortune*, sloop, Commander William Hotham (1).

The most interesting of the French privateers at sea at that date was François Thurot.[2] Thurot was appointed to the command of a regularly constituted squadron, and sailed from St. Malo on July 16th, 1757, with two 36-gun frigates, the *Maréchal de Belleisle* and *Chauvelin,* both with a main-deck armament of 12-prs., and with two sloops. On July 25th he fell in, off Portland, with the *Southampton*, 32, Captain James Gilchrist, then on her way to Plymouth with stores and money, and, after a brisk action, was beaten off.

"As the action is one which Thurot's French biographer considers especially glorious, it is well to point out that the French frigates were each of them more than a nominal match for the *Southampton.* The point is that Thurot, with two frigates against one, each larger, heavier, and with a more numerous crew, did not capture the one ; and, with the best will in the world, it is difficult to see the great glory which, from this non-capture, redounds to the French Navy. It looks indeed as if M. Thurot had conceived his special work to be plundering comparatively helpless merchant-ships, rather than fighting sturdily defended men-of-war ; and that, when he found the *Southampton* no easy capture, he stomached his loss—amounting, on board the *Belleisle* alone, to fourteen killed, twenty-six wounded—and hauled to the wind. That

---

[1] Captain Rawling was mortally wounded, and died on May 18th, 1757.

[2] See pp. 196, 223, 224, 229–231 *antea.*

this is the correct view to take of Thurot's conduct seems confirmed by the facts of another action which he fought off Flushing on 1st August, with the *Seahorse*, a 24-gun frigate, carrying 9-pounders.   After an engagement lasting three hours and a half, the *Seahorse* was almost dismantled and had eight men killed, and seventeen badly wounded.   She was of much smaller force than either the *Belleisle* or the *Chauvelin*, and ought to have been captured.   That she was not, was due not so much to her material strength as to the moral weakness of her opponents." [1]

The *Southampton* was afterwards attached to the grand fleet under Hawke's orders, and was sent to look into Brest.   On September 21st, Gilchrist saw a ship in chase of him, and promptly made sail towards her.   The wind fell light, and it was not till the afternoon that the ships drew close together.   The action which then took place was very bloody.   The enemy lost sixty men killed and wounded, chiefly in an unavailing attempt to board, and the loss in the *Southampton* was twenty killed and thirty wounded. The Frenchman, having lost both her first and second captains, hauled down her colours, and was found to be the royal frigate *Emeraude*, 28.   She was bought into the British Navy under the name of the *Emerald*.   On November 23rd a night action was fought by the *Hussar*, 28, Captain John Elliot, and *Dolphin*, 24, Captain Benjamin Marlow, with a French two-decked ship.   Who the stranger was did not appear at the time, but the frigates so handled her that at the end of two hours she sank.   None of her crew could be picked up.   It was learned afterwards that she was the *Alcion*, 50.

It has already been stated that Hawke and Boscawen cruised during the year to intercept M. Dubois de La Motte's squadron on its way home from Louisbourg,[2] and that they failed to meet with it.   Two only of the French ships, the frigates *Bien Acquise*, 36, and *Hermione*, 28, fell in with the British cruisers ; and they were taken possession of without difficulty.

If 1758 was a year of great successes for the British Navy, it was nevertheless not without its disasters.   The earliest of these, the loss of the *Invincible*, needs no further notice than it has already received,[3] but the burning of the *Prince George*, 90, in the Bay of Biscay on April 13th, merits some detail of description.[4]   A letter from the ship's chaplain gives a good account of the mishap, though

[1] J. K. Laughton : 'Studies in Naval History,' pp. 333–35.
[2] See p. 172 *antea*.
[3] See p. 182 *antea*.
[4] P. R. O. Minutes of Courts-martial, vol. 38, May 10th, 1758.

it does not suggest its cause. At half-past one in the afternoon
word was passed that the fore part of the ship was on fire. The
people assembled on the quarter deck ; it was ascertained that the fire
had begun in the boatswain's storeroom, buckets were passed, and
all possible measures were taken to get the flames under, but without
effect. A considerable sea was running, and it was hoped that the
opening of the lower deck ports would be of avail ; but even this
was useless. Presently, although the magazine had been flooded,
it appeared that there was no possible chance of saving the ship.
The barge was, therefore, ordered to be got out, to put the Rear-
Admiral, Thomas Broderick, in a place of safety. But he, seeing
forty men in her, preferred to trust himself to the waves, and, after
swimming about for an hour, was saved by a boat from one of the
convoy. The captain, Joseph Peyton (1), was also picked up, as
were most of the officers ; but, either by the over-setting of boats,
or in the flames, no fewer than four hundred and eighty-five men
perished as against two hundred and sixty who were saved. The
merchantmen, it was complained, held aloof to windward ; and their
boats were busier in salving gear than in saving lives.

There were many prizes made during the year 1758, and, while as
before a large proportion were heavily armed privateers, many were
ships of war. On the North American station, the *Boreas*, Captain
the Hon. Robert Boyle, took the *Diane*, 36 ; and in European waters
the *Loire*, 36, was taken by the *St. Albans* and *Favourite*, and the
Rose, 36, was driven ashore at Malta by the *Monmouth* and *Lyme*,
and was burnt where she lay. One of the most interesting of the
actions was a brush between the *Solebay*, 28, Captain Robert Craig,
and *Dolphin*, 24, Captain Benjamin Marlow, and Thurot's ship,
the *Maréchal de Belleisle*, the armament of which he had
increased to 44 guns by cutting a few extra ports on the lower
deck. The vessel was thus no longer a frigate proper ; on the other
hand she was not a two-decked ship at all comparable to the
English 44's. Perhaps the only other instance of a ship being
similarly armed is that of Paul Jones's *Bonhomme Richard*. In the
Belleisle's case, however, the change seems to have been beneficial,
and Thurot is credited with having made a number of prizes before
he was brought to action by the *Dolphin* and *Solebay* on May 26th.
The *Dolphin* was first in action ; but, having the slings of her
main-yard shot away, she dropped astern ; and the *Solebay* came
up and in her turn occupied the Frenchman's attention while the

Dolphin was getting her main-yard up. In due time the *Dolphin* again got close; but, about three and a half hours from the beginning of the action, the *Belleisle* wore and made sail away. Both the British frigates were much damaged aloft, and, probably, even if they had not been they would have stood no chance against Thurot in sailing. The story of Thurot's final cruise has been already told.[1]

On May 29th the *Raisonnable*, 64, then on her way to Louis-bourg, was sighted by Captain Edward Pratten, who, in the *Intrepid*, was cruising off the French coast with a small squadron. He detached the *Dorsetshire*, 70, Captain Peter Denis, and the *Achilles*, 60, Captain the Hon. Samuel Barrington, in chase. The *Dorsetshire* had beaten the enemy to a standstill before the *Achilles* came up, and had killed sixty-one Frenchmen and wounded one hundred more, while she herself had lost but fifteen killed and twenty wounded. The arrival of the *Achilles* settled the matter; and the prize, being a fine ship, was bought into the Royal Navy.

In July the *Shrewsbury*, 74, Captain Hugh Palliser, was detached by Anson, together with the *Unicorn*, 20, and *Lizard*, 28, to cruise as near Brest as possible and watch the French fleet in the road. On September 12th the British vessels sighted a fleet of coasters, which, under convoy of the *Thétis* and *Calypso* frigates, were working so close in shore that it was a matter of great difficulty to cut them off. Captain Brodrick Hartwell, in the *Lizard*, managed, nevertheless, to get between the frigates and part of the convoy, the result being that the *Calypso* was driven ashore and destroyed at the entrance to Audierne Bay, and that of the coasters many were either taken or destroyed. On October 2nd the *Lizard* did a further piece of service by capturing the *Duc d'Hanovre*, privateer, 14; and, a little later, the *Torbay*, Captain the Hon. Augustus Keppel, took the *Rostan*, a privateer of twenty-six guns and three hundred and twenty men. This prize was bought into the Royal Navy under the name of the *Crescent*. Beatson says[2] that the French concealed ninety men in her hold in the hopes of recapturing her from her prize crew, but that the people below betrayed themselves too soon and were overpowered.

In extra-European waters, the *Winchelsea*, 20, Captain John Hale, while on her way home from Carolina, was taken on October 11th by the *Bizarre*, 60. The *Winchelsea* attacked in

---

[1] See pp. 229–231 *antea*.   [2] Beatson, ii. 191.

order to cover her convoy, and, till the *Bizarre* ran out her lower deck guns, did not realise the immense superiority of the enemy's force. When she did so, she hauled her wind and tried to get away; but, as she was under a jury mainmast, she stood no chance of accomplishing her purpose, and, after a little firing, hauled down her colours.

On the Jamaica station, in 1758, there was little for British cruisers to do save to cut up the enemy's commerce, and to capture his small privateers. The only action of any note was between the *Dreadnought*, 60, Captain Maurice Suckling, and the *Assistance*, 50, Captain Robert Wellard, on the one hand, and the *Palmier*, 74, which had previously taken the *Stork*, 10, on the other. On the morning of September 2nd, the British ships came up with the Frenchman off Port au Prince; but, unfortunately, a calm prevented the *Assistance* from seconding her consort; and the *Palmier*, having disabled the *Dreadnought*, made sail and escaped. On the Leeward Islands' station much the same state of affairs prevailed; but, on November 3rd, Captain Richard Tyrrell, in the *Buckingham*, 70,[1] cruising off St. Eustatia to intercept a French convoy from Martinique, was sharply engaged with the *Florissant*, 74, which, with two frigates,[2] had charge of the merchantmen. The frigates took some part in the action, but were soon beaten off; and the ships of the line fought on from about three o'clock till dark. It was claimed that the *Florissant* struck; and it is possible that she did so; but the *Buckingham* was much disabled,[3] and the Frenchman, taking advantage of the fact, made sail away from her.

The interest of 1759 was almost entirely confined to the actions of the main fleets; and, although it was the decisive year of the war, there were few actions by detached cruisers. The first and most stubborn of these was fought between the *Vestal*, 32, Captain Samuel Hood (1), and the *Bellone* of equal force. The *Vestal* had been cruising for a year, chiefly in the Soundings, but, on February 12th, had sailed with Rear-Admiral Holmes for North America. On the 21st, being then in advance of the squadron, she sighted a sail ahead. It was soon seen that the stranger was an enemy; and, signalling this fact to Holmes, Hood made sail

---

[1] The *Weazel*, 14, being in company.

[2] *Aigrette*, 38, and *Atalante*, 28.

[3] She lost seven killed and forty-six wounded, among the latter being Captain Tyrrell.

in chase. The Rear-Admiral detached the *Trent*, 28, reputed to be a fine sailer, to support the *Vestal ;* but it may here be said that the *Trent* had no share at all in the engagement, she being still four miles astern when the enemy struck. The action lasted from two in the afternoon until six, when the *Bellone* had lost forty men in killed alone, and was totally dismasted. The *Vestal* [1] had only her lower masts standing. She returned to Spithead with her prize, which was bought into the Navy and renamed *Repulse*.

On March 19th, the *Isis*, 50, Captain Edward Wheeler, and *Æolus*, 32, Captain John Elliot, cruising off Isle Dieu, fought an engagement with four French frigates which were employed on convoy service. Only two of the enemy were closely engaged, and of these one, the *Blonde*, 32, escaped ; but the other, the *Mignonne*, 20, lost fifty-five killed and wounded out of a crew of one hundred and fifty, and was taken possession of. On the 27th, the *Windsor*, 60, Captain Samuel Faulknor (2), took, off Lisbon, the French East Indiaman *Duc de Chartres*, mounting twenty-four 12-prs., but pierced for sixty guns. There were four East India ships in company, but the other three made off.

On the following day there was fought a much more interesting little action. The *Southampton*, 32, Captain James Gilchrist, and *Mélampe*, 24, Captain William Hotham (1), cruising in the North Sea, fell in with and engaged two French frigates. The *Mélampe* fought them both for three-quarters of an hour before the *Southampton* could come up; and she suffered so much aloft that she dropped astern. One of the French ships made sail away while the *Southampton* was engaging the other, and while the *Mélampe* was refitting. When Hotham drew up again, the French ship struck. She proved to be the *Danaé*, 40; and she had lost her captain, second captain, and about thirty men killed, besides a great number wounded. She was added to the Royal Navy as the *Danae*. Gilchrist was himself severely wounded by a grape shot, and lost the use of an arm. He was given a pension of £300 a year for life, and could not be employed again ; but, a generation later, the martial ardour of his family again showed itself in the career of Thomas Cochrane, tenth Earl of Dundonald, a son of Gilchrist's sister.

On April 4th, Captain the Hon. Samuel Barrington, in the *Achilles*, 60, took, to the westward of Cape Finisterre, the very large privateer, *Comte de St. Florentine*, also mounting sixty guns. This

---

[1] Which lost five killed and twenty wounded.

prize, too, was bought into the Navy, as also was the *Aréthuse*, 36, which was taken by the *Venus*, 36, Captain Thomas Harrison (2), on the coast of Brittany on May 18th.

When M. de La Clue's fleet had been shattered and dispersed, the *Souverain*, 74, made for the Canaries, whence she returned to Rochefort. On her way thither she fell in on October 10th with the *Hercules*, 74, Captain Jervis Henry Porter, which engaged her in a running fight till the British ship fell astern owing to the loss of her maintopmast. Another French ship of the line, which was met with and brought to action during the year 1759, was the *Palmier*, 74, which, having a frigate in company, fell in, when on her way home from the West Indies, with the *Thames*, 32, and *Coventry*, 28. The British frigates attacked her ; and as the sea was rough and she could not use her lower deck guns, they had her somewhat at a disadvantage. They shot away her foretopmast and did her other considerable damage, and, but for the assistance which her frigate was able to give her, would have stood some chance of taking her.[1] As it was, they hung on to her in the hope of falling in with some other British cruiser, keeping out of gun-shot by day, and pouring in broadsides by night. They had not, however, the fortune to meet with a friend ; and, after a long chase, they had the mortification of seeing the *Palmier* run into Brest.

In March, 1760, the French fitted out the *Malicieuse*, 32, and *Opale*, 32, in order to intercept the Portuguese trade, which, they had heard, was to be convoyed by a single sloop. Near the Bayona Islands [2] they fell in with the *Penguin*, 20, Captain William Harris, which tried to get away, but which they overhauled and took. They judged her not worth keeping, set fire to her, and continued their cruise, till it was spoilt on April 4th by the *Flamborough*, 20, Captain Archibald Kennedy,[3] and *Biddeford*, 20, Captain Lancelot Skynner (1), which, though not powerful enough to take them, hung on to them in a most dogged manner and eventually put them to flight.[4] Meanwhile the convoy reached Lisbon in safety. Of other little successes in European waters, perhaps not the least complete was that of Captain the Hon. Augustus John Hervey of the *Dragon*, 74, who, while attached to Boscawen's fleet, on

---

[1] Beatson, ii. 351.

[2] P. R. O. Courts-martial, vol. 40.

[3] Later Earl of Cassilis.

[4] In this gallant action, both Captain Skynner and his lieutenant were mortally wounded, the latter surviving, however, until April 10th.

July 12th, being then close in shore off Isle Groix, was fired on by a small fort. That evening he went ashore with his boats, surprised the guard, dismounted the guns of the battery, tumbled the pieces over the rocks, and eventually went off to his ship with the whole of the guard and with not a single man hurt.[1]

Of Boscawen's cruisers, the *Centaur*, 74, which had been taken the year before in the action with M. de La Clue, fell in off Cape Finisterre with the *Vaillant*, 64, and *Améthyst*, 32, homeward bound from the West Indies. Deceived by her appearance they let her come close up; and it was not till they saw that she was clearing for battle that they realised that she was no longer a French ship. They made all possible sail, and got away by night into Corunna. Another of Boscawen's cruisers, the *Niger*, 32, Captain John Albert Bentinck, fell in with the *Diadème*, 74, escorting store-ships to Martinique. For some days the frigate hung on to the Frenchman, both in the hope of cutting off some of the convoy, and of meeting a ship of the line that could deal with the seventy-four. In the course of her attempts on the convoy, she ventured close enough to be severely mauled, and so had to leave the enemy in order to make good her damages. A few days afterwards, the *Diadème* was sighted and chased by the *Shrewsbury*, 74, *Pallas*, 36, and *Argo*, 28. The *Shrewsbury* sailed very badly, the *Argo* was busy with the convoy, and it was left to the *Pallas*, Captain Michael Clements, to attack single handed. She was but a frigate, and fought only in the hope of knocking away a spar or two and enabling the *Shrewsbury* to come up. Unfortunately she exposed herself to the enemy's broadside, and very soon had to be content to leave the big ship alone. This voyage of the *Diadème* bears a certain resemblance to the last cruise of the *Glorioso*. She was annoyed by frigates all along her route, and she ended with an affair with a heavy ship of the line. The *Glorioso*, of course, had been harder put to it, and was ultimately taken. The French ship was more fortunate. The *Royal William*, 80, which chased her at the conclusion of her voyage, had not time to come up with her before she found safety in Corunna.

The loss of the *Cumberland*, 56, Captain Robert Kirk, which sank at her anchors near Goa, on the night of November 2nd, 1760, was adjudged to have " proceeded from her being entirely decayed,

[1] P. R. O. Admiral's Dispatches, Channel, vol. 4, July 27th, 1760.

and not in a condition to have proceeded to sea." [1] There was nothing extraordinary in the loss of the ship, save that it resulted from the fact that she was one of the rather numerous vessels which were at the time kept on service when they ought to have been in the ship-breaker's yard. In many cases, no doubt, the fault lay with the Admiralty ; but it must be borne in mind that ships were not then built under cover, and that the decay of vessels built in the open was often so irregular as to baffle calculation.

On January 8th, 1761, the *Unicorn*, 28, Captain Joseph Hunt, cruising off Penmarck, fought a sharp action with, and captured, the *Vestale*, 32, which later became the *Flora* in the British Navy. The captains of both ships were mortally wounded. On the following day the *Unicorn* chased, but could not come up with, the *Aigrette*, 32, and, on the 10th, saw her engage the *Seahorse*, 20, Captain James Smith, then carrying out astronomers to India to observe the transit of Venus. Again she tried to come up, but could not ; and the *Aigrette*, having mauled the *Seahorse* [2] considerably, refused to be further detained and forced to fight at a disadvantage.

In January, the *Félicité*, 32, left Cherbourg for Martinique ; but no sooner was she outside than she met the *Richmond*, 32, Captain John Elphinstone (1). The ships sighted one another in the evening, but the action did not begin till half-past ten the next morning (January 24th), when they engaged broadside to broadside, standing in for the land. Still close together, they both ran ashore near Scheveningen, and continued serving their guns in that position. Presently the *Richmond* floated, and was set to leeward by the tide. The Frenchmen seized their opportunity and escaped to the shore. They had lost very heavily, and their captain had been killed ; but the casualties on board the *Richmond* amounted only to three killed and thirteen wounded. Next day, when the *Félicité* was boarded, the dispatches which she had been carrying to Martinique were found to be still in her. They were taken out, and the ship was set on fire.

On the same day, but in the Mediterranean, the *Warwick*, the ex-British 60-gun ship, with, however, only thirty-four guns mounted, was attacked, while on her way to the East Indies, by Captain

---

[1] P. R. O. Courts-martial, vol. 41.

[2] Which was, in consequence, obliged to return to port. When she sailed again she was commanded by Charles Cathcart Grant, Captain James Smith having been appointed to the *Guernsey*, 50.

Alexander Arthur Hood in the *Minerva*, 32.   The wind was fresh
from the east, and the sea was heavy.   The enemy lost her mainmast
and foretopmast, but Hood waited for her to come up again, and
presently the ships fell foul of one another.   The *Minerva* in turn
lost her foremast and bowsprit, and fell astern; but she cleared
away the wreck very promptly, stood off to the *Warwick* and forced
her to strike.   The loss was curiously even, fourteen killed and
thirty-two wounded in the *Warwick* as against fourteen killed and
thirty-four wounded in the *Minerva*.   No sooner had the *Warwick*
struck, than the *Minerva* rolled away her remaining masts.   The
capture of the *Brune*, 36, a week later, in the Soundings, by the
Venus and *Juno*, presented no unusual feature.   She was added to
the Navy.

On March 9th, the *Ripon*, 60, Captain Edward Jekyll, one of
Commodore Buckle's squadron off Brest, chased a French sixty-four
and a frigate.   They bore away from him, and during the night
he lost sight of them; but, on the following day, with a fresh breeze
aft and a heavy sea, he overhauled a sixty-four, which proved to
be the *Achille*.   The ships engaged at half-past nine at night yard-
arm to yard-arm, running before the wind at a great rate; and the
Ripon was half swamped by the water that came on board through
her lower-deck ports, which could only be opened from time to time.
To make matters worse, one of her lower-deck guns burst, killing
and wounding many men and throwing the whole deck into
confusion.   After this all her mid-ship and forward ports on that
deck were kept shut, yet she managed to shoot away the enemy's
foreyard and foretopmast.   The *Ripon* then came to the wind to
wait for the Frenchman, and the enemy ran down under the stern
of the British ship.   Fortunately the *Achille* was in such great
confusion that she missed the opportunity of raking the *Ripon*.   As
soon as the Frenchman had passed to leeward, Jekyll gave orders
to wear ship and follow her, but his rigging was so much cut that
the manœuvre took a long time, and when it was complete the
enemy's lights were no longer visible.

There were other single-ship actions at about the same time.
On March 13th, 1761, the *Vengeance*, 26, Captain Gamaliel Nightingale, took the *Entreprenant*, an armed ship of force equal if not
superior to her own.   On March 16th, the *Bedford*, 64, took the
frigate *Comète*, 32, off Ushant; and on April 3rd, the *Hero* and
Venus took the *Bertin*, an East India ship pierced for sixty-four

guns, but then armed *en flûte* and outward bound with soldiers on
board.   On April 1st, the *Oriflamme*, 40, really a 50-gun ship,
was taken in the Mediterranean, after a short action, by the *Isis*, 50,
whose captain, Edward Wheeler, was killed in the fight.   Another
easy capture was that of the *Ste. Anne*, a heavily-armed merchantman, which was taken on the Jamaica station by the *Centaur*, 74,
Captain Arthur Forrest, on June 5th.   She was pierced for sixty-
four guns, but had at the time only forty on board.   When,
however, she was added to our Navy, her full number of guns
was mounted.

On July 14th, the *Thunderer*, 74, Captain Charles Proby, cruising
with the *Modeste*, 64, Captain the Hon. Robert Boyle Walsingham,
Thetis, 32, Captain John Moutray, and *Favourite*, sloop, Commander
Philemon Pownall, for the purpose of intercepting the *Achille*, 64,
and *Bouffonne*, 32, which it was believed were ready to sail from
Cadiz, discovered that those ships had slipped out of port.   The
squadron fell in with them, however, on the 16th, brought them
to action on the 17th, and in due course took them both,[1] the
Achille being carried by a boarding party from the *Thunderer*, which
had had a great part of her poop blown up by the bursting of an
upper-deck gun.   The *Bouffonne* struck to the *Thetis*.   The *Thunderer*
lost seventeen killed, and one hundred and fourteen, including
Captain Proby, wounded, most of the casualties being due, however,
to the accident to the gun.

The most brilliant of the actions fought between cruising ships
in 1761 remains to be described.   On August 13th, the *Bellona*, 74,
Captain Robert Faulknor (2), and the *Brilliant*, 36, Captain James
Loggie, met the *Courageux*, 74, and the two 32-gun frigates, *Malicieuse*
and *Hermione*, off Vigo.   The meeting took place in the evening;
but it was bright moonlight, and the ships kept sight of each other
till morning, when the enemy, who up to that time had been trying
to escape, decided to engage.   On the 13th, it had been believed that
the British vessels were both ships of the line; on the 14th, however, the French commodore fell into the opposite error of taking
the *Bellona* for a 50-gun ship.   He signalled to the frigates to
engage the *Brilliant*, while he himself closed with the *Bellona*.   The
Brilliant accepted her share with alacrity, and gave the frigates
so much to do that they were unable to interfere in the combat
between the seventy-fours.   The duel between the *Bellona* and

[1] Troude denies it, i. 427.

Courageux was fought out in a fine breeze and a smooth sea. The first broadside was fired from the Frenchman when the ships were within musket-shot; and so good was the gunnery under the favourable conditions that prevailed, that, in nine minutes from the start, the *Bellona's* mizen-mast went over the side and the rigging was so much cut that the ship became unmanageable. Faulknor was afraid that the enemy might get away, and promptly called for boarders; but the *Courageux* sheered off, and the attempt had to be abandoned. With great difficulty, Faulknor managed to wear ship, a manœuvre which brought him up on the Frenchman's starboard quarter. A few broadsides fired from his new position settled the fate of the day. The *Courageux*, much damaged, and with about two hundred men killed and another hundred wounded, struck, and was taken possession of. The frigates made sail away. The total duration of the action was no more than forty minutes. It was much the fashion to speak of the French as always firing at the rigging, and as seizing the earliest opportunity to escape. Certainly this is stated to have been the procedure in many instances where the facts will not support such an assertion; but in this case something of the sort does seem to have happened, owing partly no doubt to the enemy's having accepted battle through a misunderstanding of the force he had before him. It is not easy to suggest any other explanation for the condition of the *Bellona*, and for the *Courageux*, which lost more than three hundred men, having killed and wounded only four-and-thirty.

The new year, 1762, opened with affairs in a peculiar condition. Great Britain was paramount at sea, whereas France was exhausted. There was, indeed, nothing new in this; it had been the prevailing state of things since the action in Quiberon Bay. What was strange was that France, having received a new ally in virtue of the Family Compact, gained no real accession of force, although the Spaniards entered upon the war with a considerable number of ships. Why this happened was because, as has been already noticed, the French ports were so closely watched that nothing could get out without running the risk of immediate capture, and because the Spaniards concentrated all their naval forces for the protection of their colonies and lost them, *en masse*, in distant seas. The result, as far as Spain was concerned, was, that she was hopelessly beaten without anything worthy the name of a naval battle having taken place in European waters. The French, too, were so utterly exhausted that there was not only no fleet action fought but also not even a ship of the line to be taken.

Short accounts of a few frigate actions will, therefore, finish the story. Captain Thomas Harrison (2), in the *Venus*, 36, had a large share of good fortune. On January 6th, he took, after a short action, the *Boulogne*, 20, on her homeward journey from the Isle of France, with a valuable cargo on board, and, amongst other passengers, the Comte d'Estaing. On March 17th, he took a 14-gun privateer out of San Sebastian ; on May 6th, he captured another privateer of the same force out of Bayonne ; and on June 4th, a large Spanish privateer of sixteen guns, twenty swivels, from Bilbao, struck to him. These were by no means all the privateers he took, either Spanish or French, but the cases supply typical instances of the force of the ships he had to deal with. Another somewhat notable capture of a privateer was made on the night of March 7th. The *Milford*, 28, Captain Robert Mann, fell in with the *Gloire*, a French letter of marque, mounting sixteen 6-prs., besides swivels, and bound to San Domingo, and took her after a sharp action. The *Milford* lost only four killed and thirteen wounded, but among the former were Captain Robert Mann,[1] and his first lieutenant. The richest capture of the war was made by the *Active*, Captain Herbert Sawyer (1), and the *Favourite*, sloop, Commander Philemon Pownall, two of Sir Piercy Brett's cruisers, which, on May 21st, intercepted the register-ship *Hermione*, bound from Lima for Cadiz. The summons to surrender was the first intimation to the Spaniards that war had broken out ; there was no resistance whatsoever ; and in this easy manner did treasure to the value of about half a million pass into British hands. On the Jamaica station, the *Fowey*, 24, (9-prs.), Captain Joseph Mead, fell in, off Cape Tiberon, with the Spanish royal frigate *Ventura*, 26 (12-prs.), and fought her for an hour and a half, when the ships separated, much damaged. On the following morning the action was resumed with vigour, and continued till the *Ventura* struck. The *Fowey* lost ten killed and twenty-four wounded, and the *Ventura*, forty in killed alone.

On August 18th, the *Rochester*, cruising in the Channel, in company with the *Maidstone* and *Renommée*, took the *Guirlande*, 26, a French frigate ; and on September 1st, the *Lion*, 60, one of a small

---

[1] Commander, 1756 ; Captain, 1757. His name is very consistently spelt Mann in the Navy Lists of the period, whereas that of his contemporary Robert Man (2), presently to be mentioned, who died an Admiral in 1783, is spelt with one *n* only.—W. L. C.

squadron detached, under Commodore Robert Man (2), by Hawke to cruise off Brest, took the *Zéphyr*, 32, which had, however, only twenty-six guns mounted, and which was then carrying troops and stores to Newfoundland. The last capture made from the French during the war was that of the *Oiseau*, 26, which struck to the *Brune*, 32, Captain George Anthony Tonyn, in the Mediterranean, on October 23rd.

APPENDIX TO CHAPTERS XXVII. AND XXVIII.

LOSSES OF THE BELLIGERENT POWERS.

L. CARR LAUGHTON.

NOTE.—These lists, like tnose on p. 535 *et seq.* of Vol. II., are tentative ; but they are not so meagre as the lists given by the best-known historians of the period, *e g.*, Charnock, Peatson, and Troude. Those authorities have been largely checked by reference to Captains' Letters, Muster Books, Minutes of Courts-Martial, and other papers of like nature , but it is an almost impossible task to ensure completeness.

(a.) LOSSES OF H.M. SHIPS FROM 1714 TO 1763.

Year.	Date.	Ships.	Guns.	Commander. [* Lost his life on the occasion.]	Fate.
1716	Nov. 10	*Auguste*	60	Capt. Robert Johnson.	Wrecked in the Baltic.
		Hazardous	..		Lost at sea.
1717		*Sorlings*	42		Lost.
1719	Jan. 29	*Crown*	50	,, John Roberts.	Lost at entrance of Tagus.
	Feb. 14	*Burford*	70	,, Charles Vanbrugh.	Lost in the Mediterranean.
	Mar. 28	*Blandford*	..	*Capt. Erasmus Phillips.	Foundered in the Bay.
1720	Nov. 24	*Monck*	50	,, Hon. George Clinton.	{Lost in Yarmouth Roads. {Crew saved.
		Milford	20		Lost.
1721		*Royal Anne*	40		Lost.
	Dec. 7	*Hind*	..	*Capt. John Furzer.	Wrecked off Guernsey.
1722	April 15	*Greyhound*	20		Taken by guarda costas : restored.
	?	*Bedford*	20		Sunk.
1724	?	*Cruiser* (prize) . .	12		Lost.
1729	Nov. 10	*Royal Anne,* galley. .	..	*Capt. Francis Willis.	Foundered off the Lizard.
1736	Dec.	*Princess Louisa* . .	40		Lost (ex-*Launceston*).
1740	Jan. ?	*Triumph* (prize). . .	18		Foundered off Sambala Keys.
1741	Jan. 13	*Otter*	8	Com. John Gage.	Wrecked in the South Seas.
	Mar.	*Wolf*	†14		Wrecked on coast of Florida.
	Apr. 16	*Galicia* (prize) . . .	70	Capt. Daniel Hoare.	Burnt as useless at Cartagena.
	May 14	*Wager*	28	,, David Cheap.	Wrecked in the South Seas.
	Aug.	*Anna* (pink) . . .	{ st. { sh.		}Broken up at Juan Fernandez.
	Oct. 4	*Tryal* (brig-sloop) . .	14	Com. Charles Saunders.	Scuttled by order.
1742	Jan. 12	*Tiger*	50	Capt. Edw. Herbert (1).	Wrecked on a key near Tortuga.
	June 14	*Duke* (f.s.)	8	Com. Smith Callis.	Expended at St. Tropez.
	Aug. 15	*Gloucester*	50	Capt. Matthew Michell.	Burnt by order in the South Seas.
	Sept. 21	*Tilbury*	60	,, Peter Lawrence.	Accidentally burnt in W. Indies.
		Drake	†14		Lost in the Channel (?).
		Grampus	†14		Lost.
		Saltash	†14	Com. Peter Toms.	Lost in the W. Indies.
1743		*Looe*	44	Capt. Ashby Utting.	Lost in America.
		Astræa, 3.s. . . .	..	Com. R. bert Swanton.	Accidentally burnt at Piscataqua.
1744	Jan.	*Orford*	70	Capt. Perry Mayne.	Wrecked in Gulf of Mexico.
	Feb. 11	*Anne Galley,* f.s. . .	8	*Com. —— Mackie.	Expended off Toulon.
	May 8	*Northumberland* . .	70	*Capt. Thomas Watson (1).	Taken by the French.
	Summer	*Solebay*	20	,, Thomas Bury (1).	Taken by the French ; retaken.
	,,	*Seaford*	20	,, Thomas Pye.	}Taken by the French.
	,,	*Grampus*	16	Com. Richard Collins (1).	
	Oct. 5	*Victory*	100	{*Ad. Sir John Balchen. {*Capt. Samuel Faulknor (1).	}Lost in the Channel.
	,, 20	*St. Albans*	50	*Capt. William Knight.	
	,, ,,	*Greenwich*	50	*Capt. Edward Allen.	
	,, ,,	*Bonetta*	14	*Com. William Lea.	}Wrecked in a hurricane at Jamaica.
	,, ,,	*Thunder,* bomb . . .	8	Com. Thomas Gregory (2).	
	,, ,,	*Lark* (hulk)	..		
		Colchester	50	Capt. Sir Wm. Hewett, Bt.	Wrecked on the Kentish Knock.
		Hornet	14		Taken by the French ; retaken.

† These sloops are usually spoken of as carrying 14 guns. Sometimes, however. they are credited with 20, sometimes with only 8. The explanation seems to be that they often carried 8 guns and 12 swivels or patercroes ; thus the 14 would be arrived at by rating a swivel conventionally as half a gun. But in reality their armament was rather haphazard.

Year.	Date.	Ships.	Guns.	Commander. [* Lost his life on the occasion.]	Fate.
1744		*Swallow*	16		Wrecked.
		Salisbury	50		Taken by the French ; retaken.
1745	Feb. 16	*Weymouth*	60	Capt. Warwick Calmady.	Wrecked in Leeward Islands.
	Mar. 28	*Anglesey*	44	* ,, Jacob Elton.	Taken by *Apollon*, 50.
	June	*Blandford*	20	,, Edward Dodd.	Taken by French in W. Indies.
	Nov. 14	*Fox*	20	* ,, Edmund Beavor.	Foundered off Dunbar ; all lost.
		Lyme	20		Foundered in the Atlantic.
		Mercury.	14		Taken by the French.
		Wolf	14	Com. George Vachell.	Taken by the French ; retaken.
		Fame	14		Foundered.
		Sapphire's Prize . .	14		Wrecked.
		Hazard	12		Taken by the rebels ; retaken.
		Mediator	10		Sunk.
		Blast, bomb	8		} Taken by two Spaniards near Jamaica.
		Achilles	8		
		Falcon	8		Taken by the French.
1746	Oct. 19	*Severn*.	50	Capt. William Lisle.	Taken by M. de Conflans ; retaken 1747.
	Dec.	*Hornet*	14		Taken by the French.
		Albany	14	Com. Stephen Colby.	Taken by the French.
		Saltash	14		Wrecked in the Channel.
		Lightning, bomb . .	8	,, William Martin (2).	Capsized near Leghorn ; 45 drowned.
		Louisbourg, f.s. . . .	8		Taken by the French.
1747	July 7	*Maidstone*	50	Capt. Hon. Augustus Keppel	Wrecked on Belle Isle.
	Sept.	*Whitehaven*, armed sp.	14	Com. Carr Scrope.	Burnt by accident off Irish coast.
	Oct. 8	*Dartmouth*	50	*Capt. James Hamilton (2).	Blown up in action with *Glorioso*.
1748		*Fowey*.	20	,, Francis William Drake	Wrecked in G. of Florida.
		Savage	14		Wrecked on the Lizard.
1749	Jan.	*Wolf*	14	*Com. George Vachell.	Wrecked off Ireland.
	April 12	*Namur*	74	{ R.-Ad. Hon. Edward Bos-cawen. { Capt. Samuel Marshall (1).	} Wrecked in E. Indies ; 600 lost.
	,, ,,	*Apollo*, hosp. sh. . .	18		Wrecked in E. Indies.
	,, 13	*Pembroke*	60	* ,, Thomas Fincher.	Wrecked in E. Indies ; 330 lost.
1755	June	*Mars*	64	,, John Amherst.	Wrecked at Halifax.
	Aug. 13	*Blandford*	20	,, Richard Watkins.	Taken off Brest ; restored.
1756	Mar. 11	*Warwick*	60	,, Molyneux Shuldham.	Taken at Martinique.
		Adventure	6	Lieut. James Orrok.	Taken by privateer *Infernal*.
		Oswego	sloop		} Surrendered at Oswego.
		Ontario	sloop		
1757	Mar. 18	*Greenwich*	50	Capt. Robert Roddam.	Taken in W. Indies.
	April 19	*Merlin*	10	Com. John Cleland (1).	Taken off Brest ; retaken.
	Sept. 24	*Tilbury*	60	*Capt. Henry Barnsley.	} Lost in a hurricane off Louisbourg.
	,, ,,	*Ferret*	10	*Com. Arthur Upton.	
1758	Feb. 19	*Invincible*	74	Capt. John Bentley.	Lost near St. Helen's.
	April 13	*Prince George* . . .	90	{ R.-Ad. Thomas Broderick. { Capt. Joseph Peyton (1).	} Burnt at sea ; 485 lost.
	,, 28	*Triton*.	24	,, John Stanton.	} Destroyed in the E. Indies.
	,, ,,	*Bridgewater*. . . .	24	,, Thomas Manning.	
	,, 29	*London* (buss) . . .	. .		Wrecked in R. Sénégal.
	Aug.	*Stork*	10	,, William Tucker.	Taken in W. Indies.
	Oct. 11	*Winchelsea*	20	,, John Hale.	Taken by French ; retaken.
	Nov. 29	*Lichfield*	50	,, Matthew Parton.	Wrecked on African coast ; 130 lost.
1759	May	*Tartar's Prize* . . .	24	,, Thomas Baillie (1).	Sprang a plank in Mediterranean.
	Nov. 20	*Resolution*	74	,, Henry Speke.	} Wrecked on Four Bank in Quiberon Bay.
	,, 21	*Essex*	64	,, Lucius O'Brien.	
		Mermaid	20	,, James Hackman.	Wrecked among the Bahamas.
		Hawke	12		Taken off C. Clear ; retaken 1761.
		Falcon (bomb) . . .	8	Com. Mark Robinson (1).	Wrecked on the Saintes, Guadeloupe.
1760	Feb. 15	*Ramillies*.	90	*Capt. Wittewronge Taylor.	Wrecked on Bolt Head.
	Mar. 28	*Penguin*	20	,, William Harris.	Taken and burnt.
	May 17	*Lowestoft*.	28	,, Joseph Deane.	Wrecked in the St. Lawrence.
	,,	*Virgin*	12	Com. Edward St. Loe (2).	Taken by French ; retaken, Sept.
	Oct. 4	*Harwich*	50	Capt. William Marsh.	Wrecked on the Isle of Pines.
	,,	*Griffin*	20	,, Thomas Taylor (1).	Wrecked near Barbuda.
	Nov. 2	*Cumberland*	56	,, Robert Kirk.	Foundered near Goa.
		Lyme	28	,, Sir Edward Vernon (2)	Wrecked in North Sea.
		Eurus.	20	,, John Elphinstone (1)	Wrecked in St. Lawrence.
		Conqueror	70		Wrecked on St. Nicholas Island.
		Newcastle. . . .	50	,, Digby Dent (3).	} Lost in a hurricane off Pondicherry ; crews saved.
		Queenborough . .	20		
1761	Jan. 1	*Protector*, f.s. . . .	8		
		Duc d'Aquitaine . .	64	* ,, Sir William Hewitt, Bt.	} Lost in a hurricane off Pondicherry ; crews lost.
		Sunderland	60	* ,, Hon. James Colville.	
		Duke (store-ship) . .	10		
	Mar.	*Pheasant* (cutter) . .	16	{ *Com. Bartholomew (?) Nel-son.	} Foundered in the Channel.
	April 4	*Speedwell*.	10	Lieut. James Allen.	Taken at Vigo by *Achille*.
	Dec. 30	*Biddeford*	20	*Capt. Thomas Gordon (2).	Wrecked near Flamborough Head.
1762	Feb.	*Raisonnable*	64	,, Molyneux Shuldham.	Lost at Martinique.
		Epreuve	14	Com. Peter Blake.	Lost in returning from South Carolina.
		Savage	9		Lost in Torbay.

Year.	Date.	Ships.	Guns.	Commander. [* Lost his life on the occasion.]	Fate.
1762	May 24	*Hussar*	28	Capt. Robert Carkett.	Lost in the W. Indies.
	July 24	*Chesterfield* . . .	40		Lost in Old Strait of Bahama.
	Nov. 29	*Marlborough*. . . .	70	,, Thomas Burnett.	}Foundered on passage home from
	Dec. 18	*Temple*	70	,, Thomas Collingwood.	Havana.
		Southsea Castle . . .	40	,, William Newsom.	Lost at Manilla.
		Humber	40	,, Richard Onslow.	Lost on Hazeboro' Sands.
		Gramont	18	Com. Patrick Mouat.	Taken at St. John's, Newfoundland.
		Scorpion	16		Lost in Irish Sea.
		Peregrine	16	*Com. Edward Knowles.	Foundered on way to W. Indies.
1763	Jan.	*San Genaro*	60		Wrecked in the Downs.
		Basilisk (bomb). . .	8	Com. —— Lowfield.	Taken by *Audacieux*, privateer.

(*b.*) LOSSES OF THE FRENCH NAVY, 1744–48, 1755–62.

NOTE.—French East Indiamen, if serving with, or in lieu of ships of, the French Navy, are, in a few instances, included below.

Year.	Date.	Ships.	Guns.	Fate.
1744	Apr. 4	*Médée*	26	Taken by *Dreadnought* and *Grampus*.
1745	Jan. 10	*Fleuron*	64	Accidentally burnt at Brest.
	Feb. 20	*Eléphant*	20	Taken by *Chester* and *Sunderland*.
	Mar. 26	*Panthère*	26	Taken by V.-Adm. Martin in the Channel.
	May 19	*Vigilante*.	64	Taken by Commodore Warren at Louisbourg.
1746	Feb. 9	*Auguste*	50	Taken by *Portland*. Renamed *Portland's Prize*.
	Apr. 4	*Volage*	32	Taken ; retaken next day.
	Aug. 4	*Mercure* (en flûte)	56	Taken by *Namur*.
	,, 4	*Ferme*	54	Taken by *Pembroke*.
	Oct. 11	*Mars* . . . . . . * .	64	Taken by *Nottingham*.
	,, 14	*Duc d'Orléans* *	30	Wrecked in E. Indies.
	Nov. 19	*Subtile*	26	Taken by *Portland*. Renamed *Amazon*.
		Ardent	64	Captured and burnt.
	,,	*Casaubon*.	60	}Accidentally burnt at Chebucto.
		Parfait	54	
		Embuscade	40	Taken by *Defiance*.
		Fine	30	Wrecked at Montrose.
		Flore	24	Taken by *Greyhound*, privateer.
		Maligne (sloop)	? 8	Taken.
1747	May 3	*Invincible*	74	Taken by Anson.
	,, 3	*Sérieux*	64	Taken by Anson. Renamed *Intrepid*.
	,, 3	*Diamant*	52	Taken by Anson. Renamed *Isis*.
	,, 3	*Jason*	50	Taken by Anson.
	,, 3	*Gloire*.	40	Taken by Anson.
	,, 3	*Rubis* (flûte)	26	Taken by Anson.
	June 21	*Etoile*.	46	Destroyed by Warren.
	Sept. 13	*Renommée*	32	Taken by *Dover*.
	Oct. 14	*Monarque*	74	Taken by Hawke.
	,, 14	*Terrible*	74	Taken by Hawke.
	,, 14	*Neptune*	70	Taken by Hawke.
	,, 14	*Fougueux*	64	Taken by Hawke.
	,, 14	*Trident*	64	Taken by Hawke.
	,, 14	*Severne*	50	Taken by Hawke.
	,, 14	*Castor*.	28	Taken by Hawke.
		Bellone	36	Taken.
		Lys	26	Taken.
1748	Jan. 31	*Magnanime*	74	Taken by *Nottingham* and *Portland*.
1755	June 8	*Lys* (en flûte)	64	}Taken off Louisbourg.
	,, 8	*Alcide*.	64	
	Nov. 13	*Espérance* (en flûte) . . .	74	Taken and burnt.
1756	Mar.	*Chariot Royal*	36	Taken by *Lichfield* and *Norwich*.
	July 12	*Arc en Ciel*	50	Taken by *Torbay*.
1757	May 14	*Aquilon*	50	Destroyed by *Antelope*.
	,, 30	*Duc d'Aquitaine*	50	Taken by *Eagle* and *Medway*.
	Sept. 21	*Emeraude*	28	Taken by *Southampton*.
	Nov. 23	*Alcion*	50	Sunk by *Hussar* and *Dolphin*.
	,,	*Bien Acquise*.	36	Taken.
	,,	*Hermione*	24	Taken.
	Autumn	*Merlin*	10	Retaken by *Lancaster* and *Dunkirk*.

* Really a ship of the East India Company, but was serving with the fleet.

Year.	Date.		Ships.	Guns.	Fate.
1757			*Nymphe*	36	Destroyed at Majorca.
			Escarboucle	16	Taken by *Isis.*
			A sloop	16	Taken by *Phœnix*, privateer.
1758	Feb.	28	*Foudroyant*	80	Taken by *Monmouth.*
	,,	28	*Oriflamme*	50	Destroyed by *Monarch* and *Montagu.*
	,,	28	*Orphée*	64	Taken by *Revenge* and *Berwick.*
	Apr.	7	*Galatée*	22	Taken by *Essex* and *Pluto.*
	,,	30	*Bien Aimé*	58	Wrecked in E. Indies.
	,,		*Diane*	36	Taken by *Boreas.*
	May	29	*Raisonnable*	64	Taken by *Dorsetshire* and *Achilles.*
	,,		*Echo*	26	Taken by *Juno.*
			Apollon	50	
	June	28	*Chèvre*	16	Sunk by French at Louisbourg.
			Biche	16	
			Fidèle	26	
	,,	29	*Guirlande*	24	Taken by *Rochester* and *Renown.*
			Entreprenant	74	
	July	21	*Capricieux* } en flûte	64	Burnt by accident at Louisbourg.
			Célèbre }	64	
	,,	25	*Prudent*	74	Cut out by boats at Louisbourg.
	,,		*Bienfaisant*	64	
	Sept.		*Rhinocéros*	36	Taken and burnt by *Isis.*
	,,	12	*Calypso*	..	Driven ashore and destroyed in Audierne Bay.
	Oct.	2	*Duc d'Hanovre*	14	Taken by *Lizard* off Brest.
	,,	31	*Belliqueux*	64	Taken by *Antelope* off Ilfracombe.
	Dec.		*Opiniâtre*	64	
	,,		*Outarde*	44	Wrecked near Brest.
	,,		*Greenwich*	50	
			Robuste (en flûte)	74	Taken by *Alcide* and *Actæon.*
			Loire	44	Taken by *St. Albans* in Mediterranean.
			Rose	36	Destroyed at Malta by *Monmouth.*
	Aug.		4 ships building	..	Burned at St. Servand.
1759	Feb.	21	*Bellone*	32	Taken by *Vestal.*
	Mar.	19	*Mignonne*	20	Taken by *Æolus* and *Isis.*
	,,	27	*Duc de Chartres*	60	Taken by *Windsor.*
	,,	28	*Danaé*	46	Taken by *Southampton* and *Mélampe.*
	May	18	*Aréthuse*	36	Taken by *Chatham*, *Venus* and *Thames.*
	Aug.	13	*Berkeley*	20	Taken by *Crescent.*
	,,	? 16	*Hermione*	26	Taken by Cotes at Jamaica.
			Océan	80	Destroyed by Boscawen.
			Redoutable	74	
	,,	18	*Téméraire*	74	Taken by Boscawen.
			Centaure	74	
			Modeste	64	Destroyed by Boscawen.
			Soleil Royal	80	Burnt by Hawke.
			Formidable	80	Taken by Hawke.
	Nov. 20–		*Héros*	74	Taken and burnt by Hawke.
	22		*Thésée*	74	Sunk by Hawke.
			Superbe	70	Sunk by Hawke.
			Juste	70	Wrecked at mouth of Loire.
			Inflexible	64	Wrecked in Vilaine.
1760	May	16	*Pomone*	36	Destroyed at Quebec by Swanton.
			Atalante	32	
			Machault	32	
	July	8	*Bienfaisant*	22	Destroyed at Chaleur Bay by Byron.
			Marquis de Marloze	16	
	Sept.		*Vierge* (ex *Virgin*)	12	Retaken by *Temple* and *Griffin*
			Sirène	32	Taken by *Boreas.*
	Oct.	18	*Prince Edouard*	32	Destroyed by Holmes.
			Valeur	20	Taken by *Lively.*
	,,	19	*Fleur-de-Lys*	32	Destroyed by Holmes.
	,,		*Hermione*	36	Cut out at Pondicherry.
			Baleine	32	
			Epreuve	14	Taken by *Niger.*
1761	Jan.	8	*Vestale*	32	Taken by *Unicorn.*
	,,	24	*Félicité*	..	Taken and destroyed by *Richmond.*
			Warwick (en flûte 34)	60	Taken by *Minerva.*
	,,	30	*Brune*	32	Taken by *Venus* and *Juno.*
	Mar.	16	*Comète*	32	Taken by *Bedford.*
	Apr.	1	*Oriflamme* (en flûte)	50	Taken by *Isis.*
	,,	3	*Bertin* (en flûte 28)	64	Taken by *Hero* and *Venus.*
	,,		*Faisan*	16	Taken by *Albany.*
	June	5	*Ste. Anne* (en flûte 40)	64	Taken by Admiral Holmes's squadron on Jamaica station.
	July	17	*Bouffonne*	32	Taken by *Thetis* and *Modeste.*
			Achille	62	Taken by *Thunderer.*
	Aug.	13	*Courageux*	74	Taken by *Bellona.*
			Anémone	14	Taken by *Mars* and *Oxford* in Bay of Biscay.
			Sardoine	14	
			Léopard	60	Burnt at Quebec with plague on board.
1762	Aug.	18	*Guirlande*	26	Taken.
	Sept.	1	*Zéphyr*	26	Taken by *Lion.*
	Oct.	15	*Crozon* (schooner)	6	Taken by *Venus.*

Year.	Date.	Ships.	Guns.	Fate.
1762	Oct. 23	Oiseau	26	Taken by *Brune.*
		Opale	24	Taken by *Phœnix.*
		Ecureuil	10	Taken by *Fame* and *Lion.*
		Dragon	64	Lost at Cape François.
		Junon	40	Lost off Mahon.
		Hermione	32	Lost coming out of Dunquerque.
		Zénobie	26	Lost off Portland.
		Mutine	24	Lost on the Doggersbank.
		Minerve	24	Lost near Villa Franca.
		Aigle	50	Lost in Strait of Belle Isle.

(c.) LOSSES OF THE SPANISH NAVY, 1718–19, 1739–48, 1762.

NOTE.—It is possible that a few of the small craft mentioned may have belonged to the Caraccas Company.

		Ships.	Guns.	Fate.
1718	Aug. 11	Real San Felipe	74	Taken by Byng in the battle off Cape Passaro.
		Principe de Asturias	70	
		San Carlos	60	
		Santa Isabela	60	
		Santa Rosa	60	
		Volante	44	
		Juno	36	
	Aug. 11	Real	60	Taken by Walton's division.
		San Isidoro	46	
		Sorpresa	36	
		Aguila	24	
	Aug. 11	A 4th rate	54	Burnt after capture.
		Esperança	46	Burnt by Mari.
		A 4th rate	44	Burnt.
	Aug.	S. Juan Menor	20	Taken.
	,,	Hermione	44	Burnt at Messina.
	,,	Conde de Toulouse	30	Taken at Messina.
	,,	San Fernando	60	Sunk at Messina.
		Tigre	26	Taken.
	Aug. 11	2 bombs	10	Burnt by Mari.
		1 bomb	10	Taken by Walton's division.
		1 fireship	..	Burnt by Mari.
		4 storeships	..	Taken.
		1 settee	..	Burnt.
1719		Santa Rosalia	64	Driven ashore.
		San Pedro	60	Lost in Bay of Taranto.
	Jan. 16	A frigate	..	Taken by *Royal Oak.*
1727	Mar. 11	N. S. del Rosario	46	Taken by *Royal Oak.*
1739	Dec. 6	2 storeships	.	Taken by *Sheerness.*
	Nov. 23	Astræa	20	Taken at Puerto Bello.
		Triunfo	20	
1740	Apr. 8	Princesa	64	Taken by *Kent, Lenox* and *Orford.*
	,, 28	1 sloop*	8	Taken near St. Augustine by *Squirrel.*
	Oct. 23	2 storeships	..	Taken by *Diamond.*
1741	Feb.	Guipuscoa	74	Lost off Santa Martha.
	Mar. ? 6	Hermione	54	Foundered at sea.
		1 patache	20	Broken up at St. Catherine's.
		Galicia	70	Taken at Cartagena; afterwards burnt.
	,, 25	San Carlos	70	Scuttled at Cartagena by Spaniards.
	etc.	Africa	60	Scuttled at Cartagena by Spaniards.
		Conquistador	60	Scuttled at Cartagena by Spaniards.
		San Felipe	80	Burnt at Cartagena by Spaniards.
	,, 30	Dragón	60	Burnt at Cartagena by Spaniards.
	Aug.	1 frigate*	24	Taken by *Worcester.*
1742	Feb.	Fuerte	60	Wrecked while trying to take the ship's company of the *Tiger.*
	June 14	San Juan		Burnt at St. Tropez.
		Santa Teresa		
		Soledad	galleys.	
		San Felipe		
		S. Genaro		
		Invencibile	70	Burnt at Havana.
? 1742		S. Juan Bautista (35 men)†	..	Taken or destroyed.
? 1742		San Joaquin (110 men)†	..	
? 1742		San José (32 men)†	..	

* These may perhaps be identified with some of the ships on which head-money was paid in 1746, and which are given at the end of the losses for 1742.

† The only record of these ships is that they were men-of-war taken or destroyed, but not at Puerto Bello or Cartagena. Head-money was being paid for them in 1746, at the same time as for the *Princesa* and other ships taken before 1742; hence it may be inferred that their loss was prior to the earlier date. See note * above.

Year.	Date.	Ships.	Guns.	Fate.
1743	June 20	*N. S. de Cabadonga**	56	Taken by *Centurion.*
		S. Isidoro	70	Burnt at Ajaccio.
1744	Feb. 11	*Poder*	60	Taken by *Berwick ;* afterwards burnt.
		Conde de Chincan	24	Taken by *Ripon* in W. Indies.
1745		*Concepción* (treasure ship)	.	Taken by *Rose.*
1746		*Forte de Nantz* (?)	32	Taken.
1747	Oct. 9	*Glorioso*	74	Taken by *Russell.*
1748	Oct. 1	*Conquistador*	64	Taken by Knowles in W. Indies.
	,, 3	*Africa*	70	Burnt by Knowles in W. Indies.
1762	May 28	*Fénix,* f.s.	18	Taken by *Alarm.*
	,, 28	*Venganza*	24	Taken by *Defiance.*
	,, 28	*Marte*	18	Taken by *Defiance.*
	June 3	*Thetis*	22	Taken by *Alarm.*
	,,	*Neptuno*	70	
	,,	*Asia*	64	Sunk at the entrance to Havana.
	,,	*Europa*	60	
		Tigre	70	
		Reina	70	
		Soberano	70	
		Infante	70	
	Aug. 13	*Aquilón*	70	Surrendered with Havana.
		America	60	
		Conquistador	60	
		San Genaro	60	
		San Antonio	60	
	Aug.	2 ships (building)	..	Destroyed at Havana.
	Oct. 31	*Santisima Trinidad*	22	Taken at Manilla.
		Ventura	26	Taken by the *Fowey.*

* Not a man-of-war.

CHAPTER XXIX.

VOYAGES AND DISCOVERIES, 1714–1762.

SIR CLEMENTS MARKHAM, K.C.B.

Clipperton and Shelvocke to the Pacific—Voyages to Hudson's Bay —Expeditions of
Barlow, Vaughan, Scroggs, and Middleton—The search for a North-West Passage
—Henry Ellis's Voyage—Coats's book on Hudson's Bay—Anson's Voyage—The
value of naval Exploration.

 IN 1718 there was war between the German
Emperor and Spain; and some London
adventurers obtained a commission from the
government at Vienna to cruise against the
Spaniards in the Pacific. The commission
was received from the authorities at Ostend;
and the ships, fitted out in the Thames, were named the *Prince
Eugene* and the *Starhemberg*. A retired naval lieutenant named
Shelvocke was to have had the former, a ship with thirty-six guns
and a complement of one hundred and eighty men; while the *Starhemberg*, mounting twenty-four guns, was to have been entrusted to
John Clipperton, the man who had deserted Captain Dampier. But
the owners were displeased with Shelvocke for his extravagance
when he went to Ostend for the commissions, so they disrated
him, giving Clipperton the chief command in the *Prince Eugene*,
and transferring Shelvocke to the *Starhemberg*. Meanwhile war
broke out with Spain, so the names of the ships were changed to
Success and *Speedwell*, the Ostend commissions were returned with
thanks, and the expedition sailed under British colours. Shelvocke
for the time stifled his resentment at having been superseded; and
the ships sailed from Plymouth on February 13th, 1719. Soon
afterwards a gale of wind gave Shelvocke an opportunity of parting
company with his superior officer, with all the wine and brandy on
board his ship. His chief mate was Simon Hatley, who had been
with Woodes Rogers, and William Betagh was his " captain of

marines."   With both these officers Shelvocke, who was a free
drinker, had constant quarrels.   In rounding Cape Horn the ship
was driven down to 61° 30' S., where the cold was intense.   " We
had continued squalls of sleet, snow, and rain," says Shelvocke ;
and the only sea bird was a disconsolate black albatross.   Simon
Hatley thought it was a bird, of ill-omen which brought the snow
and mist; and he shot the albatross.   He believed that this act
would bring a fair wind : but, on the contrary, it continued foul
and tempestuous for another month.   Shelvocke touched at the
island of Chiloe, plundered and burnt the town of Payta, on
the Peruvian coast, and arrived at Juan Fernandez on May
4th, 1720.   There the *Speedwell* parted her cable, was driven on
shore, and became a total wreck.   The crew worked hard at a
new vessel, of 20 tons, which was launched on the 5th of October
and named the *Recovery*.   Shelvocke embarked with forty-six men,
leaving eleven Englishmen on the island.   He shaped a course
to the Peruvian coast and captured a fine vessel of 200 tons at
Pisco, leaving his own little craft for the Spanish crew.   Sailing
northward, they encountered the *Success* off Quibo, but they parted
company almost immediately.   The two vessels met again three times
on the coast of Mexico, but without exchanging a word.   Shelvocke
named his prize the *Happy Return*.   Clipperton sailed for China in
May, 1721, and sold the *Success* at Macao on account of the owners,
returning home with his crew in June, 1722.   Shelvocke captured
a rich prize called the *Concepción*, with 108,636 dollars on board, and
then steered for California, anchoring in Puerto Seguro, near Cape
San Lucas, for which port he gives some sailing directions.   Having
left California for China in August, 1721, Shelvocke states that on
the 21st he sighted an island one hundred and ten leagues from
Cape San Lucas, at a distance of two leagues.   This he judged to be
seven or eight leagues in circumference.   It was named Shelvocke
Island.   Burney thinks that it is the *Roca Partida* seen by Villa-
lobos, and afterwards by Spilbergen in about 20° N.   When the
present writer was serving as a midshipman on board the flagship of
Sir George Francis Seymour in the Pacific, the *Collingwood* sailed
over the position of Shelvocke Island on the old chart; and we had
orders to enter the visibility of distant objects in the log at each bell,
so as to judge the space our eyes covered on either side of our track.
But no Shelvocke's Island was ever seen.   That worthy made the
best of his way across the Pacific to China, where he sold his

ship. He reached England in July, 1722, and was prosecuted for piracy and other misdemeanours ; but the evidence was insufficient. Shelvocke published his account of the voyage in 1726, and two years afterwards his " captain of marines," William Betagh, published a refutation of Shelvocke's statements.   The unfortunate English-men who were left by Shelvocke at Juan Fernandez were captured by a certain Captain Salavarria, who was given the command of a ship fitted out by two wealthy Lima merchants in consequence of the arrival of Clipperton and Shelvocke on the coast.   Their fate is unknown.

The British vessels which cruised in the Pacific Ocean during the forty years from 1680 to 1720 were all employed either for piratical or for warlike purposes.   Yet they are properly noticed in a chapter on discovery and exploration, because they made the west coast of South America and the Pacific Ocean known to English seamen, and familiarised them with the navigation.   Surveys were executed, especially of the Galapagos and Bashee Islands, and some few discoveries were made.   Above all, they kept alive that spirit of maritime enterprise which has ever been the mainstay of our Navy.

The Arctic voyages to Hudson's Bay were of practical importance, for they led to the formation of a company to trade for furs and skins, with a charter, granted in 1669, which conferred rights and privileges over all the lands in that direction.   In the previous year one Gillam, in the *Nonsuch*, had been sent on a voyage of discovery, and had reached a latitude of 75° up Davis Strait, then passing through Hudson's Strait, and wintering in the southern extreme of Hudson's Bay.   Gillam had there formed a settlement called Fort Charles. The French were at Fort Bourbon, on the western side of the bay, from 1697 to 1714 ; but after the peace of Utrecht they departed and their settlement became Fort York on the Hayes River.   The Company's most northern fort was on the Churchill River.   Ships were sent out every year, returning with valuable cargoes of furs and skins ; but a strict monopoly was maintained, and discovery was discouraged.   Nevertheless, it could not be altogether sup-pressed, especially as a general belief prevailed that the north-west passage was to be discovered by following up the opening named Sir Thomas Roe's Welcome by Button.

In 1719 two vessels named the *Albany* and *Discovery* sailed from the Thames, under masters Barlow and Vaughan, to discover a passage, but they never returned.   A man named Scroggs, in a ship called the *Whalebone*, was sent from Fort Churchill in search of them in 1722. He went up the "Welcome" as far as 64° 15', heard news from the Eskimos of a very rich copper mine, and named a point of land after his ship—Whalebone Point. Then followed an expedition, the despatch of which was due to the representations of Mr. Arthur Dobbs, who had studied the subject with great care. He spoke to Sir Robert Walpole, and eventually he induced Admiral Sir Charles Wager, the First Lord of the Admiralty, to supply two vessels for the discovery of the north-west passage, the *Furnace*, sloop, and *Discovery*, pink. Christopher Middleton, who had commanded ships of the Hudson's Bay Company, was induced by Mr. Dobbs to take command, and he had good officers under him, but a rascally crew, consisting of the sweepings of the jails. There were not three seamen amongst them.

Middleton did his work well. Starting from England late in the season of 1741, it was necessary to winter at the Churchill River. In 1742 Middleton left Churchill on the 1st of July, and proceeded up Sir Thomas Roe's Welcome. He reached a headland in 65° 10' N., which he named Cape Dobbs, and on the northern side of which there was a wide opening. But, after a careful examination, Middleton came to the conclusion that it was merely an estuary, and gave it the name of the Wager River, after the First Lord of the Admiralty. Pressing onwards he came to another headland, which he named Cape Hope, anticipating that the passage was on the other side of it. But there was again disappointment. Repulse Bay showed no opening. The Frozen Strait then turns south-east. As there was much scurvy on board the ship, Middleton resolved to return. In the circumstances he had done excellently, but Mr. Dobbs was so bitterly disappointed that he made a violent and unjustifiable attack on the commander of the expedition. The Admiralty called upon Middleton for a detailed reply to the accusations against him ; and he made it to the satisfaction of their lordships.

In 1745 an Act was passed for giving "a public reward of £20,000 to such person or persons as shall discover a north-west passage through Hudson's Strait to the western and southern ocean of America." Subscribers came forward to fit out an expedition. A sum of £10,000 was raised, and a North-West Committee was formed, and purchased the *Dobbs*, galley, of 100 tons, and the *Caliofrnia* of 160 tons. They were well equipped,

William Moor commanding the *Dobbs* and Francis White the *California*. Mr. Henry Ellis, an able and experienced seaman, also went out as the Committee's agent, with instructions to make charts, to record bearings, distances, soundings, and variations, to collect specimens, and to keep a journal. The expedition left Gravesend on May 20th, 1746, was off Cape Digges on August 2nd, and wintered at York Factory. On June 24th, 1747, it left its winter quarters, entered the Welcome, and sent northward a boat, which rounded Cape Dobbs. The conclusion of Ellis was in agreement with that of Middleton, that the Wager River was not a strait; but that the passage would probably be found through Frozen Strait. Ellis returned home in October; and this con-cluded the attempts to find a passage by Hudson's Bay during the eighteenth century. But William Coats, a master in the Hudson's Bay Company's service, who had made many voyages, acquired an intimate knowledge of the great inland sea, and wrote in 1750 " The Geography of Hudson's Bay," a very useful treatise, which was first printed for the Hakluyt Society in 1852.

The expedition of Commodore George Anson was despatched for belligerent purposes when the war with Spain broke out in 1739. It is, however, properly looked upon as a voyage of discovery, so far as the Navy is concerned, because Anson's was the first naval expedition which ever crossed the Pacific Ocean. Anson received his orders in June, 1740; but the ships were manned with great difficulty, and at last the complement was made up by five hundred superannuated invalids, out-pensioners of Chelsea Hospital, who all died during the voyage. The Commodore was on board the *Centurion*, 60; and the other vessels were the *Gloucester*, 50, Captain Richard Norris; the *Severn*, 50, Captain the Hon. Edward Legge; the *Pearl*, 40, Captain Matthew Michell; the *Wager*, 28, Captain Dandy Kidd; the *Tryal*, sloop, Commander the Honourable George Murray; and two store ships, the *Anna* and *Industry*. Anson's expedition finally sailed from St. Helen's on September 18th, 1740. At Madeira the captain of the *Gloucester* was invalided, and was succeeded by Captain Michell, whose place in the *Pearl* was given to Captain Kidd; and Lieutenant David Cheap, of the *Centurion*, received command of the *Tryal*. At Port St. Julian, the captain of the *Pearl* having died, the Honourable Captain Murray succeeded him, and Captain Cheap was given the *Wager*, and Lieutenant Charles Saunders, the *Tryal*. Running through the Strait of Le

Maire in March, 1741, the squadron encountered a succession of furious gales off the Horn, and the *Pearl* and *Severn* returned home. The scurvy broke out in a most malignant form, so that the *Centurion* alone buried forty-three men, the mortality in the other ships being equally serious. Driven down to 60° 5′ S., the remaining ships were dispersed.

The *Centurion* did not reach Juan Fernandez until June 10th, 1741, having one hundred and thirty men in the sick-list, and having buried two hundred during the voyage. She was anchored in Cumberland Bay; and the *Tryal* arrived on the same afternoon. On the 21st, the *Gloucester* came in sight, having lost two-thirds of her crew from scurvy. The sick were landed and placed in tents, twelve dying while they were being carried from the ship to the shore. The fresh vegetables of the island, and the healthier surroundings, soon began to restore the survivors. A prize named the *Monte Carmelo* was captured, and equipped as a cruiser; and, in September, the *Centurion, Tryal*, and prize, the last commanded by Lieutenant Philip de Saumarez, sailed for the South American coast. The *Gloucester*, not being ready, was to join them at Payta. Soon afterwards another fine prize was captured; and, the *Tryal* having become unseaworthy, her crew was turned over to the new vessel, which was armed and received the name of the *Tryal's Prize*. After cruising along the coasts of Chile and Peru, and capturing some other prizes, Commodore Anson anchored on November 13th in Payta Bay and surprised the town. The plunder amounted in value to £32,000, besides stores of wine and brandy, fresh provisions, and live stock. The town was set on fire, and six vessels in the bay were sunk. Two days after leaving Payta the *Gloucester* joined, with prizes containing specie and plate worth £18,000; and in December the squadron arrived safely off the island of Quibo.

Meanwhile misfortune had attended the voyage of the remaining vessel. The *Wager*, commanded by Captain David Cheap, had parted company with the Commodore in a gale off Cape Horn on April 23rd, 1741. Out of one hundred and thirty men on board, only thirteen officers and men were fit for duty. The rest were down with scurvy, and the captain had dislocated his shoulder. Being off the southern coast of Chile, on May 15th, the ship struck on a rock; and she was wrecked within musket-shot of the land. Captain Cheap was navigating by Narbrough's chart, which had been supplemented from faulty Spanish surveys. In reality this part of the coast of Patagonia was unknown. The *Wager* was deeply embayed in the Gulf of Peñas, and was lost off the south coast of the peninsula of Tres Montes. Masts were cut away, boats were got out, and the sick were landed. The land was precipitous, but well wooded. The men declared that as soon as the ship was lost their pay ceased, and that they were no longer amenable to naval discipline. A few, however, remained loyal, provisions were landed, and a guard was placed over them. The captain shot a midshipman named Cozens, who was in open mutiny; but this increased the discontent, and an insubordinate feeling was aroused. The long boat was lengthened and rigged as a schooner. The mutineers insisted upon being taken back to England by Magellan's Strait; and, when Captain Cheap refused, they surprised him at night, tied his hands, and deposed him, as they said, for having killed Cozens. They then prepared to depart in the long boat, barge, and cutter, altogether eighty-one men, leaving the Captain behind. Lieutenant Hamilton, of the Marines, and the surgeon, with seven men, remained faithful, the mutineers leaving the yawl and some provisions for them. Soon after the departure of the boats the barge returned with two midshipmen, the Honourable John Byron and Alexander Campbell, and eight more men, who were also true to the Captain.

On December 15th, the forlorn party embarked in the barge and yawl. After enduring fearful hardships and sufferings, they were obliged to give up the voyage, and, in February, 1742, they returned to the place where the *Wager* was wrecked, which had been called "Cheap's Bay." At last some natives arrived in two canoes, and undertook to pilot the fourteen survivors in the barge to the Island of Chiloe. They started; but, soon afterwards, the men deserted with the barge and were never heard of again, leaving behind Captain Cheap, Lieutenant Hamilton, the surgeon, and the two midshipmen. The surgeon died, and the rest were taken by the natives in canoes. After the most terrible privations they reached Chiloe, and were kindly received by the Spanish governor, who sent them as prisoners of war to Valparaiso. They were eventually embarked on board a French ship, arrived in France, and were released in April, 1746. Campbell and Byron both wrote narratives of their wonderful adventures. The mutineers made their way through Magellan's Strait to the Portuguese settlement of Rio Grande, whence they got passages to Lisbon.

The Commodore had, of course, given the *Wager* up as lost. Leaving Quibo, he cruised off Acapulco to intercept the return galleon from that port to Manilla. The squadron consisted of the *Centurion, Gloucester,* and three armed prizes. Anson released all his prisoners, giving them the prizes, and made sail for China, with the *Gloucester* in company, on May 5th, 1742. In August it was found necessary to abandon the *Gloucester,* owing to her leaky condition. She was set on fire, and her officers and crew were taken on board the *Centurion.* During the voyage the scurvy broke out afresh, and for a long time several men died every day. On August 27th, the *Centurion* anchored in Tinian Road, in one of the Ladrone Islands, after an unusually prolonged voyage. The sick were landed to the number of one hundred and twenty-eight, and placed in a large thatched building on shore. Live-stock and vegetables were obtained in abundance. About thirty of the sick died, but the rest rapidly recovered, and were soon convalescent. The ship was repaired, and on October 21st Commodore Anson sailed for China, anchoring off Macao in November. There the *Centurion* wintered; and on April 29th, 1743, Anson put to sea, announcing to his people that he intended to make another attempt to intercept the Manilla galleon. Although officers and men had been so long away, and had gone through such fearful sufferings, they all cheerfully concurred. On May 5th, they sighted the Bashee Islands of Dampier, and for a month Anson cruised off the island of Samar without sighting any vessel. At length, on June 20th, a midshipman named Charles Proby [1] shouted from his station at the top-masthead, " A sail to windward ! " She was soon seen from the deck, coming down before the wind towards the *Centurion.* It was the long-sought galleon, *N. S. de Cavadonga.* Both ships cleared for the action, which lasted an hour and twenty minutes, at the end of which the Spaniard struck her colours. Anson lost only two men killed and seventeen wounded; but the loss of the Spaniards was sixty-seven killed and eighty-four wounded. The cargo of the galleon included $1,313,843, besides 35,682 ounces of silver, and merchandise. The prize was commissioned and entrusted to the command of Lieutenant Philip de Saumarez. Next day they again made the Bashee Islands, and on July 10th they entered the river of Canton. In December the prize was sold at Macao, and the *Centurion*

---

[1] Brother of the first Lord Carysfort. Afterwards Commissioner at Chatham Dockyard.

was homeward bound on December 15th, 1743. She anchored at
Spithead, after an absence of nearly four years, on June 15th, 1744.

Commodore George Anson's expedition is correctly looked upon
as an exploring expedition, although with warlike objects. It
was the first purely naval exploring expedition of modern times;
and it is memorable for having been—quite as much, if not
more, than those which succeeded it—a most successful nursery of
valuable naval officers. Many of the best men in the Navy, during
the Seven Years' War, had learnt their first lessons, and gained
invaluable experience, during their hard service in Anson's exploring
squadron. There were Piercy Brett (1),[1] and John Campbell,[2]
who was Lord Hawke's flag-captain at the battle of Quiberon
Bay; there were Charles Saunders,[3] Charles Proby, de Keppel,[4]
Philip de Saumarez,[5] Peter Denis,[6] the Hon. John Byron,[7] and
Hyde Parker (1). No doubt, the voyage of Anson, remarkable
as it was for its early misfortunes, for the thrilling stories of
suffering and shipwreck connected with it, and yet notable for the
way in which the patience and resolution of its commander were
rewarded with final success, was the incentive for the despatch of
the expeditions which, in due time, followed in its wake. It is still
more noteworthy that Anson's expedition was, perhaps, the best
example of a naval exploring voyage, forming a splendid and
prolific nursery for training the best and most valuable class of
naval officers.

[1] Lieutenant in the *Centurion*.
[2] A petty officer in the *Centurion*.
[3] First lieutenant of the *Centurion*.
[4] Midshipman in the *Centurion*.
[5] Third lieutenant of the *Centurion*.
[6] Lieutenant in the *Centurion*.
[7] Midshipman in the *Wager*.

CHAPTER XXX.

THE CIVIL HISTORY OF THE ROYAL NAVY, 1763–1792.

Administration of the Navy—First Lords—Secretaries of the Admiralty—Navy Board officials, etc.—Naval Expenditure—Seamen and Marines— Strength of the Fleet—Rigging of a First-Rate—New classes of men-of-war—The carronade—Establishments of guns—Gun-locks—Typical ships of the period—Condition of the Dockyards—Ships in ordinary—Coppering—Pumps—Distillation of water—Sanitation—Lighting and buoying—Lightning conductors—The longitude—Harrison's time-keepers — The Nautical Almanac — Desertion — Discontent — Mutiny—Bounties to seamen—Officers' halfpay—Officers in peace-time—Prizemoney—The Marine Society—The Hibernian Marine Society—The Marine School at Hull—Dockyard artificers—The King and the Navy—Promotion to the flag—Superannuation—Naval uniform—Naval law—Coffin's case—The right of search —The right of the flag—International courtesies.

SIGNATURE OF RICHARD, EARL HOWE, ADMIRAL OF THE FLEET.

NO changes of great importance were made in the administrative machinery of the Navy during the comparatively short period which is covered by the present chapter. Even the lessons of the War of American Independence produced few reforms, save in the management of the Dockyards. The succession of the more important administrative officers was as follows :—

FIRST LORD OF THE ADMIRALTY.

George Grenville.

Apr. 10, 1763.	John, Earl of Egmont.
Apr. 23, 1763.	John, Earl of Sandwich.
Sept. 10, 1763.	John, Earl of Egmont.
Sept. 16, 1766.	Sir Charles Saunders, K.B., Vice-Admiral.
Dec. 1766.	Sir Edward Hawke, K.B., Admiral.
Jan. 12, 1771.	John, Earl of Sandwich.
Mar. 30, 1782.	Hon. Augustus Keppel, Admiral.
Jan. 30, 1783.	Richard, Viscount Howe, Admiral.
Apr. 10, 1783.	Augustus, Viscount Keppel, Admiral.
Dec. 31, 1783.	Richard, Viscount Howe, Admiral.
July 1788.	John, Earl of Chatham.

SECRETARY OF THE ADMIRALTY.

John Clevland.

1763. Philip Stephens (later, Sir P. Stephens, Bart.).

1785. (As Assistant) John Ibbetson.

TREASURER OF THE NAVY.

William Wildman, Viscount Barrington.

	1665.	Richard, Viscount Howe, Captain, R.N.
	1670.	Sir Gilbert Elliot, Bart., later Lord Minto.
	1777.	Welbore Ellis.
Apr.	1782.	Isaac Barré.
July	1782.	Henry Dundas.
Apr.	5, 1783.	Charles Townsend.
Dec.	30, 1783.	Henry Dundas.[1]

CONTROLLER OF THE NAVY.

George Cockburne, Captain, R.N.

Aug.	1770.	Hugh Palliser, Captain, R.N.
Apr.	1775.	Maurice Suckling, Captain, R.N.
July	1778.	Sir Charles Middleton, Captain and Rear-Admiral.[2]
Mar.	1790.	Sir Henry Martin (2), Bart., Captain, R.N.

SURVEYOR OF THE NAVY.

{Thomas Slade.
{William Bateley.

June	1765.	{Sir Thomas Slade, Kt. {John Williams.
	1771.	Sir John Williams, Kt.
Mar.	1778.	{Sir John Williams, Kt. {Edward Hunt.
	1785.	{Edward Hunt. {John Henslow.

CLERK OF THE ACTS.

Edward Mason.

July	1773.	George Marsh.

CONTROLLER OF THE TREASURER'S ACCOUNTS.

Timothy Brett.

	1782.	George Rogers.

CONTROLLER OF THE VICTUALLING ACCOUNTS.

Robert Osborne.

June	1771.	Charles Proby, Captain, R.N.
Oct.	1771.	Thomas Hanway, Captain, R.N.
Oct.	1772.	George Marsh.
July	1773.	James Gambier (1), Captain, R.N.
Aug.	1773.	William Palmer.

CONTROLLER OF THE STOREKEEPER'S ACCOUNTS.

Hon. William Bateman, Captain, R.N.

	1783.	William Campbell.
Jan.	1790.	William Bellingham.

EXTRA COMMISSIONERS.

Sir Richard Temple.

Sir John Bentley, Kt., Captain, R.N. (till 1763).

Jan.	1778.	Edward Le Cras, Captain, R.N. (till 1783).
Oct.	1782.	Samuel Wallis, Captain, R.N. (till 1783).
	1787.	Samuel Wallis, Captain, R.N. (again).

COMMISSIONERS AT H.M. DOCKYARDS, ETC.

Chatham.

Thomas Hanway, Captain, R.N.

Oct.	1771.	Charles Proby, Captain, R.N.

Portsmouth.

Richard Hughes (2), Captain, R.N. (Bart. 1773).

Aug.	1773.	James Gambier (1), Captain, R.N.
Jan.	1778.	Sir Samuel Hood, Bart., Captain, R.N.[3]

---

[1] Created Viscount Melville, 1802.   [2] Created Lord Barham, 1805.

[3] Created Lord Hood, 1782.

Oct.   1780.   Henry Martin (2), Captain,
                 R.N. (later a Baronet).
Mar.   1791.   Sir Charles Saxton, Kt.,
                 Captain, R.N. (a Bart.
                 1794).

Plymouth.

        Frederick Rogers, Cap-
        tain, R.N. (a Baronet,
        1773).
Jan.   1775.   Paul Henry Ourry, Cap-
                 tain, R.N.
        1783.   Edward Le Cras, Cap-
                 tain, R.N.
Apr.   1784.   John Laforey, Captain,
                 R.N.
        1789.   Robert Fanshawe (1),
                 Captain, R.N.

Gibraltar and Minorca.

        Charles Colby, Captain,
        R.N. (retired, 1763).

Halifax, Nova Scotia.

July   1775.   Marriot Arbuthnot, Cap-
                 tain, R.N.
Feb.   1778.   Sir Richard Hughes (2),
                 Bart., Captain, R.N.
Oct.   1780.   Sir Andrew Snape Ha-
                 mond, Bart., Captain,
                 R.N.
        1784.   Henry Duncan (1), Cap-
                 tain, R.N.

Leeward Islands.

Sept.   1779.   John Laforey, Captain,
                 R.N. (till 1783).
Apr.   1784.   John Moutray, Captain,
                 R.N. (till 1785).

Jamaica.

        1782.   Robert Alexander Lam-
                 bert, Captain, R.N.
                 (till 1784).

The " extra " and " ordinary " expenditure, as voted by Parliament from year to year, and the number of seamen and Marines authorised, are shown below in a table which is a continuation of the one on p. 5 of the present volume :—

Year.	" Extra."	" Ordinary."	No. of Seamen and Marines.[1]	Year.	" Extra."	" Ordinary."	No. of Seamen and Marines.[1]
	£	£			£	£	
1763	100,000	380,661	30,000	1778	488,695	389,200	60,000
1764	200,000	398,568	16,000	1779	579,187	369,882	70,000
1765	200,000	407,734	16,000	1780	697,903	385,381	85,000
1766	277,300	412,983	16,000	1781	670,016	286,261	90,000
1767	328,144	409,177	16,000	1782	953,519	409,766	100,000
1768	274,954	416,403	16,000	1783	311,843[2]	451,989	110,000
1769	282,413	410,255	16,000	1784	1,100,000	701,869	26,000
1770	283,687	406,380	16,000	1785	940,000	675,307	18,000
1771	423,747	378,752	40,000	1786	800,000	692,320	18,000
1772	375,939	394,725	25,000	1787	650,000	700,000	18,000
1773	421,554	424,019	20,000	1788	600,000	700,000	18,000
1774	420,729	444,188	20,000	1789	575,570	713,000	20,000
1775	297,379	444,680	18,000	1790	490,360	703,276	20,000
1776	339,151	426,904	28,000	1791	506,010	689,395	24,000
1777	465,500	400,805	45,000	1792	350,000[3]	672,482	16,000

[1] The cost of these was in addition to the sums specified in the " Extra " and " Ordinary " columns.

[2] This was £1,000,000 short of the estimated expense : but it was considered that the deficiency would be balanced by the number of men to be discharged owing to the peace.

[3] For work in the Royal Yards only. No money was voted for work in private yards, the estimate for which, with fittings and stores for the ships, was £81,820.

The fluctuations in the strength of the fleet are indicated in the appended table, which, though it goes into less detail, and omits to notice vessels possessed of no distinct fighting value, is, in effect, a continuation of the table on p. 7.

ABSTRACT OF THE FIGHTING SHIPS OF THE ROYAL NAVY AT FOUR DIFFERENT DATES, 1762–1792.

(From Derrick, pp. 148–197, with corrections.)

Rate.	Class of Ship.	Nov. 3rd, 1762. (End of War.)	Jan. 1st, 1775. (End of Peace.)	Jan. 20th, 1783. (End of War.)	Dec. 1st, 1792. (End of Peace.)
	Guns.	No.	No.	No.	No.
First[1]	100	5	4	5	5
Second	98 and 90	15	16	19	16
,,	84	1	1	1	..
Third	80	7	3	4	1
,,	76	..	..	1	1
,,	74	37	57	81	66
,,	70	11	7	4	..
,,	68 and 66	3	..	2	..
,,	64	30	32	49	39
Fourth	60	32	11	8	1
TOTAL OF THE LINE:—		141[2]	131	174[3]	129[4]
Fourth	56	..	..	2	..
,,	52	..	..	1	1
,,	50	24	12	20	16
Fifth	44	21	4	28	21
,,	40	..	..	2	1
,,	38	2	..	7	7
,,	36	4	3	17	14
,,	34	..	..	1	..
,,	32	32	35	59	47
,,	30	1	..	1	..
,,	24	1	..	..	..
,,	22	..	..	1	..
Sixth	30	1	..	..	..
,,	28	22	24	33	28
,,	26	..	..	1	..
,,	24	21	7	11	6
,,	22 and 20	13	13	14	7
Sloops	18 to 8	57	38	85	42
Bombs	..	14	2	4	2
Fireships	..	11	1	17	9
GENERAL TOTAL .		365	270	468	330[5]

[1] It having been suggested, in the course of the progress of this work, that some description of the rigging o a man-of-war in the heroic age of the British Navy would be useful to the reader, a plate, showing the rigging, etc., of a first-rate in 1775 is here inserted. Explanatory references to it will be found on the page opposite.

[2] Besides 7 prizes which, though taken, had not then been purchased for the Navy.

[3] Besides 4 prizes which, though taken, had not then been purchased for the Navy.

[4] Including 47 needing repair.

[5] Besides 18 building or ordered.

The 50-gun ship had ceased about the year 1756 to rank as of the line. Another class of ship ranking between the ship of the line

REFERENCES TO THE PLATE,

Showing the Rigging, etc., of a First-rate of 1775.

1 BOWSPRIT.
  2 Yard and sail.
  3 Gammoning.
  4 Horse.
  5 Bobstay.
  6 Spritsail sheets.
  7 Pendants.
  8 Braces and pendants.
  9 Haliards.
  10 Lifts.
  11 Clewlines.
  12 Spritsail horses.
  13 Buntlines.
  14 Standing lifts.
  15 Spritsail top.
  16 Flying jib-boom.
  17 Flying jib stay and sails.
  18 Haliards.
  19 Sheets.
  20 Horses.

21 SPRITSAIL TOPMAST.
  22 Shrouds.
  23 Yard and sail.
  24 Sheets.
  25 Lifts.
  26 Braces and pendants.
  27 Cap.
  28 Jack staff.
  29 Truck.
  30 Jack flag.

31 FORE MAST.
  32 Runner and tackle.
  33 Shrouds.
  34 Lanyards.
  35 Stay and lanyard.
  36 Preventer stay and lanyard.
  37 Wooldings of the mast.
  38 Yard and sail.
  39 Horses.
  40 Top.
  41 Crowfoot.
  42 Jeers.
  43 Yard tackles.
  44 Lifts.
  45 Braces and pendants.
  46 Sheets.
  47 Fore tacks.
  48 Bowlines and bridles.
  49 Fore buntlines.
  50 Fore leechlines.
  51 Fore top-rope.
  52 Futtock shrouds.

53 FORE TOPMAST.
  54 Shrouds and lanyards.
  55 Yard and sail.
  56 Stay and sail.
  57 Runner.
  58 Backstays.
  59 Haliards.
  60 Lifts.
  61 Braces and pendants.
  62 Horses.
  63 Clewlines.
  64 Bowlines and bridles.
  65 Reef-tackles.
  66 Sheets.
  67 Buntlines.

  68 Crosstrees.
  69 Cap.

70 FORE TOPGALLANT-MAST.
  71 Shrouds and lanyards.
  72 Yard and sail.
  73 Backstays.
  74 Stay.
  75 Lifts.
  76 Clewlines.
  77 Braces and pendants.
  78 Bowlines and bridles.
  79 Flag staff.
  80 Truck.
  81 Flag staff stay.
  82 Flag of Lord High Admiral.

83 MAIN MAST.
  84 Shrouds.
  85 Lanyards.
  86 Runner and tackle.
  87 Pendant of the gornet.
  88 Guy of ditto.
  89 Fall of ditto.
  90 Stay.
  91 Preventer stay.
  92 Stay tackle.
  93 Woolding of the mast.
  94 Jeers.
  95 Yard tackles.
  96 Lifts.
  97 Braces and pendants.
  98 Horses.
  99 Sheets.
  100 Tacks.
  101 Bowlines and bridles.
  102 Crowfoot.
  103 Top-rope.
  104 Top.
  105 Buntlines.
  106 Leechlines.
  107 Yard and sail.

108 MAIN TOPMAST.
  109 Shrouds and lanyards.
  110 Yard and sail.
  111 Futtock shrouds.
  112 Backstays.
  113 Stay.
  114 Staysail and stay and haliard.
  115 Runners.
  116 Haliards.
  117 Lifts.
  118 Clewlines.
  119 Braces and pendants.
  120 Horses.
  121 Sheets.
  122 Bowlines and bridles.
  123 Buntlines.
  124 Reef-tackles.
  125 Crosstrees.
  126 Cap.

127 MAIN TOPGALLANT-MAST.
  128 Shrouds and lanyards.
  129 Yard and sail.

  130 Backstays.
  131 Stay.
  132 Stay sail and haliards.
  133 Lifts.
  134 Braces and pendants.
  135 Bowlines and bridles.
  136 Clewlines.
  137 Flagstaff.
  138 Truck.
  139 Flagstaff stay.
  140 Royal Standard.

141 MIZEN MAST.
  142 Shrouds and lanyards.
  143 Pendants and burtons.
  144 Yard and sail.
  145 Crowfoot.
  146 Sheet.
  147 Pendant lines.
  148 Peakbrails.
  149 Staysail.
  150 Stay.
  151 Derrick and span.
  152 Top.
  153 Crossjack yard.
  154 Crossjack lifts.
  155 Crossjack braces.
  156 Crossjack slings.

157 MIZEN TOPMAST.
  158 Shrouds and lanyards.
  159 Yard and sail.
  160 Backstays.
  161 Stay.
  162 Haliards.
  163 Lifts.
  164 Braces and pendants.
  165 Bowlines and bridles.
  166 Sheets.
  167 Clewlines.
  168 Staysail.
  169 Crosstrees.
  170 Cap.
  171 Flagstaff.
  172 Flagstaff stay.
  173 Truck.
  174 Union Flag.
  175 Ensign staff.
  176 Truck.
  177 Ensign.
  178 Poop ladder.
  179 Bower cable.

HULL.

A Cat head.
B Fore channels.
C Main channels.
D Mizen channels.
E Entering port.
F Hawse holes.
G Poop lanterns.
H Chesstree.
I Head.
K Stern.

and the frigate proper was the two-decked 44-gun class. When these vessels had nearly all died out, a new class, the 38-gun frigate, appeared in 1780. Of this class the *Minerva*, launched on June 3rd, 1780, was the first. She originally carried, on her main deck, twenty-eight 18-pounders, and on her quarterdeck and forecastle ten 9-pounders, eight 18-pounder carronades and fourteen swivels ; but slight modifications were afterwards made and the swivels were omitted. In 1780, also, the 36-gun frigate was revived, with, however, 18 and 9-pounders in lieu of the 12 and 6-pounders of the older ships of the same class. In 1775 a new so-called 24-gun class was introduced, carrying twenty-two 9-pounders on the main deck and four 3-pounders, later two 6-pounders, on the quarterdeck. Thenceforward there were no proper frigates of less than 24 guns, though post ships of 22 and even 20 guns continued to be commissioned. These corresponded roughly with the vessels which, in the French navy, were called corvettes. Below them came the sloops, which, with bombs, fireships, armed ships and store ships, were commanded by Masters and Commanders.[1] Below these again came cutters, schooners, brigs, armed vessels, armed transports, armed store-ships and surveying sloops, which were commanded by Lieutenants. All yachts were commanded by Post Captains, and the larger of them were sometimes entrusted to Captains of long standing who, in consideration of the honour, either temporarily or permanently surrendered their right to promotion to flag-rank, when it fell to them in the ordinary course of seniority.[2]

The introduction of the carronade was by far the most important development of naval ordnance during the period under review.

" So long," says Mr. William James, " as that species of ordnance, called gun by the English and *canon* by the French, continued in exclusive possession of the decks of a fighting ship, no difference existed between the number of carriage pieces she actually mounted and the number which stood as a sign of her class in the published lists. In process of time, however, the nominal, or rated, and the real force of a ship lost their synonymous signification, and that in a manner, and to an extent, too important, in every point of view, to be slightly passed over.

" In the early part of 1779, a piece of carriage ordnance, the invention, by all accounts, of the late scientific General Robert Melville, was cast, for the first time, at the ironworks of the Carron Company, situated on the banks of the river Carron, in

---

[1] The " Master-and-Commander " was equivalent to the modern Commander, and is, in fact, usually called Commander in these pages, for the sake of brevity.

[2] *E.g.*, Captain Sir Alexander Schomberg, Kt., who, posted in 1757, would, in the ordinary course, have obtained his flag in 1787, but who, accepting in 1771 the command of the Irish Viceroy's yacht, retained it until his death in 1804.

Scotland.   Although shorter than the navy 4-pounder, and lighter, by a trifle, than the navy 12-pounder, this gun equalled, in its cylinder, the 8-inch howitzer.   Its destructive effects, when tried against timber, induced its ingenious inventor to give it the name of *smasher.*

" As the smasher was calculated chiefly, if not wholly, for a ship-gun, the Carron Company made early application to have it employed in the British Navy, but, owing to some not well-explained cause, were unsuccessful.   Upon the supposition that the size and weight of the smasher, particularly of its shot, would operate against its general employment as a sea-service gun, the proprietors of the foundry ordered the casting of several smaller pieces, corresponding in their calibre with the 24, 18, and 12-pounder guns in use, or rather, being of a trifle less bore, on account of the reduced windage very judiciously adopted in carronades, and which might be extended to long guns with considerable advantage.   These new pieces became readily disposed of among the captains and others, employed in fitting out private armed ships to cruise against America, and were introduced, about the same time, on board a few frigates and smaller vessels belonging to the Royal Navy.

" The new gun had now taken the name of *carronade,* and its several varieties became distinguished, like those of the old gun, by the weight of their respective shot. This occasioned the smasher to be called, irrevocably, a 68-pounder, whereas, repeated experiments had shown that a hollow, or cored shot, weighing 50 or even 40 lbs., would range further in the first graze, or that at which the shot first strikes the surface of the water, and the only range worth attending to in naval gunnery.   The hollow shot would, also, owing to its diminished velocity in passing through a ship's side, and the consequent enlargement of the hole and increased splintering of the timbers, produce more destructive effects than the shot in its solid form, one of the principal objections against which, was, and still continues to be, its being so cumbrous to handle.

" Before half the expiration of the year in which the first carronade had been cast, a scale was drawn up by the Navy Board and sanctioned by the Lords of the Admiralty,[1] for arming the different rates in the service with the 18 and 12-pounder

---

[1] Carronades assigned to each class of ship in the Royal Navy, by Admiralty Order of July 13th, 1779 :—

Rate.	Class of Ship. Guns.	Quarterdeck.		Forecastle.		Poop.		Actual number of carriage guns mounted.
		No.	Prs.	No.	Prs.	No.	Prs.	
First	100	..	..	2	12	8	12	110
Second	98	..	..	4	12	6	12	108
,,	90	..	..	4	12	6	12	100
Third	74	..	..	2	12	6	12	82
,,	64	..	..	2	12	6	12	72
Fourth	50	2	24	2	24	6	12	60
Fifth	44	8	18	2	18	..	..	54
,,	38	6	18	4	18	..	..	48
,,	36	4	18	4	18	..	..	44
,,	32	6	18	2	18	..	..	40
Sixth	28	4	18	2	18	..	..	34
,,	24	6	12	4	12	..	..	34
,,	20	6	12	2	12	..	..	28
Sloops [1]	18	6	12	2	12	..	..	26
,,	16	6	12	2	12	..	..	24
,,	14	6	12	2	12	..	..	22

[1] Ship-rigged.

calibres. In consequence of the first, second, and third-rate ships having their quarter-decks as fully supplied with guns as there was room for ports on each side, no additional pieces could be placed there; but it was found that the forecastle would generally admit the opening of a pair of extra ports, and that the poop, which for nearly a century past had served chiefly as a roof to the captain's cabin, would if timbered up on each side, afford space for three pairs of ports, making, in the whole, eight additional ports for the]reception of carronades. The 50-gun ship was found to have room for a pair of additional ports on her quarterdeck, besides a pair on her forecastle, and three pairs on her poop, when the latter was barricaded, making altogether ten ports. The 44-gun ship had no poop, and no armament on the quarterdeck. By furnishing the latter with a barricade, and cutting through it four pairs of ports, besides an extra pair on the forecastle, this ship might mount the same additional number of pieces as the 50. The three remaining classes of the fifth, and the first two classes of the sixth rate, would also admit of additional ports being cut through the sides of their forecastles and quarterdecks. The third class of the sixth rate, and the quarterdecked ship-sloop class, being, in respect to their quarterdecks and forecastles, in a similar state to the 44, would require to be similarly built up before they could mount the eight carronades assigned to them.[1]

" Several captains complained of the carronade ; some, of its upsetting after being heated by successive discharges; others, that, owing to its shortness, its fire scarcely passed clear of the ship's side, and that its range was too confined to be useful. The captains of some of the 32-gun frigates, in particular, represented that one pair of their quarterdeck carronades was so much in the way of the rigging as to endanger the lanyards of the shrouds, and begged to have their established number reduced from six to four. As the principal objection to carronades appeared to have arisen from defects in the manner of mounting them, some additional instructions on that head were prepared and forwarded by Mr. Gascoigne, the chief proprietor of the Carron foundry. Some alterations were also made in the piece itself.[2] Still the Board of Ordnance, in repeated conferences with the Navy Board, maintained the superiority of the old gun, resting their arguments chiefly on the comparative length of its range ; while the Navy Board urged that a vessel, able to carry 4-pounders of the common construction, might, with equal ease, bear 18-pounders of the new; that its shot was far more formidable and destructive; and that its range was quite sufficient for the purpose required. . . .

" According to an official list, dated on the 9th of January, 1781, there were then 429 ships in the Navy mounting carronades, among which the 32-pounder carronade appears, and was the first of that calibre which had been used. The total of the carronades employed was 604, namely, eight 32-pounders, four 24-pounders, three hundred and six 18-pounders, and two hundred and eighty-six 12-pounders. In December of this year, a recommendation to use 68-pounder carronades on the fore-castle of large ships, and 42 and 32-pounders on the same deck of some of the smaller rates, induced the Navy Board to order the old *Rainbow*, 44, to be fitted, by way of experiment, wholly with carronades of the largest description. Sir John Dalrymple proposed the casting of some that should carry a ball of 100 or 130 lbs. weight; but the Board resolved to confine themselves to the heaviest of the pieces already cast, the 68-pounder.

" The necessary carronades were ordered from the foundry, and some of the foremen belonging to the works attended to see them properly fitted. It was not, however, until February or March, 1782, that the *Rainbow* could be completed in her

---

[1] Establishment of 1762.

[2] *E.g.*, increasing its length by two calibres.

equipment. What additional force she acquired by this change in her armament the following table will show :—

	Old Armament.				New Armament.		
	Long Guns.		Broadside weight of metal.		Carronades.		Broadside weight of metal.
	No.	Prs.			No.	Prs.	
			Lbs.				Lbs.
First deck	20	18	} 318		20	68	} 1238
Second deck	22	12			22	42	
Quarterdeck	..	..			4	32	
Forecastle	2	6			2	32	
	44				48		

"In the beginning of April, the *Rainbow*, thus armed, and commanded by Captain . . . Henry Trollope, who, with Captain Keith Elphinstone (the late Admiral Lord Keith) and the late Rear-Admiral Macbride, was among the earliest patrons of the carronade, sailed on a cruise. All the well-known skill and enterprise of her captain failed, however, to bring him within gunshot of a foe worth contending with until the 4th of the succeeding September, when, being off Isle de Bas, he came suddenly upon a large French frigate. Owing to the latter's peculiar bearing, one of the *Rainbow's* forecastle 32-pounders was first discharged at her. Several of the shot fell on board, and discovered their size. The French captain, rationally concluding that, if such large shot came from the forecastle of the enemy's ship, much larger ones would follow from her lower batteries, fired his broadside 'pour l'honneur du pavillon,' and sur-rendered to the *Rainbow*. . . .

"In the course of 1782, a few of the larger sorts of the carronade were mounted on board some of the receiving ships in order that the seamen of such vessels as were in port refitting might be exercised at handling and firing this, to them, novel piece of ordnance. As one proof of many that carronades were gaining ground in the Navy, the captains of the few 38 and 36-gun frigates in commission applied for and obtained 24-pounder carronades, in lieu of the 18s with which their ships had been established. The termination of the war in January, 1783, put a stop to any further experiments with the carronade; but its merits were now too generally acknowledged to admit a doubt of its becoming a permanent favourite : in the British Navy, at least, where a short range is ever the chosen distance."

It does not, however, appear that foreign powers adopted the carronade until after 1783.[1]

The establishment of long guns underwent various modifications, the most important of which may be shown thus :—

---

[1] Nor is it quite certain that the innovation was altogether beneficial. Mr. Henry Carey Baird, of Philadelphia, has laid before the author reasons for attributing some at least of the British failures during the War of 1812–15 to an excessive confidence in the value of the carronade.

ESTABLISHMENT OF GUNS (other than Carronades in 1792, and half-pounder Swivels in 1762) CARRIED by some of the PRINCIPAL CLASSES OF SHIPS of the ROYAL NAVY in 1762 and 1792 respectively:—

Classes of Ships.	Date.	Lower Deck.		Middle Deck.		Upper Deck.		Quarter-deck.		Forecastle.	
		No.	Prs.	No.	Prs.	No.	Prs.	No.	Prs.	No.	Prs.
100 guns (large). .	1762	30	42	28	24	30	12	10	6	2	6
100 ,, ,, . .	1792	30	32 or 42	28	24	30	18	10	12	2	12
100 ,, (smaller) .	1762	28	42	28	24	28	12	12	6	4	6
100 ,, ,, .	1792	28	32 or 42	28	24	28	12	12	12	4	12
90 ,, ...	1762	26	32	26	18	26	12	10	6	2	6
90 ,, ...	1792	26	32	26	18	26	12	10	12	2	12
80 ,, (3-decker).	1762	26	32	26	18	24	9	4	6	..	..
80 ,, (2-decker).	1792	30	32	..	..	32	24	14	12	4	12
74 ,, (larger) .	1762	28	32	..	..	30	24	12	9	4	9
74 ,, ,, .	1792	28	32	..	..	30	24	14	9	2	9
74 ,, (smaller) .	1762	28	32	..	..	28	18	14	9	4	9
74 ,, ,, .	1792	28	32	..	..	30	18	12	9	4	9
64 ,, ...	1762	26	24	..	..	26	18	10	9	2	9
64 ,, ...	1792	26	24	..	..	26	18	10	9	2	9
50 ,, ...	1762	22	24	..	..	22	12	4	6	2	6
50 ,, ...	1792	22	24	..	..	22	12	4	6	2	6
44 ,, ...	1762	20	18	..	..	22	9	..	..	2	6
44 ,, ...	1792	20	18	..	..	22	12	..	..	2	6
36 ,, ...	1762	..	..	..	..	26	12	8	6	2	6
36 ,, ...	1792	..	..	..	..	26	18	8	9	2	12
32 ,, ...	1762	..	..	..	..	26	12	4	6	2	6
32 ,, ...	1792	..	..	..	..	26	18	4	6	2	6
28 ,, ...	1762	..	..	..	..	24	9	4	3	..	..
28 ,, ...	1792	..	..	..	..	24	9	4	6	..	..
24 ,, ...	1762	2	9	..	..	20	9	2	3	..	..
24 ,, ...	1792	..	..	..	..	22	9	2	6	..	..
20 ,, ...	1762	..	..	..	..	20	9	..	..	..	..
20 ,, ...	1792	..	..	..	..	20	9	..	..	..	..
14-gun sloops . .	1762	..	..	..	..	14	6	..	..	..	..
14-gun ,, . .	1792	..	..	..	..	14	6	..	..	..	..

Gun-locks and tin firing-tubes had been used in a few ships during the latter part of the Seven Years' War; but, the general feeling of the service being against them, the old match was reverted to until after 1780, when the flint lock, with an improved tube, became common, though the match-tub was retained for use in case of breakdown.

As in Chap. XXVI., particulars of some typical ships of war of the period under review are given:—

TYPICAL BRITISH SHIPS OF WAR, 1763–92, INCLUDING BOTH PRIZES AND BRITISH-BUILT VESSELS;—

Ship.	Guns.	Date of Launch.	Length of Gun Deck.		Length of Keel.		Beam.		Depth.		Burthen in Tons.	Where, and by whom Built.
			Ft.	in.	Ft.	in.	Ft.	in.	Ft.	in.		
Victory	100	1765	186	0	151	3⅜	52	0	21	6	2162	Chatham, E. Allen, after Sir T. Slade.
Ville de Paris	104	*1782	185	7½	153	0	53	8½	22	2	2347	*Taken from the French.
Queen Charlotte	100	1789	190	0	156	5	52	4	22	4	2279	Chatham.
Barfleur	98	1768	177	8	144	0½	50	5	21	0	1947	Chatham, J. Harris.
Gibraltar (ex *Fénix*)	80	*1780	178	10¾	144	6	53	3¾	22	4	2184	*Taken from the Spaniards.
Cæsar	80	1793	181	0	148	3¾	51	3	22	4	1991	Plymouth.
Ramillies	74	1763	168	6	138	2	46	11⅜	19	9	1619	Chatham, E. Allen.
Ramillies	74	1785	170	0	140	1⅛	47	2	19	11	1669	Thames, Randall & Co.
Brunswick	74	1790	176	2½	145	3	48	9	19	6	1836	Deptford, M. Ware.
Augusta	64	1763	159	0	130	6⅛	44	7½	18	10	1381	Thames, Wells & Co.
Protée	64	*1780	164	1	140	0⅞	44	7	19	0	1480	*Taken from the French.
Prince William	64	*1780	153	2½	130	3⅝	44	1	19	9½	1346	*Taken from the Spaniards.
Argonaut	64	*1782	163	0	136	0	45	4	18	1	1521	*Taken from the French.
Warwick	50	1765	151	0	122	9	40	2	18	3	1053	Portsmouth, J. Bucknall.
Roebuck	44	1774	140	0	116	4⅜	37	10¾	16	4	886	Chatham.
Princess Caroline	44	*1781	129	1	107	5	38	10	15	6	862	*Taken from the Dutch.
Prudente	38	*1779	136	0	118	11	37	9¾	10	10	897	*Taken from the French.
Minerva	38	1780	141	0	117	3⅜	38	10	13	9	940	Woolwich, J. Jenner,
Hébé	38	*1782	150	1½	125	4½	39	11	12	10	1062	*Taken from the French.
Oiseau	36	*1779	146	3	126	9⅜	34	1	9	10¾	783	*Taken from the French.
Thalia	36	1782	137	1	113	3¾	38	3	13	3	881	Bursledon, H. Parsons.
Melampus	36	1786	141	3	117	0⅜	38	10	13	9	939	Bristol.
Glory	32	1763	125	0	103	4	35	2	11	0½	679	Hull, J. Hodgson.
Iris (later *Hancock*)	32	*1777	137	1	116	6	34	3¾	10	11	730	*Taken from the Americans.
Clinton (ex *Espérance*)	32	*1780	134	0	113	0	35	0	13	9	736	*Taken from the French.
Heroine	32	1783	130	11½	107	10⅜	36	0¼	13	3	779	Bucklershard.
Castor	32	1786	126	0	104	0	35	0	12	2	678	Harwich.
Hussar	28	1763	114	4	102	8½	33	10⅜	11	0	627	Thames, R. Inwood.
Sartine	28	*1778	132	6	118	0	35	9	15	3	802	*Taken from the French.
Virginia	28	*1778	132	6	108	0	34	6	10	7	802	*Taken from the Americans.
Rose	28	1785	120	6	99	6	33	6	11	0	594	Sandgate.
Amphitrite	24	1776	114	3	94	3½	32	0	10	3½	513	Deptford, A. Hayes.
Squirrel	24	1785	119	0	99	0	32	5	10	3	553	Liverpool.
Ariadne	20	1776	108	0	89	8	30	0	9	8	429	Chatham, J. Pownall.
Charleston (ex *Boston*)	20	*1780	114	3	94	3½	32	0	10	3	514	*Taken from the Americans.
Cygnet	18	1776	110	11	90	9¼	28	3¼	9	0	385	
Zebra	18	1780	98	0½	80	0	27	5¼	13	4	320	Gravesend, Cleverly.
Brisk	16	1774	101	4	83	4	27	7	12	10	337	Sandgate.
Swift	14	1763	91	6	74	3⅛	26	2½	13	3¼	271	Thames, H. Bird.
Servent	14	1789	100	0	82	9¼	27	0	13	0	321	Plymouth.
Childers, brig	14	1778	78	7	60	8	25	0	11	0	202	Thames.
Ferret, cutter	6	1763	50	0	39	0	20	0	7	10	83	Chatham, E. Allen.
Cockatrice, cutter	10	1781	69	4	52	0	25	7	10	9	181	Dover.
Alecto, fireship	12	1781	108	9	90	6¾	29	7½	9	0	423	Dover.
Ætna, bomb	8	1776	91	9½	74	5	27	8	12	1	303	Thames.
Augusta, yacht	8	reblt. 1770	80	6	64	11⅜	23	1¼	10	11	184	Deptford.

During the peace which preceded the war with the American Colonies, the condition of the dockyards, and of the ships in ordinary, was much neglected; and when, in 1771, the First Lord of the Admiralty had occasion to demand of the Surveyor of the Navy a return of the number of vessels fit for service, he received a reply which, he presently found, conveyed an entirely misleading impression. The store of oak timber was also discovered to be at a dangerously low ebb. Upon this, it was ordered in Council that for the future His Majesty's Navy and Yards throughout the kingdom should be inspected by the Board of Admiralty every two years. A little later, in 1775, the practice of paying by piece-work was introduced in the dockyards. After the war, the Admiralty, on July 10th, 1783, appointed twenty-four Masters [1] from the half-pay list to superintend the ships in ordinary; eight at Portsmouth, six at Plymouth, eight at Chatham and Sheerness, and two at Woolwich. To each Master a division of ships was entrusted; and to every ship was assigned a proportion of men, besides warrant officers and servants, as follows · ships of 100 guns and upwards, 36 men; ships of 90 or 98 guns, 32 men; ships of 70 or 74 guns, 26 men; ships of 64 guns, 20 men; ships of 50 guns, 14 men; ships of 44 guns, 12 men; ships of 28 or 38 guns, 10 men · ships of 24 guns, 8 men; sloops, 6 men; and cutters, 4 men.

Ships fit for service were ordered to have their lower masts in; their bowsprits, lower yards, topmasts and topsail yards on board; and a roof over their upper decks to protect them from the weather. In 1784, revised rules were issued for the appropriation and laying aside of gear and stores for ships under construction, with a view to ensuring that the former should be ready as soon as the latter; and better arrangements were made for the accumulation of reserve and spare stores at the dockyards and the naval stations abroad. It has been mentioned in a previous chapter that the first British man-of-war to be coppered was the *Alarm*, 32. This was in 1761. A second ship was not similarly treated till 1764, when the *Dolphin*, 24, was coppered. Then followed the *Jason*, 32, and in 1776, the *Daphne*, 20. Between that time and 1784 or 1785 nearly every vessel in the Navy was dealt with in the same way. It was still asserted that the ships in ordinary deteriorated very rapidly in consequence of the action set up between the copper on their bottoms and the iron on their bolts. An inquiry into the matter was instituted in 1786; but it did not result in the condemnation of the practice of laying up ships with their copper on. An improved method of copper fastening had been, however, introduced a little before that time; [2] and this, doubtless, had the effect of diminishing, if not of altogether preventing, the galvanic action which had been complained of.

About the year 1764 some improvements in ships' pumps were

---

[1] The Master, it need scarcely be explained, was then only a warrant officer, although he was nearly equivalent to the Navigating Lieutenant of a later date. He was totally distinct from the commissioned Master-and-Commander,—the Commander of to-day.

[2] In November, 1783.

introduced by a Mr. Coles; and in that year the Admiralty ordered a 60-gun ship to be experimentally fitted with pumps of Mr. Coles's pattern. In the following year a similar pump was fitted on board the *Seaford*, 20, at Portsmouth; and it was then found that, whereas the old pump required seven men to pump out a ton of water in 76 seconds, the new pump, with but four men, would pump out a ton of water in 43½ seconds; and that, whereas two men could not move the old pump at all, two men could with the new pump pump out a ton of water in 55 seconds. It was also found that, when choked with single ballast, the new pump could be cleared in four minutes, while the old could not be cleared at all so long as water remained in the ship's hold. Experiments continued; and it would appear that, for some years, Coles's pump was largely used in the Navy; but it was from time to time improved, notably in 1787, and, in 1791, by a Mr. Hill, a carpenter R.N., who was also the inventor of a machine for drawing bolts out of ships' sides, and of an apparatus for stopping shot-holes below the water-line.

The distillation of fresh water from salt was not usually practised on shipboard during the period; but it was carried out occasionally. In 1772 the Admiralty directed all ships of war to be fitted with a still and other necessary apparatus. The process appears to have been the invention of one Dr. Lynn; but a Frenchman, M. de St. Poissonnière, devised a somewhat similar process at about the same time. It was, however, impossible in those days to distil sufficient water for the whole ordinary consumption of a ship's crew. At best only relatively small quantities could be prepared; and, looking to the invariable foulness of shore water after it has been for some time in a ship's casks or tanks, it is astonishing that it was ever possible for even the most careful captains to keep their crews in fair health during long voyages. Yet some at least of them certainly managed to do so. In the course of Cook's second voyage, with the *Resolution* and *Adventure*, between April, 1772, and July, 1774, only four men, exclusive of a boat's crew who were murdered in New Zealand by the natives, died; and of these but one died of sickness. In Cook's last voyage the *Resolution* lost but five by sickness, three of these having been in ill-health when they left England; and the *Adventure* lost not so much as a single man in the four years and two months during which she was absent from home.

Progress, but not very rapid progress, was made between 1763 and 1792 in lighting and buoying the coasts of the United Kingdom. The Smalls Rock light was first shown from a wooden structure which was built by Mr. Henry Whiteside in 1778, and which was not removed until 1861. The Needles' and St. Catherine's lighthouses were established in 1780. The Longships' lighthouse, off Land's End, was begun in September, 1791. A 21-inch aperture facet reflector, used at Liverpool in 1763 ; a facet parabolic reflector, used in the Scots lighthouses about the year 1787 ; and a plano-convex lens, used at Portland in 1789, were shown at the Royal Naval Exhibition, 1891.

Lightning conductors were, at Anson's instance, supplied to ships soon after that officer's death in 1762 ; but they were not permanently fitted, and were merely directed to be set up when a storm threatened. In consequence, they were often not used at all, and many accidents resulted.

Efforts to arrive at some satisfactory method of discovering the longitude at sea continued to be made. In 1764, Mr. William Harrison, with one of his timekeepers, was received on board the *Tartar*, 28, Captain John Lindsay. She sailed from Spithead on March 28th, and arrived at Madeira on April 19th. Captain Lindsay made Porto Santo exactly as he had been led to believe that he would make it by Mr. Harrison, who had taken two altitudes of the sun on the 18th. The ship proceeded ; and on May 12th, Harrison was able accurately to discover her distance from Barbados, which was sighted on the 13th. Harrison returned to England in a merchantman, arriving in London on July 18th. The timekeeper was then only fifteen seconds slow, allowing for the variations of the thermometer, as chronicled in the inventor's journal. In 1765 the Board of Longitude approved a scheme of marine tables, designed by Mr. Witchell, for finding the longitude at sea by the lunar method ; and it awarded the inventor £1000 to enable him to carry out his plans. In consequence, with Mr. Isaac Lyons, junior, Mr. Wales, of Greenwich, and Mr. Mapson, Mr. Witchell became responsible, under the direction of the Astronomer Royal, Neville Maskelyne, for the compilation of a nautical ephemeris for the use of navigators and astronomers. This was the origin of the ' Nautical Almanac,' a publication which has since remained at the head of all works of the kind.

In the course of the war which ended in 1763 the number of seamen and Marines employed in the Navy was 184,893. Of these only 1512 were returned as having been killed in action or by accident : yet, at the conclusion of the war, no more than 49,673 remained on the books of the Navy Office.   The number, therefore, of those who had died by sickness or were missing reached the extraordinarily large total of 133,708.   These figures incline one to believe that there must have been an enormous amount of desertion.

Another return, issued in 1780, shows the number of men raised for H.M. Navy between September 29th, 1774, and September 29th, 1780, and the number killed in action, and who died or deserted, between January 1st, 1776, and September 29th, 1780.   This casts much light upon the discontent which in those days must have prevailed upon the lower deck of the Navy.   The number of men raised in the six years was 175,990.   Of these, in the four years covered by the second part of the return, only 1243 had been killed, and no more than 18,541 had perished from sickness or disease ; but as many as 42,069 had run.   The discontent thus indicated did not lead during the period, as it did later, to any general outbreak, but it produced several isolated disturbances.   For instance, at the peace in 1783, when the Channel fleet was ordered into port to be reduced and paid off, the men in many ships became riotous and even mutinous, owing to their intolerance of delay in liberating them. On that occasion the discontent in the *Raisonnable*, 64, was quashed by the captain, Lord Hervey, who, having appealed in vain to his crew to behave themselves, went forward armed, with his officers, and, having seized the ringleaders, soon compelled the rest to obey. When the ship arrived at Sheerness several men were tried by court-martial, and four of them were condemned to death.   Three of them were executed on August 11th, on board the *Carnatic*, *Scipio*, and *Dictator* respectively.   The fourth, who was to have suffered on board the *Thetis*, was reprieved immediately before the moment fixed for his execution.   The mutiny of the *Bounty* is described elsewhere.   There were also mutinous outbreaks in the *Narcissus*, 20, Captain Edward Edwards, in 1782, and, at different times, in other vessels.

During this period it was on several occasions found necessary to offer government bounties to seamen ; and, as often, special bounties were also offered to them by corporations and cities. In 1770, at the time of the Falkland Islands' scare, the King, by proclamation, offered a bounty of 30s. to every able seaman ; and the following cities offered additional bounties : *i.e.*, London, 40s. to every able seaman; Bristol, 20s. to every able seaman; Montrose and Edinburgh, each 2 guineas to every able, and 1 guinea to every ordinary seaman; Aberdeen, 1 guinea to every able, and 15s. to every ordinary seaman; and Lynn, 1 guinea to every able seaman. In 1773, again, the King offered to every able seaman £3, to every ordinary seaman £2, and to every landsman £1. In 1779 the East India Company, besides building at its own expense three 74-gun ships, the *Ganges*, *Carnatic*, and *Bombay Castle*, provided the necessary bounty for the raising of 6000 seamen. In 1791 bounties were offered on the same scale as in 1773.

The position of the seamen of the Navy was but little improved, and the failure of the authorities to care sufficiently for the lower deck led a little later to mutinies which, at one time, threatened to be extremely serious. The status of many of the officers was, however, from time to time considerably bettered. For example, in 1773, in consequence of a petition presented to Parliament by Lord Howe, Captains were granted an addition of 2s. a day to their half-pay, so that, thereafter, the first thirty Captains on the list received 10s., the next 8s., and the rest 6s. per day. In the same year the number of Surgeons entitled to half-pay was increased from fifty to a hundred, half to receive 2s. 6d. and half 2s. The number of Masters entitled to half-pay was increased to the same extent, the half-pay being the same as in the case of the Surgeons. In 1779 the twenty senior Masters, if qualified for first or second-rate ships, were given half-pay at the rate of 3s. 6d. a day, and the next seventy-five at the rate of 3s. a day. In 1781, the list of Surgeons entitled to half-pay was increased to one hundred and twenty-five, they being Surgeons of not less than five years' actual service. The first fifty on the list received 2s. 6d., and the next seventy-five 2s. a day.

But the attractions of the Navy in peace time were never great enough to induce anything like the whole body of officers to rest content with their position, which was indeed then a very unsatisfactory one. In 1771, Admiral Sir Charles Knowles solicited and obtained the King's permission to enter the Russian navy, in which he remained until 1774, when, upon his return to England, he was reinstated in his rank. During the next peace many officers of inferior position also lent their services to Russia; and in the battles of 1788–90, between the Russians and the Swedes, British captains, some of whom had been only lieutenants or masters in their own service, commanded ships on both sides. Indeed, Admiral Samuel

Grieg,[1] who was at one time commander-in-chief of the Russian fleet, was a Scot. Among the captains, Trevenen,[2] Denison, and Marshall, who were killed, and Elphinstone,[3] Miller, and Aiken, deserve to be remembered. Sir William Sidney Smith, then a captain, R.N., served as a volunteer with the Swedes. In wartime, adventures and the prospect of prize-money seem to have satisfied British naval officers as a body : and there was very little agitation in favour of increased pay, although the pay, all things considered, was miserably small. But in peace, many officers either found work for their swords in the service of foreign states, or accepted employment in command of merchant vessels.[4]

It may be mentioned in connection with the subject of prize-money that in 1781 an old dispute between Vice-Admiral John Campbell, who had been Keppel's Captain of the Fleet in 1778, and Sir Hugh Palliser, who had been Keppel's third in command, was decided. Campbell claimed a flag-officer's share of the prize-money arising from captures made by the fleet : Palliser resisted the claim ; and the matter was referred to arbitration. The arbitrator decided against Campbell, and, incidentally, against Kempenfelt, upon whose behalf there was a similar claim ; and this in spite of the fact that as early as 1672 an order of the Duke of York had directed that the First Captain to the Commander-in-Chief of the Fleet should rank as a flag-officer. But, although the decision was thus adverse, the King, on January 9th, 1782, by proclamation, ordered that for the future the First Captain to the Commander-in-Chief of the Fleet or to any flag-officer commanding twenty ships in the line of battle, whether British only, or British and their allies, should rank as a flag-officer, and should be entitled to share prize-money on the same scale as the junior flag-officer in the fleet. It was at the same time ordered that the Physician of the Fleet should share prize-money on the same scale as the lieutenants. A seaman's share of prize-money

---

[1] Samuel Grieg, born, 1736 ; served with the British fleet at Quiberon, 1759 ; joined the Russian navy, 1764. Mainly responsible for the victory off Tchesme, July, 1770. Commanded in the action off Gogland. Died, 1788. A Russian man-of-war still bears his name.

[2] Had been a midshipman and lieutenant in the *Resolution* in Cook's last voyage. Mortally wounded at Wyborg, 1789.

[3] Samuel Williams Elphinstone, second son of Captain John Elphinstone (1), R.N., who entered the Russian service in 1769, and became an admiral. He returned to active service in the British Navy in 1775, and died in 1785. Captain S. W. Elphinstone married a daughter of Admiral Cruse, a Scotsman in the Russian service.

[4] Among those who commanded merchant ships was Sir Home Riggs Popham.

was of course always very small ; but a slight concession to the lower deck was made in 1771, when an Act of Parliament authorised Greenwich Hospital, in certain specified cases, to refund unclaimed shares of prize-money or bounty-money within a limited time after payment of such into the funds of the hospital.

Indirectly, something more was done for the seamen by the action of the Marine Society, which, in 1763, immediately after the peace, resolved to receive, and make provision for, all boys under sixteen years of age, who had been, or might.be, discharged from the service, by putting them as apprentices into the mercantile marine, on their presenting certificates of good behaviour from their former officers, or by apprenticing them into some trade. Thus 295 boys were at once benefited. Again, in 1775 the Hibernian Marine Society in Dublin was incorporated under letters patent, for the maintenance, education, and apprenticing of orphans and children of decayed mariners ; and in 1787 a Marine School at Hull was opened by the Corporation of Trinity House, for the education and clothing of boys intended for the sea service.

A little more was done for the artificers in the Dockyards. In 1764 one man out of every fifty of those who had served with good character for thirty years, was made entitled to a pension of £20 per year. In 1771 this privilege was extended to one in forty, instead of one in fifty ; and the men, for pension purposes, were divided into three classes, *i.e.*, joiners, shipwrights,[1] blockmakers, plumbers, braziers, blacksmiths, and armourers, £20 a year ; house carpenters, sailmakers, smiths, and bricklayers, £15 ; pitch-heaters, bricklayers' labourers, riggers, and riggers' labourers, £10 a year. When the King was at Portsmouth in 1773 he, moreover, ordered £1500 to

[1] Number of shipwrights borne in H.M. Dockyards on January 14th of each year, 1763–1792 :—

Year.	No.	Year.	No.	Year.	No.
1763	2941	1773	3195	1783	3260
1764	2723	1774	3260	1784	3141
1765	3060	1775	3236	1785	3130
1766	3143	1776	3145	1786	3125
1767	3155	1777	3140	1787	3082
1768	3003	1778	3126	1788	3059
1769	2974	1779	3246	1789	3023
1770	2928	1780	3260	1790	2965
1771	5383	1781	3290	1791	3082
1772	3202	1782	3248	1792	3060

be distributed among the artificers, workmen, and labourers of the Dockyard, Victualling Office, and Gunwharf.

The King's visit on that occasion took place in order that His Majesty might review the fleet then lying at Spithead. On June 22nd, the King went on board the *Barfleur*, flagship of Vice-Admiral Thomas Pye, dined there, and, in the evening, knighted the Vice-Admiral, Rear-Admiral Richard Spry, Captain Joseph Knight, senior captain in the fleet, Captain Edward Vernon (2), of the *Barfleur*, and Captain Richard Bickerton, of the *Augusta*, yacht. He also conferred baronetcies on Captain Hugh Palliser, Controller of the Navy, and Captain Richard Hughes (2), Commissioner of the Dockyard. He directed the promotion of such commanders of sloops, first lieutenants of flagships, and lieutenants commanding cutters, as were present, as well as of the lieutenant of the *Augusta*, yacht, and of two midshipmen from each of certain ships. He further gave £350 to the crews of the *Barfleur*, of the *Augusta*, yacht, and of the royal barge.

This was not the only time when George III. visited his Navy in the earlier part of his reign. In 1781 he reviewed Vice-Admiral Sir Hyde Parker's fleet at the Nore, after its return from the battle of the Doggersbank, and went on board the *Fortitude*. In 1789, the King and Queen, with some of the princes, reviewed such ships as were in Portland Road; and, during their residence at Weymouth, they went for several short sea cruises in the *Southampton*, 32, Captain Andrew Snape Hamond, and the *Magnificent*, 74, Captain Richard Onslow. Later in the same summer they proceeded to Plymouth and visited the *Impregnable*, 90, Rear-Admiral Sir Richard Bickerton. Indeed, King George III. always took a great personal interest in the Navy, in which served two of his brothers [1] and one of his sons. [2]

The subject of promotion to the flag, which had for some time previously been a little unsystematic, attracted much attention in 1787. Early in the eighteenth century it had been the custom for the Crown to promote to the flag by selection, tempered by seniority. In the middle of the century, seniority gradually strengthened its claim; and soon after the conclusion of the American War, when a captain, upon reaching the top of the captains' list, instead of being given a flag was put upon the list

[1] Edward Augustus, Duke of York, and Henry Frederick, Duke of Cumberland.
[2] William Henry, Duke of Clarence, afterwards William IV.

of Superannuated Rear-Admirals, or was altogether passed over, he thought himself aggrieved. Things came to a crisis in 1787. On March 5th of that year, Sir Matthew White Ridley moved in the House of Commons an address to the King on behalf of Captain David Brodie,[1] who had been several times passed over. The motion, being strongly opposed by the Ministry, was defeated by a majority of seventeen in a house of one hundred and eighty-three. But the subject was not left there. On February 20th, 1788, Lord Rawdon took up the matter in the House of Lords.

It should be explained that by an Order in Council, dated in 1718 and addressed to the Lords Commissioners of the Admiralty, it was directed that their Lordships, in the advancement of officers to the rank of rear-admiral, should promote according to the seniority of the captains on the list, regard only being had to the officers being qualified for the rank to which they were otherwise eligible for promotion. By a subsequent order of 1747, the Lords of the Admiralty were authorised to superannuate such captains of long and meritorious service as, in their Lordships' opinion, should be disqualified by age or infirmity from serving as flag-officers, and that such officers should have the title of Superannuated Rear-Admirals. In the vulgar speech of the day these were usually called " Yellow Admirals." In a promotion made by the Board of Admiralty on September 24th, 1787, sixteen captains had been advanced to the flag, while upwards of forty had been passed over. The greater number of these last had been offered transfer to the superannuated list ; but, believing themselves fully competent to serve as active flag-officers ; and believing, also, that their past services fully entitled them to promotion on the active list, they refused the retirement that was offered them, and sought to be reinstated in the line of active promotion. The policy which had been pursued by the Admiralty occasioned great dissatisfaction amongst naval officers, who discovered with misgiving that their expectations of rank, as a reward for long and meritorious service, might be altogether dependent upon the caprice of a First Lord of the Admiralty. It was for this reason that Lord Rawdon brought the case before the House of Lords.

He moved " that a humble address be presented to His Majesty,

---

[1] A captain of March 9th, 1748, who, in the ordinary course, would have become a Rear-Admiral in 1778 or 1779; yet, though he had lost an arm in action, he was neither promoted nor superannuated. He appears to have died in 1788.

praying that he will be graciously pleased to take into his royal consideration the services of such captains of His Majesty's Navy as were passed over in the last promotion of admirals." Lord Howe, as First Lord, rose at once to oppose the motion, and to justify his own action. He pointed out that there were several reasons, which might reasonably excuse an official in his position for passing over a number of captains. Those who were likely to be entrusted with the care of our fleets ought to be men sound in mind and body, and capable of enduring the hard service which would lie before them in war time. It did not necessarily follow that an officer, who had served ably and meritoriously in a subordinate position, was fit to be entrusted with the care of a fleet. A sergeant of grenadiers, though an able and excellent soldier, might not be qualified to command a body of troops on a forlorn hope. The First Lord was responsible for the good conduct and well-being of the service ; and, having such responsibility, he was necessarily justified in exercising his judgment and discretion in the appointment of officers by whom the fleet was to be led. At the same time he could not, in any public assembly, state the particular reasons which had influenced his judgment in coming to a conclusion on each case. He could only say that he had acted with the strictest impartiality. Had the officers who had been passed over been advanced, as was suggested, and had they been called into active service, as would probably have been the case, they must have gone on being promoted from time to time, subject only to the contingency of death ; and they might thus have stood in the way of many officers from whose services the country would have derived the highest degree of advantage. Finally, he pointed out that the principles which had governed the late promotion were not without precedent.[1]

The Earl of Sandwich also opposed the motion. It had been found, he said, at different periods extremely inconvenient and detrimental to the service that promotions to the flag should be governed merely by seniority. In the year 1747 a promotion had been necessary ; and those then on the Board of Admiralty had been aware that there were then on the list of captains several officers who were in an eminent degree qualified for the command of fleets ; but they had not, at first, known how to get at them without loading the public with unjustifiable expense. They had

---

[1] Instancing a promotion made in 1770, when Lord Hawke had been First Lord.

therefore planned the superannuation list, the object of which was
to provide an income for such captains as the Board of Admiralty,
not meaning to call them out for further service, omitted to appoint
to the flag in the rota of seniority.   At the time of instituting the
establishment the object was to make eight flag-officers only ; and, in
order to do that, nineteen captains were passed over.   Yet the
matter had not been taken notice of in the House of Commons,
nor had there been any complaint of injustice or partiality.   Those
captains who had been put upon the superannuation list were not
in any wise disgraced nor even stigmatised ; they merely entered
what was an honourable retirement from service.

Lord Rawdon's motion was negatived without a division.   But
on April 12th the subject was again brought forward in the House
of Commons by Mr. Bastard, who particularly devoted himself to
the cases of Captains Balfour [1] and Thompson,[2] who, although
they had received the thanks of the House for their behaviour
on April 12th, 1782, had, when they reached the top of the
captains' list, been passed over.   Naval opinion in the House was
divided, Captain Sir George Collier and Captain John Macbride
contending that such a principle as had been followed by Lord
Howe in 1787 must inevitably lead to the ruin of the service, and
Captain Lord Mulgrave and Vice-Admiral Lord Hood being of
opinion that any interference on the part of the House might
eventually prove more detrimental than advantageous to the Navy.
At the same time it seemed to be admitted on all sides that several
officers who had been passed over did not appear to be in any
respect disqualified for the rank to which, in the ordinary course
of advancement, they were entitled.   Finding, however, that the
wording of his motion did not meet with favour, Mr. Bastard
withdrew it, promising to bring forward the subject later in some
other shape.

Accordingly, on April 18th he moved " that the House resolve
itself into a committee of the whole House to inquire into the
conduct of the Board of Admiralty touching the late promotion
to the flag."   In support of his motion Mr. Bastard cited the
cases not only of Captains Balfour and Thompson, but also those

---

[1] George Balfour, Captain, July 26th, 1758 ; superannd. Rear-Admiral, 1787 ; died,
June 28th, 1794.
[2] Samuel Thompson, Captain, November 4th, 1760 ; superannd. Rear-Admiral,
1788 ; died, August 13th, 1813.

of Captains Samuel Uvedale, Thomas Shirley, John Bray, and John Laforey, most of whom had served with distinction in war; and he pointed out that, although it might be alleged that Captain Bray had not been promoted because, during the last war, he had been employed on shore in the impress service, and that Captain Laforey [1] had been set aside because he had previously accepted the post of Commissioner of the Navy at Antigua, and, later, at Plymouth, Sir Charles Middleton, even while actually serving in a civil capacity, [2] had been promoted, apparently, as a matter of course. Both Pitt and Fox took part in the debate. The latter, who supported the motion, urged that the rank of flag-officer ought to be considered from two points of view. The principal view was undoubtedly prospective, and looked to future service; and, from that point of view, selection was proper and justifiable. But the rank might also be looked upon as an honour and reward for past services; and, from that point of view, the promotion of 1787 could not be defended for a moment, and was most scandalously partial and unjust. And, he said, as proof that the Admiralty, at least in some cases, considered promotion as a reward for past services, he might cite the advancement of Sir John Lindsay, who, though an officer of first-rate reputation, was well known to be in so bad a state of health that there was no hope of his ever being able to resume an active career. [3] Upon the question being put, the House divided, and the motion was lost by sixteen votes in a House of two hundred and eighty-four.

The smallness of the majority encouraged Mr. Bastard to make a third attempt; and on April 29th he moved "that it is highly injurious to the service, and unjust, to set aside from promotion to the flag meritorious officers of approved services, who are not precluded by the orders of His Majesty in Council." On that occasion the motion was defeated by a majority of fifty-one in a House of three hundred and eighty-nine.

The institution of a naval uniform for certain officers has been noticed in a previous chapter. As early as 1767, within twenty

---

[1] Laforey was eventually promoted, his commission as a flag-officer being ante-dated so as not to deprive him of any seniority.

[2] *i.e.*, as Controller. Sir Charles was afterwards created Lord Barham.

[3] In point of fact, he died on June 4th, 1788, having been promoted only on September 24th, 1787.

years of that institution, alterations were made by an Admiralty order of July 18th of that year, worded as follows :—

It is His Majesty's pleasure that the embroidered uniform clothing of flag officers, and the full dress uniform of Captains, Commanders, and Lieutenants of His Majesty's fleet, be discontinued, and that the frock uniform clothing of the said officers be likewise altered and worn as follows: The Admiral's frock to have narrow lappels down to the waist; small boot cuffs ; a single lace instead of treble lace down to the skirts—a plain musquetaire lace; but in all other respects the same as now worn.   The Captains' and Commanders' frocks to have narrow lappels down to the waist, and in all other respects as they are now worn.   The Lieutenants' frocks to have narrow lappels down to the waist, flash cuffs like the commanders', without lace, instead of roll cuffs, and in all other respects as now worn.

Another modification was made in January, 1768, when the King signified his pleasure that the lappels and cuffs of the military uniform frocks appointed to be worn by the Lieutenants should be thenceforth of white, instead of blue cloth, and the waistcoat, etc., of plain white cloth, with gilt buttons of the pattern previously worn, without any lace.   In 1774 another alteration was made in the uniform of Captains and Commanders ; and it was directed that the uniforms so altered should be considered as full dress, and that a blue frock with embroidered button-holes, conformable to a pattern lodged at the Navy Office, might be worn upon common occasions.   The altered uniform was thus described :—

The lace on the coat to return round the pockets and sleeves; the lappels and cuffs to be two inches and a half broad ; the lace upon the upper part of the lappels to run even with the bottom lace of the collar; the buttons to be flat, with an anchor and cable engraved thereon, according to the pattern lodged at the Navy Office ; the waistcoat to be plain instead of laced ; the breeches to be of the same colour as the waistcoat, instead of blue, and both to have buttons of the same pattern as those on the coat.   The undress uniform was to have blue frock lappels, and collar and cuffs of the same ; but the collar was to button on to the lappels and lap over behind ; the lining to be of white shalloon ; the buttons to be the same as on the dress coat, and the buttonholes to be gold embroidered according to the following scheme : for Captains who had taken post three years or upwards, twelve holes in the lappels, by threes, three on the flaps, and three on the sleeves ; for Post Captains of less than three years' standing, twelve holes in the lappels, by twos, four holes on the flaps, and three on the sleeves ; and for Commanders, twelve holes in the lappels disposed regularly, with three holes on the flaps and three on the sleeves ; and waistcoat and breeches to be the same as for the dress uniform.

In 1783 there was another alteration, the uniforms then being—

For Admirals, blue cloth coat, with white cuffs, white waistcoat and breeches.   The coat and waistcoat to be embroidered with gold, in pattern and description the same as that worn by generals in the army, with three rows of embroidery on the cuffs.   For Vice-Admirals the same, but with embroidery the same as worn by lieutenant-generals in the army, and with two rows of embroidery on the cuffs.   For Rear-Admirals the same, but with embroidery similar to that worn by major-generals in the army, and with one row of embroidery on the cuffs. The buttons were to remain as before.

The above were the full dress uniforms. The undress uniforms were—

For Admirals, a blue cloth frock with blue cuffs and blue lappels; embroidered buttonholes, like those previously in use, from the top to the bottom of the lappels, and three holes on the cuffs; for Vice-Admirals, the same, with buttonholes arranged three and three; for Rear-Admirals, the same, with buttonholes arranged two and two. All to wear plain white waistcoat and breeches.

On November 17th, 1787, more extensive changes were made, in accordance with the following instructions:—

Admirals' frocks; blue cloth, with blue lappels and cuffs; gold-lace holes, three, pointing at the end, with the same distinction in the disposition for the different ranks as before; stand-up collar, with one hole on each side; three holes in the flaps, three on the outside cuffs, and three behind; white lining, and new anchor buttons with laurel.

Post Captains of three years' standing; full dress: blue cloth coat with white lappels and cuffs, laced with gold lace; the pockets double laced; round cuffs with two laces; three buttons to the pockets and cuffs; blue stand-up collar, double laced; white lining; new buttons with anchor in an oval; white cloth waistcoat, and breeches plain. Frocks: blue cloth coat with blue lappels and round cuffs; fall-down collar; gold laced holes square at both ends, regular in the lappels; two to the pockets and two to the cuffs; none behind; white lining; buttons the same as in full dress; white cloth waistcoat, and breeches plain.

Post Captains of under three years' standing; full dress: blue coat with white lappels and cuffs, laced with gold lace; pockets with one lace; round cuffs with one lace; three buttons to the pockets and cuffs; blue stand-up collar double laced; white lining; buttons as before-mentioned; white cloth waistcoat, and breeches plain. Frocks: blue cloth coat; blue lappels; blue round cuffs; fall-down collar; gold laced holes square at both ends; nine holes in the lappel by threes, two to the pockets, and two to the cuffs; none behind; white lining; buttons the same as in full dress; white cloth waistcoat, and breeches plain.

Masters and Commanders; full dress: blue cloth coat with blue lappels and round cuffs, laced with gold lace; the pockets once laced, with one lace on the cuffs; three buttons to each; stand-up collar, double laced; white lining; buttons as before; white cloth waistcoat, and breeches plain. Frocks: blue coat, with blue lappels; round cuffs, and fall-down collar; gold laced holes, square at each end; ten holes in the lappels by two and two; two to the pockets, and two to the cuffs; none behind; white lining; buttons as before; white cloth waistcoat, and breeches plain.

Lieutenants; full dress: blue cloth coat, with white lappels; blue round cuffs; holes regular in the lappels; three buttons to the pockets, and three to the cuffs; stand-up collar; white lining; buttons as for the Captains; white cloth waistcoat, and breeches plain. Undress: blue cloth coat, edged with white cloth; blue lappels, and blue round cuffs; three buttons to the pockets and cuffs; stand-up collar; buttons as above; white cloth waistcoat, and breeches plain.

Warrant officers: blue cloth coat, with blue lappels and round cuffs; fall-down collar; three buttons to the pockets and cuffs; white lining, but not edged with white; buttons with an anchor, like the buttons previously worn by Captains; white cloth waistcoat and breeches.

Masters' Mates: blue cloth coat, edged with white; no lappels; blue round cuffs, with three buttons; three to the pockets; fall-down collar; white lining; buttons as for the warrant officers; white cloth waistcoat and breeches.

Midshipmen: blue cloth coat; no lappels; blue round cuffs, with three buttons, and three to the pockets; stand-up collar, with small white turn back as before; white lining, but not edged; buttons as for the warrant officers; white cloth waistcoat and breeches.

The expedition of Commodore Johnstone in 1781 led up to some interesting problems in naval law. Johnstone caused Captain Evelyn Sutton, of the *Isis*, to be tried by court-martial on a charge of misconduct during the action in Porto Praya Bay. Sutton, being honourably acquitted, brought a civil action for damages against Johnstone in the Court of Exchequer, and obtained a verdict for £5000. A new trial was demanded and Sutton thereupon secured a verdict for £6000. Johnstone procured a reversal of the judgment on a writ of error; and Sutton ultimately took the case to the House of Lords, which, in May, 1787, affirmed the reversal of the judgment, Lord Howe declaring that to establish the verdict would be to subvert the good order and discipline of the Navy. Sutton in consequence lost his case.

Another problem, arising out of the captures made by Johnstone in Saldanha Bay, was determined in June, 1786, when, on an appeal from the Court of Admiralty to the Lords of the Council, it was decided that, since the destination of Johnstone's force had been the Cape of Good Hope, and, seeing that a considerable land force, under General Meadows, had been on board and had shared in the action, the capture did not come under the provisions of the Prize Act. The whole of the property was claimed by, and would go to, the Crown; and the captors must relinquish all hope of prize-money in respect of it, and look merely to the royal bounty for any compensation which they might eventually obtain.

Yet another interesting and rather celebrated point in naval law was threshed out in 1788. In May of that year Captain Isaac Coffin, of the *Thisbe*, had been tried by court-martial at Halifax, N.S., on a charge of making false musters, in that he had kept on his ship's books one of his own nephews and two sons of Lord Dorchester, who had, it appeared, not been actually on board, conformably with the rules of the Navy. The charge had been proved; but as it had seemed to the court that it had been brought forward mainly in consequence of private pique and resentment, and that the accused officer had not intended to defraud His Majesty, Coffin had been sentenced only to be dismissed from the command of the *Thisbe*. When the officer arrived in England, Earl Howe, who was then First Lord of the Admiralty, so strongly disapproved of the sentence, which he believed to be not in accordance with the spirit of the 31st Article of War, that he induced the Board to strike Coffin's name off the list of post captains. The Article in question declared, " Every officer, or other person in the fleet, who shall knowingly make or sign a false muster, or muster-book, etc., upon proof of any such offence being made before a court-martial, shall be cashiered and rendered incapable of further employment in his Majesty's naval service." Coffin laid his case before the King, who, with the assent of the Privy Council, directed the twelve judges to give their opinion as to whether the Admiralty had the power to set aside the judgment of the court-martial. The judges decided that the Admiralty's sentence was not legal, and that the punishment directed to be inflicted by the Act of 22 George II., cap. 33, upon persons convicted of the offence set forth in the 31st Article of War established by the said Act, could not be inflicted, nor judgment thereon be pronounced or supplied, by any other authority than that of the court-martial which tried the offender. Coffin was thereupon reinstated in his rank, and after having served as Commissioner in Corsica, at Sheerness, etc., died an Admiral and a Baronet in 1839, in his eighty-first year.

Questions concerning the right of search and the honour of the flag cropped up as in previous periods. In 1780, a squadron which, under Captain Charles Feilding (1), had been despatched for the purpose, intercepted, west of the Isle of Wight, a Dutch convoy escorted by two sail of the line and two frigates, under Rear-Admiral Count Lodewijk van Bylandt. Feilding demanded to examine the merchantmen, which were suspected of having on board naval stores for France. Van Bylandt resisted, and fired at some boats which had been sent to board the convoy. Feilding thereupon fired a shot ahead of the Dutch rear-admiral, who replied by discharging a broadside at the *Namur*, and, when it was returned, struck. Seven of the merchantmen were detained.

In 1791, Commodore the Hon. William Cornwallis, having received intelligence that some neutral ships under French colours were expected on the Malabar coast, with supplies for Tippoo Sultan, found two of them in Mahé Road. They refused to be examined, pleading in particular that they were then in their own port ; but

Commander Edward James Foote, of the *Atalanta*, 14, sent a party, which broke open the hatchways.   The examination, however, seems to have been considered by the Commodore to be inconclusive ; and, a little later, when the two French vessels sailed in company with the French frigate *Résolu*, 32, they were followed by the *Phœnix*, 36, and *Perseverance*, 36.   The former got up with the French frigate off Mangalore, and was hailed to know what she wanted.   Captain Sir Richard John Strachan replied that he had orders to board the merchantmen.   While his boats were occupied on that service they were fired at by the *Résolu*, which presently also discharged a broadside at the *Phœnix*.   An action resulted ; and in twenty-five minutes the Frenchman struck, having lost 25 killed and 40 wounded.   The *Phœnix* lost only 6 killed and 11 wounded.   A renewed examination of the merchantmen showed that they had no contraband of war on board ; and they were suffered to proceed on their voyage.

A noteworthy case of the insistance of the right of the flag happened in 1769, when a French frigate anchored in the Downs and neglected to pay the usual compliment.   Captain John Hollwell sent a lieutenant to demand the salute.   The French captain refused compliance, whereupon Hollwell ordered the *Hawke*, 10, to fire two shots over her.   This induced her to concede the point without further dispute.

Though the British Navy was thus jealous of its privileges, the relations between it and other countries upon the high seas were in some respects courteous and pleasant.   In 1779, the French court chivalrously issued orders that the British circumnavigators, James Cook and Charles Clark, were on no account to be molested, although a state of war existed at the time.   In 1785, when La Pérouse[1] set out from Brest on his great voyage of discovery, the Admiralty and Royal Society furnished him with copies of all such observations and charts as could be of use to him, and gave him also Cook's timekeeper and azimuth compass.

---

[1] Jean François de Galaup, Comte de La Pérouse.   Born, 1741.   Attacked British settlements in Hudson's Bay, 1782.   Perished off Vanicoro Island, 1788.   His fate was not ascertained until 1827, by Dumont d'Urville.

CHAPTER XXXI.

MAJOR OPERATIONS OF THE ROYAL NAVY, 1762–1783.*

Decisive Influence of Control of the Water in the American Revolution—The Lake Campaign of 1776—Attack upon Charleston, S. C.—Combined Military and Naval Operations about New York and Philadelphia, 1776–1778—Howe and d'Estaing, 1778—Battle of Ushant, July, 1778—Barrington at St. Lucia, December, 1778 —Byron off Grenada, July, 1779—Franco-Spanish Fleet in the Channel, 1779— Rodney and Langara, January, 1780—Rodney at Gibraltar, and in the West Indies, 1780—Combined Naval and Military Operations in Southern States, 1779–1781—Arbuthnot and des Touches off the Chesapeake, March, 1781—Hood and de Grasse off Martinique, April, 1781—Graves and de Grasse off the Chesapeake, September, 1781, and Capitulation of Yorktown—Relief of Gibraltar, and Allied Fleet in the Channel, 1781—Hyde Parker's Action with the Dutch Fleet, August, 1781—Kempenfelt and de Guichen, December, 1781—Hood and de Grasse at St. Kitts, January, 1782—Rodney's Victory over de Grasse, April, 1782—Howe's Relief of Gibraltar, October, 1782—Military and Naval Operations in India, 1778–1783—Suffren's Campaign in India, and Actions with Johnstone and Hughes, 1781–1783.

COMMEMORATIVE MEDAL OF KEPPEL'S ACTION OFF USHANT, 1778.

(From an original lent by Capt. H. S. H. Prince Louis of Battenberg, R. N.)

AT the time when hostilities began between Great Britain and her American Colonies, the fact was realised generally, being evident to reason and taught by experience, that control of the water, both ocean and inland, would have a preponderant effect upon the contest. It was clear to reason, for there was a long seaboard with numerous interior navigable watercourses, and at the same time scanty and indifferent communications by land. Critical portions of the territory involved were yet an unimproved wilderness. Experience, the rude but efficient schoolmaster of that large portion of mankind which gains knowledge only by hard knocks, had confirmed through the preceding French wars the inferences of the thoughtful. Therefore, conscious of the great superiority of the

British Navy, which, however, had not then attained the unchallenged supremacy of a later day, the American leaders early sought the alliance of the Bourbon kingdoms, the hereditary enemies of Great Britain.   There alone could be found the counterpoise to a power which, if unchecked, must ultimately prevail.

Nearly three years elapsed before the Colonists accomplished this object, by giving a demonstration of their strength in the enforced surrender of Burgoyne's army at Saratoga.   This event has merited the epithet " decisive," because, and only because, it decided the intervention of France.   It may be affirmed, with little hesitation, that it was at once the result of naval force, and the cause that naval force, entering further into the contest, transformed it from a local to a universal war, and assured the independence of the Colonies. That the Americans were strong enough to impose the capitulation of Saratoga, was due to the invaluable year of delay, secured to them by their little navy on Lake Champlain, created by the indomitable energy, and handled with the indomitable courage, of the traitor, Benedict Arnold.   That the war spread from America to Europe, from the English Channel to the Baltic, from the Bay of Biscay to the Mediterranean, from the West Indies to the Mississippi, and ultimately involved the waters of the remote peninsula of Hindostan, is traceable, through Saratoga, to the rude flotilla which in 1776 anticipated its enemy in the possession of Lake Champlain. The events which thus culminated merit therefore a clearer understanding, and a fuller treatment, than their intrinsic importance and petty scale would justify otherwise.

In 1775, only fifteen years had elapsed since the expulsion of the French from the North American continent.   The concentration of their power, during its continuance, in the valley of the St. Lawrence, had given direction to the local conflict, and had impressed upon men's minds the importance of Lake Champlain, of its tributary Lake George, and of the Hudson River, as forming a consecutive, though not continuous, water line of communications from the St. Lawrence to New York.   The strength of Canada against attack by land lay in its remoteness, in the wilderness to be traversed before it was reached, and in the strength of the line of the St. Lawrence, with the fortified posts of Montreal and Quebec on its northern bank.   The wilderness, it is true, interposed its passive resistance to attacks from Canada, as well as to attacks upon it ; but when it had been traversed, there were to the southward no such strong natural

positions confronting the assail-
ant.   Attacks from the south
fell upon the front, or at best
upon the flank, of the line of
the St. Lawrence. Attacks from
Canada took New York and its
dependencies in the rear.

These elements of natural
strength, in the military conditions of the North, were impressed upon the minds of the
Americans by the prolonged resistance of Canada to the greatly
superior numbers of the British
Colonists in the previous wars.
Regarded, therefore, as a base
for attacks, of a kind with which
they were painfully familiar, but
to be undergone now under
disadvantages of numbers and
power never before experienced,
it was desirable to gain possession of the St. Lawrence and its
posts before they were strengthened and garrisoned.   At this
outset of hostilities, the American insurgents, knowing clearly
their own minds, possessed the
advantage of the initiative over
the British government, which
still hesitated to use against
those whom it styled rebels the
preventive measures it would
have taken at once against a
recognised enemy.

Under these circumstances,
in May, 1775, a body of two hundred and seventy Americans, led
by Ethan Allen and Benedict
Arnold, seized the posts of Ti-

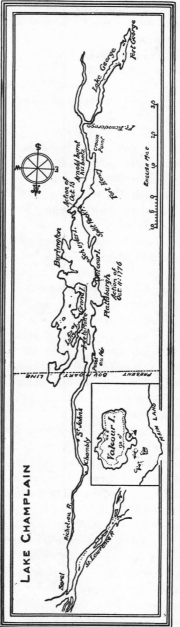

LAKE CHAMPLAIN.

conderoga and Crown Point, which were inadequately garrisoned. These are on the upper waters of Lake Champlain, where it is less than a third of a mile wide; Ticonderoga being on a peninsula formed by the lake and the inlet from Lake George, Crown Point on a promontory twelve miles lower down. They were recognised positions of importance, and advanced posts of the British in previous wars. A schooner being found there, Arnold, who had been a seaman, embarked in her and hurried to the foot of the lake. The wind failed him when still thirty miles from St. John's, another fortified post on the lower narrows, where the lake gradually tapers down to the Richelieu River, its outlet to the St. Lawrence. Unable to advance otherwise, Arnold took to his boats with thirty men, pulled throughout the night, and at six o'clock on the following morning surprised the post, in which were only a sergeant and a dozen men. He reaped the rewards of celerity. The prisoners informed him that a considerable body of troops was expected from Canada, on its way to Ticonderoga; and this force in fact reached St. John's on the next day. When it arrived, Arnold was gone, having carried off a sloop which he found there and destroyed everything else that could float. By such trifling means two active officers had secured the temporary control of the lake and of its southern approaches. There being no roads, the British, debarred from the water line, were unable to advance. Sir Guy Carleton, Governor and Commander-in-Chief in Canada, strengthened the works at St. John's, and built a schooner; but his force was inadequate to meet that of the Americans.

The seizure of the two posts, being an act of offensive war, was not at once pleasing to the American Congress, which still clung to the hope of reconciliation; but events were marching rapidly, and ere summer was over the invasion of Canada was ordered. On September 4th, General Montgomery, appointed to that enterprise, embarked at Crown Point with two thousand men, and soon afterwards appeared before St. John's, which, after prolonged operations, capitulated on the 3rd of November. On the 13th Montgomery entered Montreal, and thence pressed down the St. Lawrence to Pointe aux Trembles, twenty miles above Quebec. There he joined Arnold, who in the month of October had crossed the northern wilderness, between the head waters of the Kennebec River and the St. Lawrence. On the way he had endured immense privations, losing five hundred men of the twelve hundred with whom he started; and upon arriving opposite Quebec, on the 10th of November, three days had been unavoidably spent in collecting boats to pass the river. Crossing on the night of the 13th, this adventurous soldier and his little command climbed the Heights of Abraham by the same path that had served Wolfe so well sixteen years before. With characteristic audacity he summoned the place. The demand of course was refused; but that Carleton did not fall at once upon the little band of seven hundred that bearded him shows by how feeble a tenure Great Britain then held Canada. Immediately after the junction Montgomery advanced on Quebec, where he appeared on the 5th of December. Winter having already begun, and neither his numbers nor his equipments being adequate to regular siege operations, he very properly decided to try the desperate chance of an assault upon the strongest fortress in America. This was made on the night of December 31st, 1775. Whatever possibility of success there may have been, vanished with the death of Montgomery, who fell at the head of his men.

The American army retired three miles up the river, went into winter-quarters, and established a land blockade of Quebec, which was cut off from the sea by the ice. "For five months," wrote Carleton to the Secretary for War, on the 14th of May, 1776, "this town has been closely invested by the rebels." From this unpleasant position it was relieved on the 6th of May, when signals were exchanged between it and the *Surprise*, the advance ship of a squadron under Captain Charles Douglas,[1] which had sailed from England on the 11th of March. Arriving off the mouth of the St. Lawrence, on the morning of April 12th, Douglas found ice extending nearly twenty miles to sea, and packed too closely to admit of working through it by dexterous steering. The urgency of the case not admitting delay, he ran his ship, the *Isis*, 50, with a speed of five knots, against a large piece of ice about ten or twelve feet thick, to test the effect. The ice, probably softened by salt water and salt air, went to pieces. "Encouraged by this experiment," continues Douglas, somewhat magnificently, "we thought it an enterprise worthy an English ship of the line in our King and country's sacred cause, and an effort due to the gallant defenders of Quebec, to make the attempt of pressing her by force of sail, through the thick, broad, and closely connected fields of ice, to which we saw no bounds towards the western part of our horizon. Before night (when blowing a snow-storm,

[1] Father of the late Sir Howard Douglas. He died a Rear-Admiral and Baronet in 1789.

we brought-to, or rather stopped), we had penetrated about eight leagues into it, describing our path all the way with bits of the sheathing of the ship's bottom, and sometimes pieces of the cutwater, but none of the oak plank; and it was pleasant enough at times, when we stuck fast, to see Lord Petersham exercising his troops on the crusted surface of that fluid through which the ship had so recently sailed." It took nine days of this work to reach Anticosti Island, after which the ice seems to have given no more trouble; but further delay was occasioned by fogs, calms, and head winds.

Upon the arrival of the ships of war the Americans at once retreated. During the winter, though reinforcements must have been received from time to time, they had wasted from exposure, and from small-pox, which ravaged the camp. On the 1st of May the returns showed nineteen hundred men present, of whom only a thousand were fit for duty. There were then on hand but three days' provisions, and none other nearer than St. John's. The inhabitants would of course render no further assistance to the Americans after the ships arrived. The Navy had again decided the fate of Canada, and was soon also to determine that of Lake Champlain.

When two hundred troops had landed from the ships, Carleton marched out, "to see," he said, "what these mighty boasters were about." The sneer was unworthy a man of his generous character, for the boasters had endured much for faint chances of success; and the smallness of the reinforcement which encouraged him to act shows either an extreme prudence on his part, or the narrow margin by which Quebec escaped. He found the enemy busy with preparations for retreat, and upon his appearance they abandoned their camp. Their forces on the two sides of the river being now separated by the enemy's shipping, the Americans retired first to Sorel, where the Richelieu enters the St. Lawrence, and thence continued to fall back by gradual stages. It was not until June 15th that Arnold quitted Montreal; and at the end of June the united force was still on the Canadian side of the present border line. On the 3rd of July it reached Crown Point, in a pitiable state from small-pox and destitution.

Both parties began at once to prepare for a contest upon Lake Champlain. The Americans, small as their flotilla was, still kept the superiority obtained for them by Arnold's promptitude a year before. On the 25th of June the American General Schuyler, commanding the Northern Department, wrote: " We have happily such a naval superiority on Lake Champlain, that I have a confident hope the enemy will not appear upon it this campaign, especially as our force is increasing by the addition of gondolas, two nearly finished. Arnold, however," — whose technical knowledge caused him to be intrusted with the naval preparations, — " says that 300 carpenters should be employed and a large number of gondolas, row-galleys, etc., be built, twenty or thirty at least. There is great difficulty in getting the carpenters needed." Arnold's ideas were indeed on a scale worthy of the momentous issues at stake. " To augment our navy on the lake appears to me of the utmost importance. There is water between Crown Point and Pointe au Fer for vessels of the largest size. I am of opinion that row-galleys are the best construction and cheapest for this lake. Perhaps it may be well to have one frigate of 36 guns. She may carry 18-pounders on the Lake, and be superior to any vessel that can be built or floated from St. John's."

Unfortunately for the Americans, their resources in men and means were far inferior to those of their opponents, who were able eventually to carry out, though on a somewhat smaller scale, Arnold's idea of a sailing ship, strictly so called, of force as yet unknown in inland waters. Such a ship, aided as she was by two consorts of somewhat similar character, dominated the Lake as soon as she was afloat, reversing all the conditions. To place and equip her, however, required time, invaluable time, during which Arnold's two schooners exercised control. " If we could have begun our expedition four weeks earlier," wrote Baron Riedesel, the commander of the German contingent with Carleton, after examining the American position at Ticonderoga, " I am satisfied that everything would have been ended this year (1776); but, not having shelter nor other necessary things, we were unable to remain at the other [southern] end of Champlain." So delay favours the defence, and changes issues. What would have been the effect upon the American cause if, simultaneously with the loss of New York, August 20th–September 15th, had come the news that Ticonderoga, whose repute for strength stood high, had also fallen? Nor was this all; for in that event, the plan which was wrecked in 1777 by Sir William Howe's ill-conceived expedition to the Chesapeake, would doubtless have been carried out in 1776. In a contemporary English paper occurs the following significant item: " London, September 26th, 1776. Advices have been received here from Canada, dated August 12th, that General Burgoyne's army has found it impracticable to get across the lakes this season. The naval force of the Provincials is too great for them to contend with at present. They must build larger vessels for this purpose, and these cannot be ready before next summer. The design *was* [1] that the two armies commanded by Generals Howe and Burgoyne should co-operate ; that they should both be on the Hudson River at the same time ; that they should join about Albany, and thereby cut off all communication between the northern and southern Colonies." [2]

As Arnold's more ambitious scheme could not be realised, he had to content himself with gondolas and galleys, for the force he was to command as well as to build. The precise difference between the two kinds of rowing vessels thus distinguished by name, the writer has not been able to ascertain. The gondola was a flat-bottomed boat, and inferior in nautical qualities — speed, handiness, and seaworthi-ness — to the galleys, which probably were keeled. The latter cer-tainly carried sails, and may have been capable of beating to windward. Arnold preferred them, and stopped the building of gondolas. " The galleys," he wrote, " are quick moving, which will give us a great advantage in the open lake."   The complements of the galleys were eighty men, of the gondolas forty-five; from which, and from their batteries, it may be inferred that the latter were between one third and one half the size of the former. The armaments of the two were alike in character, but those of the gondolas much lighter. American accounts agree with Captain Douglas's report of one galley captured by the British. In the bows, an 18 and a 12-pounder ; in the stern, 2 nines ; in broadside, from 4 to 6 sixes. There is in this a some-what droll reminder of the disputed merits of bow, stern, and broadside fire, in a modern iron-clad; and the practical conclusion is much the same. The gondolas had one 12-pounder and 2 sixes. All the vessels of both parties carried a number of swivel guns.

Amid the many difficulties which lack of resources imposed upon all American undertakings, Arnold succeeded in getting afloat with three schooners, a sloop, and five gondolas, on the 20th of August. He cruised at the upper end of Champlain till the 1st of September, when he moved rapidly north, and on the 3rd anchored in the lower narrows, twenty-five miles above St. John's, stretching his line from shore to shore. Scouts had kept him informed of the progress of the British naval preparations, so that he knew that there was no immediate danger; while an advanced position, maintained with a bold front, would certainly prevent reconnoissances by water, and

---

[1] Author's italics.   [2] *Remembrancer*, iv. 291.

possibly might impose somewhat upon the enemy. The latter, however, erected batteries on each side of the anchorage, compelling
Arnold to fall back to the broader Lake. He then had soundings
taken about Valcour Island, and between it and the western shore;
that being the position in which he intended to make a stand. He
retired thither on the 23rd of September.

The British on their side had contended with no less obstacles
than their adversaries, though of a somewhat different character.
To get carpenters and materials to build, and seamen to man, were
the chief difficulties of the Americans, the necessities of the seaboard conceding but partially the demands made upon it; but their
vessels were built upon the shores of the Lake, and launched into
navigable waters. A large fleet of transports and ships of war in
the St. Lawrence supplied the British with adequate resources, which
were utilised judiciously and energetically by Captain Douglas; but
to get these to the Lake was a long and arduous task. A great
part of the Richelieu River was shoal, and obstructed by rapids.
The point where Lake navigation began was at St. John's, to which
the nearest approach, by a hundred-ton schooner, from the St. Lawrence, was Chambly, ten miles below. Flat-boats and long-boats
could be dragged up stream, but vessels of any size had to be transported by land; and the engineers found the roadbed too soft in
places to bear the weight of a hundred tons. Under Douglas's directions, the planking and frames of two schooners were taken down
at Chambly, and carried round by road to St. John's, where they
were again put together. At Quebec he found building a new hull,
of one hundred and eighty tons. This he took apart nearly to the
keel, shipping the frames in thirty long-boats, which the transport
captains consented to surrender, together with their carpenters, for
service on the Lake. Drafts from the ships of war, and volunteers
from the transports, furnished a body of seven hundred seamen for
the same employment, — a force to which the Americans could oppose nothing equal, commanded as it was by regular naval officers.
The largest vessel was ship-rigged, and had a battery of eighteen
12-pounders; she was called the *Inflexible*, and was commanded by
Lieutenant John Schanck. The two schooners, *Maria*, Lieutenant
Starke, and *Carleton*, Lieutenant James Richard Dacres, carried respectively fourteen and twelve 6-pounders. These were the backbone
of the British flotilla. There were also a radeau, the *Thunderer*, and
a large gondola, the *Loyal Convert*, both heavily armed; but, being

equally heavy of movement, they do not appear to have played any important part.   Besides these, when the expedition started, there were twenty gunboats, each carrying one fieldpiece, from twenty-fours to 9-pounders; or, in some cases, howitzers.[1]

" By all these means," wrote Douglas on July 21st, "our acquiring an absolute dominion over Lake Champlain is not doubted of." The expectation was perfectly sound.   With a working breeze, the *Inflexible* alone could sweep the Lake clear of all that floated on it. But the element of time remained.   From the day of this writing till that on which he saw the *Inflexible* leave St. John's, October 4th, was over ten weeks; and it was not until the 9th that Carleton was ready to advance with the squadron.   By that time the American troops at the head of the Lake had increased to eight or ten thousand.   The British land force is reported [2] as thirteen thousand, of which six thousand were in garrison at St. John's and elsewhere.

Arnold's last reinforcements reached him at Valcour on the 6th of October.   On that day, and in the action of the 11th, he had with him all the American vessels on the Lake, except one schooner and one galley.   His force, thus, was two schooners and a sloop, broadside vessels, besides four galleys and eight gondolas, which may be assumed reasonably to have depended on their bow guns; there, at least, was their heaviest fire.   Thus reckoned, his flotilla, disposed to the best advantage, could bring into action at one time, 2 eighteens, 13 twelves, 1 nine, 2 sixes, 12 fours, and 2 2-pounders, independent of swivels; total, 32 guns, out of eighty-four that were mounted in fifteen vessels.   To this the British had to oppose, in three broadside vessels, 9 twelves and 13 sixes, and in twenty gunboats, 20 other brass guns, "from twenty-fours to nines, some with howitzers;" [3] total, 42 guns.   In this statement the radeau and gondola have not been included, because of their unmanageableness.   Included as broadside vessels, they would raise the British armament — by 3 twenty-fours, 3 twelves, 4 nines, and a howitzer — to a total of 53 guns.   Actually, they could be brought into action only under exceptional circumstances, and are more properly omitted.

---

[1] The radeau had six 24-pounders, six 12's, and two howitzers; the gondola, seven 9-pounders.   The particulars of armament are from Douglas's letters.

[2] By American reports.   Beatson gives the force sent out, in the spring of 1776, as 13,357.   ('Mil. and Nav. Memoirs,' vi. 44.)

[3] Douglas's letters.

These minutiæ are necessary for the proper appreciation of what Captain Douglas justly called " a momentous event." It was a strife of pigmies for the prize of a continent, and the leaders are entitled to full credit both for their antecedent energy and for their dispositions in the contest ; not least the unhappy man who, having done so much to save his country, afterwards blasted his name by a treason unsurpassed in modern war. Energy and audacity had so far preserved the Lake to the Americans ; Arnold determined to have one more try of the chances. He did not know the full force of the enemy, but he expected that " it would be very formidable, if not equal to ours." [1] The season, however, was so near its end that a severe check would equal a defeat, and would postpone Carleton's further advance to the next spring. Besides, what was the worth of such a force as the American, such a flotilla, under the guns of Ticonderoga, the Lake being lost? It was eminently a case for taking chances, even if the detachment should be sacrificed, as it was.

Arnold's original purpose had been to fight under way ; and it was from this point of view that he valued the galleys, because of their mobility. It is uncertain when he first learned of the rig and battery of the *Inflexible ;* [1] but a good look-out was kept, and the British squadron was sighted from Valcour when it quitted the narrows. It may have been seen even earlier; for Carleton had been informed, erroneously, that the Americans were near Grand Island, which led him to incline to that side, and so open out Valcour sooner. The British anchored for the night of October 10th, between Grand and Long [2] Islands. Getting under way next morning, they stood up the Lake with a strong north-east wind, keeping along Grand Island, upon which their attention doubtless was fastened by the intelligence which they had received ; but it was a singular negligence thus to run to leeward with a fair wind, without thorough scouting on both hands. The consequence was that the American flotilla was not discovered until Valcour Island, which is from one hundred and twenty to one hundred and eighty feet high throughout its two miles of length, was so far passed that the attack had to be made from the south, — from leeward.

---

[1] Douglas thought that the appearance of the *Inflexible* was a complete surprise; but Arnold had been informed that a third vessel, larger than the schooners, was being set up. With a man of his character, it is impossible to be sure, from his letters to his superior, how much he knew, or what he withheld.

[2] Now called North Hero.

When the British were first made out, Arnold's second in command, Waterbury, urged that in view of the enemy's superiority the
flotilla should get under way at once, and fight them "on a retreat
in the main Lake ; " the harbor being disadvantageous " to fight a
number so much superior, and the enemy being able to surround us
on every side, we lying between an island and the main." With
sounder judgment, Arnold decided to hold on.   A retreat before
square-rigged sailing vessels having a fair wind, by a heterogeneous
force like his own, of unequal speeds and batteries, could result
only in disaster.   Concerted fire and successful escape were alike
improbable ; and besides, escape, if feasible, was but throwing up the
game.   Better trust to a steady, well-ordered position, developing
the utmost fire.   If the enemy discovered him, and came in by the
northern entrance, there was a five-foot knoll in mid-channel which
might fetch the biggest of them up; if, as proved to be the case,
the island should be passed, and the attack should be made from
leeward, it probably would be partial and in disorder, as also happened.   The correctness of Arnold's decision not to chance a retreat
was shown in the retreat of two days later.

Valcour is on the west side of the Lake, about three quarters
of a mile from the main ; but a peninsula projecting from the island
at mid-length narrows this interval to a half-mile.   From the accounts, it is clear that the American flotilla lay south of this peninsula.   Arnold had, therefore, a reasonable hope that it might be
passed undetected.   Writing to Gates, the commander-in-chief at
Ticonderoga, he said : " There is a good harbor, and if the enemy
venture up the Lake it will be impossible for them to take advantage of our situation.   If we succeed in our attack upon them, it
will be impossible for any to escape.   If we are worsted, our retreat
is open and free.   In case of wind, which generally blows fresh at
this season, our craft will make good weather, while theirs cannot
keep the Lake."   It is apparent from this, written three weeks before the battle, that he then was not expecting a force materially
different from his own.   Later, he describes his position as being
" in a small bay on the west side of the island, as near together as
possible, and in such a form that few vessels can attack us at the
same time, and those will be exposed to the fire of the whole
fleet."   Though he unfortunately gives no details, he evidently had
sound tactical ideas.   The formation of the anchored vessels is described by the British officers as a half-moon.

When the British discovered the enemy, they hauled up for them. Arnold ordered one of his schooners, the *Royal Savage*, and the four galleys, to get under way; the two other schooners and the eight gondolas remaining at their anchors. The *Royal Savage*, dropping to leeward, — by bad management, Arnold says, — came, apparently unsupported, under the distant fire of the *Inflexible*, as she drew under the lee of Valcour at 11 A.M., followed by the *Carleton*, and at greater distance by the *Maria* and the gunboats. Three shots from the ship's 12-pounders struck the *Royal Savage*, which then ran ashore on the southern point of the island. The *Inflexible*, followed closely by the *Carleton*, continued on, but fired only occasionally; showing that Arnold was keeping his galleys in hand, at long bowls, — as small vessels with one eighteen should be kept, when confronted with a broadside of nine guns. Between the island and the main the north-east wind doubtless drew more northerly, adverse to the ships' approach; but, a flaw off the cliffs taking the fore and aft sails of the *Carleton*, she fetched "nearly into the middle of the rebel half-moon, where Lieutenant J. R. Dacres intrepidly anchored with a spring on her cable." The *Maria*, on board which was Carleton, together with Commander Thomas Pringle, commanding the flotilla, was to leeward when the chase began, and could not get into close action that day. By this time, seventeen of the twenty gunboats had come up, and, after silencing the *Royal Savage*, pulled up to within point-blank range of the American flotilla. "The cannonade was tremendous," wrote Baron Riedesel. Lieutenant Edward Longcroft, of the radeau *Thunderer*, not being able to get his raft into action, went with a boat's crew on board the *Royal Savage*, and for a time turned her guns upon her former friends; but the fire of the latter forced him again to abandon her; and it seemed so likely that she might be retaken that she was set on fire by Lieutenant Starke of the *Maria*, when already "two rebel boats were very near her. She soon after blew up." The American guns converging on the *Carleton* in her central position, she suffered severely. Her commander, Lieutenant Dacres, was knocked senseless; another officer lost an arm; only Mr. Edward Pellew, afterwards Lord Exmouth, remained fit for duty. The spring being shot away, she swung bows on to the enemy, and her fire was thus silenced. Captain Pringle signalled to her to withdraw; but she was unable to obey. To pay her head off the right way, Pellew himself had to get out on the bowsprit under a heavy fire of musketry, to bear the jib over to

windward; but to make sail seems to have been impossible. Two
artillery boats were sent to her assistance, "which towed her off
through a very thick fire, until out of farther reach, much to the
honour of Mr. John Curling and Mr. Patrick Carnegy, master's mate
and midshipman of the *Isis*, who conducted them; and of Mr.
Edward Pellew, mate of the *Blonde*, who threw the tow-rope from
the *Carleton's* bowsprit." [1] This service on board the *Carleton* started
Pellew on his road to fortune; but, singularly enough, the lieutenancy
promised him in consequence, by both the First Lord and Lord Howe,
was delayed by the fact that he stayed at the front, instead of going
to the rear, where he would have been " within their jurisdiction." [2]
The *Carleton* had two feet of water in the hold, and had lost eight
killed and six wounded, — about half her crew, — when she anchored
out of fire. In this small but stirring business, the Americans, in
addition to the *Royal Savage*, had lost one gondola. Besides the
injuries to the *Carleton*, a British artillery boat, commanded by a
German lieutenant, was sunk. Towards evening the *Inflexible* got
within point-blank shot of the Americans, " when five broadsides,"
wrote Douglas, " silenced their whole line." One fresh ship, with
scantling for sea-going, and a concentrated battery, has an unques-
tioned advantage over a dozen light-built craft, carrying one or two
guns each, and already several hours engaged.

At nightfall the *Inflexible* dropped out of range, and the British
squadron anchored in line of battle across the southern end of the
passage between the island and the main; some vessels were extended also to the eastward, into the open Lake. "The best part
of my intelligence," wrote Burgoyne next day from St. John's, to
Douglas at Quebec, " is that our whole fleet was formed in line
above the enemy, and consequently they must have surrendered this
morning, or given us battle on our own terms. The Indians and
light troops are abreast with the fleet; they cannot, therefore, escape
by land." The British squadron sharing this confidence, a proper
look-out was not kept. The American leader immediately held a
conference with his officers, and decided to attempt a retreat, "which
was done with such secrecy," writes Waterbury, " that we went
through them entirely undiscovered." The movement began at
7 P.M., a galley leading, the gondolas and schooners following, and
Arnold and his second bringing up the rear in the two heaviest galleys. This delicate operation was favoured by a heavy fog, which

---

[1] Douglas's letter.   [2] Sandwich to Pellew.

did not clear till next morning at eight. As the Americans stole
by, they could not see any of the hostile ships. By daylight they
were out of sight of the British. Riedesel, speaking of this event,
says, " The ships anchored, secure of the enemy, who stole off
during the night, and sailing round the left wing, aided by a
favourable wind, escaped under darkness." The astonishment next
morning, he continues, was great, as was Carleton's rage. The latter started to pursue in such a hurry that he forgot to leave orders
for the troops which had been landed; but, failing to discover the
fugitives, he returned and remained at Valcour till nightfall, when
scouts brought word that the enemy were at Schuyler's Island, eight
miles above.

The retreat of the Americans had been embarrassed by their
injuries, and by the wind coming out ahead. They were obliged to
anchor on the 12th to repair damages, both hulls and sails having
suffered severely. Arnold took the precaution to write to Crown
Point for bateaux, to tow in case of a southerly wind; but time was
not allowed for these to arrive. Two gondolas had to be sunk on
account of their injuries, making three of that class so far lost. The
retreat was resumed at 2 P.M., but the breeze was fresh from the
southward, and the gondolas made very little way. At evening the
British chased again. That night the wind moderated, and at daybreak the American flotilla was twenty-eight miles from Crown
Point, — fourteen from Valcour, — having still five miles' start.
Later, however, by Arnold's report, " the wind again breezed up to
the southward, so that we gained very little either by beating or rowing. At the same time the enemy took a fresh breeze from north-
east, and, by the time we had reached Split Rock, were alongside of
us." The galleys of Arnold and Waterbury, the *Congress* and the
Washington, had throughout kept in the rear, and now received the
brunt of the attack, made by the *Inflexible* and the two schooners,
which had entirely distanced their sluggish consorts. This fight was
in the upper narrows, where the Lake is from one to three miles
wide; and it lasted, by Arnold's report, for five glasses (two hours
and a half),[1] the Americans continually retreating, until about ten
miles from Crown Point. There, the *Washington* having struck
some time before, and final escape being impossible, Arnold ran his
own galley and four gondolas ashore in a small creek on the east
side; pulling to windward, with the cool judgment that had marked

---

[1] Beatson, ' Nav. and Mil. Memoirs,' says two hours.

all his conduct, so that the enemy could not follow him — except in small boats with which he could deal.   There he set his vessels on fire, and stood by them until assured that they would blow up with their flags flying.   He then retreated to Crown Point through the woods, " despite the savages ; " a phrase which concludes this singular aquatic contest with a quaint touch of local colour.

In three days of fighting and retreating the Americans had lost one schooner, two galleys, and seven gondolas, — in all, ten vessels out of fifteen.   The killed and wounded amounted to over eighty, twenty odd of whom were in Arnold's galley.   The original force, numbering seven hundred, had been decimated.   Considering its raw material and the recency of its organisation, words ,can scarcely exaggerate the heroism of the resistance, which undoubtedly depended chiefly upon the personal military qualities of the leader.   The British loss in killed and wounded did not exceed forty.

The little American navy on Champlain was wiped out; but never had any force, big or small, lived to better purpose or died more gloriously ; for it had saved the Lake for that year.   Whatever deductions may be made for blunders, and for circumstances of every character, which made the British campaign of 1777 abortive and disastrous, and so led directly to the American alliance with France in 1778, the delay, with all that it involved, was obtained by the Lake campaign of 1776.   On October 15th, two days after Arnold's final defeat, Carleton dated a letter to Douglas from before Crown Point, whence the American garrison was withdrawn.   A week later Riedesel arrived, and wrote that, " were our whole army here it would be an easy matter to drive the enemy from their entrenchments," at Ticonderoga, and — as has been quoted already — four weeks sooner would have insured its fall.   It is but a coincidence that just four weeks had been required to set up the *Inflexible* at St. John's ; but it typifies the whole story.   Save for Arnold's flotilla, the two British schooners would have settled the business.   " Upon the whole, Sir," wrote Douglas in his final letter from Quebec before sailing for England, " I scruple not to say, that had not General Carleton authorised me to take the extraordinary measure of sending up the *Inflexible* from Quebec, things could not this year have been brought to so glorious a conclusion on Lake Champlain."   Douglas further showed the importance attached to this success by men of that day, by sending a special message to the British ambassador at Madrid, " presuming that the early knowledge of this great event in the southern parts of Europe may be of advantage to His Majesty's service." That the opinion of the government was similar may be inferred from the numerous rewards bestowed. Carleton was made a Knight of the Bath, and Douglas a baronet.

In no case where the British and the Americans have met upon the water, has a serious charge of personal misconduct been proved against any individual; and the gallantry shown upon occasion by both sides upon Lake Champlain in 1776, is evident from the foregoing narrative. With regard to the direction of movements, — the skill of the two leaders, — the same equal credit cannot be assigned. It was a very serious blunder, on October 11th, to run to leeward, passing a concealed enemy, undetected, upon waters so perfectly well known as those of Champlain were; it having been the scene of frequent British operations in previous wars. Owing to this, "the *Maria*, because of her distant situation (from which the *Inflexible* and *Carleton* had chased by signal) when the rebels were first discovered, and baffling winds, could not get into close action." [1] For the same reason the *Inflexible* could not support the *Carleton*. The Americans, in the aggregate distinctly inferior, were thus permitted a concentration of superior force upon part of their enemies. It is needless to enlarge upon the mortifying incident of Arnold's escape that evening. To liken small things to great, — always profitable in military analysis, — it resembled Hood's slipping away from de Grasse at St. Kitts.

In conduct and courage, Arnold's behaviour was excellent throughout. Without enlarging upon the energy which created the flotilla, and the breadth of view which suggested preparations that he could not enforce, admiration is due to his recognition of the fact — implicit in deed, if unexpressed in word — that the one use of the navy was to contest the control of the water; to impose delay, even if it could not secure ultimate victory. No words could say more clearly than do his actions that, under the existing conditions, the navy was useless, except as it contributed to that end; valueless, if buried in port. Upon this rests the merit of his bold advance into the lower narrows; upon this his choice of the strong defensive position of Valcour; upon this his refusal to retreat, as urged by Waterbury, when the full force of the enemy was disclosed, — a

---

[1] Douglas's letters. The sentence is awkward, but carefully compared with the copy in the author's hands. Douglas says, of the details he gives, that " they have been collected with the most scrupulous circumspection."

decision justified, or rather, illustrated, by the advantages which the accidents of the day threw into his hands. His personal gallantry was conspicuous there as at all times of his life. " His countrymen," said a generous enemy of that day, "chiefly gloried in the dangerous attention which he paid to a nice point of honour, in keeping his flag flying, and not quitting his galley till she was in flames, lest the enemy should have boarded, and struck it." It is not the least of the injuries done to his nation in after years, that he should have silenced this boast and effaced this glorious record by so black an infamy.

With the destruction of the flotilla ends the naval story of the Lakes during the War of the American Revolution. Satisfied that it was too late to proceed against Ticonderoga that year, Carleton withdrew to St. John's and went into winter-quarters. The following year the enterprise was resumed under General Burgoyne; but Sir William Howe, instead of co-operating by an advance up the Hudson, which was the plan of 1776, carried his army to Chesapeake Bay, to act thence against Philadelphia. Burgoyne took Ticonderoga and forced his way as far as Saratoga, sixty miles from Ticonderoga and thirty from Albany, where Howe should have met him. There he was brought to a stand by the army which the Americans had collected, found himself unable to advance or to retreat, and was forced to lay down his arms on October 17th, 1777. The garrisons left by him at Ticonderoga and Crown Point retired to Canada, and the posts were re-occupied by the Americans. No further contest took place on the Lake, though the British vessels remained in control of it, and showed themselves from time to time up to 1781. With the outbreak of war between Great Britain and France, in 1778, the scene of interest shifted to salt water, and there remained till the end.

The opening conflict between Great Britain and her North American Colonies teaches clearly the necessity, too rarely recognised in practice, that when a state has decided to use force, the force provided should be adequate from the first. It is better to be much too strong than a little too weak. Seeing the evident temper of the Massachusetts Colonists, force would be needed to execute the Boston Port Bill and its companion measures of 1774; for the Port Bill especially, naval force. The supplies for 1775 granted only 18,000 seamen, — 2,000 less than for the previous year. For 1776, 28,000 seamen were voted, and the total appropriations rose from £5,556,000 to £10,154,000; but it was then too late. Boston was evacuated by the British army, 8,000 strong, on the 17th of March, 1776; but already, for more than half a year, the spreading spirit of revolt in the thirteen Colonies had been encouraged by the sight of the British army cooped up in the town, suffering from want of necessaries, while the colonial army blockading it was able to maintain its position, because ships laden with stores for the one were captured, and the cargoes diverted to the use of the other. To secure free and ample communications for one's self, and to interrupt those of the opponent, are among the first requirements of war. To carry out the measures of the British government a naval force was needed, which should not only protect the approach of its own transports to Boston Bay, but should prevent access to all coast ports whence supplies could be carried to the blockading army. So far from this, the squadron was not equal, in either number or quality, to the work to be done about Boston; and it was not until October, 1775, that the Admiral was authorised to capture colonial merchant vessels, which therefore went and came unmolested, outside of Boston, carrying often provisions which found their way to Washington's army.

After evacuating Boston, General Howe retired to Halifax, there to await the coming of reinforcements, both military and naval, and of his brother Vice-Admiral Lord Howe, appointed to command the North American Station. General Howe was commander-in-chief of the forces throughout the territory extending from Nova Scotia to West Florida; from Halifax to Pensacola. The first operation of the campaign was to be the reduction of New York.

The British government, however, had several objects in view, and permitted itself to be distracted from the single-minded prosecution of one great undertaking to other subsidiary, and not always concentric, operations. Whether the control of the line of the Hudson and Lake Champlain ought to have been sought through operations beginning at both ends, is open to argument; the facts that the Americans were back in Crown Point in the beginning of July, and that Carleton's 13,000 men got no farther than St. John's that year, suggest that the greater part of the latter force would have been better employed in New York and New Jersey than about Champlain. However that may be, the diversion of a third body, respectable in point of numbers, to the Carolinas, is scarcely to be defended on military grounds. The government was induced to it by the expectation of local support from royalists. That there were con-

siderable numbers of these in both Colonies is certain; but while
military operations must take account of political conditions, the
latter should not be allowed to overbalance elementary principles
of the military art.   It is said that General Howe disapproved of
this ex-centric movement.

The force destined for the Southern coasts assembled at Cork
towards the end of 1775, and sailed thence in January, 1776.   The
troops were commanded by Lord Cornwallis, the squadron by Nelson's early patron, Commodore Sir Peter Parker, whose broad pennant was hoisted on board the *Bristol*, 50, Captain John Morris.
After a boisterous passage, the expedition arrived in May off Cape
Fear in North Carolina, where it was joined by 2,000 men under Sir
Henry Clinton, Cornwallis's senior, whom Howe had detached to the
southward in January, by the government's orders.   Upon his appearance, the royalists in North Carolina had risen, headed by the hus-
band of Flora Macdonald, whose name thirty years before had been
associated romantically with the escape of the young Pretender, but
who had afterwards emigrated to America.   The rising, however,
had been put down, and Clinton had not thought it expedient to try
a serious invasion, in face of the large force assembled to resist him.
Upon Parker's coming, it was decided to make an attempt upon
Charleston, South Carolina.   The fleet therefore sailed from Cape
Fear on the 1st of June, and on the 4th anchored off Charleston Bar.

Charleston Harbour opens between two of the Sea-Islands which
fringe the coasts of South Carolina and Georgia.   On the north is
Sullivan's Island, on the south James Island.   The bar of the main
entrance was not abreast the mouth of the port, but some distance
south of it.   Inside the bar, the channel turned to the northward,
and thence led near Sullivan's Island, the southern end of which
was therefore chosen as the site of the rude fort hastily thrown up
to meet this attack, and afterwards called Fort Moultrie, from the
name of the commander.   From these conditions, a southerly wind
was needed to bring ships into action.   After sounding and buoying
the bar, the transports and frigates crossed on the 7th and anchored
inside; but as it was necessary to remove some of the *Bristol's* guns,
she could not follow until the 10th.   On the 9th Clinton had landed
in person with five hundred men, and by the 15th all the troops had
disembarked upon Long Island, next north of Sullivan's.   It was
understood that the inlet between the two was fordable, allowing the
troops to co-operate with the naval attack, by diversion or otherwise;

but this proved to be a mistake.   The passage was seven feet deep
at low water, and there were no means for crossing ; consequently a
small American detachment in the scrub wood of the island was sufficient to check any movement in that quarter.   The fighting therefore was confined to the cannonading of the fort by the ships.

Circumstances not fully explained caused the attack to be fixed
for the 23rd; an inopportune delay, during which the Americans
were strengthening their still very imperfect defences.   On the 23rd
the wind was unfavourable.   On the 25th the *Experiment*, 50, Captain Alexander Scott, arrived, crossed the bar, and, after taking in
her guns again, was ready to join in the assault.   On the 27th, at
10 A.M., the ships got under way with a south-east breeze, but this
shifted soon afterwards to north-west, and they had to anchor again,
about a mile nearer to Sullivan's Island.   On the following day the
wind served, and the attack was made.

In plan, Fort Moultrie was square, with a bastion at each angle.
In construction, the sides were palmetto logs, dovetailed and bolted
together, laid in parallel rows, sixteen feet apart, and the interspace
filled with sand.   At the time of the engagement, the south and west
fronts were finished ; the other fronts were only seven feet high, but
surmounted by thick planks, to be tenable against escalade.   Thirty-
one guns were in place, eighteen and nine pounders, of which twenty-
one were on the south face, commanding the channel.   Within was
a traverse running east and west, protecting the gunners from shots
from the rear ; but there was no such cover against enfilading fire,
in case an enemy's ship passed the fort and anchored above it.   " The
general opinion before the action," Moultrie says, " and especially
among sailors, was that two frigates would be sufficient to knock the
town about our ears, notwithstanding our batteries."   Parker may
have shared this impression, and it may account for his leisure-
liness.   When the action began, the garrison had but twenty-eight
rounds for twenty-six cannon, but this deficiency was unknown to
the British.

Parker's plan was that the two 50's, *Bristol* and *Experiment*, and
two 28-gun frigates, the *Active*, Captain William Williams, and the
Solebay, Captain Thomas Symonds, accompanied by a bomb-vessel, the
Thunder, 8, Captain James Reid, should engage the main front;
while two frigates of the same class, the *Actæon*, Captain Christopher
Atkins, and the *Syren*, Captain Christopher Furneaux, with a 20-gun
corvette, the *Sphinx*, Captain Anthony Hunt, should pass the fort,

anchoring to the westward, up-channel, to protect the heavy vessels against fire-ships, as well as to enfilade the main battery. The order to weigh was given at 10.30 A.M., when the flood-tide had fairly made; and at 11.15 the *Active*, *Bristol*, and *Experiment*, anchored in line ahead, in the order named, the *Active* to the eastward. The *Solebay* lay outside the others, abreast the interval between the 50's. The ships seem to have taken their places skilfully and without confusion, and their fire, which opened at once, was rapid, well-sustained, and well-directed; but their disposition suffered under the radical defect that, whether from actual lack of water, or only from fear of grounding, they were too far from the works to use grape effectively. The sides of ships being much weaker than those of shore works, while their guns were much more numerous, the secret of success was to get near enough to beat down the hostile fire by a multitude of projectiles. The bomb-vessel *Thunder* anchored ahead, and outside, of the *Active*, south-east by south from the east bastion of the engaged front. Her shells, though well aimed, were ineffective. "Most of them fell within the fort," Moultrie reported, "but we had a morass in the middle, which swallowed them instantly, and those that fell in the sand were immediately buried." During the action, the mortar bed broke, disabling the piece.

Owing to the scarcity of powder, the garrison had positive orders not to engage at ranges exceeding four hundred yards. Four or five shots were thrown at the *Active*, while still under sail, but with this exception the fort kept silence until the ships anchored, at a distance estimated by the Americans to be 350 yards. The word was then passed along the platform, "Mind the Commodore; mind the two 50-gun ships," — an order which was strictly obeyed, as the losses show. The protection of the work proved to be almost perfect, — a fact which doubtless contributed to the coolness and precision of fire vitally essential with such deficient resources. The texture of the palmetto wood suffered the balls to sink smoothly into it without splintering, so that the facing of the work held well. At times, when three or four broadsides struck together, the merlons shook so that Moultrie feared they would come bodily in; but they withstood, and the small loss inflicted was chiefly through the embrasures. The flagstaff was shot away, falling outside into the ditch, but a young sergeant, named Jasper, distinguished himself by jumping after it, fetching back and rehoisting the colours under a heavy fire.

In the squadron an equal gallantry was shown under circum-

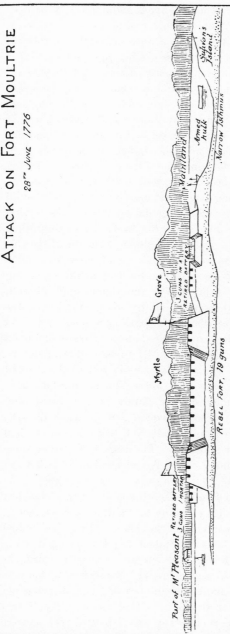

ATTACK ON FORT MOULTRIE.
From a Sketch by a British officer on the Spot.
(In "Admirals' Despatches." N. Amer. Stat. Vol. 7. Record Office.)

stances which made severe demands upon endurance. Whatever
Parker's estimate of the worth of the defences, no trace of vain-con-
fidence appears in his dispositions, which were thorough and careful,
as the execution of the main attack was skilful and vigorous. But
the ships' companies had expected an easy victory, and they found
themselves confronted with a resistance and a punishment as severe
as were endured by the leaders at Trafalgar, and far more prolonged.
Such conditions impose upon men's tenacity the additional test of
surprise and discomfiture. The *Experiment*, though very small for
a ship of the line, lost 23 killed and 56 wounded, out of a total probably not much exceeding 300, while the *Bristol*, having the spring
shot away, swung with her head to the southward and her stern to
the fort, undergoing for a long time a raking fire to which she could
make little reply. Three several attempts to replace the spring
were made by Mr. James Saumarez, — afterwards the distinguished
admiral, then a midshipman, — before the ship was relieved from this
grave disadvantage. Her loss was 40 killed and 71 wounded ; not a
man escaping of those stationed on the quarter-deck at the beginning
of the action. Among the injured was the Commodore himself,
whose cool heroism must have been singularly conspicuous, from the
notice it attracted in a service where such bearing was not rare. At
one time when the quarter-deck was cleared and he stood alone upon
the poop-ladder, Saumarez suggested to him to come down ; but he
replied, smiling, " You want to get rid of me, do you ? " and refused
to move. The captain of the ship, John Morris, was mortally
wounded. With commendable modesty Parker only reported himself as slightly bruised ; but deserters stated that for some days he
needed the assistance of two men to walk, and that his trousers had
been torn off him by shot or splinters. The loss in the other ships
was only one killed, 14 wounded. The Americans had 37 killed and
wounded.

The three vessels assigned to enfilade the main front of the fort
did not get into position. They ran on the middle ground, owing,
Parker reported, to the ignorance of the pilots. Two had fouled
each other before striking. Having taken the bottom on a rising
tide, two floated in a few hours, and retreated ; but the third, the
Actæon, 28, sticking fast, was set on fire and abandoned by her officers. Before she blew up, the Americans boarded her, securing her
colours, bell, and some other trophies. " Had these ships effected
their purpose," Moultrie reported, " they would have driven us from
our guns."

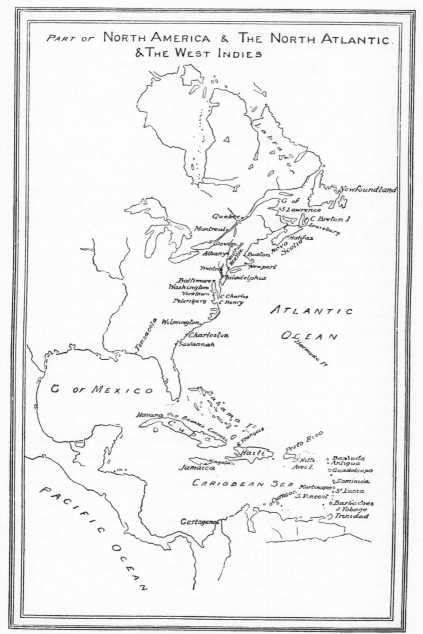

PART OF NORTH AMERICA AND THE NORTH ATLANTIC AND THE WEST INDIES.

The main division held its ground until long after nightfall,
firing much of the time, but stopping at intervals. After two hours
it had been noted that the fort replied very slowly, which was attributed to its being overborne, instead of to the real cause, the necessity for sparing ammunition. For the same reason it was entirely
silent from 3.30 P.M. to 6, when fire was resumed from only two or
three guns, whence Parker surmised that the rest had been dismounted. The Americans were restrained throughout the engagement by the fear of exhausting entirely their scanty store.

"About 9 P.M.," Parker reported, "being very dark, great part
of our ammunition expended, the people fatigued, the tide of ebb
almost done, no prospect from the eastward (that is, from the army),
and no possibility of our being of any further service, I ordered the
ships to withdraw to their former moorings." Besides the casualties
among the crew, and severe damage to the hull, the *Bristol's* mainmast, with nine cannon-balls in it, had to be shortened, while the
mizzen-mast was condemned. The loss of the frigates was immaterial, owing to the garrison's neglecting them.

The fight in Charleston Harbour, the first serious contest in
which ships took part in this war, resembles generically the battle of
Bunker's Hill, with which the regular land warfare had opened a
year before. Both illustrate the difficulty and danger of a front
attack, without cover, upon a fortified position, and the advantage
conferred even upon untrained men, if naturally cool, resolute, and
intelligent, not only by the protection of a work, but also, it may be
urged, by the recognition of a tangible line up to which to hold, and
to abandon which means defeat, dishonour, and disaster. It is much
for untried men to recognise in their surroundings something which
gives the unity of a common purpose, and thus the coherence which
discipline imparts. Although there was in Parker's dispositions
nothing open to serious criticism, — nothing that can be ascribed to
undervaluing his opponent, — and although, also, he had good reason
to expect from the army active co-operation which he did not get, it
is probable that he was very much surprised, not only at the tenacity
of the Americans' resistance, but at the efficacy of their fire. He
felt, doubtless, the traditional and natural distrust — and, for the
most part, the justified distrust — with which experience and practice regard inexperience. Some seamen of American birth, who had
been serving in the *Bristol*, deserted after the fight. Her crew,
they reported, said, " We were told the Yankees would not stand

two fires, but we never saw better fellows; " and when the fire of
the fort slackened and some cried, " They have done fighting," others
replied, " By God, we are glad of it, for we never had such a drub-
bing in our lives."   " All the common men of the fleet spoke loudly
in praise of the garrison," — a note of admiration so frequent in
generous enemies that we may be assured that it was echoed on the
quarter-deck also.   They could afford it well, for beyond the natural
mortification of defeat, there was no stain upon their own record, no
flinching under the severity of their losses, although a number of
their own men were comparatively raw, volunteers from the transports, whose crews had come forward almost as one man when they
knew that the complements of the ships were short through sickness.
Burke, a friend to both sides, was justified in saying that "never did
British valour shine more conspicuously, nor did our ships in an
engagement of the same nature experience so serious an encounter."
There were several death-vacancies for lieutenants ; and, as the battle
of Lake Champlain gave Pellew his first commission, so did that of
Charleston Harbour give his to Saumarez, who was made lieutenant
of the *Bristol* by Parker.   Two years later, when the ship had gone
to Jamaica, he was followed on her quarter-deck by Nelson and Collingwood, who also received promotion in her from the same hand.

The attack on Fort Moultrie was not resumed.   After necessary
repairs, the ships of war with the troops went to New York, where
they arrived on the 4th of August, and took part in the operations
for the reduction of that place under the direction of the two Howes.

The occupation of New York Harbour, and the capture of the
city were the most conspicuous British successes of the summer and
fall of 1776.   While Parker and Clinton were meeting with defeat
at Charleston, and Arnold was hurrying the preparation of his flotilla
on Champlain, the two brothers, General Howe and the Admiral,
were arriving in New York Bay, invested not only with the powers
proper to the commanders of great fleets and armies, but also with
authority as peace commissioners, to negotiate an amicable arrangement with the revolted Colonies.

General Howe had awaited for some time at Halifax the arrival
of the expected reinforcements, but wearying at last he sailed thence
on the 10th of June, 1776, with the army then in hand.   On the
25th he himself reached Sandy Hook, the entrance to New York
Bay, having preceded the transports in a frigate.   On the 29th, the

day after Parker's repulse at Fort Moultrie, the troops arrived; and
on July 3rd, the date on which the Americans, retreating from Canada, reached Crown Point, the British landed on Staten Island, which
is on the west side of the lower Bay.   On the 12th of July the *Eagle*,
64, came in, carrying the flag of Admiral Lord Howe.   This officer
was much esteemed by the Americans for his own personal qualities,
and for his attitude towards them in the present dispute, as well as
for the memory of his brother, who had endeared himself greatly to
them in the campaign of 1758, when he had fallen near Lake Champlain; but the decisive step of declaring their independence had
been taken already, on July 4th, eight days before the Admiral's
arrival.   A month was spent in fruitless attempts to negotiate with
the new government, without recognising any official character in its
representatives.   During that time, however, while abstaining from
decisive operations, cruisers were kept at sea to intercept American
traders, and the Admiral, immediately upon arriving, sent four vessels of war twenty-five miles up the Hudson River, as far as Tarrytown.   This squadron was commanded by Hyde Parker, afterwards,
in 1801, Nelson's commander-in-chief at Copenhagen.   The service
was performed under a tremendous cannonade from all the batteries
on both shores, from the lower Bay to far above the city, but the ships
could not be stopped.   Towards the middle of August it was evident
that the Americans would not accept any terms in the power of the
Howes to offer, and it became necessary to attempt coercion by arms.

In the reduction of New York in 1776, the part played by the
British Navy, owing to the nature of the campaign in general and of
the enemy's force in particular, was of that inconspicuous character
which obscures the fact that without the Navy the operations could
not have been undertaken at all, and that the Navy played to them
the part of the base of operations and line of communications.   Like
the foundations of a building, these lie outside the range of superficial attention, and therefore are less generally appreciated than the
brilliant fighting that goes on at the front, to the maintenance of
which they are indispensable.   Consequently, whatever of interest
may attach to any, or to all, of the minor affairs, which in the aggregate constitute the action of the naval force in such circumstances,
the historian of the major operations is confined perforce to indicating the broad general effect of naval power upon the issue.   This
will be done best by tracing in outline the scene of action, the combined movements, and the Navy's influence in both.

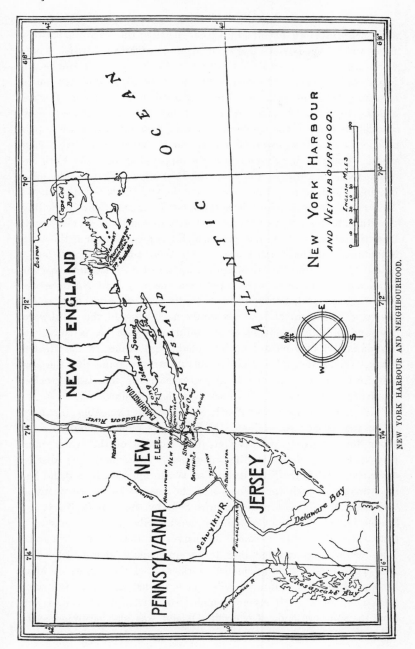

NEW YORK HARBOUR AND NEIGHBOURHOOD.

The harbour of New York divides into two parts — the upper and lower Bays — connected by a passage called the Narrows, between Long and Staten Islands, upon the latter of which the British troops were encamped.   Long Island, which forms the eastern shore of the Narrows, extends to the east-north-east a hundred and ten miles, enclosing between itself and the continent a broad sheet of water called Long Island Sound, that reaches nearly to Narragansett Bay. The latter, being a fine anchorage, entered also into the present plan of operations, as an essential feature in a coastwise maritime campaign.   Long Island Sound and the upper Bay of New York are connected by a passage, known as the East River, eight or ten miles in length, and at that time nearly a mile wide [1] abreast the city of New York.   At the point where the East River joins New York Bay, the Hudson River, an estuary there nearly two miles wide, also enters from the north, — a circumstance which has procured for it the alternative name of the North River.   Near their confluence, and half a mile below the town, is Governor's Island, centrally situated to command the entrances to both.   Between the East and North rivers, with their general directions from north and east-north-east, is embraced a long strip of land gradually narrowing to the southward. The end of this peninsula, as it would otherwise be, is converted into an island, of a mean length of about eight miles, by the Harlem River, — a narrow and partially navigable stream connecting the East and North rivers.   To the southern extreme of this island, called Manhattan, the city of New York was then confined.

As both the East and North rivers were navigable for large ships, the former throughout, the latter for over a hundred miles above its mouth, it was evident that control of the water must play a large part in warlike operations throughout the district described.   With the limited force at Washington's disposal, he had been unable to push the defences of the city as far to the front as was desirable.   The lower Bay was held by the British Navy, and Staten Island had been abandoned, necessarily, without resistance, thus surrendering the strong defensive position of the Narrows. The lines were contracted thus to the immediate neighbourhood of New York itself.   Small detached works skirted the shores of Manhattan Island, and a line of redoubts extended across it, following the course of a small stream which then partly divided it, a mile from the southern end.   Governor's Island was also occupied as an

---

[1] At the present day reduced by reclaimed land.

outpost.   Of more intrinsic strength, but not at first concerned,
strong works had been thrown up on either side of the North River,
upon commanding heights eight miles above New York, to dispute
the passage of ships.

The crucial weakness in this scheme of defence was that the
shore of Long Island opposite the city was much higher than that
of Manhattan.   If this height were seized, the city, and all below it,
became untenable.   Here, therefore, was the key of the position and
the chief station for the American troops.   For its protection a line
of works was thrown up, the flanks of which rested upon Wallabout
Bay and Gowanus Cove, two indentations in the shores of Long
Island.   These Washington manned with 9,000 of the 18,000 men
under his command.   By the arrival of three divisions of Hessian
troops, Howe's army now numbered over 34,000 men, to which
Clinton brought 3,000 more from before Charleston.[1]

On the 22nd of August the British crossed from Staten Island to
Gravesend Bay, on the Long Island shore of the Narrows.   The
Navy covered the landing, and the transportation of the troops was
under the charge of Commodore William Hotham, who, nineteen
years later, was Nelson's commander-in-chief in the Mediterranean.
By noon 15,000 men and forty field-guns had been carried over and
placed on shore.   The force of the Americans permitted little opposition to the British advance; but General Howe was cautious and
easy-going, and it was not till the 27th that the army, now increased
to 25,000, was fairly in front of the American lines, having killed,
wounded, and taken about 1,500 men.   Hoping that Howe would be
tempted to storm the position, Washington replaced these with 2,000
drawn from his meagre numbers; but his opponent held back his
troops, who were eager for the assault.   The Americans now stood
with their backs to a swift river, nearly a mile wide, with only a
feeble line of works interposing between them and an enemy more
than double their number.

On the morning of the 27th, Sir Peter Parker, with a 64, two
50's, and two frigates, attempted to work up to New York, with a
view of supporting the left flank of the army; but the wind came
out from the north, and, the ebb-tide making, the ships got no nearer
than three miles from the city.   Fortunately for the Americans, they
either could not or would not go farther on the following two days.

---

[1] Beatson's 'Military and Naval Memoirs,' vi. 44, give 34,614 as the strength of
Howe's army.   Clinton's division is not included in this.   vi. 45.

After dark of the 28th, Howe broke ground for regular approaches. Washington, seeing this, and knowing that there could be but one result to a siege under his condition of inferiority, resolved to withdraw. During the night of the 29th ten thousand men silently quitted their positions, embarked, and crossed to Manhattan Island, carrying with them all their belongings, arms, and ammunition. The enemy's trenches were but six hundred yards distant, yet no suspicion was aroused, nor did a single deserter give treacherous warning. The night was clear and moonlit, although a heavy fog towards daybreak prolonged the period of secrecy which shrouded the retreat. When the fog rose, the last detachment was discovered crossing, but a few ineffectual cannon shot at it were the only harassment experienced in the course of this rapid and dexterous retirement. The garrison of Governor's Island was withdrawn at the same time.

The unmolested use of the water, and the nautical skill of the fishermen who composed one of the American regiments, were essential to this escape; for admirable as the movement was in conception and execution, no word less strong than escape applies to it. By it Washington rescued over half his army from sure destruction, and, not improbably, the cause of his people from immediate collapse. An opportunity thus seized implies necessarily an opportunity lost on the other side. For that failure both army and Navy must bear their share of the blame. It is obvious that when an enemy is cornered, his line of retreat should be watched. This was the business of both commanders-in-chief, the execution of it being primarily the duty of the Navy, as retreat from the American position could be only by water. It was a simple question of look-out, of detection, of molestation by that means; not of arresting the retreat. To the latter, sailing ships were inadequate, for they could not have remained at anchor under the guns of Manhattan Island, either by day or night; but a few boats with muffled oars could have watched, could have given the alarm, precipitating a British attack, and such a movement interrupted in mid-course brings irretrievable disaster.

Washington now withdrew the bulk of his army to the line of the Harlem. On his right, south of that river and commanding the Hudson, was a fort called by his name; opposite to it on the Jersey shore was Fort Lee. A garrison of four thousand men occupied New York. After amusing himself with some further peace negotiations, Howe determined to possess the city. As a diversion from the main effort, and to cover the crossing of the troops, two detach-

ments of ships were ordered to pass the batteries on the Hudson and
East rivers. This was done on the 13th and the 15th of September,
the North River division commanded by Captain Francis Banks, the
East River by Captain Hyde Parker. The latter suffered severely,
especially in spars and rigging; [1] but the success of both, following
upon that of Hyde Parker a few weeks earlier, in his expedition to
Tarrytown, confirmed Washington in the opinion which he expressed
five years later to de Grasse, that batteries alone could not stop ships
having a fair wind. This is now a commonplace of naval warfare.
On the 15th Howe's army crossed under cover of Parker's ships,
Hotham again superintending the boat work. The garrison of New
York slipped along the west shore of the island and joined the main
body on the Harlem; favoured again, apparently, in this flank movement a mile from the enemy's front, by Howe's inertness, and fondness for a good meal, to which a shrewd American woman invited
him at the critical moment.

Despite these various losses of position, important as they were,
the American army continued to elude the British general, who
apparently did not hold very strongly the opinion that the most
decisive factor in war is the enemy's organised force. As control of
the valley of the Hudson, in connection with Lake Champlain, was,
very properly, the chief object of the British government, Howe's
next aim was to loosen Washington's grip on the peninsula north of
the Harlem. The position seeming to him too strong for a front
attack, he decided to strike for its left flank and rear by way of Long
Island Sound. In this, which involved the passage of the tortuous
and dangerous channel called Hell Gate, with its swift conflicting
currents, the Navy again bore an essential part. The movement
began on October 12th, the day after Arnold was defeated at Valcour. So far as its leading object went it was successful, Washington
feeling obliged to let go the line of the Harlem, and change front to
the left. As the result of the various movements and encounters of
the two armies, he fell back across the Hudson into New Jersey,
ordering the evacuation of Fort Washington, and deciding to rest his
control of the Hudson Valley upon West Point, fifty miles above
New York, a position of peculiar natural strength, on the west bank
of the river. To these decisions he was compelled by his inferiority
in numbers, and also by the very isolated and hazardous situation
in which he was operating, between two navigable waters, abso-

---

[1] Admiral James's Journal, p. 30. (Navy Records Society.)

lutely controlled by the enemy's shipping. This conclusion was further forced upon him by another successful passage before the guns of Forts Washington and Lee by Hyde Parker, with three ships, the *Phœnix,* 44, *Roebuck,* 44, and *Tartar,* 28, on the 9th of October. On this occasion the vessels, two of which were frigates of the heaviest class, suffered very severely, losing nine killed and eighteen wounded; but the menace to the communications of the Americans, whose supplies came mostly from the west of the Hudson, could not be disregarded.

It was early in November that Washington crossed into New Jersey with five thousand men; and soon afterwards he directed the remainder of his force to follow. At that moment the blunder of one subordinate, and the disobedience of another, brought upon him two serious blows. Fort Washington not being evacuated when ordered, Howe carried it by storm, capturing not only it but its garrison of 2,700 men, a very heavy loss to the Americans. On the other hand, the most explicit orders failed to bring the officer left in command on the east of the Hudson to rejoin the commander-in-chief. This criminal perverseness left Washington with only 6,000 men in New Jersey, 7,000 being in New York. Under these conditions nothing remained but to put the Delaware also between himself and the enemy. He therefore retreated rapidly through New Jersey, and on the 8th of December crossed into Pennsylvania with an army reduced to 3,000 by expiry of enlistments. The detachment beyond the Hudson, diminishing daily by the same cause, gradually worked its way to him, its commander luckily being captured on the road. At the time it joined, a few battalions also arrived from Ticonderoga, released by Carleton's retirement to the foot of Champlain. Washington's force on the west bank of the Delaware was thus increased to 6,000 men.

In this series of operations, extending from August 22nd to December 14th, when Howe went into winter-quarters in New Jersey, the British had met with no serious mishaps, beyond the inevitable losses undergone by the assailants of well-chosen positions. Nevertheless, having in view the superiority of numbers, of equipment, and of discipline, and the command of the water, the mere existence of the enemy's army as an organised body, its mere escape, deprives the campaign of the claim to be considered successful. The red ribbon of the Bath probably never was earned more cheaply than by Sir William Howe that year. Had he displayed anything like the energy of his two elder brothers, Washington, with all his vigilance, firmness, and enterprise, could scarcely have brought off the force, vastly diminished but still a living organism, around which American resistance again crystallised and hardened. As it was, within a month he took the offensive, and recovered a great part of New Jersey.

Whatever verdict may be passed upon the merit of the military conduct of affairs, there is no doubt of the value, or of the unflagging energy, of the naval support given. General Howe alludes to it frequently, both in general and specifically; while the Admiral sums up his always guarded and often cumbrous expressions of opinion in these words: " It is incumbent upon me to represent to your Lordships, and I cannot too pointedly express, the unabating perseverance and alacrity with which the several classes of officers and seamen have supported a long attendance and unusual degree of fatigue, consequent of these different movements of the army."

The final achievement of the campaign, and a very important one, was the occupation of Rhode Island and Narragansett Bay by a combined expedition, which left New York on the 1st of December, and on the 8th landed at Newport without opposition. The naval force, consisting of five 50-gun ships, — the *Chatham* (broad pennant), Captain Toby Caulfield ; *Preston* (Commodore W. Hotham), Captain Samuel Uppleby ; *Centurion*, Captain Richard Brathwaite; *Renown*, Captain Francis Banks ; and *Experiment*, Captain James Wallace, and eight smaller vessels, — was commanded by Sir Peter Parker ; the troops, seven thousand in number, by Lieutenant-General Sir Henry Clinton. The immediate effect was to close a haven of privateers, which centred in great numbers around an anchorage that flanked the route of all vessels bound from Europe to New York. The possession of the bay facilitated the control of the neighbouring waters by British ships of war, besides giving them a base, central for coastwise operations, and independent of tidal considerations for entrance or exit. The position was abandoned somewhat precipitately three years later, and Rodney then deplored its loss in the following terms: " The evacuating Rhode Island was the most fatal measure that could possibly have been adopted. It gave up the best and noblest harbour in America, capable of containing the whole Navy of Britain, and where they could in all seasons lie in perfect security ; and from whence squadrons, in forty-eight hours, could blockade the three capital cities of America; namely, Boston, New York, and Philadelphia."

At the end of 1776 began the series of British reverses which characterised the year 1777, and made it the decisive period of the war, because of the effect thus produced upon general public opinion abroad, and especially upon the governments of France and Spain. On the 20th of December, Howe, announcing to the Ministry that he had gone into winter-quarters, wrote : " The chain, I own, is rather too extensive, but I was induced to occupy Burlington to cover the county of Monmouth ; and trusting to the loyalty of the inhabitants, and the strength of the corps placed in the advanced posts, I conclude the troops will be in perfect security." Of this unwarranted security Washington took prompt advantage. On Christmas night a sudden descent, in a blinding snow-storm, upon a British outpost at Trenton, swept off a thousand prisoners ; and although for the moment the American leader again retired behind the Delaware, it was but to resume the offensive four days later. Cornwallis, who was in New York on the point of sailing for England, hurried back to the front, but in vain. A series of quick and well-directed movements recovered the State of New Jersey ; and by the 5th of January the American headquarters, and main body of the army, were established at Morristown in the Jersey hills, the left resting upon the Hudson, thus recovering touch with the strategic centre of interest. This menacing position of the Americans, upon the flank of the line of communications from New York to the Delaware, compelled Howe to contract abruptly the lines he had extended so lightly ; and the campaign he was forced thus reluctantly to reopen closed under a gloom of retreat and disaster, which profoundly and justly impressed not only the opinion of the public, but that of military critics as well. " Of all the great conquests which his Majesty's troops had made in the Jersies," writes Beatson, " Brunswick and Amboy were the only two places of any note which they retained ; and however brilliant their successes had been in the beginning of the campaign, they reaped little advantage from them when the winter advanced, and the contiguity of so vigilant an enemy forced them to perform the severest duty." With deliberate or unconscious humour he then immediately concludes the chronicle of the year with this announcement: " His Majesty was so well pleased with the abilities and activity which General Howe had displayed this campaign, that on the 25th of October he conferred upon him the Most Honourable Order of the Bath."

The leading purpose of the British government in the campaign of 1777 was the same as that with which it had begun in 1776, — the control of the line of the Hudson and Lake Champlain, to be mastered by two expeditions, one starting from each end, and both working towards a common centre at Albany, near the head of navigation of the River. Preliminary difficulties had been cleared away in the previous year, by the destruction of the American flotilla on the Lake, and by the reduction of New York. To both these objects the Navy had contributed conspicuously. It remained to complete the work by resuming the advance from the two bases of operations secured. In 1777 the fortifications on the Hudson were inadequate to stop the progress of a combined naval and military expedition, as was shown in the course of the campaign.

The northern enterprise was intrusted to General Burgoyne. The impossibility of creating a naval force able to contend with that put afloat by Carleton had prevented the Americans from further building. Burgoyne therefore crossed the Lake without opposition to Ticonderoga, before which he appeared on the 2nd of July. A position commanding the works was discovered, and this the Americans had neglected to occupy. It being seized, and a battery established, the fort had to be evacuated. The retreat being made by water, the British Lake Navy, under Captain Skeffington Lutwidge, with whom Nelson had served a few years before in the Arctic seas, had a conspicuous part in the pursuit; severing the boom blockading the river, and joining impetuously in an attack upon the floating material, the flat-boat transports, and the few relics of Arnold's flotilla which had escaped the destruction of the previous year. This affair took place on the 6th of July. From that time forward the progress of the army was mainly by land. The Navy, however, found occupation upon Lake George, where Burgoyne established a dépôt of supplies, although he did not utilise its waterway for the march of the army. A party of seamen under Edward Pellew, still a midshipman, accompanied the advance, and shared the misfortunes of the expedition. It is told that Burgoyne used afterwards to chaff the young naval officer with being the cause of their disaster, because he and his men, by rebuilding a bridge at a critical moment, had made it possible to cross the Hudson. Impeded in its progress by immense difficulties, both natural and imposed by the enemy, the army took twenty days to make twenty miles. On the 30th of July it reached Fort Edward, forty miles from Albany, and there was compelled to stay till the middle of September.

Owing to neglect at the War Office, the peremptory orders to Sir William Howe, to move up the Hudson and make a junction with Burgoyne, were not sent forward.   Consequently, Howe, acting upon the discretionary powers which he possessed already, and swayed by political reasons into which it is not necessary to enter, determined to renew his attempt upon Philadelphia.   A tentative advance into New Jersey, and the consequent manœuvres of Washington, satisfied him that the enterprise by this route was too hazardous.   He therefore embarked 14,000 men, leaving 8,000 with Sir Henry Clinton to hold New York and make diversions in favour of Burgoyne ; and on the 23rd of July sailed from Sandy Hook, escorted by five 64-gun ships, a 50, and ten smaller vessels, under Lord Howe's immediate command. The entire expedition numbered about 280 sail.   Elaborate pains were taken to deceive Washington as to the destination of the armament ; but little was needed to prevent a competent soldier from supposing a design so contrary to sound military principle, having regard to Burgoyne's movements and to the well-understood general purpose of the British ministry.   "Howe's in a manner abandoning Burgoyne is so unaccountable a matter," wrote the American general, " that till I am fully assured of it, I cannot help casting my eyes continually behind me."   He suspected an intention to return upon New York.

On the 31st of July, just as Burgoyne reached Fort Edward, where he stuck fast for six weeks, Howe's armament was off the Capes of the Delaware.   The prevailing summer wind on the American coast is south-south-west, fair for ascending the river ; but information was received that the enemy had obstructed the channel, which, for some distance below Philadelphia, lends itself to such defences.   Therefore, although the free navigation of the river, to the sea, was essential to maintaining a position at Philadelphia, — for trial had shown that the whole army could not assure communications by land with New York, the other sea base, — Howe decided to prosecute his enterprise by way of the Chesapeake, the ascent of which, under all the conditions, could not be seriously impeded.   A fortnight more was consumed in contending against the south-west winds and calms, before the fleet anchored on the 15th of August within the Capes of the Chesapeake ; and yet another week passed before the head of the Bay was reached.   On the 25th the troops landed.   Washington, though so long in doubt, was on hand to dispute the road, but in inferior force ; and Howe had no great difficulty in fighting his way to Philadelphia, which was occupied on the 26th of September.   A week earlier Burgoyne had reached

Stillwater, on the west bank of the Hudson, the utmost point of his progress, where he was still twenty miles from Albany. Three weeks later, surrounded by overwhelming numbers, he was forced to capitulate at Saratoga, whither he had retreated.

Lord Howe held on at the head of the Chesapeake until satisfied that his brother no longer needed him. On the 14th of September he started down the Bay with the squadron and convoy, sending ahead to the Delaware a small division, under Captain Andrew Snape Hamond, to aid the army, if necessary. The winds holding southerly, ten days were required to get to sea; and outside further delay was caused by very heavy weather. The Admiral there quitted the convoy and hastened up river. On the 6th of October he was off Chester, ten miles below Philadelphia. Hamond had already been at work for a week, clearing away obstructions, of which there were two lines, both commanded by batteries on the farther, or Jersey, shore of the Delaware. The lower battery had been carried by troops; and when Howe arrived, Hamond, though meeting lively opposition from the American galleys and fire-rafts, had freed the channel for large ships to approach the upper obstructions. These were defended not only by a work at Red Bank on the Jersey shore, but also, on the other side of the stream, by a fort called Fort Mifflin, on Mud Island.[1] As the channel at this point, for a distance of half a mile, was only two hundred yards wide, and troops could not reach the island, the position was very strong, and it detained the British for six weeks. Fort Mifflin was supported by two floating batteries and a number of galleys. The latter not only fought, offensively and defensively, but maintained the supplies and ammunition of the garrison.

On the 22nd of October, a concerted attack, by the army on the works at Red Bank, and by the Navy on Fort Mifflin, resulted disastrously. The former was repulsed with considerable loss, the officer commanding being killed. The squadron, consisting of a 64, the *Augusta*, Captain Francis Reynolds, later Earl of Ducie, three frigates, and a sloop, the *Merlin*, 16, Commander Samuel Reeve, went into action with Mud Island at the same time; but, the channel having shifted, owing possibly to the obstructions, the *Augusta* and the sloop grounded, and could not be floated that day. On the 23rd the Americans concentrated upon the two their batteries, galleys, and fire-rafts; but, in the midst of the preparations

[1] Sometimes called Fort Island; it was just below the mouth of the Schuylkill.

for lightening her, the *Augusta* took fire and blew up. The *Merlin* was then set on fire and abandoned.

So long as this obstacle remained, all supplies for the army had to be carried by boats to the shore, and transported considerable distances by land. As direct attacks had proved unavailing, more deliberate measures were adopted. The army built batteries, and the Navy sent ashore guns to mount in them; but the decisive blow to Mud Island was given by a small armed ship, the *Vigilant*, 20, Lieutenant Hugh Cloberry Christian, which was successfully piloted through a channel on the west side of the river, and reached the rear of the work, towing with her a floating battery with three 24-pounders. This was on the 15th of November. That same night the Americans abandoned Fort Mifflin. Their loss, Beatson says, amounted to near 400 killed and wounded; that of the British to 43. If this be correct, it should have established the invincibility of men who under such prodigious disparity of suffering could maintain their position so tenaciously. After the loss of Mud Island, Red Bank could not be held to advantage, and it was evacuated on the 21st, when an attack was imminent. The American vessels retreated up the river; but they were cornered, and of course ultimately were destroyed. The obstructions were thus removed, and the British communications by the line of the Delaware were established.

While these things were passing, Howe's triumph was marred by the news of Burgoyne's surrender on the 17th of October. For this he could not but feel that the home government must consider him largely responsible; for in the Chesapeake, too late to retrieve his false step, he had received a letter from the Minister, saying that, whatever else he undertook, support to Burgoyne was the great object to be kept in view.

During the operations round Philadelphia, Sir Henry Clinton in New York had done enough to show what strong probabilities of success would have attended an advance up the Hudson, by the 20,000 men whom Howe could have taken with him. Starting on the 3rd of October with 3,000 troops, accompanied by a small naval division of frigates, Clinton in a week had reached West Point, fifty miles up the river. The American fortifications along the way were captured, defences levelled, stores and shipping burned; while an insignificant detachment, with the light vessels, went fifty miles further up, and there destroyed more military stores without encountering any resistance worth mentioning. Certainly, had Howe taken the same line of operations, he would have had to reckon with Washington's ten thousand men which confronted him on the march to Philadelphia; but his flank would have been covered, up to Albany, by a navigable stream, on either side of which he could operate by that flying bridge which the presence and control of the Navy continually constituted. Save the fortifications, which Clinton easily carried, there was no threat to his communications or to his flank, such as the hill country of New Jersey had offered and Washington had skilfully utilised.

The campaign of 1777 thus ended for the British with a conspicuous disaster, and with an apparent success which was as disastrous as a failure. At its close they held Narragansett Bay, the city and harbour of New York, and the city of Philadelphia. The first was an admirable naval base, especially for sailing ships, for the reasons given by Rodney. The second was then, as it is now, the greatest military position on the Atlantic coast of the United States ; and although the two could not communicate by land, they did support each other as naval stations in a war essentially dependent upon maritime power. Philadelphia served no purpose but to divide and distract British enterprise. Absolutely dependent for maintenance upon the sea, the forces in it and in New York could not co-operate ; they could not even unite except by sea. When Clinton relieved Howe as commander-in-chief, though less than a hundred miles away by land, he had to take a voyage of over two hundred miles, half of it up a difficult river, to reach his station; and troops were transferred by the same tedious process. In consequence of these conditions, the place had to be abandoned the instant that war with France made control of the sea even doubtful. The British held it for less than nine months.

During 1777 a number of raids were made by combined British land and sea forces, for the purpose of destroying American dépôts and other resources. Taken together, such operations are subsidiary to, and aid, the great object of interrupting or harassing the communications of an enemy. In so far, they have a standing place among the major operations of war ; but taken singly they cannot be so reckoned, and the fact, therefore, is simply noted, without going into details. It may be remarked, however, that in them, although the scale was smaller, the Navy played the same part that it now does in the many expeditions and small wars undertaken by Great Britain in various parts of the world; the same that it did in the Peninsular War. The land force depended upon the water, and the water was controlled by the Navy.

The events of 1777 satisfied the French government that the Americans had strength and skill sufficient seriously to embarrass Great Britain, and that the moment, therefore, was opportune for taking steps which scarcely could fail to cause war. On the 6th of February, 1778, France concluded with the United States an open treaty of amity and commerce; and at the same time a second secret treaty, acknowledging the independence of the late Colonies, and contracting with them a defensive alliance. On the 13th of March, the French Ambassador in London communicated the open treaty to the British government, with the remark that " the United States were in full possession of the independence proclaimed by their declaration of July 4th, 1776." Great Britain at once recalled her Ambassador, and both countries prepared for war, although no declaration was issued. On the 13th of April, a French fleet of twelve ships of the line and five frigates, under the command of the Count d'Estaing,[1] sailed from Toulon for the American coast. It was destined to Delaware Bay, hoping to intercept Howe's squadron. D'Estaing was directed to begin hostilities when forty leagues west of Gibraltar.

The British ministry was not insensible of the danger, the imminence of which had been felt during the previous year; but it had not got ready betimes, owing possibly to confident expectations of success from the campaign of 1777. The ships, in point of numbers and equipment, were not as far forward as the Admiralty had represented; and difficulty, amounting for the moment to impossibility, was experienced in manning them. The vessels of the Channel fleet had to be robbed of both crews and stores to compose a proper reinforcement for America. Moreover, the destination of the Toulon squadron was unknown, the French government having given out that it was bound to Brest, where over twenty other ships of the line were in an advanced state of preparation. Not until the 5th of June, when d'Estaing was already eight weeks out, was certain news brought by a frigate, which had watched his fleet after it

---

[1] Charles H., Comte d'Estaing. Born, 1729. Served in India under Lally Tollendal, 1758. After having been taken prisoner at Madras in 1759, exchanged into the navy. Commanded in North America, 1778–80. Guillotined, 1794.

had passed Gibraltar, and which had accompanied it into the Atlantic
ninety leagues west of the Straits.   The reinforcement for America
was then permitted to depart.   On the 9th of June, thirteen ships of
the line sailed for New York under the command of Vice-Admiral
the Hon. John Byron.[1]

These delays occasioned a singular and striking illustration of
the ill effects upon commerce of inadequate preparation for manning
the fleet. A considerable number of West India ships, with stores
absolutely necessary for the preservation of the islands, waited at
Portsmouth for convoy for upwards of three months, while the
whole fleet, of eighty sail, was detained for five weeks after it had
assembled; " and, although the wind came fair on the 19th of May,
it did not sail till the 26th, owing to the convoying ships, the *Boyne*
and the *Ruby*, not being ready."   Forty-five owners and masters
signed a letter to the Admiralty, stating these facts. " The convoy,"
they said, "was appointed to sail April 10th."   Many ships had
been ready as early as February. " Is not this shameful usage, my
Lords, thus to deceive the public in general?   There are two hundred ships loaded with provisions, etc., waiting at Spithead these
three months.   The average expense of each ship amounts to £150
monthly, so that the expense of the whole West India fleet since
February amounts to £90,000."

The West Indies before the war had depended chiefly upon their
fellow Colonies on the American continent for provisions, as well as

[1] List of the fleet sent to North America under Vice-Admiral Byron: —

Princess Royal	90 {	Vice-Admiral the Hon. J. Byron (B.). Captain William Blair.
Royal Oak	74 {	Rear-Admiral Hyde Parker (B.). Captain Henry Francis Evans.
Invincible	74 {	Commodore John Evans. Captain Anthony Parrey.
Bedford	74	Captain Edmund Affleck.
Albion	74	Captain George Bowyer.
Conqueror	74	Captain Thomas Graves.
Cornwall	74	Captain Timothy Edwards.
Culloden	74	Captain George Balfour.
Fame	74	Captain Stephen Colby.
Grafton	74	Captain Thomas Wilkinson.
Russell	74	Captain Francis Samuel Drake.
Sultan	74	Captain John Wheelock.
Monmouth	64	Captain Thomas Collingwood.
Guadaloupe	28	Captain Hugh Robinson.

Beatson, vi. 106 (corrected).   W. L. C.

for other prime necessaries.   Not only were these cut off as an incident of the war, entailing great embarrassment and suffering, which
elicited vehement appeals from the planter community to the home
government, but the American privateers preyed heavily upon the
commerce of the islands, whose industries were thus smitten root
and branch, import and export.   In 1776, salt food for whites and
negroes had risen from 50 to 100 per cent, and corn, the chief support of the slaves, — the labouring class, — by 400 per cent.   At the
same time sugar had fallen from 25 to 40 per cent in price, rum over
37 per cent.   The words "starvation" and "famine" were freely
used in these representations, which were repeated in 1778.   Insur-
ance rose to 23 per cent; and this, with actual losses by capture,[1]
and by cessation of American trade, with consequent fall of prices,
was estimated to give a total loss of £66 upon every £100 earned
before the war.   Yet, with all this, the outward West India fleet
in 1778 waited six weeks, April 10th–May 26th, for convoy.   Immediately after it got away, a rigorous embargo was laid upon all shipping in British ports, that their crews might be impressed to man the
Channel fleet.   Market-boats, even, were not allowed to pass between Portsmouth and the Isle of Wight.

Three days after Byron had sailed, Admiral the Hon. Augustus
Keppel also put to sea with twenty-one ships of the line, to cruise
off Brest.   His instructions were to prevent the junction of the

---

[1] The Secretary of Lloyd's, for the purposes of this work, has been so good as to
cause to be specially compiled a summary of the losses and captures during the period
1775–1783.   This, so far as it deals with merchantmen and privateers, gives the following results.

	BRITISH VESSELS.				ENEMY'S VESSELS.			
	Merchantmen.		Privateers.		Merchantmen.		Privateers.	
	Taken.*	Re-taken or Ransomed.	Taken.*	Re-taken or Ransomed.	Taken.*	Re-taken or Ransomed.	Taken.*	Re-taken or Ransomed.
1775 . .	—	—	—	—	—	—	—	—
1776 . .	229	51	—	—	19	—	6	—
1777 . .	331	52	—	—	51	1	18	—
1778 . .	359	87	5	—	232	5	16	—
1779 . .	487	106	29	5	238	5	31	—
1780 . .	581	260	15	2	203	3	34	1
1781 . .	587	211	38	6	277	10	40	—
1782 . .	415	99	1	—	104	1	68	—
1783 . .	98	13	1	1	11	2	3	—

* Including those re-taken or ransomed.

W. L. C.

Toulon and Brest divisions, attacking either that he might meet. On the 17th of June, two French frigates were sighted. In order that they might not report his force or his movements, the British Admiral sent two of his own frigates, with the request that they would speak him. One, the *Belle Poule*, 36, refused; and an engagement followed between her and the British ship, the *Arethusa*, 32, Captain Samuel Marshall.[1] Although both Keppel's and d'Estaing's orders prescribed acts of hostility, no formal war yet existed. The King of France subsequently declared that this occurrence fixed the date of the war's beginning.

Byron had a very tempestuous passage, with adverse winds, by which his vessels were scattered and damaged. On the 18th of August, sixty-seven days from Plymouth, the flagship arrived off the south coast of Long Island, ninety miles east of New York, without one of the fleet in company. There twelve ships were seen at anchor to leeward (north), nine or ten miles distant, having jury masts, and showing other signs of disability. The British vessel approached near enough to recognise them as French. They were d'Estaing's squadron, crippled by a very heavy gale, in which Howe's force had also suffered, though to a less extent. As he was alone, and ignorant of existing conditions, Byron thought it inexpedient to continue on for either New York or Narragansett Bay. The wind being southerly, he steered for Halifax, which he reached August 26th. Some of his ships also entered there. A very few had already succeeded in joining Howe in New York, being fortunate enough to escape the enemy.

So far as help from England went, Lord Howe would have been crushed long before this. He owed his safety partly to his own celerity, partly to the delays of his opponent. Early in May he received advices from home, which convinced him that a sudden and rapid abandonment of Philadelphia and of Delaware Bay might become necessary. He therefore concentrated his ships of the line from New York and Narragansett at the mouth of the Bay, while the transports embarked all stores, except those needed for a fortnight's supply of the army in a hostile country. The threatening contingency of a superior enemy's appearing off the coast might, and did, make it imperative not to risk the troops at sea, but to choose instead the alternative of a ninety-mile march through New Jersey, which a year before had been rejected as too hazardous for an even larger force.

[1] For an account of the single-ship actions of the war, see Chap. XXXII.

Thus prepared, no time was lost when the evacuation became neces-sary. Sir William Howe, who had been relieved on the 24th of May by Sir Henry Clinton, escaped the humiliation of giving up his dearly bought conquest. On the 18th of June the British troops, 12,000 in number, were ferried across the Delaware, under the super-vision of the Navy, and began their hazardous march to New York. The next day the transports began to move down the river ; but, owing to the difficult navigation, head winds, and calms, they did not get to sea until the 28th of June. On the 8th of July, ten days too late, d'Estaing anchored in the mouth of the Delaware. " Had a passage of even ordinary length taken place," wrote Washington, " Lord Howe with the British ships of war and all the transports in the river Delaware must inevitably have fallen ; and Sir Henry Clinton must have had better luck than is commonly dispensed to men of his profession under such circumstances, if he and his troops had not shared at least the fate of Burgoyne."

Had Howe's fleet been intercepted, there would have been no naval defence for New York ; the French fleet would have sur-mounted the difficulties of the harbour bar at its ease ; and Clinton, caught between it and the American army, must have surrendered. Howe's arrival obviated this immediate danger ; but much still needed to be done, or the end would be postponed only, not averted. A fair wind carried the fleet and the whole convoy from the Dela-ware to Sandy Hook in forty-eight hours. On the morning of the 29th, as Howe was approaching his port, he spoke a packet from England, which not only brought definite news of d'Estaing's sailing, but also reported that she herself had fallen in with him to the south-ward, not very far from the American coast, and had been chased by his ships. His appearance off New York, therefore, was imminent.

Howe's measures were prompt and thorough, as became his great reputation. To watch for d'Estaing's approach, a body of cruisers was despatched, numerous enough for some to bring frequent word of his movements, while others kept touch with him. The ships at New York were ordered down to Sandy Hook, where the defence of the entrance was to be made. Clinton, who had been hard pressed by Washington throughout his march, arrived on the 30th of June — the day after Howe himself — on the heights of Navesink, on the sea-coast, just south of Sandy Hook. During the previous winter the sea had made a breach between the heights and the Hook, convert-ing the latter into an island. Across this inlet the Navy threw a

bridge of boats, by which the army on the 5th of July passed to the
Hook, and thence was conveyed to the city.

On the same day the French fleet was sighted off the coast of
Virginia by a cruiser, which reached Howe on the 7th; and two days
later another brought word that the enemy had anchored on the 8th
off the Delaware.   There d'Estaing again tarried for two days, which
were diligently improved by the British Admiral, who at the same
time sent off despatches to warn Byron, of whose coming he now had
heard.   Despite all his energy, his preparations still were far from
complete, when on the morning of the 11th a third vessel arrived,
announcing that the French were approaching.   That evening they
anchored outside, four miles south of Sandy Hook.   Howe, who
during all those days was indefatigable, not only in planning but also
in personal supervision of details, hastened at once to place his vessels according to the disposition which he had determined, and which
he had carefully explained to his captains, thus insuring an intelligent co-operation on their part.

The narrow arm of land called Sandy Hook projects in a northerly direction from the New Jersey coast, and covers the lower bay
of New York on the south side.   The main ship-channel, then as
now, ran nearly east and west, at right angles to the Hook and close
to its northern end.   Beyond the channel, to the north, there was no
solid ground for fortification within the cannon range of that day.
Therefore such guns as could be mounted on shore, five in number,
were placed in battery at the end of the Hook.   These formed the
right flank of the defence, which was continued thence to the westward by a line of seven ships, skirting the southern edge of the
channel.   As the approach of the French, if they attacked, must be
with an easterly wind and a rising tide, the ships were placed with
that expectation; and in such wise that, riding with their heads to
the eastward, each successive one, from van to rear, lay a little outside — north — of her next ahead.   The object of this indented formation was that each ship might bring her broadside to bear east, and
yet fire clear of those to the east of her.   In order to effect this concentration of all the batteries in an easterly direction, which would
rake the approach of the enemy, a spring was run from the outer, or
port quarter of every ship, except the leader.[1]   These springs were

---

[1] The leader, the *Leviathan*, Commander Joseph Tathwell, was excepted, evidently
because she lay under the Hook, and her guns could not bear down channel.   She
was not a fighting ship of the squadron, but an armed storeship, although originally

not taken to the bow cable or anchor, as was often done, but to anchors of their own, placed broad off the port bows. If, then, the enemy attacked, the ships, by simply keeping fast the springs and veering the cables, would swing with their broadsides to the east. If the enemy, which had no bow fire, survived his punishment, and succeeded in advancing abreast the line, it was necessary only to keep fast the cables and let go the springs; the ships would swing head again to the east, and the broadsides would once more bear across the channel, instead of along it. These careful arrangements were subject, of course, to the mischance of shot cutting away cables or springs; but this was more than offset by the probable injury to the enemy's spars and rigging, before he could use his batteries at all.

Such was the main defence arranged by Howe; with which New York stood or fell. In the line were five sixty-fours, one fifty, and an armed storeship. An advanced line, of one fifty with two smaller vessels, was placed just inside the bar — two or three miles outside the Hook — to rake the enemy as he crossed, retiring as he approached; and four galleys, forming a second line, were also stationed for the same purpose, across the channel, abreast of the Hook. The retreat of these was secure into the shoal water, where they could not be followed. One sixty-four and some frigates were held as a reserve, inside the main line, to act as occasion might require. The total available force was, six sixty-fours,[1] three fifties, and six frigates. D'Estaing's fleet, in detail, consisted of one ninety-gun ship, one eighty, six seventy-fours, three sixty-fours, and one fifty. Great as was this discrepancy between the opponents, it was counterbalanced largely by Howe's skilful dispositions, which his enemy could not circum-

a ship of war, and therefore by her thickness of side better fitted for defence than an ordinary merchant vessel. Placing her seems to have been an afterthought, to close the gap in the line, and prevent even the possibility of the enemy's ships turning in there and doubling on the van. Thus Howe avoided the fatal oversight made by Brueys twenty years later, in Aboukir Bay.

[1] These were : —

Eagle	64	Vice-Admiral Lord Howe (R.).
		Captain Henry Duncan (1st).
		Captain Roger Curtis (2nd).
Trident	64	Commodore John Elliot.
		Captain Anthony James Pye Molloy.
Somerset	64	Captain George Ourry.
Nonsuch	64	Captain Walter Griffith.
Ardent	64	Captain George Keppel.
St. Albans	64	Captain Richard Onslow.

W. L. C.

vent. If the latter once got alongside, there was little hope for the
British ; but it was impossible to evade the primary necessity of
undergoing a raking fire, without reply, from the extreme range of
their cannon up to the moment of closing. The stake, however, was
great, and the apparent odds stirred to the bottom the fighting blood
of the British seamen. The ships of war being short-handed, Howe
called for volunteers from the transports. Such numbers came forward
that the agents of the vessels scarcely could keep a watch on board ;
and many whose names were not on the lists concealed themselves in
the boats which carried their companions to the fighting ships. The
masters and mates of merchantmen in the harbour in like manner
offered their services, taking their stations at the guns. Others
cruised off the coast in small boats, to warn off approaching vessels ;
many of which nevertheless fell into the enemy's hands.

Meanwhile d'Estaing was in communication with Washington,
one of whose aides-de-camp visited his flagship. A number of New
York pilots also were sent. When these learned the draught of the
heavier French ships, they declared that it was impossible to take
them in ; that there was on the bar only twenty-three feet at high-
water. Had that been really the case, Howe would not have needed
to make the preparations for defence that were visible to thousands
of eyes on sea and on shore ; but d'Estaing, though personally brave
as a lion, was timid in his profession, which he had entered very late
and without serving in the lower grades. The assurances of the
pilots were accepted after an examination by a lieutenant of the
flagship, who could find nothing deeper than twenty-two feet.[1] Fortune's favours are thrown away, as though in mockery, on the incompetent or the irresolute. On the 22nd of July a fresh north-east
wind concurred with a spring tide to give the highest possible water
on the bar.

" At eight o'clock," wrote an eye-witness in the British fleet, " d'Estaing with
all his squadron appeared under way. He kept working to windward, as if to gain
a proper position for crossing the bar by the time the tide should serve. The wind
could not be more favourable for such a design ; it blew from the exact point from
which he could attack us to the greatest advantage. The spring tides were at the
highest, and that afternoon thirty feet on the bar. We consequently expected the
hottest day that had ever been fought between the two nations. On our side all
was at stake. Had the men-of-war been defeated, the fleet of transports and

---

[1] A letter to the Admiralty, dated October 8th, 1779, from Vice-Admiral Marriot
Arbuthnot, then commander-in-chief at New York, states that " at spring tides there
is generally thirty feet of water on the bar at high water."

victuallers must have been destroyed, and the army, of course, have fallen with us. D'Estaing, however, had not spirit equal to the risk ; at three o'clock we saw him bear off to the southward, and in a few hours he was out of sight."

Four days later, Howe, reporting these occurrences, wrote : " The weather having been favourable the last three days for forcing entrance to this port, I conclude the French commander has desisted." It is clear that the experienced British admiral did not recognise the impossibility of success for the enemy.

After the demonstration of the 22nd, d'Estaing stood to the southward, with the wind at east.   The British advice-boats brought back word that they had kept company with him as far south as the Capes of the Delaware, and there had left him ninety miles from land.   When their departure freed him from observation, he turned, and made for Narragansett Bay, an attack on which, in support of an American land force, had been concerted between him and Washington.   On the 29th he anchored three miles south of Rhode Island, and there awaited a suitable moment for forcing the entrance.

Narragansett Bay contains several islands.   The two largest, near the sea, are Rhode Island and Conanicut, the latter being the more westerly.   Their general direction, as that of the Bay itself, is north and south ; and by them the entrance is divided into three passages.   Of these, the eastern, called Seakonnet, is not navigable above Rhode Island.   The central, which is the main channel, is joined by the western above Conanicut, and thus the two lead to the upper Bay.   The town of Newport is on the west side of Rhode Island, four miles from the main entrance.

On the 30th of July, the day after the French fleet had arrived, two of its ships of the line, under command of the afterwards celebrated Suffren, went up the western channel, anchoring within it near the south end of Conanicut.   One of them, as she passed, was hulled twice by the British batteries.   At the same time, two frigates and a corvette entered Seakonnet ; whereupon the British abandoned and burned a sloop of war, the *Kingfisher*, 16, and some galleys there stationed.   The British general, Sir Robert Pigot, now withdrew his detachments from Conanicut, disabling the guns, and concentrated the bulk of his force in the southern part of Rhode Island and about Newport.   Goat Island, which covers the inner harbour of the town, was still occupied, the main channel being commanded by its batteries, as well as by those to the north and south of it upon Rhode Island.   On the 5th of August, Suffren's two ships got under way, sailed through the western passage, and anchored in the main channel, north of Conanicut; their former positions being taken by two other ships of the line.[1] The senior British naval officer, Captain John Brisbane, seeing retreat cut off in both directions, now destroyed those ships of war[2] which could not enter the inner harbour, sinking two between Goat and Rhode Islands, to prevent any enemy passing there. Five transports also were sunk north of Goat Island, between it and Coaster's Harbour, to protect the inside anchorage in that direction. These preliminary operations thus cost the British five frigates and two sloops, besides some galleys. Guns and ammunition taken from them went to increase the defences; and their officers and crews, over a thousand in number, served in the fortifications.

On the 8th of August the eight remaining French ships of the line ran the batteries on Rhode and Goat Islands, anchoring above the latter, between it and Conanicut, and were rejoined there by the four previously detached to the western passage. Ten thousand American troops having by this time crossed from the mainland to the northern part of Rhode Island, d'Estaing immediately landed four thousand soldiers and seamen from the fleet upon Conanicut, for a preliminary organisation; after which they also were to pass to Rhode Island and join in the operations. For the moment, therefore, the British garrison, numbering probably six thousand men,[3] was hemmed in by vastly superior forces, by land and by water. Its embarrassment, however, did not last long. On the following morning Lord Howe appeared, and anchored off Point Judith, seven miles from the entrance to the Bay, and twelve from the position then occupied by the French fleet. He brought a stronger force than he had been able to gather for the defence of New York, having now one seventy-four, seven sixty-fours, and five fifties, besides several smaller vessels; but he still was greatly inferior to his opponent, by any rational mode of naval reckoning.

Howe's energies in New York had not been confined to preparations for resisting the entrance of the enemy, nor did they cease with the latter's departure. When he first arrived there from Phila-

---

[1] These four ships were among the smallest of the fleet, being one 74, two 64's, and a 50. D'Estaing very properly reserved his heaviest ships to force the main channel.

[2] *Flora*, 32 ; *Juno*, 32 ; *Lark*, 32 ; *Orpheus*, 32; *Falcon*, 16.

[3] I have not been able to find an exact statement of the number ; Beatson gives eight regiments, with a reinforcement of five battalions.

delphia, he had hastened to get his ships ready for sea, a pre-occupation which somewhat, but not unduly, delayed their taking their positions at Sandy Hook. Two, for instance, had been at the watering-place when the approach of the French was signalled. Owing to this diligence, no time was lost by his fault when the new destination of the enemy was made known to him, on the 28th or 29th of July, by the arrival of the *Raisonnable*, 64,[1] Captain Thomas Fitzherbert, from Halifax. This ship narrowly escaped the French fleet, having passed it on the evening of the 27th, steering for Rhode Island.   The *Renown*, 50, Captain George Dawson (Act'g), which on the 26th had reached New York from the West Indies, had a similar close shave, having passed unnoticed through the rear of the enemy the night before. Besides these two, Howe was joined also by the *Centurion*, 50, Captain Richard Brathwaite, from Halifax, and by the *Cornwall*, 74, Captain Timothy Edwards ; the latter, which crossed the bar on the 30th, being the first of Byron's fleet to reach New York. The three others belonged to Howe's own squadron. For the two Halifax ships which helped to make this most welcome reinforcement, the Admiral was indebted to the diligence of the officer there commanding, who hurried them away as soon as he learned of d'Estaing's appearance on the coast. The opportuneness of their arrival attracted notice.   " Had they appeared a few days sooner," says a contemporary narrative, " either they must have been prevented from forming a junction with our squadron, and forced again to sea, or we should have had the mortification to see them increase the triumph of our enemy."

On the 1st of August, forty-eight hours after the *Cornwall* had come in from a stormy passage of fifty-two days, the squadron was ready for sea, and Howe attempted to sail ; but the wind hauled foul immediately after the signal to weigh had been made. It did not become fair at the hour of high water, when alone heavy ships could cross the bar, until the morning of the 6th. " Rhode Island was of such importance," says the narrator already quoted, " *and the fate of so large a portion of the British army as formed the garrison was of such infinite consequence to the general cause,* that it was imagined the Admiral would not lose a moment in making some attempt for their relief." He had learned of the detachments made from the French fleet, and hoped that some advantage might be taken of this division.

---

[1] It may be interesting to recall that this was the ship on the books of which Nelson's name first was borne in the navy, in 1771.

In short, he went, as was proper and incumbent on him in such critical circumstances, to take a great risk, in hope of a favourable chance offering. On the 9th, as before stated, he anchored off Point Judith, and opened communications with the garrison, from which he learned the events that had so far occurred, and also that the enemy was well provided with craft of all kinds to make a descent upon any part of the Island.

As de Grasse at Yorktown, when rumour announced the approach of a British fleet, was deterred only by the most urgent appeals of Washington from abandoning his control of the Chesapeake, essential to the capture of Cornwallis, so now d'Estaing, in Narragansett Bay, was unwilling to keep his place, in face of Howe's greatly inferior squadron.[1] The influence exerted upon these two admirals by the mere approach of a hostile fleet, when decisive advantages depended upon their holding their ground, may be cited plausibly in support of the most extreme view of the effect of a " fleet in being ; " but the instances also, when the conditions are analysed, will suggest the question : Is such effect always legitimate, inherent in the existence of the fleet itself, or does it not depend often upon the characteristics of the man affected? The contemporary British narrative of these events in Narragansett Bay, after reciting the various obstacles and the inferiority of the British squadron, says : " The most skilful officers were therefore of opinion that the Vice-Admiral could not risk an attack ; and it appears by his Lordship's public letter that this was also his own opinion : under such circumstances, he judged it was impracticable to afford the General any essential relief." In both these instances, the admirals concerned were impelled to sacrifice the almost certain capture, not of a mere position, but of a decisive part of the enemy's organised forces, by the mere contingency of action, the moral effect, of a fleet greatly inferior to their own, and which in neither case would have attacked, as things stood. What does this prove?

Immediately upon Howe's appearance, the French seamen who had landed the day before on Conanicut were recalled to their ships. The next morning, at 7 A.M., the wind came out strong at northeast, which is exceptional at that season. D'Estaing at once put to sea, cutting the cables in his haste. In two hours he was outside,

---

[1] Troude attributes d'Estaing's sortie to a sense of the insecurity of his position; Lapeyrouse Bonfils, to a desire for contest. Chevalier dwells upon the exposure of the situation.

steering for the enemy. Howe, of course, retired at once; his inferiority [1] did not permit an engagement except on his own terms. To insure these, he needed the weather-gage, the offensive position of that day, which he expected, by keeping south, to gain, when the usual wind from that quarter should set in. The French Admiral had the same object, hoping to crush his agile opponent; and, as the sea breeze did not make that day, he succeeded in keeping the advantage with which he had started, despite Howe's skill. At nightfall, and during the night, both fleets steered to the southward,

[1] Howe's fleet consisted of : —

SHIPS.	GUNS.	MEN.	COMMANDERS.
Eagle	64	522	Vice-Adm. Lord Howe (R.). Capt. Henry Duncan (1st). Capt. Roger Curtis (2nd).
Trident	64	517	Com. John Elliot. Capt. Anthony James Pye Molloy.
Preston	50	367	Com. William Hotham. Capt. Samuel Uppleby
Cornwall	74	600	Capt. Timothy Edwards.
Nonsuch	64	500	Capt. Walter Griffith.
Raisonnable	64	500	Capt. Thomas Fitzherbert.
Somerset	64	500	Capt. George Ourry.
St. Albans	64	500	Capt. Richard Onslow.
Ardent	64	500	Capt. George Keppel.
Centurion	50	350	Capt. Richard Brathwaite.
Experiment	50	350	Capt. Sir James Wallace.
Isis	50	350	Capt. John Rayner.
Renown	50	350	Capt. George Dawson (Act'g).
Phœnix	44	280	Capt. Hyde Parker (2).
Roebuck	44	280	Capt. Andrew Snape Hamond.
Venus	36	240	Capt. William Peere Williams.
Richmond	32	220	Capt. John Lewis Gidoin.
Pearl	32	220	Capt. John Linzee.
Apollo	32	220	Capt. Philemon Pownall.
Sphinx	20	160	Capt. Alexander Græme.
Nautilus	16	125	Com. John Becher.
Vigilant (a. s.) . . .	20	150	Com. Hugh Cloberry Christian.
Strombolo (f. s.) . . .		45	Com. Peter Aplin.
Sulphur (f. s.)		45	Com. James Watt.
Volcano (f. s.)		45	Com. William Henry King O'Hara.
Thunder (bmb.) . . .	8	80	Com. James Gambier (2).
Carcass (bmb.)	8	80	Lieut. Edward Edwards. (Act'g).
Philadelphia *			Lieut. —— Paterson.
Hussar *			Lieut. Sir James Barclay, Bart.
Ferret *			Lieut. Edward (?) O'Bryen.
Cornwallis *			Lieut. —— Spry.

* Galleys.

on the port tack, with the wind variable at east. At daybreak of
the 11th they occupied nearly the same relative positions, — the
French north-east to north from the British, but somewhat more
distant than the night before, having apparently kept closer to the
wind, which by this had steadied at east-north-east. (See Plan: aa,
aa.)

Howe now shifted his flag from the *Eagle*, 64, to the *Apollo*, 32,
and placed himself between the two fleets, the better to decide the
movements of his own. Finding it impossible to gain the weather-
gage, and unwilling, probably, to be drawn too far from Rhode
Island, he formed his line on the other tack, heads to the northward.

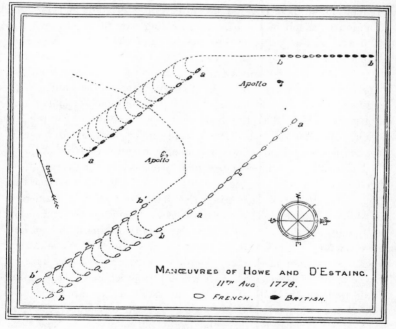

MANŒUVRES OF HOWE AND D'ESTAING.

The French continued on the port tack, under short canvas, heading
to the southward and eastward, so that their bearing changed from
east-north-east — directly to windward — at 6 A.M., to south-south-east
at 4 P.M., which would be nearly astern of the British. (See Plan:
bb, bb.) At this time their van was estimated by Howe to be two
or three miles from the British rear, and, according to his reading of

their manœuvres, d'Estaing began to form his line for the same tack as the British, with a view of "engaging the British squadron to leeward," whereby he would obtain over it the advantage of using the lower-deck guns, the wind and sea having become much heavier. As the French admiral, in this new disposition, had put his heaviest ships in the van, and his line was nearly in the wake of the British, Howe inferred an attack upon his rear. (See Plan: bb.) He therefore ordered his heaviest ship, the *Cornwall*, 74, to go there from the centre, exchanging places with the *Centurion*, 50, and at the same time signalled the fleet to close *to the centre*, — a detail worth remembering in view of Rodney's frustrated manœuvre of April 17th, 1780. It now remained simply to await firmly the moment when the French should have covered the intervening ground, and brought to action so much of his rear as d'Estaing saw fit to engage; the conditions of the sea favouring the speed of the bulkier ships that composed the hostile fleet. The latter, however, soon abandoned the attempt, and "bore away to the southward, apparently from the state of the weather, which, by the wind freshening much, with frequent rain, was now rendered very unfavourable for engaging." It may be added that the hour was very late for beginning an action. At sundown the British were under close-reefed topsails, and the sea such that Howe was unable to return to the *Eagle*.

The wind now increased to great violence, and a severe storm raged on the coast until the evening of the 13th, throwing the two fleets into confusion, scattering the ships, and causing numerous disasters. The *Apollo* lost her foremast, and sprung the mainmast, on the night of the 12th. The next day only two ships of the line and three smaller vessels were in sight of the Admiral. The latter, when the weather moderated, went on board the *Phœnix*, 44, and thence to the *Centurion*, 50, with which he "proceeded to the southward, and on the 15th discovered ten sail of the French squadron, some at anchor in the sea, about twenty-five leagues east from Cape May." [1] Leaving there the *Centurion*, to direct to New York any of Byron's ships that might come on the coast, he departed thither himself also, and on the evening of the 17th rejoined the squadron off Sandy Hook, the appointed rendezvous. Many injuries had been received by the various ships, but they were mostly of a minor character; and on· the 22nd the fleet again put to sea in search of the enemy.

[1] At the mouth of Delaware Bay.

The French had suffered much more severely. The flagship *Languedoc*, 90, had carried away her bowsprit, all her lower masts followed it overboard, and her tiller also was broken, rendering the rudder unserviceable. The *Marseillais*, 74, lost her foremast and bowsprit. In the dispersal of the two fleets that followed the gale, each of these crippled vessels, on the evening of the 13th, encountered singly a British 50-gun ship; the *Languedoc* being attacked by the *Renown*, Captain George Dawson (Act'g), and the *Marseillais* by the *Preston*, Commodore W. Hotham, Captain Samuel Uppleby. The conditions in each instance were distinctly favourable to the smaller combatant; but both unfortunately withdrew at nightfall, making the mistake of postponing to the morrow a chance which they had no certainty would exist after to-day. When morning dawned, other French ships appeared, and the opportunity passed away. The *Isis*, 50, Captain John Rayner, also was chased and overtaken by the *César*, 74. In the action which ensued, the French ship's wheel was shot away, and she retired; — two other British vessels, one of the line, being in sight. The latter are not mentioned in the British accounts, and both sides claimed the advantage in this drawn action. The French captain lost an arm.

After making temporary repairs, at the anchorage where Howe saw them on the 15th of August, the French fleet had proceeded again towards Newport. It was in the course of this passage that they were seen by Byron's flagship[1] on the 18th, to the southward of Long Island. The *Experiment*, 50, Captain Sir James Wallace, which Howe had sent to reconnoitre Narragansett Bay, was chased by them into Long Island Sound, and only reached New York by the East River; being the first ship of the line or 50-gun ship that ever passed through Hell Gate. On the 20th d'Estaing communicated with General Sullivan, the commander of the American land forces on Rhode Island; but it was only to tell him that in his own opinion, and in that of a council of war, the condition of the squadron necessitated going to Boston to refit. Whatever may be thought of the propriety of this decision, its seriousness can be best understood from the report sent by Pigot to Howe. " The rebels had advanced their batteries within fifteen hundred yards of the British works. He was under no apprehensions from any of their attempts in front; but, should the French fleet come in, it would make an alarming change. Troops might be landed and advanced in his

rear; and in that case he could not answer for the consequences."
Disregarding Sullivan's entreaties that he would remain, d'Estaing
sailed next day for Boston, and reached it on August 28th. On the
31st the indefatigable Howe came in sight; but the French had
worked actively in the three days. Forty-nine guns, 18 and 24-
pounders, with six mortars, were already in position covering the
anchorage; and " the French squadron, far from fearing an attack,
desired it eagerly." [1] The withdrawal of the fleet was followed by
that of the American troops before Newport.

Howe had quitted New York the instant he heard of d'Estaing's
reappearance off Rhode Island. He took with him the same number
of vessels as before, — thirteen of the line, — the *Monmouth*, 64,
Captain Thomas Collingwood, of Byron's squadron, having arrived
and taken the place of the *Isis*, crippled in her late action. Before
reaching Newport, he learned that the French had started for Boston.
He hoped that they would find it necessary to go outside George's
Bank, and that he might intercept them by following the shorter
road inside. In this he was disappointed, as has been seen, and the
enemy's position was now too strong for attack. The French retreat
to Boston closed the naval campaign of 1778 in North American
waters.

The inability or unwillingness of d'Estaing to renew the enterprise against Rhode Island accords the indisputable triumph in this
campaign to Howe, — an honor he must share, and doubtless gladly
would have shared, with his supporters in general. That the British
fleet, for the most part two years from home, in a country without
dockyards, should have been able to take the sea within ten days
after the gale, while their opponents, just from France, yet with three
months' sea practice, were so damaged that they had to abandon the
field and all the splendid prospects of Rhode Island, — as they already
had allowed to slip the chance at New York, — shows a decisive
superiority in the officers and crews of the former. The incontestable merits of the rank and file, however, must not be permitted to
divert attention from the great qualities of the leader, but for
which the best material would have been unavailing. The conditions were such as to elicit to the utmost Howe's strongest qualities,
— firmness, endurance, uninterrupted persistence rather than celerity,
great professional skill, ripened by constant reflection and ready at
an instant's call. Not brilliant, perhaps, but absolutely clear, and

[1] Chevalier : ' Marine Française,' 1778.

with mind replete with expedients to meet every probable contingency, Howe exhibited an equable, unflagging energy, which was
his greatest characteristic, and which eminently fitted him for the
task of checkmating an enemy's every move — for a purely defensive
campaign.   He was always on hand and always ready; for he never
wearied, and he knew his business.   To great combinations he was
perhaps unequal.   At all events, such are not associated with his
name.   The distant scene he did not see; but step by step he saw
his way with absolute precision, and followed it with unhesitating
resolution.   With a force inferior throughout, to have saved, in one
campaign, the British fleet, New York, and Rhode Island, with the
entire British army, which was divided between those two stations
and dependent upon the sea, is an achievement unsurpassed in the
annals of naval defensive warfare.

Howe's squadron had been constituted in 1776 with reference to
the colonial struggle only, and to shallow water, and therefore was
composed, very properly, of cruisers, and of ships of the line of the
smaller classes; there being several fifties, and nothing larger than
a sixty-four.   When war with France threatened, the Ministry, having long warning, committed an unpardonable fault in allowing such
a force to be confronted by one so superior as that which sailed from
Toulon, in April, 1778.   This should have been stopped on its way,
or, failing that, its arrival in America should have been preceded
by a British reinforcement.   As it was, the government was saved
from a tremendous disaster only by the efficiency of its Admiral.   As
is not too uncommon, gratitude was swamped by the instinct of self-
preservation from the national wrath, excited by this, and by other
simultaneous evidences of neglect.   An attempt was made to dis-
parage Howe's conduct, and to prove that his force was even superior to that of the French, by adding together the guns in all his
ships, disregarding their classes, or by combining groups of his small
vessels against d'Estaing's larger units.   The instrument of the
attack was a naval officer, of some rank but slender professional
credit, who at this most opportune moment underwent a political
conversion, which earned him employment on the one hand, and the
charge of apostasy on the other.   For this kind of professional arith-
metic, Howe felt and expressed just and utter contempt.   Two and
two make four in a primer, but in the field they may make three, or
they may make five.   Not to speak of the greater defensive power
of heavy ships, nor of the concentration of their fire, the unity of

direction under one captain possesses here also that importance
which has caused unity of command and of effort to be recognised
as the prime element in military efficiency, from the greatest things
to the smallest. Taken together, the three elements — greater defensive power, concentration of fire, and unity of direction — constitute
a decisive and permanent argument in favour of big ships, in Howe's
days as in our own. Doubtless, now, as then, there is a limit; most
arguments can be pushed to an *absurdum*, intellectual or practical.
To draw a line is always hard; but, if we cannot tell just where the
line has been passed, we can recognise that one ship is much too big,
while another certainly is not; and between the two we can make
an approximation to an exact result.

On his return to New York on September 11th, Howe found there
Rear-Admiral Hyde Parker [1] with six ships of the line of Byron's
squadron. Considering his task now accomplished, Howe decided
to return to England, in virtue of a permission granted some time
before at his own request. The duty against the Americans, lately
his fellow-countrymen, had been always distasteful to him, although
he did not absolutely refuse to undertake it, as did Admiral Keppel.
The entrance of France into the quarrel, and the coming of d'Estaing,
refreshed the spirits of the veteran, who moreover scorned to
abandon his command in the face of such odds. Now, with the
British positions secure, and superiority of force insured for the time
being, he gladly turned over his charge and sailed for home, burning against the Admiralty with a wrath common to most of the
distinguished seamen of that war. He was not employed afloat again
until a change of Ministry took place, in 1782.

During the same two months that saw the contest between
d'Estaing and Howe in America, the only encounter between nearly
equal fleets in 1778 took place in European waters. Admiral the
Hon. Augustus Keppel, having returned to Spithead after the affair
between the *Belle Poule* and the *Arethusa*, again put to sea on the
9th of July, with a force now increased to thirty ships of the line.
He had been mortified by the necessity of avoiding action, and of
even retiring into port, with the inadequate numbers before under

---

[1] Later Vice-Admiral Sir Hyde Parker, Bart., who perished in the *Cato* in 1783.
He was father of that Admiral Sir Hyde Parker, who, in 1801, was Nelson's com-
mander-in-chief at Copenhagen, and who in 1778 commanded the *Phœnix*, 44, in
Howe's fleet.

his command, and his mind was fixed now to compel an engagement, if he met the French.

The Brest fleet also put to sea, the day before Keppel, under the command of Admiral the Comte d'Orvilliers. It contained thirty-two ships of the line. Of these, three — a sixty-four, a sixty, and a fifty — were not considered fit for the line of battle, which was thus reduced to twenty-nine sail, carrying 2,098 guns. To these the British opposed an aggregate of 2,278 ; but comparison by this means only is very rough. Not only the sizes of the guns, but the classes and weight of the vessels need to be considered. In the particular instance the matter is of little importance ; the action being indecisive, and credit depending upon manœuvres rather than upon fighting.

The French admiral was hampered by vacillating instructions, reflections of the unstable impulses which swayed the Ministry. Whatever his personal wishes, he felt that he must avoid action, unless under very favourable circumstances. At the moment of sailing he wrote : " Since you leave me free to continue my cruise, I will not bring the fleet back to Brest, unless by positive orders, until I have fulfilled the month at sea mentioned in my instructions, and known to all the captains. Till then I will not fly before Admiral Keppel, whatever his strength ; only, if I know him to be too superior, I will avoid a disproportionate action as well as I can ; but if the enemy really seeks to force it, it will be very hard to shun." These words explain his conduct throughout the next few days.

On the afternoon of July 23rd the two fleets sighted each other, about a hundred miles west of Ushant, the French being then to leeward. Towards sunset, the latter were standing south-west, with the wind at west-north-west, and bore north-east from the British, who were lying-to, heads to the northward. The latter remaining nearly motionless throughout the night, and the wind shifting, d'Orvilliers availed himself of the conditions to press to windward, and in the morning was found to bear north-west from his opponent.[1] Their relative positions satisfied for the moment both admirals ; for Keppel found himself interposed between Brest and the French, while d'Orvilliers, though surrendering the advantage of open retreat to his port, had made it possible, by getting the weather-gage, to fulfil his promise to keep the sea and yet to avoid action. Two of

---

[1] Testimony of Captains Hood, Robinson, and Macbride, and of Rear-Admiral Campbell, captain of the fleet to Keppel.

his ships, however, the *Duc de Bourgogne*, 80, and a seventy-four, were still to leeward, not only of their own main body, but also of the British. Keppel sent chasers after them, for the expressed purpose of compelling d'Orvilliers to action in their support,[1] and it was believed by the British that they were forced to return to Brest, to avoid being cut off. They certainly quitted their fleet, which was thus reduced to twenty-seven effective sail. From this time until July 27th the wind continued to the westward, and the wariness of the French admiral baffled all Keppel's efforts to get within range. The latter, having no doubts as to what was expected of him, pursued vigorously, watching his chance.

On the morning of the 27th the two fleets were from six to ten miles apart, wind west-south-west, both on the port tack, steering north-west, the French dead to windward. The latter were in line ahead, the British in bow-and-quarter line ; that is, nearly abreast each other, but so ranged that, if they went about together, they should have been in line ahead. Both fleets were irregularly formed, the British especially so ; for Keppel rightly considered that he would not accomplish his purpose, if he were pedantic concerning the order of his going. He had therefore signalled a " General Chase," which, by permitting much individual freedom of movement, facilitated the progress of the whole. At daylight, the division commanded by Sir Hugh Palliser — the right wing, as then heading — had dropped astern ; and at 5.30 A. M. the signal was made to seven of its fastest sailers to chase to windward, the object being so to place them, relatively to the main body, as to support the latter, if an opportunity for action should offer.

At 9 A. M. the French admiral, wishing to approach the enemy and to see more clearly, ordered his fleet to wear in succession, — to countermarch. As the van ships went round under this signal, they had to steer off the wind, parallel to their former line, on which those following them still were, until they reached the rear ship, when they could again haul to the wind. This caused a loss of ground to leeward, but not more than d'Orvilliers could afford, as things stood. Just after he had fairly committed himself to the manœuvre, the wind hauled to the southward two points,[2] which favoured the British, allowing them to head more nearly towards the enemy. Keppel therefore continued on the port tack, until all the French were on the starboard, and at 10.15, being nearly in their

---

[1] See note on preceding page.   [2] Twenty-two degrees.

List of the British and French Fleets in the action off Ushant, July 27th, 1778, chiefly from Beatson, vi. 129–132, and Guérin, v. 24, 25 ; corrected from the Navy List, the *Gazette de France*, the dispatches of d'Orvilliers to Sartine (Arch. de la Marine), and the Proceedings of the C. M., 7 Jan. to 11 Feb., 1779, and April 12 to May 5, 1779. — W. L. C.

	SHIPS.	GUNS.	COMMANDERS.	SHIPS.	GUNS.	COMMANDERS.
VAN.	Monarch.	74	Capt. Joshua Rowley.			
	Hector.	74	Capt. Sir John Hamilton, Bart.	Couronne.	80	Lieut.-Gen. Comte Duchaffault.
	Centaur.	74	Capt. Phillips Cosby.			Capt. Baron de Kermadec.
	Exeter.	64	Capt. John Neale Pleydell Nott.	Duc de Bourgogne.	80	Vicomte de Rochechouart (chef d'esc.).
	Duke.	90	Capt. William Brereton.			
	Queen.	90	Vice-Admiral Sir Robert Harland (R.).	Glorieux.	74	Capt. de Beaunes (chef d'esc.).
			Capt. Isaac Prescott.	Palmier.	74	Capt. de Réals.
				Bien-Aimé.	74	Capt. d'Aubenton.
	Shrewsbury.	74	Capt. Sir John Lockhart Ross, Bart.	Dauphin Royal.	70	Capt. de Nieuil.
				Vengeur.	64	Capt. d'Amblimont.
	Cumberland.	74	Capt. Joseph Peyton (1).	Alexandre.	64	Capt. de Trémigon (1).
	Berwick.	74	Capt. the Hon. Keith Stewart.	Indien.	64	Capt. de la Grandière.
	Stirling Castle.	64	Capt. Sir Charles Douglas, Bart.	Saint Michel.	60	Capt. Mithon de Genouilli.
				Amphion.	50	Capt. de Trobriand.
CENTRE.	Courageux.	74	Capt. Lord Mulgrave.			
	Thunderer.	74	Capt. the Hon. Robert Boyle Walsingham.	Bretagne.	110	Lieut.-Gen. Comte d'Orvilliers.
						Capt. Duplessis Perseault.
	Sandwich.	90	Capt. Richard Edwards (2).	Ville de Paris.	100	Comte de Guichen (chef d'esc.).
	Valiant.	74	Capt. the Hon. John Leveson Gower.	L'Orient.	74	Capt. Hector (chef d'esc.).
				Fendant.	74	Capt. de Vaudreuil.
	Bienfaisant.	64	Capt. John Macbride.	Magnifique.	74	Capt. de Brach.
			Adm. the Hon. A. Keppel (B).	Actif.	74	Capt. Thomas d'Orves.
	Victory.	100	Rear-Admiral John Campbell (1st Capt.).	Réfléchi.	64	Capt. Cillart de Suville.
				Eveillé.	64	Capt. de Bot-Deru.
			Capt. Jonathan Faulknor (1) (2nd).	Artésien.	64	Capt. des Touches.
				Actionnaire.	64	Capt. de Proissi.
	Foudroyant.	80	Capt. John Jervis.			
	Prince George.	90	Capt. Sir John Lindsay, K. B.			
	Vigilant.	64	Capt. Robert Kingsmill.			
	Terrible.	74	Capt. Sir Richard Bickerton, Bart.			
	Vengeance.	74	Capt. Michael Clements.			
REAR.	Worcester.	64	Capt. Mark Robinson (1).			Lieut.-Genl. Duc de Chartres.
	Elizabeth.	74	Capt. the Hon. Fredk. Lewis Maitland.	Saint Esprit.	80	Capt. La Motte-Picquet (1st).
						Capt. de Monperoux.
	Robust.	74	Capt. Alexander Arthur Hood.	Robuste.	74	Capt. de Grasse-Tilli (chef d'esc.).
	Formidable.	90	Vice-Admiral Sir Hugh Palliser (B).	Conquérant.	74	Capt. de Monteil (chef d'esc.).
				Intrépide.	74	Capt. de Beaumier.
			Capt. John Bazely (1).	Zodiaque.	74	Capt. de la Porte-Vezins.
	Ocean.	90	Capt. John Laforey.	Diadème.	74	Capt. de la Cardonnie.
	America.	64	Capt. Lord Longford.	Solitaire.	64	Capt. de Bricqueville.
	Defiance.	64	Capt. Samuel Granston Goodall.	Roland.	64	Capt. de l'Archantel.
	Egmont.	74	Capt. John Carter Allen.	Sphinx.	64	Capt. de Soulanges.
	Ramillies.	74	Capt. Robert Digby.	Triton.	64	Capt. de Ligondès.
				Fier.	50	Capt. de Turpin.
FRIGATES, ETC.	Arethusa	32	Capt. Samuel Marshall.	Sensible.	32	
	Proserpine.	28	Capt. Evelyn Sutton.	Andromaque.	32	
	Milford.	28	Capt. Sir William Burnaby, Bt.	Sincère.	32	Capt. de la Clocheterie.
	Fox.	28	Capt. the Hon. Thos. Windsor.	Junon.	32	
	Andromeda.	28	Capt. Henry Bryne.	Iphigénie.	32	Capt. Comte de Kersaint (2).
	Lively.	20	Capt. Robert Biggs.	Nymphe.	32	
	Pluto (f. s.).	8	Com. James Bradby (1).	Surveillante.	16	
	Vulcan (f. s.)	8	Com. —— Lloyd.	Perle.	16	
	Alert (cutter).	12	Com. William George Fairfax.	Ecureuil.	14	
				Hirondelle.	16	
				Serin	14	Capt. de la Pérouse.
				Curieuse.	10	
				Lunette.	4	
				Favorite.	10	

wake, he ordered his own ships to tack together. At this moment a
thick rain-squall came up, concealing the fleets one from another for
three quarters of an hour. With the squall the wind shifted back,
favouring the British on this tack, as it had on the other, and enabling them to lay up for the enemy's rear. When the weather cleared,
at 11, the French were seen to have gone about again, and were still
in the confusion of a partly executed manœuvre. Their admiral had
doubtless recognised, from the change of wind, and from the direction
of the enemy when last visible, that an encounter could not be
avoided. If he continued on the starboard tack, the van of the
pursuing enemy, whose resolve to force battle could not be misunderstood, would overtake his rear ships, engaging as many of them
as he might choose. By resuming the port tack, the heads of the
columns would meet, and the fleets pass in opposite directions, on
equal terms as regarded position. Therefore he had ordered his
ships to go about, all at the same time ; thus forming column again
rapidly, but reversing the order so that the rear became the van.

Keppel so far had made no signal for the line of battle, nor did
he now. Recognising from the four days' chase that his enemy was
avoiding action, he judged correctly that he should force it, even at
some risk. It was not the time for a drill-master, nor a parade.
Besides, thanks to the morning signal for the leewardly ships to
chase, these, forming the rear of the disorderly column in which he
was advancing, were now well to windward, able therefore to support their comrades, if needful, as well as to attack the enemy. In
short, practically the whole force was coming into action, although
much less regularly than might have been desired. What was to
follow was a rough-and-ready fight, but it was all that could be had,
and better than nothing. Keppel therefore simply made the signal
for battle, and that just as the firing began. The collision was so
sudden that the ships at first had not their colours flying.

The French also, although their manœuvres had been more
methodical, were in some confusion. It is not given to a body of
thirty ships, of varying qualities, to attain perfection of movement
in a fortnight of sea practice. The change of wind had precipitated
an action, which one admiral had been seeking, and the other shun-
ning ; but each had to meet it with such shift as he could. The
British being close-hauled, the French, advancing on a parallel line,
were four points [1] off the wind. Most of their ships, therefore, could

---

[1] Forty-five degrees.

have gone clear to windward of their opponents, but the fact that the latter could reach some of the leaders compelled the others to support them. As d'Orvilliers had said, it was hard to avoid an enemy resolute to fight. The leading three French vessels [1] hauled their wind, in obedience to the admiral's signal to form the line of battle, which means a close-hauled line. The effect of this was to draw them gradually away from the British, and, if imitated by their followers, to render the affair a mere touch at a single point — indecisive. The fourth French ship began the action, opening fire soon after eleven. The vessels of the opposing fleets surged by under short canvas, firing as opportunity offered, but necessarily much handicapped by smoke, which prevented the clear sight of an enemy, and caused anxiety lest an unseen friend might receive a broadside. "The distance between the *Formidable*, 90, and the *Egmont*, 74, was so short," testified Captain John Laforey, whose three-decker, the *Ocean*, 90, was abreast and outside this interval, "that it was with difficulty I could keep betwixt them to engage, without firing upon them, and I was once very near on board the *Egmont.*" The *Formidable*, Palliser's flagship, kept her mizzen topsail aback much of the time, to deaden her way, to make room for the *Ocean*, and to allow the ships behind her to close. "At a quarter past one," testified Captain Maitland of the *Elizabeth*, 74, "we were very close behind the *Formidable*, and a midshipman upon the poop called out that there was a ship coming on board on the weather bow. I put the helm up, . . . and found, when the smoke cleared away, I was shot up under the *Formidable's* lee. She was then engaged with the two last ships in the French fleet, and, as I could not fire at them without firing through the *Formidable*, I was obliged to shoot on." [2] Captain Bazely, of the *Formidable*, says of the same incident, "The *Formidable* did at the time of action bear up to one of the enemy's ships, to avoid being aboard of her, whose jib boom nearly touched the main topsail weather leech of the *Formidable*. I thought we could not avoid being on board."

Contrary to the usual result, the loss of the rear division, in killed and wounded, was heaviest, nearly equalling the aggregate of

---

[1] Chevalier says, p. 89, "The English passed out of range" of these ships. As these ships had the wind, they had the choice of range, barring signals from their own admiral. In truth, they were obeying his order.

[2] This evidence of the captains of the *Ocean* and the *Elizabeth* contradicts Palliser's charge that his ship was not adequately supported.

the other two.[1] This was due to the morning signal to chase to windward, which brought these ships closer than their leaders. As soon as the British van, ten ships, had passed the French rear, its commander, Vice-Admiral Sir Robert Harland, anticipating Keppel's wishes, signalled it to go about and follow the enemy (Fig. 1, V). As the French column was running free, these ships, when about, fetched to windward of its wake. As the *Victory* drew out of the fire, at 1 P.M., Keppel made a similar signal, and attempted to wear,

ADMIRAL AUGUSTUS, VISCOUNT KEPPEL.

(From Ridley's engraving, after the portrait by G. Romney.)

the injuries to his rigging not permitting tacking; but caution was needed in manœuvring across the bows of the following ships, and it was not till 2 P.M., that the *Victory* was about on the other tack, heading after the French. At this time, 2 P.M., just before or just after wearing, the signal for battle was hauled down, and that for

----

[1] It was actually quite equal, but this was due to an accidental explosion on board the *Formidable*.

the line of battle was hoisted. The object of the latter was to
re-form the order, and the first was discontinued, partly because no
longer needed, chiefly that it might not seem to contradict the urgent
call for a re-formation.[1]

At this time six or seven of Harland's division were on the
weather bow of the *Victory*, to windward (westward), but a little
ahead, and standing like her after the French; all on the port tack
(Fig. 1). None of the centre division succeeded in joining the flagship at once (Fig. 1, C). At 2.30 Palliser's ship, the *Formidable*,

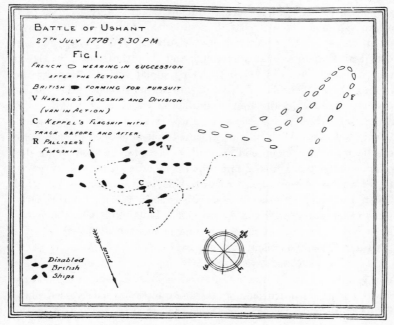

BATTLE OF USHANT.

on the starboard tack passed her to leeward, the last of the fleet
apparently out of action (Fig. 1, R). A half-hour after this the
Victory had been joined by three of the centre, which were following
her in close order, the van remaining in the same relative position.
Astern of these two groups were a number of other ships in various
degrees of confusion, — some going about, some trying to come up,

---

[1] Naval officers will observe the strong analogy to the speculative naval tactics of
to-day, — a charge through (or by), and a re-formation afterwards.

others completely disabled.   Especially, there was in the south-south-east, therefore well to leeward, a cluster of four or five British vessels, evidently temporarily incapable of manœuvring.

This was the situation which met the eye of the French admiral, scanning the field as the smoke drove away.   The disorder of the British, which originated in the general chase, had increased through the hurry of the manœuvres succeeding the squall, and culminated in the conditions just described.   It was an inevitable result of a military exigency confronted by a fleet only recently equipped. The French, starting from a better formation, had come out in better shape.   But, after all, it seems difficult wholly to remedy the disadvantage of a policy essentially defensive ; and d'Orvilliers' next order, though well conceived, was resultless.   At 1 P.M.[1] he signalled his fleet to wear in succession, and form the line of battle on the starboard tack (Fig. 1, F).   This signal was not seen by the leading ship, which should have begun the movement.   The junior French admiral, in the fourth ship from the van, at length went about, and spoke the *Bretagne*, to know what was the commander-in-chief's desire.   D'Orvilliers explained that he wished to pass along the enemy's fleet from end to end, *to leeward*, because in its disordered state there was a fair promise of advantage, and by going to leeward — presenting his weather side to the enemy — he could use the weather lower-deck guns, whereas, in the then state of the sea, the lee ports could not be opened.   Thus explained, the movement was executed, but the favourable moment had passed.   It was not till 2.30 that the manœuvre was evident to the British.

As soon as Keppel recognised his opponent's intention, he wore the *Victory* again, a few minutes after 3 P.M., and stood slowly down, on the starboard tack *off the wind*, towards his crippled ships in the south-south-east, keeping aloft the signal for the line of battle, which commanded every manageable ship to get to her station (Fig. 2, C).   As this deliberate movement was away from the enemy, Palliser tried afterwards to fix upon it the stigma of flight, — a preposterous extravagancy.   Harland put his division about at once and joined the Admiral.   On this tack his station was ahead of the *Victory*, but in consequence of a message from Keppel he fell in behind her, to cover the rear until Palliser's division could repair damage and take their places.   At 4 P.M. Harland's division was in the line.   Palliser's ships, as they completed refitting, ranged themselves in rear

---

[1] Chevalier.   Probably later by the other times used in this account.

of the *Formidable*, their captains considering, as they testified, that
they took station from their divisional commander, and not from
the ship of the commander-in-chief.   There was formed thus, on the
weather quarter of the *Victory*, and a mile or two distant, a separate
line of ships, constituting on this tack the proper rear of the fleet,
and dependent for initiative on Palliser's flagship (Fig. 2, R).   At
5 P.M. Keppel sent word by a frigate to Palliser to hasten into
the line, as he was only waiting for him to renew the action, the

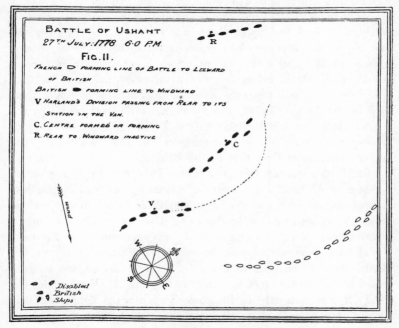

BATTLE OF USHANT.

French now having completed their manœuvre.   They had not attacked, as they might have done, but had drawn up under the lee
of the British, their van abreast the latter's centre.   At the same
time Harland was directed to move to his proper position in the van,
which he at once did (Fig. 2, V).   Palliser made no movement, and
Keppel with extraordinary — if not culpable — forbearance, refrained
from summoning the rear ships into line by their individual pennants.
This he at last did about 7 P.M., signalling specifically to each of the
vessels then grouped with Palliser (except the *Formidable*), to leave

the latter and take their posts in the line. This was accordingly
done, but it was thought then to be too late to renew the action.
At daylight the next morning, only three French ships were in sight
from the decks; but the main body could be seen in the south-east
from some of the mastheads, and was thought to be from fifteen to
twenty miles distant.

Though absolutely indecisive, this was a pretty smart skirmish;
the British loss being 133 killed and 373 wounded, that of the
French 161 killed and 513 wounded. The general result would
appear to indicate that the French, in accordance with their usual
policy, had fired to cripple their enemy's spars and rigging, the
motive-power. This would be consistent with d'Orvilliers' avowed
purpose of avoiding action except under favourable circumstances.
As the smoke thickened and confusion increased, the fleets had got
closer together, and, whatever the intention, many shot found their
way to the British hulls. Nevertheless, as the returns show, the
French hit were to the British nearly as 7 to 5. On the other hand,
it is certain that the manœuvring power of the French after the
action was greater than that of the British.

Both sides claimed the advantage. This was simply a point of
honour, or of credit, for material advantage accrued to neither.
Keppel had succeeded in forcing d'Orvilliers to action against his
will; d'Orvilliers, by a well-judged evolution, had retained a superiority of manœuvring power after the engagement. Had his next
signal been promptly obeyed, he might have passed again by the
British fleet, in fairly good order, before it re-formed, and concentrated his fire on the more leewardly of its vessels. Even under the
delay, it was distinctly in his power to renew the fight; and that
he did not do so forfeits all claim to victory. Not to speak of
the better condition of the French ships, Keppel, by running off
the wind, had given his opponent full opportunity to reach his fleet
and to attack. Instead of so doing, d'Orvilliers drew up under the
British lee, out of range, and offered battle ; a gallant defiance, but
to a crippled foe.

Time was thus given to the British to refit their ships sufficiently
to bear down again. This the French admiral should not have permitted. He should have attacked promptly, or else have retreated;
to windward, or to leeward, as seemed most expedient. Under the
conditions, it was not good generalship to give the enemy time, and
to await his pleasure. Keppel, on the other hand, being granted

this chance, should have renewed the fight; and here arose the controversy which set all England by the ears, and may be said to have immortalised this otherwise trivial incident. Palliser's division was to windward from 4 to 7 P.M., while the signals were flying to form line of battle, and to bear down in the Admiral's wake; and Keppel alleged that, had these been obeyed by 6 P.M., he would have renewed the battle, having still over two hours of daylight. It has been stated already that, besides the signals, a frigate brought Palliser word that the Admiral was waiting only for him.

The immediate dispute is of slight present interest, except as an historical link in the fighting development of the British Navy; and only this historical significance justifies more than a passing mention. In 1778 men's minds were still full of Byng's execution in 1757, and of the Mathews and Lestock affair in 1744, which had materially influenced Byng's action off Minorca. Keppel repeatedly spoke of himself as on trial for his life; and he had been a member of Byng's court-martial. The gist of the charges against him, preferred by Palliser, was that he attacked in the first instance without properly forming his line, for which Mathews had been cashiered; and, secondly, that by not renewing the action after the first pass-by, and by wearing away from the French fleet, he had not done his utmost to "take, sink, burn, and destroy"—the latter, the charge on which Byng was shot. Keppel, besides his justifying reasons for his course in general, alleged and proved his full intention to attack again, had not Palliser failed to come into line, a delinquency the same as that of Lestock, which caused Mathews's ruin.

In other words, men's minds were breaking away from, but had not thrown off completely, the tyranny of the Order of Battle, — one of the worst of tyrannies, because founded on truth. Absolute error, like a whole lie, is open to speedy detection; half-truths are troublesome. The Order of Battle was an admirable servant and a most objectionable despot. Mathews, in despair over a recalcitrant second, cast off the yoke, engaged with part of his force, was ill supported, and cashiered; Lestock escaping. Byng, considering this, and being a pedant by nature, would not break his line; the enemy slipped away, Minorca surrendered, and he was shot. In Keppel's court-martial, twenty-eight out of the thirty captains who had been in the line were summoned as witnesses. Most of them swore that if Keppel had chased in line of battle that day, there could have been no action, and the majority of them cordially approved; but there

was evidently an undercurrent still of dissent, and especially in the
rear ships, where there had been some of the straggling inevitable in
such movements, and whose commanders therefore had uncomfortable
experience of the lack of mutual support, which the line of battle was
meant to insure.

Another indication of still surviving pedantry was the obligation
felt in the rear ships to take post behind their own admiral, and to
remain there when the signals for the line of battle, and to bear down
in the admiral's wake, were flying. Thus Palliser's own inaction, to
whatever cause due, paralysed the six or eight sail with him; but it
appears to the writer that Keppel was seriously remiss in not summoning those ships by their own pennants, as soon as he began to
distrust the purposes of the Vice-Admiral, instead of delaying doing
so till 7 P. M., as he did. It is a curious picture presented to us by
the evidence. The Commander-in-Chief, with his staff and the captain of the ship, fretting and fuming on the *Victory's* quarter-deck;
the signals flying which have been mentioned; Harland's division
getting into line ahead; and four points on the weather quarter, only
two miles distant, so that "every gun and port could be counted," a
group of seven or eight sail, among them the flag of the third in command, apparently indifferent spectators. The *Formidable's* only sign
of disability was the foretopsail unbent for four hours, — a delay which,
being unexplained, rather increased than relieved suspicion, rife then
throughout the Navy. Palliser was a Tory, and had left the Board
of Admiralty to take his command. Keppel was so strong a Whig
that he would not serve against the Americans; and he evidently
feared that he was to be betrayed to his ruin.

Palliser's defence rested upon three principal points : (1), that the
signal for the line of battle was not seen on board the *Formidable ;*
(2), that the signal to get into the Admiral's wake was repeated by
himself; (3), that his foremast was wounded, and, moreover, found to
be in such bad condition that he feared to carry sail on it. As regards the first, the signal was seen on board the *Ocean*, next astern
of and "not far from" [1] the *Formidable ;* for the second, the Admiral
should have been informed of a disability by which a single ship was
neutralising a division. The frigate that brought Keppel's message
could have carried back this. Thirdly, the most damaging feature to
Palliser's case was that he asserted that, after coming out from under
fire, he wore at once towards the enemy; afterwards he wore back

---

[1] Evidence of Captain John Laforey, of the *Ocean.*

again.   A ship that thus wore twice before three o'clock, might have displayed zeal and efficiency enough to run two miles, off the wind,[1] at five, to support a fight.   Deliberate treachery is impossible.   To the writer the Vice-Admiral's behaviour seems that of a man in a sulk, who will do only that which he can find no excuses for neglecting. In such cases of sailing close, men generally slip over the line into grievous wrong.

Keppel was cleared of all the charges preferred against him ; the accuser had not thought best to embody among them the delay to recall the ships which he himself was detaining.   Against Palliser no specific charge was preferred, but the Admiralty directed a general inquiry into his course on the 27th of July.   The court found his conduct " in many instances highly exemplary and meritorious," — he had fought well, — " but reprehensible in not having acquainted the Commander-in-Chief of his distress, which he might have done either by the *Fox*, or other means which he had in his power." Public opinion running strongly for Keppel, his acquittal was celebrated with bonfires and illuminations in London ; the mob got drunk, smashed the windows of Palliser's friends, wrecked Palliser's own house, and came near to killing Palliser himself.   The Admiralty, in 1780, made him Governor of Greenwich Hospital.

On the 28th of July, the British and French being no longer in sight of each other, Keppel, considering his fleet too injured aloft to cruise near the French coast, kept away for Plymouth, where he arrived on the 31st.   Before putting to sea again, he provided against a recurrence of the misdemeanour of the 27th by a general order, that " in future the Line is always to be taken from the Centre."   Had this been in force before, Palliser's captains would have taken station by the Commander-in-Chief, and the *Formidable* would have been left to windward by herself.   At the same time Howe was closing his squadron upon the centre in America ; and Rodney, two years later, experienced the ill-effects of distance taken from the next ahead, when the leading ship of a fleet disregarded an order.

Although privately censuring Palliser's conduct, the Commander-in-Chief made no official complaint, and it was not until the matter got into the papers, through the talk of the fleet, that the difficulty began which resulted in the trial of both officers, early in the following year.

---

[1] "I do not recollect how many points I went from the wind ; I must have bore down a pretty large course."   Testimony of Captain J. Laforey, of the *Ocean*, on this point.

After this, Keppel, being dissatisfied with the Admiralty's treatment, intimated his wish to give up the command. The order to strike his flag was dated March 18th, 1779. He was not employed afloat again, but upon the change of administration in 1782 he became First Lord of the Admiralty, and so remained, with a brief intermission, until December, 1783.

It is perhaps necessary to mention that both British and French asserted, and assert to this day, that the other party abandoned the field.[1] The point is too trivial, in the author's opinion, to warrant further discussion of an episode whose historical interest is very slight, though its professional lessons are valuable. The British case has the advantage — through the courts-martial — of the sworn testimony of twenty to thirty captains, who agreed that the British kept on the same tack under short sail throughout the night, and that in the morning only three French ships were visible. As far as known to the author, the French contention rests only on the usual reports.

Conditions of weather exerted great influence upon the time and place of hostilities during the maritime war of 1778, the opening scenes of which, in Europe and in North America, have just been narrated. In European seas it was realised that naval enterprises by fleets, requiring evolutions by masses of large vessels, were possible only in summer. Winter gales scattered ships and impeded manœuvres. The same consideration prevailed to limit activity in North American waters to the summer; and complementary to this was the fact that in the West Indies hurricanes of excessive violence occurred from July to October. The practice therefore was to transfer effort from one quarter to the other in the Western Hemisphere, according to the season.

In the recent treaty with the United States, the King of France had formally renounced all claim to acquire for himself any part of the American continent then in possession of Great Britain. On the other hand, he had reserved the express right to conquer any of her islands south of Bermuda. The West Indies were then, in the value of their products, the richest commercial region on the globe; and

---

[1] "During the night (of the 27th) Admiral Keppel kept away (*fit route*) for Portsmouth." Chevalier, 'Marine Française,' p. 90. Paris, 1877. Oddly enough, he adds that " on the evening of the 28th the French squadron, *carried eastward by the currents*, sighted Ushant."

France wished not only to increase her already large possessions there, but also to establish more solidly her political and military tenure.

In September, 1778, the British Island of Dominica was seized by an expedition from the adjacent French colony of Martinique. The affair was a surprise, and possesses no special military interest; but it is instructive to observe that Great Britain was unprepared, in the West Indies as elsewhere, when the war began. A change had been

ADMIRAL THE HON. SAMUEL BARRINGTON

(From the lithograph by Ridley, after the portrait by J. S. Copley, R. A.)

made shortly before in the command of the Leeward Islands Station, as it was called, which extended from Antigua southward over the Lesser Antilles with headquarters at Barbados. Rear-Admiral the Hon. Samuel Barrington, the new-comer, leaving home before war had been declared, had orders not to quit Barbados till further instructions should arrive. These had not reached him when he learned of the loss of Dominica. The French had received their orders on the 17th of August.   The blow was intrinsically somewhat serious, so far as the mere capture of a position can be, for the fortifications were strong, though they had been inadequately garrisoned. It is a mistake to build works and not man them, for their fall transfers to the enemy strength which he otherwise would need time to create.   To the French the conquest was useful beyond its commercial value, because it closed a gap in their possessions.   They now held four consecutive islands, from north to south, Guadeloupe, Dominica, Martinique, and St. Lucia.

Barrington had two ships of the line, his flagship, the *Prince of Wales*, 74, Captain Benjamin Hill, and the *Boyne*, 70, Captain Herbert Sawyer, which, had he been cruising, would probably have deterred the French.   Upon receiving the news, he put to sea, going as far as Antigua; but he did not venture to stay away because his expected instructions had not come yet, and, like Keppel, he feared an ungenerous construction of his actions.   He remained in Barbados, patiently watching for an opportunity to act.

The departure of Howe and the approach of winter determined the transference of British troops and ships to the Leeward Islands. Reinforcements had given the British fleet a numerical superiority, which for the time imposed a check upon d'Estaing; but Byron, proverbially unlucky in weather, was driven crippled to Newport, leaving the French free to quit Boston.   The difficulty of provisioning so large a force as twelve ships of the line at first threatened to prevent the movement, supplies being then extremely scarce in the port; but at the critical moment American privateers brought in large numbers of prizes, laden with provisions from Europe for the British army.   Thus d'Estaing was enabled to sail for Martinique on the 4th of November.   On the same day there left New York for Barbados a British squadron, [1] — 2 sixty-fours, 3 fifties, and three smaller craft, — under the command of Commodore William Hotham, convoying 5,000 troops for service in the West Indies.

[1] *Preston*	50	Commodore William Hotham. Captain Samuel Uppleby.
St. Albans	64	Captain Richard Onslow.
Nonsuch	64	Captain Walter Griffith.
Isis	50	Captain John Rayner.
Centurion	50	Captain Richard Brathwaite.
Venus	36	Captain James Ferguson.
Pearl	32	Captain Alexander Græme.
Carcass (bomb)	8	Commander Edward Edwards.

Beatson, vi. 116. — W. L. C

Being bound for nearly the same point, the two hostile bodies steered parallel courses, each ignorant of the other's nearness. In the latitude of Bermuda both suffered from a violent gale, but the French most; the flagship *Languedoc* losing her main and mizzen topmasts. On the 25th of November one [1] of Hotham's convoy fell into the hands of d'Estaing, who then first learned of the British sailing. Doubtful whether their destination was Barbados or Antigua, — their two chief stations, — he decided for the latter. Arriving off it on the 6th of December, he cruised for forty-eight hours, and then bore away for Fort Royal, Martinique, the principal French dépôt in the West Indies, where he anchored on the 9th. On the 10th Hotham joined Barrington at Barbados.

Barrington knew already what he wanted to do, and therefore lost not a moment in deliberation. The troops were kept on board, Hotham's convoy arrangements being left as they were; and on the morning of December 12th the entire force sailed again, the main change being in the chief command, and in the addition of Barrington's two ships of the line. In the afternoon of the 13th the shipping anchored in the Grand Cul de Sac, an inlet on the west side of St. Lucia, which is seventy miles east-north-east from Barbados. Part of the troops landed at once, and seized the batteries and heights on the north side of the bay. The remainder were put on shore the next morning. The French forces were inadequate to defend their works; but it is to be observed that they were driven with unremitting energy, and that to this promptness the British owed their ability to hold the position.

Three miles north of the Cul de Sac is a bay then called the Carénage; now Port Castries. At its northern extremity is a precipitous promontory, La Vigie, then fortified, upon the tenure of which depended not only control of that anchorage, but also access to the rear of the works which commanded the Cul de Sac. If those works fell, the squadron must abandon its position and put to sea, where d'Estaing's fleet would be in waiting. On the other hand, if the squadron were crushed at its anchors, the troops were isolated and must ultimately capitulate. Therefore La Vigie and the squadron were the two keys to the situation, and the loss of either would be decisive.

By the evening of the 14th the British held the shore line from La Vigie to the southern point of the Cul de Sac, as well as Morne

---

[1] The French accounts say three.

Fortuné (Fort Charlotte), the capital of the island. The feeble
French garrison retired to the interior, leaving its guns unspiked,
and its ammunition and stores untouched, — another instance of the
danger of works turning to one's own disadvantage. It was Barrington's purpose now to remove the transports to the Carénage, as
a more commodious harbour, probably also better defended; but he
was prevented by the arrival of d'Estaing that afternoon. " Just as
all the important stations were secured, the French colours struck,

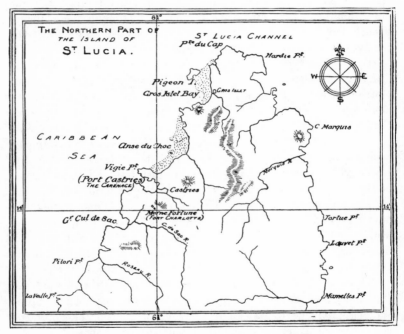

THE NORTHERN PART OF THE ISLAND OF ST. LUCIA.

and General Grant's headquarters established at the Governor's
house, the *Ariadne* frigate came in sight with the signal abroad for
the approach of an enemy." [1] The French fleet was seen soon afterwards from the heights above the squadron.

The British had gained much so far by celerity, but they still
spared no time to take breath. The night was passed by the soldiers
in strengthening their positions, and by the Rear-Admiral in rectifying his order to meet the expected attack. The transports, between

[1] Beatson : 'Military and Naval Memoirs,' iv. 390.

fifty and sixty in number, were warped inside the ships of war, and the latter were most carefully disposed across the mouth of the bay. At the northern (windward) end was placed the *Isis*, 50, Captain John Rayner, well under the point to prevent anything from passing round her; but for further security she was supported by three frigates; the *Venus*, 36, Captain William Peere Williams, the *Ariadne*, 20, Captain Thomas Pringle, and the *Aurora*, 28, Captain James Cumming, anchored abreast of the interval between her and the shore. From the *Isis* the line extended to the southward, inclining slightly outward; the *Prince of Wales*, 74, Barrington's flagship, taking the southern flank, as the most exposed position. Between her and the *Isis* were five other ships, — the *Boyne*, 70, *Nonsuch*, 64, *St. Albans*, 64, *Preston*, 50, and *Centurion*, 50. The works left by the French at the north and south points of the bay may have been used to support the flanks, but Barrington in his report does not say so.

D'Estaing had twelve ships of the line, and was able to land, two days after this, 7,000 troops. With such a superiority it is evident that, had he arrived twenty-four hours sooner, the British would have been stopped in the midst of their operation. To gain time, Barrington had sought to prevent intelligence reaching Fort Royal, less than fifty miles distant, by sending cruisers in advance of his squadron, to cover the approaches to St. Lucia; but, despite his care, d'Estaing had the news on the 14th. He sailed at once, and, as has been said, was off St. Lucia that evening. At daybreak of the 15th he stood in for the Carénage; but when he came within range, a lively cannonade told him that the enemy were already in possession. He decided therefore to attack the squadron, and at 11.30 the French passed along it from north to south, firing, but without effect. A second attempt was made in the afternoon, directed upon the lee flank, but it was equally unavailing. The British had three men killed; the French loss is not given, but is said to have been slight. It is stated that the sea breeze did not penetrate far enough into the bay, that day, to admit closing. This frequently happens, but it does not alter the fact that the squadron was the proper point of attack, and that, especially in the winter season, an opportunity to close must offer soon. D'Estaing, governed probably by the soldierly bias he more than once betrayed, decided now to assault the works on shore. Anchoring in a small bay north of the Carénage, he landed seven thousand men, and on the 18th attempted to storm the British lines at La Vigie. The neck of land connecting the promontory with the island is very flat, and the French therefore laboured under great disadvantage from the commanding position of their enemy.   It was a repetition of Bunker Hill, and of many other ill-judged and precipitate attacks.   After three gallant but ineffectual charges, led by d'Estaing in person, the assailants retired, with the loss of 41 officers and 800 rank and file, killed and wounded.

D'Estaing re-embarked his men, and stood ready again to attack Barrington, a frigate being stationed off the Cul de Sac, to give notice when the wind should serve.   On the 24th she signalled, and the fleet weighed ; but Barrington, who had taken a very great risk for an adequate object, ran no unnecessary risks through presumption.   He had employed his respite to warp the ships of war farther in, where the breeze reached less certainly, and where narrower waters gave better support to the flanks.   He had strengthened the latter also by new works, in which he had placed heavy guns from the ships, manned by seamen.   For these or other reasons d'Estaing did not attack.   On the 29th he quitted the island, and on the 30th the French governor, the Chev. de Micoud, formally capitulated.

This achievement of Barrington, and of Major-General James Grant, who was associated with him, was greeted at the time with an applause which will be echoed by the military judgment of a later age.   There is a particular pleasure in finding the willingness to incur a great danger, conjoined with a care that chances nothing against which the utmost diligence and skill can provide.   The celerity, forethought, wariness, and daring of the Hon. Samuel Barrington have inscribed upon the records of the British Navy a success whose distinction should be measured, not by the greatness of the scale, but by the perfection of the workmanship, and by the energy of the execution in the face of great odds.

St. Lucia remained in the hands of the British throughout the war.   It was an important acquisition, because at its north-west extremity was a good and defensible anchorage, Gros Ilet Bay, only thirty miles from Fort Royal.   In it the British fleet could lie, when desirable to close-watch the enemy, yet not be worried for its safety when away; for it was but an outpost, not a base of operations, as Fort Royal was.   It was thus used continually, and from it Rodney issued for his great victory in April, 1782.

During the first six months of 1779 no important incident occurred in the West Indies.   On the 6th of January, Vice-Admiral the Hon. John Byron, with ten ships of the line from Narragansett Bay, reached St. Lucia, and relieved Barrington of the chief command. Both the British and the French fleets were reinforced in the course of the spring, but the relative strength remained nearly as before, until the 27th of June, when the arrival of a division from Brest made the French numbers somewhat superior.

VICE-ADMIRAL SIR HYDE PARKER (1), BART.
(From a lithograph by H. R. Cook, after the portrait by J. Northcote, R. A.)

Shortly before this, Byron had been constrained by one of the commercial exigencies that constantly embarrassed the military action of the British admirals. A large convoy of trading ships, bound to England, was collecting at St. Kitts, and he thought necessary to accompany it part of the homeward way, until well clear of the enemy's West India cruisers. For this purpose he left St. Lucia early in June. As soon as the coast was clear, d'Estaing, informed of his object, sent a small combined expedition against St. Vincent, which was surrendered on the 18th of the month. On the 30th the French admiral himself quitted Fort Royal with his whole fleet, — twenty-five ships of the line and several frigates, — directing his course for the British Island of Grenada, before which he anchored on the 2nd of July. With commendable promptitude, he landed his troops that evening, and on the 4th the island capitulated. Except as represented by one small armed sloop, the *York*, 12, Lieutenant Daniel Dobrée, which was taken, the British Navy had no part in this transaction. Thirty richly laden merchant ships were captured in the port.

At daybreak of July 6th, Byron appeared with twenty-one sail of the line, one frigate,[1] and a convoy of twenty-eight vessels, carrying troops and equipments. He had returned to St. Lucia on the 1st, and there had heard of the loss of St. Vincent, with a rumour that the French had gone against Grenada. He consequently had put to sea on the 3rd, with the force mentioned.

---

[1] List of the British Fleet in the action off Grenada, July 6th, 1779. From Beatson, vi. 160 (corrected). — W. L. C.

SHIPS.	GUNS.	MEN.	COMMANDERS.	LOSSES.	
				Killed.	Wounded.
Suffolk	74	617	{ Rear-Adm. Joshua Rowley. { Capt. Hugh Cloberry Christian.	7	25
Boyne	70	520	Capt. Herbert Sawyer.	12	30
Royal Oak . . .	74	600	Capt. Thomas Fitzherbert.	4	12
Prince of Wales .	74	600	{ Vice-Admiral the Hon. Samuel Barrington. { Capt. Benjamin Hill.	26	46
Magnificent . .	74	600	Capt. John Elphinstone.	8	11
Trident	64	500	Capt. Anthony James Pye Molloy.	3	6
Medway . . .	60	420	Capt. William Affleck.	—	4
Fame	74	600	Capt. John Butchart.	4	9
Nonsuch . . .	64	500	Capt. Walter Griffith.	—	—
Sultan	74	600	Capt. Alan Gardner.	16	39
Princess Royal .	90	770	{ Vice-Adm. the Hon. John Byron. { Capt. William Blair.	3	6
Albion	74	600	Capt. George Bowyer.	—	2
Stirling Castle .	64	500	Capt. Robert Carkett.	2	6
Elizabeth . . .	74	600	Capt. William Truscott.	1	2
Yarmouth . . .	64	500	Capt. Nathaniel Bateman.	—	—
Lion	64	500	Capt. the Hon William Cornwallis.	21	30
Vigilant . . .	64	500	Capt. Sir Digby Dent, Kt.	—	—
Conqueror . . .	74	617	{ Rear-Adm. Hyde Parker (1). { Capt. Harry Harmood.	—	—
Cornwall . . .	74	600	Capt. Timothy Edwards.	16	27
Monmouth . . .	64	500	Capt. Robert Fanshawe.	25	28
Grafton	74	600	Capt. Thomas Collingwood.	35	63
Ariadne . . .	20	160	Capt. Thomas Pringle.	—	—

The British approach was reported to d'Estaing during the night of the 5th. Most of his fleet was then lying at anchor off George-town, at the south-west of the island; some vessels, which had been under way on look-out duty, had fallen to leeward.[1] At 4 A.M. the French began to lift their anchors, with orders to form line of battle on the starboard tack, in order of speed; that is, as rapidly as possible without regard to usual stations. When daylight had fully made, the British fleet was seen standing down from the northward, close inshore, on the port tack, with the wind free at north-east by east. It was not in order, as is evident from the fact that the ships nearest the enemy, and therefore first to close, ought to have been in the rear on the then tack. For this condition there is no evident excuse; for a fleet having a convoy necessarily proceeds so slowly that the war-ships can keep reasonable order for mutual support. Moreover, irregularities that are permissible in case of emergency, or when no enemy can be encountered suddenly, cease to be so when the probability of an imminent meeting exists. The worst results of the day are to be attributed to this fault. Being short of frigates, Byron assigned three ships of the line (a), under Rear-Admiral Rowley, to the convoy, which of course was on the off hand from the enemy, and somewhat in the rear. It was understood, however, that these would be called into the line, if needful.

When the French were first perceived by Byron, their line was forming; the long thin column lengthening out gradually to the north-north-west, from the confused cluster[2] still to be seen at the anchorage (A). Hoping to profit by their disorder, he signalled "a general chase in that quarter,[3] as well as for Rear-Admiral Rowley to leave the convoy; and as not more than fourteen or fifteen of the enemy's ships appeared to be in line, the signal was made for the ships to engage, *and form as they could get up.*"[4] It is clear from this not only that the ships were not in order, but also that

[1] To the westward. These islands lie in the trade-winds, which are constant in *general* direction from north-east.

[2] Admiral Keppel, in his evidence before the Palliser Court, gave an interesting description of a similar scene, although the present writer is persuaded that he was narrating things as they seemed, rather than — as at Grenada — as they were. "The French were forming their line exactly in the manner M. Conflans did when attacked by Admiral Hawke." (Keppel had been in that action.) "It is a manner peculiar to themselves, and to those who do not understand it, it appears like con-fusion; they draw out ship by ship from a cluster."

[3] That is, towards the ships at anchor, — the enemy's rear as matters then were.

[4] Byron's Report. The italics are the author's.

they were to form under fire. Three ships, the *Sultan*, 74, the *Prince of Wales*, 74, and the *Boyne*, 70, in the order named, — the second carrying the flag of Barrington, now a Vice-Admiral, — were well ahead of the fleet (b). The direction prescribed for the attack, that of the clustered ships in the French rear, carried the British

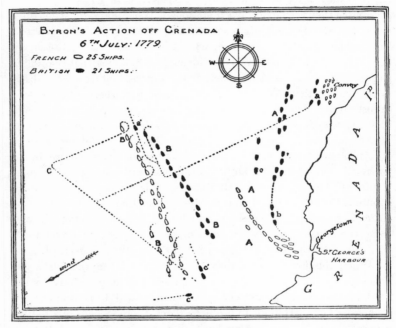

BYRON'S ACTION OFF GRENADA.

down on a south-south-west, or south by west, course; and as the enemy's van and centre were drawing out to the north-north-west, the two lines at that time resembled the legs of a " V," the point of which was the anchorage off Georgetown. Barrington's three ships therefore neared the French order gradually, and had to receive its fire for some time before they could reply, unless, by hauling to the wind, they diverged from the set course. This, and their isolation, made their loss very heavy. When they reached the rear of the French, the latter's column was tolerably formed, and Barrington's ships wore in succession, — just as Harland's had done in Keppel's action, — to follow on the other tack. In doing this, the *Sultan* kept away under the stern of the enemy's rearmost ship, to rake her; to avoid which the latter bore up. The *Sultan* thus lost time and ground, and Barrington took the lead, standing along the French line, from rear to van, and to windward.

Meanwhile, the forming of the enemy had revealed to Byron for the first time, and to his dismay, that he had been deceived in thinking the French force inferior to his own. "However, the general chase was continued, and the signal made for close engagement."[1] The remainder of the ships stood down on the port tack, as the first three had done, and wore in the wake of the latter, whom they followed; but before reaching the point of wearing, three ships (c), "the *Grafton,* 74, the *Cornwall,* 74, and the *Lion,* 64, *happening to be to leeward,*[1] sustained the fire of the enemy's whole line, as it passed on the starboard tack." It seems clear that, having had the wind, during the night and now, and being in search of an enemy, it should not have "happened" that any ships should have been so far to leeward as to be unsupported. Captain Thomas White, R.N., writing as an advocate of Byron, says,[2] "while the van was wearing . . . the sternmost ships were coming up under Rear-Admiral Hyde Parker. . . . Among these ships, the *Cornwall* and *Lion,* from being nearer the enemy than those about them (for the rear division had not then *formed into line*), drew upon themselves almost the whole of the enemy's fire." No words can show more clearly the disastrous, precipitate disorder in which this attack was conducted. The *Grafton,* White says, was similarly situated. In consequence, these three were so crippled, besides a tremendous loss in men, that they dropped far to leeward and astern on the other tack.

When the British ships in general had got round, and were in line ahead on the starboard tack, — the same as the French, — ranging from rear to van of the enemy (B), Byron signalled for the eight leading ships to close together, for mutual support, and to engage close. This, which should have been done — not with finikin precision, but with military adequacy — before engaging, was less easy now, in the din of battle and with crippled ships. A quick-eyed subordinate, however, did something to remedy the error of his chief. Rear-Admiral Rowley had been left considerably astern, having to make up the distance between the convoy and the fleet. As he followed the latter, he saw Barrington's three ships unduly separated, and doubtless visibly much mauled. Instead, therefore, of blindly

---

[1] Byron's Report. Author's italics.
[2] 'Naval Researches.' London, 1830. p. 22.

following his leader, he cut straight across (a a′) to the head of the column to support the van, — an act almost absolutely identical with that which won Nelson renown at Cape St. Vincent.   In this he was followed by the *Monmouth*, 64, the brilliancy of whose bearing was so conspicuous to the two fleets that it is said the French officers after the battle toasted " the little black ship."   She and the *Suffolk*, 74, Rowley's flagship, also suffered severely in this gallant feat.

It was imperative with Byron now to keep his van well up with the enemy, lest he should uncover the convoy, broad on the weather bow of the two fleets.   " They seemed much inclined to cut off the convoy, and had it much in their power by means of their large frigates, independent of ships of the line." [1]   On the other hand, the *Cornwall*, *Grafton*, and *Lion*, though they got their heads round, could not keep up with the fleet (c′), and were dropping also to leeward — towards the enemy.   At noon, or soon after, d'Estaing bore up with the body of his force to join some of his vessels that had fallen to leeward.   Byron very properly — under his conditions of inferiority — kept his wind; and the separation of the two fleets, thus produced, caused firing to cease at 1 P.M.

The enemies were now ranged on parallel lines, some distance apart; still on the starboard tack, heading north-north-west.   Between the two, but far astern, the *Cornwall*, *Grafton*, *Lion*, and a fourth British ship, the *Fame*, were toiling along, greatly crippled.   At 3 P.M., the French, now in good order, tacked together, which caused them to head towards these disabled vessels.   Byron at once imitated the movement, and the eyes of all in the two fleets anxiously watched the result.   Captain Cornwallis of the *Lion*, measuring the situation accurately, saw that, if he continued ahead, he would be in the midst of the French by the time he got abreast them.   Having only his foremast standing, he put his helm up, and stood broad off before the wind (c″), across the enemy's bows, for Jamaica.   He was not pursued.   The other three, unable to tack and afraid to wear, which would put them also in the enemy's power, stood on, passed to windward of the latter, receiving several broadsides, and so escaped to the northward.   The *Monmouth* was equally maltreated; in fact, she had not been able to tack to the southward with the fleet.   Continuing north (a′), she was now much separated.   D'Estaing afterwards re-formed his fleet on its leewardmost ship (BC).

Byron's action off Grenada was the most disastrous, viewed as an isolated event, that the British Navy had encountered since Beachy Head, in 1690. That the *Cornwall*, *Grafton*, and *Lion* were not captured was due simply to the strained and cautious inaptitude of the French admiral. This Byron virtually admitted. "To my great surprise no ship of the enemy was detached after the *Lion*. The *Grafton* and *Cornwall* might have been weathered by the French, if they had kept their wind, . . . but they persevered so strictly in declining every chance of close action that they contented themselves with firing upon these ships when passing barely within gunshot, and suffered them to rejoin the squadron, without one effort to cut them off." Suffren,[1] who led the French on the starboard tack, and whose ship, the *Fantasque*, 64, lost 22 killed and 43 wounded, wrote : "Had our admiral's seamanship equalled his courage, we would not have allowed four dismasted ships to escape." That the *Monmouth* and *Fame* could also have been secured is extremely probable ; and had Byron, in order to save them, borne down to renew the action, the disaster might have become a catastrophe.

That nothing resulted to the French from their great advantage is a matter for French naval history, not for British. It is otherwise as regards the causes of such a grave calamity, when twenty ships met twenty-four,[2] — a sensible but not overwhelming superiority. These facts have been shown sufficiently. Byron's disaster was due to attacking with needless precipitation, and in needless disorder. He had the weather-gage, it was early morning, and the east wind, already a working breeze, must freshen as the day advanced. The French were tied to their new conquest, which they could not abandon without humiliation, not to speak of their troops ashore ; but even had they wished to retreat, they could not have done so before a general chase, unless prepared to sacrifice their slower ships. If twenty-four ships could reconcile themselves to running from twenty, it was scarcely possible but that the fastest of these would overtake the slowest of those. There were time for fighting, an opportunity for forcing action

---

[1] Pierre A. de Suffren de Saint Tropez, a Bailli of the Order of Knights of Malta. Born 1726. Present at two naval actions before he was twenty. Participated in 1750 in the attack on Port Mahon, and in 1759 in the action off Lagos. Chef d'escadre in 1779. Dispatched to the East Indies. Fought a British squadron in the Bay of Praya, and a succession of brilliant actions with Sir Edward Hughes. Vice-Admiral, 1783. Killed in a duel, 1788. One of the greatest of French naval officers. — W. L. C.

[2] Troude says that one French seventy-four, having touched in leaving port, was not in the engagement.

which could not be evaded, and time also for the British to form in reasonable order.

It is important to consider this, because, while Keppel must be approved for attacking in partial disorder, Byron must be blamed for attacking in utter disorder. Keppel had to snatch opportunity from an unwilling foe. Having himself the lee-gage, he could not pick and choose, nor yet manœuvre; yet he brought his fleet into action, giving mutual support throughout nearly, if not quite, the whole line. What Byron did has been set forth; the sting is that his bungling tactics can find no extenuation in any urgency of the case.

The loss of the two fleets, as given by the authorities of either nation, were: British, 183 killed, 346 wounded; French, 190 killed, 759 wounded. Of the British total, 126 killed and 235 wounded, or two thirds, fell to the two groups of three ships each, which by the Vice-Admiral's mismanagement were successively exposed to be cut up in detail by the concentrated fire of the enemy. The British loss in spars and sails — in motive-power — also exceeded greatly that of the French.

After the action d'Estaing returned quietly to Grenada. Byron went to St. Kitts to refit; but repairs were most difficult, owing to the dearth of stores in which the Admiralty had left the West Indies. With all the skill of the seamen of that day in making good damages, the ships remained long unserviceable, causing great apprehension for the other islands. This state of things d'Estaing left unimproved, as he had his advantage in the battle. He did, indeed, parade his superior force before Byron's fleet as it lay at anchor; but, beyond the humiliation naturally felt by a Navy which prided itself on ruling the sea, no further injury was done.

In August Byron sailed for England. Vice-Admiral Barrington had already gone home, wounded. The station therefore was left in command of Rear-Admiral Hyde Parker (1), and so remained until the following March, when Admiral Sir George Brydges Rodney, K. B., arrived as Commander-in-Chief on the Leeward Islands Station. The North American Station was given to Vice-Admiral Marriot Arbuthnot, who had under him a half-dozen ships of the line, with headquarters at New York. His command was generally independent of Rodney's, but the latter had no hesitation in going to New York on emergency and taking charge there; in doing which he had the approval of the Admiralty.

The approach of winter in 1778 had determined the cessation of operations, both naval and military, in the northern part of the American continent, and had led to the transfer of 5,000 troops to the West Indies, already noted.   At the same time, an unjustifiable extension of British effort, having regard to the disposable means, was undertaken in the Southern States of Georgia and South Carolina.   On the 27th of November a small detachment of troops under Lieutenant-Colonel Archibald Campbell, sailed from Sandy Hook, convoyed by a division

ADMIRAL MARRIOT ARBUTHNOT.

(From a lithograph by H. R. Cook, after the portrait by Rising.)

of frigates commanded by Captain Hyde Parker (2),[1] in the *Phœnix*, 44.   It entered the Savannah River four weeks later, and soon afterwards occupied the city of the same name.   Simultaneously with this, by Clinton's orders, General Prevost moved from Florida, then a British colony, with all the men he could spare from the defence of St. Augustine.   Upon his arrival in Savannah, he took command of the whole force thus assembled.

[1] Sir Hyde Parker, Kt. Born, 1739. Captain, 1763. Rear-Admiral, 1793. Vice-Admiral, 1794. Admiral, 1799. Died, 1807. Nelson's chief at Copenhagen, in 1801.

These operations, which during 1779 extended as far as the
neighbourhood of Charleston, depended upon the control of the
water, and are a conspicuous example of misapplication of power to
the point of ultimate self-destruction. They were in 1778–79 essentially of a minor character, especially the maritime part, and will
therefore be dismissed with the remark that the Navy, by small vessels, accompanied every movement in a country cut up in all directions by water-courses, large and small. " The defence of this
province," wrote Parker, " must greatly depend on the naval force
upon the different inland creeks. I am therefore forming some galleys covered from musketry, which I believe will have a good effect."
These were precursors of the " tin-clads " of the American Civil War,
a century later. Not even an armoured ship is a new thing under
the sun.

In the Southern States, from Georgia to Virginia, the part of the
Navy from first to last was subsidiary, though important. It is therefore unnecessary to go into details, but most necessary to note that
here, by misdirection of effort and abuse of means, was initiated the
fatal movement which henceforth divided the small British army in
North America into two sections, wholly out of mutual support.
Here was reproduced on a larger, and therefore more fatal, scale,
Howe's error of 1777. This led directly, by the inevitable logic of
a false position, to Cornwallis's march through North Carolina
into Virginia, to Yorktown in 1781, and to the signal demonstration of sea power off Chesapeake Bay, which accomplished with a
crash the independence of the United States. No hostile strategist
could have severed the British army more hopelessly than did
the British government; no fate could have been more inexorable
than was its own perverse will. The personal alienation and
official quarrel between Sir Henry Clinton and Lord Cornwallis,
their divided counsels and divergent action, were but the natural
result, and the reflection, of a situation essentially self-contradictory
and exasperating.

As the hurricane season of 1779 advanced, d'Estaing, who had
orders to bring back to France the ships of the line with which he
had sailed from Toulon in 1778, resolved to go first upon the American coast, off South Carolina or Georgia. Arriving with his whole
fleet at the mouth of the Savannah, August 31st, he decided to
attempt to wrest the city of Savannah from the British. This would
have been of real service to the latter, had it nipped in the bud

their ex-centric undertaking; but, after three weeks of opened trenches, an assault upon the place failed. D'Estaing then sailed for Europe with the ships designated to accompany him, the others returning to the West Indies in two squadrons, under De Grasse and La Motte-Picquet. Though fruitless in its main object, this enterprise of d'Estaing had the important indirect effect of causing the British to abandon Narragansett Bay. Upon the news of his appearance, Sir Henry Clinton had felt that, with his greatly diminished army, he could not hold both Rhode Island and New York. He therefore ordered the evacuation of the former, thus surrendering, to use again Rodney's words, "the best and noblest harbour in America." The following summer it was occupied in force by the French.

D'Estaing was succeeded in the chief command, in the West Indies and North America, by Rear-Admiral de Guichen,[1] who arrived on the station in March, 1780, almost at the same moment as Rodney.

In June, 1779, the maritime situation of Great Britain had become much more serious by Spain's declaring war. At the same moment that d'Estaing with twenty-five ships of the line had confronted Byron's twenty-one, the Channel fleet of forty sail had seen gathering against it a host of sixty-six. Of this great number thirty-six were Spanish.

The open declaration of Spain had been preceded by a secret alliance with France, signed on the 12th of April. Fearing that the British government would take betimes the reasonable and proper step of blockading the Brest fleet of thirty with the Channel forty, thus assuming a central position with reference to its enemies and anticipating the policy of Lord St. Vincent, the French Ministry hurried its ships to sea on the 4th of June; Admiral d'Orvilliers, Keppel's opponent, still in command. His orders were to cruise off the island of Cizarga, where the Spaniards were to join. On the 11th he was at his station, but not till the 23rd of July did the bulk of the Spanish force appear. During this time, the French, insufficiently equipped from the first, owing to the haste of their departure, were consuming provisions and water, not to speak of wasting pleasant summer weather. Their ships also were ravaged by an epidemic

---

[1] Louis Urbain de Bouënic, Comte de Guichen. Born, 1712. Entered the navy, 1730. Commanded the *Illustre* with success in North America in 1756. Second in command in the action off Ushant in 1778. Thrice fought Rodney in the West Indies in 1780. Fought Kempenfelt off the Azores in 1781. Died, 1790. — W. L. C.

fever.   Upon the junction, d'Orvilliers found that the Spaniards had
not been furnished with the French system of signals, although by
the treaty the French admiral was to be in chief command.   The
rectification of this oversight caused further delay, but on the 11th
of August the combined fleet sighted Ushant, and on the 14th was
off the Lizard.   On the 16th it appeared before Plymouth, and there
on the 17th captured the *Ardent*, 64, Captain Philip Boteler.

ADMIRAL SIR CHARLES HARDY (2), KT.

(From the lithograph by H. R. Cook, after the portrait by G. Romney.)

Thirty-five ships of the Channel fleet had gone to sea on the
16th of June, and were now cruising outside, under the command
of Admiral Sir Charles Hardy (2).[1]   His station was from ten to

---

[1] Admiral Sir Charles Hardy (2), Kt.   Son of Vice-Admiral Sir Charles Hardy
(1), who died in 1744.   Born about 1716.   Entered the Navy, 1731.   Lieutenant,
1737.   Commander, 1741.   Captain, 1741.   Knighted, and Governor of New York,
1755.   Rear-Admiral, 1756.   Employed under Boscawen and Hawke.   Vice-Admiral,
1762.   Admiral, 1770.   Governor of Greenwich Hospital, 1771.   Commander-in-
Chief in the Channel, 1779.   Died, 1780. — W. L. C.

twenty leagues south-west of Scilly; consequently he had not been seen by the enemy, who from Ushant had stood up the Channel. The allies, however, now nearly double the numbers of the British, were between them and their ports, — a serious situation doubtless, but by no means desperate; not so dangerous for sailing ships as it probably will be for steamers to have an enemy between them and their coal.

The alarm in England was very great, and especially in the south. On the 9th of July a royal proclamation had commanded all horses and cattle to be driven from the coasts, in case of invasion.   Booms had been placed across the entrance to Plymouth Harbour, and orders were sent from the Admiralty to sink vessels across the harbour's mouth.   Many who had the means withdrew into the interior, which increased the panic.   Great merchant fleets were then on the sea, homeward bound.   If d'Orvilliers were gone to cruise in the approaches to the Channel, instead of to the Spanish coast, these might be taken; and for some time his whereabouts were unknown.   As it was, the Jamaica convoy, over two hundred sail, got in a few days before the allies appeared, and the Leeward Islands fleet had similar good fortune.   Eight homeward bound East Indiamen were less lucky, but, being warned of their danger, took refuge in the Shannon, and there remained till the trouble blew over.   On the other hand, the stock market stood firm.   Nevertheless, it was justly felt that such a state of things as a vastly superior hostile fleet in the Channel should not have been.   "What a humiliating state is our country reduced to!" wrote Jervis, who was with the fleet, to his sister; but he added that he laughed at the idea of invasion.

The French had placed a force of fifty thousand men at Le Havre and St. Malo, and collected four hundred vessels for their transport. Their plans were not certainly known, but enough had transpired to cause reasonable anxiety; and the crisis, on its face, was very serious. Not their own preparations, but the inefficiency of their enemies, in counsel and in preparation, saved the British Islands from invasion. What the results of this would have been is another question, — a question of land warfare.   The original scheme of the French Ministry was to seize the Isle of Wight, securing Spithead as an anchorage for the fleet, and to prosecute their enterprise from this near and reasonably secure base.   Referring to this first project, d'Orvilliers wrote: "We will seek the enemy at St. Helen's, and then, if I find that roadstead unoccupied, or make myself master of it, I will send

word to Marshal De Vaux, at Le Havre, and inform him of the
measures I will take to insure his passage, which [measures] will
depend upon the position of the English main fleet [dépendront
des forces supérieures des Anglais]. That is to say, I myself will
lead the combined fleet on that side, to contain the enemy, and
I will send, on the other side, a light squadron, with a sufficient
number of ships of the line and frigates; or I will propose to M. de
Cordova to take this latter station, in order that the passage of the
army may be free and sure. I assume that then, either by the
engagement I shall have fought with the enemy, *or by their retreat
into their ports,* I shall be certain of their situation and of the success
of the operation." [1]   It will be observed that d'Orvilliers, accounted
then and now one of the best officers of his day in the French navy,
takes here into full account the British "fleet in being." [2]   The main
body of the allies, fifty ships, was to hold this in check, while a
smaller force — Cordova had command of a special "squadron of
observation," of sixteen ships of the line — was to convoy the
crossing.

These projects all fell to pieces before a strong east wind, and a
change of mind in the French government. On the 16th of August,
before Plymouth, d'Orvilliers was notified that not the Isle of
Wight, but the coast of Cornwall, near Falmouth, was to be the scene
of landing. The effect of this was to deprive the huge fleet of any
anchorage, — a resource necessary even to steamers, and far more
to sailing vessels aiming to remain in a position. As a point to
begin shore operations, too, as well as to sustain them, such a remote
corner of the country to be invaded was absurd. D'Orvilliers duly
represented all this, but could not stay where he was long enough to
get a reply. An easterly gale came on, which blew hard for several
days and drove the allies out of the Channel. On the 25th of August
word was received that the British fleet was near Scilly. A council
of war was then held, which decided that, in view of the terrible
increase of disease in the shipping, and of the shortness of provisions,
it was expedient not to re-enter the Channel, but to seek the enemy,
and bring him to battle. This was done. On the 29th Hardy was
sighted, being then on his return up Channel. With the disparity
of force he could not but avoid action, and the allies were unable to

<hr>

[1] Chevalier, 'Marine Française,' 1778. p. 165. Author's italics.
[2] But it was not merely a "fleet in being." It was also, in all senses, a "potential
fleet." — W. L. C.

compel it. On the 3rd of September he reached Spithead. D'Orvilliers soon afterwards received orders to return to Brest, and on
the 14th the combined fleet anchored there.

The criticism to be passed on the conduct of this summer campaign by the British Ministry is twofold. In the first place, it was
not ready, according to the reasonable standard of the day, which
recognised in the probable co-operation of the two Bourbon kingdoms, France and Spain, the measure of the minimum naval force
permissible to Great Britain. Secondly, the entrance of Spain into the
war had been foreseen months before. For the inferior force, therefore,
it was essential to prevent a junction, — to take an interior position.
The Channel fleet ought to have been off Brest before the French
sailed. After they were gone, there was still fair ground for the
contention of the Opposition, that they should have been followed,
and attacked, off the coast of Spain. During the six weeks they
waited there, they were inferior to Hardy's force. Allowance here
must be made, however, for the inability of a representative government to disregard popular outcry, and uncover the main approach to
its own ports. This, indeed, does but magnify the error made in not
watching Brest betimes, for a fleet before Brest covered also the
Channel.

With regard to the objects of the war in which they had become
partners, the views of France and Spain accorded in but one point, —
the desirability of injuring Great Britain. Each had its own special
aim for its own advantage. This necessarily introduced divergence
of effort; but France, having first embarked in the contest and then
sought the aid of an ally, the particular objects of the latter naturally
obtained from the beginning a certain precedence. Until near the
close of the war, it may be said that the chief ambitions of France
were in the West Indies; those of Spain, in Europe, — to regain
Minorca and Gibraltar.

In this way Gibraltar became a leading factor in the contest, and
affected, directly or indirectly, the major operations throughout the
world, by the amount of force absorbed in attacking and preserving
it. After the futile effort in the Channel, in 1779, Spain recalled
her vessels from Brest. " The project of a descent upon England
was abandoned provisionally. To blockade Gibraltar, to have in
America and Asia force sufficient to hold the British in check,
and to take the offensive in the West Indies, — such," wrote the
French government to its ambassador in Madrid, " was the plan of

campaign adopted for 1780." Immediately upon the declaration of war, intercourse between Gibraltar and the Spanish mainland was stopped; and soon afterwards a blockade by sea was instituted, fifteen cruisers being stationed at the entrance of the Bay, where they seized and sent into Spanish ports all vessels, neutral or British, bound to the Rock. This blockade was effectively supported from Cadiz, but a Spanish force of some ships of the line and many small vessels also maintained it more directly from Algeciras, on the opposite side of the Bay of Gibraltar. The British Mediterranean squadron, then consisting only of one 60-gun ship, three frigates, and a sloop, was wholly unable to afford relief. At the close of the year 1779, flour was fourteen guineas the barrel, and other provisions in proportion. It became therefore imminently necessary to throw in supplies of all kinds, as well as to reinforce the garrison. To this service Rodney was assigned; and with it he began the brilliant career, the chief scene of which was to be in the West Indies.

Rodney was appointed to command the Leeward Islands Station on the 1st of October, 1779. He was to be accompanied there immediately by only four or five ships of the line; but advantage was taken of his sailing, to place under the charge of an officer of his approved reputation a great force, composed of his small division and a large fraction of the Channel fleet, to convoy supplies and reinforcements to Gibraltar and Minorca. On the 29th of December the whole body, after many delays in getting down Channel, put to sea from Plymouth : twenty-two ships of the line, fourteen frigates and smaller vessels, besides a huge collection of storeships, victuallers, ordnance vessels, troop-ships, and merchantmen, — the "trade" for the West Indies and Portugal.

On the 7th of January, a hundred leagues west of Cape Finisterre, the West India ships parted, under convoy of a ship of the line and three frigates. At daylight on the 8th, twenty-two sail were seen to the north-east, the squadron apparently having passed them in the night. Chase was at once given, and the whole were taken in a few hours. Seven [1] were ships of war, chiefly frigates; the remainder merchant vessels, laden with naval stores and provisions for the Spanish fleet at Cadiz. The provision ships, twelve in number, were diverted at once to the relief of Gibraltar, under charge of the Span-

---

[1] *Guipuscoana*, 64 (added to the Royal Navy as *Prince William*); *San Carlos*, 32; *San Rafael*, 30; *San Bruno*, 26; *Santa Teresa*, 24; *San Fermin*, 16; *San Vincente*, 14. Steel's 'Navy List': Beatson, vi. 233. — W. L. C.

ish sixty-four, which had been one of their convoy before capture, and had now received a British crew. Continuing on, intelligence was received from time to time by passing vessels that a Spanish squadron was cruising off Cape St. Vincent. Thus forewarned, orders were given to all captains to be prepared for battle as the Cape was neared. On the 16th it was passed, and at 1 P.M. sails in the southeast were signalled. These were a Spanish squadron of eleven ships of the line, and two 26-gun frigates. Rodney at once bore down for them under a press of canvas, making signal for the line abreast. Seeing, however, that the enemy was trying to form line of battle on the starboard tack, which with a westerly wind was with heads to the southward, towards Cadiz, a hundred miles to the south-east, he changed the orders to a " General Chase," the ships to engage as they came up; " to leeward," so as to get between the enemy and his post, and "in rotation," by which probably was meant that the leading British vessel should attack the sternmost of the Spaniards, and that her followers should pass her to leeward, successively engaging from the enemy's rear towards the van.

At 4 P.M. the signal for battle was made, and a few minutes later the four headmost of the pursuers got into action. At 4.40 one of the Spanish ships, the *Santo Domingo*, 70, blew up with all on board, and at 6 another struck. By this hour, it being January, darkness had set in. A night action therefore followed, which lasted until 2 A.M., when the headmost of the enemy surrendered, and all firing ceased. Of the eleven hostile ships of the line, only four escaped. Besides the one blown up, six were taken. These were the *Fénix*, 80, flag of the Spanish Admiral, Don Juan de Langara, the *Monarca*, 70, the *Princesa*, 70, the *Diligente*, 70, the *San Julian*, 70, and the *San Eugenio*, 70. The two latter drove ashore and were lost.[1] The remaining four were brought into Gibraltar, and were ultimately added to the Navy. All retained their old names, save the *Fénix*, which was re-named *Gibraltar*. " The weather during the night," by Rodney's report, " was at times very tempestuous, with a great sea. It continued very bad weather the next day, when the *Royal George*, 100, *Prince George*, 90, *Sandwich*, 90 (Rodney's flagship), and several other ships were in great danger, and under the necessity of making sail to avoid the shoals of San Lucar, nor did they get into deep water till the next morning."

[1] Rodney's Report. Chevalier says that one of them was retaken by her crew and carried into Cadiz.

It was in this danger from a lee shore, which was deliberately though promptly incurred, that the distinction of this action of Rodney's consists. The enemy's squadron, being only eleven ships of the line, was but half the force of the British, and it was taken by surprise ; which, to be sure, is no excuse for a body of war-ships in war-time. Caught unawares, the Spaniards took to flight too late. It was Rodney's merit, and no slight one under the conditions of weather and navigation, that they were not permitted to retrieve their mistake. His action left nothing to be desired in resolution or readiness. It is true that Rodney discussed the matter with his flag-captain, Walter Young, and that rumour attributed the merit of the decision to the latter; but this sort of detraction is of too common occurrence to affect opinion. Sir Gilbert Blane, Physician to the Fleet, gives the following account: " When it was close upon sunset, it became a question whether the chase should be continued. After some discussion between the Admiral and Captain, at which I was present, the Admiral being confined with the gout, it was decided to persist in the same course, with the signal to engage to leeward." Rodney at that time was nearly sixty-two, and a constant martyr to gout in both feet and hands.

The two successes by the way imparted a slightly triumphal character to the welcome of the Admiral by the garrison, then sorely in need of some good news. The arrival of much-needed supplies from home was itself a matter of rejoicing ; but it was more inspiriting still to see following in the train of the friendly fleet five hostile ships of the line, one of them bearing the flag of a Commander-in-Chief, and to hear that, besides these, three more had been sunk or destroyed. The exultation in England was even greater, and especially at the Admiralty, which was labouring under the just indignation of the people for the unpreparedness of the Navy. " You have taken more line-of-battle ships," wrote the First Lord to Rodney, " than had been captured in any one action in either of the two last preceding wars."

It should be remembered, too, as an element in the triumph, that this advantage over an exposed detachment had been snatched, as it were, in the teeth of a main fleet superior to Rodney's own; for twenty Spanish and four French ships of the line, under Admiral de Cordova, were lying then in Cadiz Bay. During the eighteen days when the British remained in and near the Straits, no attempt was made by Cordova to take revenge for the disaster, or to reap the benefit of superior force. The inaction was due, probably, to the poor condition of the Spanish ships in point of efficiency and equipment, and largely to their having uncoppered bottoms. This element of inferiority in the Spanish navy should be kept in mind as a factor in the general war, although Spanish fleets did not come much into battle. A French Commodore, then with the Spanish fleet in Ferrol, wrote as follows : " Their ships all sail so badly that they can neither overtake an enemy nor escape from one. The *Glorieux* is a bad sailer in the French navy, but better than the best among the Spaniards." He adds : "The vessels of Langara's squadron were surprised at immense distances one from the other. Thus they always sail, and their negligence and security on this point are incredible."

On approaching Gibraltar, the continuance of bad weather, and the strong easterly current of the Straits, set many of Rodney's ships and convoy to leeward, to the back of the Rock, and it was not till the 26th that the flagship herself anchored. The storeships for Minorca were sent on at once, under charge of three coppered ships of the line. The practice of coppering, though then fully adopted, had not yet extended to all vessels. As an element of speed, it was an important factor on an occasion like this, when time pressed to get to the West Indies ; as it also was in an engagement. The action on the 16th had been opened by the coppered ships of the line, which first overtook the retreating enemy and brought his rear to battle. In the French navy at the time, Suffren was urging the adoption upon an apparently reluctant Minister. It would seem to have been more general among the British, going far to compensate for the otherwise inferior qualities of their ships. "The Spanish men-of-war we have taken," wrote Rodney to his wife concerning these prizes, "are much superior to ours." It may be remembered that Nelson, thirteen years later, said the same. "I perceive you cry out loudly for coppered ships," wrote the First Lord to Rodney after this action ; "and I am therefore determined to stop your mouth. You shall have copper enough."

Upon the return of the ships from Minorca, Rodney put to sea again on the 13th of February, for the West Indies. The detachment from the Channel fleet accompanied him three days' sail on his way, and then parted for England with the prizes. On this return voyage it fell in with fifteen French supply vessels, convoyed by two sixty-fours, bound for the Ile de France, in the Indian Ocean. One

of the ships of war, the *Protée*, and three of the storeships were taken.
Though trivial, the incident illustrates the effect of operations in
Europe upon war in India.   It may be mentioned here as indicative
of the government's dilemmas, that Rodney was censured for having left one ship of the line at the Rock.   " It has given us the
trouble *and risk* of sending a frigate on purpose to order her home
immediately ; and if you will look into your original instructions, you
will find that there was no point more strongly guarded against than
that of your leaving any line-of-battle ship behind you."   These
words clearly show the exigency and peril of the general situation,
owing to the inadequate development of the naval force as compared
with its foes.   Such isolated ships ran the gauntlet of the fleets flanking their routes in Cadiz, Ferrol, and Brest.

When Rodney arrived at St. Lucia with his four ships of the line,
on the 27th of March, he found there a force of sixteen others, composed in about equal proportions of ships that had left England with
Byron in the summer of 1778, and of a reinforcement brought by
Rear-Admiral Rowley in the spring of 1779.

During the temporary command of Rear-Admiral Hyde Parker,
a smart affair had taken place between a detachment of the squadron
and one from the French division, under La Motte-Picquet, then
lying in Fort Royal.

On the 18th of December, 1779, between 8 and 9 A.M., the British
look-out ship, the *Preston*, 50, between Martinique and St. Lucia,
made signal for a fleet to windward, which proved to be a body of
French supply ships, twenty-six in number, under convoy of a frigate.
Both the British and the French squadrons were in disarray, sails
unbent, ships on the heel or partially disarmed, crews ashore for
wood and water.   In both, signals flew at once for certain ships to
get under way, and in both the orders were executed with a rapidity
gratifying to the two commanders, who also went out in person.
The British, however, were outside first, with five sail of the line
and a 50-gun ship.   Nine of the merchant vessels were captured
by them, and four forced ashore.   The French Rear-Admiral had
by this time got out of Fort Royal with three ships of the line, — the
Annibal, 74, *Vengeur*, 64, and *Réfléchi*, 64, — and, being to windward,
covered the entrance of the remainder of the convoy.   As the two
hostile divisions were now near each other, with a fine working
breeze, the British tried to beat up to the enemy ; the *Conqueror*, 74,
Captain Walter Griffith, being ahead and to windward of her consorts.

Coming within range at 5, firing began between her and the French flagship, *Annibal*, 74, and subsequently between her and all the three vessels of the enemy.   Towards sunset, the *Albion*, 74, had got close up with the *Conqueror*, and the other ships were within distant range ; "but as they had worked not only well within the dangers of the shoals of the bay (Fort Royal), but within reach of the batteries, I called them off by night signal at a quarter before seven."[1]   In this chivalrous skirmish, — for it was little more, although the injury to the French in the loss of the convoy was notable, — Parker was equally delighted with his own squadron and with his enemy.   "The steadiness and coolness with which on every tack the *Conqueror* received the fire of these three ships, and returned her own, work-ing his ship with as much exactness as if he had been turning into Spithead, and on every board gaining on the enemy, gave me infi-nite pleasure.   It was with inexpressible concern," he added, "that I heard that Captain Walter Griffith, of the *Conqueror*, was killed by the last broadside."[1]   Having occasion, a few days later, to exchange a flag of truce with the French Rear-Admiral, he wrote to him : "The conduct of your Excellency in the affair of the 18th of this month fully justifies the reputation which you enjoy among us, and I assure you that I could not witness without envy the skill you showed on that occasion.   Our enmity is transient, depending upon our masters ; but your merit has stamped upon my heart the greatest admiration for yourself."   This was the officer who was commonly known in his time as "Vinegar" Parker; but these letters show that the epithet fitted the rind rather than the kernel.

Shortly after de Guichen took command, he arranged with the Marquis de Bouillé, Governor of Martinique, to make a combined attack upon some one of the British West India Islands.   For this purpose 3,000 troops were embarked in the fleet, which sailed on the night of the 13th of April, 1780, intending first to accompany a convoy for Santo Domingo, until it was safely out of reach of the British.   Rodney, who was informed at once of the French departure, put to sea in chase with all his ships, twenty of the line, two of which were of 90 guns, and on the 16th came in sight of the enemy to lee-ward of Martinique, beating up against the north-east trade-winds, and intending to pass through the channel between that island and Dominica.   "A general chase to the north-west followed, and at five

---

[1] Parker's Report.

in the evening we plainly discovered that they consisted of twenty-three sail of the line, and one fifty-gun ship." [1]

As it fell dark Rodney formed his line of battle,[2] standing still to the north-west, therefore on the starboard tack ; and he was attentive to keep to windward of the enemy, whom his frigates watched diligently during the night. "Their manœuvres," he wrote, "indicated a wish to avoid battle," and he therefore was careful to coun-

[1] Rodney's Report. The French authorities give their line of battle as twenty-two ships of the line. There was no 90-gun ship among them — no three-decker ; but there were two of 80 guns, of which also the British had none.

[2] British line of battle on April 17th, 1780. The *Stirling Castle* to lead with the starboard, and the *Magnificent* with the larboard tacks on board. From Beatson, vi., 217, 218, with additions and corrections. — W. L. C.

	SHIPS.	Guns.	Men.	COMMANDERS.	Killed.	Wounded.
VAN.	Stirling Castle . .	64	500	Capt. Robert Carkett.	4	34
	Ajax	74	600	Capt. Samuel Uvedale.	4	13
	Elizabeth	74	600	Capt. Hon. Fredk. Lewis Maitland.	9	15
	Princess Royal . .	90	770	{ Rear-Admiral Hyde Parker (R). } { Capt. Harry Harmood. }	5	14
	Albion	74	600	Capt. George Bowyer.	3	2
	Terrible	74	600	Capt. John Douglas.	—	—
	Trident	64	500	Capt. Anthony James Pye Molloy.	14	26
	Greyhound, 28 .			Capt. William Dickson.	—	—
CENTRE.	Grafton	74	600	{ Commod. Thomas Collingwood. } { Capt. Thomas Newnham. }	2	30
	Yarmouth . . .	64	500	Capt. Nathaniel Bateman.	5	15
	Cornwall	74	600	Capt. Timothy Edwards.	21	49
	Sandwich	90	752	{ Adm. Sir George Brydges Rodney (W). } { Capt. Walter Young. }	18	51
	Suffolk	74	600	Capt. Abraham Crespin.	—	12
	Boyne	70	520	Capt. Charles Cotton.	2	—
	Vigilant	64	500	Capt. Sir George Home, Bart.	—	2
	Venus, 36 . .			Capt. John Fergusson.	—	—
	Pegasus, 28 . .			Capt. John Bazely (1).	—	—
	Deal Castle, 24			Capt. William Fooks.	—	—
REAR.	Vengeance	74	617	{ Commod. William Hotham. } { Capt. John Holloway. }	4	6
	Medway	60	420	Capt. William Affleck.	2	3
	Montagu	74	600	Capt. John Houlton.	9	26
	Conqueror	74	617	{ Rear-Admiral Joshua Rowley (R). } { Capt. Thomas Watson. }	13	36
	Intrepid	64	500	Capt. the Hon. Henry St. John.	7	10
	Magnificent . . .	74	600	Capt. John Elphinstone.	1	10
	Andromeda, 28			Capt. Henry Bryne.	—	—
	Centurion,* 50			Capt. Richard Brathwaite.	—	—

* To assist the Rear in case of need.

teract them. At daylight of the 17th, they were seen forming line
of battle, on the port tack, four or five leagues to leeward, — that is,
to the westward. The wind being east, or east by north, the French
would be heading south-south-east (Fig. 1, aa). The British order
now was rectified by signal from the irregularities of darkness,
the ships being directed to keep two cables'[1] lengths apart, and
steering as before to the northward and westward (a). At 7 A.M.,

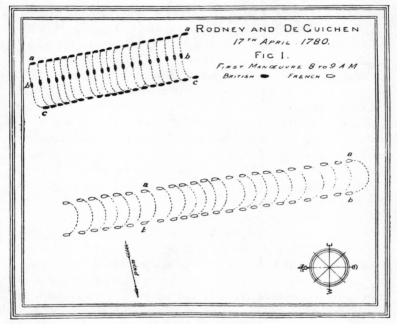

RODNEY AND DE GUICHEN.

considering this line too extended, the Admiral closed the intervals
to one cable. The two fleets thus were passing on nearly parallel
lines, but in opposite directions, which tended to bring the whole
force of Rodney, whose line was better and more compact than the
enemy's, abreast the latter's rear, upon which he intended to concentrate. At 8 A.M. he made general signal that this was his purpose;
and at 8.30, to execute it, he signalled for the ships to form line
abreast, bearing from each other south by east and north by west,
and stood down at once upon the enemy (Fig. 1, bb). The object

[1] A cable was then assumed to have a length of 120 fathoms, — 720 feet.

of the British being evident, de Guichen made his fleet wear together
to the starboard tack (bb).   The French rear thus became the van,
and their former van, which was stretched too far for prompt assistance to the threatened rear, now headed to support it.

Rodney, baulked in his first spring, hauled at once to the wind
on the port tack (Fig. 1, cc), again contrary to the French, standing
thus once more along their line, for their new rear.   The intervals
were opened out again to two cables.   The fleets thus were passing
once more on parallel lines, each having reversed its order ; but the
British still retained the advantage, on whatever course, that they
were much more compact than the French, whose line, by Rodney's
estimate, extended four leagues in length.[1]   The wariness of the two
combatants, both trained in the school of the eighteenth century, with
its reverence for the line of battle, will appear to the careful reader.
Rodney, although struggling through this chrysalis stage to the later
vigour, and seriously bent on a deadly blow, still was constrained
by the traditions of watchful fencing.   Nor was his caution extrava-
gant; conditions did not justify yet the apparent recklessness of
Nelson's tactics.   " The different movements of the enemy," he wrote,
" obliged me to be very attentive, and watch every opportunity that
offered of attacking them to advantage."

The two fleets continued to stand on opposite parallel courses —
the French north by west, the British south by east — until the flagship *Sandwich*, 90, was abreast the *Couronne*, 80, the flagship of de
Guichen.   Then, at 10.10 A.M., the signal was made to wear together,
forming on the same tack as the enemy.   There being some delay in
execution, this had to be repeated, and further enforced by the pennant of the *Stirling Castle*, which, as the rear ship, should begin the
evolution.   At half-past ten, apparently, the fleet was about (Fig. 2,
aa), for an order was then given for rectifying the line, still at two
cables.   At 11 A.M. the Admiral made the signal to prepare for
battle, " to convince the whole fleet I was determined to bring the
enemy to an engagement," [2] and to this succeeded shortly the order
to alter the course to port (bb), towards the enemy.[3]   Why he
thought that any of the fleet should have required such assurance

---

[1] A properly formed line of twenty ships, at two cables' interval, would be about
five miles long.   Rodney seems to have been satisfied that this was about the condition of his fleet at this moment.

[2] Rodney's Report.

[3] Testimony of the signal officer at the court-martial on Captain Bateman.

cannot certainly be said. Possibly, although he had so recently joined, he had already detected the ill-will, or the slackness, of which he afterwards complained; possibly he feared that the wariness of his tactics might lead men to believe that he did not mean to exceed the lukewarm and indecisive action of days scarce yet passed away, which had led Suffren to stigmatise tactics as a mere veil, behind which timidity thinks to hide its nakedness.

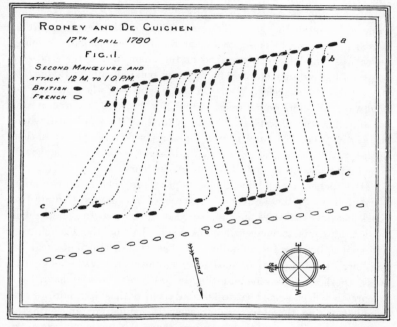

RODNEY AND DE GUICHEN.

At 11.50 A.M. the decisive signal was made "for every ship to bear down, and steer for her opposite in the enemy's line, agreeable to the 21st article of the Additional Fighting Instructions." Five minutes later, when the ships, presumably, had altered their course for the enemy, the signal for battle was made, followed by the message that the Admiral's intention was to engage closely; he expecting, naturally, that every ship would follow the example he purposed to set. The captain of the leading ship, upon whose action depended that of those near her, unfortunately understood the Admiral's signal to mean that he was to attack the enemy's leader, not the ship opposite to him at the moment of bearing away. This ship, therefore, diverged markedly from the Admiral's course, drawing after him many of the van. A few minutes before 1 P.M., one of the headmost ships began to engage at long range ; but it was not till some time after 1 P.M. that the *Sandwich*, having received several broadsides, came into close action with the second vessel astern from the French Admiral, the *Actionnaire*, 64. The latter was soon beat out of the line by the superiority of the *Sandwich's* battery, and the same lot befell the ship astern of her, — probably the *Intrépide*, 74, — which came up to close the gap. Towards 2.30 P.M., the *Sandwich*, either by her own efforts to close, or by her immediate opponents' keeping away, was found to be to leeward of the enemy's line, the *Couronne* being on her weather bow. The fact was pointed out by Rodney to the captain of the ship, Walter Young, who was then in the lee gangway. Young, going over to look for himself, saw that it was so, and that the *Yarmouth*, 64, had hauled off to windward, where she lay with her main and mizzen topsails aback. Signals were then made to her, and to the *Cornwall*, 74, to come to closer engagement, they both being on the weather bow of the flagship.

De Guichen, recognising this state of affairs, then or a little later, attributed it to the deliberate purpose of the British Admiral to break his line. It does not appear that Rodney so intended. His tactical idea was to concentrate his whole fleet on the French rear and centre, but there is no indication that he now aimed at breaking the line. De Guichen so construing it, however, gave the signal to wear together. The effect of this, in any event, would have been to carry his fleet somewhat to leeward ; but with ships more or less crippled, taking therefore greater room to manœuvre, and with the exigency of re-forming the line upon them, the tendency was exaggerated. The movement which the French called wearing together was therefore differently interpreted by Rodney. "The action in the centre continued till 4.15 P. M., when M. de Guichen, in the *Couronne*, the *Triomphant*, and the *Fendant*, after engaging the *Sandwich* for an hour and a half, bore away. The superiority of fire from the *Sandwich*, and the gallant behaviour of the officers and men, enabled her to sustain so unequal a combat ; though before attacked by them, she had beat three ships out of their line of battle, had entirely broke it, and was to leeward of the French Admiral." Possibly the French accounts, if they were not so very meagre, might dispute this prowess of the flagship ; but there can be no doubt that Rodney had set an example, which, had it been followed by all, would have made this engagement memorable, if not decisive. He reported that the captains, with very few exceptions, had not placed their ships properly (cc). The *Sandwich* had eighty shot in her hull, had lost her foremast and mainyard, and had fired 3,288 rounds, an average of 73 to each gun of the broadside engaged. Three of her hits being below the water line, she was kept afloat with difficulty during the next twenty-four hours. With the wearing of the French the battle ceased.

In the advantage offered by the enemy, whose order was too greatly extended, and in his own plan of attack, Rodney always considered this action of April 17th, 1780, to have been the great opportunity of his life; and his wrath was bitter against those by whose misconduct he conceived it had been frustrated. " The French admiral, who appeared to me to be a brave and gallant officer, had the honour to be nobly supported during the whole action. It is with concern inexpressible, mixed with indignation, that the duty I owe my sovereign and my country obliges me to acquaint your Lordships that during the action between the French fleet, on the 17th inst., and his Majesty's, the British flag was not properly supported." Divided as the Navy then was into factions, with their hands at each other's throats or at the throat of the Admiralty, the latter thought it more discreet to suppress this paragraph, allowing to appear only the negative stigma of the encomium upon the French officers, unaccompanied by any on his own. Rodney, however, did not conceal his feelings in public or private letters; and the censure found its way to the ears of those concerned. Subsequently, three months after the action, in a public letter, he bore testimony to the excellent conduct of five captains, Walter Young of the flagship, George Bowyer of the *Albion*, John Douglas of the *Terrible*, John Houlton of the *Montagu*, and A. J. P. Molloy[1] of the *Trident*. " To them I have given certificates, under my hand," " free and unsolicited." Beyond these, " no consideration in life would induce " him to go; and the two junior flag-officers were implicitly condemned in the words, " to inattention to signals, both in the van and rear divisions, is to be attributed the loss of that glorious opportunity (perhaps never to be recovered) of terminating the naval contest in these seas." These junior admirals were Hyde

---

[1] Singularly enough, this officer was afterwards court-martialled for misbehaviour, on the 1st of June, 1794, of precisely the same character as that from all share in which Rodney now cleared him.

Parker and Rowley; the latter the same who had behaved, not only
so gallantly, but with such unusual initiative, in Byron's engagement.
A singular incident in this case led him to a like independence of
action, which displeased Rodney.   The *Montagu*, of his division, when
closing the French line, wore against the helm, and could only be
brought into action on the wrong (port) tack.   Immediately upon
this, part of the French rear also wore, and Rowley followed them of
his own motion.   Being called to account by Rodney, he stated the
facts, justifying the act by the order that " the greatest impression
was to be made on the enemy's rear."   Both parties soon wore back.

Hyde Parker went home in a rage a few weeks later.   The certificates of Bowyer and Douglas, certainly, and probably of Molloy, all
of his division, bore the stinging words that these officers " meant
well, and would have done their duty had they been permitted."   It
is stated that their ships, which were the rear of the van, were going
down to engage close, following Rodney's example, when Parker
made them a signal to keep the line.   If this be so, as Parker's
courage was beyond all doubt, it was simply a recurrence of the old
superstition of the line, aggravated by a misunderstanding of Rodney's
later signals.   These must be discussed, for the whole incident is part
of the history of the British Navy, far more important than many an
indecisive though bloody encounter.

One of the captains more expressly blamed, Carkett of the *Stirling Castle*, wrote to Rodney that he understood that his name had
been mentioned, unfavourably of course, in the public letter.   Rodney's reply makes perfectly apparent the point at issue, his own plan,
the ideas running in his head as he made his successive signals, the
misconceptions of the juniors, and the consequent fiasco.   It must be
said, however, that, granting the facts as they seem certainly to have
occurred, no misunderstanding, no technical verbal allegation, can
justify a military stupidity so great as that of which he complained.
There are occasions in which not only is literal disobedience permissible, but literal obedience, flying in the face of the evident conditions,
becomes a crime.

At 6.45 in the morning, Rodney had made a general signal of his
purpose to attack the enemy's rear.   This, having been understood
and answered, was hauled down ; all juniors had been acquainted
with a general purpose, to which the subsequent manœuvres were to
lead.   How he meant to carry out his intention was evidenced by
the consecutive course of action while on that tack, — the starboard ;

when the time came, the fleet bore up together, in line abreast, standing for the French rear. This attempt, being balked then by de
Guichen's wearing, was renewed two hours later; only in place of
the signal to form line abreast, was made one to alter the course to
port, — towards the enemy. As this followed immediately upon that
to prepare for battle, it indicates, almost beyond question, that Rodney
wished, for reasons of the moment, to run down at first in a slanting
direction, — not in line abreast, as before, — ships taking course and
interval from the flagship. Later again, at 11.50, the signal was
made, "agreeable to the 21st Article of the Additional Fighting
Instructions, for every ship to steer for her opposite in the enemy's
line;" and here the trouble began. Rodney meant the ship opposite
when the signal was hauled down. He had steered slanting, till he
had gained as nearly as possible the position he wanted, probably till
within long range; then it was desirable to cover the remaining
ground as rapidly and orderly as possible, for which purpose the ship
then abreast gave each of his fleet its convenient point of direction.
He conceived that his signalled purpose to attack the enemy's rear,
never having been altered, remained imperative; and further, that
the signal for two cables' length interval should govern all ships, and
would tie them to him, and to his movements, in the centre. Carkett
construed "opposite" to mean opposite in numerical order, British
van ship against French van ship, wherever the latter was. Rodney
states — in his letter to Carkett — that the French van was then two
leagues away. "You led to the van ship, notwithstanding you had
answered my signals signifying that it was my intention to attack the
enemy's rear; which signal I had never altered. . . . Your leading in
the manner you did, induced others to follow so bad an example ; and
thereby, forgetting that the signal for the line was only at two cables'
length distance from each other, the van division was led by you to
more than two leagues' distance from the centre division, which was
thereby not properly supported." [1]

[1] The words in Rodney's public letter, suppressed at the time by the Admiralty,
agree with these, but are even more explicit. " I cannot conclude this letter without acquainting their Lordships that had Captain Carkett, who led the van, properly
obeyed my signal for attacking the enemy, and agreeable to the 21st Article of the
Additional Fighting Instructions, bore down instantly to the ship at that time
abreast of him, instead of leading as he did to the van ship, the action had com-
menced much sooner, and the fleet engaged in a more compact manner. . . ." This
clearly implies that the *Additional* Fighting Instructions prescribed the direction
which Rodney expected Carkett to take. If these Additional Instructions are to be
found, their testimony would be interesting.

Carkett was the oldest captain in the fleet, his post commission being dated March 12th, 1758. How far he may have been excusable in construing as he did Fighting Instructions, which originated in the inane conception that the supreme duty of a Commander-in-Chief was to oppose ship to ship, and that a fleet action was only an agglomeration of naval duels, is not very material, though historically interesting. There certainly was that in the past history of the British Navy which extenuated the offence of a man who must have then been well on in middle life. But since the Fighting Instructions had been first issued, there had been the courts-martial, also instructive, on Mathews, Lestock, Byng, Keppel, and Palliser, all of which turned more or less on the constraint of the line of battle, and the duty of supporting ships engaged, — above all, an engaged Commander-in-Chief. Rodney perhaps underestimated the weight of the Fighting Instructions upon a dull man ; but he was justified in claiming that his previous signals, and the prescription of distance, created at the least a conflict of orders, a doubt, to which there should have been but one solution, namely : to support the ships engaged, and to close down upon the enemy, as near as possible to the Commander-in-Chief. And in moments of actual perplexity such will always be the truth. It is like marching towards the sound of guns, or, to use Nelson's words, " *In case* signals cannot be understood, no captain can do very wrong if he places his ship alongside that of an enemy." The " In Case," however, needs also to be kept in mind ; and that it was Nelson who said it. Utterances of to-day, like utterances of all time, show how few are the men who can hold both sides of a truth firmly, without exaggeration or defect. Judicial impartiality can be had, and positive convictions too; but their combination is rare. A two-sided man is apt also to be double-minded.

The loss of men in this sharp encounter was : British, killed, 120, wounded, 354 ; [1] French, killed, 222, wounded, 537. [2] This gives three French hit for every two British, from which, and from the much greater damage received aloft by the latter, it may be inferred that both followed their usual custom of aiming, the British at

[1] Among the killed was Captain the Hon. Henry St. John, of the *Intrepid.* Among the wounded were Captains John Houlton, of the *Montagu*, and Thomas Newnham, of the *Grafton*. — W. L. C.

[2] Lapeyrouse Bonfils, ' Histoire de la Marine Française,' iii. 132. Chevalier gives much smaller numbers, but the former has particularised the ships.

the hull, the 'French at the spars. To the latter conduced also the
lee-gage, which the French had. The British, as the attacking party,
suffered likewise a raking fire as they bore down.

Rodney repaired damages at sea, and pursued, taking care to
keep between Martinique and the French. The latter going into
Guadeloupe, he reconnoitred them there under the batteries, and
then took his station off Fort Royal. " The only chance of bringing
them to action," he wrote to the Admiralty on the 26th of April,
" was to be off that port before them, where the fleet now is, in
daily expectation of their arrival." The French represent that he
avoided them, but as they assert that they came out best on the
17th, and yet admit that he appeared off Guadeloupe, the claim is
not tenable. Rodney here showed thorough tenacity of purpose.
De Guichen's orders were " to keep the sea, so far as the force
maintained by England in the Windward Islands would permit,
without too far compromising the fleet intrusted to him." [1] With
such instructions, he naturally and consistently shrunk from decisive
engagement. After landing his wounded and refitting in Guadeloupe, he again put to sea, with the intention of proceeding to St.
Lucia, resuming against that island the project which both he and
De Bouillé continuously entertained. The latter and his troops
remained with the fleet.

Rodney meantime had felt compelled to return momentarily to
St. Lucia. " The fleet continued before Fort Royal till the condition of many of the ships under my command, and the lee currents,[2]
rendered it necessary to anchor in Choque Bay, St. Lucie, in order
to put the wounded and sick men on shore, and to water and refit
the fleet, frigates having been detached both to leeward and to
windward of every island, in order to gain intelligence of the motions
of the enemy, and timely notice of their approach towards Martinique,
the only place they could refit at in these seas." In this last clause
is seen the strategic idea of the British Admiral : the French must
come back to Martinique.

From the vigilance of his frigates it resulted, that when the
look-outs of de Guichen, who passed to windward of Martinique on
the 7th of May, came in sight of Gros Ilet on the 9th, it was simply
to find the British getting under way to meet the enemy. During
the five following days both fleets were engaged in constant move-

---

[1] Chevalier, ' Marine Française,' 1778, p. 185.

[2] A lee current is one that sets with the wind, in this case the trade-wind.

ments, upon the character of which the writers of each nation put
different constructions. Both are agreed, however, that the French
were to windward throughout, except for a brief hour on the 15th,
when a fleeting change of wind gave the British that advantage,
only to lose it soon again. They at once used it to force action.
As the windward position carries the power to attack, and as the
French were twenty-three to the British twenty, it is probably not a
strained inference to say that the latter were chasing to windward,
and the former avoiding action, in favour, perhaps, of that ulterior
motive, the conquest of St. Lucia, for which they had sailed. Rodney states in his letter that, when the two fleets parted on the 20th
of May, they were forty leagues to windward of Martinique, in
sight of which they had been on the 10th.

During these days de Guichen, whose fleet sailed the better,
according to Rodney, and certainly sufficiently well to preserve the
advantage of the wind, bore down more than once, generally in the
afternoon, when the breeze is steadiest, to within distant range of
the British. Upon this movement, the French base the statement
that the British Admiral was avoiding an encounter; it is equally
open to the interpretation that he would not throw away ammunition
until sure of effective distance. Both admirals showed much skill
and mastery of their profession, great wariness also, and quickness
of eye ; but it is wholly untenable to claim that a fleet having the
weather-gage for five days, in the trade-winds, was unable to bring
its enemy to action, especially when it is admitted that the latter
struck the instant the wind permitted him to close.

On the afternoon of May 15th, about the usual hour, Rodney
" made a great deal of sail upon the wind." The French, inferring
that he was trying to get off, which he meant them to do, approached
somewhat closer than on the previous days. Their van ship had
come within long range, abreast the centre of the British, who were
on the port tack standing to the south-south-east, with the wind at
east (a, a). Here the breeze suddenly hauled to south-south-east.
The heads of all the ships in both fleets were thus knocked off to
south-west, on the port tack, but the shift left the British rear, which
on that tack led the fleet, to windward of the French van. Rodney's
signal flew at once, to tack in succession and keep the wind of the
enemy; the latter, unwilling to yield the advantage, wore all together,
hauling to the wind on the starboard tack, and, to use Rodney's
words, "fled with a crowd of sail " (a', a').

The British fleet tacking in succession after their leaders, the immediate result was that both were now standing on the starboard tack, — to the eastward, — the British having a slight advantage of the wind, but well abaft the beam of the French (b, b). The result, had the wind held, would have been a trial of speed and weatherliness. "His Majesty's fleet," wrote Rodney, "by this manœuvre had gained the wind, and would have forced the enemy to battle, had it not at once changed six points when near the enemy, and enabled

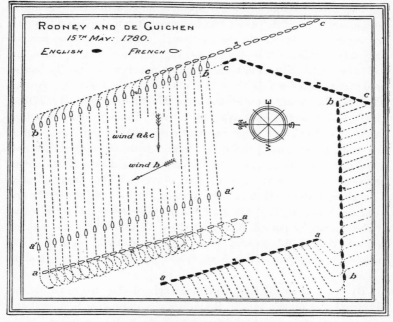

RODNEY AND DE GUICHEN.

them to recover that advantage." When the wind thus shifted again, de Guichen tacked his ships together and stood across the bows of the advancing British (c, c). The leader of the latter struck the enemy's line behind the centre, and ran along to leeward, the British van exchanging a close cannonade with the enemy's rear. Such an engagement, two lines passing on opposite tacks, is usually indecisive, even when the entire fleets are engaged, as at Ushant; but where, as in this case, the engagement is but partial, the result is naturally less. The enemy's van and centre, having passed the head of the British, diverged at that point farther and farther from the track of the on-coming ships, which, from the centre rearwards, did not fire. "As the enemy were under a press of sail, none but the van of our fleet could come in for any part of the action without wasting his Majesty's powder and shot, the enemy wantonly expending theirs at such a distance as to have no effect." Here again the French were evidently taking the chance of disabling the distant enemy in his spars. The British loss in the action of May 15th was 21 killed and 100 wounded.

The fleets continued their respective movements, each acting as before, until the 19th,[1] when another encounter took place, of exactly the same character as the last, although without the same preliminary manœuvring. The British on that occasion lost 47 killed and 113 wounded. The result was equally indecisive, tactically considered; but both by this time had exhausted their staying powers. The French, having been absent from Martinique since the 13th of April, had now but six days' provisions.[2] Rodney found the *Conqueror*, *Cornwall*, and *Boyne* so shattered that he sent them before the wind to St. Lucia, while he himself with the rest of the fleet stood for Barbados, where he arrived on the 22nd. The French anchored on the same day at Fort Royal. "The English," says Chevalier, "stood on upon the starboard tack, to the southward, after the action of the 19th, and the next day were not to be seen." " The enemy," reported Rodney, " stood to the northward with all the sail they could possibly press, and were out of sight the 21st inst. The condition of his Majesty's ships was such as not to allow a longer pursuit."

By their dexterity and vigilance each of the two admirals had thwarted the other's aims. Rodney, by a pronounced, if cautious, offensive effort, had absolutely prevented the " ulterior object " of the French, which he clearly understood to be St. Lucia. De Guichen had been successful in avoiding decisive action, and he had momentarily so crippled a few of the British ships that the fleet must await their repairs before again taking the sea. The tactical gain was his, the strategic victory rested with his opponent; but that his ships also had been much maltreated is shown by the fact that half a dozen

---

[1] Previous to which date the *Triumph*, 74, Captain Philip Affleck, and the *Preston*, 50, Captain William Truscott, had joined Rodney. In the action of the 19th, Captain Thomas Watson, of the *Conqueror*, was mortally wounded. — W. L. C.

[2] Chevalier, p. 91.

could not put to sea three weeks later. The French admiral broke down under the strain, to which was added the grief of losing a son, killed in the recent engagements. He asked for his recall. " The command of so large a fleet," he wrote, " is infinitely beyond my capacity in all respects. My health cannot endure such continual fatigue and anxiety." Certainly this seems a tacit testimony to Rodney's skill, persistence, and offensive purpose. The latter wrote to his wife : " For fourteen days and nights the fleets were so near each other that neither officers nor men could be said to sleep. Nothing but the goodness of the weather and climate would have enabled us to endure so continual a fatigue. Had it been in Europe, half the people must have sunk under it. For my part, it did me good."

Rodney stated also in his home letters that the action of his subordinates in the last affairs had been efficient; but he gave them little credit for it. " As I had given public notice to all my captains, etc., that I expected implicit obedience to every signal made, under the certain penalty of being instantly superseded, it had an admirable effect, as they were all convinced, after their late gross behaviour, that they had nothing to expect at my hands but instant punishment to those who neglected their duty. My eye on them had more dread than the enemy's fire, and they knew it would be fatal. No regard was paid to rank : admirals as well as captains, if out of their station, were instantly reprimanded by signals, or messages sent by frigates ; and, in spite of themselves, I taught them to be, what they had never been before, — *officers.*" It will be noticed that these words convey an implication of cowardice as well as of disaffection, and hint not obscurely at Byng's fate. Rodney told his officers also that he would shift his flag into a frigate, if necessary, to watch them better. It is by no means necessary to accept these gross aspersions as significant of anything worse than the suspiciousness prevalent throughout the Navy, traceable ultimately to a corrupt administration of the Admiralty. The latter, like the government of 1756, was open to censure through political maladministration , every one feared that blame would be shifted on to him, as it had been on to Byng, — who deserved it; and not only so, but that blame would be pushed on to ruin, as in his case. The Navy was honeycombed with distrust, falling little short of panic. In this state of apprehension and doubt, the tradition of the line of battle, resting upon men who did not stop to study facts or analyse impressions, and who had seen officers censured, cashiered, and shot, for errors of judgment or of

action, naturally produced hesitations and misunderstandings. An
order of battle is a good thing, necessary to insure mutual support
and to develop a plan. The error of the century, not then exploded,
was to observe it in the letter rather than in the spirit; to regard the
order as an end rather than a means; and to seek in it not merely
efficiency, which admits broad construction in positions, but precise-
ness, which is as narrowing as a brace of handcuffs. Rodney himself,
Tory though he was, found fault with the administration. With all
his severity and hauteur, he did not lose sight of justice, as is shown
by a sentence in his letter to Carkett. " Could I have imagined your
conduct and inattention to signals had proceeded from anything but
error in judgment, I had certainly superseded you, but God forbid I
should do so for error in judgment only," — again an allusion, not
obscure, to Byng's fate.

In Barbados, Rodney received certain information that a Spanish squadron of twelve ships of the line, with a large convoy of
10,000 troops, had sailed from Cadiz on April 28th for the West
Indies. The vessel bringing the news had fallen in with them on
the way. Rodney spread a line of frigates " to windward, from Barbados to Barbuda," to obtain timely warning, and with the fleet put
to sea on the 7th of June, to cruise to the eastward of Martinique to
intercept the enemy. The latter had been discovered on the 5th by a
frigate, fifty leagues east of the island, steering for it; but the Spanish
admiral, seeing that he would be reported, changed his course, and
passed north of Guadeloupe. On the 9th he was joined in that neighbourhood by de Guichen, who was able to bring with him only fifteen
sail, — a fact which shows that he had suffered in the late brushes quite
as severely as Rodney, who had with him seventeen of his twenty.

Having evaded the British, the allies anchored at Fort Royal;
but the Spanish admiral absolutely refused to join in any undertaking against the enemy's fleet or possessions. Not only so, but he
insisted on being accompanied to leeward. The Spanish squadron
was ravaged by an epidemic, due to unsanitary conditions of the
ships and the uncleanliness of the crews, and the disease was communicated to their allies. De Guichen had already orders to leave
the Windward Islands when winter approached. He decided now
to anticipate that time, and on the 5th of July sailed from Fort
Royal with the Spaniards. Having accompanied the latter to the
east end of Cuba, he went to Cap François, in Haïti, then a principal French station. The Spaniards continued on to Havana.

At Cap François, de Guichen found urgent entreaties from the French Minister to the United States, and from Lafayette, to carry his fleet to the continent, where the clear-sighted genius of Washington had recognised already that the issue of the contest depended upon the navies. The French admiral declined to comply, as contrary to his instructions, and on the 16th of August sailed for Europe, with nineteen sail of the line, leaving ten at Cap François. Sealed orders, opened at sea, directed him to proceed to Cadiz, where he anchored on the 24th of October. His arrival raised the allied force there assembled to fifty-one sail of the line, besides the ninety-five sugar and coffee ships which he had convoyed from Haïti. It is significant of the weakness of Great Britain then in the Mediterranean, that these extremely valuable merchant ships were sent on to Toulon, only five ships of the line accompanying them past Gibraltar. The French government had feared to trust them to Brest, even with de Guichen's nineteen sail.

The allied operations in the Windward Islands for the season of 1780 had thus ended in nothing, notwithstanding an incontestable inferiority of the British to the French alone, of which Rodney strongly complained. It was, however, contrary to the intentions of the Admiralty that things so happened. Orders had been sent to Vice-Admiral Marriot Arbuthnot, at New York, to detach ships to Rodney; but the vessel carrying them was driven by weather to the Bahamas, and her captain neglected to notify Arbuthnot of his whereabouts, or of his dispatches. A detachment of five ships of the line under Commodore the Hon. Robert Boyle Walsingham was detained three months in England, wind-bound. They consequently did not join till July 12th. The dispositions at once made by Rodney afford a very good illustration of the kind of duties that a British Admiral had then to discharge. He detailed five ships of the line to remain with Hotham at St. Lucia, for the protection of the Windward Islands. On the 17th, taking with him a large merchant convoy, he put to sea with the fleet for St. Kitts, where the Leeward Islands "trade" was collecting for England. On the way he received precise information as to the route and force of the Franco-Spanish fleet under de Guichen, of the sickness on board it, and of the dissension between the allies. From St. Kitts the July "trade" was sent home with two ships of the line. Three others, he wrote to the Admiralty, would accompany the September fleet, "and the remainder of the ships on this station, which are in

want of great repair and are not copper-bottomed, shall proceed with
them, or with the convoy which their Lordships have been pleased
to order shall sail from hence in October next." If these arrived
before winter, he argued, they would be available by spring as a
reinforcement for the Channel fleet, and would enable the Admiralty
to send him an equivalent number for the winter work on his
station.

As de Guichen had taken from Martinique to Cap François the
whole French homeward merchant fleet, and as the height of the
hurricane season was near, Rodney reasoned that but a small French
force would remain in Haïti, and consequently that Jamaica would
not require all the British fleet to save it from any possible attack.
He therefore sent thither ten sail of the line, notifying Vice-Admiral
Sir Peter Parker that they were not merely to defend the island,
but to enable him to send home its great trade in reasonable
security.

These things being done by July 31st, considering that the allies
had practically abandoned all enterprises in the West Indies for
that year, and that a hurricane might at any moment overtake the
fleet at its anchors, possibly making for it a lee shore, Rodney went
to sea, to cruise off Barbuda. His mind, however, was inclined
already to go to the continent, whither he reasoned, correctly but
mistakenly, that the greater part of de Guichen's fleet would go,
as it should. His purpose was confirmed by information from an
American vessel that a French squadron of seven ships of the line,
convoying 6,000 troops, had anchored in Narragansett Bay on the
12th of July. He started at once for the coast of South Carolina,
where he communicated with the army in Charleston, and thence,
" sweeping the southern coast of America," anchored with fourteen
ships of the line at Sandy Hook, on the 14th of September, unexpected and unwelcome to friends and foes alike.

Vice-Admiral Arbuthnot, being junior to Rodney, showed plainly
and with insubordination his wrath at this intrusion into his command, which superseded his authority and divided the prize-money of
a lucrative station. This, however, was a detail. To Washington,
Rodney's coming was a death-blow to the hopes raised by the arrival
of the French division at Newport, which he had expected to see
reinforced by de Guichen. Actually, the departure of the latter
made immaterial Rodney's appearance on the scene; but this Washington did not know then. As it was, Rodney's force joined to

Arbuthnot's constituted a fleet of over twenty sail of the line, before which, vigorously used, there can be little doubt that the French squadron in Newport must have fallen. But Rodney, though he had shown great energy in the West Indies, and unusual resolution in quitting his own station for a more remote service, was sixty-two, and suffered from gout. " The sudden change of climate makes it necessary for me to go on shore for some short time," he wrote ; and although he added that his illness was " not of such a nature as shall cause one moment's delay in his Majesty's service," he probably lost a chance at Rhode Island. He did not overlook the matter, it is true, but he decided upon the information of Arbuthnot and Sir Henry Clinton, and did not inspect the ground himself. Nothing of consequence came of his visit; and on the 16th of November he sailed again for the West Indies, taking with him only nine sail of the line.

The arrival of de Ternay's seven ships at Newport was more than offset by a British reinforcement of six ships of the line under Rear-Admiral Thomas Graves (1),[1] which entered New York on July 13th, — only one day later. Arbuthnot's force was thus raised to ten of the line, one of which was of 98 guns. After Rodney had come and gone, the French division was watched by cruisers, resting upon Gardiner's Bay, — a commodious anchorage at the east end of Long Island, between thirty and forty miles from Rhode Island. When a movement of the enemy was apprehended, the squadron assembled there, but nothing of consequence occurred during the remainder of the year.

The year 1780 had been one of great discouragement to the Americans, but the injury, except as the lapse of time taxed their staying power, was more superficial than real. The successes of the British in the Southern States, though undeniable, and seemingly substantial, were involving them ever more deeply in a ruinously ex-centric movement. They need here only to be summarised, as steps in the process leading to the catastrophe of Yorktown, — a disaster which, as Washington said, exemplified naval rather than military power.

The failure of d'Estaing's attack upon Savannah in the autumn of 1779 had left that place in the possession of the British as a base

---

[1] Thomas, Lord Graves. Born, 1725. Commander, 1754. Captain, 1755. Rear-Admiral, 1779. Vice-Admiral, 1787. Admiral, 1794. Raised to an Irish peerage for his share in the victory of the Glorious First of June. Died, 1802. — W. L. C.

for further advances in South Carolina and Georgia; lasting success
in which was expected from the numbers of royalists in those States.
When the departure of the French fleet was ascertained, Sir Henry
Clinton put to sea from New York in December, 1779, for the Savannah River, escorted by Vice-Admiral Arbuthnot. The details of the
operations, which were leisurely and methodical, will not be given
here; for, although the Navy took an active part in them, they
scarcely can be considered of major importance. On the 12th of
May, 1780, the city of Charleston capitulated, between six and seven
thousand prisoners being taken. Clinton then returned to New
York, leaving Lord Cornwallis in command in the south. The
latter proposed to remain quiet during the hot months; but the
activity of the American partisan troops prevented this, and in July
the approach of a small, but relatively formidable force, under General Gates, compelled him to take the field. On the 16th of August
the two little armies met at Camden, and the Americans, who were
much the more numerous, but largely irregulars, were routed decisively. This news reached General Washington in the north nearly
at the same moment that the treason of Benedict Arnold became
known. Although the objects of his treachery were frustrated, the
sorrowful words, " Whom now can we trust? " show the deep gloom
which for the moment shadowed the constant mind of the American
Commander-in-Chief. It was just at this period, too, that Rodney
arrived.

Cornwallis, not content with his late success, decided to push on
into North Carolina. Thus doing, he separated himself from his
naval base in Charleston, communication with which by land he had
not force to maintain, and could only recover effective touch with
the sea in Chesapeake Bay. This conclusion was not apparent from
the first. In North Carolina, the British general, who had expected
substantial support by the inhabitants, failed to secure it, and found
himself instead in a very difficult and wild country, confronted by
General Greene, the second in ability of all the American leaders.
Harassed and baffled, he was compelled to order supplies to be sent by
sea to Wilmington, North Carolina, an out-of-the-way and inferior
port, to which he turned aside, arriving exhausted on the 7th of April,
1781. The question as to his future course remained to be settled.
To return to Charleston by sea was in his power, but to do so would
be an open confession of failure, — that he could not return through
the country by which he had come. To support him in his distress

by a diversion, Sir Henry Clinton had sent two successive detachments to ravage the valley of the James River in Virginia. These were still there, under the command of General Phillips; and Cornwallis, in the circumstances, could see many reasons that thither was the very scene to carry the British operations. On the 25th of April, 1781, he left Wilmington, and a month later joined the division at Petersburg, Virginia, then commanded by Benedict Arnold; Phillips having died. There, in touch now with his fate, we must leave him for the moment.

To complete the naval transactions of 1780, it is necessary to mention briefly two incidents, trivial in themselves, but significant, not only as associated with the greater movements of the campaign, but as indicative of the naval policy of the states which were at war. The two, though not otherwise connected, have a certain unity of interest, in that the same British officer commanded on both occasions.

It will be remembered that in Byron's action off Grenada, in July, 1779, the 64-gun ship *Lion* received such injuries that her commander, Captain the Hon. William Cornwallis, had been compelled to run down before the trade-winds to Jamaica, in order to save her from capture. Since that time she had remained there, as one of the squadron of Vice-Admiral Sir Peter Parker. In March, 1780, still commanded by Captain Cornwallis, she was making an ordinary service cruise off the north side of Haïti, having in company the *Bristol*, 50, Captain Toby Caulfield, and the *Janus*, 44, Captain Bonovier Glover. On the 20th of March, off Monte Christi, a number of sail were sighted to the eastward, which proved to be a French convoy, on its way from Martinique to Cap François, protected by La Motte-Picquet's squadron of 2 seventy-fours, 1 sixty-four, 1 fifty, and a frigate. The French merchant ships were ordered to crowd sail for their port, while the men-of-war chased to the north-west. La Motte-Picquet's flagship, the *Annibal*, 74, got within range at 5 P.M., when a distant cannonade began, which lasted till past midnight, and was resumed on the following morning. From it the *Janus* was the chief sufferer, losing her mizzen topmast and foretopgallant mast. It falling nearly calm, the *Bristol* and *Lion* got out their boats and towed to her support. The two other French ships of the line got up during the forenoon of the 21st, so that the action that afternoon, though desultory, might be called general.

The two opposing commodores differ in their expressed opinions

as to the power of the French to make the affair more decisive.
Some of La Motte-Picquet's language seems to show that he felt the
responsibility of his position. "The *Janus*, being smaller and more
easily worked, lay upon our quarter and under our stern, where she
did considerable damage. A little breeze springing up enabled us
(the *Annibal*) to stand towards our own ships, which did everything
possible to come up and cover us, without which we should have
been *surrounded*." It is easy to see in such an expression the reflection
of the commands of the French Cabinet, to economise the ships. This
was still more evident in La Motte-Picquet's action next day. On
the morning of the 22nd, "at daylight we were within one and a half
cannon-shot, breeze fresh at east-north-east, and I expected to overtake
the British squadron in an hour, when we perceived four ships in
chase of us. At 6.30 A.M. three were seen to be men-of-war. This
superiority of force compelled me to desist, and to make signal to
haul our wind for Cap François." These three new-comers were
the *Ruby*, 64, and two frigates, the *Pomona*, 28, and *Niger*, 32. The
comparison of forces, therefore, would be: French, 2 seventy-fours,
1 sixty-four, 1 fifty, and 1 frigate, opposed to, British, 2 sixty-fours,
1 fifty, and 3 frigates. La Motte-Picquet evidently did not wait
to ascertain the size of the approaching ships. His courage was
beyond all dispute, and, as Hyde Parker had said, he was among the
most distinguished of French officers; but, like his comrades, he was
dominated by the faulty theory of his government.

The captain of the *Janus* died a natural death during the encounter. It may be interesting to note that the ship was given to Nelson,
who was recalled for that purpose from the San Juan expedition.
His health, however, prevented this command from being more than
nominal, and not long afterwards he returned to England with Cornwallis, in the *Lion*.

Three months later, Cornwallis was sent by Parker to accompany
a body of merchant ships for England as far as the neighbourhood of
Bermuda. This duty being fulfilled, he was returning towards his
station, having with him 2 seventy-fours, 2 sixty-fours, and 1 fifty,[1]
when, on the morning of June 20, a number of sail were seen from

[1] *Lion*	64	Captain the Hon. William Cornwallis.
Sultan	74	Captain Alan Gardner.
Hector	74	Captain Sir John Hamilton, Bart.
Ruby	64	Captain John Cowling.
Bristol	50	Captain Toby Caulfield.
Niger	32	Captain John Brown.

north-east to east; the squadron then steering east, with the wind at
south-south-east.   The strangers were a body of French transports,
carrying the 6,000 troops destined for Rhode Island, and convoyed
by a division of seven ships of the line — 1 eighty, 2 seventy-fours,
and 4 sixty-fours — under the command of Commodore de Ternay.
Two of the ships of war were with the convoy, the remainder very
properly to windward.   The latter therefore stood on, across the bows
of the British, to rejoin their consorts (aa), and then all hauled their

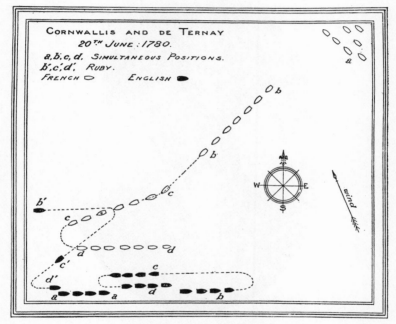

CORNWALLIS AND DE TERNAY.

wind to the south-west, standing in column towards the enemy.
Cornwallis on his part had kept on to reconnoitre the force opposed
to him (a); but one of his ships, the *Ruby*, 64, was so far to leeward
that the enemy, by keeping near the wind, could pass between her and
him (b, b, b').   She therefore went about and steered south-west, on
the port tack, close to the wind.   The French, who were already heading the same way, were thus brought on her weather quarter in chase.
Cornwallis then wore his division, formed line of battle on the same
tack as the others, and edged down towards the *Ruby* (c).   If the

French now kept their wind, either the *Ruby* (c′) must be cut off, or Cornwallis, to save her, must fight the large odds against him. De Ternay, however, did not keep his wind (c). "The enemy," wrote Cornwallis, "kept edging off and forming line, though within gunshot. At 5.30 P.M., seeing we had pushed the French ships to leeward sufficiently to enable the *Ruby*, on our lee bow, to join us, I made the signal to tack." As the British squadron went about to

ADMIRAL THE HON. SIR WILLIAM CORNWALLIS, G. C. B.

(From the lithograph by Ridley, after the portrait by D. Gardner, painted in 1775, when Cornwallis was a Post-Captain, æt. 31.)

stand east again, the French, heading west-south-west, hoisted their colours and opened fire in passing. The *Ruby* kept on till she fetched the wake of the British column, when she too tacked. The French then tacked also, in succession, and the two columns stood on for awhile in parallel lines, exchanging shots at long range, the British to windward. Cornwallis very properly declined further engagement with so superior a force. He had already done much in saving a ship so greatly exposed.

The account above followed is that of the British commander, but it does not differ in essentials from the French, whose captains were greatly incensed at the cautious action of their chief. A French *commissaire* in the squadron, who afterwards published his journal, tells that de Ternay a few days later asked the captain of one of the ships what English admiral he thought they had engaged, and received the reply, " We have lost our opportunity of finding out." He gives also many details of the talk that went on in the ships, which need not be repeated. Chevalier points out correctly, however, that de Ternay had to consider that an equal or even a superior force might be encountered as Narragansett Bay was approached, and that he should not risk crippling his squadron for such a contingency. The charge of 6,000 troops, under the then conditions, was no light responsibility, and at the least must silence off-hand criticism now. Comment upon his action does not belong to British naval history, to which the firmness and seamanship of Captain Cornwallis added a lasting glory. It may be noted that fifteen years later, in the French Revolution, the same officer, then a Vice-Admiral, again distinguished himself by his bearing in face of great odds, bringing five ships safe off, out of the jaws of a dozen. It illustrates how luck seems in many cases to characterise a man's personality, much as temperament does. Cornwallis, familiarly known as " Billy Blue " to the seamen of his day, never won a victory, nor had a chance of winning one; but in command both of ships and of divisions, he repeatedly distinguished himself by successfully facing odds which he could not overcome.

The year was uneventful also in European waters, after Rodney's relief of Gibraltar in January. The detachment of the Channel Fleet which accompanied him on that mission returned safely to England. The " Grand Fleet," as it still was styled occasionally, cruised at sea from June 8th to August 18th, an imposing force of thirty-one ships of the line, eleven of them three-deckers of 90 guns and upwards. Admiral Francis Geary was then Commander-in-Chief, but, his health failing, and Barrington refusing to take the position, through professed distrust of himself and actual distrust of the Admiralty, Vice-Admiral George Darby succeeded to it, and held it during the year 1781.

The most notable maritime event in 1780 in Europe was the capture on August 9th of a large British convoy, two or three hundred miles west of Cape St. Vincent, by the allied fleets from Cadiz. As out of sixty-three sail only eight escaped, and as of those taken sixteen were carrying troops and supplies necessary for the West India garrisons, such a disaster claims mention among the greater operations of war, the success of which it could not fail to influence. Captain John Moutray, the officer commanding the convoy, was brought to trial and dismissed his ship; but there were not wanting those who charged the misadventure to the Admiralty, and saw in the captain a victim. It was the greatest single blow that British commerce had received in war during the memory of men then living, and "a general inclination prevailed to lay the blame upon some individual, who might be punished according to the magnitude of the object, rather than in proportion to his demerit." [1]

During the year 1780 was formed the League of the Baltic Powers, known historically as the Armed Neutrality, to exact from Great Britain the concession of certain points thought essential to neutral interests. The accession of Holland to this combination, together with other motives of dissatisfaction, caused Great Britain to declare war against the United Provinces on the 20th of December. Orders were at once sent to the East and West Indies to seize Dutch possessions and ships, but these did not issue in action until the following year.

Towards the end of 1780 the French Government, dissatisfied with the lack of results from the immense combined force assembled in Cadiz during the summer months, decided to recall its ships, and to refit them during the winter for the more extensive and aggressive movements planned for the campaign of 1781. D'Estaing was sent from France for the purpose; and under his command thirty-eight ships of the line, in which were included those brought by de Guichen from the West Indies, sailed on the 7th of November for Brest. Extraordinary as it may seem, this fleet did not reach its port until the 3rd of January, 1781.

Rodney, returning to the West Indies from New York, reached Barbados on December 6th, 1780. There he seems first to have learned of the disastrous effects of the great October hurricanes of that year. Not only had several ships — among them two of the line — been wrecked, with the loss of almost all on board, but the greater part of the survivors had been dismasted, wholly or in part, as well as injured in the hull. There were in the West Indies no docking facilities; under-water damage could be repaired only by careening or heaving-down. Furthermore, as Barbados, St. Lucia, and

---

[1] Beatson, 'Military and Naval Memoirs.'

Jamaica, all had been swept, their supplies were mainly destroyed.[1] Antigua, it is true, had escaped, the hurricane passing south of St. Kitts; but Rodney wrote home that no stores for refitting were obtainable in the Caribbee Islands. He was hoping then that Sir Peter Parker might supply his needs in part; for when writing from St. Lucia on December 10th, two months after the storm, he still was ignorant that the Jamaica Station had suffered to the full as severely as the eastern islands. The fact shows not merely the ordinary slowness of communications in those days, but also the paralysis that fell upon all movements in consequence of that great disaster. "The most beautiful island in the world," he said of Barbados, "has the appearance of a country laid waste by fire and sword."

Hearing that the fortifications at St. Vincent had been almost destroyed by the hurricane, Rodney, in combination with General Vaughan, commanding the troops on the station, made an attempt to reconquer the island, landing there on December 15th; but the intelligence proved erroneous, and the fleet returned to St. Lucia. "I have only nine sail of the line now with me capable of going to sea," wrote the Admiral on the 22nd, "and not one of them has spare rigging or sails." In the course of January he was joined by a division of eight ships of the line from England, under the command of Rear-Admiral Sir Samuel Hood. These, with four others refitted during that month, not improbably from stores brought in Hood's convoy of over a hundred sail, raised the disposable force to twenty-one ships of the line: 2 nineties, 1 eighty, 15 seventy-fours, and 3 sixty-fours.

---

[1] List of H. M. ships lost in the hurricane in the West Indies in October, 1780, with the names of their commanders, such of the latter as perished being indicated with an asterisk (*). Chiefly from Steel's ' Navy List.' — W. L. C.

SHIPS.	GUNS.	COMMANDERS.
Thunderer	74	{ Com. the Hon. R. B. Walsingham.* { Capt. Robert Boyle Nicholas.*
Stirling Castle	64	Capt. Robert Carkett.*
Phœnix	44	Capt. Sir Hyde Parker (2).
Blanche	42	Capt. Samuel Uppleby.*
Laurel	28	Capt. Thomas Lloyd.*
Andromeda	28	Capt. Henry Bryne.*
Deal Castle	24	Capt. James Hawkins (afterwards Whitshed).
Scarborough	20	Capt. Samuel Hood Walker.*
Beaver's Prize	16	Com. John Auriol Drummond.*
Barbados	14	Com. Ralph Milbanke.
Chameleon	14	Com. James Johnstone.*
Endeavour	14	Lieut. Francis Wooldridge.
Victor	10	Lieut.

On the 27th of January, an express arrived from England, directing the seizure of the Dutch possessions in the Caribbean, and
specifying, as first to be attacked, St. Eustatius and St. Martin, two
small islands lying within fifty miles north of the British St. Kitts.
St. Eustatius, a rocky patch six miles in length by three in breadth,
had been conspicuous, since the war began, as a great trade centre,
where supplies of all kinds were gathered under the protection of its
neutral flag, to be distributed afterwards in the belligerent islands
and the North American continent. The British, owing to their
extensive commerce and maritime aptitudes, derived from such an
intermediary much less benefit than their enemies; and the island
had been jealously regarded by Rodney for some time. He asserted
that when de Guichen's fleet could not regain Fort Royal, because of
its injuries received in the action of April 17th, it was refitted to meet
him by mechanics and materials sent from St. Eustatius.   On the other
hand, when cordage was to be bought for the British vessels after the
hurricanes of 1780, the merchants of the island, he said, alleged that
there was none there; although, when he took the island soon afterwards, many hundred tons were found that had been long in stock.

Rodney and Vaughan moved promptly.   Three days after their
orders arrived, they sailed for St. Eustatius.   There being in Fort
Royal four French ships of the line, six British were left to check

COMMEMORATIVE MEDAL OF THE CAPTURE OF ST. EUSTATIUS BY RODNEY, 1781.
(From an original lent by Capt. H. S. H. Prince Louis of Battenberg, R. N.)

them, and on the 3rd of February the fleet reached its destination.   A
peremptory summons from the commander of a dozen ships of the
line secured immediate submission.   Over a hundred and fifty merchant ships were taken; and a convoy of thirty sail, which had left
the island two days before, was pursued and brought back.   The
merchandise found was valued at over £3,000,000.   The neighbouring islands of St. Martin and Saba were seized also at this time.

Rodney's imagination, as is shown in his letters, was greatly impressed by the magnitude of the prize and by the defenceless condition of his capture. He alleged these as the motives for staying in person at St. Eustatius, to settle the complicated tangle of neutral and belligerent rights in the property involved, and to provide against the enemy's again possessing himself of a place now so equipped for transactions harmful to Great Britain. The storehouses and conveniences provided for the particular traffic, if not properly guarded, were like fortifications insufficiently garrisoned. If they passed into the hands of the enemy, they became sources of injury. The illicit traffic could start again at once in full force, with means which elsewhere would have first to be created. There were a mile and a half of storehouses in the lower town, he said, and at the least he must leave these roofless, if not wholly demolished.

For such reasons he remained at St. Eustatius throughout February, March, and April. The amount of money involved, and the arbitrary methods pursued by him and by Vaughan, gave rise to much scandal, which was not diminished by the King's relinquishing all the booty to the captors, nor by the latters' professed disinterestedness. Men thought they did protest too much. Meanwhile, other matters arose to claim attention. A week after the capture, a vessel arrived from the Bay of Biscay announcing that eight or ten French sail of the line, with a large convoy, had been seen on the 31st of December steering for the West Indies. Rodney at once detached Sir Samuel Hood with eleven ships of the line, directing him to take also under his command the six left before Fort Royal, and to cruise with them to windward of Martinique, to intercept the force reported. Hood sailed February 12th. The particular intelligence proved afterwards to be false, but Hood was continued on this duty. A month later he was ordered to move from the windward to the leeward side of the island, and to blockade Fort Royal closely. Against this change he remonstrated, and the event showed him to be right ; but Rodney insisted, saying that from his experience he knew that a fleet could remain off Fort Royal for months without dropping to leeward, and that there ships detached to St. Lucia, for water and refreshments, could rejoin before an enemy's fleet, discovered to windward, could come up. Hood thought the Admiral's object was merely to shelter his own doings at St. Eustatius ; and he considered the blockade of Fort Royal to be futile, if no descent upon the island were intended. " It would doubtless have been fortunate for the

public," he remarked afterwards, "had Sir George been with his
fleet, as I am confident he would have been to windward instead of
to leeward, when de Grasse made his approach."

The preparations of the French in Brest were completed towards the
end of March, and on the 22nd of that month Rear-Admiral de Grasse
sailed, having a large convoy under the protection of twenty-six ships
of the line. A week later six of the latter parted company, five under
Suffren for the East Indies, and one for North America. The remaining twenty continued their course for Martinique, which was sighted
on the 28th of April. Before sunset, Hood's squadron also was discovered to leeward of the island, as ordered by Rodney to cruise, and
off the southern point, — Pointe des Salines. De Grasse then hove-to
for the night, but sent an officer ashore both to give and to obtain intelligence, and to reach an understanding for concerted action next day.

The French fleet consisted of one ship of 110 guns, 3 eighties, 15
seventy-fours, and 1 sixty-four, in all 20 of the line, besides three
armed *en flûte*, which need not be taken into account, although they
served to cover the convoy. Besides these there were the four in
Fort Royal, 1 seventy-four and 3 sixty-fours, whose junction with the
approaching enemy it was one of Hood's objects to prevent. The force
of the British was 1 ninety, 1 eighty, 12 seventy-fours, 1 seventy, and
2 sixty-fours : total, 17.[1] Thus both in numbers and in rates of ships

---

[1] List of the fleet under Rear-Admiral Sir S. Hood, Bart., on April 29th, 1781.
Chiefly from Beatson, vi. 264, and Steel's 'Navy List.' This includes the 64-gun
ship, which joined from St. Lucia at 9.20 A.M. — W. L. C.

Alfred	74	Captain William Bayne.
Belliqueux	64	Captain James Brine.
Alcide	74	Captain Charles Thompson.
Invincible	74	Captain Sir Richard Bickerton, Bart.
Monarch	74	Captain Francis Reynolds (later F. R. Moreton).
Barfleur	90	{ Rear-Admiral Sir Samuel Hood, Bart. (B). { Captain John Knight (2).
Terrible	74	Captain James Ferguson.
Princesa	70	Captain Sir Thomas Rich, Bart.
Ajax	74	Captain John Symons.
Resolution	74	Captain Lord Robert Manners.
Montagu	74	Captain John Houlton.
Gibraltar	80	{ Rear-Admiral Francis Samuel Drake (B). { Captain Charles Knatchbull.
Centaur	74	Captain John Neale Pleydell Nott.
Russell	74	Captain Andrew Sutherland.
Prince William	64	Captain Stair Douglas (1).
Torbay	74	Captain John Lewis Gidoin.
Intrepid	64	Captain Anthony James Pye Molloy.
Shrewsbury	74	Captain Mark Robinson (1).

Lizard, 28, as repeater.   *Pocahontas*, 14, as repeater.

Hood was inferior to the main body alone of the French; but he had the advantage of ships all coppered, owing to Rodney's insistence with the Admiralty. He also had no convoy to worry him; but he was to leeward.

Early in the morning of the 29th, de Grasse advanced to round the southern point of the island, which was the usual course for sailing ships. Hood was too far to leeward to intercept this movement,

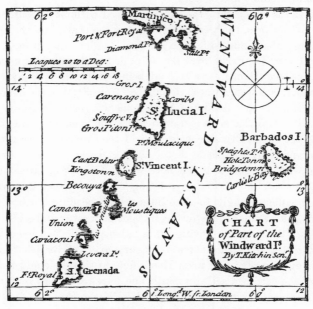

CHART OF PART OF THE WINDWARD ISLANDS.

for which he was blamed by Rodney, who claimed that the night had not been properly utilised by beating to windward of Pointe des Salines.[1] Hood, on the other hand, said in a private letter: "I never once lost sight of getting to windward, but it was totally impossible. . . . Had I fortunately been there, I must have brought the enemy to close action upon more equal terms, or they must have given up

---

[1] Rodney said that Hood "lay-to" for the night. This is antecedently incredible of an officer of Hood's character, and is expressly contradicted by Captain Sutherland of the *Russell*. "At 6 P.M. (of the 28th) our fleet tacked to the north, and *kept moving* across the bay (Fort Royal) for the right (*sic*), in line of battle." Ekins, 'Naval Battles,' p. 136. The word "right" is evidently a misprint for "night." Rodney's criticisms seem to the author captious throughout.

their transports, trade, etc." Hood's subsequent career places it beyond doubt that had he been to windward there would have been a
severe action, whatever the result; but it is not possible to decide
positively between his statement and Rodney's, as to where the fault
of being to leeward lay. The writer believes that Hood would have
been to windward, if in any way possible. It must be added that the
British had no word that so great a force was coming. On this point
Hood and Rodney are agreed.

Under the conditions, the French passed without difficulty round
Pointe des Salines, the transports hugging the coast, and the ships of
war being outside and to leeward of them. Thus they headed up to
the northward for Fort Royal Bay (Cul de Sac Royal), Hood standing
to the southward until after 10, and being joined at 9.20 by a sixty-
four (which is counted in the list above) from St. Lucia, making his
force eighteen. At 10.35 the British tacked together to the northward. The two fleets were now steering the same way, the French
van abreast of the British centre. At 11 the French opened their fire,
to which no reply was made then. At 11.20, the British van being
close in with the shore to the northward of the Bay, Hood tacked
again together, and the enemy, seeing his convoy secure, wore, also
together, which brought the two lines nearer, heading south. At this
time the four French ships in the Bay got under way and easily joined
the rear of their fleet, it having the weather-gage. The French were
thus 24 to 18. As their shot were passing over the British, the latter
now began to reply. At noon Hood, finding that he could not close
the enemy, shortened sail to topsails and hove-to, hoping by this defiance to bring them down to him. At 12.30 the French admiral was
abreast of the British flagship, and the action became general, but at
too long range. " Never, I believe," wrote Hood, " was more powder
and shot thrown away in one day before." The French continuing
to stand on, Hood filled his sails again at 1 P.M., as their van had
stretched beyond his.

As the leading ships, heading south, opened the channel between
St. Lucia and Martinique, they got the breeze fresher, which caused
them to draw away from the centre. Hood, therefore, at 1.34 made
the signal for a close order, and immediately afterwards ceased firing,
finding not one in ten of the enemy's shot to reach. The engagement, however, continued somewhat longer between the southern
ships, where, by the account of Captain Sutherland, who was in that
part of the line, four of the British were attacked very smartly by

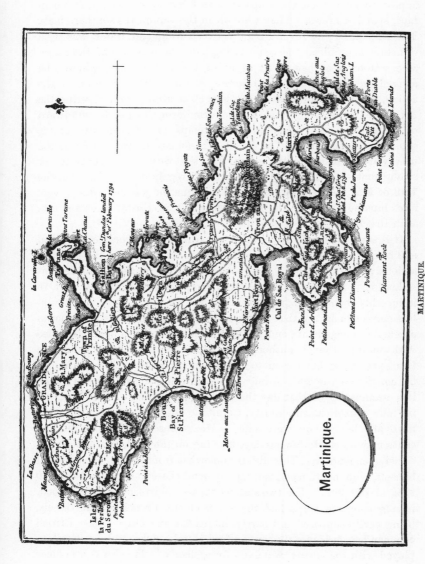

MARTINIQUE.

(From a map published by J. Gold in 1805.)

eight of the French.   The *Centaur*, *Russell*, *Intrepid*, and *Shrewsbury*
appear to have been the ships that suffered most heavily, either in
hull, spars, or crews.   They were all in the van on the southern tack.
The *Russell*, having several shot between wind and water, was with
difficulty kept afloat, the water rising over the platform of the magazine.   Hood sent her off at nightfall to St. Eustatius, where she
arrived on the 4th of May, bringing Rodney the first news of the
action, and of the numbers of the French reinforcement.   During the
30th Hood held his ground, still endeavouring to get to windward
of the enemy; but failing in that attempt, and finding two of his
squadron much disabled, he decided at sunset to bear away to the
northward, because to the southward the westerly currents set so
strong that the crippled ships could not regain St. Lucia.   On the
11th of May, between St. Kitts and Antigua, he joined Rodney, who,
after hurried repairs to the *Russell*, had left St. Eustatius on the 5th,
with that ship, the *Sandwich*, and the *Triumph*.

It is somewhat difficult to criticise positively the conduct of Hood
and of de Grasse in this affair.   It is clear that Hood on the first day
seriously sought action, though his force was but three-fourths that
of his foe.   He tried first to take the offensive, and, failing that, to
induce his enemy to attack frankly and decisively.   Troude is doubtless correct in saying that it was optional with de Grasse to bring on
a general engagement; and the writer finds himself in agreement also
with another French authority, Captain Chevalier, that "Count de
Grasse seems to have been too much preoccupied with the safety of
his convoy on the 29th, Admiral Hood having shown himself much
less circumspect on that day than he was on the next.   Notwithstanding our numerical superiority, Count de Grasse kept near the land
until all the convoy were safe."   He represents Hood as fencing
cautiously on the following day, keeping on the field, but avoiding a
decisive encounter.   This differs somewhat from the version of Hood
himself, who mentions signalling a general chase to windward at 12.30
P. M. of the 30th.   The two statements are not irreconcilable.   Hood,
having coppered ships, had the speed of the French, whose vessels,
being partly coppered and partly not, sailed unevenly.   The British
commander consequently could afford to take risks, and he therefore
played with the enemy, watching for a chance.   Hood was an officer
of exceptional capacity, much in advance of his time.   He thoroughly
understood a watching game, and that an opportunity might offer to
seize an advantage over part of the enemy, if the eagerness of pursuit,

or any mishap, caused the French to separate. From any dilemma that ensued, the reserve of speed gave him a power of withdrawal, in relying upon which he was right. The present writer adopts here also Chevalier's conclusion : " Admiral Hood evidently had the very great advantage over his enemy of commanding a squadron of coppered ships. Nevertheless, homage is due to his skill and to the confidence shown by him in his captains. If some of his ships had dropped behind through injuries received, he would have had to sacrifice them, or to fight a superior force." This means that Hood, for an adequate gain ran a great risk; that he thoroughly understood both the advantages and the disadvantages of his situation; and that he acted not only with great skill, but warily and boldly, — a rare combination. The British loss in this affair was 39 killed, including Captain Nott, of the *Centaur*, and 162 wounded. The French loss is given by Chevalier as 18 killed and 56 wounded; by Beatson, as 119 killed and 150 wounded.

Rodney, having collected his fleet, proceeded south, and on the 18th of May put into Barbados for water. Much anxiety had been felt at first for St. Lucia, which Hood's retreat had uncovered. As was feared, the French had attacked it at once, their fleet, with the exception of one or two ships, going there, and 1,200 troops landing at Gros Ilet Bay; but the batteries on Pigeon Island, which Rodney had erected and manned, kept them at arms' length. The works elsewhere being found too strong, the attempt was abandoned.

At the same time, two ships of the line and 1,300 troops had sailed from Martinique against Tobago. When de Grasse returned from the failure at St. Lucia, he learned that the British were at sea, apparently bound for Barbados. Alarmed for his detachment before Tobago, he again sailed with the fleet for that island on the 25th of May, accompanied by 3,000 more troops. Rodney learned at Barbados of the attempt on Tobago, and on the 29th dispatched a squadron of six sail of the line, under Rear-Admiral Francis Samuel Drake, to support the defence. On the following day he heard that the French main fleet had been seen to windward of St. Lucia, steering south, evidently for Tobago. On the 30th also Drake and de Grasse encountered one another off the latter island, the French being to leeward, nearest the land. Drake necessarily retired, and on the morning of June 3rd was again off Barbados, whereupon Rodney at once sailed for Tobago with the whole fleet. On the 4th the island was sighted, and next morning information was received that it had capitulated on the 2nd.

The two fleets returning north were in presence of one another on
the 9th; but no engagement took place. Rodney, who was to windward, having twenty sail to twenty-three,[1] was unwilling to attack
unless he could get a clear sea. The strength of the currents, he
said, would throw his fleet too far to leeward, in case of reverse, into
the foul ground between St. Vincent and Grenada, thus exposing
Barbados, which had not recovered sufficiently from the hurricane
to stand alone. He put into Barbados, and de Grasse went to Martinique to prepare the expedition to the American continent, which
resulted in the surrender of Cornwallis. On the 5th of July he sailed
from Fort Royal, taking with him the " trade " for France, and on
the 26th anchored with it at Cap François, where he found a division
of four ships of the line which had been left the year before by
de Guichen. There also was a frigate, which had left Boston on
the 20th of June, and by which he received dispatches from Washington, and from Rochambeau, the general commanding the French
troops in America. These acquainted him with the state of affairs
on the continent, and requested that the fleet should come to either
the Chesapeake or New York, to strike a decisive blow at the British
power in one quarter or the other.

It is expedient here to resume the thread of events on the continent.

It has been said that, to support the operations of Cornwallis in
the Carolinas, Clinton had begun a series of diversions in the valley
of the James River. The first detachment so sent, under General
Leslie, had been transferred speedily to South Carolina, to meet the
exigencies of Cornwallis's campaign. The second, of 1,600 troops
under Benedict Arnold, left New York at the end of December, and
began its work on the banks of the James at the end of January, 1781.
It advanced to Richmond, nearly a hundred miles from the sea, wasting the country round about, and finding no opposition adequate to
check its freedom of movement. Returning down stream, on the
20th it occupied Portsmouth, south of the James River, near the sea,
and valuable as a naval station.

Washington urged Commodore des Touches, who by de Ternay's
death had been left in command of the French squadron at Newport,
to interrupt these proceedings, by dispatching a strong detachment
to Chesapeake Bay; and he asked Rochambeau also to let some troops

_____
[1] One French ship had left the fleet, disabled.

accompany the naval division, to support the scanty force which he himself could spare to Virginia. It happened, however, that a gale of wind just then had inflicted severe injury upon Arbuthnot's squadron, three of which had gone to sea from Gardiner's Bay upon a report that three French ships of the line had left Newport to meet an expected convoy. One seventy-four, the *Bedford*, was wholly dismasted ; another, the *Culloden*, Captain George Balfour, drove ashore on Long Island, and was wrecked. The French ships had returned to port the day before the gale, but the incident indisposed des Touches to risk his vessels at sea at that time. He sent only a sixty-four, with two frigates. These left Newport on February 9th, and entered the Chesapeake, but were unable to reach the British vessels, which, being smaller, withdrew up the Elizabeth River. Arbuthnot, hearing of this expedition, sent orders to some frigates off Charleston to go to the scene. The French division, when leaving the Bay, met one of these, the *Romulus*, 44, Captain George Gayton, off the Capes, captured her, and returned to Newport on February 25th. On the 8th of March, Arnold reported to Clinton that the Chesapeake was clear of French vessels.

On the same day Arbuthnot also was writing to Clinton, from Gardiner's Bay, that the French were evidently preparing to quit Newport. His utmost diligence had failed as yet to repair entirely the damage done his squadron by the storm, but on the 9th it was ready for sea. On the evening of the 8th the French had sailed. On the 10th Arbuthnot knew it, and, having taken the precaution to move down to the entrance of the bay, he was able to follow at once. On the 13th he spoke a vessel which had seen the enemy and gave him their course. Favoured by a strong north-west wind, and his ships being coppered, he outstripped the French, only three of which had copper on them. At 6 A.M. of the 16th the latter were reported by a frigate to be astern — to the north-east — about a league distant, a thick haze preventing the British from seeing them even at that distance (A A).[1] Cape Henry, the southern point of the entrance to the Chesapeake, then bore south-west by west, distant forty miles. The wind as stated by Arbuthnot was west; by the French, south-west.

The British admiral at once went about, steering in the direction reported, and the opposing squadrons soon sighted one another. The British being between them and their port, the French hauled to the wind, which shifted between 8 and 9 to north by west, putting them to windward. Some preliminary manœuvres then followed, both

---

[1] Reference is to Mahan's " Influence of Sea Power Upon History," Plate XII.

parties seeking the weather-gage. The weather remained thick and squally, often intercepting the view; and the wind continued to shift until towards noon, when it settled at north-east. The better sailing, or the better seamanship, of the British had enabled them to gain so far upon their opponents that at 1 P.M. they were laying nearly up in their wake, on the port tack, overhauling them; both squadrons in line of battle, heading east-south-east, the French bearing from their pursuers east by south, — one point on the weather bow (B B).[1] The wind was rising with squalls, so that the ships lay over well to their canvas, and the sea was getting big.

As the enemy now was threatening his rear, and had the speed to overtake, des Touches felt it necessary to resort to the usual parry to such a thrust, by wearing his squadron and passing on the other tack. This could be done together, reversing the order, or in succession; depending much upon the distance of the enemy. Having room enough, des Touches chose the latter, but, as fighting was inevitable, he decided also to utilise the manœuvre by surrendering the weather-gage, and passing to leeward. The advantage of this course was that, with the existing sea and wind, and the inclination of the ships, the party that had the opponent on his weather side could open the lower-deck ports and use those guns. There was thus a great increase of battery power, for the lower guns were the heaviest. Des Touches accordingly put his helm up, his line passing in succession to the southward (c), across the head of the advancing British column, and then hauling up so as to run parallel to the latter, to leeward, with the wind four points free.

Arbuthnot accepted the position offered, stood on as he was until nearly abreast of the French, and at 2 P.M. made the signal to wear. It does not appear certainly how this was executed; but from the expression in the official report, "the van of the squadron wore in the line," and from the fact that the ships which led in the attack were those which were leading on the port tack, — the tack before the signal was made, — it seems likely that the movement was made in succession (a). The whole squadron then stood down, but with the customary result. The ships in the van and centre were all engaged by 2.30, so Arbuthnot states; but the brunt of the action had already fallen upon the three leading vessels, which got the first raking fire, and, as is also usual, came to closer action than those which followed them (C). They therefore not only lost most heavily

---

[1] Reference is to Mahan's "Influence of Sea Power Upon History," Plate XII.

in men, but also were so damaged aloft as to be crippled. The British Vice-Admiral, keeping the signal for the line flying, and not hoisting that for close action, appears to have caused a movement of indecision in the squadron, — an evidence again of the hold which the line then still had upon men's minds. Of this des Touches cleverly availed himself, by ordering his ships to wear in succession. The French column filed by the three disabled British vessels (d), gave them their broadsides one by one, and then hauled off to the eastward, quitting

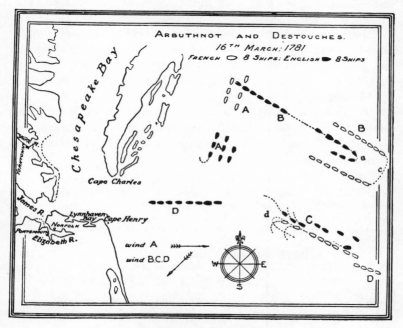

ARBUTHNOT AND DES TOUCHES.

the field (D). Arbuthnot made signal to wear in pursuit, but the *Robust* and *Prudent*, two of the van ships, were now wholly unmanageable from the concentration of fire upon them caused by des Touches's last movement; and the maintopsail yard of the *London*, the only British three-decker, had been shot away. The chase therefore was abandoned, and the squadron put into Chesapeake Bay, for which the wind was fair (D). The French returned to Newport. The respective losses in men were: British, 30 killed, 73 wounded; French, 72 killed, 112 wounded.

Both sides had eight ships, besides smaller craft, in this encounter. From the table [1] given below it is evident that the advantage in force was distinctly with the British. For this reason, probably, the action was considered particularly discreditable by contemporaries, and the more so because several vessels did not engage closely, — a fault laid to the Vice-Admiral's failure to make the signal for close action, hauling down that for the line. This criticism is interesting, for it indicates how men's minds were changing ; and it shows also that Arbuthnot had not changed, but still lived in the middle of the century. The French commodore displayed very considerable tactical skill ; his squadron was handled neatly, quickly, and with precision. With inferior force he carried off a decided advantage by sheer intelligence and good management. Unluckily, he failed in resolution to pursue his advantage. Had he persisted, he doubtless could have controlled the Chesapeake.

His neglect to do so was justified by Commodore de Barras, who on the 10th of May arrived in Newport from France to command the squadron. This officer, after pointing out the indisputable tactical success, continued thus : —

"As to the advantage which the English obtained, in fulfilling their object, that is a necessary consequence of their superiority, and, *still more*, of their purely defensive attitude. *It is a principle in war that one should risk much to defend one's own positions, and very little to attack those of the enemy.* M. des Touches, whose object was purely offensive, could and should, when the enemy opposed to him

[1] List of the British and French squadrons in the action of March 16th, 1781. The British list gives Arbuthnot's line of battle ; the *America* to lead with the starboard, and the *Robust* with the larboard tacks on board. Beatson, vi. 273 (corrected). — W. L. C.

SHIPS.	GUNS.	COMMANDERS.	SHIPS.	GUNS.	COMMANDERS.
America . .	64	Capt. Samuel Thompson.	*Neptune*	74	{ M. des Touches. } { Capt. de Médine. }
Bedford . .	74	Capt. Edmund Affleck.			
Adamant. .	50	Capt. Gideon Johnstone.	*Duc de Bourgogne* .	84	Capt. Baron de Durfort.
London . .	98	{ Rear-Adm. Thomas Graves (2), (R). } { Capt. David Graves. }	*Conquérant* . . .	74	Capt. de la Grandière.
			Provence	64	Capt. Lambart.
Royal Oak .	74	{ Vice-Adm. Marriot Arbuthnot. } { Capt. William Swiney. }	*Ardent*	64	Capt. de Marigny.
			Jason	64	Capt. de la Clocheterie.
Prudent . .	64	Capt. Thomas Burnett.	*Éveillé*	64	Capt. de Tilly.
Europe . .	64	Capt. Smith Child.	†*Romulus*	44	Capt. de Villebrune.
Robust . .	74	Capt. Phillips Cosby.			
FRIGATES : —			FRIGATES : —		
Guadalupe .	28	Capt. Hugh Robinson.	*Hermione*	36	Capt. de la Touche.
Pearl . . .	32	Capt. George Montagu.	*Gentille*	32	
Iris . . .	32	Capt. George Dawson.	*Fantasque* (en flûte)	64	Capt. de Vaudoré.
Medea . .	28	Capt. Henry Duncan (1).			

* These ships were coppered.
† Late British. Though only a 44-gun ship, she was a two-decker.

superior forces, renounce a project which could no longer succeed, unless, *contrary to all probability*, it ended not only in beating, but also in *destroying entirely*, that superior squadron."

This exaltation of the defensive above the offensive, this despairing view of probabilities, this aversion from risks, go far to explain the French want of success in this war. No matter how badly the enemy was thrashed, unless he were entirely destroyed, he was still a fleet " in being," a paralysing factor.

The retreat of des Touches and the coming of Arbuthnot restored to the British the command of Chesapeake Bay. Clinton, as soon as he knew that the two squadrons had sailed, had sent off a reinforcement of 2,000 troops for Arnold, under General Phillips. These arrived on March 26th in Lynnhaven Bay, and thence proceeded at once to Portsmouth, Virginia. It is unnecessary to speak of the various operations of this land force. On the 9th of May, in consequence of letters received from Cornwallis, it moved to Petersburg. There on the 13th Phillips died, the command reverting momentarily to Arnold. On the 20th Cornwallis joined, and Arnold soon after returned to New York.

Cornwallis now had with him about 7,000 troops, including the garrison at Portsmouth ; but a serious difference of opinion existed between him and Clinton, the Commander-in-Chief. The latter had begun the conquest of South Carolina, and he did not welcome the conclusion of his lieutenant that the conquest could not be maintained, away from the seaboard, unless Virginia also were subdued; for from the latter, a rich and populous region, men and supplies supported the American cause in the south. Cornwallis had tested the asserted strength of the Royalists in the Carolinas, and had found it wanting. Offensive operations in Virginia were what he wished ; but Clinton did not approve this project, nor feel that he could spare troops enough for the purpose. Between October, 1780, and June, 1781, he said, 7,724 effectives had been sent from New York to the Chesapeake ; and he could not understand the failure to cut off the greatly inferior force of the enemy in Virginia. This at least did not indicate probable success for a renewed offensive. The garrison of New York was now short of 11,000, and could not be diminished further, as he was threatened with a siege. In short, the British position in America had become essentially false, by the concurring effect of insufficient force and ex-centric — double — operations. Sent to conquer, their numbers now were so divided that they could barely maintain the defensive. Cornwallis therefore was ordered to occupy a defensive position, which should control an anchorage for ships of the line, and to strengthen himself in it. After some discussion, which revealed further disagreement, he placed himself at Yorktown, on the peninsula formed by the James and York rivers. Portsmouth was evacuated, the garrison reaching Yorktown on the 22nd of August. Cornwallis's force was then 7,000 troops; and there were with him besides about a thousand seamen, belonging to some half-dozen small vessels, which had been shut up in the York by the coming of the French fleet.

On the 2nd of July Arbuthnot sailed for England, leaving the command at New York to Rear-Admiral Thomas Graves (2). The latter on the same day wrote to Rodney, by the brig *Active*, that intercepted dispatches of the enemy had revealed that a large division from the West Indies was to arrive on the American coast during the summer, to co-operate with the force already in Newport. Rodney, on the other hand, dispatched to New York on the 7th the *Swallow* sloop, 16, with word that, if he sent reinforcements from the West Indies, they would be ordered to make the Capes of the Chesapeake, and to coast thence to New York. He asked, therefore, that cruisers with information might be stationed along that route. Two days later, having then certain news that de Grasse had sailed for Cap François, he sent the intelligence to Vice-Admiral Sir Peter Parker at Jamaica, and gave Rear-Admiral Sir Samuel Hood preparatory orders to command a reinforcement destined for the continent. This, however, was limited in numbers to fifteen sail of the line, Rodney being misled by his intelligence, which gave fourteen ships as the size of the French division having the same destination, and which reported that de Grasse himself would convoy the trade from Cap François to France. On the 24th instructions were issued for Hood to proceed on this duty. He was first to convoy the Jamaica trade as far as the passage between Cuba and Haïti, and thence to make the utmost speed to the Chesapeake. A false report, of French ships reaching Martinique from Europe, slightly delayed this movement. The convoy was dispatched to Jamaica with two ships of the line, which Sir Peter Parker was directed to send at once to America, and requested to reinforce with others from his own squadron. Hood was detained until the report could be verified. On the 1st of August Rodney sailed for England on leave of absence. On the 10th Hood left Antigua with fourteen ships of the line, direct for the Capes. He had already received, on the 3rd, Graves's letter by the *Active*, which he sent back on the 6th with his answer and with a notification of his speedy departure.

The *Swallow* and the *Active* should have reached Graves before Hood; but neither got to him at all. The *Swallow*, Commander Thomas Wells, arrived safely in New York on the 27th of July; but Graves had sailed with all his squadron on the 21st, for Boston Bay, hoping there to intercept an expected convoy from France, concerning which a special caution had been sent him by the Admiralty. The sloop was at once sent on by the senior naval officer, but was attacked by hostile vessels, forced ashore on Long Island, and lost. The *Active* was captured before she reached New York. Graves, in happy ignorance of the momentous crisis approaching, continued cruising until the 16th of August, when he returned to Sandy Hook. There he found the duplicates of the *Swallow's* letters, but they only notified him of the course a reinforcement would take, not that Hood had started. On August 25th the latter, being then off the Chesapeake, sent duplicates of the *Active's* dispatches, but these preceded by little his own arrival on the 28th. That evening news was received in New York that de Barras had sailed from Newport on the 25th, with his whole division. Hood anchored outside the Hook, where Graves, who was the senior officer, undertook to join him at once. On the 31st five sail of the line and a fifty-gun ship, all that could be got ready in time, crossed the bar, and the entire body of nineteen ships of the line started at once for the Chesapeake, whither it was now understood that both the French fleet and the united armies of Washington and Rochambeau were hurrying.

Count de Grasse upon his arrival at Cap François had found that many things must be done before he could sail for the continent. Measures needed to be taken for the security of Haïti; and a large sum of money, with a considerable reinforcement of troops, was required to insure the success of the projected operation, for which but a short time was allowed, as it was now August and he must be again in the West Indies in October. It was not the least among the fortunate concurrences for the American cause at that moment, that de Grasse, whose military capacity was not conspicuous, showed then a remarkable energy, politic tact, and breadth of view. He decided to take with him every ship he could command, postponing the sailing of the convoys; and by dexterous arrangement

with the Spaniards he contrived to secure both the funds required
and an efficient corps of 3,300 French troops, without stripping
Haïti too closely.   On the 5th of August he left Cap François, with
twenty-eight ships of the line, taking the route through the Old
Bahama Channel,[1] and anchored in Lynnhaven Bay, just within the
entrance of the Chesapeake, on the 30th, the day before Graves sailed
from New York for the same place.   The troops were landed instantly
on the south side of the James River, and soon reached La Fayette,
who commanded the forces so far opposed to Cornwallis, which were
thus raised to 8,000 men.   At the same time Washington, having
thrown Clinton off his guard, was crossing the Delaware on his way
south, with 6,000 regular troops, 2,000 American and 4,000 French,
to join La Fayette.   French cruisers took position in the James River,
to prevent Cornwallis from crossing, and escaping to the southward
into Carolina.   Others were sent to close the mouth of the York.
By these detachments the main fleet was reduced to twenty-four sail
of the line.

On the 5th of September, at 8 A.M., the French look-out frigate,
cruising outside Cape Henry, made the signal for a fleet steering for
the Bay.   It was hoped at first that this was de Barras's squadron
from Newport, known to be on its way, but it was soon evident from
the numbers that it must be an enemy.   The forces now about to be
opposed, nineteen British sail of the line to twenty-four French, were
constituted as follows : British, 2 ninety-eights (three-deckers) ; 12
seventy-fours, 1 seventy, 4 sixty-fours, besides frigates ;[2] French, 1
one hundred and four (three-decker),[3] 3 eighties, 17 seventy-fours,
3 sixty-fours.

The mouth of the Chesapeake is about ten miles wide, from Cape
Charles on the north to Cape Henry on the south.   The main channel is between the latter and a shoal, three miles to the northward,
called the Middle Ground.   The British fleet, when the French were
first seen from it, was steering south-west for the entrance, under
foresails and topgallant sails, and it so continued, forming line as it
approached.   The wind was north-north-east. At noon the ebb-tide
made, and the French began to get under way, but many of their
ships had to make several tacks to clear Cape Henry.   Their line was

---

[1] Along the north coast of Cuba, between it and the Bahama Banks.
[2] See note on opposite page.
[3] The *Ville de Paris*, to which Troude attributes 104 guns.   She was considered
the biggest and finest ship of her day.

consequently late in forming, and was by no means regular or closed as they got outside.

At 1 P.M. Graves made the signal to form on an east and west line, which would be the closehauled line heading out to sea, on the other tack from that on which his fleet still was. At 2 P.M. the French van, three miles distant by estimate, bore south from the *London*, Graves's flagship, and was therefore abreast of the centre of the British line. As the British van came near the Middle Ground, at 2.13 P.M., the ships wore together. This put them on the same tack as the French, Hood's division, which had been leading, being now the rear in the reversed order; and the fleet brought-to, in order to allow the centre

---

NOTE. — British line of battle in the action of Sept. 5, 1781. Mainly from Beatson, vi. 284; corrected by Steel's 'Navy List' of the period, and from MS. notes by Henry Wise Harvey in Ed's. edition of Schomberg, iv. 377, 378. The *Alfred* was to lead with the starboard, and the *Shrewsbury* with the larboard tacks on board. — W. L. C.

SHIPS.	GUNS.	COMMANDERS.
Alfred	74	Capt. William Bayne.
Belliqueux	64	Capt. James Brine.
Invincible	74	Capt. Charles Saxton.
Barfleur	98	{ Rear-Admiral Sir Samuel Hood (B). { Capt. Alexander Hood.
Monarch	74	Capt. Francis Reynolds (later Lord Ducie).
Centaur	74	Capt. John Nicholson Inglefield.
Santa Margaritta, 36 .		Capt. Elliot Salter.
Richmond, 32 . . .		Capt. Charles Hudson.
America	64	Capt. Samuel Thompson.
Resolution	74	Capt. Lord Robert Manners.
Bedford	74	Capt. Thomas Graves (3).
London	98	{ Rear-Admiral Thomas Graves (2), (R). { Capt. David Graves.
Royal Oak	74	Capt. John Plummer Ardesoif.
Montagu	74	Capt. George Bowen (1).
Europe	64	Capt. Smith Child.
Solebay, 28		Capt. Charles Holmes Everitt (later Calmady).
Nymphe, 36		Capt. John Ford.
Adamant, 50 . . .		Capt. Gideon Johnstone.
Terrible	74	Capt. Hon. William Clement Finch.
Ajax	74	Capt. Nicholas Charrington.
Princesa	70	{ Rear-Admiral Francis Samuel Drake (B). { Capt. Charles Knatchbull.
Alcide	74	Capt. Charles Thompson.
Intrepid	64	Capt. Anthony James Pye Molloy.
Shrewsbury	74	Capt. Mark Robinson (1).
Salamander (f. s.) . .		Commander Edward Bowater.
Sibyl, 28		Capt. Lord Charles Fitzgerald (?).
Fortunée, 40		Capt. Hugh Cloberry Christian.

of the enemy to come abreast of the centre of the British (a a). The
two lines now were nearly parallel, but the British, being five ships
fewer, naturally did not extend so far as the rear of the French, which
in fact was not yet clear of the Cape. At 2.30 Graves made the
signal for the van ship (the *Shrewsbury*), to lead more to starboard —
towards the enemy. As each ship in succession would take her course
to follow the leader, the effect of this was to put the British on a line

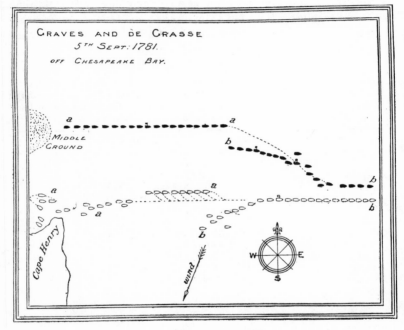

GRAVES AND DE GRASSE.

inclined to that of the enemy, the van nearest, and as the signal was
renewed three quarters of an hour later, — at 3.17, — this angle became
still more marked (b b).[1] This was the original and enduring cause
of a lamentable failure, by which seven of the rear ships, in an inferior
force undertaking to attack, never came into battle at all. At 3.34
the van was ordered again to keep still more towards the enemy.

At 3.46 the signal was made for ships to close to one cable, followed almost immediately by that to bear down and engage the

---

[1] This reproduced the blunder of Byng, between whose action and the one now
under discussion there is a marked resemblance.

enemy, — the signal for the line still flying. Graves's flagship, which was hove-to, filled and bore down. Under the conditions, the van ships of course got first under fire, and the action gradually extended from them to the twelfth in the order, two ships astern of the *London*. According to the log of the latter, at 4.11 the signal for the line ahead was hauled down, that it might not interfere with that for close action, but at 4.22 it was rehoisted, " the ships not being sufficiently extended." The meaning of this expression may be inferred from Beatson's account : —

" The *London*, by taking the lead, had advanced farther towards the enemy than some of the ships stationed immediately ahead of her in the line of battle ; and upon luffing up, to bring her broadside to bear, they having done the same thing, her second ahead was brought nearly upon her weather beam. The other ships ahead of her were likewise too much crowded together."

As the ship on the *London's* weather beam could not fire upon the enemy unless she drew ahead, this condition probably accounts for the flagship being again hove-to, while firing, as Hood says that she was. Readers will remember a similar incident occurring with Byng's flagship. The signal for the line was hauled down again at 4.27, by the *London's* log, that for close action being up, and repeated at 5.20, when Hood at last bore down with his division, but the French ships bearing up also, he did not near them. Firing ceased shortly after sunset. The loss of the British was 90 killed, 246 wounded; that of the French is given only in round numbers, as about 200 killed and wounded.

Hood's statement introduces certain important qualifications into the above account : —

" Our centre began to engage at the same time as the van, at four, but at a most *improper* distance, and our rear, being barely within random shot, did not fire while the signal for the line was flying. The *London* had the signal for close action flying, as well as the signal for the line ahead at *half a cable* was under her topsails, with the main topsail to the mast,[1] though the enemy's ships were pushing on."

As showing the improper distance at which the *London* brought-to to fire, he says : —

" The second ship astern of her (of the *London*) received but trifling damage, and the third astern of her received no damage at all, which most clearly proves [at] how much too great a distance was the centre division engaged."

The day after the action Hood made a memorandum of his criticisms upon it, which has been published. The gist of this is as

---

[1] *I. e.,* she had stopped.

follows. As the French stood out, their line was not regular or connected. The van was much separated from the centre and rear, and
it appears also, from the French narratives, that it was to windward
of the rest of the fleet. From these causes it was much exposed to
be attacked unsupported. There was, by Hood's estimate, " a full
hour and a half to have engaged it before any of the rear could have
come up." The line of battle on the port tack, with the then wind,
was east and west, and Graves had first ranged his fleet on it, as the
French were doing; but afterwards, owing to his method of approach,
by the van bearing down and the other ships following in its wake, the
two lines, instead of being parallel, formed an angle, the British
centre and rear being much more distant from the enemy than the
van was. This alone would cause the ships to come into battle successively instead of together, a fault of itself ; but the Commander-
in-Chief, according to Hood, committed the further mistake that he
kept the signal for the line of battle flying until 5.30 P.M., near to
sunset. The line of battle at any moment ran, of course, from the
van ship through that of the Commander-in-Chief ; those two points
determined it for all in the rear, where Hood was. Hence the latter's
criticism, which is marked by much acerbity towards his superior, but
does not betray any consciousness that he himself needed any justification for his division not having taken part.

" Had the centre gone to the support of the van, and the signal for the line
been hauled down, or the Commander-in-Chief had set the example of close action,
even with the signal for the line flying, the van of the enemy must have been cut
to pieces, and the rear division of the British fleet would have been opposed to
those ships the centre division fired at, and at the proper distance for engaging, or
the Rear-Admiral who commanded it [1] would have a great deal to answer for." [2]

So much for the tactical failure of that day. The question remained
what next was to be done. Graves contemplated renewing the
action, but early in the night was informed that several of the van

[1] Hood himself.

[2] Concerning the crucial fact of the signal for the line of battle being kept flying
continuously until 5.30 P.M., upon which there is a direct contradiction between Hood
and the log of the *London*, it is necessary to give the statement of Captain Thomas
White, who was present in the action in one of the rear ships. " If the *London's* log,
or the log of any other individual ship in the fleet, confirm this statement," (that
Hood was dilatory in obeying the order for close action), " I shall be induced to fancy
that what I that day saw and heard was a mere chimera of the brain, and that what
I believed to be the signal for the line was not a union jack, but an *ignis fatuus* con-
jured up to mock me." White and Hood also agree that the signal for the line was
rehoisted at 6.30. (White : ' Naval Researches,' London, 1830.)

ships were too crippled to permit this. He held his ground, however, in sight of the French, until dark on the 9th, when they were
seen for the last time. They were then under a cloud of sail, and
on the morning of the 10th had disappeared. From their actions
during this interval, Hood had inferred that de Grasse meant to get
back into the Chesapeake without further fighting; and he implies
that he advised Graves to anticipate the enemy in so doing. Though
some ships were crippled aloft, the British batteries were practically
intact, nor had men enough been disabled to prevent any gun in
the fleet from being fought. Could but a single working day
be gained in taking up an anchorage, a defensive order could be
assumed, practically impregnable to the enemy, covering Cornwallis,
and not impossibly intercepting the French ships left in the Bay. In
the case of many men such comment might be dismissed as the idle
talk of the captious fault-finder, always to the fore in life; but in the
case of Hood it must be received with deference, for, but a few
months later, when confronted with greater odds, he himself did the
very thing he here recommended, for an object less vital than the
relief of Cornwallis. Having regard to the character of de Grasse, it
is reasonable to believe that, if he had found the British fleet thus
drawn up at anchor in Chesapeake Bay, as he found Hood at St.
Kitts in the following January, he would have waited off the
entrance for de Barras, and then have gone to sea, leaving Washington
and Rochambeau to look at Cornwallis slipping out of their grasp.

On the 10th of September Graves decided to burn the *Terrible*, 74,
which had been kept afloat with difficulty since the action. This
done, the fleet stood towards the Chesapeake, a frigate going ahead
to reconnoitre. On the 13th, at 6 A.M., Graves wrote to Hood that
the look-outs reported the French at anchor above the Horse Shoe
(shoal) in the Chesapeake, and desired his opinion what to do with
the fleet. To this Hood sent the comforting reply that it was no
more than what he had expected, as the press of sail the (French)
fleet carried on the 9th, and on the night of the 8th, made it very
clear to him what de Grasse's intentions were. He "would be very
glad to send an opinion, but he really knows not what to say in the
truly lamentable state [to which] we have brought ourselves." [1] On
the 10th de Barras had reached the Bay, where he was joined by de
Grasse on the 11th, so that there were then present thirty-six French
ships of the line. Graves, therefore, returned to New York, reach-

---

[1] 'Letters of Lord Hood.' N. R. S., p. 35.

ing Sandy Hook on the 19th.   On the 14th Washington had arrived
before Yorktown, where he took the chief command; and the armies
closed in upon Cornwallis by land as the French fleets had done
already by water.   On the 19th of October the British force was
compelled to surrender, 7,247 troops and 840 seamen laying down
their arms.   During the siege the latter had served in the works,
the batteries of which were largely composed of ships' guns.

After Graves's return to New York, Rear-Admiral the Hon. Robert
Digby arrived from England on the 24th of September, to take command of the station in Arbuthnot's place.   He brought with him
three ships of the line; and the two which Sir Peter Parker had been
ordered by Rodney to send on at once had also reached the port.   It
was decided by the land and sea officers concerned to attempt the
relief of Cornwallis, and that it was expedient for Graves to remain
in command until after this expedition.   He could not start, however, until the 18th of October, by which time Cornwallis's fate was
decided.   Graves then departed for Jamaica to supersede Sir Peter
Parker.   On the 11th of November Hood sailed from Sandy Hook
with eighteen ships of the line, and on the 5th of December anchored
at Barbados.   On the 5th of November de Grasse also quitted the
continent with his whole fleet, and returned to the West Indies.

In Europe, during the year 1781, the two leading questions which
dominated the action of the belligerents were the protection, or
destruction, of commerce, and the attack and defence of Gibraltar.
The British Channel Fleet was much inferior to the aggregate sea
forces of France and Spain in the waters of Europe; and the Dutch
navy also was now hostile.   The French government represented to
its allies that by concentrating their squadrons near the entrance of
the Channel they would control the situation in every point of view;
but the Spaniards, intent upon Gibraltar, declined to withdraw their
fleet from Cadiz until late in the summer, while the French persisted
in keeping their own at Brest.   The Channel Fleet was decisively
superior to the latter, and inferior to the Spaniards in numbers
only.

No relief having been given Gibraltar since Rodney had left it in
February, 1780, the question of supplying the fortress became pressing.   For this purpose, twenty-eight ships of the line, under Vice-
Admiral George Darby, sailed from St. Helen's on the 13th of March,
1781, with a large convoy.   Off Cork a number of victuallers joined,

and the whole body then proceeded for Gibraltar, accompanied by
five ships of the line which were destined for the East Indies, as well
as by the West India and American "trade." These several attach-
ments parted from time to time on the way, and on the 11th of April
the main expedition sighted Cape Spartel. No attempt to intercept
it was made by the great Spanish fleet in Cadiz; and on the 12th of
April, at noon, the convoy anchored in the Bay of Gibraltar. That
night thirteen sail of transports, under the charge of two frigates,
slipped out and made their way to Minorca. The ships of war
remained under way, cruising in the Bay and Gut of Gibraltar.

As the convoy entered, the besiegers opened a tremendous cannonade, which was ineffectual, however, to stop the landing of the
stores. More annoyance was caused by a flotilla of gunboats, specially
built for this siege, the peculiar fighting power of which lay in one
26-pounder, whose great length gave a range superior to the batteries of ships of the line. Being moved by oars as well as by sails,
these little vessels could choose their own distance in light airs and
calms, and were used so actively to harass the transports at anchor
that Darby was obliged to cover them with three ships of the line.
These proved powerless effectually to injure the gunboats; but, while
the latter caused great annoyance and petty injury, they did not
hinder the unloading nor even greatly delay it. The experience
illustrates again the unlikelihood that great results can be obtained by
petty means, or that massed force, force concentrated, can be effectually counteracted either by cheap and ingenious expedients, or by
the co-operative exertions of many small independent units. "They
were only capable of producing trouble and vexation. So far were
they from preventing the succours from being thrown into the garrison, or from burning the convoy, that the only damage of any
consequence that they did to the shipping was the wounding of the
mizen-mast of the *Nonsuch* so much that it required to be shifted."[1]
On the 19th of April — in one week — the revictualling was completed, and the expedition started back for England. The fleet
anchored at Spithead on the 22nd of May.

While Darby was returning, La Motte Picquet had gone to sea
from Brest with six ships of the line and some frigates to cruise in
the approaches to the Channel. There, on the 2nd of May, he fell
in with the convoy returning from the West Indies with the spoils of
St. Eustatius. The ships of war for the most part escaped, but La

[1] Beatson : ' Military and Naval Memoirs,' v. 347.

Motte Picquet carried twenty-two out of thirty merchant ships into Brest before he could be intercepted, although a detachment of eight sail sent by Darby got close upon his heels.

After a long refit, Darby put to sea again, about the 1st of August, to cover the approach of the large convoys then expected to arrive. Being greatly delayed by head winds, he had got no further than the Lizard, when news was brought him that the Franco-Spanish grand fleet, of forty-nine ships of the line, was cruising near the Scilly Isles. Having himself but thirty of the line, he put into Torbay on the 24th of August, and moored his squadron across the entrance to the Bay.

This appearance of the allies was a surprise to the British authorities, who saw thus unexpectedly renewed the invasion of the Channel made in 1779. Spain, mortified justly by her failure even to molest the intrusion of succours into Gibraltar, had thought to retrieve her honour by an attack upon Minorca, for which she asked the co-operation of France. De Guichen was sent in July with nineteen ships of the line; and the combined fleets, under the chief command of the Spanish admiral Don Luis de Cordova, convoyed the troops into the Mediterranean beyond the reach of Gibraltar cruisers. Returning thence into the Atlantic, de Cordova directed his course for the Channel, keeping far out to sea to conceal his movements. But though thus successful in reaching his ground unheralded, he made no attempt to profit by the advantage gained. The question of attacking Darby at his anchors was discussed in a council of war, at which de Guichen strongly advocated the measure; but a majority of votes decided that Great Britain would be less hurt by ruining her fleet than by intercepting the expected convoys. Even for the latter purpose, however, de Cordova could not wait. On the 5th of September he informed de Guichen that he was at liberty to return to Brest; and he himself went back to Cadiz with thirty-nine ships, nine of which were French. "This cruise of the combined fleet," says Chevalier, "diminished the consideration of France and Spain. These two powers had made a great display of force, without producing the slightest result." It may be mentioned here that Minorca, after a six months' siege, capitulated in February, 1782.

While Darby was beating down Channel in the early days of August, Vice-Admiral Hyde Parker (1), lately Rodney's second in command in the West Indies, was returning from the Baltic to England convoying a large merchant fleet. On the 5th of August, at daylight, a Dutch squadron, also with a convoy, was discovered in the south-west, near the Doggersbank.   Heading as the two enemies then were, their courses must shortly intersect.   Parker, therefore, ordered his convoy to steer to the westward for England, while he himself bore down for the enemy.   The Dutch Rear-Admiral, Johan Arnold Zoutman, on the contrary, kept the merchant vessels with him, under his lee, but drew out the ships of war from among them, to form his order on the side towards the enemy.   Each opponent put seven sail into the line.[1]   The British vessels, besides being of such different rates, were chiefly very old ships,[2] dragged out from Rotten Row to meet the pressing emergency caused by the greatly superior forces which were in coalition against Great Britain. Owing to the decayed condition of some of them, their batteries

[1] Fleets engaged in the action off the Doggersbank, August 5th, 1781.

BRITISH.			DUTCH.		
SHIPS.	GUNS.	COMMANDERS.	SHIPS.	GUNS.	COMMANDERS.
IN THE LINE: —					
Berwick	74	Capt. John Fergusson.	Erfprins	54	Capt. A. Braak.
Dolphin	44	Capt. William Blair.	Admirtal Generaal	74	Capt. van Kinsbergen.
Buffalo	60	Capt. William Truscott.	Argo	40	Capt. A. C. Staering.
Fortitude . . .	74	{ V.-Adm. Hyde Parker (1) { Capt. George Robertson.	Batavier	54	Capt. W. J. Bentinck.
Princess Amelia .	80	Capt. John Macartney.*	Admiraal de Ruijter	68	{ Rear-Adm. Zoutman. { Capt. Staringh.
Preston	50	Capt. Alexander Græme.	Admiraal Piet Heijn	54	Capt. W. van Braam.
Bienfaisant . .	64	Capt. Richard Brathwaite.	Holland	68	Capt. S. Dedel.
FRIGATES WITH THE FLEET: —					
Surprise (cutter).	14	Lieut. P. Rivett.	Bellona	36	Capt. Haringcarspel Decker.
Cleopatra . . .	32	Capt. George Murray.	Dolphijn	24	Capt. Mulder.
Latona	38	Capt. Sir Hyde Parker (2).	Ajax (cutter) . .	20	Capt. Grave van Welderen.
Belle Poule . .	36	Capt. Philip Patton.	Eensgezindheit . .	36	Capt. Bouritius.
Artois	40	Capt. John Macbride.	Zephijr	36	Capt. Wiertz.
			Amphitrite . . .	36	Capt. van Woensel.
WITH THE CONVOY: —					
Iphigenia . . .	32	Capt. Charles Hope.	Medemblik . . .	36	Capt. van Rijneveld.
Tartar	28	Capt. Robert Sutton.	Venus	24	Capt. Grave van Regteren.
Cabot	14	Com. Henry Cromwell.	Spion	16	Com. Stutzer.
Alert	14	Com. James Vashon.	Zwaluw	10	Com. Butger.
Leith (armed ship).	20	Com. Peter Rothe.			
Busy (cutter) . .	14	Lieut. William Furnivall.			
Sprightly (cutter)	14	Lieut. J. B. Swan.			

* Killed.

The vessels in the two lines are given above in the respective orders of battle. The British list is founded on one in Beatson, vi. 315, compared with the 'Navy Lists' of 1781, the dispatches, etc.   The Dutch list is founded on a MS. of Capt. Count van Bylandt, compared with the dispatches, and with the plan and particulars in De Jonge, iv. 508-561.   The gun-power of each ship is taken from official papers, British and Dutch. — W. L. C.

[2] The *Bienfaisant* had been captured in 1758, and the *Buffalo* in 1748; and the *Princess Amelia* and *Preston* were both built in 1757.

had been lightened, to the detriment of their fighting power. The
two seventy-fours, however, were good and new ships. The *Dolphin*
also was new. It is probable that the Dutch vessels, after a long
peace, were not much better than their antagonists. In fact, each
squadron was a scratch lot, in the worst sense of the phrase. The
conduct of the affair by the two admirals, even to the very intensity
of their pugnaciousness, contributes a tinge of the comic to the
history of a desperately fought action.

The breeze was fresh at north-east, and the sea smooth. The
Dutch, being to leeward, awaited attack, forming line on the port
tack, heading south-east by east, a point off the wind, under topsails
and foresails, a cable's length apart. There is little room to doubt
that an adversary who thus holds his ground means to make a
stand-up fight, but Parker, although the sun of a midsummer day
had scarcely risen, thought advisable to order a general chase. Of
course, no ship spared her canvas to this, while the worse sailers had
to set their studdingsails to keep up; and the handling of the sails
took the men off from the preparations for battle. Parker, who doubtless was still sore over Rodney's censure of the year before, and who
moreover had incurred the Admiralty's rebuke, for apparent hesitation to attack the enemy's islands while temporarily in command in
the West Indies, was determined now to show the fight that was in
him. "It is related that, upon being informed of the force of the
Dutch squadron in the morning, he replied (pulling up his breeches),
' It matters little what their force is; we must fight them if they are
double the number.'" At 6.10 A.M. the signal was made for line
abreast, the ships running down nearly before the wind. This of
course introduced more regularity, the leading ships taking in their
lighter sails to permit the others to reach their places; but the pace
still was rapid. At 6.45 the order was closed to one cable, and at
7.56 the signal for battle was hoisted. It is said that at that moment
the 80-gun ship was still securing a studdingsail-boom, which indicates how closely action trod on the heels of preparation.

The Dutch admiral was as deliberate as Parker was headlong.
An English witness writes: —

" They appeared to be in great order; and their hammocks, quarter-cloths, etc.,
were spread in as nice order as if for show in harbour. Their marines also were
well drawn up, and stood with their muskets shouldered, with all the regularity
and exactness of a review. Their politeness ought to be remembered by every man
in our line: for, as if certain of what happened, we came down almost end-on upon
their broadsides; yet did not the Dutch admiral fire a gun, or make the signal to

engage, till the red flag was at the *Fortitude's* masthead, and her shot finding their way into his ship.   This was a manœuvre which Admiral Zutman should not be warmly thanked for by their High Mightinesses; as he had it in his power to have done infinite mischief to our fleet, coming down in that unofficer-like manner. Having suffered Admiral Parker to place himself as he pleased, he calmly waited till the signal was hoisted on board the *Fortitude*, and at the same time we saw the signal going up on board Admiral Zutman's ship."

The British, thus unmolested, rounded-to just to windward of the enemy.   A pilot who was on board their leading ship was for some reason told to assist in laying her close to her opponent.   " By close," he asked, " do you mean about a ship's breadth?"   "Not a gun was fired on either side," says the official British report, "until within the distance of half musket-shot."   Parker, whom an on-looker describes as full of life and spirits, here made a mistake, of a routine character, which somewhat dislocated his order.   It was a matter of tradition for flagship to seek flagship, just as it was to signal a general chase, and to bear down together, each ship for its opposite, well extended with the enemy.   Now Parker, as was usual, was in the centre of his line, the fourth ship; but Zoutman was for some reason in the fifth.   Parker therefore placed his fourth by the enemy's fifth.   In consequence, the rear British ship overlapped the enemy, and for a time had no opponent; while the second and third found themselves engaged with three of the Dutch.   At 8 A.M. the signal for the line was hauled down, and that for close action hoisted, — thus avoiding a mistake often made.

All the vessels were soon satisfactorily and hotly at work, and the action continued with varying phases till 11.35 A.M.   The leading two ships in both orders got well to leeward of the lines, and the British vessels had to tack to regain their places to windward. Towards the middle of the engagement the Dutch convoy bore away for the Texel, as the British had steered for England before it began; the difference being that the voyage was abandoned by one, and completed by the other.   At eleven o'clock Parker made sail, and passed with the flagship between the enemy and the *Buffalo*, his next ahead and third in the British order; the three rear ships following close in his wake, in obedience to the signal for line ahead, which had been rehoisted at 10.43.[1]   A heavy cannonade attended this evolution, the

[1] Sir John Ross, in his ' Life of Saumarez,' who was a lieutenant in the flagship, says that the flagship only passed ahead of the *Buffalo*, and that the rear ships closed upon the latter.   The version in the text rests upon the detailed and circumstantial statement of another lieutenant of the squadron, in Ekins's ' Naval Battles.'   As Ekins

Dutch fighting gloriously to the last. When it was completed, the British fleet wore and the action ceased. "I made an effort to form the line, in order to renew the action," wrote Parker in his report, "but found it impracticable. The enemy appeared to be in as bad a condition. Both squadrons lay-to a considerable time near each other, when the Dutch, with their convoy, bore away for the Texel. We were not in a condition to follow them."

This was a most satisfactory exhibition of valour, and a most unsatisfactory battle; magnificent, but not war. Except as regards the sailings of the convoys, the *status quo* remained much as before, although one of the Dutch ships sank next day; yet the British loss, 104 killed and 339 wounded, was nearly as great as in Keppel's action, where thirty ships fought on each side, or in Rodney's of April 17th, 1780, where the British had twenty sail; greater than with Graves off the Chesapeake, and, in proportion, fully equal to the sanguinary conflicts between Suffren and Hughes in the East Indies. The Dutch loss is reported as 142 killed, 403 wounded. Both sides aimed at the hull, as is shown by the injuries; for though much harm was done aloft, few spars were wholly shot away. The *Buffalo*, a small ship, had 39 shot through and through her, and a very great number pierced between wind and water; in the British van ship as many as 14, another proof that the Dutch fired low.

With the rudimentary notions of manœuvring evinced, it is not surprising that Parker was found an unsatisfactory second by an enlightened tactician like Rodney. The Vice-Admiral, however, laid his unsuccess to the indifferent quality of his ships. George III. visited the squadron after the action, but Parker was not open to compliments. "I wish your Majesty better ships and younger officers," he said. "For myself, I am now too old for service." No rewards were given, and it is asserted that Parker made no secret that none would be accepted, if offered, at the hands of the then Admiralty. He voiced the protest of the Navy and the nation against the mal-administration of the peace days, which had left the country unprepared for war. The gallant veteran was ordered soon afterwards to command in the East Indies. He sailed for his station in the *Cato*, and was never heard of again.

Though unfruitful in substantial results, Parker's action merits commemoration, for, after all, even where skill does its utmost,

also was present as a midshipman, this gives, as it were, the confirmation of two witnesses.

staunchness such as his shows the sound constitution of a military body.

The year 1781 closed with an incident more decisive in character than most of the events that occurred in European waters during its course; one also which transfers the interest, by natural transition, again to the West Indies. The French government had felt throughout the summer the necessity of sending de Grasse reinforcements both of ships and of supplies, but the transports and material of war needed could not be collected until December. As the British probably would attempt to intercept a convoy upon which the next campaign so much depended, Rear-Admiral de Guichen was ordered to accompany it clear of the Bay of Biscay, with twelve ships of the line, and then to go to Cadiz. Five ships of the line destined to de Grasse, and two going to the East Indies, raised to nineteen the total force with which de Guichen left Brest on the 10th of December. On the afternoon of the 12th, the French being then one hundred and fifty miles to the southward and westward of Ushant, with a southeast wind, the weather, which had been thick and squally, suddenly cleared and showed sails to windward. These were twelve ships of the line, one 50, and some frigates,[1] under Rear-Admiral Richard Kempenfelt (B), who had left England on the 2nd of the month, to cruise in wait for this expedition. The French numbers should have been amply sufficient to frustrate any attack, but de Guichen, ordinarily a careful officer, had allowed his fleet to be to leeward and ahead of the convoy. The latter scattered in every direction, as the British swooped down upon it, but all could not escape; and the French ships of war remained helpless spectators, while the victims were hauling down their flags right and left. Night coming on,

[1] Fleet under Rear-Admiral Richard Kempenfelt, December, 1781. From Beatson, vi. 317, checked by Steel's 'Navy List' of Dec. 31st, 1781. — W. L. C.

SHIPS.	GUNS.	COMMANDERS.	SHIPS.	GUNS.	COMMANDERS.
Victory	100	{ Rear-Adm. Richard Kempenfelt (B). / Capt. Henry Cromwell.	Courageux	74	Capt. Hon. Chas. Phipps (Actg.).
			Agamemnon	64	Capt. Benjamin Caldwell.
Edgar	74	{ Commod. John Elliot. / Capt. Thomas Boston.	Medway	60	Capt. Harry Harmood.
			Renown	50	Capt. John Henry.
Britannia	100	Capt. James Bradby (1).			
Duke	98	Capt. Sir Walter Stirling, Kt.	FRIGATES, etc.		
Queen	98	Capt. Hon. Fredk. Lewis Maitland.	Arethusa	38	Capt. Sir Richard Pearson, Kt.
Union	90	Capt. John Dalrymple.	Monsieur	36	Capt. Hon. Seymour Finch.
Ocean	90	Capt. George Ourry.	Prudente	36	Capt. Hon. William Waldegrave.
Alexander	74	Com. Thomas Farnham (Actg.).	Tartar	28	Capt. Robert Manners Sutton.
Valiant	74	Capt. Samuel Granston Goodall.	Tisiphone (f. s.)	8	Com. James Saumarez.

some prizes could not be secured, but Kempenfelt carried off fifteen, laden with military and naval stores of great money value and greater military importance.   A few days later a violent storm dispersed and shattered the remainder of the French body.   Two ships of the line only, the *Triomphant*, 84, and *Brave*, 74, and five transports, could pursue their way to the West Indies.   The rest went back to Brest.

Kempenfelt, before returning to England, sent off express to Hood in the West Indies the fireship *Tisiphone*, 8, Commander James Saumarez,[1] — afterwards the distinguished admiral, — with news of the French approach.   Saumarez, having been first to Barbados, joined Hood on the 31st of January, 1782, in Basse Terre Roads, on the lee side of St. Kitts.   The campaign for the year 1782 had opened already with an attack upon that island by the French army and navy; and the enemy's fleet was even then cruising close at hand to leeward, between St. Kitts and Nevis.

The original intention of de Grasse and de Bouillé had been to capture Barbados, the most important of the Eastern Antilles still remaining to the British; but the heavy trade-winds, which in those days made a winter passage to windward so long and dreary a beat, twice drove him back to port.   "The whole French fleet," wrote Hood, "appeared off St. Lucia on the 17th of last month, endeavouring to get to windward, and having carried away many topmasts and yards in struggling against very squally weather, returned to Fort Royal Bay on the 23rd, and on the 28th came out again with forty transports, manœuvring as before."   On the 2nd of January it disappeared from St. Lucia, and, after a short stay at Martinique, proceeded on the 5th to St. Kitts, anchoring in Basse Terre Roads on the 11th.   The British garrison retired to Brimstone Hill, a fortified position at the north-west of the island, while the inhabitants surrendered the government to the French, pledging themselves to neutrality.   The adjacent island of Nevis capitulated on the same terms on the 20th.

On the 14th of the month an express sent by General Shirley, governor of St. Kitts, informed Hood that a great fleet approaching had been seen from the heights of Nevis on the 10th.   The Rear-

<hr />

[1] James Saumarez, Lord de Saumarez, G. C. B.   Born, 1757.   Commander, 1781. Captain, 1782.   Captain of *Russell* in Rodney's action, 1782.   Knighted for capture of frigate *Réunion*, 1793.   Captain of *Orion* in Bridport's action, at St. Vincent, and at the Nile (when he was second in command).   Rear-Admiral and Baronet, 1801. Defeated French and Spaniards off Algeciras, July 12th, 1801.   Vice-Admiral, 1805. Vice-Admiral of England and a peer, 1831.   Died, 1836.

Admiral at once put to sea, though short of bread and flour, which could not be had, and with the material of his ships in wretched condition. " When the *President* joins," he wrote the Admiralty, " I shall be twenty-two strong, with which I beg you will assure their Lordships I will seek and give battle to the Count de Grasse, be his numbers as they may." On the 16th a ship reached him with word that the French fleet had invested St. Kitts. On the 21st Hood anchored at Antigua for repairs and supplies, indispensable for keeping the sea in the operations which he contemplated, the duration of which could not be foreseen. About a thousand troops also were embarked, which, with the Marines that could be spared from the squadron, would give a landing force of 2,400 men.

St. Kitts being less than fifty miles from Antigua, Hood doubtless now got accurate information of the enemy's dispositions, and could form a definite, well-matured plan. This seems to have been carefully imparted to all his captains, as was the practice of Nelson, who was the pupil of Hood, if of any one. "At 9.15 A.M. the Admiral made the signal for all flag-officers," says the log of the *Canada;* "and at 4 P.M. the Admirals and Commodore made the signals for all captains of their divisions." At 5 P.M. of the same day, January 23rd, the fleet weighed and stood over for Nevis, round the southern point of which Basse Terre must be approached; for, the channel between the two islands being impracticable for ships of the line, they virtually were one, and, their common axis lying north-west and south-east, the trade-wind is fair only when coming from the south.

Basse Terre, where de Grasse then was, is about fifteen miles from the south point of Nevis. The roadstead lies east and west, and the French fleet, then twenty-four of the line and two fifties, were anchored without attention to order, three or four deep, the eastern ships so placed that an enemy coming from the southward could reach them with the prevailing wind, against which the western ships could not beat up quickly to their support. This being so, we are told that Hood, starting shortly before sunset with a fair, and probably fresh wind, from a point only sixty miles distant, hoped to come upon the French by surprise at early daybreak, to attack the weather ships, and from them to pass along the line so far as might seem expedient. His column, thus passing in its entirety by a certain exposed fraction of the enemy, the latter would be cut up in detail by the concentration upon it. The British then, wearing to the southward, would haul their wind, tack, and again stand up to the assault, if the enemy continued to await it.

This reasonable expectation, and skilful conception, was thwarted by a collision, during the night, between a frigate, the *Nymphe*, 36, and the leading ship of the line, the *Alfred*, 74. The repairs to the latter delayed the fleet, the approach of which was discovered by daylight. De Grasse therefore put to sea. He imagined Hood's purpose was to throw succours into Brimstone Hill; and moreover the position of the enemy now was between him and the four ships of the line momentarily expected from Martinique, one of which joined him on the same day. The French were all under way by sunset, standing to the southward under easy sail, towards the British, who had rounded the south point of Nevis at 1 P.M. Towards dark, Hood went about and stood also to the southward, seemingly in retreat.

During the following night the British tacked several times, to keep their position to windward. At daylight of January 25th, the two fleets were to the westward of Nevis; the British near the island, the French abreast, but several miles to leeward. Foiled in his first spring by an unexpected accident, Hood had not relinquished his enterprise, and now proposed to seize the anchorage quitted by the French, so establishing himself there, — as he had proposed to Graves to do in the Chesapeake, — that he could not be dislodged. For such a defensive position St. Kitts offered special advantages. The anchorage was on a narrow ledge, dropping precipitately to very deep water; and it was possible so to place the ships that the enemy could not easily anchor near them.

At 5.30 A.M. of the 25th Hood made the signal to form line of battle [1] on the starboard tack, at one cable interval. [2] It is mentioned in the log of the *Canada*, 74, Captain the Hon. William Cornwallis, that that ship brought-to in her station, fourth from the rear, at 7 o'clock. By 10 o'clock the line was formed, and the ships hove-to in it. At 10.45 the signal was made to fill [to go ahead], the van ships to carry the same sail as the Admiral, — topsails and foresails, — followed, just before noon, by the order to prepare to anchor, with springs on the cables. The French, who were steering south, on the

---

[1] See note on opposite page.

[2] The times and general movements are put together from Hood's Journal and the Log of the *Canada*, published by the Navy Records Society. 'Letters of Lord Hood,' pp. 64, 86.

port tack, while the British were hove-to, went about as soon as the latter filled, and stood towards them in bow and quarter line.

At noon the British fleet was running along close under the high land of Nevis; so close that the *Solebay*, 28, Captain Charles Holmes Everitt, one of the frigates inshore of the line, grounded and was wrecked.   No signals were needed, except to correct irregularities in the order, for the captains knew what they were to do.   The French were approaching steadily, but inevitably dropping astern with reference to the point of the enemy's line for which they were heading. At 2 P.M. de Grasse's flagship, the *Ville de Paris*, fired several shot at the British rear, which alone she could reach, while his left wing was nearing the *Barfleur*, Hood's flagship, and the vessels astern of her, which opened their fire at 2.30.   Hood, trusting to his captains, disregarded this threat to the rear half of his force.   Signals flew for the van to crowd sail and take its anchorage, and at 3.30 P.M. the leading ships began to anchor in line ahead, covered as they did so by the broadsides of the rear and the rear centre.   Upon the latter the French were now keeping up a smart fire.   Between the *Canada* and her next astern, the *Prudent*, 64, — which was a dull sailer, — there was a considerable interval.   Towards it the French admiral pressed, aiming to cut off the three rear vessels; but Cornwallis threw

NOTE. — List of the fleet under Rear-Admiral Sir Samuel Hood, Bart., on Jan. 25th, 1782. (Intended line of battle as the fleet stood in. It was slightly modified by accidental circumstances ; and on the 26th the ships were anchored in the order indicated by the numbers prefixed to them, the *Bedford* being nearest to Basse Terre.)

SHIPS.	GUNS.	COMMANDERS.	SHIPS.	GUNS.	COMMANDERS.
4. *St. Albans* .	64	Capt. Charles Inglis.	22. *Alfred* . .	74	Capt. William Bayne.
5. *Alcide* . . .	74	Capt. Charles Thompson.	*Pegasus*, 28		Capt. John Stanhope.
7. *Intrepid* . .	64	Capt. Anthony Jas. Pye Molloy.	*Fortunée*, 40		Capt. Hugh Cloberry Christian.
8. *Torbay* . .	74	Capt. John Lewis Gidoin.	*Lizard*, 28		Capt. Edmund Dod.
9. *Princesa* . .	70	{ Rear-Admiral Francis Samuel Drake (B).	*Champion*, 24		Capt. Thomas West.
		Convert, 32		Capt. Henry Harvey.
		{ Capt. Charles Knatchbull.	*Triton*, 28 .		Capt. John M'Laurin.
10. *Prince George*	98	Capt. James Williams.	2. *Russell* . .	74	Capt. Hon. Henry Edwyn Stan-
11. *Ajax* . . .	74	Capt. Nicholas Charrington.			hope.
Eurydice, 24		Capt. George Wilson.	19. *Resolution* .	74	Capt. Lord Robert Manners.
12. *Prince William*	64	Capt. George Wilkinson.	1. *Bedford* . .	74	{ Commod. Edmund Affleck.
13. *Shrewsbury* .	74	Capt. John Knight.			{ Capt. Thomas Graves (3).
14. *Invincible* .	74	Capt. Charles Saxton.	21. *Canada* . .	74	Capt. Hon. William Cornwallis.
15. *Barfleur* . .	98	{ Rear-Adm. Sir Samuel Hood, Bart. (R).	20. *Prudent* . .	64	Capt. Andrew Barkley.
		3. *Montagu* . .	74	Capt. George Bowen (1).
		{ Capt. Alexander Hood.	6. *America* . .	64	Capt. Samuel Thompson.
16. *Monarch* . .	74	Capt. Francis Reynolds.	*Sibyl*, 28 .		Capt. John Rodney (?).
18. *Belliqueux* .	64	Capt. Lord Cranstoun.	*Solebay*, 28		Capt. Charles Holmes Everitt.
17. *Centaur* . .	74	Capt. John Nicholson Inglefield.			

From a list in Schomberg, iv. 396, as corrected in MS. by Henry Wise Harvey ; checked by Steel's 'Navy List' of Dec. 31st, 1781, and March 31st, 1782, and compared with dispatches, etc. — W. L. C.

everything aback and closed down upon his consort, — a stirring
deed in which he was imitated by the *Resolution* and *Bedford*, 74's,
immediately ahead of him.   De Grasse was thus foiled, but so narrowly, that an officer, looking from one of the ships which had
anchored, asserted that for a moment he could perceive the *Ville de
Paris's* jib inside the British line.   As the rear of the latter pushed
on to its place, it cleared the broadsides of the now anchored van and
centre, and these opened upon the enemy, a great part of whom were

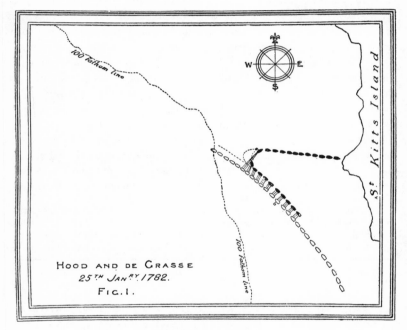

HOOD AND DE GRASSE
25ᵀᴴ JANʳʸ 1782.
FIG. I.

HOOD AND DE GRASSE.

strung out behind the British column, without opponents as yet, but
hastening up to get their share of the action.   The *Barfleur*, which
anchored at 4.03, opened fire again at 4.40 P.M.   Thus, as the
Canada and her few companions, who bore the brunt of the day,
were shortening sail and rounding-to, still under a hot cannonade,
the batteries of their predecessors were ringing out their welcome,
and at the same time covering their movements by giving the enemy
much else to think about.   The *Canada*, fetching up near the tail
of the column, and letting go in a hurry, ran out two cables on end,

and found upon sounding that she had dropped her anchor in a hundred and fifty fathoms of water.   The French column stood on, off
soundings, though close to, firing as it passed, and then, wearing to
the southward in succession, stood out of action on the port tack, its
ineffectual broadsides adding to the grandeur and excitement of the
scene, and swelling the glory of Hood's successful daring, of which
it is difficult to speak too highly.   The captain of the *Resolution*,
Lord Robert Manners, writing a week later, passed upon this achieve-

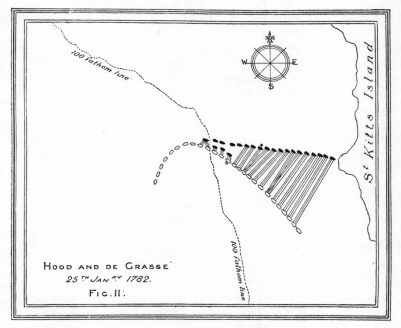

HOOD AND DE GRASSE.

ment a verdict, which posterity will confirm.   " The taking possession of this road was well judged, well conducted, and well executed,
though indeed the French had an opportunity — which they missed
— of bringing our rear to a very severe account.   The van and centre
divisions brought to an anchor under the fire of the rear, which was
engaged with the enemy's centre (Fig. 1); and then the centre, being
at an anchor and properly placed, covered us while we anchored
(Fig. 2), making, I think, the most masterly manœuvre I ever saw."
Whether regard be had to the thoughtful preparation, the crafty

management of the fleet antecedent to the final push, the calculated
audacity of the latter, or the firm and sagacious tactical handling
from the first moment to the last, Nelson himself never did a more
brilliant deed than this of Hood's.[1]   All firing ceased at 5.30.

Naturally, an order taken up under such conditions needed some
rectifying before further battle.   As the proper stationing of the fleet
depended in great measure upon the position of the van ship, Hood
had put a local pilot on board her; but when the action ceased, he
found that she was not as close to the shore as he had intended.
The rear, on the other hand, was naturally in the most disorder, owing
to the circumstances attending its anchorage.   Three ships from the
rear were consequently directed to place themselves ahead of the van,
closing the interval, while others shifted their berths, according to
specific directions.   The order as finally assumed was as follows.
The van ship was anchored so close to the shore that it was impossible
to pass within her, or, with the prevailing wind, even to reach her,
because of a point and shoal just outside, covering her position.
From her the line extended in a west-north-west direction to the
fifteenth ship, — the *Barfleur*, 98, Hood's flagship, — when it turned
to north, the last six ships being on a north and south line.   These
six, with their broadsides turned to the westward, prevented a
column passing from south to north, the only way one could pass,
from enfilading the main line with impunity.   The latter covered
with its guns the approach from the south.

At daylight on the following morning, January 26th, the ships
began changing their places, the French being then seven or eight
miles distant in the south-south-east.   At 7 A.M. they were seen to
be approaching in line of battle, under a press of sail, heading for
the British van.   The *Canada*, which had begun at 5 A.M. to tackle
her 200-odd fathoms of cable, was obliged to cut, whereby "we lost
the small bower anchor and two cables with one 8-inch and one 9-inch
hawsers, which were bent for springs."   The ship had to work to
windward to close with the fleet, and was therefore ordered by the
Rear-Admiral to keep engaging under way, until 10.50, when a message was sent her to anchor in support of the rear.   The action
began between 8.30 and 9 A.M., the leading French ship heading for
the British van, seemingly with the view of passing round and inside
it.   Against this attempt Hood's precautions probably were suffi-

---

[1] Illustrations of other phases of this battle can be found in Mahan's 'Influence
of Sea Power upon History,' pp. 470, 472.

cient; but as the enemy's vessel approached, the wind headed her, so
that she could only fetch the third ship. The latter, with the vessels
ahead and astern, sprung their batteries upon her. "The crash occasioned by their destructive broadsides was so tremendous on board
her that whole pieces of plank were seen flying from her off side,
ere she could escape the cool concentrated fire of her determined
adversaries." [1] She put her helm up, and ran along outside the
British line, receiving the first fire of each successive ship. Her

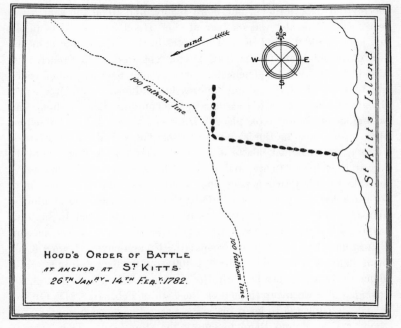

HOOD'S ORDER OF BATTLE.   AT ANCHOR AT ST. KITTS.

movement was imitated by her followers, some keeping off sooner,
some later; but de Grasse in his flagship not only came close, but
pointed his after yards to the wind,[2] to move the slower. As he
ported his helm when leaving the *Barfleur*, this brought these sails
aback, keeping him a still longer time before the British ships thrown
to the rear. "In this he was supported by those ships which were
astern, or immediately ahead of him. During this short but tre-

---

[1] White : 'Naval Researches.'

[2] Sharp up by the starboard braces, the wind being on the starboard quarter.

mendous conflict in that part of the field of battle, nothing whatever could be seen of them for upwards of twenty minutes, save de Grasse's white flag at the main-topgallant masthead of the *Ville de Paris*, gracefully floating above the immense volumes of smoke that enveloped them, or the pennants of those ships which were occasionally perceptible, when an increase of breeze would waft away the smoke." [1]

Though most gallantly done, no such routine manœuvre as this could shake Hood's solidly assumed position. The attempt was repeated in the afternoon, but more feebly, and upon the centre and rear only. This also was ineffectual; and Hood was left in triumphant possession of the field. The losses in the several affairs of the two days had been: British, 72 killed, 244 wounded; French, 107 killed, 207 wounded. Thenceforth the French fleet continued cruising to leeward of the island, approaching almost daily, frequently threatening attack, and occasionally exchanging distant shots; but no serious encounter took place. Interest was centred on Brimstone Hill, where alone on the island the British flag still flew. De Grasse awaited its surrender, flattering himself that the British would be forced then to put to sea, and that his fleet, increased by successive arrivals to thirty-two of the line, would then find an opportunity to crush the man who had outwitted and out-manœuvred him on January 25th and 26th. In this hope he was deceived by his own inaptness and his adversary's readiness. Hood was unable to succour Brimstone Hill, for want of troops; the French having landed 6,000 men, against which the British 2,400 could effect nothing, either alone or in co-operation with the garrison, which was but 1,200 strong. The work capitulated on the 13th of February. De Grasse, who had neglected to keep his ships provisioned, went next day to Nevis and anchored there to empty the storeships. That evening Hood called his captains on board, explained his intentions, had them set their watches by his, and at 11 P.M. the cables were cut one by one, lights being left on the buoys, and the fleet silently decamped, passing round the north end of St. Kitts, and so towards Antigua. When De Grasse opened his eyes next morning, the British were no longer to be seen. "Nothing could have been more fortunately executed," wrote Lord Robert Manners, "as not one accident happened from it. Taking the whole in one light, though not successful in the point we aimed at, nevertheless it was well conducted, and

[1] White : ' Naval Researches.'

has given the enemy a pretty severe check; and if you give him half
the credit the enemy does, Sir Samuel Hood will stand very high in
the public estimation."

Hood's intention had been to return to Barbados; but on the
25th of February he was joined, to windward of Antigua, by Admiral
Sir George Rodney, who had arrived from England a week earlier,
bringing with him twelve ships of the line. The new Commander-in-
Chief endeavoured to cut off de Grasse from Martinique, but the
French fleet got in there on the 26th. Rodney consequently went to
St. Lucia, to refit Hood's ships, and to prepare for the coming campaign, in which it was understood that the conquest of Jamaica was
to be the first object of the allies. An important condition to their
success was the arrival of a great convoy, known to be on its way
from Brest to repair the losses which Kempenfelt's raid and subsequent bad weather had inflicted in December. Hood suggested to
Rodney to halve the fleet, which then numbered thirty-six of the
line, letting one part cruise north of Dominica, between that island
and Deseada, while the other guarded the southern approach, between
Martinique and St. Lucia. Rodney, however, was unwilling to do
this, and adopted a half-measure, — Hood's division being stationed
to windward of the north end of Martinique, reaching only as far
north as the latitude of Dominica, while the centre and rear were
abreast of the centre and south of Martinique; all in mutual touch
by intermediate vessels. It would seem — reading between the lines
— that Hood tried to stretch his cruising ground northwards, in
pursuance of his own ideas, but Rodney recalled him. The French
convoy consequently passed north of Deseada, convoyed by two ships
of the line, and on the 20th of March reached Martinique safely.
De Grasse's force was thus raised to thirty-five of the line, including
two fifty-gun ships, as against the British thirty-six. At the end of
the month Rodney returned to St. Lucia, and there remained at
anchor, vigilantly watching the French fleet in Fort Royal by means
of a chain of frigates.

The problem now immediately confronting de Grasse — the first
step to the conquest of Jamaica — was extremely difficult. It was to
convoy to Cap François the supply vessels essential to his enterprise,
besides the merchant fleet bound for France; making in all one
hundred and fifty unarmed ships to be protected by his thirty-five sail
of the line, in face of the British thirty-six. The trade-wind being
fair, he purposed to skirt the inner edge of the Caribbean Sea; by

which means he would keep close to a succession of friendly ports, wherein the convoy might find refuge in case of need.

With this plan the French armament put to sea on the 8th of April, 1782. The fact being reported promptly to Rodney, by noon his whole fleet[1] was clear of its anchorage and in pursuit. Then was evident the vital importance of Barrington's conquest of St. Lucia; for, had the British been at Barbados, the most probable alternative, the French movement not only would have been longer unknown, but pursuit would have started from a hundred miles distant, instead of thirty. If the British had met this disadvantage by cruising before Martinique, they would have encountered the difficulty of keeping their ships supplied with water and other necessaries, which St. Lucia afforded. In truth, without in any degree minimising the faults of the loser, or the merits of the winner, in the exciting week that fol-

---

[1] British fleet under Admiral Sir George Brydges Rodney, and line of battle on April 12th, 1782. From lists in Beatson, vi. 324, and Schomberg (revised in MS. of H. W. Harvey), iv. 399 ; compared with dispatches and with Steel's ' Navy Lists.' — W. L. C.

SHIPS.	GUNS.	COMMANDERS.	SHIPS.	GUNS.	COMMANDERS.
Royal Oak . . .	74	Capt. Thomas Burnett.	*Resolution* . . .	74	Capt. Lord Robert Manners.‡
Alfred	74	Capt. William Bayne.†	*Protée* . . .	64	Capt. Charles Buckner.
Montagu . . .	74	Capt. George Bowen (1).	*Hercules*	74	Capt. Henry Savage.
Yarmouth . . .	64	Capt. Anthony Parrey.	*America*	64	Capt. Samuel Thompson.
Valiant	74	Capt. Samuel Granston Goodall.	*Fortunée,** 40 .		Capt. Hugh Cloberry Christian.
			Endymion, 44 .		Capt. Edward Tyrrel Smith.
Barfleur	98	⎰ Rear-Admiral Sir Samuel Hood, Bart. (B). ⎱ Capt. John Knight.	*Flora,* 36 . . .		Capt. Samuel Marshall.
			*Convert,** 32 . .		Capt. Henry Harvey.
			Alarm, 32 . .		Capt. Charles Cotton.
Monarch	74	Capt. Francis Reynolds.	*Andromache,* 32		Capt. George Anson Byron.
Warrior	74	Capt. Sir James Wallace, Kt.	*Sibyl,* 28 . . .		Capt. John Rodney.
Belliqueux . . .	64	Capt. Andrew Sutherland.	*Pegasus,** 28 . .		Capt. John Stanhope.
Centaur	74	Capt. John Nicholson Inglefield.	*Alert,* 14 . . .		Com. James Vashon.
			*Salamander**(f. s.), 8.		Com. Richard Lucas.
Magnificent . . .	74	Capt. Robert Linzee.			
Prince William .	64	Capt. George Wilkinson.	*Russell*	74	Capt. James Saumarez.
*Nymphe,** 36 .		Capt. John Ford.	*Prudent** . . .	64	Capt. Andrew Barkley.
*Lizard,** 28 .		Capt. Edmund Dod.	*Fame*	74	Capt. Robert Barbor.
Champion, 24 .		Capt. Thomas West.	*Anson*	64	Capt. William Blair. §
*Zebra,** 16 .		Com. John Bourchier.	*Torbay* . . .	74	Capt. John Lewis Gidoin.
Bedford	74	⎰ Commod. Edmund Affleck. ⎱ Capt. Thomas Graves (3).	*Prince George* . .	98	Capt. James Williams.
Ajax	74	Capt. Nicholas Charrington.	*Princesa*	70	⎰ Rear-Adm. Francis Samuel Drake (B). ⎱ Capt. Charles Knatchbull.
Repulse	64	Capt. Thomas Dumaresq.			
Canada	74	Capt. Hon. Wm. Cornwallis.	*Conqueror* . . .	74	Capt. George Balfour.
St. Albans . . .	64	Capt. Charles Inglis.	*Nonsuch*	64	Capt. William Truscott.
Namur	90	Capt. Robert Fanshawe (1).	*Alcide*	74	Capt. Charles Thompson.
Formidable . . .	98	⎰ Adm. Sir George Brydges Rodney (W). ⎰ Capt. Sir Chas. Douglas (1st) ⎱ Capt. John Symons (2nd).	*Arrogant* . . .	74	Capt. Sam. Pitchford Cornish.
			Marlborough . .	74	Capt. Taylor Penny.
			*Santa Monica,** 36		Capt. John Linzee.
			Triton, 28 . .		Capt. John M'Laurin.
Duke	98	Capt. Alan Gardner.	*Eurydice,* 24 .		Capt. George Wilson.
Agamemnon . .	64	Capt. Benjamin Caldwell.	*Germaine,** 16 .		Com. Geo. Augustus Keppel.
			Blast (f. s.),* 8 .		Com. John Aylmer.

* These vessels were not in the action.   ‡ Mortally wounded on April 12th.
† Killed on April 9th.   § Killed on April 12th.

lowed, the opening situation may be said to have represented on either side an accumulation of neglects or of successes, which at the moment of their occurrence may have seemed individually trivial.   De Grasse was tremendously handicapped from the outset by the errors of his predecessors and of himself.   That the British had St. Lucia as their outpost was due not only to Barrington's diligence, but also to d'Estaing's slackness and professional timidity; and it may be questioned whether de Grasse himself had shown a proper understanding of strategic conditions, when he neglected that island in favour of Tobago and St. Kitts.   Certainly, Hood had feared for it greatly the year before.   That the convoy was there to embarrass his movements, may not have been the fault of the French admiral; but it was greatly and entirely his fault that, of the thirty-six ships pursuing him, twenty-one represented a force that he could have crushed in detail a few weeks before, — not to mention the similar failure of April, 1781.

Large bodies of ships commonly will move less rapidly than small. By 2.30 P.M. of the day of starting, Rodney's look-outs had sighted the French fleet; and before sundown it could be seen from the mastheads of the main body.   At 6 next morning, the 9th, the enemy, both fleet and convoy, was visible from the deck of the *Barfleur*, the flagship of Hood's division, then in the van.   The French bore north-east, distant four to twelve miles, and extending from abreast of the centre of Dominica northwards towards Guadeloupe.   The British therefore had gained much during the night, and were now off Dominica, to leeward of the enemy's rear, which was becalmed under the land (b).   Some fourteen or fifteen of the French van, having opened out the channel between Dominica and Guadeloupe, felt a fresh trade-wind, against which they were beating; and their number was gradually increased as individual ships, utilising the catspaws, stole clear of the high land of Dominica (b).   Hood's division in like manner, first among the British, got the breeze, and, with eight ships, the commander of the van stood north in order of battle.   To the north-west of him were two French vessels, separated from their consorts and threatened to be cut off (i).   These stood boldly down and crossed the head of Hood's column; one passing so close to the leading ship, the *Alfred*, that the latter had to bear up to let her pass.   Rodney had hoisted a signal to engage at 6.38 A.M., but had hauled it down almost immediately, and Hood would not fire without orders.   These ships therefore rejoined the main body un-

harmed.   At 8.30 the French hoisted their colours, and shortly afterwards their whole fleet tacked and stood south, opposite to Hood.

De Grasse now had recognised that he could not escape action, if
the convoy kept company.   He therefore directed the two fifty-gun
ships, *Expériment* and *Sagittaire*, to accompany it into Guadeloupe,
where it arrived safely that day; and he decided that the fleet should
ply to windward through the channel between Dominica and
Guadeloupe, nearly midway in which lies a group of small islands

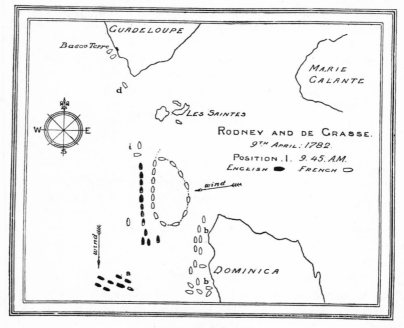

RODNEY AND DE GRASSE.

called The Saintes, — a name at times given to the battle of April
12th.   By this course he hoped not only to lead the enemy away
from the convoy, but also to throw off pursuit through his superior
speed, and so to accomplish his mission unharmed.   The French
ships, larger, deeper, and with better lines than their opponents, were
naturally better sailers, and it may be inferred that even coppering
had not entirely overcome this original disadvantage of the British.

At the very moment of beginning his new policy, however, a
subtle temptation assailed de Grasse irresistibly, in the exposed posi-

tion of Hood's column; and he met it, not by a frank and hearty acceptance of a great opportunity, but by a half-measure. Hood thoroughly crushed, the British fleet became hopelessly inferior to the French; Hood damaged, and it became somewhat inferior: possibly it would be deterred from further pursuit. De Grasse decided for this second course, and ordered half his fleet to attack. This operation was carried out under the orders of the Marquis de Vaudreuil, the second in command. The ships engaged in it bore

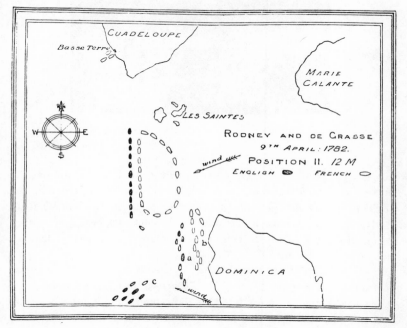

RODNEY AND DE GRASSE.

down from the windward, attacked Hood's rear ships, stood along on the weather side of his column at long range, and, having passed ahead, tacked in succession and formed again in the rear, whence they repeated the same manœuvre (Position I.). Thus a procession of fifteen ships kept passing by eight, describing a continuous curve of elliptical form. They were able to do this because Hood was condemned to a low speed, lest he should draw too far away from the British centre (a) and rear (c), still becalmed under Dominica. The French, having choice of distance, kept at long gunshot, because they

were deficient in carronades, of which the British had many.   These
guns, of short range but large calibre, were thus rendered useless.
Could they have come into play, the French rigging and sails would
have suffered severely.   This first engagement lasted, by Hood's log,
from 9.48 to 10.25 A.M.   It was resumed in stronger force at 14
minutes past noon, and continued till 1.45 P.M. (Position II.), when
firing ceased for that day; Rodney hauling down the signal for battle

MEDAL COMMEMORATIVE OF RODNEY'S VICTORY, APRIL 12TH, 1782.
(From an original kindly lent by Capt. H. S. H. Prince Louis of Battenberg, R. N.)

at 2.   Between the two affairs, which were identical in general
character, Hood's column was reinforced, and great part of the
British centre also got into action with some of the French main
body, though at long range only.   "Except the two rear ships,"
wrote Rodney to Hood that night, "the others fired at such a distance
that I returned none."

The injuries to the British ships engaged were not such as to compel them to leave the fleet.   The *Royal Oak* lost her main topmast,
and that of the *Warrior* fell two days later, not improbably from
wounds; but in these was nothing that the ready hands of seamen
could not repair so as to continue the chase.   Rodney therefore contented himself with reversing the order, putting Hood in the rear,
whereby he was able to refit, and yet follow fast enough not to be out
of supporting distance.   One of the French ships, the *Caton*, 64, was
so injured that de Grasse detached her into Guadeloupe.   It must be
remembered that a crippled ship in a chased fleet not only embar-
rasses movement, but may compromise the whole body, if the latter
delay to protect it; whereas the chaser keeps between his lame birds
and the enemy.

During the night of the 9th the British lay-to for repairs.   The
next morning they resumed the pursuit, turning to windward after

the enemy, but upon the whole losing throughout the 10th and the 11th. At daylight of the 10th the French, by the logs of Hood and Cornwallis, were "from four to five leagues distant," "just in sight from the deck." During that night, however, the *Zélé*, 74, had collided with the *Jason*, 64; and the latter was injured so far as to be compelled to follow the *Caton* into Guadeloupe. At sunset of that day Rodney signalled a general chase to windward, the effect of which was to enable each ship to do her best according to her captain's judgment during the dark hours. Nevertheless, on the morning of the 11th the French seem again to have gained; for Hood, who, it will be remembered, was now in the rear, notes that at 10 A.M. twenty-two French sail (not all the fleet) could be counted *from the masthead;* Cornwallis, further to windward, could count thirty-three. Troude, a French authority, says that at that time nearly all the French had doubled The Saintes, and it looked as though de Grasse might succeed in throwing off his pursuer. Unluckily, two ships, the *Magnanime*, 74, and the *Zélé*, 74, the latter of which had lost her main topmast, were several miles to leeward of the French main body. It was necessary to delay, or to drop those vessels. Again, trivial circumstances conspired to further a great disaster, and de Grasse bore down to cover the crippled ships; losing so much of his hard-won ground, and entailing a further misfortune that night. Rodney hung doggedly on, relying on the chapter of accidents, as one who knows that all things come to him who endures. To be sure, there was not much else he could do; yet he deserves credit for unremitting industry and pluck. During the afternoon, the signals noted in the logs — to call in all cruisers and for the fleet to close — attest mutely the movement of de Grasse in bearing down.

During the night, at 2 A.M. of April 12th, the *Zélé* and de Grasse's flagship, the *Ville de Paris*, 110, crossing on opposite tacks, came into collision. The former lost both foremast and bowsprit. It has been stated by John Paul Jones, who served on board the French fleet a few months later, that this accident was due to the deficiency of watch-officers in the French navy; the deck of the *Zélé* being in charge of a young ensign, instead of an experienced lieutenant. It was necessary to rid the fleet of the *Zélé* at once, or an action could not be avoided; so a frigate was summoned to tow her, and the two were left to make their way to Guadeloupe, while the others resumed the beat to windward. At 5 A.M. she and the frigate were again

under way, steering for Guadeloupe, to the north-west, and making
from five to six miles an hour (a); but in the interval they had been
nearly motionless, and consequently when day broke at 5.30 they
were only two leagues from the *Barfleur,* which, still flagship of the
British rear, was then standing south on the port tack.   The body
of the French was at about the same distance as on the previous
evening, — ten to fifteen miles, — but the *Ville de Paris* not more
than eight (A).   Just before 6 A.M. Rodney signalled Hood, who was

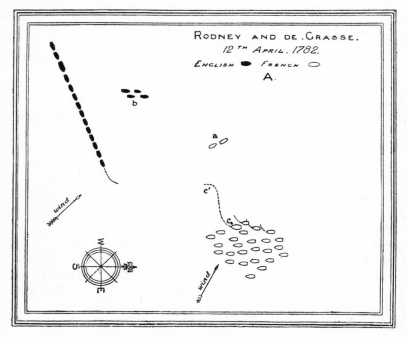

RODNEY AND DE GRASSE.

nearest, to chase the *Zélé* (a); and four of the rearmost ships of the
line were detached for that purpose (b).   De Grasse, seeing this,
signalled his vessels at 6 A.M. to close the flagship, making all sail;
and he himself bore down (c) on the port tack, but running free, to
frighten away Rodney's chasers.   The British Admiral kept them
out until 7 o'clock, by which time de Grasse was fairly committed to
his false step.   All cruisers were then called in, and the line was
closed to one cable.   Within an hour were heard the opening guns of

the great battle, since known by the names of the 12th of April, or of The Saintes, and, in the French navy, of Dominica.

The British appear to have been standing to the south on the port tack at daylight; but, soon after sending out the chasers, Rodney had ordered the line of bearing (from ship to ship) to be north-north-east to south-south-west, evidently in preparation for a close-hauled line of battle on the starboard tack, heading northerly, to an

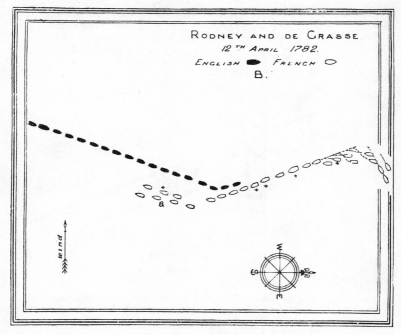

RODNEY AND DE GRASSE.

east wind. Somewhat unusually, the wind that morning held at south-east for some time, enabling the British to lie up as high as east-north-east on the starboard tack, on which they were when the battle joined; and this circumstance doubtless led to the annulling of the signal for the line of bearing, half an hour after it was made, and the substitution for it of the line of battle ahead at one cable. It is to be inferred that Rodney's first purpose was to tack together, thus restoring Hood to the van, his natural station; but the accident of the wind holding to the southward placed the actual van — regu-

larly the rear — most to windward, and rendered it expedient to tack
in succession, preserving to the full the opportunity which chance had
extended for reaching the enemy. In the engagement, therefore,
Hood commanded in the rear, and Rear-Admiral Drake in the van.
The wind with the French seems to have been more to the eastward
than with the British, — not an unusual circumstance in the neighbourhood of land.

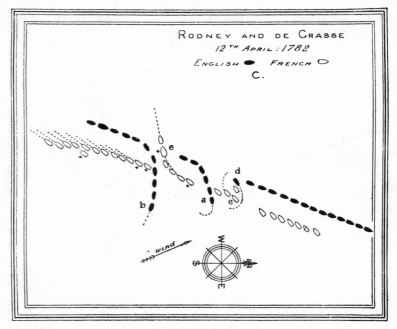

RODNEY AND DE GRASSE.

    As Rodney, notwithstanding his haste, had formed line from time
to time during the past three days, his fleet was now in good order,
and his signals were chiefly confined to keeping it closed. The
French, on the other hand, were greatly scattered when their commander-in-chief, in an impulse of hasty, unbalanced judgment,
abandoned his previous cautious policy and hurried them into action.
Some of them were over ten miles to windward of the flagship.
Though they crowded sail to rejoin her, there was not time enough
for all to take their stations properly, between daylight and 8 A.M.,
when the firing began. "Our line of battle was formed under the

fire of musketry,"[1] wrote the Marquis de Vaudreuil,[2] the second in command, who, being in the rear of the fleet on this occasion, and consequently among the last to be engaged, had excellent opportunity for observation.   At the beginning it was in de Grasse's power to postpone action, until the order should be formed, by holding his wind under short canvas; while the mere sight of his vessels hurrying down for action would have compelled Rodney to call in the ships chasing the *Zélé,* whose rescue was the sole motive of the

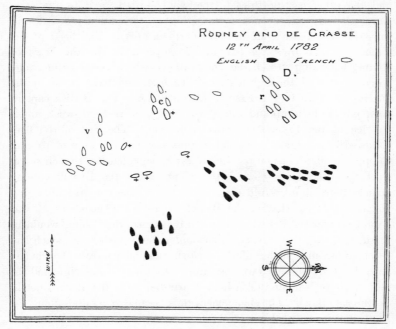

RODNEY AND DE GRASSE.

French manœuvre.   Instead of this, the flagship kept off the wind; which precipitated the collision, while at the same time delaying the preparations needed to sustain it.   To this de Grasse added another fault by forming on the port tack, the contrary to that on which the British were, and standing towards Dominica.   The effect of this was to bring his ships into the calms and baffling winds which cling to the shore-line, thus depriving them of their power of manœuvre.

[1] Probably not over one or two hundred yards.

[2] His brother, the Comte de Vaudreuil, was also with the fleet, as chef d'escadre, in the *Sceptre,* 74.

His object probably was to confine the engagement to a mere pass-by on opposite tacks, by which in all previous instances the French had thwarted the decisive action that Rodney sought. Nevertheless, the blunder was evident at once to French eyes. "What evil genius has inspired the admiral?" exclaimed du Pavillon, Vaudreuil's flag-captain, who was esteemed one of the best tacticians in France, and who fell in the battle.

As the two lines drew near to one another, standing, the one south, and the other east-north-east, the wind shifted back to the east-ward, allowing the French to head higher, to south-south-east, and knocking the British off to north-north-east (B). The head of the French column thus passed out of gunshot, across the bows of Rodney's leading vessel, the *Marlborough*, which came within range when abreast of the eighth ship. The first shots were fired by the *Brave*, 74, ninth in the French line, at 8 A.M. The British captain then put his helm up and ran slowly along, north-north-west, under the lee of the French, towards their rear. The rest of the fleet followed in his wake. The battle thus assumed the form of passing in opposite directions on parallel lines; except that the French ships, as they successively cleared the point where the British column struck their line, would draw out of fire, their course diverging thenceforth from that of the British approach. The effect of this would be that the British rear, when it reached that point, would be fresh, and with that advantage encounter the French rear, which had received already the fire of the British van and centre. To obviate this, by bringing his own van into action, de Grasse signalled the van ships to lead south-south-west, parallel with the British north-north-east (B, a). The engagement thus became general all along the lines; but it is probable that the French van was never well formed. Its commander, at all events, reached his post after the commander of the rear did his.[1]

At five minutes past eight, Rodney made a general signal for close action, followed immediately by another for the leading ships to head one point to starboard — towards the enemy — which indicates that he was not satisfied with the distance first taken by the *Marlborough*. The *Formidable*, his flagship, eighteenth in the column, began to fire at 8.23;[2] but the *Barfleur*, Hood's flagship, which was

---

[1] The position, in the French order, of the ships taken in the battle, is shown by the crosses in Figures B, C, D.

[2] *Canada's* log, 8.15 ; reduced to Hood's times, which are generally followed.

thirty-first, not till 9.25.   This difference in time is to be accounted
for chiefly by the light airs near Dominica, contrasted with the fresh
trades in the open channel to the northward, which the leading
British vessels felt before their rear.   De Grasse now, too late, had
realised the disastrous effect which this would have upon his fleet.
If he escaped all else, his ships, baffled by calms and catspaws while
the British had a breeze, must lose the weather-gage, and with it
the hope of evading pursuit, hitherto his chief preoccupation.   Twice
he signalled to wear, — first, all together, then in succession, — but,
although the signals were seen, they could not be obeyed with the
enemy close under the lee.   "The French fleet," comments Chevalier
justly, "had freedom of movement no longer.   A fleet cannot wear
with an enemy's fleet within musket-range to leeward."

The movement therefore continued as described, the opposing
ships slowly "sliding by" each other until about 9.15, when the
wind suddenly shifted to south-east again.   The necessity of keeping
the sails full forced the bows of each French vessel towards the
enemy, destroying the order in column, and throwing the fleet into
échelon, or, as the phrase then was, into bow and quarter line (C).
The British, on the contrary, were free either to hold their course or
to head towards the enemy.   Rodney's flagship (C, a) luffed, and
led through the French line just astern of the *Glorieux*, 74, which
was the nineteenth in their order.   She was followed by five ships;
and her next ahead also, the *Duke* (d), seeing her chief's movement,
imitated it, breaking through the line astern of the twenty-third
French.   The *Glorieux*, on the starboard hand of Rodney's little
column, received its successive broadsides.   Her main and mizzen
masts went overboard at 9.28, when the *Canada*, third astern of
the *Formidable*, had just passed her; and a few moments later her
foremast and bowsprit fell.   At 9.33 the *Canada* was to windward
of the French line.   The *Formidable* was using both broadsides as
she broke through the enemy's order.   On her port hand, between
her and the *Duke*, were four French ships huddled together (c), one
of which had paid off the wrong way; that is, after the shift of wind
took her aback, her sails had filled on the opposite tack from that of
the rest of her fleet.[1]   These four, receiving the repeated broadsides,
at close quarters, of the *Formidable*, *Duke*, and *Namur*, and having
undergone besides the fire of the British van, were very severely
mauled.   While these things were happening, the *Bedford*, the sixth

---

[1] This mishap occurred to three French vessels.

astern of the *Formidable*, perhaps unable to see her next ahead in the smoke, had luffed independently (b), and was followed by the twelve rearmost British ships, whom she led through the French order astern of the *César*, 74, twelfth from the van. This ship and her next ahead, the *Hector*, 74, suffered as did the *Glorieux*. The *Barfleur*, which was in the centre of this column of thirteen, opened fire at 9.25. At 10.45 she "ceased firing, having passed the enemy's van ships;" that is, she was well on the weather side of the French fleet. Some of the rearmost of Hood's division, however, were still engaged at noon; but probably all were then to windward of the enemy.

The British ships ahead of the *Duke*, the van and part of the centre, in all sixteen sail, had continued to stand to the northward. At the time Rodney broke the line, several of them must have passed beyond the French rear, and out of action. One, the *America*, the twelfth from the van, wore without signals, to pursue the enemy, and her example was followed at once by the ship next ahead, the *Russell*. No signal following, the *America* again wore and followed her leaders, but the *Russell* continued as she was, now to windward of the French; by which she was able to take a conspicuous share in the closing scenes. At 11.33 Rodney signalled the van to tack, but the delay of an hour or more had given the *Russell* a start towards the enemy which could not be overcome.

The effect of these several occurrences had been to transfer the weather-gage, the position for attack, to the British from the French, and to divide the latter also into three groups, widely separated and disordered (D). In the centre was the flagship *Ville de Paris* with five ships (c). To windward of her, and two miles distant, was the van, of some dozen vessels (v). The rear was four miles away to leeward (r). To restore the order, and to connect the fleet again, it was decided to re-form on the leewardmost ships; and several signals to this effect were made by de Grasse. They received but imperfect execution. The manageable vessels succeeded easily enough in running before the wind to leeward, but, when there, exactitude of position and of movement was unattainable to ships in various degrees of disability, with light and baffling side airs. The French were never again in order after the wind shifted and the line was broken; but the movement to leeward left the dismasted *Glorieux*, *Hector*, and *César*, motionless between the hostile lines.

It has been remarked, disparagingly, that the British fleet also was divided into three by the manœuvre of breaking the line. This is true; but the advantage remained with it incontestably, in two respects.   By favour of the wind, each of the three groups had been able to maintain its general formation in line or column, instead of being thrown entirely out, as the French were; and passing thus in column along the *Glorieux*, *Hector*, and *César*, they wrought upon these three ships a concentration of injury which had no parallel among the British vessels.   The French in fact had lost three ships, as well as the wind.   To these certain disadvantages is probably to be added a demoralisation among the French crews, from the much heavier losses resultant upon the British practice of firing at the hull. An officer present in the action told Sir John Ross[1] afterwards that the French fired very high throughout; and he cited in illustration that the three trucks[2] of the *Princesa* were shot away.   Sir Gilbert Blane, who, though Physician to the Fleet, obtained permission to be on deck throughout the action, wrote ten days after it, "I can aver from my own observation that the French fire slackens as we approach, and is totally silent when we are close alongside."   It is needless to say that a marked superiority of fire will silence that of the bravest enemy; and the practice of aiming at the spars and sails, however suited for frustrating an approach, substantially conceded that superiority upon which the issue of decisive battle depends.   As illustrative of this result, the British loss will be stated here.   It was but 243 killed and 816 wounded[3] in a fleet of thirty-six sail.   The highest in any one ship was that of the *Duke*, 73 killed and wounded. No certain account, or even very probable estimate, of the French loss has ever been given.   None is cited by French authorities.   Sir Gilbert Blane, who was favourably placed for information, reckoned that of the *Ville de Paris* alone to be 300.   There being 5,400 troops distributed among the vessels of the fleet, the casualties would be proportionately more numerous; but, even allowing for this, there can be no doubt that the loss of the French, to use Chevalier's words, "was certainly much more considerable" than that reported by the British.   Six post-captains[4] out of thirty were killed, against two[5] British out of thirty-six.

[1] Ross: 'Life of Saumarez.'

[2] Circular pieces of wood which cap the top of the masts.

[3] Beatson, vi. 324, 325.   Beatson's additions are slightly incorrect.

[4] Captain de La Clocheterie, of the *Hercule;* Captain de Saint-Césaire, of the *Northumberland;* Captain de La Vicomté, of the *Hector;* Captain Bernard de Marigny, of the *César ;* Captain Comte d'Escars, of the *Glorieux;* and Captain du Pavillon, of the *Triomphant.*   Rapport du Marquis de Vaudreuil. — W. L. C.

[5] Captain William Blair, of the *Anson;* and Captain Lord Robert Manners, —

Rodney did not make adequate use of the great opportunity, which accident rather than design had given him at noon of April 12th.   He did allow a certain liberty of manœuvre, by discontinuing the order for the line of battle; but the signal for close action, hoisted at 1 P.M., was hauled down a half-hour later.   Hood, who realised the conditions plainly visible, as well as the reasonable inferences therefrom, wished the order given for a general chase, which would have applied the spur of emulation to every captain present, without surrendering the hold that particular signals afford upon indiscreet movements.   He bitterly censured the Admiral's failure to issue this command.   Had it been done, he said: —

" I am very confident we should have had twenty sail of the enemy's ships before dark.   Instead of that, he pursued only under his topsails (sometimes his foresail was set and at others his mizzen topsail aback) the greatest part of the afternoon, though the *flying* enemy had all the sail set their very shattered state would allow."

To make signal for a general chase was beyond the competence of a junior admiral; but Hood did what he could, by repeated signals to individual ships of his own division to make more sail, by setting all he could on the *Barfleur*, and by getting out his boats to tow her head round.   Sir Gilbert Blane unintentionally gives a similar impression of laxity.

" After cutting the French line, the action during the rest of the day was partial and desultory, the enemy never being able to form, and several of the [our] ships being obliged to lie by and repair their damages.   As the signal for the line was now hauled down, every ship annoyed the enemy as their respective commanders judged best."

For this indolent abandonment of the captains to their own devices, the correctest remedy was, as Hood indicated, the order for a general chase, supplemented by a watchful supervision, which should check the over-rash and stimulate the over-cautious.   If Hood's account of the sail carried by Rodney be correct, the Commander-in-Chief did not even set the best example.   In this languid pursuit, the three crippled French ships were overhauled, and of course had to strike; and a fourth, the *Ardent*, 64, was taken, owing to her indifferent sailing.   Towards sunset the flagship *Ville de Paris*, 110,[1] the finest ship of war afloat, having been valiantly defended against a host of

who, though mortally wounded, survived for some days, — of the *Resolution*.   But Captain William Bayne, of the *Alfred*, had fallen in the action of April 9th.

[1] She is thus rated in the British Navy Lists published between the time of her capture and the receipt of news of her loss ; but she seems to have carried 120 guns.

enemies throughout great part of the afternoon, and having expended all her ammunition, hauled down her colours. The two British vessels then immediately engaged with her were the *Russell* and the *Barfleur*, Hood's flagship, to the latter of which she formally surrendered; the exact moment, noted in Hood's journal, being 6.29 P.M.

At 6.45 Rodney made the signal for the fleet to bring-to (form line and stop) on the port tack, and he remained lying-to during the night, while the French continued to retreat under the orders of the Marquis de Vaudreuil, who by de Grasse's capture had become commander-in-chief. For this easy-going deliberation also Hood had strong words of condemnation.

> "Why he should bring the fleet to because the *Ville de Paris* was taken, I cannot reconcile. He did not pursue under easy sail, so as never to have lost sight of the enemy in the night, which would clearly and most undoubtedly have enabled him to have taken almost every ship the next day. . . . Had I had the honour of commanding his Majesty's noble fleet on the 12th, I may, without much imputation of vanity, say the flag of England should now have graced the sterns of *upwards* of twenty sail of the enemy's ships of the line."

Such criticisms by those not responsible are to be received generally with caution; but Hood was, in thought and in deed, a man so much above the common that these cannot be dismissed lightly. His opinion is known to have been shared by Sir Charles Douglas, Rodney's Captain of the Fleet;[1] and their conclusion is supported by the inferences to be drawn from Rodney's own assumptions as to the condition of the French, contrasted with the known facts. The enemy, he wrote, in assigning his reasons for not pursuing, "went off in a *close connected body*,[2] and might have defeated, by rotation, the ships that had come up with them." "The enemy *who went off in a body of twenty-six ships of the line*,[2] might, by ordering two or three of their best sailing ships or frigates to have shown lights at times, and by changing their course, have induced the British fleet to have followed them, while the main of their fleet, by hiding their lights, might have hauled their wind, and have been far to windward by daylight, and intercepted the captured ships, and the most crippled ships of the English;" and he adds that the Windward Islands even might have been endangered. That such action was in a remote degree possible to a well-conditioned fleet may be guardedly con-

---

[1] See letter of Sir Howard Douglas, son to Sir Charles; 'United Service Journal,' 1834, Part II., p. 97.

[2] Author's italics; Mundy: 'Life of Rodney,' ii. 248.

ceded; but it was wildly improbable to a fleet staggering under such a blow as the day had seen, which had changed its commander just as dark came on, and was widely scattered and disordered up to the moment when signals by flags became invisible.

The facts, however, were utterly at variance with these ingenious suppositions. Instead of being connected, as Rodney represents, de Vaudreuil had with him next morning but ten ships; and no others during the whole of the 13th. He made sail for Cap François, and was joined on the way by five more, so that at no time were there upwards of fifteen [1] French ships of the line together, prior to his arrival at that port on April 25th. He there found four others of the fleet. The tale of twenty-five survivors, from the thirty engaged on April 12th, was completed by six which had gone to Curaçao, and which did not rejoin until May. So much for the close connected body of the French. It is clear, therefore, that Rodney's reasons illustrate the frame of mind against which Napoleon used to caution his generals as "making to themselves a picture" of possibilities; and that his conclusion at best was based upon the ruinous idea, which a vivid imagination or slothful temper is prone to present to itself, that war may be made decisive without running risks. That Jamaica even was saved was not due to this fine, but indecisive action, but to the hesitation of the allies. When de Vaudreuil reached Cap François, he found there the French convoy safely arrived from Guadeloupe, and also a body of fifteen Spanish ships of the line. The troops available for the descent upon Jamaica were from fifteen to twenty thousand. Well might Hood write: "Had Sir George Rodney's judgment, after the enemy had been so totally put to flight, borne any proportion to the high courage, zeal and exertion, so very manifestly shown by every captain, *all* difficulty would now have been at an end. We might have done just as we pleased, instead of being at this hour upon the defensive."

The allies, however, though superior in numbers, did not venture to assume the offensive. After the battle, Rodney remained near Guadeloupe until the 17th of April, refitting, and searching the neighbouring islands, in case the French fleet might have entered some one of them. For most of this time the British were becalmed, but Hood remarks that there had been wind enough to get twenty leagues to the westward; and there more wind probably would have

---

[1] Troude. Chevalier says sixteen, differing with Troude as to the whereabouts of the *Brave.*

been found. On the 17th Hood was detached in pursuit with ten sail of the line; and a day or two later Rodney himself started for Jamaica. Left to his own discretion, Hood pushed for the Mona Passage, between Puerto Rico and Santo Domingo, carrying studding-sails below and aloft in his haste. At daybreak of the 19th he sighted the west end of Puerto Rico; and soon afterwards a small French squadron was seen. A general chase resulted in the capture of the *Jason* and *Caton*, sixty-fours, which had parted from their fleet before the battle and were on their way to Cap François. A frigate, the *Aimable*, 32, and a sloop, the *Cérès*, 18, also were taken. In reporting this affair to Rodney, Hood got a thrust into his superior. "It is a very mortifying circumstance to relate to you, Sir, that the French fleet which you put to flight on the 12th went through the Mona Channel on the 18th, only the day before I was in it." A further proof of the utility of pursuit, here hinted at, is to be found in the fact that Rodney, starting six days later than de Vaudreuil, reached Jamaica April 28th, only three days after the French got into Cap François. He had therefore gained three days in a fortnight's run. What might not have been done by an untiring chase! But a remark recorded by Hood summed up the frame of mind which dominated Rodney: "I lamented to Sir George on the 13th that . . . he did not continue to pursue so as to keep sight of the enemy all night, to which he only answered, ' Come, we have done very handsomely as it is.' "

Rodney stayed at Jamaica until the 10th of July, when Admiral Hugh Pigot arrived from England to supersede him. This change was consequent upon the fall of Lord North's ministry, in the previous March, and had been decided before the news of the victory could reach England. Rodney sailed for home from Port Royal on the 22nd of July; and with his departure the war in the West Indies and North America may be said to have ended. Pigot started almost immediately for New York, and remained in North American waters until the end of October, when he returned to Barbados, first having detached Hood with thirteen ships of the line from the main fleet, to cruise off Cap François. It is of interest to note that at this time Hood took with him from New York the frigate *Albemarle*, 28, then commanded by Nelson, who had been serving on the North American station. These various movements were dictated by those of the enemy, either actually made or supposed to be in contemplation; for it was an inevitable part of the ill-effects of Rodney's most imperfect success, that the British fleet was thenceforth on the defensive purely, with all the perplexities of him who waits upon the initiative of an opponent. Nothing came of them all, however, for the war now was but lingering in its death stupor. The defeat of de Grasse, partial though it was; the abandonment of the enterprise upon Jamaica; the failure of the attack upon Gibraltar; and the success of Howe in re-victualling that fortress, — these had taken all heart out of the French and Spaniards; while the numerical superiority of the allies, inefficiently though it had been used heretofore, weighed heavily upon the imagination of the British Government, which now had abandoned all hope of subduing its American Colonies. Upon the conclusion of peace, in 1783, Pigot and Hood returned to England, leaving the Leeward Islands' Station under the command of Rear-Admiral Sir Richard Hughes, Bart., (2)[1] an officer remembered by history only through Nelson's refusing to obey his orders not to enforce the Navigation Acts, in 1785.

The change in the Ministry, besides occasioning the recall of Rodney, drew Lord Howe out of his long retirement, to command the Channel Fleet. He hoisted his flag on the 20th of April, 1782, on board the *Victory*, 100. Owing to the various directions in which the efforts of Great Britain had to be made, either to defend her own interests or to crush the movements of the many enemies now combined against her, the operations of the fleet were for some months carried on by detached squadrons, — in the North Sea, in the Bay of Biscay, and at the entrance of the Channel; Howe having under him several distinguished subordinates, at the head of whom, in professional reputation, were Vice-Admiral the Hon. Samuel Barrington and Rear-Admiral Richard Kempenfelt. In the North Sea, the Dutch were kept in their ports; and a convoy of near 400 merchant ships from the Baltic reached England unmolested. In the Bay of Biscay, Barrington, having with him twelve of the line, discovered and chased a convoy laden with stores for the fleet in the East Indies. One of the ships of the line accompanying it, the *Pégase*, 74, surrendered, after a night action of three hours with the *Foudroyant*, 80, Captain John Jervis,[2] afterwards Earl St.

---

[1] Son of Captain Sir Richard Hughes, Bart. (1), who was for many years Commissioner at Portsmouth, and who died in 1782. The younger officer died a full Admiral in 1812.

[2] Who was made a K. B. for this service.

Vincent. Of nineteen transports, thirteen, one of which, the *Action-naire*, was a 64-gun ship armed *en flûte*,[1] were taken; a weighty blow to the great Suffren, whose chief difficulty in India was inadequate material of war, and especially of spars, of which the *Actionnaire* carried an outfit for four ships of the line. After Barrington's return, Kempenfelt made a similar but uneventful cruise of a month in the Bay.

Howe himself went first to the North Sea in the month of May. Having there held the Dutch in check during a critical moment, he was directed next to go to the entrance of the Channel, leaving only a division in the Downs. Information had been received that an allied fleet of thirty-two ships of the line, five only of which were French, had sailed from Cadiz early in June, to cruise between Ushant and Scilly. It was expected that they would be joined there by a reinforcement from Brest, and by the Dutch squadron in the Texel, making a total of about fifty of the line, under the command of the Spanish Admiral, Don Luis de Cordova. The Dutch did not appear, owing probably to Howe's demonstration before their ports; but eight ships from Brest raised the allied fleet to forty. To oppose these Howe sailed on the 2nd of July with twenty-two sail, of which eight were three-deckers. Before his return, on the 7th of August, he was joined by eight others; mostly, however, sixty-fours. With this inferiority of numbers the British Admiral could expect only to act on the defensive, unless some specially favourable opportunity should offer. The matter of most immediate concern was the arrival of the Jamaica convoy, then daily expected; with which, it may be mentioned, de Grasse also was returning to England, a prisoner of war on board the *Sandwich*.

On its voyage north, the combined fleet captured on June 25th eighteen ships of a British convoy bound for Canada. A few days later it was fixed in the chops of the Channel, covering the ground from Ushant to Scilly. On the evening of July 7th it was sighted off Scilly by Howe, who then had with him twenty-five sail. The allies prepared for action; but the British Admiral, possessing a thorough knowledge of the neighbouring coasts, either in his own person or in some of his officers, led the fleet by night through the passage between Scilly and Land's End. On the following morning he was no more to be seen, and the enemy, ignorant of the manner

---

[1] That is, with a great part of her guns dismounted, and below as cargo.

of his evasion, was thrown wholly off his track.[1] A strong gale of
wind afterwards forcing the allies to the southward, both convoy and
fleet slipped by successfully, and again reached England.

Howe was ordered now to prepare to throw reinforcements and
supplies into Gibraltar, which had not received relief since Darby's
visit, in April, 1781. For this urgent and critical service it was
determined to concentrate the whole Channel Fleet at Spithead,
where also the transports and supply-ships were directed to rendezvous. It was while thus assembling for the relief of Gibraltar that
there occurred the celebrated incident of the *Royal George*, a 100-gun
ship, while being heeled for under-water repairs, oversetting and
sinking at her anchors, carrying down with her Rear-Admiral
Kempenfelt and about 900 souls, including many women and children. This was on the 29th of August, 1782. On the 11th of
September the expedition started, 183 sail in all; thirty-four being
ships of the line, with a dozen smaller cruisers, the rest unarmed
vessels. Of the latter, 31 were destined for Gibraltar, the remainder
being trading ships for different parts of the world. With so extensive a charge, the danger to which had been emphasised by numerous
captures from convoys during the war, Howe's progress was slow.
It is told that shortly before reaching Cape Finisterre, but after a
violent gale of wind, the full tally of 183 sail was counted. After
passing Finisterre, the several "trades" probably parted from the
grand fleet.

On the 8th of October, off Cape St. Vincent, a frigate, the
Latona, 38, was sent ahead for information. It was known that a
great combined force of ships of war lay in Algeciras Bay, — opposite
Gibraltar, — and that an attack upon the works was in contemplation; but much might have happened meantime. Much, in fact,
had happened. A violent gale of wind on the 10th of September
had driven some of the allied fleet from their moorings, one vessel,
the *San Miguel*, 72, being forced under the batteries of Gibraltar,
where she had to surrender; but there still remained the formidable
number of 48 ships of the line, anchored only four miles from the point
which the relief ships must reach. This was the problem which
Howe had to solve. More important still, though of less bearing

---

[1] Chevalier, following La Motte-Picquet's report, ascribes Howe's escape to greater
speed. ('Mar. Fran. en 1778': p. 335.) It must be noted that Howe's object was
not merely to escape, up Channel, by better sailing, but to get to the westward, *past*
the allies, a feat impracticable save by a stratagem such as is mentioned.

upon his mission, was the cheering news brought by the frigate, when she rejoined on the 10th, that the long-intended attack had been made on the 13th of September, and had been repelled gloriously and decisively. The heavily protected Spanish floating batteries, from which success had been expected confidently, one and all had been set on fire and destroyed. If Howe could introduce his succours, the fortress was saved.

The admiral at once summoned his subordinate officers, gave them full and particular instructions for the momentous undertaking, and issued at the same time, to the masters of the supply-ships, precise information as to local conditions of wind and currents at Gibraltar, to enable them more surely to reach their anchorage. On the 11th of October, being now close to its destination, the fleet bore up for the Straits, which it entered at noon with a fair westerly wind. The convoy went first, — sailing before the wind it was thus to leeward of the fleet, in a position to be defended, — and the ships of war followed at some distance in three divisions, one of which was led by Howe himself. At 6 P.M. the supply-ships were off the mouth of the Bay, with a wind fair for the mole; but, through neglect of the instructions given, all but four missed the entrance, and were swept to the eastward of the Rock, whither the fleet of course had to follow them.

On the 13th the combined fleets came out, being induced to quit their commanding position at Algeciras by fears for two of their number, which shortly before had been driven to the eastward. During the forenoon of the same day the British were off the Spanish coast, fifty miles east of Gibraltar. At sunset the allies were seen approaching, and Howe formed his fleet, but sent the supply-ships to anchor at the Zaffarine Islands, on the coast of Barbary, to await events. Next morning the enemy was close to land, but visible only from the mastheads; the British apparently having headed south during the night. On the 15th the wind came to the eastward, fair for Gibraltar, towards which all the British began cautiously to move. By the evening of the 16th, eighteen of the convoy were safe at the mole; and on the 18th all had arrived, besides a fireship with 1,500 barrels of powder, sent in by the Admiral upon the governor's requisition. Throughout this critical time, the combined fleets seem to have been out of sight. Either intentionally or carelessly, they had got to the eastward and there remained; having rallied their separated ships, but allowed Gibraltar to be replenished for a year.

On the morning of the 19th they appeared in the north-east, but the relief was then accomplished and Howe put out to sea. He was not willing to fight in mid-Straits, embarrassed by currents and the land; but when outside he brought-to, to allow the enemy to attack if they would, they having the weather-gage. On the following day, the 20th, towards sunset they bore down, and a partial engagement ensued; but it was wholly indecisive, and next day was not renewed. The British loss was 68 killed and 208 wounded; that of the allies 60 killed and 320 wounded. On the 14th of November the fleet regained Spithead.

The services rendered to his country by Howe on this occasion were eminently characteristic of the special qualities of that great officer, in whom was illustrated to the highest degree the solid strength attainable by a man not brilliant, but most able, who gives himself heart and soul to professional acquirement. In him, profound and extensive professional knowledge, which is not inborn but gained, was joined to great natural staying powers; and the combination eminently fitted him for the part we have seen him play in Delaware Bay, at New York, before Rhode Island, in the Channel, and now at Gibraltar. The utmost of skill, the utmost of patience, the utmost of persistence, such had Howe; and having these, he was particularly apt for the defensive operations, upon the conduct of which chiefly must rest his well-deserved renown.

A true and noble tribute has been paid by a French officer to this relief of Gibraltar:[1] —

" The qualities displayed by Lord Howe during this short campaign rose to the full height of the mission which he had to fulfil. This operation, one of the finest in the War of American Independence, merits a praise equal to that of a victory. If the English fleet was favoured by circumstances, — and it is rare that in such enterprises one can succeed without the aid of fortune, — it was above all the Commander-in-Chief's quickness of perception, the accuracy of his judgment, and the rapidity of his decisions, that assured success."

To this well-weighed, yet lofty praise of the Admiral, the same writer has added words that the British Navy may remember long with pride, as sealing the record of this war, of which the relief of Gibraltar marked the close in European and American waters. After according credit to the Admiralty for the uniform high speed of the British vessels, and to Howe for his comprehension and use of this advantage, Captain Chevalier goes on: —

---

[1] Chevalier : ' Mar. Fran. dans la Guerre de 1778,' p. 358.

" Finally, if we may judge by the results, the Commander-in-Chief of the English fleet could not but think himself most happy in his captains. There were
neither separations, nor collisions, nor casualties ; and there occurred none of those
events, so frequent in the experiences of a squadron, which often oblige admirals
to take a course wholly contrary to the end they have in view. In contemplation
of this unvexed navigation of Admiral Howe, it is impossible not to recall the
unhappy incidents which from the 9th to the 12th of April befell the squadron of
the Count de Grasse. . . . If it is just to admit that Lord Howe displayed the
highest talent, it should be added that he had in his hands excellent instruments."

To quote another French writer: " Quantity disappeared before
quality."

The operations in India, both naval and military, stand by themselves, without direct influence upon transactions elsewhere, and
unaffected also by these, except in so far as necessary succours were
intercepted sometimes in European waters. The cause of this isolation was the distance of India from Europe; from four to six months
being required by a fleet for the voyage.

Certain intelligence of the war between Great Britain and France
reached Calcutta July 7th, 1778. On the same day the Governor-
General ordered immediate preparations to attack Pondicherry, the
principal seaport of the French. The army arrived before the place
on the 8th of August, and on the same day Commodore Sir Edward
Vernon[1] anchored in the roads to blockade by sea. A French
squadron, under Captain Tronjoly, soon after appearing in the offing,
Vernon gave chase, and on the 10th an action ensued. The forces
engaged were about equal, the French, if anything, slightly superior;
a sixty-gun ship and four smaller vessels being on each side. As
the French then went into Pondicherry, the immediate advantage
may be conceded to them; but, Vernon returning on the 20th,
Tronjoly soon after quitted the roads, and returned to the Ile de
France.[2] From that day the British squadron blockaded closely, and
on the 17th of October Pondicherry capitulated.

---

[1]. British Squadron in the East Indies under Commodore Sir Edward Vernon, Kt.,
in 1778.

Ripon	. . . . .	60	{ Commodore Sir Edward Vernon. { Capt. Benjamin Marlow.
Asia .	. . . . .	54	Capt. George Vandeput.
Coventry .	. . . .	28	Capt. John Alexander Panton.
Seahorse .	. . . .	24	Commander Alexander M'Coy.
Cormorant	. . . .	18	Commander William Owen.*

  * Who, being killed by accident, was succeeded by Commander Charles Morice Pole.
— W. L. C.

  [2] Now Mauritius.

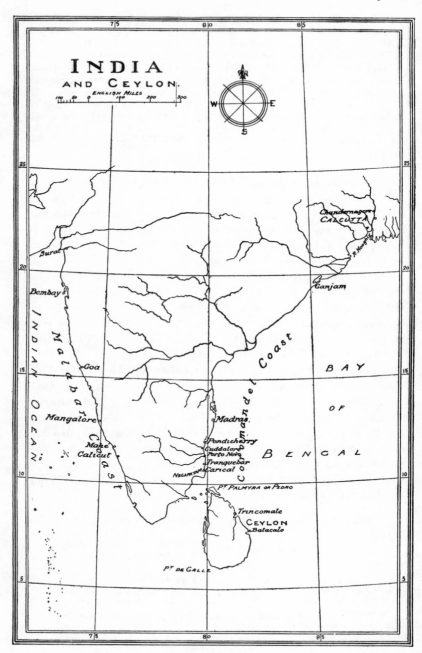

INDIA AND CEYLON.

On the 7th of March, 1779, Rear-Admiral Sir Edward Hughes, K. B., sailed for the East Indies with a small squadron.[1] The French also sent out occasional ships; but in 1779 and 1780 these went no further than the Ile de France, their naval station in the Indian Ocean. Hughes's force remained unopposed during those years. The period was critical, for the British were at war with Hyder Ali, Sultan of Mysore, and with the Mahrattas; and all depended upon command of the sea. In January, 1781, when Hughes was wintering at Bombay, the French squadron under Comte d'Orves appeared off the Coromandel coast, but, despite Hyder Ali's entreaties, it refused to co-operate with him. The different spirit of the two commanders may be illustrated from contemporary documents.

" We have advices from Fort St. George of a French squadron which appeared off that place on January 25, 26, and 27, consisting of 1 seventy-four, 4 sixty-fours, and 2 fifties. They proceeded south without making any attempt on five Indiamen then in the roads, with a number of vessels laden with grain and provisions; the destroying of which might have been easily accomplished, and would have been severely felt."

" On December 8th, off Mangalore," [2] writes Hughes, " I saw two ships, a large snow, three ketches, and many smaller vessels at anchor in the road with Hyder's flag flying; and, standing close, found them vessels of force and all armed for war. I anchored as close as possible, sent in all armed boats, under cover of three smaller ships of war, which anchored in four fathoms water, close to the enemy's ships. In two hours took and burned the two ships, one of 28 and one of 26 guns, and took or destroyed all the others, save one which, by throwing everything overboard, escaped over the bar into the port. Lost 1 lieutenant and 10 men killed, 2 lieutenants and 51 wounded."

D'Orves returned to the Ile de France.

When war with Holland began, the British government decided to attempt the capture of the Cape of Good Hope. For that object a squadron of 1 seventy-four, 1 sixty-four, and 3 fifties, with numerous smaller vessels, under Commodore George Johnstone, convoying a

---

[1] Squadron which, under Rear-Admiral Sir Edward Hughes, K. B. (B), sailed for India from St. Helens in 1779. — W. L. C.

Superb	74	Rear-Admiral Sir Edward Hughes, K. B. Capt. Robert Simonton.
Exeter	64	Capt. Richard King.
Eagle	64	Capt. Ambrose Reddall.
Burford	64	Capt. Peter Rainier (1).
Worcester	64	Capt. George Talbot.
Belleisle	64	Capt. John Brooks.
Nymph	14	Commander John Blankett.

[2] On the Malabar — western — coast.

considerable body of troops, sailed from England on the 13th of March, 1781, in company with the Channel fleet under Vice-Admiral George Darby, then on its way to relieve Gibraltar. The French government, having timely notice of the expedition, undertook to frustrate it; detailing for that purpose a division of 2 seventy-fours, and 3 sixty-fours, under the since celebrated Suffren.[1] These ships left Brest on the 22nd of March, with the fleet of de Grasse. They also carried some battalions of troops.

On April 11th the British squadron reached Porto Praya, Cape de Verde Islands. This bay is open to the southward, extending from east to west about a mile and a half, and is within the limits of the north-east trade-winds. Although aware that a French division was on his track, and conscious, by the admissions of his report, that protection could not be expected from the neutrality of the place, Johnstone permitted his vessels to anchor without reference to attack. His own flagship, the *Romney*, 50, was so surrounded by others that she could fire only with great caution through intervals. On the 16th of April, at 9.30 A.M., the *Isis*, 50, which was the outermost of the British squadron, signalled eleven sail in the north-east. Fifteen hundred persons were then ashore engaged in watering, fishing, embarking cattle, and amusing themselves. The strangers were Suffren's division. The meeting was not expected by

---

[1] Squadrons under Commodore George Johnstone and M. de Suffren in the action in Porto Praya, on April 16th, 1781.

BRITISH.			FRENCH.		
SHIPS	GUNS.	COMMANDERS.	SHIPS.	GUNS.	COMMANDERS.
Romney . . .	50	{ Commod. George Johnstone. { Capt. Roddam Home.	*Héros*	74	M. le Bailli de Suffren.
Hero	74	Capt. James Hawker.	*Annibal* . . .	74	Capt. de Trémigon, Senr.‡
Monmouth . .	64	Capt. James Alms (1).	*Artésien* . . .	64	Capt. de Cardaillac.‡
Jupiter . . .	50	Capt. Thomas Pasley.	*Sphinx*	64	Capt. du Chilleau.
Isis	50	Capt. Evelyn Sutton.	*Vengeur* . . .	64	Capt. de Forbin.
Diana	32	Capt. Sir William Chaloner Burnaby, Bart.			
Jason	32	Capt. James Pigott.			
Active	32	Capt. Thomas Mackenzie.			
Rattlesnake . .	14	Commander Peter Clements.			
Porto	16	Commander the Hon. Thomas Charles Lumley.	* Armed ships. The *Royal Charlotte* was hired.		
Infernal (f. s.) .	8	Commander Henry d'Esterre Darby.	† Armed transport.		
Terror (bomb) .	8	Commander Charles Wood.	‡ Killed.		
Tapageur (cutter)	14	Lieut. Philip d'Auvergne.			
San Carlos * . .	20	Commander John Boyle.			
Pondicherry † .	20	Lieut. Thomas Saunders Grove.			
Royal Charlotte *	20	Commander Thomas Stanhope Bennett.			
and ten East Indiamen, each of 26 guns.					

W. L. C.

the French commander, whose object in entering was simply to
complete the water of the ships; but he determined at once to attack,
and hauled round the east point of the bay in column, the two
seventy-fours at the head, his own ship, the *Héros*, leading with the
signal for battle (line ab). He luffed to the wind, and anchored five
hundred feet from the starboard beam of the British *Hero*, 74 (f),
whence he at once opened fire from both broadsides. His next
astern, the *Annibal* (b), brought up immediately ahead of him, but

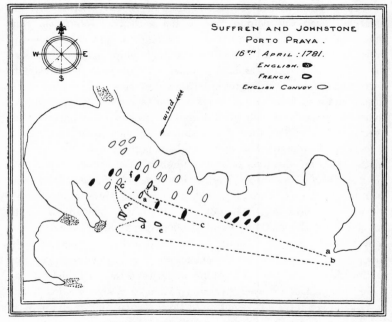

SUFFREN AND JOHNSTONE. PORTO PRAYA.

so close that the *Héros* had to veer cable and drop astern (a), which
brought her on the beam of the *Monmouth*, 64.[1] The captain of the
Annibal had thought the order for battle merely precautionary, and
had not cleared for action. He was therefore taken unawares, and
his ship did no service proportionate to her force. The third French
vessel (c) reached her station, but her captain was struck dead just

[1] I infer, from the accounts, that the *Monmouth* was well east of the *Hero*, that
the French had passed her first, and that the *Héros* was now on her port beam; but
this point is not certain.

when about to anchor, and in the confusion the anchor was not let go. The ship drifted foul of a British East Indiaman, which she carried out to sea (c' c'') The two remaining French (d, e) simply cannonaded as they passed across the bay's mouth, failing through mishap or awkwardness to reach an effective position.

The attack thus became a mere rough and tumble, in which the two seventy-fours alone sustained the French side. After three quarters of an hour, Suffren, seeing that the attempt had failed, slipped his cable and put to sea. The *Annibal* followed, but she had been so damaged that all her masts went overboard; fortunately, not until her head was pointed out of the harbour. Johnstone, thus luckily escaping the consequences of his neglect, now called his captains together to learn the condition of their ships, and then ordered them to cut their cables and pursue. All obeyed except Captain Sutton of the *Isis,* who represented that the spars and rigging of his ship could not bear sail at once. Johnstone then ordered him to come out anyhow, which he did, and his fore topmast shortly went overboard. The disability of this ship so weighed upon the Commodore that his pursuit was exceedingly sluggish; and, the *Annibal* having got a bit of canvas on a jury foremast, the French kept drawing him away to leeward. Night, therefore, was falling as he came near them; the *Isis* and *Monmouth* were two or three miles astern; the sea was increasing; if he got much further to leeward, he could not get back; he had forgotten to appoint a rendezvous where the convoy might rejoin; a night action, he considered, was not to be thought of. Yet, if he let the enemy go, they might anticipate him at the Cape. In short, Johnstone underwent the "anguish" of an undecided man in a "cruel situation," [1] and of course decided to run no risks. He returned therefore to Porto Praya, put the captain of the *Isis* under arrest, and remained in port for a fortnight. Suffren hurried on to the Cape, got there first, landed his troops, and secured the colony against attack. Johnstone arrived in the neighbourhood some time later, and, finding himself anticipated, turned aside to Saldanha Bay, where he captured five Dutch East Indiamen. He then sent the *Hero*, *Monmouth*, and *Isis*, on to India, to reinforce Hughes, and himself went back to England.

No accusation of misbehaviour lies against any of the British subordinates in this affair of Porto Praya. The captain of the *Isis* was brought to a court-martial, and honourably acquitted of all the

---

[1] Expressions in Johnstone's Report.

charges.   The discredit of the surprise was not redeemed by any exhibition of intelligence, energy, or professional capacity, on the part of the officer in charge.   It has been said that he never had commanded a post-ship [1] before he was intrusted with this very important mission, and it is reasonably sure that his selection for it was due to attacks made by him upon the professional conduct of Keppel and Howe, when those admirals were at variance with the administration.   His preposterous mismanagement, therefore, was probably not wholly bitter to the Navy at large.   In the British ships of war, the entire loss in men, as reported, was only 9 killed, 47 wounded.   Several casualties from chance shots occurred on board the convoy, bringing up the total to 36 killed and 130 wounded.[2] The French admit 105 killed and 204 wounded, all but 19 being in the *Héros* and *Annibal*.   Although precipitated by Suffren, the affair clearly was as great a surprise to his squadron as to the British. Therefore, the latter, being already at anchor and more numerous as engaged, had a distinct advantage; to which also contributed musketry fire from the transports.   Nevertheless, the result cannot be deemed creditable to the French captains or gunnery.

Suffren remained in the neighbourhood of the Cape for two months.   Then, having seen the colony secure, independent of his squadron, he departed for the Ile de France, arriving there October 25th.   On the 17th of December the whole French force, under the command of d'Orves, sailed for the Coromandel coast.   On the way the British 50-gun ship *Hannibal*, Captain Alexander Christie, was taken.   On the 9th of February, 1782, Comte d'Orves died, and Suffren found himself at the head of twelve ships of the line: 3 seventy-fours, 7 sixty-fours, and 2 fifties.[3]   On the 15th Hughes's fleet was sighted, under the guns of Madras.   It numbered nine of the line: 2 seventy-fours, 1 sixty-eight, 5 sixty-fours, and 1 fifty. Suffren stood south towards Pondicherry, which had passed into the power of Hyder Ali.   After nightfall Hughes got under way, and

---

[1] Charnock, however, says that in 1762, immediately after receiving his post-commission, he commanded in succession the *Hind*, 20, and the *Wager*, 20.   Moreover, before his appointment to the expedition of 1781, he had been Commodore on the Lisbon Station.   But he had spent comparatively little time at sea as a captain. — W. L. C.

[2] Details are in Schomberg, iv. 385. — W. L. C.

[3] One being the captured British *Hannibal*, 50, which was commissioned by Captain Morard de Galles, retaining the English form of the name, Hannibal, to distinguish her from the *Annibal*, 74, already in the squadron.

also steered south.   He feared for Trincomale, in Ceylon, recently
a Dutch port, which the British had captured on the 5th of January.
It was a valuable naval station, and as yet most imperfectly defended.

At daylight the British saw the French squadron [1] twelve miles
east (A, A) and its transports nine miles south-west (c).   Hughes
chased the latter and took six.   Suffren pursued, but could not overtake before sunset, and both fleets steered south-east during the night.
Next morning there were light north-north-east airs, and the French
were six miles north-east of the British (B, B).   The latter formed
line on the port tack (a), heading to seaward; Hughes hoping that
thus the usual sea-breeze would find him to windward.   The breeze,
however, did not make as expected; and, as the north-east puffs were
bringing the enemy down, he kept off before the wind (b) to gain
time for his ships to close their intervals, which were too great.   At
4 P.M. the near approach of the French compelled him to form line
again, on the port tack, heading easterly.   The rear ship, *Exeter*, 64,
was left separated, out of due support from those ahead (C).   Suffren,
leading one section of his fleet in person, passed to windward of the

[1] British and French Squadrons in the action off Sadras, Feb. 17th, 1782.

BRITISH.				FRENCH.		
SHIPS.	Guns.	COMMANDERS.		SHIPS.	Guns.	COMMANDERS.
Eagle	64	Capt. Ambrose Reddall.		*Sévère*	64	Capt. de Villeneuve-Cillart.
Monmouth . .	64	Capt. James Alms (1).		*Vengeur* . . .	64	Capt. de Forbin.
Worcester . .	64	Capt. George Talbot.		*Brillant* . . .	64	Capt. de St. Félix.
Burford . . .	64	Capt. Peter Rainier (1).		*Flamand* . . .	50	Capt. de Cuverville.
Superb	74	{ Vice-Admiral Sir Edward Hughes, K. B. (B). Capt. William Stevens.		*Annibal* . . .	74	Capt. du Tromelin.
				Héros	74	{ M. de Suffren, Chef d'Esc. Capt. de Moissac.
Hero	74	Capt. Charles Wood.		*Orient*	74	Capt. de Lapallière.
Isis	50	Capt. the Hon. Thos. Chas. Lumley.		*Artésien* . . .	64	Capt. Bidé de Maurville.
				Sphinx	64	Capt. du Chilleau.
Monarca . . .	68	Capt. John Gell.		*Ajax*	64	Capt. Bouvet.
Exeter	64	{ Commod. Richard King. Capt. Henry Reynolds.		*Hannibal* . . .	50	Capt. Morard de Galles.
				Bizarre . . .	64	Capt. de Lalandelle.
Seahorse . .	24	Capt. Robert Montagu.		*Pourvoyeuse* . .	38	Capt. de Beaulieu.
Manilla . .	14	Lieut. William Robinson.		*Fine*	32	Capt. Perrier de Salvert.
				Bellone . . .	32	Capt. de Ruyter.
				Subtile	22	Capt. de Galifet.
				Sylphide . . .	16	
				Diligent . . .	10	

The British list is founded upon that in Beatson, vi. 298, Steel's ' Navy List '
(1782), and dispatches ; the French list, on Trublet : ' Hist. de la Campagne de
l'Inde ' (1801) ; ' Relation Détaillée,' etc. (1783) ; Chevalier : ' Hist. de la Mar.
Franç.' and Cunat : ' Hist. du Bailli de Suffren.'   But some of these contradict the
others.   From some it would appear that the *Pourvoyeuse* was also in the line. —
W. L. C.

British line, from the rear, as far as Hughes's flagship, which was fifth from the van.　There he stopped, and kept at half cannon-shot, to prevent the four van ships from tacking to relieve their consorts. It was his intention that the second half of his fleet should attack the other side of the English (D), but only two of them did so, engag. ing to leeward the extreme rear (C).　The result was, to use Hughes's own words, that "the enemy brought eight of their best ships to the attack of five of ours."　It will be noted with interest

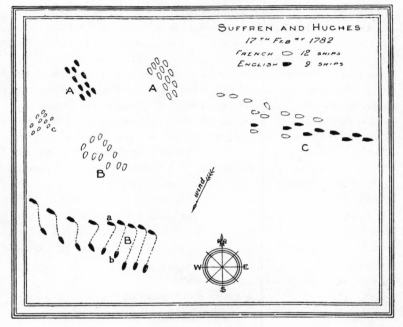

SUFFREN AND HUGHES.

that these were exactly the numbers engaged in the first act of the battle of the Nile.　The *Exeter* (like the *Guerrier* at the Nile) received the fresh broadsides of the first five of the enemy, and then remained in close action on both sides, assailed by two, and at last by three, opponents, — two fifties, and one sixty-four.　When the third approached, the master of the ship asked Commodore Richard King, whose broad pennant flew at her masthead, "What is to be done?" "There is nothing to be done," replied King, "but to fight her till she sinks."　Her loss, 10 killed and 45 wounded, was not creditable

under the circumstances to the French gunnery, which had been
poor also at Porto Praya.   At 6 P.M. the wind shifted to south-east.
throwing all on the other tack, and enabling the British van to come
into action.   Darkness now approaching, Suffren hauled off and
anchored at Pondicherry.   Hughes went on to Trincomale to refit.
The British loss had been 32 killed, among whom were Captain
William Stevens of the flagship, and Captain Henry Reynolds, of the
Exeter, and 83 wounded.   The French had 30 killed; the number of
their wounded is put by Professor Laughton at 100.

, On the 12th of March Hughes returned to Madras, and towards
the end of the month sailed again for Trincomale, carrying reinforcements and supplies.   On the 30th he was joined at sea by the *Sultan*,
74, and the *Magnanime*, 64, just from England.   Suffren had
remained on the coast from reasons of policy, to encourage Hyder
Ali in his leaning to the French; but, after landing a contingent of
troops on the 22nd of March, to assist at the siege of the British port
of Cuddalore, he put to sea on the 23rd, and went south, hoping to
intercept the *Sultan* and *Magnanime* off the south end of Ceylon.
On the 9th of April he sighted the British fleet to the south and west
of him.   Hughes, attaching the first importance to the strengthening
of Trincomale, had resolved neither to seek nor to shun action.   He
therefore continued his course, light northerly airs prevailing, until
the 11th, when, being about fifty miles to the north-east of his port, he
bore away for it.   Next morning, April 12th, finding that the enemy
could overtake his rear ships, he formed line on the starboard tack,[1]

---

[1] Line of battle of the squadron under Vice-Admiral Sir Edward Hughes, K. B.,
in the action off Providien, on April 12th, 1782.

Exeter	64	{ Commodore Richard King. { Capt. Charles Hughes.
Hero	74	Capt. James Hawker.
Isis	50	Capt. the Hon. Thos. Chas. Lumley.
Burford	64	Capt. Peter Rainier (1).
Monarca	68	Capt. John Gell.
Superb	74	{ Vice-Admiral Sir Edward Hughes, K.B. (B). { Capt. the Hon. Dunbar Maclellan (Actg.).
Monmouth	64	Capt. James Alms (1).
Worcester	64	Capt. George Talbot.
Eagle	64	Capt. Ambrose Reddall.
Sultan	74	Capt. James Watt.
Magnanime	64	Capt. Charles Wolseley.
Seahorse	24	Capt. Robert Montagu.
Combustion (f. s.)	14	Commander Henry Newcome.

The above is taken, the spelling of names being corrected, from Beatson, vi. 298;
but the order of the line was slightly modified at the last moment. — W. L. C.

at two cables' intervals, heading to the westward, towards the coast
of Ceylon, wind north by east, and the French dead to windward
(A, A).   Suffren drew up his line on the same tack, parallel to
the British (a), and at 11 A.M. gave the signal to steer west-south-
west all together; his vessels going down in a slanting direction,
each steering for one of the enemy.   Having twelve ships to eleven,
the twelfth was ordered to place herself on the off side of the rear
British, which would thus have two antagonists.

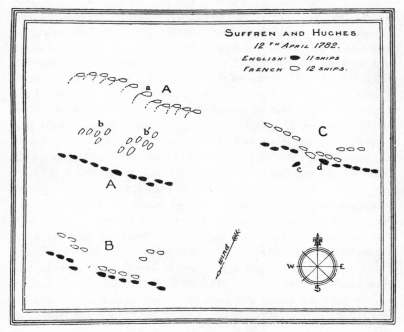

SUFFREN AND HUGHES.

In such simultaneous approach it commonly occurred that the
attacking line ceased to be parallel with the foe's, its van becoming
nearer and rear more distant.   So it was here.   Further, the British
opening fire as soon as the leading French were within range, the
latter at once hauled up to reply.   Suffren, in the centre, wishing
closest action, signalled them to keep away again, and himself bore
down wrathfully upon Hughes to within pistol-shot; in which he
was supported closely by his next ahead and the two next astern.
The rear of the French, though engaged, remained too far distant

Their line, therefore, resembled a curve, the middle of which — four
or five ships — was tangent to the British centre (B). At this point
the heat of the attack fell upon Hughes's flagship, the *Superb*, 74
(C, d), and her next ahead, the *Monmouth*, 64 (c). Suffren's ship,
the *Héros*, having much of her rigging cut, could not shorten sail,
shot by the *Superb*, and brought up abreast the *Monmouth*. The
latter, already hotly engaged by one of her own class, and losing her
main and mizzen masts in this unequal new contest, was forced at 3
P.M. to bear up out of the line. The place of the *Héros* alongside
the *Superb* was taken by the *Orient*, 74, supported by the *Brillant*,
64; and when the *Monmouth* kept off, the attack of these two ships
was reinforced by the half-dozen stern chasers of the *Héros*, which
had drifted into the British line, and now fired into the *Superb's*
bows. The conflict between these five ships, two British and three
French, was one of the bloodiest in naval annals; the loss of the
Superb, 59 killed and 96 wounded, and of the *Monmouth*, 45 killed
and 102 wounded, equalling that of the much larger vessels that
bore[1] the flags of Nelson and Collingwood at Trafalgar. The loss of
the three French was 52 killed and 142 wounded; but to this should
be added properly that of the *Sphinx*, 64, the *Monmouth's* first adversary: 22 killed and 74 wounded. At 3.40 P.M., fearing that if he
continued steering west he would get entangled with the shore,
Hughes wore his ships, forming line on the port tack. The French
also wore, and Suffren hoped to secure the *Monmouth*, which was left
between the two lines; but the quickness of a British captain,
Hawker, of the *Hero*, ran a tow-rope to her in time, and she was
thus dragged out of danger. At 5.40 Hughes anchored, and Suffren
did the same at 8 P. M. The total British loss in men on this occasion
was 137 killed and 430 wounded; that of the French 137 killed and
357 wounded.

The exhausted enemies remained at anchor in the open sea, two
miles apart, for a week, repairing. On the 19th of April the French
got under way and made a demonstration before the British, inviting
battle, yet not attacking; but the condition of the *Monmouth* forbade
Hughes from moving. Suffren therefore departed to Batacalo, in
Ceylon, south of Trincomale, where he covered his own convoys from
Europe, and flanked the approach of his adversary's. Hughes, on
the 22nd of April, got into Trincomale, where he remained till June
23rd. He then went to Negapatam, formerly a Dutch possession,
but then held by the British. There he learned that Suffren, who

meanwhile had captured several British transports, was a few miles
north of him, at Cuddalore, which had surrendered to Hyder Ali on
April 4th.   On the 5th of July, at 1 P.M., the French squadron
appeared.   At 3 P.M. Hughes put to sea, and stood south during
the night to gain the wind, — the south-west monsoon now blowing.

Next morning, at daylight, the French were seen at anchor,
seven or eight miles to leeward.   At 6 A.M. they began to get under
way.   One of their sixty-fours, the *Ajax*, had lost her main and

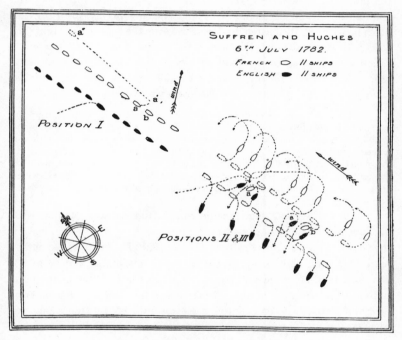

SUFFREN AND HUGHES.

mizzen topmasts in a violent squall on the previous afternoon, and
was not in the line.   There were therefore eleven ships on each side.
The action, known as that of Negapatam, began shortly before 11,
when both fleets were on the starboard tack, heading south-south-east,
wind south-west.   The British being to windward, Hughes ordered
his fleet to bear up together to the attack, exactly as Suffren had
done on the 12th of April.   As commonly happened, the rear got
less close than the van (Position I.).   The fourth ship in the French

order (a), losing her mainmast early, dropped to leeward of the line
(a'), and astern of her place (a''). At half-past noon the wind flew
suddenly to south-south-east, — the sea-breeze, — taking the ships a
little on the port bow. Most of them, on both sides, paid off from
the enemy, the British to starboard, the French to port; but between
the main lines, which were in the momentary confusion consequent
upon such an incident, were left six ships — four British and two
French — that had turned the other way (Position II.). These were
the *Burford*, *Sultan* (s), *Worcester*, and *Eagle*, fourth, fifth, eighth,
and tenth, in the British order; and the *Sévère* (b), third in the
French, with the dismasted *Brillant*, towards the rear of the fight (a).
Under these conditions, the *Sévère*, 64, underwent a short but close
action with the *Sultan*, 74; and with two other British ships, according to the report of the *Sévère's* captain. The remainder of the
incident shall be given in the latter's own words.

> "Seeing the French squadron drawing off, — for all the ships except the
> *Brillant* had fallen off on the other tack, — Captain de Cillart thought it useless to
> prolong his defence, and had the flag hauled down. The ships engaged with him
> immediately ceased their fire, and the one on the starboard side moved away. At
> this moment the *Sévère* fell off to starboard, and her sails filled. Captain de Cillart
> then ordered the fire to be resumed by his lower-deck guns, the only ones which
> remained manned, and he rejoined his squadron" (Position III.).

When the *Sévère's* flag came down, Suffren was approaching with
his flagship. The *Sultan* wore to rejoin her fleet, and was raked by
the *Sévère* in so doing (Position III.). The *Brillant*, whose mainmast had been shot away in conflict with either the *Sultan* or the
Burford, both much heavier ships, had at this later phase of the fight
fallen under the guns of the *Worcester* and the *Eagle*. Her captain,
de Saint-Félix, was one of the most resolute of Suffren's officers.
She was rescued by the flagship, but she had lost 47 killed and 136
wounded, — an almost incredible slaughter, being over a third of the
usual complement of a sixty-four; and Suffren's ships were under-
manned.

These spirited episodes, and the fact that his four separated ships
were approaching the enemy, and being approached by them, caused
Hughes to give the orders to wear, and for a general chase; the flag
for the line being hauled down. Two of his fleet, however, made
signals of disability; so he annulled the orders, and at 1.30 formed
on the port tack, recalling the engaged vessels. Both squadrons
now stood in shore, and anchored at about 6 P.M.; the British near

Negapatam, the French some ten miles north.   The loss in the action had been: British, 77 killed, 233 wounded; French, 178 killed, 601 wounded.   Among the slain was Captain the Hon. Dunbar Maclellan of Hughes's flagship.

On the following day Suffren sailed for Cuddalore.   There he received word that two ships of the line — the *Illustre*, 74, and *St. Michel*, 60, with a convoy of supplies and 600 troops — were to be expected shortly at Pointe de Galle, then a Dutch port, on the south-west side of Ceylon.   It was essential to cover these, and on the 18th he was ready for sea; but the necessity of an interview with Hyder Ali delayed him until the 1st of August, when he started for Batacalo.   On the 9th he arrived there, and on the 21st the reinforcement joined him.   Within forty-eight hours the supply-ships were cleared, and the squadron sailed again with the object of taking Trincomale.   On the 25th he was off the port, and, the operation being energetically pushed, the place capitulated on the 31st of August.

It is difficult to resist the impression that greater energy on Hughes's part might have brought him up in time to prevent this mishap.   He reached Madras only on July 20th, a fortnight after the late action; and he did not sail thence until the 20th of August, notwithstanding that he apprehended an attempt upon Trincomale. Hence, when he arrived there on the 2nd of September, not only had it passed into the hands of the enemy, but Suffren had re-embarked already the men and the guns that had been landed from his fleet. When Hughes's approach was signalled, all preparations for sea were hastened, and the following morning, at daybreak, the French came out.   Hughes had been joined since the last action by the *Sceptre*, 64, Captain Samuel Graves, so that the respective forces in the action fought off Trincomale on September 3rd were twelve of the line to fourteen, viz.: British, 3 seventy-fours, 1 seventy, 1 sixty-eight, 6 sixty-fours, 1 fifty; French, 4 seventy-fours, 7 sixty-fours, 1 sixty, 2 fifties.   Suffren had also put into the line a 36-gun ship, the *Consolante*.[1]

While the French were getting under way, the British fleet was standing towards the entrance, closehauled on the starboard tack, a fresh south-west monsoon blowing.   When Hughes made out the hostile flags on the works, he kept away four points,[2] and steered east-south-east, still in column, under short canvas.   Suffren pursued,

---

[1] Previously the British East Indiaman, *Elizabeth.*
[2] Forty-five degrees.

being to windward yet astern, with his fleet on a line of bearing; that is, the line on which the ships were ranged was not the same as the course which they were steering. This formation, wherein the advance is oblique to the front, is very difficult to maintain. Wishing to make the action, whatever the immediate event, decisive in results, by drawing the French well to leeward of the port, Hughes, who was a thorough seaman and had good captains, played with his eager enemy. "He kept avoiding me without taking flight," wrote Suffren; "or rather, he fled in good order, regulating his canvas by his worst sailers; and, keeping off by degrees, he steered from first to last ten or twelve different courses." Hughes, on his part, while perfectly clear as to his own object, was somewhat perplexed by the seeming indecision of an adversary whose fighting purpose he knew by experience. "Sometimes they edged down," he wrote; "sometimes they brought-to; in no regular order, as if undetermined what to do." These apparent vacillations were due to the difficulty of maintaining the line of bearing, which was to be the line of battle; and this difficulty was the greater, because Hughes was continually altering his course and Suffren's ships were of unequal speed.

At length, at 2 P.M., being then twenty-five miles south-east of the port, the French drew near enough to bear down. That this movement might be carried out with precision, and all the vessels come into action together, Suffren caused his fleet to haul to the wind, on the starboard tack, to rectify the order. This also being done poorly and slowly, he lost patience; and at 2.30, to spur on the laggard ships, he gave the signal to attack, specifying pistol-range (A). Even this not sufficing to fetch the delinquents promptly into line with the flag-ship, the latter fired a gun to enforce obedience. Her own side being still turned towards the British, as she waited, the report was taken by the men below to be the signal for opening fire, and her whole broadside was discharged. This example was followed by the other ships, so that the engagement, instead of being close, was begun at half cannon-shot.

Owing to his measured and deliberate retreat, Hughes had his fleet now in thoroughly good shape, well aligned and closed-up. The French, starting from a poor formation to perform a difficult evolution, under fire, engaged in utter disorder (B). Seven ships, rounding-to too soon and fore-reaching, formed a confused group, much to windward and somewhat ahead of the enemy's van. Imperfectly deployed, their fire could not be adequately developed. In the

rear a somewhat similar condition existed. Suffren, expecting the
bulk of his line to fight the British to windward, had directed
the *Vengeur*, 64, and the *Consolante*, 36, to double to leeward on the
extreme rear; but they, finding that the weather sides of the enemy
were not occupied, feared to go to leeward, lest they should be cut
off. They attacked the rear British ship, the *Worcester*, 64, Captain
Charles Wood, to windward; but the *Monmouth*, 64, Captain James
Alms (1), dropping down to her support, and the *Vengeur* catching

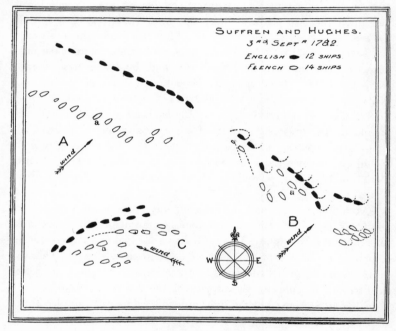

SUFFREN AND HUGHES.

fire in the mizzen top, they were compelled to haul off. Only Suffren's
own ship, the *Héros*, 74 (a), and her next astern, the *Illustre*, 74,
came at once to close action with the British centre; but subsequently
the *Ajax*, 64, succeeding in clearing herself from the snarl in
the rear, took station ahead of the *Héros*. Upon these three fell the
brunt of the fight. They not only received the broadsides of the
ships immediately opposed to them, but, the wind having now become
light yet free, the British vessels ahead and astern, by luffing or

keeping off, played also upon them. "The enemy formed a semi-circle around us," wrote Suffren's chief of staff, "and raked us ahead and astern, as the ship came up and fell off with the helm to lee-ward." The two seventy-fours were crushed under this fire. Both lost their main and mizzen masts in the course of the day, and the foretopmast of the flagship also fell. The *Ajax* arriving later, and probably drawing less attention, had only a topmast shot away.

The British total of killed and wounded was very evenly dis-tributed throughout the fleet. Only the rear ship lost an important spar, — the main topmast. It was upon her, as already mentioned, and upon the two leading ships, the *Exeter* and *Isis*, that fell the heaviest fire, proportionately, of the French. From the position of the seven van ships of the latter, such fire as they could make must needs be upon the extreme British van, and the *Exeter* was forced to leave the line. The loss of the French that day was 82 killed and 255 wounded; of which 64 killed and 178 wounded belonged to the *Héros*, *Illustre*, and *Ajax*. The British had 51 killed and 283 wounded; the greatest number of casualties in one ship being 56. Singularly enough, in such a small list of deaths, three were com-manding officers: Captains James Watt, of the *Sultan*, Charles Wood of the *Worcester*, and the Hon. Thomas Charles Lumley of the *Isis*.

At 5.30 P.M. the wind shifted suddenly from south-west to east-south-east (C). The British wore together, formed on the other tack, and continued the fight. It was during this final act, and at 6 P.M., that the mainmast of the French flagship came down. The van ships of the French had towed their heads round with boats before 4, in order to come to the support of the centre, in obedience to a signal from Suffren; but the light airs and calms had retarded them. With the shift they approached, and passed in column between their crippled vessels and the enemy. This manœuvre, and the failure of daylight, brought the battle to an end. According to Hughes's report, several of his fleet "were making much water from shot-holes so very low down in the bottom as not to be come at to be effectually stopped; and the whole had suffered severely in their masts and rigging." Trincomale being in the enemy's possession, and the east coast of Ceylon an unsafe anchorage now, at the change of the monsoon, he felt compelled to return to Madras, where he anchored on the 9th of the month. Suffren regained Trincomale on the 7th of September, but the *Orient*, 74, running ashore at the entrance and being lost, he remained outside until the 17th, saving material from the wreck.

The break-up of the south-west monsoon, then at hand, is apt to be accompanied by violent hurricanes, and is succeeded by the north-east monsoon, during which the east coast, of the peninsula and of Ceylon, is a lee shore, with heavy surf. Naval operations, there-fore, were suspended for the winter. During that season Trincomale is the only secure port. Deprived of it, Hughes determined to go to Bombay, and for that purpose left Madras on the 17th of October. Four days later a reinforcement of five ships of the line arrived from England, under Commodore Sir Richard Bickerton, Bart., who followed the Commander-in-Chief at once to the west coast. In the course of December the entire British force was united at Bombay.

In Trincomale Suffren had a good anchorage; but the insuffi-ciency of its resources, with other military considerations, decided him to winter at Acheen, at the west end of Sumatra. He arrived there on the 2nd of November, having first paid a visit to Cuddalore, where the *Bizarre*, 64, was wrecked by carelessness. On the 20th of December he left Acheen for the Coromandel coast, having shortened his stay to the eastward for reasons of policy. On the 8th of January, 1783, he was off Ganjam, on the Orissa coast, and thence reached Trincomale again on the 23rd of February. There he was joined on the 10th of March by three ships of the line from Europe: 2 seventy-fours and 1 sixty-four. Under their convoy came General de Bussy, with 2,500 troops, who were at once dispatched to Cuddalore.

On the 10th of April Vice-Admiral Hughes, returning from Bombay, passed Trincomale on the way to Madras. The various maritime occurrences since the battle of September 3rd had reversed the naval odds, and Hughes now had eighteen ships of the line, one of which was an eighty, opposed to fifteen under Suffren. Another important event in the affairs of India was the death of Hyder Ali, on the 7th of December, 1782. Although his policy was continued by his son, the blow to the French was serious. Under all the con-ditions, the British authorities were emboldened to attempt the reduction of Cuddalore. The army destined to this enterprise marched from Madras, passed round Cuddalore, and encamped south of it by the shore. The supply-ships and lighter cruisers anchored near, while the fleet cruised to the southward, where, being to wind-ward, for the south-west monsoon had then set in, it covered the operations against disturbance from the sea.

Towards the beginning of June the investment of the place was complete by land and by water. Intelligence of this state of things was brought on the 10th of June to Suffren, who by Bussy's direction was keeping his inferior fleet in Trincomale until its services should be absolutely indispensable. Immediately upon receiving the news he left port, and on the 13th sighted the British fleet, then at anchor off Porto Novo, a little south of Cuddalore. Upon his approach Hughes moved off, and anchored again five miles from the besieged place. For the next two days the French were baffled by the winds; but on the 17th, the south-west monsoon resumed, and Suffren again drew near. The British Vice-Admiral, not caring to accept action at anchor, got under way, and from that time till the 20th remained outside, trying to obtain the weather-gage, in which he was frustrated by the variableness of the winds. Meanwhile Suffren had anchored near the town, communicated with the general, and, being very short of men at the guns, had embarked 1,200 troops for his expected battle; for it was evident that the issue of the siege would turn upon the control of the sea. On the 18th he weighed again, and the two fleets manœuvred for the advantage, with light baffling airs, the British furthest from shore.

On the 20th of June, the wind holding at west with unexpected constancy, Hughes decided to accept the attack which Suffren evidently intended. The latter, being distinctly inferior in force, — fifteen to eighteen, — contemplated probably an action that should be decisive only as regarded the fate of Cuddalore; that is, one which, while not resulting in the capture or destruction of ships, should compel his opponent to leave the neighbourhood to repair damages. The British formed line on the port tack, heading to the northward. Suffren ranged his fleet in the same manner, parallel to the enemy, and was careful to see the order exact before bearing down.[1] When the signal to attack was given, the French kept away together, and brought-to again on the weather beam of the British, just within point-blank range. The action lasted from shortly after 4 P.M. to nearly 7, and was general throughout both lines; but, as always experienced, the rears were less engaged than the centres and vans. No ship was taken; no very important spars seem to have been shot away. The loss of the British was 99 killed, 434 wounded; of the French, 102 killed, 386 wounded.

As the ships' heads were north, the course of the action carried

[1] See note on next page.

them in that direction. Suffren anchored next morning twenty-five miles north of Cuddalore. There he was sighted on the 22nd by Hughes, who had remained lying-to the day after the fight. The British Vice-Admiral reported several ships much disabled, a great number of his men — 1,121 — down with scurvy, and the water of the fleet very short. He therefore thought it necessary to go to Madras, where he anchored on the 25th. Suffren regained Cuddalore on the afternoon of the 23rd. His return and Hughes's departure completely changed the military situation. The supply-ships, upon which the British scheme of operations depended, had been forced to take flight when Suffren first approached, and of course could not come back now. "My mind is on the rack without a moment's rest since the departure of the fleet," wrote the commanding general on the 25th, "considering the character of M. de Suffren, and the infinite superiority on the part of the French now that we are left to ourselves."

The battle of June 20th, 1783, off Cuddalore, was the last of the maritime war of 1778. It was fought, actually, exactly five months

---

NOTE. — List of the British and French fleets in the action off Cuddalore, on June 20th, 1783: —

BRITISH.			FRENCH.		
SHIPS.	GUNS.	COMMANDERS.	SHIPS.	GUNS.	COMMANDERS.
Cumberland . .	74	Capt. William Allen.	*Héros*	74	
Monmouth . .	64	Capt. James Alms (1).	*Fendant* . . .	74	
Bristol	50	Capt. James Burney.	*Annibal* . . .	74	
Hero	74	{ Commod. Richard King. { Capt. Theophilus Jones.	*Illustre* . . . *Argonaute* . .	74 74	
Eagle	64	Capt. William Clark.	*Vengeur* . . .	64	
Magnanime . .	64	Capt. Thomas Mackenzie.	*Sphinx* . . .	64	
Sceptre . . .	64	Capt. Samuel Graves.	*Artésien* . . .	64	
Burford . . .	64	Capt. Peter Rainier (1).	*Ajax*	64	
Monarca . . .	68	Capt. John Gell.	*Sévère*. . . .	64	
Superb	74	{ Vice-Admiral Sir Edward Hughes, { K. B. (B). { Capt. Henry Newcome.	*Brillant* . . . *Hardi* . . . . *St. Michel* . .	64 64 60	
Sultan	74	Capt. Andrew Mitchell.	*Flamand* . . .	50	
Africa	64	Capt. Robert M'Douall.	*Hannibal*. . .	50	
Worcester . . .	64	Capt. Charles Hughes.	*Apollon* . .	40	
Exeter	64	Capt. John Samuel Smith.	*Cléopâtre* .	36	
Inflexible . . .	64	Capt. the Hon. John Whitmore Chetwynd.	*Coventry* .	28	
Gibraltar . . .	80	{ Commodore Sir Richard Bickerton, Bart. { Capt. Thomas Hicks.			
Isis	50	Capt. Christopher Halliday.			
Defence . . .	74	Capt. Thomas Newnham.			
Juno . . .	32	Capt. James Montagu.			
Medea . .	28	Capt. Erasmus Gower.			
Seahorse. .	20				

W. L. C.

after the preliminaries of peace had been signed.[1] Although the relative force of the two fleets remained unchanged, it was a French victory, both tactically and strategically: tactically, because the inferior
fleet held its ground, and remained in possession of the field: strategically, because it decided the object immediately at stake, the fate
of Cuddalore, and with it, momentarily at least, the issue of the
campaign.   It was, however, the triumph of one commander-in-chief
over another; of the greater man over the lesser.   Hughes's reasons
for quitting the field involve the admission of his opponent's greater
skill.   "Short of water," — with eighteen ships to fifteen that should
not have happened; "injury to spars," — that resulted from the action;
"1,121 men short," — Suffren had embarked just that number — 1,200
— because Hughes let him communicate with the port without fighting.   This is not the place, nor is there room, for enlargement upon
the merits of Suffren; upon the difficulties he surmounted, and the
genius he showed.   He was a great sea-captain, Hughes was not;
and with poorer instruments, both in men and ships, the former over-
came the latter.

On the 29th of June a British frigate, the *Medea*, bearing a flag of
truce, reached Cuddalore.   She brought well-authenticated intelligence of the conclusion of peace; and hostilities ceased by common
consent.

[1] January 20, 1783.

PUBLISHER'S NOTE
In the original edition the four photogravure plates and
the first full-page illustration faced the text pages as
listed on page XVII. In this edition these illustrations
are collected on the following pages in the order in
which they appeared in the first edition. The original
position indicators have been retained.

H.M.S. *GRAFTON*, FITTED WITH A JURY RUDDER, &c., FOR HER VOYAGE TO ENGLAND, AFTER THE STORM OFF LOUISBOURG, 1757.

(*From Hervey's 'Naval History.'*)

[*To face page* 169.

Semircierg ravure   Printed in Paris

George Brydges Rodney, Lord Rodney, K. B. Admiral,
Vice-Admiral of England

From the Engraving by G. Dupont, after the Portrait by Gainsborough

Sampson Low Marston and Company L.ᵈ London

Lemercier gravure   Printed in Paris

James Cook, F.R.S., Captain, R.N.

From the Engraving by J.K.Sherwin, after Dance.

Sampson Low Marston and Company L.td London

Lemerciergravure

Printed in Paris

Richard, Earl Howe, K. G.,
Admiral of the Fleet, and General of Marines.
From the Engraving by Dunkerton, after the Portrait by Copley.

Sampson Low Marston and Company L.ᵗᵈ London.

Lemerciergravure Printed in Paris.

Sir Edward Hughes, K.B., Admiral.

From the Engraving by Jones, after the Portrait by Reynolds.

Sampson Low Marston and Company Ltd. London.

APPENDIX TO CHAPTER XXXI.

LIST OF BRITISH FLAG-OFFICERS ON THE ACTIVE LIST AT THE PROMOTION OF OCTOBER 21ST, 1762, and of all Officers who were subsequently promoted to flag-rank on the active list, up to the eve of the outbreak of war with France, in 1793.

NAME AND TITLES.	BORN.	POST CAPTAIN.	REAR-ADMIRAL.			VICE-ADMIRAL.			ADMIRAL.		ADMIRAL OF THE FLEET.	
			Blue.	White.	Red.	Blue.	White.	Red.	Blue.	White.		
Sir William Rowley, K.B.	1690	26-4-1716		22-12-1743		23-6-1744	23-4-1745		15-7-1747	12-5-1748	1762	Died 1-1-1768.
Isaac Townsend (2)		9-2-1720			23-6-1744	23-4-1745			15-7-1747	12-5-1748		Died 22-11-1765.
Henry Osborn (2)		4-1-1728				12-5-1748		2-1757	2-1757	21-10-1762		Died 4-2-1771.
Thomas Griffin (1)		1-4-1731					6-1-1755		2-1757	21-10-1762		Died 1771.
Sir Edward Hawke, K.B. (Baron, 1776)	1705	20-3-1734				12-5-1748	6-1-1755		2-1757	21-10-1762	1768	Died V.-Adm. of England 17-10-1781
Charles Knowles (Bt. 1765)	1714	4-2-1737	16-7-1747			2-1757	2-1757	5-2-1758	5-2-1758	18-10-1770		Died 9-12-1777.
Hon. John Forbes	1706	7-3-1737				2-1757	2-1757	5-2-1758	5-2-1758	18-10-1770	1781	Died 10-3-1796.
Sir George Pocock, K.B.	1706	1-8-1738				5-2-1758	5-2-1758	5-2-1758	21-10-1762			Retired 1766; died 3-4-1792.
Hon. George Townshend	29-10-1716	30-1-1739				14-2-1759	21-10-1762	21-10-1762				Died Aug. 1769.
Francis Holburne		15-2-1740	5-1755			14-2-1759	21-10-1762	21-10-1762	18-10-1770	18-10-1770		Died 15-7-1771.
Thomas Cotes		12-5-1740	5-1755		4-6-1756	14-2-1759	21-10-1762	21-10-1762				Died Oct. 1767.
Thomas Frankland (Bt. 1768)		15-7-1740	5-1755		4-6-1756	14-2-1759	21-10-1762	21-10-1762	18-10-1770	18-10-1770		Died 20-11-1784.
Lord Harry Powlett (Duke of Bolton)	1720	15-7-1740		4-6-1756		14-2-1759	21-10-1762	21-10-1762	1773			Died 25-12-1791.
Harry Norris	1704	26-4-1740		4-6-1756								Died 13-6-1764.
Thomas Broderick	1716	25-3-1741		4-6-1756	4-6-1756	14-2-1759	21-10-1762	21-10-1762				Died 1-1-1769.
Sir Charles Hardy (2), Kt.	1715	10-8-1741	4-6-1756	5-2-1758	18-10-1770	18-10-1770	18-10-1770	18-10-1770	18-10-1770	29-1-1778		Died 18-5-1780.
George, Earl of Northesk	1720	25-8-1741	4-6-1756	5-2-1758	18-10-1770	18-10-1770	18-10-1770	18-10-1770	18-10-1770	29-1-1778		Died 22-1-1792.
Sir Charles Saunders, K.B.		26-9-1741		1758		14-2-1759	21-10-1762	21-10-1762	18-10-1770			Died 7-12-1775.
Thomas Pye[1] (Kt. 1773)		[13-4-1741]	8-7-1758		14-3-1759			18-10-1770	18-10-1770	31-3-1775		Died 1785.
Philip Durell (1)		6-2-1742	8-7-1758		14-2-1759	21-10-1762						Died Aug. 1766.
Samuel Cornish (Bt. 1766)	1709	12-3-1742	11-2-1759	14-2-1759		21-10-1762	21-10-1762	21-10-1762				Died 30-10-1770.
Francis Geary (Bt. 1782)	19-2-1718	30-6-1742	19-5-1759		21-10-1762	21-10-1762	18-10-1770	18-10-1770	29-1-1778	29-1-1778		Died 7-2-1796.
George Brydges Rodney (Bt. 1764; K.B. 1780; Baron, 1782)		9-11-1742			18-10-1770	18-10-1770		31-3-1775	29-1-1778	29-1-1778		Died 24-5-1792.
H.R.H. Edward Augustus, Duke of York	25-3-1739	14-6-1759	8-4-1761									Died 14-9-1767.
Sir William Burnaby, Kt. (Bt. 1754)		9-12-1742										Died 1776.
James Young (1), Kt.		16-5-1743		21-10-1762	18-10-1770	24-10-1770	24-10-1770		29-1-1778	29-1-1778		Died 24-1-1789.
Sir Piercy Brett (1), Kt.		30-9-1743		21-10-1762	18-10-1770	24-10-1770	24-10-1770		29-1-1778	29-1-1778		Died 12-10-1781.
John Moore (1) (Bt. 1766)	24-3-1718	24-12-1743		21-10-1762	18-10-1770	24-10-1770	24-10-1770		29-1-1778	29-1-1778		Died 24-3-1778.
Richard Tyrrell		26-12-1743	21-10-1762									Died 27-6-1766.
Alexander, Lord Colville		19-3-1744	21-10-1762	21-10-1762		24-10-1770	24-10-1770					Died 21-5-1770.
Sir James Douglas (1), Kt.		1-8-1744	Commr.	21-10-1762	18-10-1770	18-10-1770	24-10-1770	24-10-1770	5-2-1776	8-4-1782		Died 2-11-1787.
Sir John Bentley, Kt.[2]		4-8-1744		[28-12-1763]		18-10-1770	24-10-1770	24-10-1770				Died 14-12-1772.
William Gordon		19-8-1744	21-10-1762	21-10-1762	18-10-1770							Died 25-4-1768.
George, Lord Edgcumbe (Visct.; Mount Edgcumbe, 1781; Earl, 1789.)		27-8-1744	21-10-1762	21-10-1762	18-10-1770	24-10-1770	24-10-1770	24-10-1770	5-2-1776	8-4-1782		D'ed 4-2-1795.
Robert Swanton (1)	1713	11-9-1744	21-10-1762	21-10-1762								Died 1-8-1765.
Samuel Graves (1)		2-10-1744	21-10-1762	21-10-1762	18-10-1770	31-3-1775	31-3-1775	5-2-1776	5-2-1776	8-4-1782		Died 8-3-1787.
William Parry[2]			[-1763]			18-10-1770	31-3-1775	31-3-1775	5-2-1776			Died 29-4-1779.
Hon. Aug. Keppel (Visct. Keppel, 1782)	2-4-1725	11-12-1744	21-10-1762	21-10-1762	18-10-1770	31-3-1775	31-3-1775	5-2-1776	5-2-1776	8-4-1782		Died 2-10-1786.

Flag-List on October 21st, 1762.

1 Promotion to flag-rank delayed, in consequence of the officer being under suspension when his turn came.   2 Passed over when their turn came, but promoted later.

FLAG-OFFICERS, 1762–1793.

NAME AND TITLES.	BORN.	POST CAPTAIN.	REAR-ADMIRAL. Blue	White	Red	VICE-ADMIRAL. Blue	White	Red	ADMIRAL. Blue	White	ADMIRAL OF THE FLEET.	
John Amherst	1718	29-12-1744	1764	18-10-1770		24-10-1770	5-2-1776		29-1-1778			Died 14-2-1778.
H.R.H. Henry Frederick, Dk. of Cumberland	1745	28-10-1768		18-10-1770		24-10-1770	5-2-1776		29-1-1778	8-4-1782		Died 1790.
Sir Peter Denis, Bt.		9-2-1745	18-10-1770	18-10-1770		31-3-1775	5-2-1776	29-1-1778				Died 12-6-1778.
Robert Hughes [2]	1716	2-4-1745	18-10-1770	18-10-1770								Died 12-5-1774.
Matthew Buckle (1)		29-5-1745			24-10-1770	31-3-1775	5-2-1776	29-1-1778	26-9-1780			Died 19-7-1784.
Robert Man (2)		22-6-1745	18-10-1770		24-10-1770	31-3-1775	5-2-1776	29-1-1778	26-9-1780			Died 1783.
Clark Gayton [2]		6-7-1745			24-10-1770	31-3-1775	5-2-1776	29-1-1778	8-4-1782			Died ca. 1787.
John Barker (1) [2]		19 9-1745	18-10-1770	24-10-1770	31-3-1775							Died 26-5-1776.
Richard Spry (Kt. 1773)		23-9-1745	18-10-1770	24-10-1770	31-3-1775							Died 12-1775.
Lucius O'Brien [2]		3-12-1745		24-10-1770	31-3-1775							Died 17-12-1770..
John Montagu [2]		15-1-1746	24-10-1770		31-3-1775	5-2-1776	18-4-1777	29-1-1778	8-4-1782	24-9-1787		Died 7-9-1795.
Thomas Craven [2]		8-2-1746	24-10-1770		31-3-1775	5-2-1776			8-4-1782			Died 14-12-1772.
Robert Harland (2) (Bt. 1771)		19-3-1746	18-10-1770		31-3-1775	5-2-1776						Died 28-2-1783.
James Sayer [2]	1721	22-3-1746	24-10-1770		31-3-1775	5-2-1776						Died 15-10-1777.
Richard, Visct. Howe (Earl, 1788; K.G. 1797)	1726	10-4-1746	18-10-1770	31-3-1775		5-2-1776			8-4-1782	24-9-1787	1796	Died 5-8-1799.
Washington, Earl Ferrers		19-4-1746		31-3-1775								Died 1-10-1778.
Hugh Pigot (1)		22-4-1746		31-3-1775		5-2-1776	29-1-1778	26-9-1780	24-4-1782	24-9-1787		Died 15-12-1792.
Molyneux Shuldham (Baron Shuldham, 1776)		12-5-1746		31-3-1775		5-2-1766	29-1-1778	26-9-1780	24-9-1787			Died 1798.
Sir Joseph Knight, Kt.		31-7-1746		31-3-1775			29-1-1778	26-9-1789	24-9-1787			Died 8-9-1775.
John Vaughan		11-8-1746	31-3-1775	31-3-1775			29-1-1778		24-9-1787			Died 7-1-1789.
John Lloyd (2)		4-9-1746	31-3-1775	31-3-1775		29-1-1778		26-9-1780				Died 8-3-1778.
Robert Duff		23-10-1746	31-3-1775		5-2-1776	29-1-1778		26-9-1780				Died 6-6-1787.
John Reynolds (1)		30-10-17.6	31-3-1775	5-2-1776		29-1-1778						Died 1788.
Sir Hugh Palliser, Bt.		25-11-1746	31-3-1775	5-2-1776	23-1-1778	29-1-1778	29-1-1778		24-9-1787	1-2-1793		Died 19-3-1796.
Hon. John Byron	26-2-1722	30-12-1746	31-3-1775	20-5-1777	23-1-1778	29-1-1778			24-9-1787			Died 10-4-1786.
Aug. John, Earl of Bristol	8-11-1723	15-1-1747	31-3-1775	20-5-1777	23-1-1778	29-1-1778						Died 23-12-1779.
George Mackenzie	19-5-1724	24-1-1747	31-3-1775	23-1-1778	29-1-1778	29-1-1778						Died 1781.
Matthew Barton	1716	7-2-1747	20-5-1777	23-1-1778	29-3-1779	29-3-1779			24-9-1787	1-2-1793		Died 30-12-1795.
Sir Peter Parker (1), Kt. (Bt. 1782)	1715	6-5-1747	20-5-1777	23-1-1778	29-3-1779	29-3-1779			24-9-1787	12-4-1794	1799	Died 21-12-1811.
Hon. Samuel Barrington	1729	29-5-1747	20-5-1777	23-1-1778	29-3-1779	29-3-1779			24-9-1787	12-4-1794		Died 16-8-1800.
Marriot Arbuthnot	1719	22-6-1747		23-1-1778	29-3-1779	29-3-1779			1-2-1793	12-4-1794		Died 31-1-1794.
Robert Roddam		9-7-1747	23-1-1778	23-1-1778		29-3-1779	26-9-1780	24-9-1787	1-2-1793			Died 31-1-1808.
George Darby		12-9-1747	23-1-1778	23-1-1778		29-3-1779	26-9-1780	24-9-1787				Died 26-11-1790.
John Campbell (1)	1723	23-11-1747	23-1-1778	23-1-1778		29-3-1779	26-9-1780	24-9-1787				Died 16-12-1790.
Christopher Hill		5-12-1747	23-1-1778	29-1-1778		26-9-1780	26-9-1780					Died 4-7-1778.
James Gambier (1)	1725	12-1-1748	23-1-1778	29-1-1778	29-3-1779	26-9-1780	26-9-1780	24-9-1787	1-2-1793			Died 8-1-1789.
William Lloyd (1)		12-1-1748			29-3-1779	26-9-1780	26-9-1780	24-9-1787	1-2-1793			Died 19-7-1796.
Francis William Drake		6-2-1748	23-1-1778		29-3-1779	26-9-1780		24-9-1787	1-2-1793	1-6-1795		Died 1789.
Sir Edward Hughes, Kt. (K.B. 1778)	22-8-1724	6-2-1748	23-1-1778		29-3-1779	26-9-1780		24-9-1787	1-2-1793	1-6-1795		Died 17-2-1794.
Hyde Parker (1) (Bt. 1782)	1717	24-3-1748		29-3-1779		26-9-1780	24-9-1787	21-9-1790	1-2-1793			(Drowned 1783, in Cato.)
John Evans		20-4-1748		29-3-1779		26-9-1780	24-9-1787	21-9-1790	1-2-1793			Died 15-7-1794.
Mark Milbanke		21-5-1748		29-3-1779		26-9-1780	24-9-1787	21-9-1790	1-2-1793	1-6-1795		Died 10-6-1805.

[2] Passed over when their turn came, but promoted later.

FLAG-OFFICERS, 1762-1793.

Name and Titles	Born	Post Captain	Rear-Admiral Blue	Rear-Admiral White	Rear-Admiral Red	Vice-Admiral Blue	Vice-Admiral White	Vice-Admiral Red	Admiral Blue	Admiral White	Admiral of the Fleet	
Nicholas Vincent		5-7-1748		29-3-1779	26-9-1780		24-9-1787	1-2-1793	12-4-1794	1-6-1795		Died 1809.
John Storr		1-11-1748		29-3-1779	26-9-1780							Died 1-1783.
Sir Edward Vernon (2), Kt.		3-4-1753		29-3-1779	26-9-1780		24-9-1787	1-2-1793	12-4-1794			Died 7-1794.
Joshua Rowley (Bt. 1786)	5-1734	14-12-1753	29-3-1779		26-9-1780		24-9-1787	1-2-1793	12-4-1794			Died 26-2-1790.
Richard Edwards (2)		27-12-1753	29-3-1779		26-9-1780		24-9-1787	1-2-1793				Died 1794.
Thomas Graves (2) (Baron Graves, 1794)	23-10-1725	8-7-1755		29-3-1779	26-9-1780	24-9-1787	21-9-1790	1-2-1793	12-4-1794	1-6-1795		Died 9-2-1802.
Hon. Robert Digby	11-11-1721	5-8-1755	29-3-1779		26-9-1780	24-9-1787	21-9-1790	1-2-1793	12-4-1794	1-6-1795		Died 1814.
Sir John Lockhart Ross, Bt.		23-3-1756	29-3-1779		26-9-1780	24-9-1787	21-9-1790					Died 9-6-1790.
Charles Webber	1711	5-4-1756		26-9-1780								Died 1783.
William Langdon		5-6-1756		26-9-1780								Died 29-6-1785.
Benjamin Marlow		6-6-1756		26-9-1780		24-9-1787	21-9-1790	1-2-1793	12-4-1794			D ed 1795.
Alexander Arthur Hood (K.B. 1788; Baron Bridport, 1794)	1727	10-6-1756		26-9-1780		24-9-1787	21-9-1790	1-2-1793	12-4-1794	1-6-1795		Died 2-5-1814.
Alexander Innes		25-6-1756		26-9-1780								Died 1785.
Sir Chaloner Ogle (2), Kt. (Bart. 1816)	1738	30-6-1756	26-9-1780		24-9-1787	24-9-1787		1-2-1793	12-4-1794	14-2-1799		Died 27-8-1816.
Sir Samuel Hood (1), Bt. (Baron Hood, 1782; Visct. G.C.B. 1815)	12-1724	22-7-1756	26-9-1780			24-9-1787		1-2-1793	12-4-1794	14-2-1799		Died 27-1-1816.
Matthew Moore		20-8-1756	26-9-1780									Died 4-7-1787.
Sir Richard Hughes (3), Bt.		10-11-1756	26-9-1780		24-9-1787	21-9-1790	1-2-1793	12-4-1794		14-2-1799		Died 4-1-1812.
Francis Samuel Drake (Bt. 1782)		15-11-1756	26-9-1780		24-9-1787							Died 19-10-1789.
Richard Kempenfelt	1718	17-1-1757	26-9-1780									Drowned 29-8-1782, in Royal George.
Sir Edmund Affleck, Bt.	19-4-1735	23-3-1757	1784		24-9-1787							Died 19-11-1788.
John Elliot		5-4-1757		[24-9-1787²]	24-9-1787	21-9-1790	1-2-1793	12-4-1794	14-2-1799			Died 20-9-1808.
William Hotham (1) (Baron Hotham, 1797)		17-8-1757		24-9-1787	24-9-1787	21-9-1790	1-2-1793	12-4-1794	14-2-1799			Died 2-5-1813.
Sir John Lindsay, K.B.	1737	29-9-1757			24-9-1787							Died 4-6-1788.
Joseph Peyton (1)	1725	2-12-1757		24-9-1787	21-9-1790		1-2-1793	12-4-1794				Died 22-9-1804.
John Carter Allen		21-3-1758		24-9-1787	21-9-1790		1-2-1793	12-4-1794				Died 1801.
Sir Charles Middleton, Bt. (Lord Barham, 1805)	10-1726	22-5-1758		24-9-1787	21-9-1790	1-2-1793	1-2-1793	12-4-1794	1-6-1795	14-2-1799		Died 17-6-1813.
John Laforey (Bt. 1789)	1729	26-7-1758	Commr.	[24-9-1787²]	21-9-1790	21-9-1790	1-2-1793	12-4-1794	1-6-1795			Died 14-6-1796.
John Dalrymple		18-10-1758		24-9-1787	21-9-1790	21-9-1790	1-2-1793	12-4-1794	1-6-1795			Died 8-1798.
Herbert Sawyer (1)		26-12-1758		24-9-1787	21-9-1790	21-9-1790	1-2-1793	4-7-1794	1-6-1795			Died 6-1798.
Sir Richard King (1), Kt. (Bt. 1792)	10-8-1730	29-1-1759		24-9-1787	21-9-1790	21-9-1790	1-2-1793	12-4-1794	1-6-1795	14-2-1799		Died 11-1806.
Jonathan Faulknor (1)		9-7-1759		24-9-1787	21-9-1790	1-2-1793	1-2-1793	4-7-1794	1-6-1795			Died 24-6-1795.
Philip Affleck		20-8-1759		24-9-1787	21-9-1790	1-2-1793	1-2-1793	4-7-1794	1-6-1795	14-2-1799		Died 22-12-1799.
Sir Richard Bickerton, Bt.		21-8-1759		24-9-1787	21-9-1790							Died 28-2-1792.
Hon. John Leveson Gower	11-7-1740	30-6-1760		24-9-1787	21-9-1790							Died 15-8-1792.
Sir John Jervis, K.B. (Earl St. Vincent, 1797²)	1-1734	13-10-1760		24-9-1787	21-9-1790	1-2-1793	12-4-1794		1-6-1795	14-2-1799	19-7-1821	Died 1823.

² Passed over when their turn came, but promoted later.

FLAG-OFFICERS, 1762–1793.

NAME AND TITLES.	BORN.	POST CAPTAIN.	REAR-ADMIRAL.			VICE-ADMIRAL.			ADMIRAL.		ADMIRAL OF THE FLEET.	
			Blue.	White.	Red.	Blue.	White.	Red.	Blue.	White.		
Adam Duncan (Visct. Duncan, 1797)	1-7-1731	25-2-1761	24-9-1787	21-9-1790	—	1-2-1793	12-4-1794	—	1-6-1795	14-2-1799	—	Died 4-8-1804.
Sir Charles Douglas, Bt.		13-3-1761	24-9-1787									Died 10-3-1789.
Richard Braithwaite	1725	6-4-1761	—	21-9-1790		1-2-1793	12-4-1794	1-6-1795	14-2-1799	1-1-1801		Died 28-6-1805.
Phillips Cosby	1730	19-5-1761	—	21-9-1790		1-2-1793	12-4-1794	1-6-1795	14-2-1799	1-1-1801		Died 10-1-1808.
Thomas Fitzherbert		10-7-1761	21-9-1790		1-2-1793	12-4-1794	4-7-1794					Died 1794.
Samuel Pitchford Cornish	1739	24-8-1761	21-9-1790		1-2-1793	12-4-1794	4-7-1794	1-6-1795	14-2-1799	1-1-1801		Died 3-4-1816.
John Brisbane		24-9-1761	21-9-1790		1-2-1793	12-4-1794	4-7-1794	1-6-1795	14-2-1799	1-1-1801		Died 10-12-1807.
John Houlton	1740	4-11-1761	21-9-1790	—								Died 1792.
Charles Wolseley	1741	4-11-1761	21-9-1790	—	1-2-1793	12-4-1794	4-7-1794	1-6-1795	14-2-1799	1-1-1801		Died 1808.
Charles Inglis (1)		15-12-1761	21-9-1790	—								Died 10-10-1791.
Samuel Granston Goodall		13-1-1762	21-9-1790		1-2-1793	12-4-1794	4-7-1794	1-6-1795	14-2-1799	1-1-1801		Died 1801.
Hon. Keith Stewart (1)	1739	7-4-1762	10-1790					—				Died 1795.
H.R.H. William Henry, Duke of Clarence	21-8-1765	10-4-1786	3-12-1790		1-2-1793	12-4-1794	4-7-1794	1-6-1795	14-2-1799	1-1-1801	24-12-1811	Died King William IV. 20-6-1837.

NOTE.—Some of the above officers were promoted to the rank of Admiral of the Red (created in 1805); but it is unnecessary to indicate them here. A table of the flag-list as it stood in 1793, and of subsequent promotions to it, will be given later.

INDEX.

VOLUME III.

—◆—

NOTE—*British naval officers in the following are described as of the rank to which they attained upon the completion of their active service.*

Bryne, Captain Henry, 415, 454 n., 479 n.
Buccaneers, 61, 79
Buckingham, 40 n., 63, 96, 148 n., 151 n., 201 n., 234 n., 236 and n., 300
Buckle, Admiral Matthew (1), 139, 185, 212 n., 215, 218 n., 222, 234, 235 and n., 286, 305, 566
Bucklershard, 335
Bucknall, J., shipbuilder, 335
Buckner, Admiral Charles, 520 n.
Buenos Ayres, 251, 252
Buffalo, 505 n., 507 and n., 508
Bunker's Hill, 378
Buoys, 338
Burchett, Josiah, 3, 264
Burford, 34, 46 n., 55, 56, 57 n., 59, 62, 70 n., 75 n., 86, 87, 88, 96, 201 n., 202, 218 n., 234 n., 310, 545 n., 550 n., 552 n., 556, 563 n.
Burgoyne, Lieutenant-General John, 354, 359, 360, 366, 370, 389, 390, 391, 392, 398
Burke, Edmund, quoted, 379
Burlington, 388
Burnaby, Vice-Admiral Sir William, Bart., 250, 292, 415, 565
Burnaby, Captain Sir William Chaloner, Bart., 546 n.
Burnett, Captain Thomas, 201 n., 202, 227 n., 242 n., 246 n., 312, 492 n., 520 n.
Burrish, Captain George, 96, 103
Bursledon, 335
Burslem, Captain Francis, 218 n.
Burton, Richard, 3
Bury, Captain Thomas (1), 310
Busses, 187
Bussy, General de, 561, 562
Busy, 505 n.
Butchart, Captain John, 434
Butger, Commander, 505 n.
Button, the navigator, 318
Bylandt, Rear-Admiral Count Lodewijk van, 351
Byng, Sir George: see Torrington, Admiral of the Fleet Sir George Byng, Viscount
Byng, Admiral Hon. John, 105, 106, 113, 123, 124, 130, 137, 142, 146–160, 196 n., 289, 290 and n., 292, 293, 423, 467, 468, 498 n., 499
Byng, Hon. Henry Pattee, 3, 33 n.
Byng, Robert, 3, 4
Byron, Captain George Anson, 520 n.
Byron, Vice-Admiral Hon. John, 190 n., 224, 228, 235 n., 313, 322, 324, 395 and n., 396, 399, 404, 408, 409, 410, 412, 428, 433, 434–440, 443, 452, 460, 473, 566

CABLES, 9
Cabot, 505 n.
Cadiz, 31, 38, 39, 47, 62, 65, 66, 67, 107, 116, 212 and n., 215, 280, 285, 306, 308, 448, 449, 450, 452, 468, 469, 477, 478, 502, 503, 504, 509, 539

Cæsar, 335
Caimamera, 76 n.
Calabria, 33
Calais, 112
Calcutta, 201
Calcutta, 160, 161–163, 543
Caldwell, Admiral Benjamin, 509 n., 520 n.
California, 317
California, 319, 320
Callis, Rear-Admiral Smith, 86, 211, 212 n., 273, 285 n., 310
Calmady, Admiral Charles Holmes Everitt (*formerly* Charles Holmes Everitt), 497 n., 513 and n.
Calmady, Captain Warwick, 115, 311
Calypso, 218 n., 244 n., 299, 313
Cambridge, 96, 101, 201 n., 202, 246 n., 248
Camden, 472
Camilly, Vice-Admiral Blouet de, 91
Cammock, Captain George (Rear-Admiral in the Spanish Navy), 34, 35 and n., 38
Campbell, Captain Alexander (1), 322
Campbell, Colonel Archibald, 441
Campbell, Captain James (1), 41 n.
Campbell, Captain James (2), 167 n., 206 n., 242 n., 245 n., 246 n.
Campbell, Vice-Admiral John (1), 218 n., 222, 324, 341, 413 n., 415, 566
Campbell, William, 326
Campeche, 263
Canada, 511, 512 and n., 513 and n., 514, 516, 520 n., 530, 531
Canada, 117, 118, 139, 140, 164, 196, 197, 204–210, 226–228, 242, 253, 354, 355, 356, 370, 380, 539
Canary Islands, The, 188, 302
Cancale Bay, 192, 193
Candia, 229
Candles in lighthouses, 14, 15
Canoa, Point, 68 n.
Canso, 109, 113, 115
Canterbury, 33, 34, 35, 133 n., 135 n., 136
Canton, 323
Cape Breton, 109, 115, 116, 124, 166–168, 184, 191, 206, 253
Cape Cabron, San Domingo, 294
Cape Charles, 496
Cape Clear, 282, 311
Cape Coast Castle, 169, 287
Cape de Gata, 189
Cape de Verde Islands, 546
Cape Digges, 320
Cape Dobbs, 319, 320
Cape Fear, 372
Cape Finisterre, 283, 301, 303, 448, 540
Cape François, 123, 165, 225, 245, 246, 314, 468, 469, 470, 473, 474, 488, 492, 495, 496, 519, 536, 537
Cape Henry, 489, 496
Cape Hope, 319
Cape Horn, 267, 317, 321
Cape Lopez, 260
Cape May, 408